THE NEW COOKS' CATALOGUE

THE NEW COOKS' CATALOGUE

Edited by Burt Wolf,
Emily Aronson, and Florence Fabricant

ALFRED A. KNOPF   NEW YORK   2000

This Is a Borzoi Book
Published by Alfred A. Knopf

www.aaknopf.com

Knopf, Borzoi Books, and the colophon are registered trademarks
of Random House, Inc.

Owing to limitations of space, permissions acknowledgments
can be found on pages 505–8, which constitute an extension
of this copyright page.

Library of Congress Cataloging-in-Publication Data
The new cooks' catalogue / edited by Burt Wolf, Emily Aronson,
    and Florence Fabricant—1st ed.
        p.   cm.
    Includes bibliographical references and index.
    ISBN 0-375-40673-5 (alk. paper)
      1. Kitchen utensils—Catalogs.   I. Wolf, Burton.

TX656.N49 2000
016.683'82—dc21   00-034914

Manufactured in the United States of America
First Edition

This book is dedicated to Ted Aronson, a good friend who has supported my work in a brotherly way for many years.

—BW

CONTENTS

Introduction ix

1 Measuring Devices 1

2 Bowls 24

3 Knives, Sharpeners, & Cutting Boards 34

4 Cutting Instruments Other Than Knives 65

5 Refiners, Grinders, Crushers, Mashers, & Extractors 89

6 Colanders, Strainers, & Separators 118

7 Handheld Utensils for Beating, Mixing, Whisking, Stirring & Lifting 128

8 Electric Blenders, Mixers, & Food Processors 149

9 Pots & Pans 165

10 Griddles, Grill Pans, & Irons 231

11 Toasters & Toaster Ovens 246

12 Roasting Equipment 250

13 Baking Dishes & Molds 263

14 Pasta-Making Equipment 289

15 Bread- & Pizza-Making Equipment 302

16 Baking & Pastry Equipment 321

17 Ice Cream Makers, Scoops, & a Yogurt Machine 369

18   Wine Tools   376

19   Coffee- & Tea-Making Equipment   389

20   Preserving & Canning Devices   419

Appendices   429

A   Universal Tools   431

B   Cooks' Reference Library   435

C   Product Index   443

D   Manufacturer & Distributor Information   465

About the Contributors   477

Acknowledgements   485

Recipe Index   487

Index   491

Permissions Acknowledgments   505

INTRODUCTION

The Mythic Origin of the Gadget Drawer

When it comes to eating and drinking there are two great truths: if you don't eat and drink you will soon depart for the great beyond, and no matter how much you eat and drink at one time you will soon be hungry again. As a result, eating and drinking are at the center of all life, and layered with social significance far beyond nutritional value. We have also extended those symbolic values to the equipment we use in preparing our food. Each year billions of dollars are spent equipping our kitchens, collecting utensils like cookie cutters, copper sauté pans, or ice cream makers that are well outside our basic culinary needs.

The Cooks' Catalogue Project

My grandmother owned a small cooking equipment shop in New York City and I considered much of her inventory to be part of my toy chest—a large enamel-over-steel roaster was my boat, a 14″ wooden spatula my paddle, and the blue strip of linoleum that ran down the center of the shop played the part of the Hudson, Amazon, and Nile Rivers.

But it wasn't until 1969 that pots and pans became a serious part of my life. That was the year that the Bonnier Group, in Stockholm, asked me to find out if a line of cooking equipment could be developed in coop-eration with the three-star chefs of France. I visited thirteen outstanding restaurants, interviewed dozens of talented chefs, and gained twenty-three pounds, eventually concluding that there was no agreement as to what constituted the "best" cooking tools. In almost every case a chef's favorite tool was the one he had become comfortable with over the years; there was very little in the way of objective, comparative testing.

My research soon came to an end, leaving me with a desire to lose weight and have my questions answered: What made a good knife? How do I pick the right pot for each cooking method? Are the metals and coatings used in cooking equipment safe? Which equipment do I need and how do I get my money's worth? The project that became the original edition of *The Cooks' Catalogue* was under way.

Milton Glaser (the renowned graphic designer and serious eater) and James Beard (one of the most important food authorities of the past century) helped me put together and execute a five-year plan for testing thousands of pieces of equipment and compiling the book. Author and food expert Barbara Kafka took over the operations of the project and gave the book its underlying structure. Her diligence, knowledge, and desire to make the book a significant work were essential to its success. After its publication in 1975, the research continued to be updated and was used for a paperback edition, a second volume that addressed ethnic equipment (*The International Cooks' Catalogue*), a syndicated column for the *Washington Post,* a series of television reports on CNN, and more than two hundred cooking equipment shops in leading department stores throughout the United States.

For more than three decades I have been reporting on the excellent, the necessary, and the unique in cooking equipment and utensils that prove to be the "best." And each year I find new materials, new technology, new versions of old tools, old versions of new tools, and new tools that are already old and should quickly be forgotten. I have tried to bring some science and order to this chaos through our ongoing work on *The Cooks' Catalogue.* To mark the twenty-fifth anniversary of the first edition, a group of the world's leading food authorities have once again come together to collaborate on *The New Cooks' Catalogue.* Thousands of pieces of equipment were evaluated and tested and finally narrowed down to those presented in the book. *The New Cooks' Catalogue* is an independent publication and the content was developed free of any affiliation with manufacturers, distributors, or retailers.

How to Use This Book

Each chapter begins with a general introduction to the equipment being covered. The introduction sets up the criteria for selection and the "What to Look For" sections tell you what you need to know before you make a purchase. The individual pieces of equipment that met our criteria are shown, accompanied by a descriptive text and photograph.

There were some excellent tools that met all our criteria but could not be included due to space limitations. Moreover, some of the tools in the book will cease to be manufactured in the future, while new models and inventions will be introduced. However, the basic criteria for selection will remain the same, and we believe that once you know what to look for in a category, the specific item you purchase is a matter of personal taste.

As the manuscript developed we added informative sidebars written by leading experts and recipes that are related to the equipment being reviewed so you can see how the tools might be used. You can also see demonstrations of equipment use in *Local Flavors,* a nationally syndicated television series for public broadcasting, which shares content with *The Cooks' Catalogue.* Finally, we reprinted a series of food-related cartoons that I had seen over the years in *The New Yorker* magazine.

You will notice that we have not included the prices of the equipment reviewed. The 1975 edition of *The Cooks' Catalogue* contained prices for each item, but within weeks they were inaccurate. Thanks to twenty-first century technology we were able to develop a website that lists present prices for almost all of the items in the book and offers continual updates on availability and new products. This site is at www.burtwolf.com.

Our desire was to produce a book about cooking equipment that would inform you, make the selection process easier and more reliable, and help you get the most for your money. I hope you find it both useful and enjoyable.

—BURT WOLF

Up-to-date prices for the equipment in
The New Cooks' Catalogue
can be found online at
www.burtwolf.com

THE NEW COOKS' CATALOGUE

1

MEASURING DEVICES

WHEN WE TALK ABOUT COOKING, eventually the questions become the same: How much? How hot? For how long? Take a few carrots—how many? Add some stock—how much? Cook it over a low flame—for how long? The saying that "Anyone who can read can cook" relies for its validity on a commonly accepted system of measurements.

What do we measure? We measure volume, weight, temperature, density, time, and distance. All are of ancient origin, and hints of their great age remain in our terminology. When an Englishman weighs himself or his child or his dog in *stones,* he is looking back to the time in ancient Egypt when stones were placed on a balance with gold. And *grain,* a term still in use for quantities of precious metals and pharmaceuticals, comes from the Babylonian practice of weighing out gold using seeds of grain. Even the division of hours into 60 minutes, and of minutes into 60 seconds, comes from the fact that 60 was the Babylonian unit of counting.

The earliest units of measurement were produced for commercial reasons and corresponded to easily available standards—the finger, the foot, the length of a stride, the seed of a carob plant. From these rough beginnings we have evolved more or less precise standards of measurement.

Essentially, measuring is an agreement among people about certain standards. A U.S. gallon, which we consider an absolute, is in fact a formula made up for 231 cubic inches. What we call a 5° rise in temperature is really the change in heat that is necessary to make a column of liquid in a tube rise or fall a given distance. Even a calorie is a unit of measurement: not of gaining or losing weight, but, in physics, the amount of energy needed to raise the temperature of a liter of water by 1°C.

The most common of our kitchen measurements is volume, the answer to the constant question: How much? We think of cups and teaspoonfuls, but in fact the basic unit of this standard is the cube—a virtual cubic inch of air. On this structure we have built all of the formulas that we use to illustrate capacity. A dry pint, for example, is 33.6 cubic inches, while a liquid pint is 28.875 cubic inches. And cups and half-cups and teaspoonfuls all express a relationship to these cubic inches of air.

The United Kingdom and Canada use units of their Old Imperial system and the modern metric one. Most other countries are now using the metric system, but the United States continues to use its own forms of measurement. It is the only industrialized country in the world not using the metric system, and some say that the government's long-standing effort to persuade Americans to convert to it is gaining new urgency. If history is any indication it will be no easy task. In 1866, Congress officially authorized the use of the metric system and supplied each state with a set of standard weights and measures. Since then, Americans have largely ignored the initiative, but officials at the National Institute of Standards and Technology in

Maryland, the torchbearers of this decimal-based system, say they're not giving up. Indeed, they're convinced that the increasing competitiveness of other nations and the demands of today's global marketplace will do much to jump-start the American conversion to the metric system. As proof, they point to the fact that metric units are already widely used in the design and manufacture of everything from automobiles to pharmaceutical products to soft drinks and, increasingly, on containers of food—especially those that are imported.

Still, it may be some time before such a switch will find its way into American cooking, since the average home cook is more concerned with the pressures of getting dinner on the table than a product on the global market. Should metric numbers (237 milliliters, for example, equals 1 cup) begin creeping into recipes, cooks in this country can rely on many tools that are marked with both systems and on the conversion tables included in good cookbooks.

Still, there is no question that things are better than they used to be, when cooking directions were given according to such measures as different sizes of wine glasses, teacups, or coffee cups. The only vestige of that system is the teaspoon-tablespoon nomenclature, and these measures are now standardized in the United States at $\frac{1}{6}$ and $\frac{1}{2}$ fluid ounce. In trying to follow an old recipe, you might be able to "add butter the size of a hazelnut," or "as much brown sugar as a walnut," but your end result might not be the same as that of the recipe's author.

MEASURING CUPS & SPOONS
Measuring Volume the American Way

TODAY IN THE United States we use volume measurements for both dry and liquid ingredients. Dry measurement is done in containers that hold exactly the amount wanted, whether a cupful or half a teaspoonful. You take the back of your knife and scrape it across the top of the cup or spoon to remove the excess flour or baking powder, and there you are. For liquid measurement we use containers marked to hold various quantities. Glass measuring pitchers are best, because (until you drop them) they will hold their exact shape and allow you to check the level of the liquid at eye level with the marking. Plastic can melt and change its shape, while metal can dent and can't be seen through.

It's not in your best interest to measure dry ingredients in a liquid measure due to the difference in the way liquids and granulated solids (sugar or flour, for example) fill a space. When a liquid is placed in a container it occupies the entire area. When a granulated solid goes into a container the shape and size of the grains cause the substance to settle in an unpredictable way. Measuring a dry ingredient in a liquid measuring container therefore results in a different quantity of the ingredient than measuring it in a dry measure. We tried it with sugar and were quite surprised at the variance.

We also recommend that you measure your liquid ingredients in a 1-cup liquid measure even though larger capacity containers may be more convenient. The bigger containers are usually wider and offer a broader surface area. If you make a small error in reading the height of the ingredient on that larger surface the result will be a larger error in volume. Large, wide-mouth measures for liquids are therefore less accurate.

Buying enough good measuring equipment is worth the extra expense if only for those moments when, because you have extra measures, you will not have to wash the vanilla extract out of the teaspoon before dipping it into the baking powder. Dry measuring cups and spoons should be of sturdy construction. Considerable pressure is placed on the joint between the handle and the cup as you sweep it through a container of flour; you want the bond between handle and cup to be strong so that the handle doesn't bend. In addition to the dry measures you will need a few pitcher-shaped glass cups for liquid measure. Be sure that everything is easily washable.

Cooking is often one disaster after another. What you learn is the only thing you can't fix is a soufflé.
—JULIA CHILD

1.1 ENDURANCE SPICE SPOONS

How often have you fumbled—tapping, shaking, and spilling spices—while trying to measure a level tablespoon or teaspoon because the appropriate spoon didn't fit through the neck of the spice jar? Here is the commonsense solution: a set of sleek rectangular measuring spoons that are designed to fit easily into the narrow openings of commercial spice jars or cans. That's reason enough to choose this stainless steel set, but you'll also be glad of its other unique features: comfortable long-handled design, equivalent metric milliliter markings on each spoon, and an unusual ¾-teaspoon measure, in addition to the 1-tablespoon, 1-teaspoon, ½-teaspoon, ¼-teaspoon, and ⅛-teaspoon capacities.

1.2 OXO MEASURING SPOONS

We applaud the excellent utilitarian design of this set of heavy-duty nesting measuring spoons. First of all, they're made of sturdy stainless steel that won't snap, bend, or break as cheaper metals eventually will. The handles are covered with a sheath of dishwasher-safe rubber so they feel very secure and comfy in hand (if you have big hands, however, you may wish you could stretch their 3½″ length). Best of all, each handle of the four spoons is inlaid with a different-colored measurement to indicate the capacity of the bowl— ¼ teaspoon, ½ teaspoon, 1 teaspoon, or 1 tablespoon. This permanent size marking appears at the end of the handle nearest the bowl, so it's not covered up by your hand while measuring—a worthwhile feature that just might alert the distracted cook who unwittingly reaches for the wrong size spoon.

1.3 OXO MEASURING CUPS

It's hardly fair to recommend any particular set of measuring cups, since there are many good brands in the marketplace. However, we can show you a few we especially like to use as a standard for choosing your own. This dry-measuring set, with its sturdy brushed stainless steel construction and soft, non-slip rubber-coated handles, excels in the category. As with OXO's measuring spoons, the handles of these four cups have different-colored inlays indicating their capacities—¼ cup, ⅓ cup, ½ cup, and 1 cup. With their protective handles the cups could, in a pinch, be used for warming or melting ingredients over the pilot light of your stove.

1.4 AMCO MEASURING CUPS

Go into any professional test kitchen and you'll find an array of measuring cups just like these: strong, durable, dishwasher safe, constructed of 18/8 stainless steel, and with clear size markings that make the job of controlling amounts to be measured practically foolproof. They also nest together for easy storage. You should avoid flimsy dime-store plastic measuring cups and opt for a basic set that gives you the necessary ¼-, ⅓-, ½-, and 1-cup measures. Another word of advice: parents of young children may need to buy an extra set for the playroom—kids think they make a terrific set of miniature cooking pots.

CURRANT–DRIED CHERRY BUTTERMILK SCONES

3¼ cups batter; 8 scones (3½" diameter)

Traditional scones are often made with dried currants. For a change, as well as extra color and flavor, I like to add dried cherries as well. Buttermilk makes scones especially tender. These are quickly mixed in a food processor, but they can also be prepared by hand in a bowl.

FOR GOOD MEASURE

• If you don't have liquid buttermilk, you can substitute the powdered form sold in supermarkets and natural-food shops; follow directions on the package, adding the powdered buttermilk with the dry ingredients and mixing the water with the eggs.
• For a less sweet scone, reduce sugar to ¼ cup. For a slightly darker color, substitute packed light or dark brown sugar.
• For greater richness, you can increase butter up to 8 tablespoons (1 stick).

SPECIAL EQUIPMENT

Baking sheet, baking parchment or wax paper, food processor, pastry brush

ADVANCE PREPARATION

Scones are best when freshly baked but will keep well for several days when stored or tightly double-wrapped and keep frozen up to one month. Serve warm.

TIME & TEMPERATURE

10 to 12 minutes at 425°F

FOR THE SCONES

2 cups sifted all-purpose flour
⅓ cup granulated sugar
2½ teaspoons baking powder
¼ teaspoon baking soda
1 teaspoon salt
6 tablespoons (¾ stick) cold unsalted butter, cut up
1 large egg, at room temperature
½ cup buttermilk
½ cup packed dried currants or raisins
½ cup dried tart or bing cherries (or use all currants, or seedless gold or black raisins)

FOR THE GLAZE

2 tablespoons buttermilk
2 teaspoons granulated sugar

1 Position a rack in the center of the oven and preheat it to 425°F. Cover the baking sheet with parchment or wax paper.
2 In the workbowl of a food processor, combine the flour, sugar, baking powder, baking soda, and salt. Pulse twice just to combine. Add the butter and pulse ten to twelve times, just until the butter forms pea-size pieces. In a cup, lightly beat together the egg and buttermilk, then pour it into the processor, add the fruit, and pulse four to six times, only to combine. Don't overwork the batter or the scones will be tough instead of tender.
3 Remove the workbowl. Use a flexible spatula to scoop out the thick, sticky batter, placing eight irregular mounds on the prepared sheet. In a cup, stir together the glaze ingredients, then paint it on scones with a pastry brush. Bake 10 to 12 minutes, until golden brown. Cool the scones on a wire rack

The Family Baker, by Susan Purdy

1.5 AMCO ODD-SIZE MEASURING CUPS

Sure, you could make do with a basic measuring set of ¼-, ⅓-, ½-, and 1-cup capacities and continue to add up fractions in your head, but why not indulge in an additional trio of handy odd-size measuring cups like this one that includes ⅔-, ¾-, and 1½-cup sizes. This set is sister to the Amco standard set and is made with the same commercial-quality stainless steel, clear markings, and long, unbreakable handles. Unfortunately, though, you can't nest both sets together for efficient storage; the ½-cup measure does not fit inside the ⅔-cup size.

1.6 CATAMOUNT MEASURE–BATTER BOWL

Made from borosilicate glass, the same material used for those beakers that endured your high school chemistry experiments, this crystal clear, ultralight 6-cup measuring utensil is ovenproof, microwave safe, and dishwasher friendly, like the venerable Pyrex. It also displays the list of ½- and ⅓-cup increments, fluid ounces, and milliliter measurements. But this measure offers one advantage the classic cup doesn't: it can be used on the stovetop to melt or heat ingredients. (NOTE: On electric ranges, it is best to use a heat diffuser between the element and the glassware.) This flameproof feature, combined with its oversize capacity, allows you to melt, measure, and mix certain recipes all in this one vessel. We made a batch of brownies in it and didn't dirty another bowl. Its light weight and big size also make it great for watering houseplants.

1.7 PYREX STACKABLE MEASURING CUP SET

The ubiquitous Pyrex measuring pitcher for liquid ingredients is to measuring what the wooden spoon is to stirring: timeless, practical, and essential. Made of Corning's thick, ovenproof glass, this archetypal measuring cup is hard to break and easy to clean, and its large, bright-red markings are a cinch to read. Shown here in a family of three, holding 4 cups, 2 cups, and 1 cup, each measure gives a scale with ½- and ⅓-cup increments, fluid ounces, and a ladderlike display of metric milliliter capacities on the opposite side.

1.8 EMSA PERFECT BEAKER

This model belongs as much in the classroom as in the kitchen, for it is a veritable billboard of measurement scales, including tablespoons, teaspoons, ounces, pints, cups, and milliliters. Imprinted with black number markings, this vaselike plastic beaker is an ideal tool for demonstrating that 1 cup equals ½ a pint, 16 tablespoons, 8 ounces, or 48 teaspoons! Beyond its instructional value, we like this unbreakable 2-cup capacity measure because it allows you to perform the timesaving trick of combining quantities all in one vessel. For example, a salad dressing that combines ⅓ cup peanut oil, 2 tablespoons sesame oil, ¼ cup rice vinegar, and 2 tablespoons soy sauce can be measured one ingredient after another in this beaker—no fussing with tablespoon measures and different-size cups. What's more, the Frieling model comes with a tight-fitting plastic lid, so you can also shake and store mixtures in it.

FANNIE FARMER'S INFLUENCE ON MEASURING
⚜ MARION CUNNINGHAM ⚜

Home cooks owe a debt to Fannie Farmer. She was a passionate cook with a fine palate (she asked every student who had completed a dish to taste and tell her if it could be improved). She was also committed to the new field of domestic science. Her biographers wrote of her plainness, but when teaching she had a great charisma that made her the most popular cooking teacher of her day.

Her greatest achievement was the systemization of recipes, converting measurements that had commonly been expressed in terms like "hazelnut-size," "a wine glass," or "a few handfuls" to calibrated spoons and cups. She taught that successfully replicating a recipe meant measuring each ingredient exactly.

Born in Boston in 1857, Fannie Merritt Farmer might have become a schoolteacher like her three younger sisters but for a paralyzing illness, probably polio, that prevented her from completing her education. She recovered with a limp and began doing domestic work, including baking, for which she had a talent. She had just turned thirty when her parents sent her to Mrs. Lincoln's Cooking School in Boston. She eventually became its director. Her first cookbook, written in 1896, was a perennial best-seller, second only to *The Joy of Cooking*.

As the "Mother of Level Measurements" she influenced every succeeding generation of American cooks, who wouldn't be able to function without her accomplishment, especially when baking. But fine cooks also know that her other attributes—passion and a fine palate—can often do more for a recipe than a perfectly measured spoonful of salt.

1.9 KITCHENART ADJUSTABLE TABLESPOON

Challenging the traditional concept of individual size-specific measuring spoons, we have this all-in-one gadget that is actually a sensible means of measurement. It is a 6"-long narrow plastic scoop, into which has been set a sliding barrier that works like a dam. In the middle of the handle is a scale of five measure markings, from 1 teaspoon incrementally up to 1 tablespoon (with metric equivalents), along which you set the slide depending on the quantity desired. What we like best about this system is that it allows for a quick, accurate measurement of odd-size amounts such as 1½, 2, or 2½ teaspoons. Plus, the 1¼" width of the scoop fits inside any spice jar that accommodates a standard teaspoon. The company also makes an adjustable teaspoon that works by the same mechanism. Both snap apart for easy cleaning and are dishwasher safe.

1.10 ENDURANCE HANDY SCOOPS

These shovel-like implements rest inside canisters of flour, sugar, and grain where they are used to gather

heaping amounts of dry ingredients as needed. Though not meant to be used as a precise measuring device, their sizes approximate 1 cup, ½ cup, and ¼ cup. If you're a muffin maker, you may want to keep an extra set handy, as the smallest scoop will measure just enough batter to fill a mini-muffin cup, the medium size will fill a standard muffin cup, and the large scoop holds the amount of batter for one of those Texas-size muffins. They are well constructed of 18/8 stainless steel and are dishwasher safe.

SCALES & BALANCES

MEASURING BY WEIGHT is both more exact and more sensible than measuring by volume or number. "Take two eggs": a superficially precise instruction, but one that is dependent on the highly variable size of eggs. As for a cup measure, it can vary remarkably depending on the way in which the flour is placed in the cup: was it sifted first, until airy and light, or was it compacted in the canister and lifted into the cup in near-solid spoonfuls? In contrast, a given number of grams of flour or salt will always yield the same amount.

In European recipes, as well as in most professional chef's recipes, the ingredients are listed by weight in grams if they are solids, or in liters if they are liquids. Opened at random, a French cookbook in our office calls for 200 grams of butter and 4 deciliters of cognac. With one of the American- and metric-marked measuring pitchers you'd have no trouble measuring the cognac, but if you don't own a scale with metric markings, you will have a problem with the butter.

Of course, there are conversion tables available in cookbooks, and they give you approximate equivalents so that you can cope with a recipe; they can tell you, for example, that 100 grams of flour will measure ⅔ of a U.S. cup. But if you think that you might be using international cookbooks, you'd be wise to invest in a good kitchen scale with metric markings. You may consider eventually converting all your American recipes to weight to achieve more consistent results and to save yourself time. As you prepare a favorite recipe by

volume, simply jot down the weight equivalent for future use. This is particularly helpful for bakers.

Kitchen scales fall into two categories—mechanical and electronic. The most common form of mechanical scale measures weight using a spring. An ingredient is placed on the scale's holding tray, and the holding tray presses down on the spring, which is attached to a dial that moves in response to the spring's compression and indicates the weight of the item on the tray. A second type of mechanical scale is the balance. A horizontal beam sits over a central support, with a pan at each end. The ingredient is placed in one pan, and weights are placed in the other. When the beam is horizontal the weight of the ingredient is read off the measuring face. This system has been in use for more than five thousand years but it is inconvenient and time consuming. And if you lose any of the measuring weights, you're in big trouble. A third form of mechanical scale is known as a "beam balance." It works on the same principle as the scale in a doctor's office. You simply slide the small weights across the beam and read the measure.

An electronic scale has a base plate that is locked in place and electrically connected to a second plate that sits above the base plate at a fixed distance. When an ingredient (or bowl) is placed on the weighing platform, the internal base plate begins to measure the pressure being applied to it. It converts the pressure into a digital signal, which is displayed as a numerical measurement of weight.

WHAT TO LOOK FOR

The criteria for the selection of a scale, either mechanical or electronic, are the same:

- Will the scale be able to hold all of the food you want to weigh?
- Will it be large enough to hold the bowl you do your preparation in?
- Will it measure with maximum accuracy?
- Can you read the display easily?
- Will it convert from the American system to the metric system?
- Does it measure in units small enough or large enough to meet your needs?
- Is it easy to store and clean?

In addition, you may want a tare feature that allows you to reset the scale to zero while ingredients are still in the bowl or on the tray. With this option you can place an ingredient into the bowl, check its weight, zero the scale, add the next ingredient, check its weight, and so on; all the ingredients are added to the same bowl, yet the weight of each is individually measured. (However, if you put too much of an ingredient into the bowl and need to take some out you may find that the foods have mixed together, making correction difficult.) Good scales should also have an overload protection to safeguard the mechanism if the user exceeds the maximum capacity. Scales without it will become inaccurate. Electronic scales should have an automatic shutoff in order to conserve the battery.

Mechanical scales often have a dial face with lines that are tightly spaced and difficult to read when it comes to small amounts. They also tend to be less accurate, but they can measure weights up to 25 pounds and don't require batteries. In the end, however, we weigh in on the side of electronic scales; they're easier to read, better for measuring smaller amounts, more accurate, and more compact.

1.11 SOEHNLE VITA SCALE

Leave it to the Europeans, who have always measured ingredients by weight, to design a superb electronic kitchen scale. This Swiss-made model has every important feature we look for: big capacity (11 pounds/ 5 kilograms); both American- and metric-system measurements; small increments (0.1 ounces/2 grams); a high degree of accuracy; a large, dishwasher-safe mixing bowl; a tare function that allows you to "add-and-weigh" ingredients; an automatic shutoff that conserves the battery; a display indicating when the battery needs to be replaced; an easy-to-use single-press bar design rather than multiple buttons; and the ability to be stored neatly, because the scale fits inside the bowl. Our only gripe with this otherwise perfect model is its relatively small numerical display. Bigger *is* better, at least when it comes to reading numbers. Requires a 9-volt battery.

1.12 SALTER BAKER'S DREAM SCALE

The sleek, compact design of this model belies its generous capacity— 11 pounds/5 kilograms, in ¼-ounce/5- gram increments—which means you can weigh ingredients as large as a leg of lamb or as small as a square of chocolate. The scale's wide platform supports any size mixing bowl. We also give this model high marks for accuracy: a big, easy-to-read display; a kilogram-pound conversion button; a durable body that can be stored flat or on end; the tare function; and a very thoughtful automatic shutoff feature that works either when zero has been displayed for 1 minute or when the same weight has appeared on the display for 5 minutes. (Most other scales shut off after a minute or so—invariably while you're in the middle of a recipe.) We chose to ignore the Baker's Dream's special milliliter–fluid ounce button and corresponding hype for measuring fluid ounces and instead simply used the kilogram-pound button for weighing everything—liquid or solid. (An ounce of weight, after all, is an ounce—right?) Do, however, note the accompanying conversion chart that translates the volume of many standard ingredients into weight in ounces. This scale comes with a lithium battery.

1.13 PELOUZE SCALE

Designed for food service portion control, this basic spring scale is not too pretty, but it is dependable, maintenance free, easy to read, and built for long life and accuracy in weighing up to 5 pounds (2.27 kilograms). It reads in ½-ounce and 10-gram increments, with a bright red pointer and well-spaced lines. To offset the weight of a bowl or plate, or to "add-and-weigh" ingredients, the dial rotates clockwise so the pointer can be repeatedly lined up with zero. To maintain the precision of this instrument it's important not to *drop* loads onto the weighing platform, but rather to *place* them on the scale.

1.14 COMPONENT DESIGN SCALEMAN

At first glance, we nearly rejected this model because it has such a puny, straight-sided bowl—not easy to empty or clean and certainly not

---

POUND CAKE

9–10"/23–25cm cake

In old-fashioned recipes for pound cake, the eggs were used as weights on one side of the scale and balanced with equal weights of butter, sugar, and flour. The most familiar version is flavored simply with vanilla, orange-flower water, or grated orange or lemon zest. Rich but light, with outstanding flavor when butter is used, pound cake is popular in many countries. In France you will find *quatre quarts*, in Germany *sandkuchen*, in Finland *murokakku*, and in Britain Madeira cake (which does not contain Madeira but is intended as an accompaniment to it).

Variations of pound-cake mixtures include spiced cakes such as caraway-seed cake, American antebellum cake with allspice and cloves, and Whitby nun's cake with rose water and spices.

A French variation of pound cake includes fresh fruit such as strawberries or pitted cherries; the cake will need a few more minutes' baking time.

FOR THE CAKE
2 cups/250 grams flour
1 tablespoon baking powder
pinch of salt
1 cup/250 grams unsalted butter
1¼ cups/250 grams sugar
4 eggs
1 teaspoon vanilla extract or grated zest of 1 lemon or 1 orange

FOR THE TOPPING:
confectioners' sugar or sugar glaze made with ½ cup/100 gram confectioners' sugar and 5-6 tablespoons/ 70-90 milliliters water, lemon, or orange juice

9–10-inch/23-25 centimeter round or springform pan

1 Grease the pan and line the base with paper. Grease the paper and coat it with flour and sugar. Heat the oven to 350°F/175°C. Sift the flour with the baking powder and salt.
2 Cream the butter and sugar. Beat in the eggs one by one, beating thoroughly after each addition. Beat in the flavoring. Fold the flour mixture into the batter in three batches, then spoon the batter into the prepared pan.
3 Bake the cake in the preheated oven for 40 to 50 minutes or until the cake tests done. Transfer the cake to a rack to cool.
4 Shortly before serving, sprinkle the cake with confectioners' sugar or top it with sugar glaze.

La Varenne Pratique, by Anne Willan

---

roomy enough for piling a batch of ingredients (though it does have 10-pound measuring capacity!). But since you can always substitute your own bowl, we gave this scale a second chance and discovered that it has all the likable functions of an electronic scale plus two unique features not seen in the other nonprofessional kitchen scales. One is a plug for a 9-volt DC adapter, so you have the choice of plugging into the nearest outlet or operating under battery power. (Be advised, though, that neither the adapter nor the battery is included with the scale.) Second, the

Scaleman has a "Target Monitoring" function that allows you to preset a target weight for your ingredients and then sounds an alarm (three beeps) when the amount you've added reaches this target, the advantage being that you don't have to continuously monitor the display. It's quite a useful function if you're scaling dough, assembling multiple portions, or dividing up bulk food from a warehouse club. You could, for instance, purchase a 5-pound bag of dry pasta and easily weigh out 1-pound portions without even glancing at the display.

1.15 EKS MECHANICAL SCALE

Right off, we appreciated that the measuring base and needle, which work in tandem, were tightly fitted so that even with a little jiggle the needle kept its reading. Next, we found it to be highly accurate as well as easy to read, even at low increments. Add to these fine features the scale's hefty 11-pound/5-kilogram capacity, its tare function, plus an extra-large mixing bowl that the scale fits into for storage, and you'll know why we think this one really measures up.

1.16 PELOUZE BAKER'S SCALE

This item from Pelouze is the Rolls-Royce of beam-balance scales—you may, in fact, need to store this one in your garage since it takes up as much counter space as a microwave. The scale mechanism is 20″ long, and with its capacious measuring trough in place, the whole affair can be about 2′ long and 16″ deep. Yes, it's big, but it's also exquisitely made with a glossy enameled base and sparkling stainless steel plat-forms that silently, gracefully "float" in midair when you've achieved match-

ing weights. (That's a lovely visual metaphor about things in harmony.) To work this machine as the professional baker would, you place the measuring vessel on the left side and its stainless steel counterweight on the right; the scale should be balanced at zero. You can also forego the vessel and counterweight and weigh directly on the stainless steel plates. To measure an ingredient, tell the scale the desired weight by placing the appropriate cast-iron weights (4-, 2-, and 1-pounders come with the scale—don't lose them!) on the right platform and/or by sliding another weight that moves across a bar notched with ¼-pound increments up to 1 pound. (You can weigh up to 8 pounds, in ¼-pound increments, using all these weights.) Now fill the vessel with your ingredient, watching intently for the moment when the right platform ascends and the left one descends as they seek to balance. There's your measure.

1.17 SALTER ANTIQUE SCALE

If you're the low-tech sort who values old-fashioned good looks over modern practicality, this reproduction antique balance scale may be just the thing. Part of the family of antique-style products from Salter, an English company, this cast-metal scale, with its accompanying solid brass scoop, allows you to weigh up to 1¾ pounds using a collection of seven solid brass weights (they're handsome enough to display along with your scale). Primitive as it appears, we found the scale to be remarkably sensitive and accurate—

"Actually, he's not so bad, considering that he's recipe-dependent."

even to ¼ ounce. The obvious disadvantage of this scale is that you cannot weigh anything quickly. If you misplace any of the weights, additional ones can be purchased separately.

> The accepted way to test the heat of an oven was to thrust in the hand and count seconds till one had to pull it out with a faint scream.
>
> —J. C. FURNAS

THERMOMETERS

TEMPERATURE IN COOKING brings to mind ovens and freezers, but room temperature is also important—just try making a pastry crust or chocolate curls on a hot summer day—although there is not much that we can do to change it. As the comedian Steven Wright says, "Whatever the temperature of the room is, it's always room temperature." On the other hand, there is a lot that we can do about the temperature of the oven, freezer, and food. We can heat and chill them for the best effect, but in order to do so we need to be able to detect just how hot or cold they are.

Professional chefs often carry a penlike instant thermometer, ready to be whipped out at any moment to get an immediate reading of the temperature of a food. The home cook doesn't need to be so vigilant, but the success of certain recipes depends on the food's reaching and maintaining the correct temperature. Of course, there are still the subjective tests, like flicking drops of water onto a griddle to see if it is hot enough, or watching to see when the butter foam subsides in a frying pan to indicate the right moment for the food to be added. Fortunately, we no longer need to test an oven by putting a piece of paper in and watching to see how long it takes to brown, or check what stage the candy has reached by dropping sugar syrup into cold water and then judging the quality of the ball that forms. It is far better to have at your disposal a good set of cooking thermometers.

OVEN THERMOMETERS

No matter how good your oven is, we are willing to bet that the temperature that you set it for is not the temperature that it actually reaches. Considering how important oven temperature is to the success of your cooking, and especially your baking, it's an outrageous situation. You can set the controls at 350°F or 500°F, but there is no way to be sure your oven is actually reaching and holding the temperature you want unless you test the interior space. One option is to have the oven professionally tested and calibrated. We suggest that instead you buy a good oven thermometer and put it into your heated oven, moving it through the four quadrants of each rack level so that you can identify the hot spots. Then adjust subsequent oven settings to achieve the heat that you actually want.

Although they function well, mercury thermometers for oven use are becoming increasingly rare, and we do not recommend thermometers made with mercury substitutes (see item 1.19). Now the most common oven thermometers function through the action of a spring made of two different metals that expand at variable rates with the application of heat. As the spring heats up, it moves an attached pointer around the face of the thermometer dial to indicate the temperature. All oven thermometers must respond quickly to changes in temperature, but not so quickly that opening the oven door changes the reading before you note it. They must also be safely encased in a metal form and sit securely on the rack.

1.18 PYREX OVEN THERMOMETER

The top of the line in spring-action oven thermometers, this gleaming, heavy-duty stainless steel model sits or hangs securely on your oven rack and registers temperatures from 100°F to 600°F. The bright-red pointer is well fitted, so it doesn't shake or rattle when tapped. White numbers against a black background make for high contrast that's easy to read, even at the back of the oven. We were impressed that it reacted to heat almost instantly; other spring thermometers seem to take some time to warm up. While this is an excellent thermometer, it is also a large one—more than 3″ wide, 4″ high, and 1½″ deep, it takes up more oven space than most. The tempered glass lens should be hand washed.

1.19 COMPONENT DESIGN BULB-TYPE MERCURY THERMOMETER

Take a good look at this oven thermometer, for soon it will be practically extinct—a veritable dinosaur in the world of culinary equipment. An excellent product that works on the steadfast principle of mercury rising in a glass tube when heated, this unerring oven thermometer is the most accurate type made. Ironically, it is precisely this reliable component—mercury—that has proved to be the thermometer's downfall. Mercury, we now know, is a highly toxic liquid, and there are many government regulations covering its use. A number of leading manufacturers feel that as a result of these regulations it is no longer practical to market products containing mercury to the consumer and are therefore converting their mercury tubes to use nonmercury liquids. In our experience with these substitutes, however, the liquid tends to separate in the tube after several uses, making the device difficult to read.

REFRIGERATOR & FREEZER THERMOMETERS

Yes, you do need a freezer thermometer. Not because you will get food poisoning if you don't have one: few bacteria grow below 20°F, and almost none below 10°F. And not for the rare occasions when the power goes out for more than 36 hours: there's not much point in knowing just how high the temperature has risen when the ice cream is lying all over the floor of the freezer and the turkey doesn't resist the pressure of a probing finger. (In such cases your best bet is to leave the freezer closed as long as the power is off, keeping its contents as cold as possible—don't even look inside until the motor is humming again.) The reason you need a freezer thermometer is because the quality of frozen food is affected enormously by the temperature at which it has been held.

Preserving techniques are only as good as the palatability of the end product. There isn't much point to having a freezer if it doesn't give you food that you will be happy eating. Both nutrients and aesthetics are best preserved when the freezer temperature is kept near 0°F, or even below. Above 4°F or so, enzyme action within the frozen food will alter its flavor, color, and texture.

Commercial standards require that a freezer be kept within a range of no more than 2°F above or below zero; any higher and the quality, although not the safety, of the food is threatened. A piece of meat or a package of strawberries held for a year at zero will be of the same quality as food stored for five months at 5°F, for one month at 15°F, and for one week at 25°F. Note that at each of these temperatures the food will be hard-frozen to the touch, but just being frozen isn't good enough. That's why your refrigerator ice-cube compartment isn't cold enough to ensure good-quality frozen food.

TESTING THE ACCURACY OF YOUR THERMOMETER

In areas considered to be at sea level, water boils at 212°F. You can test your thermometer by putting the probe into boiling water to see that it registers 212°F. If you're cooking at a higher altitude, deduct 1°F from the 212°F for every 500 feet above sea level. For instance, at 2,000 feet above sea level water boils at 208°F. If your thermometer can be adjusted, make the adjustment. If your thermometer does not have an adjustment feature, remember what allowance to make for its error when next you use it. If the test shows that the thermometer is off—that it registers 215°F, for example, instead of 212°F—and the thermometer is not adjustable, then add 3° to every temperature given in the recipe.

Thermometers can also be tested with a second system that works at any altitude. Fill a cup with crushed ice, add cold water until the ice is just covered, and wait 5 minutes. The water and ice mixture will reach a temperature of 32°F. Stir the solution and place your thermometer in the ice water for 30 seconds. Do not let it touch the walls of the container. If the thermometer is accurate you will get a reading of 32°F.

Get yourself a freezer thermometer and use it. Remember that the temperature will go up in the freezer when a lot of unfrozen food is first added. Also remember that, in accordance with the rule that warm air rises, you will get a higher reading near the top of the freezer compartment than near the bottom, and it will be warmer near the door of an upright freezer than toward the back. Freezer burn, by the way, is another matter and rather a misnomer, being a result of dehydration of the food's surface due to poor wrapping in frost-free units with blowers, rather than of incorrect temperature.

Since refrigerated food should be held at less than 41°F, it's also a good idea to have a thermometer in your refrigerator. For refrigerator and freezer thermometers, fog- and frost-free dial faces are preferred.

1.20 SUNBEAM LARGE-FACE REFRIGERATOR-FREEZER THERMOMETER

Big and bold-faced, this thermometer won't get lost behind the milk cartons and marmalade jars. Its 3"-wide, color-keyed dial is practically a poster for food safety, with a DEEP FREEZE zone from 0°F to -30°F indicated by shades of blue, a FOOD zone from 32°F to 40°F in red, and a SPOILAGE zone, 50°F to 90°F, in deepening hues of orange. While the colors make it instantly readable, we question the choice of red for the food zone. Doesn't red universally signal a warning? Wouldn't it make great sense to have this safe refrigerator temperature zone indicated by, say, a bright green? Apart from this minor design flaw, the model is exemplary: stainless steel construction, established accuracy, a hang-or-stand feature, and oversized numbers.

1.21 TAYLOR REFRIGERATOR-FREEZER DIAL THERMOMETER

What makes this diminutive thermometer so appealing is its utter simplicity. Like a basic black dress, this model is reliable and always appropriate. The 2½" dial registers from -20°F to 60°F, and its teal-and-white face indicates ideal refrigerator and freezer temperatures with two simple pie-slice designs. Mounted on a stainless steel base with an appendage that can swivel up or down for hanging or standing, this gauge is a classic you can count on.

HOW THERMOMETERS WORK

The most useful food thermometers for the home cook are those designed for instant readings. Inserted into almost any food, they will display the internal temperature in seconds. Instant-read thermometers fall into two groups: dial and digital.

A dial thermometer contains a coil that is made from two metals with different rates of expansion that have been bonded together. The coil is connected to the dial on the thermometer face. When the thermometer is inserted into a food the expanding metals cause the pointer to turn to the appropriate temperature number on the dial.

Most digital instant-read thermometers use a metal-oxide semiconductor. The electronic resistance decreases as the temperature increases, and the shifting resistance is registered on a microprocessor that reports the change as a number on a liquid crystal display. Some digital thermometers weld together two wires, each made from a different metal, to form a "hot junction." There is a second junction at the meter called the "cold junction." The difference between the temperature at the hot junction and the cold junction alters the voltage in the unit, which is measured by a microprocessor and presented as a number on the display. Thermometers that use hot and cold junctions can cover an extremely wide range of temperatures. Professionals often favor them because the probes can be very thin. The probe can also be part of an interchangeable set (including meat, grill, oven, and surface probes) that mount onto a single meter.

FOOD THERMOMETERS

Once we have tested and corrected the temperature of the oven, the refrigerator, and the freezer, we then turn to the point of the whole thing—the internal temperature of the food. In testing food temperature, thermometers all work on the same principle: the probe of the thermometer is placed into the food and a reading is taken from the center. The tip of the thermometer must not touch a bone or a pocket of fat, either of which will give a distorted reading. The pointed probe should not have to be forced into place. Thermometers are sensitive over a wide range of temperatures, according to their purpose: a dough thermometer registers only up to 120°F, but a deep-frying thermometer gives readings up to 460°F. It is essential that the face of the thermometer be particularly easy to read.

INSTANT-READ THERMOMETERS

Rare meat, like raw meat, is soft to the touch, while well-done meat is firm; between the two there is a range of resistance that is easily read by those with tactile sensitivity and long experience. They simply give the food a poke with their finger to determine the degree of doneness. Some cooks judge the doneness of meat by making a cut into it and checking the color of the juices and the inside flesh. A rare roast will produce red juices, a medium roast will give pink juices, and a well-done roast will yield colorless ones. If you don't want to risk losing moisture from the meat with repeated cuts, it may be better to time your roasts according to a chart in a cookbook, which will tell you the number of minutes per pound that each type of meat requires. Use the minimum figure for the degree of doneness you want in a preheated oven with a trusted temperature. Near the end of the cooking time—not the beginning—place the thermometer into the meat to check the temperature in the center. You can always leave a roast in the oven a little longer if it is underdone, but if it has become overcooked, there's no way to correct it.

It is not a good idea to stick a one-piece thermometer into a cold rib roast and leave it there for hours in the oven. For one thing, it will conduct heat rapidly to the center of the roast, causing it to cook unevenly in that spot; for another, it will leave an open hole out of which the juices will bleed.

When you test the temperature of meat, take into account the fact that the internal temperature of a roast can rise 10°F while it sits out of the oven for 15 to 20 minutes, resting and firming up for the carver's knife. Take the meat out of the oven before it reaches the temperature you want and let it "coast" to doneness. Malcolm Douglas, the chief engineer at Taylor Instruments, measures with both time and temperature. He uses a timer to put him near the done stage before he starts measuring internal meat temperatures, thereby reducing the number of times he needs to open the oven or puncture the food on a grill. Finally, when using recipes, regard the recommended readings with skepticism; the cookbook author's rare may not be your rare or that of our experts, who tend to come down on the side of lower "done" readings.

WHAT TO LOOK FOR

The primary selection criteria for instant-read food thermometers are: length of the stem, which controls your ability to reach the center of the food you are measuring; placement of the sensor in the stem; readability of the display; the speed at which the temperature is registered; the accuracy of the reading; and the temperature range that the model covers.

Dial models usually have a smaller temperature range than digital units because the small display faces on the dials are harder to read over a wider range. Also, dial thermometers have sensors that start at the tip and run into the probe for about 1½". For an accurate reading, you must insert them far enough into the food to cover the entire coil. If you only use your thermometer on large foods like a turkey there's no problem, but if you are checking on a shallow liquid like a baby's formula you've got trouble.

Digital thermometers have sensors that are small—within ¼" of the tip. This makes them extremely accurate at measuring shallow liquids and thin foods. They also cover a wide range of temperatures. But digitals run on batteries, which can fail at the most frustrating moments. Models that can be shut off when not in use are best, and it's helpful when the type of battery needed is easily purchased.

1.22 THERMOWORKS SUPERFAST THERMAPEN

With a vast range of temperature detection (-50°F to 572°F) and accuracy within ± 1 percent, this English import is one of the most capable tools for home thermometry. Use it to measure the internal temperature of just about anything—water for yeast, oil for deep-frying, thin fish fillets, thick roasts, sauces, barbecues, baby bottles, and more. You need only insert the tip of the sharp stainless steel probe for a fast read (4 seconds, in fact) from a giant-size digital display. When not in use, the probe folds back (automatically turning off the thermometer) and locks in place for safe storage. The odd-size 12-volt battery that is included with the Thermapen is a standard camera battery and widely available; the display will illuminate LO BAT when it needs changing. Another notable feature: every Thermapen comes with a hand-signed and dated certificate of calibration to ensure that each one leaves the factory in mint condition.

1.23 COOPER PROFESSIONAL DIGITAL TEST THERMOMETER

There is little variation among most pocket-clip digital thermometers in style or function. All have a lollipop shape that consists of a 5"-long metal stem attached to a plastic knob that holds the battery, brains, and digital display of the thermometer. The stem slides into a plastic sheath for storage, and the clip includes a loop at the end through which you can slide the thermometer and employ the sheath as a handle. When it comes to divining the temperature of your food, most of these digital look-alikes are reliable and accurate—assuming their battery is fully juiced. However, we chose this model from the crowded lot for several reasons: it reads temperatures from -40°F to 450°F (most models only go as high as 300°F), so it can also be used for deep-fry oil testing; it has a rapid response, even when its instant-update button is not used; it has an automatic shutoff; and, last but not least, changing the battery does not require special tools or extraordinary patience.

THE SAFETY VS. SUCCULENCE DEBATE
❧ MARION NESTLE & CAROL GUBER ❧

Cooking revolutionized eating, not only from the standpoint of taste, but also in terms of safety, since heat kills most of the harmful organisms that get into food. But when it comes to meat, especially red meat like beef, the question is: How much heat is needed?

The government issues clear food-safety guidelines on the subject, which recommend that beef roasts and steaks be cooked to 145°F internally for medium rare, 160°F for medium, and a whopping 170°F for well done. The same would apply to lamb or buffalo. Notice that rare is not even mentioned. The professional chefs we know are horrified at the thought of ever cooking a tenderloin to even the lowest of these temperatures. They know that good meat tastes best, is juicier, and has a better texture when the inside is rosy and cooked no higher than 135°F. Some chefs and home cooks would even opt for 10°F to 15°F less.

Finer cuts of meat that do not require slow, moist cooking to break down tough connective tissues taste best when they are cooked medium or less. They should be seared at high temperature so the meat is thoroughly cooked on the outside to a depth of about ¼". The inside can be less well done. Our experience has shown that this method of cooking intact cuts of meat, like steaks and legs of lamb, does not pose safety problems. Unless the meat has been pierced or chopped, processes that can introduce unwanted microbes into the otherwise sterile interior, any bacteria will remain on the outside of the meat and be destroyed by searing.

Hamburger, of course, is another matter. The chopping mixes any bacteria, and especially dangerous organisms like *E. coli*, throughout the meat and provides plenty of air to encourage growth. Government advice here is even more decisive: cook chopped meat to an internal temperature of 160°F. Actually, 155°F is enough, but this directive offers a margin of error. What if you don't want your hamburger so thoroughly cooked? You have to understand that you are taking a risk; we have no idea how serious, nor does anyone else. The choice is yours. But think twice before putting anyone else at risk, and never serve undercooked hamburger to small children, pregnant women, the elderly, or people with AIDS or weakened immune systems.

1.24 TAYLOR DIGITAL COOKING THERMOMETER-TIMER

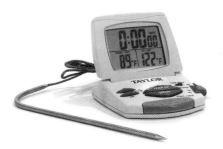

This feature-laden thermometer from Taylor lets you continuously monitor the internal temperature of your roasting meat or poultry, as well as program an alarm to ring when the food reaches the desired degree of doneness—all without ever opening the oven door. The thermometer works like this: The "command center" (i.e., the digital part) of this device sits or mounts outside the oven, attached to a thin, 36"-long metal wire that's fastened at the other end to a 7"-long L-shaped metal probe—that's the part you insert into the meat in the oven. In essence, you harpoon your food with the probe, close the oven door with the wire snaking out of it, and then wait for the moment the alarm says you've struck just the right temperature. The whole setup can be a bit cumbersome, especially when it comes time to baste, and some of us romantic cooks are put off by the laboratory-like appearance, but there's no denying that this tech wonder removes all guesswork and can help ensure perfect roasts every time. You can also use it as an ordinary timer; the display is large and easy to read. We chose this model over others because it has an on/off switch, bigger push buttons, and a temperature guide printed on the back. One precaution: the metal cord and probe should not be used when the oven temperature is higher than 392°F.

1.25 POLDER PREPROGRAMMED COOKING THERMOMETER

Built with a digital unit, thin metal wire, and attached probe that stays in the food during cooking, this sleek thermometer has an added convenience: it allows you to scroll through a menu to select beef, lamb, veal, pork, turkey, or chicken, and then to choose rare, medium rare, medium, or well done. Because it is preprogrammed based on the type of meat and degree of doneness, it will display an "alert temp" (which the alarm will ultimately respond to) plus the "cooking temp" that registers the changing internal temperature of the food. Polder programs this model using the doneness temperatures recommended by the USDA, but you can easily alter these preset options according to your own tastes by changing its memory. Note that this model has no countdown timer function.

1.26 ACU-RITE SURE-GRIP INSTANT-READ THERMOMETER

Like nearly all dial-type instant-read thermometers, this model's temperature reading was off by a few degrees when we subjected it to the boiling-water test. It was redeemed, however, by the fact that it can be easily recalibrated at home with a simple adjustment—the instructions are on the packaging—so that it gives perfect readings thereafter. (Some other dial thermometers can be adjusted too, though, curiously, not all give instructions for doing so.) The most outstanding feature of this model is its size—at 12" long it's more than twice the size of most instant-read thermometers, and it certainly won't fit in your pocket. Yet that's also why it has such likable parts: a large, easy-to-read dial; a thick grip that keeps hands far away from the hot probe; a handy display of recommended temperatures for meats and poultry on the dial; and a protective sheath. With a range from 0°F to 220°F, this mechanical thermometer is suitable for most of what you need to do in the kitchen.

1.27 COOPER COMMERCIAL TEST THERMOMETER

It's small, it's affordable, and it does the job. This model is a midget (5½") compared to the Acu-Rite, but it has the same basic ability: to register temperatures in the 0°F to 220°F range. Of course, it's not as easy to read or handle as the larger gadget, but you can store this thermometer anywhere or clip it conveniently on your buttonhole to keep it handy. We also favor the two tiny dimples etched into its metal probe that let the user know just how far the probe must be inserted (about 1¾") to get an accurate reading. Be sure to test its accuracy before using—recalibration instructions are on the package.

1.28 MAVERICK REDICHEK THERMOMETER

The RediChek is the closest thing to our idealized grill thermometer. It has a quick digital temperature readout and measures nearly 8″ long (as compared to the 5½″ size of most instant-reads). Its probe widens sharply after the first inch, however, giving it the potential to leave gaping holes in thick roasts and steaks, so use this thermometer only for less chunky cuts. The white Lexan body, designed so that you can use it with one hand, is easily cleaned.

1.29 COOPER NONCONTACT THERMOMETER

Until now, even the most experienced home cooks have had to rely on a bit of guesswork when it comes to preheating a grill pan or skillet so that a steak can be seared without sticking (about 450°F), or pancakes browned without burning (about 350°F). They rely on phenomena like "meat spattering briskly rather than hissing," or water "beading and skittering across the surface" to gauge whether a pan is ready—rough indicators at best that are not always reliable since they can occur at a fairly wide range of temperatures.

For cooks in search of thermal precision, the solution has arrived in the form of this slim, ergonomically designed device that feels and looks just like a TV remote except that it has one large red button rather than a constellation of buttons. When you aim this thermometer at your target and press a button, it instantly gives you the surface temperature of the object within the range of 0°F to 500°F. Equipped with a red laser that pinpoints exactly where you're aiming, the silent unit displays the temperature digitally and will hold the reading for 7 seconds after the button is pressed. Infrared magic is at

---

ROAST PORK LOIN

6 servings

Probably the most commonly used cut of pork is the loin. In U.S. parlance the loin is the stretch from the shoulder to the leg that takes in the ribs and the loin chops with the tenderloin. It is usually sold divided into the rib end; the center cut, which includes a small portion of the loin; and the loin end. You can also buy the entire loin. The roast may be bought boned and tied or left with the bones intact. In this case, the chine bone that runs the length of the loin should be removed or cut through to facilitate carving, and the roast should be trimmed of excess fat and securely tied.

5-pound pork loin, trimmed and tied
2 to 3 garlic cloves, peeled and cut
   into thin slivers
1 teaspoon dried thyme or
   summer savory
coarse (kosher) salt
freshly ground black pepper
12 small new potatoes, scraped
   or peeled
6 small carrots, scraped and whole, or
   3 large carrots, scraped and quartered
12 small white onions, peeled*
watercress for garnish

*If onions are dropped into boiling water for 20 seconds, their skins will slip off easily.

1 About 1 hour before roasting the pork, pierce the fat all over with the point of a small sharp knife and insert slivers of garlic into the holes. Rub the loin lightly with thyme or summer savory and then with coarse salt. Preheat the oven to 325°F.

2 Put the loin, fat side up, on a rack in a shallow roasting pan and roast at 325°F for 25 to 30 minutes per pound, about 2¼ to 2½ hours.

3 Parboil the potatoes, carrots, and onions for 5 minutes in salted water to cover (this softens them slightly, so they cook faster) and arrange them around the meat in the roasting pan for the last hour of roasting time. When you add the vegetables, baste them with the pan juices and sprinkle the loin with a little salt and pepper. Continue to roast the meat until the internal temperature reaches 165°F. Check 30 to 40 minutes after adding the vegetables to find how near the meat is to that mark, inserting the thermometer at the thickest part but not touching the bone.

4 When the meat is done, transfer it to a hot platter and let it rest in a warm place for 10 to 15 minutes before carving. Arrange the roasted vegetables around it and garnish with watercress.

5 Carve the roast downward, cutting between the bones. If the meat has been boned, cut in slices about ⅜″ thick. Skim the fat from the pan juices and serve them with the pork. A dish of sautéed, glazed apple rings is a perfect accompaniment. Wine for such a dish might be a chilled Alsatian Riesling.

James Beard's Theory and Practice of Good Cooking, by James Beard

work here, as optic sensors collect and focus the energy of your target while detectors translate it into an accurate temperature reading—accurate, that is, if the surface of your target is dark and nonreflective. Engineers at Cooper stress that shiny surfaces, like stainless steel pans, have a different "emissivity" than the dark, dull surfaces that this thermometer is programmed to read, and so it cannot be counted on to properly determine the temperature of bright reflective surfaces. Cast-iron skillets and grill pans are ideal.

Accuracy also depends on the distance between you and your target when you take the reading. The noncontact thermometer has a six to one reading ratio, meaning that if you're aiming from 6' away, the thermometer will collect thermal information from a 1' area. If your target is only 8" in size, you'll be getting energy readings from outside the target—which, of course, could make the temperature reading imprecise. Likewise, if you point from 6" away, then the thermometer reads only a 1" surface area, and that could be wrong if your target area is bigger. All of which is to say that users need to pay attention to size and distance before they press that big red button.

Testing pan heat is just one of the practical kitchen applications of this gadget; cooks can also use it to test hot spots in the oven and the temperature of refrigerated, frozen, or prepared foods. (Many large restaurants depend on infrared thermometers to ensure food safety, using them to monitor temperatures during receiving, storage, and preparation of ingredients.) It should be duly noted, however, that this highly specialized thermometer does not read internal temperatures. There is no way, for instance, that it can tell when your goose is cooked.

A NOTE ABOUT GRILL THERMOMETERS

In our opinion, the ideal grill thermometer would be an instant-read digital instrument with an illuminated temperature display and a longer-than-average probe. Being digital, it could be used to measure the internal temperature of thin cuts of meat—burgers, fish, chicken breast, steaks, etc.—that are common to grilling. Its illuminated display would be handy for all those cookouts that happen after dark (no searching for the flashlight to check the meat!), while the extra-long probe would keep hands far away from the intense, direct heat of the grill. According to our product research, such a commonsense thermometer does not yet exist. What's offered instead as "barbecue thermometers" are several kinds of oversize electronic gadgets that tell you when *they* think your meat is rare, medium, or well done, rather than telling you the internal temperature so you can decide for yourself—with the obvious problem being whether your idea of rare or medium is the same as the thermometer's. Moreover, if you're testing a particular piece of meat with one of these gadgets and it doesn't yet register done, how can you estimate how far from done the food is? Do you have to keep jabbing the meat every minute, each time losing flavorful juices? We say no thanks. We'll stick with the standard instant-read digitals.

CANDY, JELLY, & DEEP-FAT THERMOMETERS

Sugar changes its character when it is cooked. The basic aim in candy-making, jelly-making, and the production of certain frostings is to control the behavior of the sugar molecules. The old technique for measuring this involves dropping small amounts of the candy solution into a glass of cold water. Charts will tell you when the various temperatures have been reached, from the soft-ball stage to the hard-crack stage; but quite frankly this method is mostly of archaeological interest, now that there are good candy and jelly thermometers. Only when you can control the temperature of the solution can you make beautifully jelled jars of raspberry-plum jam, tins of chocolate-dipped pecan brittle; only then can you pull taffy, pour lollipops, and produce silken frostings that stand an inch deep on the top of a birthday cake.

Highly specialized techniques are involved here, with their own separate ranks of equipment and cookbooks, techniques that are all but impossible when you don't have the proper equipment and relatively simple when you do. Candy thermometers, like other thermometers, should be of the highest quality and easily read, should register with mercury or electronically, and should never be plunged into boiling syrup without a preliminary warming. A clip on the side of the thermometer should allow the sensor or mercury to be lowered into the boiling confection without touching the bottom of the pot.

The secret to deep-fat frying lies in preheating the oil to the proper temperature before adding the food; for this, a thermometer is essential. We recommend the liquid-in-glass models rather than the bimetal ones. Bimetallic deep-fat thermometers are often unable to monitor the rapid drop in temperature when food is added to the fat and the rapid return to the proper frying temperature. Deep-fat thermometers require very clear markings, sturdy construction, and a clip that holds safely to the side of the pan. And be careful: Hot fat and hot sugar are probably the most dangerous things in your kitchen.

1.30 TAYLOR CANDY-JELLY–DEEP-FRY MERCURY THERMOMETER

The basic design of candy–deep-fry thermometers has changed little over the years. Most brands are nearly identical to this one, consisting of a glass-tube thermometer that measures from 100°F to 400°F fastened to a flat, 12½"-long stainless steel frame; the frame holds the tip of the glass tube half an inch above the floor of any pan by means of a metal clip on the back that clamps on and adjusts to the height of your pan. The scales of these thermometers give markings for THREAD, SOFT BALL, HARD BALL, SOFT CRACK, and HARD CRACK stages of sugar cookery. (This model also gives markings for tempering chocolate.)

The one design feature that has recently changed in this grouping is that the once-standard column of mercury is being replaced by a blue-colored "petroleum-based mixture of mineral spirits" for reasons of liability, since uncontained mercury is toxic. In testing, we found that the new nonmercury mixture was not always accurate, and in one model the stuff separated within the tube. (Our engineer explained that this was because a bit of air had invaded the perfect vacuum of the tube during manufacture—not because the measuring mixture was faulty.) Still, if it's absolute accuracy you want, we recommend a mercury-filled device, such as this Taylor thermometer. We also found its bold, dark numbers and round (rather than beveled) glass tube easier to read.

1.31 MATFER CANDY THERMOMETER

Here's the thermometer you'll find in many professional pastry kitchens. Since it's European made, the temperature given is in Celsius (80°C to 200°C, which corresponds to about 176°F to 392°F), but the same is true of many classic pastry recipes, so it's a good choice for serious dessert makers. A large glass tube that tapers at the tip encloses a scale attached to a very slim glass column containing mercury. All this fragile hardware is positioned inside a strong stainless steel cage and fitted with small cork bumpers for protection against breakage. For cleaning, the glass thermometer insert and bumpers can be removed and the cage run through the dishwasher. To hang this apparatus on your pot or bowl, the company sells a separate metal bar that goes through the metal loop at the top of the thermometer and straddles the pot.

1.32 ACME CANDY–DEEP-FRY THERMOMETER

For the occasional user, this small (8"), simple glass thermometer is quite satisfactory. Its thick column of nontoxic, mercury-free liquid is easy to view, though the numbers (in Celsius and Fahrenheit) on its scale are smaller than we would like. On the back of its scale is a handy list of recommended temperatures for stages of sugar cookery and deep-fried foods. This model also has a sliding clip and is dishwasher safe. The one disadvantage is that this measuring tool is made of glass and therefore must be handled carefully. Likewise, cooks should be cautioned never to touch this or any hot glass thermometer with a damp cloth or pot holder; the steam created can crack the glass.

NO SMOKING IN THE KITCHEN

The oil or fat you choose for deep-frying should have a high smoking point. Olive oil smokes at a low temperature and is not suitable. The best oils for deep-frying are canola, corn, peanut, and safflower.

CHOCOLATE THERMOMETERS

To get the most intense flavor, the smoothest gloss, and the proper texture for molding or dipping, chocolate must be tempered, a process that consists of melting the chocolate and holding it at a specific temperature, adding additional chocolate, and then lowering the temperature to a precise point. Depending on the type of chocolate and the use to which it will be put, the desired temperature will fall in a range of 80°F to 120°F. The ideal chocolate thermometer will be easy to read, extremely sensitive, measure in single-degree units, and be held in a protective casing.

1.33 CORDON ROSE CHOCOLATE THERMOMETER

This highly specialized glass chocolate thermometer reads temperatures from 40°F to 130°F by means of a mercury column marked with single-degree units. Its scale is printed with well-spaced lines and numbers on either side so that it can be read either left- or right-handed. It reminds us of the old-fashioned thermometers that the school nurse inserted under your tongue and held there interminably, testing whether you were really sick or just trying to avoid the math exam. In fact, that's one of the tests we conducted to judge the accuracy of this tool; since we couldn't subject it to either the ice-slurry bath (32°F) or the boiling-water test (212°F), one of the testers took her own temperature. After several minutes under the tongue it clearly registered 98°F—close enough to the 98.6°F instant reading that the digital medical thermometer gave us. (By the way, this is not a recommendation to use such a glass thermometer for taking body temperatures at home since it is filled with potentially toxic mercury.)

TURNING A CHOCOLATE LEAF

Chocolate leaves, used as elegant dessert garnishes, are made by painting a thick layer of tempered chocolate onto the undersides of perfect leaves. Make sure that the leaves have not been sprayed with any pesticides and that they are nonpoisonous. (We know one cook, however, who threatens to make chocolate leaves from poison ivy and serve them with a sauce of calamine lotion.) Stop the chocolate just short of the leaves' edges or you will not be able to separate the two elements. Place the coated leaves on a foil- or parchment-lined baking sheet and let them rest in a cool room for 12 hours. After they've set, separate the chocolate leaves from the natural ones.

DOUGH THERMOMETERS

Live yeast fermenting in bread dough is extremely sensitive to temperature, and serious bread bakers' abilities to manage that yeast is a critical element of their skill. Great bakers measure the temperature of both the water and the dough, as well as the ambient temperature of the room prior to the dough's rising and baking. Controlling temperature and time are two of the primary tools in their struggle for consistently superior breads as opposed to lucky breaks. Their thermometers range from 10°F to 120°F.

1.34 MATFER THERMOMÈTRE BOULANGER

Imported from France, where a well-made, crusty baguette is considered one of life's necessities, this specialized dough thermometer reads temperatures from 0°C to 60°C (32°F to 140°F), with a particular mark on its scale at 18°C (64°F)—the ideal temperature for the slow fermentation of yeast. Professional French bread bakers are zealous in their effort to keep dough cool and allow a slow rise to give their bread its characteristic flavor and texture.

This thermometer can, of course, be used for other types of yeast dough, as well as for melting and tempering chocolate. The mercury-free glass column is protected inside a sturdy plastic sheath with openings at the bottom to expose the thermometer to the matter being tested. When necessary, the glass column can be removed to thoroughly clean the plastic covering. It should be washed by hand, never in a dishwasher.

SALOMETERS & HYDROMETERS

WHEN YOU TASTE lemonade to see if it is sweet enough, you are testing the density of the sugar solution. And when you sip a spoonful of broth from a pot before you season it, you are testing the density of the salt solution. In both of these cases, your testing apparatus is the set of taste buds on your tongue, an instrument sensitive enough to tell you whether the ratio of seasoning to liquid is correct. There are, however, occasions when density is important, not because of taste, but because it will have an effect on the quality of the finished product. Jellies, for example, contain sugar for sweetness, for its preservative qualities, and also because sugar can be essential to the formation of gel and the consequent firming of the jelly. A jam made with too little sugar will be soft, while one with a great oversupply of sugar will become either crystalline or syrupy. And sherbets and ices made with too much sugar will never freeze properly, no matter how heavenly they taste in liquid form. For more guaranteed results in sugar cookery, employ a hydrometer, or water measurer. Instead of measuring temperature, a hydrometer measures the amount of water in a solution in relation to the amount of sugar. It is measured on the Baumé scale (invented by the French chemist Antoine Baumé) with units that run from 0 to 40.

Tasting a salt brine to gauge the density of the solution would not only be unpleasant, but also insufficiently exact. Salting is one of the oldest forms of food preservation, working by impregnating the food with a heavy concentration of salt; the spoilage is retarded in direct proportion to the strength of the solution. Many foods that are salted go on to be further preserved by smoking, canning, or freezing, and it is essential to be able to judge the strength of the original solution in order to carry out the next step properly. Whether you are curing vegetables, such as cucumber pickles or sauerkraut, or meat or fish products, such as corned beef, bacon, or smoked fish, you need to know the density of the brine. Old recipes, when recommending very strong brine—10 percent, we would say—describe it as one "strong enough to float an egg." Luckily, we have instruments at hand, salometers (salt measurers) and hydrometers, that help us judge salt content in a less subjective manner.

1.35 MATFER SALOMETER

This salometer works on the same principle as the old cook's advice to make brine "strong enough to float an egg." No dials or mercury or thermocoupling here; rather, a weighted glass tube that is read according to how far it sinks into a beaker filled with brine. Little salt, and the tube will sink way down, so that at water level you can read 05—a light solution. Much salt, and it will bob along the top like a swimmer in the Great Salt Lake, and at water level you will see a reading of 25 or 30. This is a simple contraption: a 7½"-long weighted and sealed glass tube with a marked piece of paper rolled up inside it to give you the readings.

1.36 MATFER SYRUP DENSITY METER

Technically known as a hydrometer, or water measurer, this item from Matfer measures the amount of sugar in a solution. The 7½" weighted and sealed glass tube is placed into a beaker filled with the solution to be tested. The more sugar in the solution, the higher the tube will float in the beaker. The measurement is registered on the Baumé scale. This is an important tool for anyone serious about canning, preserving, or sherbet-making.

Columbus discovered America, but it was pickle peddler Amerigo Vespucci who gave his name to the continent. He also discovered that crews could survive three to four months without getting scurvy if he stocked ships with pickles.

MEASURING TIME

MEASUREMENTS CAN BE MADE by cups or liters, by American or Imperial pints, by degrees Centigrade or Fahrenheit, by ounces or kilograms; we have seen that a good set of conversion tables is an essential part of your collection of kitchen tools since there is by no means a universal agreement about the standards of measurement. There is absolute agreement, however, on the measurement of time. Our recipes no longer merely advise "cook until done" or "beat until light." Now we are dependent on the standard units of time—seconds, minutes, and hours—and in cooking, as in love, timing can be everything. To be sure, once you are an experienced cook you can make time judgments for yourself, but by and large you can rely on time directions.

The most important requirement for a kitchen timer is that it keeps time accurately. In addition, it should be easy to read, show seconds as well as minutes and hours, ring loudly enough to be heard above the background noise of your kitchen or in an adjacent room, and run for at least as many hours as you need for the foods you cook longest, which for many of us is the Thanksgiving turkey. Timers that count back up after counting down are helpful. If you are testing a new recipe and want to increase the cooking time, the counting-up feature after the buzzer rings is convenient for measuring the additional time. The count-up feature will also tell you how long the cooking process has been going on past the point when you missed the bell. Some timers have an interrupt feature that allows you to stop the timer and start it again later, which is helpful but not essential. Models that time more than one function simultaneously are worth the extra cost.

Timers work off either a windup spring with a dial set to the desired time or an electronic clock. If you use a dial timer and your setting is going to be below 30 minutes, wind it to 30 and then back to the lower setting. That will build up the tension in the spring and ensure that the ring will be at its loudest. Dial timers are somewhat more durable than the electronic models and don't require batteries, but the electronics are more accurate and can offer a greater range of features. The ultimate solution is to have an electronic model and a dial backup for the day the batteries run out in the middle of your task. Finally, don't overlook the usefulness of a good, old-fashioned hourglass timer.

1.37 PROGRESSUS EGG TIMER

There is much to be said for the hourglass, free as it is from any dependence on exterior sources of energy, using only a small portion of the world's infinite supply of gravity. Perhaps a large hourglass would not be useful in the kitchen, but we can think of any number of uses for this little one, which measures a rough 3-minute chunk of time. Try it the next time that you cook a 3-minute egg. This has a heavy little wooden frame, with three supports standing around an hourglass. Inside the hourglass there is a pink granular substance that runs slowly through at—we must admit—a slightly variable pace. Still, it is inexpensive, sturdy, and has a shape so classic and evocative that it would be worth having around to look at, even if it served no function.

1.38 POLDER SQUARE MECHANICAL TIMER

Mechanical timers come in a dazzling variety of shapes, sizes, and colors, so you have the option of choosing one that suits your kitchen decor, be it ultracontemporary or classic country. The 2¾"-square model from Polder that we feature here has a neat, neutral look and the best of practical features: dependable accuracy, a clear sustained ring, an easy-to-read dial, and a smooth, white plastic surface that's a cinch to wipe clean. (We found quite a few timers had notches and grooves that would require occasional scrubbing with a toothbrush.) This sturdy timer has one more handy addition: two magnetic strips are inlaid on the back of it so you can mount the timer on the stove or refrigerator, keeping it visible and away from countertop clutter.

1.39 SUNBEAM DIGI-MASTER DELUXE

For the electronically impaired who wince at the sight of instruction manuals, we recommend this basic, no-frills digital clock-timer. It's so easy to operate that even after the inevitable day you misplace the instructions, you'll still be able to work it. Simply hit a switch to display either the clock or the timer, then set either one by pressing the HOUR/MIN/SEC buttons. Press START for the timer and the digits immediately start counting down by the seconds. A series of beeps announces that the time is up; to stop the alarm just hit any key—no need to fumble for the STOP key. We especially like the count-up feature, which begins automatically when the alarm sounds, allowing you to know how many minutes and seconds you've gone past the set time. Other attractions: a jumbo number readout; compact 2¾″ size; a 5-minute prealarm alert; and the clip, magnet, or stand-up option.

1.40 POLDER PORTABLE TIMER

This hang-around-the-neck timer won't make a fashion statement but it sure says a lot about practical design. Weighing in at a mere 1½ ounces, you'll barely know the timer is there until a soft staccato of beeps issues from its trim, slender body to signal the alarm. It counts up as well as down, measuring as much as 9 hours, 59 minutes, and 59 seconds, and when you're not using it as a timer, it functions as a clock. Reliable, comfortable, and as close as your bellybutton, this is a timer you'll use more than most others.

1.41 POLDER TRIPLE TIMER CLOCK

Given that most of us cook more than one dish at a time, it makes

---

WARM, SOFT CHOCOLATE CAKE

4 individual cakes

Undercooked chocolate cake: "A mistake," says Jean-Georges Vongerichten, that has become one of the most popular (and copied) desserts in New York. When you cut into the brownielike crust with your spoon, the warm, creamy, puddinglike center oozes out. This brings out the kid in everyone, but the barely sweet nature of the chocolate batter is too sophisticated for most children. It's best when served with a scoop of vanilla or caramel ice cream. The cakes can be prepared ahead, refrigerated, and then brought back to room temperature before baking.

½ cup (1 stick) butter, plus some for buttering the molds
4 squares (4 ounces) bittersweet chocolate, preferably Valrhona
2 eggs
2 egg yolks
¼ cup sugar
2 teaspoons flour, plus more for dusting

1 In the top of a double-boiler set over simmering water, heat the butter and chocolate together until the chocolate is almost completely melted. While that's heating, beat together the eggs, yolks, and sugar with a whisk or electric beater until light and thick.

2 Beat together the melted chocolate and butter; it should be quite warm. Pour in the egg mixture, then quickly beat in the flour, just until combined.

3 Butter and lightly flour four 4-ounce molds, custard cups, or ramekins. Tap out the excess flour, then butter and flour them again. Divide the batter among the molds. (At this point you can refrigerate the desserts until you are ready to eat, for up to several hours; bring them back to room temperature before baking.)

4 Preheat the oven to 450°F. Bake the molds on a tray for 6 to 7 minutes; the center will still be quite soft, but the sides will be set.

5 Invert each mold onto a plate and let sit for about 10 seconds. Unmold by lifting up one corner of the mold; the cake will fall out onto the plate. Serve immediately.

Jean-Georges: Cooking at Home with a Four-star Chef, by Jean-Georges Vongerichten and Mark Bittman

sense to have a timer that can clock several things simultaneously. This high-tech version can display three timers at once; slide a button and the screen changes to show a digital clock and a split-second, count-up stopwatch. It also has a MEMORY button that recalls the previous set time (very convenient if you're doing batches of cookies); a large-print display of hours, minutes, and seconds; and a smart "features reminder" note glued to its back so you can operate this virtual kitchen command center without hunting for the package instructions.

"It's a children's book, with lots and lots of interesting recipes."

1.42 WEST BEND CLOCK–DOUBLE TIMER

Of all the digital timers tested, this was our favorite. Like Goldilocks, we felt that this timer was just right—neither too many nor too few features. It offers every essential function packed into a simple design with extralarge numbers for the hours-minutes-seconds display. Equipped with two timer functions; a resounding series of alarm beeps; an instant count-up function; a memory key; a clock; and a clip, magnet, or stand option, this economical 3"-wide model leaves nothing to be desired.

1.43 COMPONENT DESIGN VOICECRAFT TALKING DIGITAL TIMER & CLOCK

This amusing gadget may be more appropriate to a catalogue of toys than one of cooking equipment, for kids seem best able to appreciate all the silly sounds it makes to signal that time's up. You can choose from a car horn honking, a school bell ringing, a very boisterous teapot, or the soft sound of a cuckoo bird (the grown-ups liked that one too). There's also the option of using the "talking timer": a robotlike voice that announces the time you punch in and then counts down each minute; when the time remaining is less than a minute, it alerts you every 10 seconds, then counts down aloud from ten to zero as if a rocket were being launched. What drama! Boiling eggs will never be the same.

2

BOWLS

BOWLS, THOSE INDISPENSABLE culinary utensils, are used for a variety of purposes, including mixing, serving, storing, and, when they're made of ovenproof materials, for cooking. Some have special properties designed to assist with specific tasks.

An unlined copper bowl is the vessel of choice for whipping egg whites and was once the mark of a professionally equipped kitchen. Stainless steel is the modern workhorse of the kitchen—unbreakable, light, and responsive to heating and chilling. Stainless steel bowls are used for hundreds of tasks, from melting chocolate over gently simmering water to chilling an egg-thickened mousse in the refrigerator. In addition to stainless steel and copper, bowls for kitchen use come in glass, ceramic, plastic, and wood. They may have flat or round bases and be designed with or without han-

dles, hanging rings, and nonskid stripping. Invest in a collection of bowls in different materials and sizes.

Always match the bowl size to the beating or mixing implement, or vice versa. A whisk should reach down into the bottom of the bowl and deal effectively with every drop of food. A small whisk in a big bowl means more energy expended and less material incorporated—in other words, great inefficiency—while a big beater in too small a bowl means, simply, an overwhelming mess. In general, it's better to select a bowl that's slightly larger than you need.

The selection criteria for bowls include: ease of storage and cleaning, durability of material, heat resistance, lack of porosity, and sometimes pouring spouts, grip comfort, and/or a specific shape (e.g., a rounded bottom for whipping egg whites, a flat bottom for marinating).

UNLINED COPPER BOWLS

COOKS HAVE BEEN beating egg whites in copper bowls for hundreds of years, but this is not merely in deference to tradition; there is a specific chemical reason for using copper. When you beat egg whites in an unlined copper bowl (as opposed to any other bowl material), the result is a closely knit foam that will stay soft and elastic when additional ingredients are folded in. There is a type of protein in egg whites known as conalbumin. When air bubbles form in egg whites, it

surrounds the bubbles and combines with copper to form copper-conalbumin, which is more stable than plain conalbumin. This copper-conalbumin foam will expand to a greater volume when it comes in contact with heat.

For the greatest effect from the interaction between egg white and copper, it's important to neutralize the inner surface of the bowl before every use. To do so, toss in 2 tablespoons of coarse salt and

¼ cup of white vinegar, slosh the mixture around, then rinse the bowl and wipe it dry. Make sure that the whites and the bowl are free from even the slightest speck of egg yolk, fat, or oil, all of which retard the whites' ability to rise. An unlined copper bowl for egg whites should be twice as wide as it is deep, with a round bottom and gently sloping sides. To retain its shape and strength, the bowl should be made of thick copper, and its edge should have a rolled rim. Beware of bowls that are lightweight and come with a protective coating: these items are intended for display only, not for use. We find that a bowl with a 12" diameter is ideal for most home cooks. A ring for hanging storage is helpful. And the same salt and vinegar you used to neutralize the bowl also makes an effective cleaner and tarnish remover.

2.1 KITCHEN SUPPLY COMPANY HEAVY COPPER BOWL

When the task is beating egg whites, whether for an impressive espresso and chocolate soufflé or a simple lemon meringue, our bowl of choice is this heavy, unlined copper 6-quart model from Kitchen Supply Company. Measuring 12½" in diameter, it is twice as wide as it is deep, and it has a round bottom and gently sloping sides. The shape of the bowl requires that it be used at a tilt, with one hand secured on its smoothly rolled rim, the other moving a balloon-shaped whisk in steady, large, circular strokes. A gleaming piece of workmanship, this bowl's shiny copper exterior has a thick brass storage ring mounted just under its rim.

ZABAGLIONE WITH STRAWBERRIES IN RED WINE

4 servings

2 pints ripe strawberries, hulled
1 cup light red wine, such as a
   California Charbono or a Chianti
½ cup plus 2 tablespoons sugar
8 large egg yolks
finely grated zest of 1 orange
⅓ cup Moscato or other
   sparkling wine
large bunch of mint

1 Put the strawberries in a pretty glass bowl, add the red wine and 2 tablespoons of the sugar up to 2 hours before serving, and stir from time to time to dissolve the sugar.

(This is best done at the beginning of dinner.)
2 Put the egg yolks in a large heat-proof bowl, add the remaining ½-cup sugar, and whisk until light and fluffy.
3 Bring a large pot of water to a boil over high heat. Whisk the orange zest and Moscato into the egg yolks. Put the bowl on top of the pot of water and whisk until the zabaglione is fluffy, stiff, and pale yellow, about 5 minutes. Divide among four shallow bowls and ladle the strawberries and wine on top. Serve with a few sprigs of mint in each bowl.

The Rose Pistola Cookbook, by Reed Hearon and Peggy Knickerbocker

A BOWL OF FRESH HERBS
❧ CLAUDIA RODEN ❧

In Persia fresh herbs are served as *mezze,* and a bowl containing a varied assortment of these is placed on the table at most meals. A Persian friend of mine grows a large variety of Persian herbs in her London garden, where they thrive throughout the English summer.

It is an ancient custom for women to eat the herbs with bread and cheese at the end of a meal. According to an old belief, this will help them to keep their husbands away from a rival. Job's tears and mandrake in particular should turn him against a "co-wife."

Wash a few sprigs of fresh parsley, mint, chives, cress, dill, coriander, tarragon, scallions—any fresh herbs you like that are available—and arrange them in a bowl. They are the perfect accompaniment to a Middle Eastern meal.

STAINLESS STEEL BOWLS

STAINLESS STEEL IS acid resistant, nonbreakable, and dishwasher safe. A metal bowl will respond more rapidly to heating and chilling than a bowl made of any other material. Use it over a pan of simmering water in lieu of a double boiler, or chill it inside a larger bowl filled with cold water and ice for whipping cream. You can fold or beat while you heat or chill the food, and the chemi-cally inert stainless steel will not influence the food's color or flavor. These are the most utilitarian bowls in the commercial kitchen and should be standard items in the home kitchen as well. Over the past twenty years, stainless steel bowls have undergone a number of changes. The steel is stronger, the bowls are deeper, and there is a greater range of styles.

2.2 HACKMAN TABLETOP ALL-STEEL MIXING BOWL

At the top of the class in big bowls is the Hackman Tabletop 12″ mixing bowl, constructed of the highest-gauge (18/10) stainless steel. Manufactured in Norway, it has a brushed satin interior finish (the better to hide scratches from a whisk or metal spoon) with etched black lines to measure volume (ideal for judging rising bread dough). This round-bodied, deep bowl has a mirror-finish exterior and a flat bottom to provide countertop stability, and it holds about 8 quarts.

2.3 AMCO NONSKID MIXING BOWLS

Amco's stainless steel, nonskid mixing bowls come with a blue rubber Plastisol coating that covers the entire bottom of the bowl and virtually glues it to the countertop. Vigorous stirring won't budge these bowls from their place. Furthermore—look, Ma, no hands!—they stay put even when both hands are needed elsewhere, to operate a rotary egg beater for instance. These deep, contoured bowls are made of 18/8 commercial-gauge brushed stainless steel. A set of three includes 2-quart, 4-quart, and 6-quart sizes.

2.4 RÖSLE DEEP BOWL SET & LIDS

Rösle is the BMW of bowl manufacturers, and this handsome German-made set of bowls with matching lids stands out. Each bowl is extra deep yet very well balanced, with a flat, stable bottom. Their brushed exteriors and mirror-finish interiors are top-quality 18/10 gauge stainless steel. The rolled rims make pouring easy and prevent drips—perfect for mixing liquids. The stainless steel lids, however, are the star features of the set; designed to hug the lip, the lids will not slip, making it possible to stack the bowls for storage. Separately, the lids may be used as trivets for hot pots and pans. A set of three bowls (2-, 3¼-, and 6-quart) comes in a sturdy wooden box. Matching lids are sold separately.

THE BIG BOWL

A wardrobe of bowls for a well-equipped kitchen should include at least one very large bowl, 7 to 9 quarts, that can be used for the biggest of jobs—mixing the stuffing for a 25-pound turkey, soaking a ham, or holding dough for a half-dozen breads. Stainless steel, light yet sturdy, is the material of choice.

2.5 GOURMET STANDARD MIXING BOWL WITH HAND GRIP

The Gourmet Standard stainless steel mixing bowl with hand grip should be a candidate for museum display with its stylish modern look: 18/10 stainless steel with a mirror-finished interior and brushed exterior. It is practical, too—deep and gently rounded, with a superior curved handle that provides a comfortable four-finger grip and great maneuverability. This bowl is not just for mixing. Take it to the table for serving: food looks beautiful when presented against a mirror finish. Though it is very durable, the polished interior will scratch if a metal utensil is used for beating or stirring. Five sizes, from 1½ quarts to 6 quarts, will nest, but there is also a rounded hook attached to the rim for hanging.

2.6 AMCO PINCH BOWLS

Order and speed are nearly as important to the cook as to the surgeon, but since there's no nurse to slap the ingredients into your hand during a pressure-filled stir-fry or sauce preparation, we recommend a set of minibowls. Also known as condiment bowls or ingredient cups, they hold premeasured amounts of liquid and dry ingredients that can be lined up in the order needed. These bowls come in wood (attractive), glass (see-through), and stainless steel (very durable). Our favorite is the Amco Pinch Bowl, a slope-sided, 1"-high, 18/8 gauge stainless steel beauty that holds 3 ounces and is sold in sets of four. They are also ideal for the presentation of garnishes for everything from gazpacho to curry.

GLASS BOWLS

HEATPROOF, AND sometimes ovenproof, glass bowl sets that can also be used at the table have been a kitchen basic for decades. Glass bowls hide no secrets, so when the fruit sinks to the bottom of your gelatin mixture and stays there you will see it and have time to correct the situation. The round shape simplifies unmolding. Glass is also nonreactive, making these bowls ideal for marinating. All glass bowls must be handled with care, not put under a broiler, set directly on a stove-top burner, or transferred from one extreme temperature to another. Do not clean them with abrasives, which will scuff and scratch the glass.

2.7 PYREX THREE-PIECE MIXING-BOWL SET

The Pyrex three-piece clear-glass mixing-bowl set has been a kitchen standard since 1915. In three practical sizes (1 quart, 1½ quarts, and 2½ quarts), these nesting bowls are made of sturdy tempered glass intended for use in food preparation, storage, heating, and serving. The bowls have a nicely rounded shape with flat bottoms (stamped with the bowl capacity) and a ½"-wide top rim, handy for securing a wrap of plastic or foil. They are ovenproof, can be put into the microwave, and are dishwasher safe. Properly handled, these glass bowls will provide long service. A 4-quart mixing-bowl size is also available.

HOLDING A BOWL STEADY

There are moments during food preparation when a third hand would be very useful; for example, when a bowl begins "walking" toward the edge of the work surface while you are pouring and stirring simultaneously. One trick to keep your bowl from traveling is to spread a moist cloth towel flat on the counter and place the bowl on it. (For medium and small bowls, a damp paper towel will do nicely.) Alternatively, dampen the cloth towel and twist it into a turban around the base of the bowl to secure it, then tilt and stir or beat.

PLASTIC BOWLS

TODAY'S TOP-QUALITY plastic bowls are non-porous, virtually nonbreakable, and dishwasher safe. They are conveniently light in weight and insulate against heat or cold. Most have pouring spouts, some have nonskid rings on their bases, and others come with snap-on lids, allowing them to double as storage containers. Plastic bowls can also be used for marinating. Some are suitable for use in the microwave oven. Melamine is the most durable plastic used to manufacture mixing bowls.

2.8 OXO NONSKID MIXING BOWLS

Stir your ingredients at any angle of tilt in these 2- or 4-quart-size OXO melamine mixing bowls—they stay in place due to a Santoprene-covered base that prevents skidding. When you're finished, pour the mixture out through the contoured spout by holding on to the handle grip that won't slip out of your hand even when wet. The bowl's comfortable oversized handle also cushions your hand while absorbing pressure during use. These lightweight mixing bowls are available in stylish bright white with black trim.

2.9 FRIELING BATTER BOWL

Large handles and wide pouring lips are the chief design features that separate batter bowls from mixing bowls. You'll see batter bowls made in earthenware and clear glass, but our pick is this sturdy plastic batter bowl from Frieling. Its best attribute is an ergonomically designed handle with a thumb groove that extends from the top of the rim down to the countertop and stabilizes the bowl while mixing. In addition, a nonslip ring base prevents the bowl from moving while you're stirring or whisking, so splatters stay inside where they belong. The batter bowl comes in white, in two sizes: 2½ quarts or 1 gallon.

NAN'S EXTRA SPECIAL MARINATED SPARERIBS

4 to 6 servings

There is so much I could say about our dear friend Nan and her wonderful spareribs. She is a one-of-a-kind spirit and makes one-of-a-kind ribs! The pineapple and the sherry in the barbecue sauce make them unusually delicious. They're just the thing when you need to serve a crowd of people. Believe me, they will disappear.

1 pound 4½-ounce can juice-packed pineapple chunks, drained and juice saved
⅓ cup soy sauce
¼ cup ketchup
3 tablespoons cider vinegar
2 tablespoons sherry
2 tablespoons light or dark brown sugar
2 tablespoons minced fresh ginger or ground ginger
1 clove garlic, crushed

4 pounds baby back ribs
½ teaspoon salt
1 cup water

1 In a large bowl, combine ½ cup of the pineapple juice, the soy sauce, ketchup, vinegar, sherry, brown sugar, ginger, and garlic. Add the ribs to the bowl and let marinate for at least 6 hours, or, even better, overnight in the refrigerator. Drain the ribs, reserving the marinade.

2 Preheat the oven to 325°F.

3 Sprinkle the ribs with the salt. Place the ribs on a rack in a jelly-roll pan containing the water. Bake for 45 minutes, turning once. Discard the drippings. Place the ribs in the pan (not on the rack) and pour on the reserved marinade. Bake for 30 minutes, turning the ribs once. Add the pineapple chunks and remaining pineapple juice. Bake for 30 minutes longer, turning the ribs once. Turn the ribs in the marinade one last time before serving.

Sylvia's Family Soul Food Cookbook, by Sylvia Woods and Family

CERAMIC BOWLS

SOME CERAMIC BOWLS feature a flat surface on one side near the base, which keeps the bowl steady while the cook tilts it for beating. It's good to have a few ceramic bowls in several sizes, especially since they are often handsome enough to go directly to the table. They should be handled and stored carefully to avoid chipping. Some are ovenproof and all of them are dishwasher safe.

2.10 CHANTAL CERAMIC BOWL SET

Chantal's five-piece ceramic bowl set mixes function and beauty. With a shiny, glazed finish in decorator colors, the deep contours of these all-purpose mixing bowls prove effective in food preparation, including oven baking, and become elegant serving bowls when brought to the table. This nesting set includes 4-ounce, 12-ounce, 3-cup, 7-cup, and 12-cup sizes (3⅜", 4¼", 6", 7⅛", and 9" in diameter), a range that provides for a delightfully broad array of uses, including serving dips and spreads, storing fruit, marinating vegetables, and stirring together the ingredients of a recipe. Chantal ceramic bowls are handcrafted in China and are free of lead and cadmium.

> Noncooks think it's
> silly to invest
> two hours' work in
> two minutes' enjoyment;
> but if cooking is evanescent,
> well, so is ballet.
>
> —JULIA CHILD

2.11 MASON CASH MIXING BOWLS

Mason Cash ceramic bowls, made in Derbyshire from local clay, have been fixtures in English kitchens since the nineteenth century. The understated cane- (Americans would say "buff" or "tan") and-white mixing bowls feature easy-to-grip rims decorated with historic relief designs unique to the company. Made of vitrified ceramic (clay that has been completely fused together so as to form a fully sealed, nonporous solid), they may be used in the oven, microwave, or freezer and are dishwasher safe. However, first and foremost, these are the bowls for making batters and dough, from simple tea cakes to a rustic artisan loaf. They are fairly wide in relation to their height, making them ideal for stirring, beating, and creaming. You'll find it helpful to have these mixing bowls in several sizes. We recommend the 10", the 8", and the 4½" minibowl.

"Your squash medley will be right out, sir."

PUDDING BOWLS

Examine any English or American cookbook written before 1920 and you will find chapters filled with recipes for puddings—dessert puddings, main-course puddings, snack puddings. The modern reader may be baffled by the number of the recipes, but in those days ovens were unreliable and convenience foods unheard of. Where today's cooks bake, our forebears would pud. Sweet or savory mixtures, heaped into basins, were steamed to custard- or cakelike consistency. Leftovers, from meats to vegetables to breads, became puddings. It was not uncommon for a meal to comprise three courses, each featuring pudding.

Pudding bowls evolved with the features necessary for successful pudding-making; they must be deep, ovenproof, flat bottomed, and ringed with a characteristic inch-deep rim. The rim permits the pudding mixture to be covered with cloth that is tied in place under the lip. A well-designed pudding bowl will have a solid, comfortable simplicity but enough of the right kind of style to take to the table. Pudding bowls come in many sizes. The 1-pint-capacity bowl works well for mixing or serving sauce, the 5-cup model for marinating shrimp. One of our experts uses a set of four to serve hors d'oeuvres at the table, family style.

2.12 MASON CASH PUDDING BASINS

Mason Cash pudding basins are made in England using traditional materials and methods. These ovenware bowls are attractively designed in eggshell white with a classic basket-weave pattern, and they exude an old-fashioned charm reminiscent of English country kitchens.

Useful for many things besides pudding, these multipurpose basins are also for mixing, storing, and serving a variety of foods. With their steep tapered sides, the basins give cooked food the necessary support for seamless unmolding. They range in size from 5" in diameter to 6¾".

STEAMED PLUM PUDDING

24 servings

A truly festive Christmas dish that needs patience in the making. The slow 6-hour cooking is necessary, so that all the suet melts before the flour particles burst. If the pudding cooks too fast and the flour grains burst before the fat melts, the pudding will be close and hard.

SIFT:
1 cup all-purpose flour

PREPARE & DREDGE LIGHTLY WITH PART OF THE FLOUR:
1 lb. chopped suet: 2 cups
1 lb. seeded raisins
1 lb. washed dried currants
½ lb. chopped citron

RESIFT THE REMAINING FLOUR WITH:
1 grated nutmeg
1 tablespoon cinnamon
½ tablespoon mace
1 teaspoon salt
6 tablespoons sugar or ½ cup brown sugar

COMBINE THE DREDGED & THE SIFTED INGREDIENTS. ADD:
7 egg yolks
¼ cup cream
½ cup brandy or sherry
3 cups grated bread crumbs, white or rye

THE LATTER HELPS MAKE THE PUDDING LIGHT. PLACE ON A PLATTER AND WHIP UNTIL STIFF:
7 egg whites

Fold the egg whites lightly into the raisin mixture. Pour the batter into a greased, covered gallon mold and steam for 6 hours. To steam pudding mixtures in a steamer, use pudding molds or cans with tightly fitting lids—like baking powder tins. First, grease insides of molds well, then sprinkle with sugar. Containers should be only ⅔ full. Place molds on a trivet in a heavy kettle over 1 inch of boiling water. Cover kettle closely. Use high heat at first, then, as the steam begins to escape, low heat for rest of cooking.

The All-Purpose Joy of Cooking, by Irma S. Rombauer and Marion Rombauer Becker

CHRISTMAS PUDDING

❧ MARGARET VISSER ❧

For festival foods to have staying power, they must make us feel that they are old and strange, yet typically ours. They should involve some time and if possible several people in their preparation, and if we can be persuaded to eat them only on the festival day itself, so much the better. For Anglo-Saxons, Christmas pudding fulfills all the conditions.

The pudding is only about two centuries old, but it feels much older. And indeed it is possible to find ancient roots for it—in meat soups and humble medieval wheat gruels. Another component in the story is a great sausage, called *hackin* because of the minced or hacked meat enclosed in its skin. French *boudin*, meaning sausage, is related to the English word *pudding*. And real Christmas pudding still must contain the meat fat, suet.

Only very recently has the western European culinary tradition habitually separated meat from sweetness. Sugar used to be classed as a spice along with salt, and fruit often accompanied meat. In the seventeenth century, Britain began importing a lot more dried fruit than formerly: prunes from France, currants from Greece (the word derives from *Corinth*), sultanas from Turkey. These were added to meat and grain soups for feasts; the result was a thick "plum porridge." Gradually it became uncommon to include prunes; the word *plum* stuck, however, as a general term for dried fruit.

A momentous invention for British cuisine was the pudding cloth (late seventeenth century). It did away with guts and paunches as bags to hold food, as they still do only for sausages and haggis. Most family meals were cooked over the hearth fire in a hanging cauldron. The meat was boiled in liquid, and to it were added vegetables and balls of pudding wrapped in buttered cloth. Savory puddings were often eaten as a separate course, after the soup and before the meat. "No broth no ball, no ball no beef," children were admonished: one had to eat soup, then carbohydrate staple, then meat, in that order. Meat was expensive—not to be gobbled down with an unblunted appetite.

"Plum porridge," stiffened, could also be boiled in a pudding cloth and eaten for dessert. Made richer, denser, and heavy with fruit, it became festive, and in the end exclusively Christmas fare. Rich people, who could afford the luxury of oven baking, also made cakes at Christmas: the Twelfth Cakes of Epiphany, January 6.

At this feast of the Magi, trinkets such as rings, money, and charms, symbolic of future events, were secreted in the cake, to be found by chance (or fate) in the portions served. A bean in one's cake made one king for the day; the custom was part of the saturnalian aspect of Christmas, where children rule and royalty can be conferred on anyone at random. In the late nineteenth century, Twelfth Cake began to die out, leaving echoes in the iced Christmas cake—and the coins buried in Christmas pudding.

The pudding was simpler and cheaper than the cake, and everyone had the equipment needed to cook it. Its shape was spherical until recently, and it was considered patriotically British. No foreigners could make it successfully (many stories tell us how they try but forget, for example, to wrap it in the pudding cloth first), nor could they stomach its stodge. There is a swaggering, even military symbolism, too: Pepys ate "a mess of brave plum porridge" to open his Christmas dinner in 1662, and Dickens in *A Christmas Carol* describes one "like a speckled cannon-ball, so hard and firm, blazing in half of half-a-quartern of ignited brandy . . ."

The burning alcohol gives the dark, rich pudding a singular, extravagant, yet elemental air; the fire lasts only a short time, as befits festival magic. Traditionally, the pudding took plenty of time to make. The ones homemade from old family recipes were prepared between July and October so they could be properly aged for Christmas; they were stirred by every member of the family, from east to west in honor of the journey of the Magi. Our own Christmas puddings are likely to be shop-bought sometime in December and enclosed in covered basins rather than pudding cloths. They can be steamed or boiled still, or callously zapped in a microwave by those of us for whom the annual roast-with-trimmings is quite enough to cope with.

Unreasonably solid, fatty, sweet, rotund, calorie laden, and lathered with brandy butter, the pudding is served once—and only once—a year. It amounts to an outrageous snub to everything thin, new, light, and mobile. An obstinate cannonball from the past, the Christmas pudding intractably sits there, mocking the very idea of modernity.

WOODEN BOWLS

WOODEN BOWLS COME in three forms: laminated, treated with a tasteless oil rub, or unfinished. The first two do not absorb food odors and flavors and, therefore, are perfect for salads. Hardwood is used in the best of these bowls; alder wood and hard rock maple are common, sometimes with a black walnut trim.

Unfinished wooden bowls are fine for preparing food—shallow ones are often made to fit a mezzaluna chopper—but we don't recommend them for salad unless the bowl has been seasoned. (See page 33.) Clean all wooden bowls quickly after use, keeping soap to a minimum, and dry them at once.

2.13 WOODARD & CHARLES RUBBERWOOD SALAD BOWL

A wooden bowl's first duties are to be beautiful and feel good to the touch. The preferred shape is wide and rela-tively shallow, since the bowl will be used primarily for tossing salads (a pair of wooden salad hands fit into the bowl almost as efficiently as one's own). This attractive bowl, made in Thailand from plantation-forested rubberwood trees (not the rain forest variety) with a Nyato wood rim, suits our description. It is generously pro-portioned at 14" across and 4½" deep, practical in the kitchen for all manner of salads, and decorative in the dining room as a serving bowl or when used as a centerpiece container.

BOWLS
❧
BERNARD CLAYTON
❧

A selection of bowls, ranging from a medium 10" to a small 5" one, that are close at hand when preparation begins makes pastry-making a joy. As the ingredients are mixed, chopped, whipped, or strained, a bowl should be there to receive the material as it awaits its turn to go into the final blend. There are containers other than bowls that can be used for vari-ous substances (a bottle, a glass, or a plastic box), but none has the graceful, sloping sides of a bowl that make stirring and mixing a pleasure and cleaning no less so.

Stoneware, earthenware, and heavy ceramic bowls, accumulated at farm sales, antique shows, and from friends' cupboards, are favo-rites in my kitchen. They are easy to hold and heavy enough to maintain an even temperature. Stainless steel bowls, such as those used with an electric mixer, and plastic bowls are usable, but be aware that they reflect tem-perature changes more readily than most others.

2.14 J. K. ADAMS HERB BOWL WITH MEZZALUNA CHOPPER

The half-moon-shaped blade of the mezzaluna works best in this curved wooden chopping bowl. Parsley, thyme, mint, and other herbs collect in the bottom of the bowl as they are chopped. The bowl, made from hard maple, rests on rubber pads to help prevent skidding. The sides are indented so you can push a plate under the edge and scrape the chopped herbs overboard. The chopping bowl is a 9¼" square that rises 2" off your work surface. The mezzaluna is 6" wide and 5" from handle to blade tip.

SEASONING A WOODEN SALAD BOWL

Some wooden salad bowls are finished with a waterproof varnish that helps to protect the surface of the wood. However, many cooks prefer to have the inside of the bowl unfinished so they can season the bowl with a light coating of vegetable oil. The great food authority James Beard often favored an unvarnished surface and would in fact rub garlic into the wood.

TABBOULEH
(CRACKED WHEAT SALAD WITH PARSLEY & TOMATOES)

4 servings

The tabbouleh that was made a hundred years ago in Aleppo and Damascus—the ways Jews preserved the recipe when they left for Egypt and the Americas at the turn of the century—is more substantial and wheaty than the very green salads you find in Lebanese restaurants, which have only specks of wheat.

1 cup (175 g) fine bulgur (cracked wheat)
1 lb. (500 g) firm ripe tomatoes, diced small (¼"—5 mm)
salt and pepper
juice of 1 lemon or more to taste
4 scallions, thinly sliced
a very large bunch of flat-leafed parsley, finely chopped, preferably by hand (1 cup)
a bunch of mint, finely chopped (¼ cup)
6 tablespoons extra-virgin olive oil
4 Bibb lettuces for serving with

Soak the cracked wheat in plenty of cold water for 10 minutes. Rinse in a colander and put in a bowl with the tomatoes. Leave for 30 minutes to absorb the tomato juices. Mix gently with the rest of the ingredients.

A traditional way of eating tabbouleh is to scoop it up with small Bibb lettuce leaves or very young vine leaves.

The Book of Jewish Food: An Odyssey from Samarkand to New York, by Claudia Roden

3

KNIVES, SHARPENERS, & CUTTING BOARDS

KNIVES ARE THE OLDEST known man-made implements, but long before our forebears learned how to make them, they used sharp stones and shells, the fundamental tools that led to the contemporary knives and related accessories—the sharpeners, racks, and cutting boards—that are reviewed in this chapter.

Pebble Choppers & Hand Axes

The first tools were small stones and pebbles sharpened by striking one stone with another to flake off fragments and form a crude cutting edge. These precursors of the knife were used to butcher game more than 2.5 million years ago. As the centuries progressed and humans evolved, so did methods of stone-tool manufacture. Roughly 1 million to 100,000 years ago, humans developed a new technique to create more efficient and finer implements. Called the "soft hammer" approach, it involved working a piece of bone or wood against a rock face at a sharp angle. This type of applied pressure, as opposed to a striking force, successively broke off small, thin, stone flakes to form a flat-edged tool. During this same early Paleolithic period, the tool variety grew to include hand axes, cleavers, scrapers, and chisels; these and other such tools have been found at archeological sites all over the world.

Modern *Homo sapiens* became masterful stone-workers who gradually fashioned fine, thin, symmetri-cal stone flakes in various finishes. Some have straight, sharp edges, while others suggest the serrated knives in use today.

Modern cutting tools have come a long way from sharpened flints and bone shards. They encompass an extensive assortment intended for many specific uses and could only have come to this point through the slow-but-steady advances made by humankind's work with different metals—first copper and tin, and later, iron and its alloys.

Iron & Steels

In order to understand knives, we must first understand iron. The fourth most common element, it comprises 5 percent of the earth's crust and is usually found as an ore, that is, in combination with other elements. One familiar ore is iron pyrite—the glittering "fool's gold" that often caught the eyes of con men and the wallets of their targets.

True metalworking is less than ten thousand years old. Copper, perhaps the first metal to be extracted from its ore, was probably smelted unwittingly from a fire's heat on a copper-bearing rock. When people discovered that this ore could be converted into tough, red nuggets, they realized that it could also be melted and cast or pounded into various shapes. Once these metalworking techniques developed, the final products were hard to come by and were considered so precious

RATATOUILLE (PROVENÇAL VEGETABLES)

8–10 servings

Here is a recipe where that extra touch, extra attention to detail, makes all the difference. Straining the juice from tomatoes that have been peeled, cored, and seeded makes for a richer, more flavorful sauce. The thought of cutting the vegetables into little matchsticks may seem like busy work—until you sample the results. The vegetables have more flavor, and though it would be a mistake to think of ratatouille as an "elegant" dish, the smaller pieces make for a more refined ratatouille in the end. Chef Joël Robuchon is opposed to disgorging vegetables, such as eggplant, with salt, a practice that makes for soggy vegetables. The tomato paste and saffron are optional boosters, to add according to taste and to season.

10 medium vine-ripened tomatoes (about 2 pounds)

2 medium onions, finely chopped

1 cup extra-virgin olive oil

sea salt to taste

1 green bell pepper, peeled and thinly sliced

1 red bell pepper, peeled and thinly sliced

bouquet garni: several parsley stems, celery leaves, and sprigs of thyme, wrapped in the green part of a leek and securely fastened with cotton twine

4 garlic cloves, minced

freshly ground white pepper to taste

1 teaspoon tomato paste (optional)

6 to 7 small zucchini (about 1¼ pounds), scrubbed, trimmed, and cut into matchsticks

2 teaspoons fresh thyme leaves

3 small eggplants (about 1½ pounds), peeled and cut into matchsticks

pinch of saffron threads (optional)

1 Prepare the tomatoes: Core, peel, and seed the tomatoes. Recuperate as much tomato juice as possible, and strain. (If the strained juice does not measure 1 cup, add enough water to make up the difference.) Finely chop the tomatoes. Set aside.

2 In a large skillet, combine the onions, ¼ cup of the oil, and a pinch of salt. Cook over low heat until soft and translucent, about 5 minutes. Add the peppers and a pinch of salt. Cover and continue cooking for about 5 minutes more. Then add the chopped tomatoes, stir, and continue cooking for another 5 minutes.

3 Stir in the tomato juice, bouquet garni, and garlic, and taste for seasoning. Cover and simmer gently for about 30 minutes. Do not overcook: the vegetables should be cooked through but not mushy. If the tomatoes lack flavor, add the tomato paste.

4 Meanwhile, in another skillet, heat ½ cup of the oil over moderate heat. When hot, add the zucchini and cook until lightly colored, about 5 minutes. (Do not salt the zucchini before cooking or flavorful liquids will be lost.) Transfer to a colander to drain any excess oil. Season with thyme and salt. Set aside.

5 In the same skillet, heat the remaining ¼ cup oil over moderate heat. When hot, add the eggplant and cook until lightly colored, about 5 minutes. Transfer to a colander to drain any excess oil. Add the eggplant and zucchini to the tomato mixture. Taste for seasoning. If desired, add a pinch of saffron. Cover and simmer gently for 30 minutes.

6 Serve warm or at room temperature, as a vegetable side dish. Ratatouille will keep fresh, covered and refrigerated, for several days.

Simply French: Patricia Wells Presents the Cuisine of Joël Robuchon, by Patricia Wells

---

that they served mainly as ceremonial objects, ornaments, and weapons.

One of the greatest metallurgical breakthroughs occurred four thousand years ago, when iron was first refined. Thousands of years of practice with simple furnaces to make pottery and to work bronze led to the development of the high-temperature furnaces necessary to work iron. Refining separates iron from the other rock materials in ore and results in crude, or cast, iron. When molten, it can be poured or cast into a form or mold; when cooled, it retains that shape. Iron objects became widespread in the Fertile Crescent of Mesopotamia and sub-Saharan Africa around 900 B.C. Cast iron has been used over the centuries for almost any purpose where a strong, malleable substance was needed.

As with all metals, iron has unique properties both good and bad. On the upside, it's abundant, strong, and takes a sharp edge; on the downside, it rusts with exposure to humidity and is either very brittle (when cooled rapidly during refining) or moderately brittle but softer from a slower cooldown. A rusty, dull knife or one that might shatter during a tough job is not much use. To eliminate iron's worst qualities and accentuate its best, the metal must be made into steel—refined iron to which other elements are added. Steel is comprised of roughly 85 percent iron and up to 15 percent other elements. *High-carbon steel* contains about 12 percent carbon and is the alloy most similar to cast iron. It can be formed in the same ways as cast iron, yet it too will rust and, though harder than cast iron, is still quite brittle. *Low-carbon steel,* which is harder, tougher, and more resilient, was invented in the Middle East more than three thousand years ago. Crude iron and grass were burned together in charcoal furnaces; when the grass charred to a nearly pure carbon state, it was combined with the molten iron. The amounts of grass and crude iron were measured to control the proportions in the resulting alloy, a technique still practiced in some nonindustrialized societies.

The feature of rust resistance in steel arrived when such alloys as nickel steel and aluminum steel developed. The most rust resistant of all is *stainless steel,* which was first produced in Europe early in the twentieth century. Stainless steel's high chromium content—4 percent or more—gives it a great tensile strength and an excellent resistance to abrasion and corrosion. Some stainless steels have other added elements, like manganese or titanium. Stainless steel can be shaped in knife production by *forging,* which involves hammering a red-hot billet (a rough steel bar) into a shaped die; by *rolling,* where red-hot ingots of metal are placed between shaped rollers to be pressed into specific forms; and by *machine forming* or *laser cutting,* in which a shape is stamped or cut from a metal sheet.

Stainless vs. Carbon Steel

For many decades, stainless steel was recommended for knives used in coastal areas or wherever humid or salty air would pit and rust other blade metals. Although it remains unsurpassed for specialty cutting tools, it was always considered a compromise steel, never the ultimate knife metal, because it could neither take a good edge nor sharpen easily. Its successor, *high-carbon stainless steel* (sometimes called stainfree or no-stain), was developed in the 1920s and quickly became the fine knife–maker's favorite metal. Little wonder for this preference: with the addition of molybdenum and vanadium to the basic iron-carbonchromium mix, the blades made from this steel take and hold a sharper edge than the older stainless mixes; resist rust, pitting, and abrasion; recover from bending without breaking; and, with proper maintenance and sharpening, can maintain a keen cutting edge.

Some remain devoted to low carbon-steel knives, and this prejudice was once justified. It is easier to get a sharper edge on carbon-steel blades than on harder stainless ones, which can be too hard to sharpen. Perhaps you've seen knives that claim to "never need sharpening"; this may seem more convenient, but be wary, because what it really means is that you'll never be able to get and keep a sharp edge on the blade. Knife edges should be maintained on a steel every time they're used and occasionally sharpened on a stone. A good blade can be kept in fine condition for many years.

Decide on which metal you want for each of your kitchen knives individually, and bear in mind where they will be used and for what purpose. Although a matching set of knives may look outstanding on a wall rack, the same metal and shape might not provide the qualities needed for such widely diverse kitchen tasks as slicing rare roast beef, mincing cilantro, or filleting fish.

Strengthening Blades

A knife is only as good as the properly processed metal in its blade. Blade-destined steel must be made hard, tough, and strong through a heat treatment that includes tempering and annealing. In *tempering,* the metal is heated slowly to a desired temperature, then cooled rapidly in an air or chemical bath. This initial treatment hardens the steel but leaves it somewhat brittle, so a subsequent *annealing* is conducted. In this process, the steel is heated to a lower temperature and then air cooled at a controlled, slow rate; this relieves the internal stress on the metal and strengthens it.

Once blade metal has been treated and shaped, it's ground with successively finer abrasives to produce the desired surface finish and create a sharp edge. Forged blades are machine-ground to create a taper from spine to edge and from handle to tip. This taper-grinding produces a strong, well-balanced blade with the straight cutting edge evident on cook's knives. Fine-quality stamped and laser-cut blades are also taper-ground, but they have no bolster (sometimes called the shoulder)—the thick, perpendicular steel band that lies between the blade and the handle, contributing weight and balance. Different grindings create different edges, like the less tapered, more bowed "channel edge" on cleavers; the staggered fluting—the "hollow-ground" or "Granton edge"—on slicers; and the single-side grind visible on Japanese and serrated bread knives.

What Is a Knife?

Every knife is the sum of three parts: blade, handle, and tang. Examine any promising knife for the quality and construction of each part before you decide which one to buy. One-piece construction from the tip of the blade to the butt of the handle is the strongest and most desirable. The thickest part of the blade or tang shows you the quality and thickness of the blank of steel from which the knife was made. In a good knife, the thickness of the blade spine continues into the tang.

A *blade* should be judged by how well it will do the job and how easily it can be sharpened, since it should be sharpened regularly. A blade that's too hard can't be sharpened, and one that's too soft will lose its edge so quickly you'll spend more time sharpening than using it. Hardness is measured in degrees on the Rockwell scale, which gauges precisely the surface-depth penetration of a diamond (the hardest-known mineral). The most desirable hardness for a knife blade ranges between 55° and 58° Rockwell; knives of these hardnesses will take an edge readily and hold it for a reasonable length of time. Metal with a Rockwell number higher than 58° will hold an edge longer but will be too hard to sharpen; metal below 55° will be too soft. Good blades have been tempered, annealed, and ground carefully.

Judge a *handle* by how it feels and the quality of its finish. It should invite the grip and feel secure, like an extension of your hand. Beware of elaborately shaped handles; ostensibly designed to fit every curve of your fist, they are less likely to fit a particular grip than a more generic shape. Look instead to the slight distinctions in handle width. They are so critical in creating a comfortable feel that manufacturers frequently produce different lines to provide a bigger handle for larger grips as well as a standard one for the more common hand sizes. Handles are made of natural and impregnated woods, plastics, synthetic-rubber compounds, or stainless steel and vary in their degrees of durability. Among the more common wooden-handled knives, natural rosewood remains the most popular for its beauty and, among woods, strong resistance to splitting and cracking. (However, no wood should ever be left soaking in water.) If you're looking for the most durable and sanitary selection, opt for plastic, rubber, or stainless steel.

The *tang* is the part of the blade that extends into and forms part of the handle. A full tang is the same length and shape as the handle and is often visible sandwiched between the two capping handle halves. A rattail tang is, as its name implies, long and skinny; it extends the full length of the handle but is only a fraction of the width. A part or half-tang is as wide as a full tang but it extends only partially into the handle.

Rivets, tubelike "snaps" that must be machine attached, secure a handle cap to its tang. Their heads should be so completely smooth and flush with the surface of the handle that they are indistinguishable by feel. Some (usually inexpensive) knives forgo the rivets in favor of handle caps that are glued to their half-tangs; they usually loosen with washing and should be avoided. If there is a wooden handle and even a part tang, you should be able to see that tang and two or three rivets. Remember that a tang's length contributes balance and support to the knife.

A Word of Caution

Remember that knives are dangerous tools and that people are seldom hurt by those things which they fear; more often than not, they are hurt by those things of which they feel sure. Similarly, never work with a dull blade.

Place a knife on a work counter so that the entire implement rests on the surface; it's far too easy for someone passing by to brush a protruding handle off a table or counter and onto the floor.

Dry knife blades from the spine to the cutting edge, not from handle to tip. *Never* test the sharpness of a blade by running your finger along the edge!

Always store knives in racks, sheaths, or in-drawer trays. Never put an unsheathed knife in a drawer where it might carelessly be picked up blade first or where its edge may be nicked or dulled by contact with other knives or utensils.

What's in a Name?

Sheffield, Solingen, and Sabatier were once the three *S*'s of knife-making, but these days neither sites nor names guarantee anything. Both Sheffield, England, and Solingen, Germany, have been famous since the fourteenth century for their cutlery, produced originally by skilled guild craftsmen. Both cities house large metalworking factories, as do Thiers, France; Tokyo, Japan; and Shelburne Falls, Massachusetts. In France, Sabatier was once the name of a specific manufacturing firm. During the middle of the 1900s the firm leased its established name to other smaller factories. Quality control at some facilities became lax and standards sank; the licenses were eventually revoked, and the high quality returned. When choosing a knife, consider its individual qualifications for the job you want it to do—not the name of the town or the factory where it was produced.

A "Wardrobe" of Knives

Knives can be divided into three basic categories, according to whether their function is to chop, butcher, or slice and cut. Some, like small paring and utility knives, can both chop and slice, while others, like frozen-food and clam knives, have a very specific use. From the most minimal standpoint, you could get by with a good cook's knife and a parer. A more complete knife "wardrobe" would consist of several parers in different lengths, at least one cook's knife, a basic slicing knife, and a serrated bread knife.

Care of Knives

After months and months of chopping, cutting, and slicing with the knives in this chapter, we've concluded that every knife should be straightened or sharpened to some degree after use, depending upon how hard it's worked. (See the end of this chapter to choose your straightening steels and sharpeners.) When a knife is used, the microscopic teeth that form the edge of the blade are rolled back, dulling the edge. Strokes on a steel realign the edge and bring back the blade's sharpness.

All blades should be washed in hot soapy water as soon as possible after use, then rinsed and wiped dry with a cloth. Coat carbon-steel blades with a flavor-free vegetable oil if they're not in constant use. It's best to avoid using a dishwasher even for knives that tote the "dishwasher-safe" claim because eventually they will be knocked around and their blade edges will get nicked.

Never soak a knife; it's especially harmful to knives with wooden handles that, with time, will loosen and separate from their tang. Soaking shouldn't be necessary anyway, because there should never be caked-on food on a knife blade. If a wooden handle loses its sheen, restore it by wiping with a cloth dipped in a flavor-free vegetable oil; be sure to wipe the oil residue off prior to using the knife.

Do store knives in slotted blocks or on magnetic racks. If you store them in drawers, make sure to use sturdy polystyrene sheaths or in-drawer trays.

Do not hold knives in a flame or dip them into a pot of hot food; don't use them to pry jar lids; and never use a lightweight tool for a heavy-duty task. Not only is it bad for the knife, it's dangerous for you.

COOK'S KNIVES

ONE BRILLIANTLY TALENTED, New York–based French chef once said, "I came to this country as a cook—then became a chef." His statement refers to the difference between an accomplished cook and a creative chef, a difference that may account for why the once-used term *chef's knife* has been almost categorically replaced by the *cook's knife*. Verbiage aside, both indicate this tool's importance in professional and home kitchens alike.

Chopping is this kind of knife's primary purpose, and skilled hands use it with a smooth, rolling motion. It is a rhythmic rock that begins with the knife handle held up by one hand as the knuckles of the other, the guiding hand, rest lightly on the back of the blade tip. The blade is brought down in a series of rock-chops, a method that suits most foods, from firm vegetables for a *mirepoix* to delicate mushrooms for duxelles to ripe tomatoes for a fresh pasta sauce. Sometimes a chop-ping technique with greater impact is needed. Hold the knife parallel to the work surface, cutting edge raised slightly above the chopping block or board, then lower firmly and raise slightly several times in rapid succession in a drop-chop motion.

Since a cook's knife mainly chops, its every facet is built to support the blade impact on the chopping surface. The bolster, the thick band at the handle end of forged blades, supplies extra leverage and deters fingers from riding up on the blade. In many knives, the rear part of the handle curves downward to support and cushion the hand when chopping. Most fine cook's knives have a full tang. However, because construction within molded knives varies greatly, it is not completely accurate to say that a knife with a full tang is a better knife or that a tang should be visible within the handle. Design differences and different manufacturers make it difficult to generalize. Since the impact from chopping reverberates throughout this tool, the blade must be firmly anchored at the handle end. A weighty tang balances the long, heavy blade and increases its power.

A cook's knife blade is rigid and tapers evenly, with a smooth, even curve on the broad blade surface enhancing its proper balance. Blades range from 5″ to 14″ lengths and have considerable weight variations. You'll probably want at least two different sizes, a small and a large to tackle various tasks. Don't be afraid to handle the seemingly big, heavy cook's knives—their weight helps you do the job, and their length means fewer pauses to bring foods back to the central spot where you are doing the chopping.

3.1 WÜSTHOF-TRIDENT CLASSIC COOK'S KNIFE

This is an exceptional knife and one that many professionals are pleased to own. It has a 10″-long gently bowed cutting edge that is wider than a standard cook's knife. The extra ¼″ of knuckle clearance supplies enough razor-sharp surface to make short work of mincing herbs or julienning carrots, while its heft provides ample power for quartering chickens or halving lobsters. Its visible tang, like a Formula One's spoiler, ensures a beautifully balanced tool.

3.2 LAMSONSHARP GOLD COOK'S KNIFE

We see so many extraordinary German, French, and Japanese knives that it's almost surprising to discover superb American blades, of which this high-carbon, stainless steel 8″ knife is one. With a full tang securely riveted with solid brass to a black Delrin handle, the Lamsonsharp Gold has a good balance and well-proportioned grip. It's long, broad, and hefty enough to tackle many a tough task—try it the next time you need to gut a chicken, julienne celery root, or milk a corn cob.

3.3 J. A. HENCKELS FOUR-STAR COOK'S KNIFE

For some reason we have yet to uncover, the majority of cook's knives available in the United States come in even-inch blade lengths. That's not the case abroad, where knives like this 9″ one are in far greater demand. That popularity is not surprising: once you wield one, you'll find it's inviting and inordinately comfortable. This knife is a fine, formidable tool and a delight to dice onions, peel rutabagas, and core and slice pineapples with.

3.4 REGENT-SHEFFIELD INFINITY EDGE COOK'S KNIFE

If budget concerns restrict you from investing in a costlier forged knife, look carefully at this stamped blade from England; it caught our eye for quality and good performance. Made of stainless steel, the blade is coated with tungsten carbide to craft its fine edge. Its 8″ length supplies enough surface to finely chop parsley, while its moderately broad 1⅝″ depth easily cubes big bell peppers. It may be light, but it makes short work of splitting ducks and squab.

"Our cook is working through a lot of stuff."

THE 8" CHEF'S KNIFE

❧ MICHAEL LOMONACO ❧

Because I am a professional chef, people repeatedly ask me about the latest kitchen tools that can make their cooking just like mine. I have a ready answer: my favorite kitchen tool is sleek and shiny, with space-tech design and hypercyber abilities. This industrial-strength, silent sous-chef will never ask for a day off or leave me to open another restaurant.

It is steel, bright and gleaming, with the glint of the future and the glow of history. It is an impressive piece of work, the result of thousands of years of design and redesign, with a constant reformulation of its basic shape, style, and materials. It keeps going, day in and day out, under the most trying of conditions, without outside power sources other than the guidance of a steady hand. My perfect and most favorite tool is the 8", stainless steel, full-tang chef's knife. O simple glory that it is. From the Ice Age to the Steel Age to the Cyber Age, nothing serves a chef as well as a hard, straight edge. This tool is often overlooked, mistreated, and neglected. Many chefs, professional or otherwise, fail to honor their own cooking and culinary expertise by not investing, both monetarily and emotionally, in the purchase and proper use of a truly good knife. With my chef's knife and its proper balance, durability, and reliability, I can prepare almost anything as skillfully and quickly as you can imagine.

All good cooking begins with the ingredients you choose. And there is often no better way to prepare those same ingredients than with the simplest and most direct of cooking methods. For me that process always begins with a properly honed and sharpened knife, the most basic and essential of culinary inventions.

Make the commitment to your own cooking and get off to the proper start with the one tool that will last for years and have an impact on every dish you cook.

3.5 SABATIER AU CARBONE COOK'S KNIFE

The Sabatier au Carbone doesn't possess the smoothest bolster we've ever pressed against our fingers, but it is perhaps the best carbon-steel knife made. The very look of this firm, heavy 8" knife calls to mind all the high-toqued commanders of bygone restaurant kitchens. Unlike many cook's knives that carry the modern, bowed cutting edge, this one sports the classic French profile—narrower and more triangular, with a round, versus an angular, collar (the metal link between the handle and blade).

Because this is a carbon, not stainless, steel blade, remember to wipe it dry after washing and, when it stains on contact with acidic foods, clean it with a damp cork dipped in scouring powder. Simply rub the cork against both blade sides and rinse; the blade will nearly recover its fresh-from-the-factory shine, though the stains will never come out entirely.

PARING KNIVES

Paring knives look somewhat like cook's knives, but on a smaller scale. Larger parers—having blades longer than 4"—are called "utility knives" and carry the same curved cutting edge found on most cook's knives. Although it can be used in the same way as a cook's knife, the parer is not an impact tool. Instead, it functions more like an extension of the hand.

You may be tempted to buy the paring knives sold in discount stores, but a cheap knife with a poor blade and an uncomfortable handle is a bad investment. Its thin, hard blade will chip, and its handle will eventually split.

In order to use any paring knife, grip its handle so that your thumb is pressed against the near side of the blade. Then crook your index finger so that it is curved against the opposite side of the blade, and rest the heel of your hand atop the handle. This grip permits an easy range of motion and enough blade control to scoop out potato eyes, scrape zucchini, trim turnips, and perform other tasks. Foreshortening the blade by holding it in this fashion also lets you feel the food you're working with, so you'll have more control and be less likely to cut yourself.

3.6 J. A. HENCKELS FOUR-STAR PARING KNIFE

Our knife experts proclaimed, "If we had to go out in the world with one knife, this is the knife we'd choose." It is short enough and long enough, sharp enough and strong enough, to do almost anything. A well-balanced beauty, it has a rigid, 3"-long blade that curves gently up to a nice, tapered tip and an extremely smooth handle-to-blade joint, so there's virtually no chance of food or bacteria lodging between them.

3.7 SESHIN DIVA PARING KNIFE

From Korea's major flatware manufacturer comes this 3¼" knife with a nearly flat edge and a coped tip. Some call it a "sheep's-foot" knife because of the similarly hoofed profile and, unique or not, it's a fine peeling and paring tool. A number of our authorities felt it had the most satisfying grip of all the knives we tested. It is roughly 20 percent heavier than most parers, partly because of its broad, comfortable grip: a plus when paring piles of potatoes.

3.8 GLOBAL PARING KNIFE

More tapered than a standard parer in its overall profile, this Japanese import resembles a tiny slicer rather than a cook's knife. Its narrower 3¼" blade still does the trick when paring, trimming, or turning. But unlike other knives, it's not the blade's size but its handle that determines balance. At Global, the two halves of the handle are manufactured hollow and then filled with just enough steel to achieve the desired weight for excellent balance. The knife has a slick look and a leaner, cushion-free handle, which some people—especially those with smaller grips—like, because it prompts a greater hand-to-food contact, heightening cutting awareness.

3.9 WÜSTHOF-TRIDENT GRAND PRIX PARING KNIFE

With its elegantly arced back and cutting edge, this is one handsomely styled, rather sexy little blade. Alternately called a "bird's beak" knife, it does, in fact, look like a cutlerer's concept of a heron's bill. Wüsthof labels it a peeling knife, a task it does exceptionally well. Its rigid, high-carbon, stain-free steel 3" blade profile is perfectly suited to trimming small spherical vegetables like baby beets and Brussels sprouts.

3.10 LAMSONSHARP WIDE PARING KNIFE

The gentle, upwardly curved cutting edge on this American-made blade may mirror that of the classic parer, but its dropped spine creates a longer, slimmer tip—a clip point that can't be beat for piercing and paring. Like many clip-point parers, this knife is stamped. The blade, made of high-carbon stain-free steel, is 3¼" long, inflexible, and ideal for eyeing potatoes and removing bruises from apples and pears.

3.11 J. A. HENCKELS FIVE-STAR PARING KNIFE

Quite unlike the standard parer, this one looks like a baby boning knife. Its maker considers it a "vegetable knife," but we think that's entirely too limiting a name. Look at its nearly 3", delicate, S-shape contour: what could be better to bone quail or trim barbecued ribs? And that ergonomic handle! This parer is a true pleasure to use.

3.12 LAMSONSHARP GOLD LINE FLUTING PARER

This smallest of paring knives was once called a "French parer" because it was produced mainly in the French cities of Nogent and Thiers. No longer, as this fine American-made example proves. Shaped like a short, stout isosceles triangle, its bare 3" length brings the hand into the closest cutting contact with food to promote ultimate tip control. Use it to score or flute mushroom caps and turn carrots.

KNIFE FOLKLORE

When a knife is given as a gift in the English-speaking world, a small token is added, often a coin. The additional present is included in order to avoid having the knife cut the friendship.

CLEAVERS

According to the *Oxford English Dictionary*, to *cleave* is to "separate or sever by dividing or splitting." The easiest way to accomplish said act is to use the heftiest knife available: the cleaver. This is one rare instance when you want a blade-heavy knife: the heft does the splitting for you.

A cleaver's main function is to go through bones, but it can occasionally be used for some general work.

After chopping or slicing, simply slip the blade under the cut-up pieces, scoop them onto the flat side, and transfer them to your pot or mixing bowl. You can also use its substantial side to smash garlic or pound meat for scallopini or braciola.

When shopping for a cleaver, select a larger, heavier one than you think you might be comfortable with. You'll get accustomed to the weight, and be happy you did.

3.13 WÜSTHOF-TRIDENT CLASSIC CLEAVER

This is one handsome implement. It's purposefully heavy, thick, and finished with a distinct, 6"-long channel edge—a trio of characteristics that will stand up to decades of hacking and cracking. It's a fine tool to zip through soon-to-be-braised oxtail or to quarter chicken for sauté or duck destined for confit.

3.14 J. A. HENCKELS FOUR-STAR CLEAVER

The blade of a good cleaver accounts for 65 percent of its total weight, as it does with this nearly 5-pound example. When you pick it up, you'll sense its forward drop, which means that the knife will practically do the job for you. It has a full tang, a necessary feature to withstand the shock and reverberation from chopping.

3.15 SABATIER COMMERCIAL CLEAVER

Slightly smaller than the German-made cleavers, this nearly 6"-long French cleaver from Sabatier, which has a full tang and high-carbon stainless steel blade, is still proportionately thick and heavy. We especially like its scaled-to-size, pistol-grip molded Delrin handle, which creates a firm, comfortable grip for smaller hands.

ASIAN KNIVES

Confucius once said that one "must not eat what has been crookedly cut," and for centuries his words have been heeded, knowingly or not, throughout the Far East by those who value the look and flavor of food.

Throughout China, rectangular-shaped cleavers in varying sizes and weights became the cook's all-purpose knives of choice, while their Japanese counterparts favored a broad, blocklike shape for cutting and chopping and a longer, distinctly slender blade variety for slicing. Chinese cleavers come in three sizes: no. 1 (large), no. 2 (medium), and no. 3 (small), and each size is available in two weights—light and heavy. Although one cleaver is usually sufficient for most tasks, you might consider a long, thin, rectangular blade for mincing and a wide, rectangular blade for slicing and chopping.

The Japanese, like the Chinese, developed three variations on a knife theme designed to contend with their three most prominent foods: the broad, triangular *deba* (to fillet fish); the narrower, rectangular *usuba* (to chop vegetables); and the long and slim *yanagi* (to slice sashimi); an all-purpose *santoku* subsequently came into being. The blades are manufactured in carbon steel, stainless steel, or a layered combination of the two, a process perfected centuries ago by samurai swordsmiths for their warrior clients. These knives are ground on one side for precision slicing; they are then sharpened, polished, and finished with a metal, plastic, or horn ring cap and an oak, sandalwood, or ebony handle.

When buying any fine Asian knife, inspect it as you would a Western one; it should be carefully crafted and feel comfortable and well balanced in your hand.

3.16 JOYCE CHEN CHINESE ALL-IN-ONE KNIFE

If you're looking to slice Peking duck, grilled chicken, or sugar snap peas, look at this knife. It's quite adept at dealing with involved slicing tasks. It measures 7½" by 1¾", and looks like an American company's take on the light Chinese cleaver combined with the classic Japanese *usuba* vegetable knife. It's an attractive little thing made of chrome molybdenum stainless steel finished with a bobinga— African rosewood—handle.

3.17 RUSSELL HARRINGTON'S DEXTER CHINESE CHEF'S KNIFE

Walk into the kitchen of any fine Szechuan or Cantonese restaurant and you're likely to find this American-made blade. An excellent lightweight knife, its 8" by 3¼" blade may initially seem cumbersome, but once you get used to it, you'll discover how manageable it can be. It minces and slices—and can it shred lettuce! Don't use it to sever bones, because you may chip the fine cutting edge, but *do* use it to crush garlic, tenderize meat, and slice scallions, carrots, and anything else that might find its way into your next Mandarin hot pot.

3.18 WÜSTHOF-TRIDENT GRAND PRIX *SANTOKU*

CUTTING WITH A CHINESE CLEAVER
❧ KEN HOM ❧

Rapid cooking demands that every ingredient in a dish be properly prepared beforehand. Foods that have been chopped into smallish, well-shaped pieces can be cooked for a minimum of time, ensuring that they retain their natural texture and taste. Careful cutting also enhances the visual appeal of a dish. For these reasons, Chinese cooks are very specific about cutting techniques, particularly where vegetables are concerned. The Chinese always use a cleaver to cut and chop, but if you are more comfortable with a large sharp knife, by all means use it.

Slicing: Hold the food firmly on the chopping board with one hand and cut straight down to make very thin slices. Meat is always sliced across the grain to break up the fibers, so it will be more tender when cooked. If you are using a cleaver, grasp the handle with your thumb and index finger on either side, close to the blade. Always keep the fingers of the hand holding the food tucked under for safety. Your knuckles should act as a guide for the blade.

Horizontal or Flat Slicing: The cleaver, with its wide blade, is particularly suitable for splitting an ingredient into two thinner pieces while retaining that ingredient's overall shape. Hold the blade of the cleaver or knife parallel to the chopping board. Place your free hand on top of the piece of food to keep it steady. Using a gentle cutting motion, slice sideways into the food. Depending on the recipe, you may need to repeat this process, cutting the two halves into even thinner flat pieces.

Roll-Cutting: This technique is used for larger vegetables such as zucchini, large carrots, eggplant, and daikon (Chinese white radish). Roll-cutting allows more of the surface of the ingredient to be exposed to the heat, thereby speeding up the cooking time. Begin by making one diagonal slice at one end of the vegetable. Then roll it over 180° and make the next diagonal slice. Continue in this way until you have chopped the entire vegetable into evenly sized, diamond-shaped chunks.

Mincing: Chefs use two cleavers to mince, rapidly chopping them in unison for fast results. One cleaver or knife is easier for the less experienced, although the process will of course take a little longer. First slice the food and then, using a sharp knife or cleaver, rapidly chop the food, letting it spread out over the chopping board. Scrape it into a pile and chop again. Continue this process until the ingredient is minced. You may find it easier to hold the knife or cleaver with two hands by the top of the blade (rather than by the handle), as though you were chopping parsley. A food processor may also be used to mince, but be careful not to over-mince the food or you will lose out on texture and taste. I find that using the pulse function of the food processor is more effective in mincing ingredients for Chinese food.

What a joy it was to discover this knife! While single-task *debas, usubas*, and *yanagis* are prominent in professional Japanese kitchens, this all-purpose knife appears in virtually every other kitchen in the country. Little wonder: it slices, dices, cubes, and, with the nearly 7"-long Granton edge (hollow-ground) added by its German manufacturer, it tackles the tasks very cleanly. You'll find it in our kitchen.

JAPANESE KNIVES

The blades of Japanese knives are honed on one side only, usually the right side for right-handed use (left-handed knives can be specially ordered). Manufacturing methods for Japanese style knives can be classified as *honyaki*, *hongasumi*, and *kasumi*. These classifications are made according to a knife's *kirenaga*, or the period of time that the knife remains sharp. The intended use of the knife and the level of experience of the user are important factors to consider when choosing a knife. *Honyaki* knives are the highest quality; they maintain sharp edges over long periods of time and don't lose their original shapes even after repeated sharpening. The hardness of the *honyaki* knives makes sharpening difficult and should be left to experienced hands. *Hongasumi* and *kasumi* knives are made of high-carbon steel and soft iron. Though they're easier to sharpen than the *honyaki* knives, the blades don't maintain the same sharpness.

3.20 MASAMOTO SOHONTEN KASUMI *YANAGI*

Like an attenuated slicing knife, this 10½" blade is perfect for slicing raw fish. It's long, so it can cut clear across a big piece of tuna, swordfish, or sea bass for sashimi or sushi.

3.21 MASAMOTO SOHONTEN KASUMI *USUBA*

At first glance, it may look like a simple long, steel rectangle, but this high-carbon blade with a soft-iron outer layer is *the* Japanese vegetable knife. Its 7½" length will crosscut a big bok choy or turnip in one clean sweep, and its 2" depth will supply the extra strength to power through daikons and yams. It's finished with a smoothly sanded octagonal wooden handle for a sure, comfortable grip.

3.19 GLOBAL *DEBA*

This may resemble a chef's knife with a clipped tip, but the 7" edge's sharper upward curve is purely Japanese. It is broad—roughly 2" deep from edge to spine—and though it can be used for many purposes, the *deba* is prized in Japan for the ease with which it slips between the flesh and bones of a fish. Its breadth lifts and supports newly filleted flesh, which allows the guiding hand to perform its task with complete dispatch. Global knives often stay sharper longer because the "face" of the edge is sharpened straight, covering more surface area than just beveling the tip. We're partial to this one's sensitive, light weight.

BUTCHERING KNIVES

Butchering knives are designed to cut, trim, and finish raw meat. These are not impact knives, so they don't need a full tang or collar. Many fine butchering knives have handles whose shoulder end—the one nearest the blade—is enlarged to enhance leverage and also to protect your hand in case of slippage. The modest weight makes large, long cutting easier to execute.

3.22 DEXTER/RUSSELL'S SANI-SAFE BUTCHER KNIFE

This is the knife of choice among butchers for cutting shell and porterhouse steaks, lamb and pork chops, and for splitting a hind of beef in half. It's rigid and broad so it can't buckle when piercing or cutting though large meat cuts. It's also a full 10" long, so it can section loins and saddles. The handle is made of sanitary plastic.

3.23 MONTANA COLLEZIONE MAÎTRE BUTCHER KNIFE

This is the quintessential butcher's knife. Its cutting edge sweeps up

"I've never gotten the hang of hunting. Luckily, we're invited out a lot."

to create a broadened tip that can first pierce and then allow for a smooth drop-and-draw-through cutting stroke. Its 8" blade is 1½" deep and well balanced, a combination that makes it ideal not only for coping with larger cuts of meat but also for finely filleting and slicing.

SCIMITAR KNIVES

With their exaggerated, upwardly curved blade tips, these knives suggest formidable ancient swords rather than tools to steak out large carcasses or quarter smaller ones. To use a scimitar, pierce the point into the side of the meat farthest from you, then rock it down and back on the handle in a strong, definitive motion to cut directly through; watch an experienced butcher and you'll see the ease of movement that these blades provide.

3.24 DEXTER/RUSSELL'S SANI-SAFE SCIMITAR KNIFE

A dependable, commercial workhorse, this broad, 10"-long blade performs the same tasks as the butcher knife. It, too, steaks out sectioned meat, but whereas a butcher's blade cuts with a pierce-and-draw stroke, the scimitar is handled like a saw, with back and forth motions. In a professional's hand it creates smooth, clean slices; novices tend to leave somewhat rough edges along the sides of their steaks. However, this scimitar knife is good for both restaurant and home use.

THE KNIVES OF NOBU

NOBU MATSUHISA

Nobu Matsuhisa owns or is a partner in nine Nobu and Matsuhisa restaurants in the United States, London, and Tokyo. His knife wardrobe is worth more than $25,000.

A sushi chef needs good hands. But he also needs a good knife. My favorite knife is like a samurai sword. It's handmade of special steel with a blade that's sharp on one side. The handle is black wood. I paid $500 for it. I have three other knives like it, each with a different blade. There is one for saltwater fish, one for freshwater fish, one for eels, and one just for fugu.

Actually I have more than fifty knives. I bought my first knife more than thirty years ago and still treasure it, although the blade of the knife is worn down to ⅓ of its original size. Even the most expensive knife can be ruined if not cared for properly. I keep my knives sharp on a stone, working the blade with a little water. A sushi chef's knives are his most important tools and he always owns his own set. I have nine restaurants with a set of my knives in each. I also have another twenty in my house for my personal sushi bar.

Give me the provisions and whole apparatus of a kitchen, and I would starve.

—MONTAIGNE

BONING & FILLETING KNIVES

MOST OF THE TIME, butchers and fishmongers will bone any meat, poultry, or finfish you select; yet there are instances when you might want to enjoy the challenge, economy, and satisfaction of doing the task yourself. Sometimes, especially if there's an able hunter or fisher in the family, you'll have fresh game and fish on hand but not a butcher, so the undertaking could fall to you and the trustiest possible blade. If you plan to stuff or to simply sauté the focus of your feast, it's important to know that meat's configuration in order to get the greatest possible yield.

There's a rule of thumb about boning and filleting knives: blade rigidity should be proportional to the size of the furred, feathered, or finned beast you are dealing with. The larger the animal, bird, or fish, the stronger and more rigid that blade must be to tackle it; a flexible knife striking against hard bone could snap back or even break off, while a rigid blade used on fragile bones might mangle them and rip the flesh. A flexible knife that's more responsive to gentle contours is best for delicate poultry and fish; it would be difficult to feel the tiny bone structure otherwise.

3.25 DEXTER/RUSSELL'S SANI-SAFE BONING KNIFE

If you were to poll butchers on their preferred blade, chances are that this would be their knife of choice: it's durable, economic, and gets the job done simply and efficiently. It's the Mack truck they drive versus the Rolls-Royce they rev in their dreams. This knife is constructed of stain-free high-carbon steel, with a plastic handle. It measures 6" long to effectively deal with larger meat cuts and is a shade under an inch from edge to spine, the most minimal surface for quick and efficient boning. The flexible blade allows for more "give" around bones and joints.

3.26 CHEF'SCHOICE TRIZOR PROFESSIONAL 10X BONING KNIFE

This nearly rigid, 5½"-long boning knife blade is, perhaps, the narrowest one we've seen. Many butchers like its ⅝" depth. In fact, they will grind off some of the edge of a broader blade to achieve that slight profile; they say the narrowness enhances dexterity and speeds up their cutting pace.

3.27 VICTORINOX HAM BONING KNIFE

A highly specialized tool for boning hams and other cuts of meat with a large center bone, this knife reflects the practicality for which central Europeans are famed. The 8½"-long stainless steel blade is curved to fit around a bone, so its razor-sharp cutting edge—1¼" wide at the end of the knife—will scrape as much meat as possible off the bone. The tang,

---

OPEN-FACED BROOK TROUT

4 servings

I use this satisfying method with any roundfish up to 2½ pounds (a 1½-pound fish is best). It produces boneless servings with all the freshness and flavor of whole-fish cookery.

4 brook trout (12 to 14 ounces each), gutted only
4 teaspoons unsalted butter, softened, for broiling
salt and freshly ground black pepper
1 lemon, quartered (optional)

1 Preheat the broiler.

2 Butterfly the trout by splitting each fish through the belly from head to tail. Cut through the bones, but do not sever the fish completely. Open the fish like a book, and using a small sharp knife, trim away the skeleton on both halves. Pull out any pinbones. (This procedure may be done by your fish seller.)

3 Rub the flesh with the butter and season with the salt and pepper.

4 Place as many fish on your broiler tray as it can hold without crowding. Broil 3 to 4 inches from the heat source until the flesh is just cooked through, about 4 minutes. Serve immediately with lemon wedges or a flavored butter of your choice.

The Modern Seafood Cook, by Ed Brown

which extends two-thirds of the way up the wooden handle, is held by three nickel-silver rivets, and the cylindrical handle partly balances the long, heavy blade. A sturdy, handsome implement, this boning knife will certainly fulfill its singular purpose: to pick a bone clean.

3.28 SABATIER AU CARBONE BONING KNIFE

This boning knife's narrow, sturdy-yet-flexible 5″ carbon steel blade is just as ideal for working around a chicken's fine contours as it is for boning a breast of veal or butterflying a leg of lamb. It likewise gets our vote for preparing a Boston

shoulder roast and crown roast. The smooth protective bolster prevents your hand from riding onto the blade and the long handle makes a comfortable grip.

3.29 DEXTER/RUSSELL'S SANI-SAFE FILLET KNIFE

Slightly longer, nearly as curvaceous, and almost as flexible as the Sabatier boning knife, this American-made fillet blade's similar shape suggests a comparable use: removing flesh from bone. Yet there are distinctions, and here they are designed to better deal with a more streamlined fishbone structure versus that of a complex chicken or lamb shoulder. The blade,

blanked from stainless steel, is designed for the purpose: it's rigid—for quick, precise strokes—and fitted with a textured grip to prevent slippage, even when wet.

3.30 MONTANA COLLEZIONE MAÎTRE FILLET KNIFE

If you consider that flat fishes—like a sole, flounder, or brill—are elliptically shaped and somewhat deep bodied, it's easy to understand why this knife works so well to fillet them. Its sharp tip penetrates flesh easily, and its flexibility promotes sensitivity to underlying carcass contours, while its 7″ length can cut cleanly across them in one rapid sweep.

SLICING KNIVES

WHEN WE TALK about slicing knives we mean those blades designed to cut through every kind of cooked meat, poultry, and fish. These knife blades vary distinctly in their width from cutting edge to spine, in their tip profile, in flexibility, and in their smooth, serrated, or beveled edge. The words *slicing* and *carving* are used interchangeably, but to be truly accurate about it, carving is a subsection of slicing.

Carving is the kind of cutting done frequently at the table, and the knives designed to do so have moderately thin, barely flexible blades. Generally speaking, more rigid knives are used to slice hot, juicy meats, like roast beef. More flexible knives are used for poultry, and even more pliable ones are meant to slice smoked fish and ham. Knives with pointed tips are designed to cut bone-in meats because that tip can penetrate and free the meat surrounding its bone; rounded-tip blades are great for slicing large, boned meats and fish.

3.31 GLOBAL SLICER

As light and narrow as a fine slicer should be, this supersleek knife does a terrific job on roasted loins, fillets, and hanger steaks. Its seamless construction allows no place for bacteria to get trapped, and its steel handle will not absorb a food's flavor. The

handle, which has been intentionally weighted for better balance, has a textured surface that makes it easy to grip even when your hand is wet and slippery. There's just one caveat about this carver: since it's only 7″ long, it has a bit of a tough time with larger cuts of meats, like silver tip and rib roasts, such that it can't quite crosscut in one sweep. For those jobs, you'll need Global's 10″ or 11″ slicer.

3.32 REGENT-SHEFFIELD INFINITY EDGE SLICER

Because it's stamped, this blade is lighter and more rigid than a forged slicer, but it's equally suited to the task. The 8″ blade is sharply tipped to neatly pierce cooked meat and relatively narrow to slip deftly through it.

Its nice, sizable, brass-riveted handle provides a thick grip that would be quite comfortable for a cook with a larger hand.

3.33 WÜSTHOF-TRIDENT GRAND PRIX SLICER

This is an all-purpose slicer. Its 9" length supplies enough surface to crosscut small meat cuts in one stroke. Its moderate flexibility makes it superb for negotiating around a turkey carcass or the bones of a roast, while its sharp, narrow tip is perfectly designed to penetrate and rapidly free meat from bone.

3.34 HAM RACK

Consider the elegant prospect of having an entire, sweet, delicate *prosciutto di Parma,* and then needing an authentic Italian ham rack to hold it while you carve its paper-thin slices. The polished white marble and gleaming stainless steel of this rack should meet the challenge admirably, although it will certainly work as well for less ambitious hams. The elongated horseshoe-shaped rack grips the ham with three pairs of prongs, while a flexible knife makes a neat job of slicing. A notched crossbar can be set to adjust the space within the horseshoe so that hams of any size or shape can be accommodated. The marble base, 17½" long by 9¾" wide and ¾" high, is very heavy and needs clamping to stay in place on a table or sideboard. The steel grip stands about 7" high on three sturdy legs.

MEAT AND FISH SLICERS

There's a broad range of knives designed to cut slices from cooked roasts, smoked meat, and cured fish, and they all have one thing in common: they are longer than all-purpose slicers in order to reach across these generally larger cuts. Some have a thinner profile to contend with the drier, more compact texture of smoked ham, prosciutto, or salmon, while others have a broader, heftier blade to better slip through juicier roasts. Some knives are finished with a sharp tip to maneuver around a central bone while others are round-tipped for slicing boneless meat or fish. Again, the texture of the meat is the rationale behind flexibility (for firmer flesh) and rigidity (for moister meat) in these particular blades.

3.35 SABATIER COMMERCIAL HAM SLICER

Long, narrow, rigid, and round-tipped, this is the ultimate knife to slice boneless roast ham, braised shoulder, or poached loin. Its 10" length is more than enough to cross-slice large hams, its barely 1" width limits surface drag during a draw stroke. The blade is constructed of high-carbon steel; the handle is made of molded Delrin.

3.36 MONTANA COLLEZIONE MAÎTRE SALAMI SLICER

Peck's market in Milan is made up of a series of shops, each specializing in a group of ingredients—from fish and meat to cheese and chocolate. They are grouped next to one another in a three-block area.

If you walked into their main shop and waltzed over to their impressive *salumeria* section, you'd surely see the counterman wielding this neat, rectangular stainless steel blade. Little wonder: it's 9" long, to slice a wide mortadella or Toscana; nearly rigid; 1⅝" deep, to slip through a compact pepperoni or *saucisson fumé;* and square-tipped, since there's no need to pierce flesh or prod around bones.

3.37 J. A. HENCKELS FOUR-STAR ROAST BEEF SLICER

Long, wide, inflexible, and finished with a Granton edge, this high-carbon no-stain steel knife is tailor-made to slice large, juicy roasts. The generous 10" edge can cut across a large standing rib roast; its sturdy, 1¼" depth won't buckle or bow when driving through juicy flesh; and that Granton finish—which is a series of alternating ovals ground from both blade sides to produce the thinnest possible edge—creates air pockets during slicing to prevent meat from sticking to the blade and causing sloppy slices.

3.38 WÜSTHOF-TRIDENT CLASSIC SALMON SLICER

Sporting one of the longest blades in this category, this knife is the hands-down favorite for slicing smoked salmon, gravlax, and such cured hams as prosciutto and Serrano. These richly flavored fish and meats are best savored when served in paper-thin slices, and that's the task this knife does so well. Its limber 12″ length can equally cross-slice thick or thin, broad or narrow fish and meat contours, while its narrow Granton edge creates clean slices. This knife is also available without the hollow-ground edge, but we're partial to this version.

3.39 DEXTER/RUSSELL'S SANI-SAFE NARROW SLICER

For those who feel more secure with a thick, textured grip, pick up this knife, a delicatessen workhorse. It is 2″ shorter and less pliant than the Wüsthof salmon slicer, but that stoutness and rigidity translate into a long lifespan. And because it's finished with the Granton edge that promotes clean, even slicing, you'll find this blade equally adept at carving boiled ham or roast turkey breast.

---

⑥

GRAVLAX WITH MUSTARD SAUCE

10 servings

FOR THE GRAVLAX

3½ pounds fresh salmon, center cut
2 large bunches fresh dill, washed and patted dry
¼ cup kosher salt
¼ cup sugar
2 tablespoons crushed black pepper

FOR THE MUSTARD SAUCE

8 tablespoons olive oil
2½ tablespoons white wine vinegar
2½ tablespoons prepared mustard
½ teaspoon salt
½ teaspoon white pepper
¼ cup sugar
pinch ground cardamom (optional)

TO MAKE THE GRAVLAX

1 Ask the fish dealer to cut the salmon in half, remove the backbone and small bones, and leave the skin on.

2 Set half of the salmon, skin side down, in a glass or enamel rectangular dish. Place the dill over the fish. In a small mixing bowl, combine the salt, sugar, and pepper, then sprinkle this mixture evenly over the dill. Set the other salmon half, skin side up, over the dill.

3 Cover the fish with plastic wrap and place a baking sheet on it that is larger than the dish that contains the fish. Set weights, such as heavy cans, on the baking sheet and refrigerate the salmon for up to 3 days, turning the fish over every 12 hours and basting it with the liquid that accumulates in the bottom of the dish. After basting, replace the weights each time.

TO MAKE THE MUSTARD SAUCE

In a medium bowl, combine all of the ingredients and blend thoroughly. Cover the sauce and place in the refrigerator for at least 2 hours. Before serving, beat with a whisk or fork.

TO FINISH & SERVE

Remove the salmon from the marinade and discard the dill and seasonings. Pat the fish dry and set it skin side down on a cutting board. Cut wafer-thin slices on the diagonal and away from the skin. Serve with the mustard sauce.

 ⑥

Operakällaren, Stockholm, Sweden

3.40 SABATIER COMMERCIAL STEAK KNIVES

Until the seventeenth century, guests brought their own knives to dine in the home of another, but that changed when individual tableware became available. Excellent steak knives, like these, would have been much appreciated. The knives are narrow and nearly rigid, with 5½″ blades that gently sweeps upward to a sharp tip. The bowed edge, ¾″ depth, and rigidity of each blade are the characteristics necessary to properly slice tender steaks. And that sleek tip! It's ideal to deftly free every morsel of meat surrounding a T-bone.

3.41 MONTANA OPTIMA DOUGH KNIFE

Before we get to bread knives, we need to slip in a special-purpose blade for dough. Pasta dough, that is.

Of course homemade pasta can be cut into noodles with a machine, but for purists who like the complete hands-on experience of creating tagliatelle, fettuccine, and lasagna, this long, broad, inflexible blade is a pleasure to own. Nearly 9½″ long and 2″ deep, it will draw across lengthy folded dough sheets while its shape—broader at the grip with a slight taper to tip—eases the quick draw-and-pull slicing motion.

Using a knife like this to cut home-made pasta will give each strand a slightly different width, adding to its handmade look. It will also produce a pasta with texture on its surface and along its edges so that each strand will hold more sauce.

SERRATED KNIVES

THE DESIGN OF many contemporary serrated knife blades is drawn directly from old woodworking tools, whose varied teeth, shape, and pitch enabled them to cut across or with the grain of the wood. The serrations on these edges are formed by two successive processes. First, the wave or toothed profile is cut out from the metal blank. Then the metal along one side of the cutout is ground down to produce a very thin, sharp edge, which will create the cleanest, most narrow path while cutting.

THE ORIGIN OF CUTLERY IN THE U.S.

In 1818, Henry Harrington, a New England craftsman and inventor, established the first cutlery company in the United States in Southbridge, Massachusetts. Harrington manufactured surgical equipment and shoe knives, as well as firearms. As his cutlery line expanded, he stopped making firearms. In 1884, Harrington introduced the Dexter trade name. In 1834, another New Englander, John Russell, founded the Green River Works. By paying much higher wages than English cutlers, Russell was able to attract skilled European craftsmen to his factory, which produced large quantities of quality hunting knives to supply America's western frontier.

In 1933, a new company came into existence when the Harrington Cutlery Company and the John Russell Cutlery Company merged. Russell Harrington Cutlery Company offered a broad range of cutlery products, from the famous knives that won the West to cutlery for the professional and industrial markets, and they still do.

BREAD KNIVES

Two distinct sawlike edges appear frequently on bread knives—the broad-set scallop edge and a somewhat toothier piranha edge. Some teeth are more closely set than others (even within the same edge style), yet all angle directly downward in order to cut during push and pull strokes; both strokes smoothly slice through firmer exteriors and more fragile interiors without crushing or compacting the food. It's for this same reason that most fine tomato, fruit, and vegetable knives are also serrated.

3.42 MONTANA OPTIMA ADJUSTABLE BREAD KNIFE

This is a prime example of the fact that the bread knife need not be forged to be exemplary. This 10″ blade, with its scallop edge, quickly bites though a loaf's hard crust, then rips though the softer crumb without compressing it. And if your aim is to cut identically thick or thin slices for sandwiches or canapés, use this knife's adjustable cutting guide to do just that.

3.43 J. A. HENCKELS FOUR-STAR BREAD KNIFE

Whether you fancy yourself an artisanal bread-maker or one who's proud to produce a loaf from a well-used bread machine, you'll want to present the tempting result at the table along with a handsome knife that's fit for the task. That would be this blade: it is 8″ long, to cross-slice peasant loaves, broad brioches, or smaller boules; admirably rigid, to ensure straight cuts; and finished with a superb scallop edge to easily slip through the crispiest crusts. As any baker worth his or her weight in yeast knows, bread will stay much fresher when it's cut immediately before serving.

3.44 LAMSONSHARP GOLD BREAD KNIFE

Another knife that you can proudly bring to the table is this one from the town of Shelburne Falls, Massachusetts, where fine, forged cutlery has been produced for nearly two centuries. It has short, rather tightly set teeth along its 8″ edge, which makes for smooth, slow cuts. Nicely rigid, well balanced, and fitted with brass rivets, it's an American dream.

3.45 OXO GOOD GRIPS BREAD KNIFE

At first glance, this knife's profile seems very odd, but why shouldn't a bread knife be shaped like a saw? This one's upwardly set handle prompts the most natural, comfortable hand positioning for cutting on both push and pull strokes and at the same time raises your hand so that when a slice is complete, there's no chance of knocking your knuckles on the underlying cutting board. Like the more conventional bread knives, this scallop-edged model is 8″ long and will cross-slice broader *ciabattas* or narrower *pains de mie.*

3.46 BEST SANDWICH SPATULA

Here's an implement that should be found in more kitchens. It is simple to use, inexpensive, and very good at producing the one thing that nearly all Americans enjoy: sandwiches. The rounded 3¾″ stainless steel blade, serrated on one side and smooth on the other, is a double-duty utensil. Use the smooth edge to spread butter, cream cheese, anchovy paste, and the like, then turn the blade over and cut the bread with its sharp serrated side. The blade is flexible enough to smooth on filling without tearing the bread, yet firm enough to cut the sandwich in two. Just 7½″ in length with a handle of smooth Asian raim wood, this little helper could really make life a bit easier—especially for the lunch box chef.

FRUIT & VEGETABLE KNIVES

Among the most useful serrated knives are those tailor-made to cut and slice fruits and vegetables. They're especially good for tomatoes, where the resistant skin must be pierced without crushing the tender flesh that lies beneath. They are equally fine in slicing lemons and limes without squeezing out a drop of juice. You'll also find these knives handy to cut *ficelle,* slice sausage, and julienne bell peppers.

Citrus knives—occasionally called bar knives—are also included in this category. As their name indicates, they cut fruit but can tackle a number of other tasks as well.

3.47 LAMSONSHARP TOMATO KNIFE

What nice, evenly spaced sharp teeth this knife has! More angular in profile than the below blades' serration, they nonetheless do an equally neat job of slicing soft-fleshed fruits. This knife's straight 5″ edge gently sweeps up to a two-pronged tip, which contributes to a slick draw stroke and can be used as a fork to move the fruit to a plate.

3.48 WÜSTHOF-TRIDENT CLASSIC TOMATO KNIFE

This is a handy knife to have around when you need to segment small lemons and limes, zip through kaiser rolls and baguettes, and slice German sausage. In other words, this knife excels at sweeping through double-textured foods that have hard exteriors and delicate interiors. Made of nearly rigid, scallop-edged, no-stain steel, this 5½″-long blade has a nice two-pronged tip for spearing and transferring new slices from board to plate; its full tang contributes balance and leverage.

3.49 MONTANA COLLEZIONE MAÎTRE CITRUS KNIFE

Long, narrow, finished with tightly set teeth and a sharp, centered tip, this knife is superb for slipping through tough lemon or lime peels and then cutting the underlying flesh without relinquishing a drop of juice. It is narrow because little blade depth is needed to slice such fruits, and its 5½″ length is sufficient to cross-slice a big navel orange or Star White grapefruit. It's a perfect bar knife that can also slice bread and sausage.

3.50 KYOCERA MING TSAI CERAMIC FRUIT KNIFE

A newcomer to professional and home kitchens, this harder-than-steel blade from Japan's largest producer of industrial ceramics is a nice adjunct to a well-rounded kitchen. Its 4½″-long edge can quarter apples, slice carambola, and peel persimmons. Shorter and broader than other fruit knives, it can also be used to mince cilantro. The ceramic blade is manufactured like porcelain, through a high-temperature, long firing process that creates a dense, durable material—its maker calls it zirconium oxide—that requires little sharpening. Furthermore, 90 percent of the impurities that make porcelain brittle are taken out of this knife. Unlike porcelain, if the knife is dropped it will not shatter, although it can chip depending on the angle at which it lands. Luckily it can be repaired or replaced by the company.

WHY OUR TABLE KNIVES HAVE BLUNT ENDS

It is to Cardinal Richelieu, archenemy of the Three Musketeers, that we owe the blunt-ended table knife. Richelieu once saw a guest at one of his dinner parties picking his teeth with the point of a knife and was so upset by the sight that he ordered all the knives in his household to have their points ground down to a round end. Eventually, a law was passed making it illegal for French knife manufacturers to produce dinner knives with points. The only exception was the steak knife.

GRAPEFRUIT KNIVES

A special category of fruit knives exists for preparing grapefruit. While you can loosen each section of flesh from its pocket of membrane, most prefer to completely remove the edible fruit from its surrounding peel. For the former technique, you'll need a straight, serrated knife (like one of the preceding tomato knives), but if you like your Ruby Marsh sectioned cleanly and completely, you'll want a rigid, upwardly curved, double-edged blade.

3.51 WÜSTHOF-TRIDENT GRAPEFRUIT KNIFE

Look at this blade's saw-and-racker

This grapefruit knife is a delight. Its saw-like edges slip though pith and flesh, its curve mirrors that of a grapefruit's profile, and its dull point won't pierce flesh and unnecessarily drain juices. Its ease-of-use makes you want to load up on vitamin C.

3.52 LAMSONSHARP GRAPEFRUIT KNIFE

Although this product from Lamsonsharp bears all the characteristics of a classic grapefruit knife, we also like its unusual tip, which is not quite blunt, but tapered to a point. Not only does the shape contribute to sectioning out halved grapefruits, but the tip lets you pierce and hollow out onions or small melons like Galias and Cavaillons.

FROZEN-FOOD KNIVES

Well-designed, tailored-to-task, serrated frozen-food knives are the only blades that can saw though an iced food block. There are great savings if you buy frozen vegetables in bulk and then use amounts as needed. If you freeze your own vegetables, it is often easier to pack them in big blocks than in individual packets. And if you bake several hearty loaves but intend to use a portion of a loaf at a time, you'll need to cut through a hard-frozen crust. With a frozen-food knife, blade strength and a heavily toothed edge are essential.

3.53 WÜSTHOF-TRIDENT FROZEN-FOOD KNIFE

Look at this blade's saw-and-racker teeth: they're rough enough to advance through a frozen-food block but relatively wide-set to prevent the clogging that happens from a buildup of ice shards. The blade on this knife is extremely rigid, so it can't buckle on the push or pull motions that make headway through ice, while its generous 10″ length can slice across most frozen-food packages.

THE BIRTH OF THE SANDWICH

The Earl of Sandwich lived in England during the first half of the eighteenth century. He was so devoted to playing cards that he often refused to interrupt his games for meals. Eventually he developed a technique for holding his food between two pieces of bread which left one hand free to continue his play. His new dining method was immediately accepted by his fellow players and made him a hero among gamesmen.

SHELLFISH KNIVES

IT'S BEEN SAID that "an oyster is a fish built like a nut"; in response to that thought, manufacturers have designed nutcracker-like devices and knives to open oysters, clams, scallops, and hard-shell crabs. If you are looking for a shellfish knife, you'll discover they all have two prominent features: rigidity and shortness. The former provides the leverage needed to pry open the most incalcitrant creature, while the latter permits the close contact needed to open shellfish carefully. There are, however, variations on the theme: some blades flash a tapered, not rounded, tip; some have a cutting edge while others are dull; and some, like the crab knife, have a curious, peekaboo central hole with which to extract every morsel from a steamed blue. So, if those armored oysters or any of their kin are indeed shaped like a nut, they won't be tough ones to crack (or open) with the appropriate tools that we present in this section.

3.54 WÜSTHOF-TRIDENT ARROW-SHAPED OYSTER KNIFE

Pity the poor oyster that comes up against this strong, sharp, stout 2½" blade, because it would make short work of any Apalachicola, Olympia, or Wellfleet. It has a keen tip that slips between tightly closed shells and sharp cutting edges to quickly separate oyster from shell. This blade is an inch wide, so it can pry open broader belons as easily as more compact and plumper Willapa Bays. Some oyster knives come with a finger guard to protect your hand from the sharp edge of the shell, but any designated opener would do best to use a sturdy oyster glove.

3.55 DEXTER/RUSSELL'S SANI-SAFE OYSTER KNIFE

In catalogues meant for commercial establishments, you'll see numerous oyster knives—some are labeled as "Providence" or "Boston" patterns to contend with the variant shell shapes from those local oyster beds—but they're all versions of this standard. A fish-house favorite from Fulton Street to Billingsgate, this 2½" "New Haven" blade is narrow, inflexible, and finished with an upwardly curved tip that creates an enhanced prying fulcrum. What's more, it has a textured and comfortable hourglass grip.

3.56 OXO GOOD GRIPS CLAM KNIFE

From the company that brought numerous ergonomic tools to the kitchen comes this thin, but strong, single-edge knife. It's 2½" long to slip between a clam's lip, where a clam's two shells meet, and a bare ⅝" wide

"The trick is in shucking them out of their shells."

so it won't overwhelm and crack a littleneck's shell. A cutting edge is present to free tender flesh from the shell once it's opened. As with the other kitchenware items produced by this firm, the handle of this knife is comfortably soft, close to the blade, and horizontally ridged to supply a nice, secure grip.

3.57 DEXTER/RUSSELL'S SANI-SAFE BAY SCALLOP KNIFE

Scallops are frequently sold shucked because, once removed from the water, they quickly gape open and dry out, but if you're lucky enough to reap and savor these glistening bivalves straight from the shell, you're in for a treat—especially if

they come complete with their delectable coral roe. To enjoy them in such a state, you'll need this strong, short, stiff opener. Its 2″ blade supplies all the length needed to open tiny bay scallops, while its razor-sharp, curved cutting edge neatly arcs

3.58 OYSTER GLOVE

This slinky accessory looks like chain mail and is indeed the first line of defense against the knife in your other hand trying to worm its way inside the clasp of the mollusk. The knife can easily slip; the glove offers a reasonable level of protection to the hand and wrist. Knit with tiny, interlocking metal links and designed to fit either hand, the mesh glove was originally intended for use with oysters but would be suitable for any dicey operation where you might injure your hand—boning or filleting meat or fish, for instance, or even just slicing bagels.

🜨

OYSTERS FRIED IN A CORNMEAL BATTER

3-4 servings

45 oysters, shucked	1 Drain and dry shucked oysters.
½ cup flour	2 Place in flour and shake off excess.
4 eggs	3 Mix eggs and milk well.
¼ cup milk	4 Dip oysters in egg and milk mixture, then in mix of cornmeal and bread crumbs.
2 cups cornmeal	
2 cups bread crumbs	
oil for deep-frying	5 Deep-fry at 375°F till golden brown.
salt and white pepper to taste	6 Serve with tartar sauce.
8 ounces tartar sauce	

🜨

The Grand Central Oyster Bar and Restaurant Seafood Cookbook, by Sandy Ingber

---

under to free meat from a barely bowed shell.

3.59 WÜSTHOF-TRIDENT CRAB KNIFE

How unique this knife is, with its halved-arrowhead profile and centered hole, and how adept it is at helping a diner to enjoy a cooked hard-shell crab! Use its tip to pry off the underlying apron and top shell and then to dig into the hollows for tender meat; the dull edge is designed to scrape off spongy gills. That funny little hole? It's ideal for separating flesh from cartilage on a leg. Less a kitchen tool than an auxiliary dining implement, this stainless steel crab knife is a rare find.

CHEESE KNIVES

There are thousands of cheeses; some are soft and creamy, others crumbly or flaky, and still others rather dense and firm to the touch. Not surprisingly, a number of radically different knives are available to properly cut or apportion these cheeses. Some blades are shaped like an aspen leaf, others like a putty knife, and still others are simply an offset blade that's either etched or replete with holes. Beyond blade profile, all are manufactured in stainless steel and range from super rigid to slightly flexible.

3.60 WÜSTHOF-TRIDENT OFFSET CHEESE KNIFE

The best cheese tray is balanced in its array of scents, tastes, and textures. If you have a creamy Brie, you'll want a spicy blue counterpoint and a tangy, nearly flaky chèvre to round out the board. To set out and sample the selection, you'll also need this offset blade: the 5½" flat length makes it easy to cut neat wedges of Gruyère and Gouda, the etched sides deter semisoft or firmer cheeses from sticking, and the stepped handle makes it impossible to knock your knuckles on the cheese board after completing a slice.

3.61 J. A. HENCKELS OFFSET CHEESE KNIFE

This perfect semisoft cheese knife is ingeniously designed. Its 5" length can slip neatly through Camembert wheels; the microserrated edge guarantees it will go cleanly through Pont l'Évêque rinds, while its skeletal structure means that the ripest *fromage d'Affinois* can't stick to it.

3.62 MONTANA PARMESAN KNIFE

We're told that there are only a few practicing *battitori di formaggio grana,* or "cheese tappers"—artists who tap the outside of a wheel of cheese and, by measuring its sound, can determine whether it's perfect or has ex-

"I'm back. The Brie's not ripe."

cessive fissures or air bubbles. Once graded and sold, the drum is scored and broken into chunks. A sturdy 5" blade, like this one with its sharp tip, easily pierces hard Parmigiano-Reggiano or pecorino, while the broadening blade surface makes it a cinch to pry and break off successive pieces of these and other hard cheese varieties.

3.63 MONTANA GORGONZOLA KNIFE

A Victorian humorist once wrote in *Punch,* "James, let loose the Gorgon-zola." And though James probably used a basic blade to unleash and serve that creamy, pungent blue, he would have done far better with this broad-bladed knife. It's sturdy and 5" long, to slip through a small semisoft wheel, and the wide and dull-edged blade, like a wedge, will slice the cheese neatly along its marbelization.

3.64 MATFER DOUBLE-HANDLED CHEESE KNIFE

With this double-handed knife you can bring all your weight to bear on a large chunk of firm cheese that would normally give you (and other knives) a hard time. The use of both hands helps you distribute all your force evenly, keeping your fingers away from the sharp edge. With a 13"-long stainless steel blade riveted to two polypropylene handles, this knife means business. Use it to cut wedges

of Emmentaler and Gruyère to make cheese fondue. Accompanied by white wine, this creamy Swiss tradition will

warm the pit of your stomach and the cockles of your heart on the coldest, dreariest winter days.

HOW TO PROPERLY CUT & SERVE STILTON

There are a couple of enduring myths about how to serve Stilton, the creamy blue-veined cheese that is formed into thick-crusted, 10"-tall cylinders weighing some 18 pounds. One is that port wine should be poured directly over the wheel of cheese. The other is that a specialized Stilton scoop is required to cut it. Both misconceptions derive from the early days of Stilton, which is made at only seven authorized creameries in the English counties of Leicestershire, Nottinghamshire, and Derbyshire and was first sold in the nearby town of Stilton in the early eighteenth century. Before refrigeration, this massive round of cheese had the propensity to harden, so the port was a softening agent and the scoop an effective instrument for chipping away the

good stuff. Old traditions die hard—particularly English ones—and though serving a whole Stilton with a fancy antique (or reproduction) scoop may be festive, it will leave you with a gutted shell of cheese doomed to drying up. Today, a wheel of Stilton is generally quartered into rings with a cheese wire, the best tool for cutting the dense wheel cleanly without crumbling. Each ring can then be sliced into neat wedges and served (or wrapped immediately and stored properly). Any good, sharp cheese knife will do the job and can be used for a multitude of other cheese needs. Don't waste your money on a scoop that's an outmoded one-trick pony. And keep the port restricted to a glass next to the Stilton.

CURVED & CRENULATED KNIVES

You'd think that the complex manipulation of metal needed to form crescent-shaped and zigzagged blades could only be done with modern technology, but it was actually produced by Old World crafting. Where there's a will, there's a way, and when late-Renaissance Italian chefs needed a double-handled mincing knife, the palace smiths found a way to create

one. Period cookbook etchings testify to the mezzaluna's early use, and later illustrations from France show vegetable decorating knives. Both were probably fashioned from carbon steel; today's knives are generally stainless steel. When selecting a knife of either kind, be sure it's inflexible, has a well-defined edge, and is fitted with a comfortable handle or handles.

3.65 J. A. HENCKELS MEZZALUNA

It's safe to say that if you walk into any kitchen in northern or central Italy you'll see a well-worn version of this beautifully curved, double-

handled blade. It's called a mezzaluna, after the arced "half-moon" profile it bears and is a fine knife for chopping and mincing. Some have two or three blades and can be longer in length, but if it's to be an auxiliary knife, this one—with its single, 6"-long edge— is fine. To use, grasp the two handles, then roll the blade back and forth without lifting it from the chopping board; you'll discover that this two-fisted technique makes you exert an even, easy pressure.

3.66 RÖSLE DOUBLE-BLADED MEZZALUNA

With double the blades and double the chopping speed, this elegant double-bladed mezzaluna fits easily into your hand. Using the natural rocking motion of your wrist, you simply roll it over the herbs you want to mince, and the razor-sharp stainless steel blades do the rest. Plastic guards slip over the blades for safe storage and to keep them from dulling. This tool is 3¼" from the blade tip to the back of the handle, 6¼" long, and 1¾" wide.

3.67 WÜSTHOF-TRIDENT DECORATING KNIFE

At first glance, this knife's zigzag blade (made of high-carbon no-stain steel) looks as though it took quite a spin in a garbage disposal, but no—its cutting edge is carefully corrugated in

deep, ⅜"-wide increments to turn vegetables evenly and quickly. Roughly an inch of edge, from tip to crenulation, it is straight and sharp for light trimming while the rest of the 4" length supplies enough surface to take on turnips and carrots. When turning vegetables, select young, crisp ones and use a deep, deliberate peeling motion to be sure of notching.

KNIFE STRAIGHTENERS & SHARPENERS

THE IMPORTANCE OF regularly straightening and sharpening is stressed throughout this chapter. It's not cutting through food that dulls a knife; it's the repeated impact of the cutting edge against a chopping block or board that causes dullness. It's always much easier to give knives a few strokes with a steel each time you put them away than to attempt to bring them back from the dead. Knives can be reworked and ground free of burrs, but this can be a painstaking task.

When straightening (that is, to eliminate the microscopic curl caused by impact cutting) you should touch the edge of the blade lightly to the steel at a 20° to 30° angle. A sharpening stone removes the first level of molecules from the blade, exposing a new edge. To sharpen, the blade should be held at a 22.5° angle to the stone.

There are three factors to consider when selecting a steel or stone: its composition, shape, and length.

Straightening steels are made from high-carbon stainless steel, the important part being the carbon, because the higher the carbon content, the harder the steel. The degree of hardness of a straightening steel should be proportionate to the hardness of the blade on which it's worked (hardness is measured on the Rockwell scale, as discussed earlier in this chapter). The higher a blade's Rockwell rating, the higher should be that of its straightening steel; straightening can occur only when a harder substance comes into contact

with a less hard one. Sharpeners are made of silicon carbide or ceramic bricks, stones, or standard steels and files coated with industrial diamond dust.

The conventional shape for a steel is cylindrical, but there are many that are elliptical—a broadened shape that extends the standard sharpening area. Stones are usually flat, although there are some oval and diamond-shaped slips and specialty stones. Shape is really a matter of personal preference, but length is not, because you need ample area on which to draw an edge down and across. It's for this reason that we favor 10" steels and 6" and larger stones for straight-edged knives.

There are many other fine sharpening devices that work just as well as handheld steels and stones. Electric or manual, the mechanism behind their design is a pair of abrasive rods set at a fixed angle for swift, easy steeling. Once considered among cutlery cognoscenti as clumsy contraptions that readily ruined an edge, these have evolved into state-of-the-art sharpeners designed to hone both straight and serrated edges.

For those knives whose manufacturers claim "never need sharpening; made of the hardest stainless steel alloy and has a permanently sharp edge," bear in mind that you can always draw that tougher-than-Tarzan blade across the edge of a porcelain plate to realign and sharpen its edge. This is because high-fired clay has a higher Rockwell rating than stainless steel.

3.68 SABATIER COMMERCIAL STRAIGHTENING STEEL

A classic hard-chromed steel, this 10" round shaft tapers to a dull tip for a gentle stroke surface. The medium-fine ridges that run its length supply enough abrasion to restore a knife's cutting edge to its dead-straight lie.

Mind you, this is a straightening steel, much like the ones that come with knife sets; when you find that your knife remains dull after using one, you'll need to sharpen, not straighten it.

3.69 ZANGER ZIP ZAP

This little tool is worth many times its weight in conventional sharpening steels. Created by Alfred Zanger, it is made of ceramic, which is harder than any of the steel used in knife sharpeners. The Zip Zap looks like a mini sharpening tool. It is held between the thumb and the forefinger and drawn across the blade at a 20° angle. The knife is held in place while the Zip Zap moves. It is so convenient that you can easily get into the habit of giving the knife a few strokes before each use. After awhile, you will notice gray steel filings building up on the surface of the Zip Zap. Simply go over it with a soapy brush, rinse, and dry. The Zip Zap is not unbreakable, but it is the most effective sharpener we know and is as inexpensive as it is handy.

3.70 EZE-LAP DIAMOND SHARPENER

Long, lean, and oval, this is one fine sharpening tool. Its 10″ length is covered with rugged industrial diamond dust to create an extremely hard, sharp surface for fast, easy honing. Use it to sharpen knives, scissors, and, according to its maker, restore drill bits, garden tool edges, and even ice skates. This particular sharpener also comes as a brick shape; we're partial to the 2″ by 6″ size.

3.71 EZE-LAP POCKET SHARPENER

In its protective sheath, this tiny pocket steel looks like a precious little penknife. But pull off that cover and you have one formidable diamond dust–coated file. The sharpening shaft measures 2¼″ long and is tapered, which makes it a good handheld sharpener for serrated blades.

But don't relegate it to those edges—it's equally fine for use on straight edges, fish hooks, and to repair nettling nicks in fine crystal.

3.72 CARBORUNDUM STONE

At one time, a carborundum stone such as this one was found in every restaurant, cabinetmaker's, and bar-

PICKY ABOUT SIZE

❧ BARBARA TROPP ❧

Cooks new to our kitchen usually go berserk with the specificity with which we cut things. A dice isn't just a dice; it's a "neat, tiny dice." A coin isn't a coin; it's a "scant ¼″ coin" or a "¹⁄₁₆″ coin." Cooks in their first days at China Moon must feel like they're in cutting kindergarten. There they are, armed with their sharp knives and the occasional diploma from a prestigious cooking school, and the short boss lady is eyeing the length and width of their julienne! "Does it really make such a difference?" they ask politely.

In classic Chinese cooking, it does. In the relatively high heat of stir-frying, for one, the difference between the harder carrot that is cut precisely ¹⁄₁₆″ thin and the softer eggplant that is cut a scant ¼″ thick means the two ingredients will cook to doneness at about the same time. Or, with a potent ingredient like fresh ginger, a threadlike julienne will steam through perfectly in the few minutes it takes to cook the fish beneath it, whereas a thick, irregular julienne would taste raw.

At least in part because of the requirements of these faster cooking methods, Chinese will judge a dish foremost on the finesse of the cutting. It is the very first thing marked by the traditional Chinese eye, way before the traditional tongue makes a comment on the flavor. Chinese writers on cooking will always note the color, size, and shape of a dish's components, and dwell on them happily and long-windedly, in advance of any discussion of the taste.

I confess there might be an element of Virgo madness in the culture. Certainly, there is one in our kitchen! My only defense is one of my favorite quotes from the whole of Chinese history. It comes from a character in an official history of first-century China: "When my mother cuts the meat, the chunks are invariably in perfect squares, and when she chops the scallions, they are always in nuggets exactly 1 inch long." What can I say? History supports me in my obsessions!

SHRIMP SAMBAL

6 servings

This sumptuous dish epitomizes Malaysian cooking, with its intoxicating blend of Chinese, Malay, Thai, and European influences.

1½ pounds medium shrimp, peeled and deveined
¾ pound snow peas, ends trimmed and strings removed
2 tablespoons canola or corn oil
1½ red onions, cut into thin julienne slices
2 tablespoons fresh lime juice (or to taste)

SEASONINGS
3 dried red chiles, seeds removed, or
1½ teaspoons dried chile flakes
2½" slices fresh ginger, peeled
6 cloves garlic
1½ teaspoons ground cumin
½ teaspoon ground turmeric

COCONUT SAUCE (MIXED TOGETHER)
1 cup light coconut milk
1 tablespoon light brown sugar
1 teaspoon salt

1 With a sharp knife, score the shrimp along the back, then rinse and drain thoroughly.

2 Drop the seasonings in descending order into a blender or the feed tube of a food processor while the machine is running and process to a paste. Turn the machine on and off several times to get a smooth mixture. Blanch the snow peas in boiling water for 15 seconds, drain in a colander, refresh under cold water, and drain again.

3 Heat a wok or skillet, add the oil, and heat until hot. Add the seasonings and cook over medium-low heat, stirring with a wooden spoon for about 2 to 3 minutes until fragrant.

4 Add the red onions and toss over medium heat until soft, about 1½ minutes. Add the premixed Coconut Sauce, and heat until boiling. Add the shrimp and lime juice and cook for about 2½ minutes, then add the snow peas and cook another minute. Remove and serve with steamed rice.

A Spoonful of Ginger, by Nina Simonds

---

bershop in the country. Carborundum is the name of several abrasives, usually composed of silicon carbide, which are pressed into bricks. We like a 2" by 6" by 1" size that has a medium-coarse side and a finer one. To use, set the stone on a flat surface, drizzle a few drops of mineral oil down its length, then anchor the stone with one hand while using the other to draw the blade across it at a 10° to 20° angle. Work the coarse-grit side first, then finish off on the (first oiled) finer surface. A carborundum stone will wear out, and when it does, replace it.

3.73 GLOBAL CERAMIC WHETSTONE

This stone is made of dense ceramic: it's harder than other stones and will show less wear. You won't see any dips or valleys develop in it, as they do in softer stones. A final plus: there's no need to soak it before using. Our favorite size, as with other stones, is a 2" by 6" brick.

3.74 CHEF'S CHOICE SERRATED BLADE DIAMOND HONE KNIFE SHARPENER

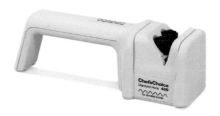

This is a terrific contraption to sharpen tomato, bread, and every other serrated knife blade. We think it's foolproof—all you do is draw the knife through its two diamond abrasives, which are not only set at the correct sharpening angle, but also dovetailed so that every facet, hollow, and point of a knife comes into contact for realignment and sharpening. Although fine-quality serrated knives are generally beveled on one side, this hone's dovetailing detail means that it can be used by both right- and left-handers with equal ease and sharp results.

3.75 CHANTRY KNIFE SHARPENER

Suppose you're of a manual-yet-mechanical mien when it comes to sharpening a blade; you hesitate to go the stone or the steel route and are not quite sure of an electric sharpener's abilities. Well, look no farther; this is the sharpener for you. Six swipes through its two interior mounted steels are generally all it takes to restore a blade to its pristine cutting condition. The steels, which are tension mounted, also revolve in their holders to prevent blade erosion. One caveat comes with this device: use a light touch.

3.76 CHEF'SCHOICE EDGESELECT DIAMOND HONE SHARPENER-PLUS

In its instructions, the manufacturer of this electric knife sharpener creates the impression that it will put the professional knife-sharpening trade out of business with this do-all device. This sharpener does offer a lot: three slots sharpen, strop, and polish straight-edge and serrated blades. A light touch, together with two swipes—one to favor each side—is recommended for straight blades, while single-sided beveled blades—such as bread, tomato, and Japanese knives—are best drawn through once along their beveled side. As with every sharpener, a slow, steady draw along these diamond-coated disks does the trick.

3.77 EZ SHARP KNIFE SHARPENER

This is the little sharpener that could. It was designed with an eye toward safety and is user-friendly. It's made of tungsten carbide, a

---

STUFFED CHICKEN BREASTS

4 servings

Russian cuisine is rich and varied, having drawn its material from the many geographic areas and cultures that have influenced its history. The most elegant Russian food was produced in the kitchens of the noble families, like the de Beausobres of St. Petersburg, who regularly imported the techniques of great French chefs. But there was also an enormous amount of plain good cooking in the homes of the farmers and peasants.

Today, however, much of the best Russian cooking takes place in restaurants. Unfortunately, those restaurants are not in Russia. A good example is the following recipe from the Russian Tea Room in New York City.

FOR THE STUFFING
2 tablespoons vegetable oil
1½ cups thinly sliced onions
1½ cups thinly sliced mushrooms
salt and freshly ground black pepper, to taste
1 tablespoon flour
½ cup red wine
1 tablespoon chopped fresh parsley

OTHER INGREDIENTS
2 whole chicken breasts, halved, skin and bones removed, then sliced almost in half through thickness and pounded thin
salt and freshly ground black pepper, to taste
½ cup flour, for dredging, placed in a shallow bowl
2 eggs beaten with 2 tablespoons milk, with salt and freshly ground black pepper to taste, placed in a shallow bowl

6 cups ½-inch-square fresh bread cubes made from coarsely textured bread, with the crust removed (don't use white bread*)
3 tablespoons vegetable oil

*NOTE It is important to use the home-made bread cubes; do not substitute croutons, as they are too crunchy and overseasoned. If you prefer, roll the chicken breasts into some *unseasoned* bread crumbs and continue as instructed below.

1 TO MAKE THE STUFFING: Place the oil in a sauté pan and sauté the onions over medium heat for 2 to 3 minutes, until softened. Add the mushrooms and sauté for another 3 minutes. Add the salt and pepper and cook for 2 minutes more. Sprinkle the tablespoon of flour over the entire mixture and stir to distribute evenly. Add the wine and continue stirring and cooking for 3 minutes. Add the parsley, combine, and remove from the heat.

2 Season the chicken breasts with salt and pepper. Lay each breast out flat and place one quarter of the stuffing mixture down the center of each. Fold each breast into thirds to enclose the stuffing. Carefully roll each breast into the flour first, tap off the excess, then dip each into the egg mixture. And last, dip each into the bread cubes. Press firmly so that the cubes adhere.

3 Preheat the oven to 350°F.

4 Heat the oil in a large sauté pan until very hot. Gently slip in the chicken breasts, seam side down. Sauté on each side until brown. Remove the chicken breasts carefully and place into an ovenproof baking dish or roasting pan. Bake for 20 to 25 minutes, until the chicken is cooked through. Allow to remain at room temperature for 5 minutes before serving.

The Russian Tea Room, New York, New York

material that is used to make the bits of rock drills. The two blades are set at a 40° angle. To use the sharpener, hold the base on your work surface and lightly draw the knife through the crook between the blades. Six light draws should be enough to shave and hone your knife. The arched handle offers a firm grip, even for people suffering from arthritis, and the front guard will shield your hand from the blade edges. Originally made for the food service industry, this sharpener functions well in the home kitchen.

KNIFE STORAGE

THERE ARE THREE methods of storing knives: blocks, racks, and sheaths. Hardwood blocks are fine if you have plenty of counter space and know your knives by the look of every handle; this should also be the case if you use in-drawer trays and heavy plastic sheaths, where the range of knife blades is partially hidden from view. However, if your whole knife selection is out in the open where you can see it, as it is on a magnetic rack, you'll be more likely to pick up the best one for the job at hand. If you're worried about a small child reaching for your knives, know that on the whole, it's probably no less safe to keep knives in or on a proper rack. No one is likely to place a rack at toddler height, near a child's chair, or alongside a stepladder. If a good rack is suitably located at adult height, it can be as safe as any other means of storing knives.

If you decide on a wall-hung rack, make sure it is well secured by installing it as you would a bookcase. These racks come complete with screws and instructions, but if you have a problem wall, you may have to use additional hardware: lead anchors for a masonry wall, toggle bolts for a hollow one. In some cases, all you need to do is locate the wooden studs in your wall and attach the rack to them. In other cases, you may have to install a wooden backboard on the wall with masonry nails and then secure the rack by screwing it to the backboard. When in doubt, consult your local hardware dealer.

3.78 MESSERMEISTER SUPER MAGNET KNIFE RACK

If your counterspace is too limited for a knife block and a large flatware and gadget collection rules out in-drawer trays and sheathed knives, this is the solution to your knife storage problem. A favorite of chefs, this rack requires no counterspace, and its two broad magnetic bands hold blades firmly in place. Another *big* plus: since the entire blade is exposed, every knife is easy to identify. This rack is meant to be wall-mounted and measures 18″ long. Be careful to select the proper screws for your particular wall surface; the ones that come with the Messermeister are fine for wood but will not work on plaster or composition board. There is also a smaller 12″ model, and a double-sided magnetic bar for slapping on the side—not the door—of a refrigerator.

3.79 J. K. ADAMS KNIFE BLOCK

Wooden knife blocks can be bigger (or smaller) than this fifteen-slot block, but its features illustrate what to look for when investing in a free-standing unit. Made of polished oak to be durable and stain-resistant, it has a full, flat base for secure placement and well-distanced slots for easy removal. It accommodates eight cook's knives, a steel, and six paring or steak knives.

3.80 J. K. ADAMS IN-DRAWER KNIFE TRAY

It was once verboten to even consider storing fine knives in a drawer, but that's no longer the case, thanks to workable in-drawer trays like this one. Crafted in ash, its twelve slots hold five large kitchen knives, six steak or paring knives, and a steel. The manufacturer calls this model The Wave, and its three gently tiered, smoothly sanded crests indeed invite a reaching hand. The tray measures 17½″ by 6¾″ by 2½″, and it fits neatly into most standard drawers.

3.81 MESSERMEISTER KNIFE SHEATH

If you have far too many knives for a knife block, rack, or tray, then slip one of these polystyrene beauties over each of those extra blades and store them in a drawer. The sheaths are made of heavy plastic, to protect both blade edges and reaching hands. They're available in progressive lengths from a 3″ model for parers to a 10″ design for cook's knives and slicers.

CLEANING CHOPPING SURFACES

The best way to clean wood is to scrape off all food residue with a bench knife, then sprinkle coarse salt over the board. Next, use half of a juiced lemon as a scouring pad to scrub and remove the stains, then rinse off with cold water. Cleaning with warm water and soap is an acceptable alternative if you don't have lemons on hand. If the wood is really discolored, use a scrubbing pad and a bit of bleach in hot soapy water. Then rinse, dry, and rub a little mineral oil into the surface. To clean plastic and rubber cutting boards, scrub with soap and hot water. Be sure to add a drop of bleach to the soapy water to disinfect and remove the stains on plastic cutting boards. In time, you'll need to relevel the surface by sanding the valleys caused by chopping on rubber boards.

CHOPPING BLOCKS & BOARDS

IN OUR OPINION, cheese boards, rustic serving planks, and meat-carving boards are really tabletop presentation pieces, not chopping-and-cutting boards on which to prepare food. The whole point of a chopping and cutting board is to receive the brunt of a working knife blade's impact, and it must therefore be both relatively soft, to protect the cutting edge, and solid, to safeguard the underlying surface. Pastry boards can be of pine or marble, and chopping bowls can be crafted in pine or plastic, but an ideal cutting board is made from one of three materials: a hardwood, such as maple; plastic; or rubber.

Wood once ruled as the cutting-board king because of its resiliency, shock absorption, and the fact that it does not impart any of its own flavor to food. It remains the finest material for freestanding chopping blocks, the best of which are made from bonded squares of end-grain wood sawn horizontally, then sanded to create a solid, even work surface. The best possible chopping surface is a freestanding block approachable from any side, but since most kitchens don't have enough space to accommodate such a block, chopping boards must be used. Wooden ones are popular and, after recent University of Wisconsin studies indicated that wood does not transfer bacteria to other surfaces—which makes it a more sanitary cutting surface than plastic, although some plastic boards are treated with antibacterial agents (which will wear away with time)—demand for wooden boards skyrocketed. Subsequent studies have contested that finding, so it remains unclear whether wood harbors or hinders salmonella, Listeria, and *E. coli* bacteria.

Aside from this issue, cutting-board composition is a matter of personal preference. Some cooks like the warm look of wood, others like the resiliency of rubber, and still others like the durability of plastic. Whichever board you choose, select the largest block or board you have room for; it should be thick, so it won't warp, and heavy, so it won't slide around on the counter as you work.

A fifteenth-century book includes this description as among the duties of "A Pantler or Butler":

In the pantry you must always keep three sharp knives, one to chop the loaves, another to pare them, and a third sharp and keen to smooth and square the trenchers with. Always cut your lord's bread, and see that it be new; and all other bread at the table one day old ere you cut it, all household bread three days old, and the trencher bread [use as plates] four days old.

3.82 JOHN BOOS PCA BUTCHER BLOCK

Weighing in at 115 pounds, this 10"-deep block of end-grain maple set on four thick, sturdy legs is one impressive chopping block. Made by the company that supplies the White House kitchen, this model stands 34" high to create a comfortable work zone, has an ample 18" by 18" surface, and comes complete with a knife rack attached securely to one side. The block is available in sizes measuring up to 30" square, as well as in lower heights, while the work surface is hand-finished with mineral oil and paraffin to provide a long life of service.

3.83 J. K. ADAMS WOODEN CUTTING BOARD

Designed to withstand the heaviest hacks of a household cleaver, this cutting board is made of solid New England sugar maple. It's 1¼" thick to absorb shocks and resist warping. Composed of sturdy, edge-grain

"You know what I love? Butcher block."

wood to supply a durable cutting board surface, it's then finished with smooth, rounded corners that won't snag a cook's sleeve. One more plus about this 14" by 20" handsome board: its flip side is grooved to catch juices and hold the Thanksgiving turkey in place, so it can double as a carving board.

3.84 TEKNOR APEX PLASTI-TUFF CUTTING BOARD

If you were to walk into any commercial kitchen across the country, you'd surely see a high-density thermoplastic cutting board like this one. It's a true workhorse in the food service industry because it can't

crack, split, chip, or swell and won't warp. Polyethylene is nonporous, so the board won't absorb moisture or odor. This board has a light, pebbly texture that helps keep food from sliding around on the surface. Some other plastic cutting boards are treated with antibacterial agents, but all are easy to sterilize with a little bleach. Measuring 15" by 20" by ½", it's a convenient countertop size.

3.85 TEKNOR APEX SANI-TUFF CUTTING BOARD

This might not be the most attractive cutting board, but it's so dependable that it has become a staple in professional kitchens. Its hard,

63

compact rubber surface absorbs shock yet still gives, so it's easier on knife edges. It's nonporous, so it won't absorb liquids or odors; heavy, so it won't shift on a counter as you work; and, because it's rubber, will reseal most cut marks over time. If you find yourself relying on this 15" by 20" by ½" cutting board and want it picture-perfect, understand that most marks can be sanded off.

3.86 CHOP & CHOP CUTTING MAT

It may look like a computer mouse pad, but this lightweight plastic cutting mat is a handy kitchen helper. Roughly the same size as an 8" by 10" sheet of paper, it takes up little space yet protects countertops when you're doing light cutting. It's flexible, so once you've chopped your onions or carrots, you can bend the mat and funnel the dice into a bowl or pot. This cutting mat is also great for campers and boaters—it packs neatly and provides a clean, viable chopping surface atop tree stumps, galley counters, and ice chests.

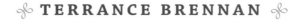

MISE EN PLACE:
ORGANIZING YOUR WORKSPACE
❧ TERRANCE BRENNAN ❧

The most important fundamental in the professional kitchen, and in the home kitchen as well, is the prep work you do before you actually start cooking. The French call this *mise en place* (literally "put in place") and it means meticulously organizing everything you are going to need for a recipe—all the equipment and all the ingredients—before you begin working. It's one of the first things they teach you in culinary school. At least 80 percent of what we do in a professional kitchen is preparation for each service. For the home cook, there is one preliminary step that's essential before you begin your *mise en place,* and that is reading the recipe through carefully, noting all the steps, all the ingredients, all the equipment, and the timing. You *must* understand the recipe before you can prepare it.

It can take a professional chef 45 minutes just to carry out his *mise en place.* We line up our equipment as we will need it—every knife, every spoon, every whisk, bowl, and pan. Then we line up the ingredients as well, measured and in the preparation called for—peeled, drained, separated, diced, minced, sliced, quartered, and so on. Each prepared and measured ingredient is then placed in a separate container, the way you see them on a television cooking show. In a restaurant, organization like this is crucial to timing; we would never succeed in feeding our customers without the prep work. If you start cooking, then stop, walk around looking for a piece of equipment or an ingredient, then come back, start again, cook, stop again, and so on, your recipe will never go smoothly.

Cooking is all about timing, and when your *mise en place* is done you're ready to concentrate 100 percent on the cooking. To me, cooking is not just knowing a recipe and putting together the elements, but is actually *nurturing* the ingredients, focusing on each and preparing it with care. With everything prepared in advance and ready in front of you, you can devote your time and attention to perfectly sweating the shallots, blanching the vegetables, sautéing the meat, poaching the fish, and reducing the sauces. You won't run the risk of scorching or overcooking while you search for the next ingredient or piece of equipment; everything is already there.

Disorganization is detrimental in the kitchen; it can throw off the timing of your whole meal and lead to anxiety. There's nothing more stressful than having guests arriving in an hour and fearing that your dishes won't be done in time. Your prep work is key to a successful meal. With everything organized, the procedure working smoothly, you'll have more time to spend with your guests and the assurance to actually enjoy the meal yourself.

4

CUTTING INSTRUMENTS OTHER THAN KNIVES

A SKILLFUL CRAFTSMAN CAN still do most of the preliminary preparation for many dishes with a good cook's knife—that is, until the recipe requires finely turned melon balls, whole pitted cherries or olives, or grated Parmigiano-Reggiano. For tasks such as these we have recourse to an array of specialized devices that accomplish the work using a blade of some form. There are tools for removing the thick skins of oranges or the barest sliver of lemon zest; for rapid-fire mechanical slicing of a boneless turkey breast or the most transparent shavings of prosciutto; for chopping onions, parsley, or potatoes; and for removing the core from an apple. Some cooks need no more than a paring knife to peel the skin from a potato or a cucumber, but most of us do better with a swiveling peeler. The characteristic that distinguishes nonknife cutters from knives is that they are specialized—each is a tool that has been developed to perform a specific task— which means that you might not know you need one until you are faced with zesting ten oranges for a dessert or hulling a few quarts of strawberries for jam.

The Relatives of the Knife

Some of the cutters in this chapter clearly show their familial relationship to knives, while others, like the egg cutter with its crisscrossed wires, hide their kinship. The essential thing in a cutter is that it possess a sharpened metal edge. This cutting edge can be set at the end of a handle or between two knobs, it can be straight or curved or round, and its use can vary according to the ways your hand can move.

Be careful when using these items. Because the often oddly shaped, permanently fixed blades in these implements are not meant to be sharpened, they are often manufactured with a razor-sharp edge. Also, these cutters are not just grasped with one hand, like a knife; they are used with a variety of hand positions and muscle movements, such as pressing down with two hands, rocking your wrist back and forth, squeezing your fingers together, or rubbing food back and forth across a blade. They can slip, so be sure the handles— and your hands—are grease-free when you use them.

MINCING DEVICES

A STEP OR TWO REMOVED from the mezzaluna is the old-fashioned rolling mincer, which looks something like a toy truck and is pushed back and forth over herbs like a child's toy over the rug. Use it or the more modern spring-mounted chopper for quick little mincings of chervil, mint, and other leafy herbs.

4.1 KÜCHENPROFI SPICE CUTTER

Actually an herb cutter, this streamlined contraption rolls over piles of parsley or mint with five circular stainless steel wheels doubling as cutting blades. On earlier versions, the rims were honed to a sharp edge that minced herbs like a dream but also nicked fingers and knuckles. The current model's blades are not as sharp, so you may have to exert some pressure as you roll them back and forth over a relatively tough herb like Italian parsley. The blades detach from the plastic holder for easy cleaning. The device is 5" long, 3½" high, and 2¼" wide.

4.2 ZYLISS CHOPPER

Although they like to boast that all they need is a knife and a cutting board, professional chefs make use of a number of inexpensive, labor-saving gadgets. This is one of them: a spring-mounted chopper that turns leafy herbs or slices of onion, apple, carrot, and nuts into confetti in a matter of seconds. Simply place slices of any firm-fleshed fruit or vegetable in the plastic container at the bottom and depress the plunger to push the zigzag-shaped stainless steel blade into the ingredient. The more times you push down the plunger, the more finely the item will be chopped, from coarse chunks to mincemeat. The base of the unit is a container that can hold the food to be chopped. The chopper is 8" high with a 3¾" diameter base and comes apart for easy cleaning.

MANDOLINES

We've talked about knife edges that are straight and serrated, flat, crescent shaped, round, and jagged; the one constant element is that they all cut food by moving over it in some fashion. However, you can also move the food over the blade. This is, of course, the principle behind the grater; it is also the principle behind the mandoline, a device widely used in restaurants for cutting vegetables into slices or strips. A mandoline is a narrow plaque, originally made of wood but now often constructed of plastic or, in the classiest professional models, stainless steel, into which have been fixed one or more cutters. Depending on the size and shape of the cutters you can slice, julienne, or produce rippled cuts of cabbage, potatoes, carrots, beets, and any other firm foods. Usually, the cutters can be removed and changed. As dependent as we may have become on our food processors, a professional mandoline slices with far greater precision and finesse. A note of caution: Always use a finger guard.

4.3 BRON CLASSIC MANDOLINE

The Bron is a tool for the professional kitchen, used in restaurants from Hong Kong to Paris. Made of stainless steel, this device works on the basic mandoline principle: the vegetable (or fruit) is held in a tray that slides into a row of blades, which does the slicing. For most uses, you place the ingredient in a kind of carriage that protects your fingers and holds the food steady, but for waffle cuts you have to remove the carriage and hold the vegetable bare-handed. The width of the slice is adjusted by a handle on the underside of the device; a knob on the side adjusts the thickness. Once you decipher the user's manual, the Bron works like the finely tuned machine that it is. However, it is bulky and hard to clean, so we recommend it only for ambitious home cooks. It measures 16" long, 4½" wide, and stands 10¼" high. The Bron also comes in a table-clamp model.

4.4 MATFER PROFESSIONAL MANDOLINE

The Bron mandoline's strongest competitor is the Matfer, which may not

4.5 FORSCHNER PERFORMANCE SHIELD CUT-RESISTANT GLOVES

Let's face facts—if you cook with regularity, you're bound to cut yourself on occasion. Even well-maintained knives and careful attention can't prevent all accidents. That's why the Forschner gloves are so valuable. Meant for workers in the food service industry, these come in handy when you do a lot of chopping, carving, or slicing. They are made of a synthetic fabric that resists the knife blade. Though thoroughly protective of your hands, the gloves are not bulky, and you can still get a good tactile sense of the ingredient you're cutting. There are four types; the one we show you is the lightest in weight and best suited to home use. Forschner  gloves are ambidextrous and come in five sizes, from extra small to extra large. They are also machine washable and bleach safe.

― ⑥ ―

A TANGLE OF TART GREENS

4 servings

This is a wonderfully simple and versatile garnish or accompaniment. We use it with duck, venison, roast pork, sausage, or even soft-shell crabs. In the winter months it can take the place of a green vegetable. The crunchy texture of the cabbage makes chewy foods seem tender.

½ head savoy cabbage
1 strip thick bacon or
  2 strips thin, diced
½ large red onion, thinly sliced
1 tablespoon mustard seeds
2 tablespoons sugar
¼ cup white wine vinegar
½ bunch watercress,
  coarse stems removed
freshly ground pepper to taste

1 Core and coarsely shred the cabbage with a sharp knife or mandoline.
2 In a 10" skillet, sauté the bacon over medium heat until lightly browned. Add the onion and cabbage and sauté until the cabbage begins to wilt. Add the mustard seeds, sugar, and vinegar and cook until the cabbage is tender but still crisp.
3 Remove the skillet from the heat. Toss in the watercress and season with pepper. Serve warm.

― ⑥ ―

The Inn at Little Washington,
by Patrick O'Connell

be quite as impressively industrial-looking, but beats its rival in ease of use. Built around a sturdy fiberglass frame, this mandoline is so simple that the user's manual is almost unnecessary. The slicer adjusts with a knob underneath that measures the thickness of your slice in both inches and millimeters. The reversible slicing blade, with a straight edge on one side and a serrated edge for waffle cuts on the other, is built into the unit. Included are three additional blades that slide into the side and lock in place. Our only criticism is that the Matfer's vegetable pusher–safety guard is not attached (as in the Bron carriage) but floats freely, increasing the risk of slips and making it difficult to hold irregularly shaped vegetables. Nevertheless, for home use, the Matfer mandoline is our most highly recommended choice. It's a good idea to use your mandoline on a large cutting board, not directly on a countertop, or to place a bowl underneath the mandoline to catch the slices as they fall from the

blade. It is approximately 15½" long, 5" wide, and stands 8½" high.

4.6 JOYCE CHEN ASIAN MANDOLINE PLUS

Like many home cooks, some professional chefs find the larger, more professional classic mandolines too awkward to use in their small kitchens. For fast slicing and fine juliennes (and easy cleaning), their secret weapon is a Japanese-made mandoline cutter like this one from Joyce Chen. A simple device compared to most French mandolines, the Mandoline Plus is nothing more than a plastic tray in the middle of which lies a razor-sharp straight blade set at an angle. To change the thickness of your slice, which can range from paper-thin to ⅛", all you

have to do is adjust a knob on the side that moves the front of the tray up or down. Simply stick the fruit or vegetable on the finger guard and slide it down the tray and over the blade; the perfect slice falls into the plastic container below. The cutter also comes with three sizes of julienning blades that produce strips ranging in width from hair-thin to ¼" wide. The Japanese use the Mandoline Plus for making garnishes as well as all kinds of salads and pickled vegetables. It is approximately 4" wide, 12¾" long, and 3" thick.

SLICING MACHINES

INSTEAD OF RUNNING the food back and forth over a straight blade, as with a mandoline, to use a slicing machine you move its round rotating knife, turned by a handle or a motor, against the food. These devices sit on the counter of your neighborhood deli, peeling off paper-thin slices of ham and roast beef, but they are also available for home use.

An electric slicer is a must-have for anyone who caters from home or entertains large crowds. However, it takes up quite a bit of countertop space and has several parts, including a razor-sharp cutting blade, to disassemble, wash by hand, and then reassemble. We don't see it as a tool for everyday use or even for slicing the occasional roast beef or the holiday ham. In these cases, you're better off using a good slicing knife.

In order to ensure that an electric slicer will fulfill its prime function—providing uniform slices—it should have a rugged structure that won't bend when a heavy food load is pressed against it. There should be a means of adjusting the thickness of the slice and—perhaps most important—a way of protecting your fingers from the sharpness of the blade.

4.7 BENRINER COOK HELP UPRIGHT TURNING SLICER

Relying on the artful arrangement of food and garnish, Japanese presentations have had a huge influence on Western restaurateurs. For sashimi, the classic garnish is a bed of fine daikon radish strings. At Japanese cooking schools, students must learn to laboriously cut the daikon by hand. At home, however, most Japanese use gadgets like this Benriner turning slicer, which produces heaps of daikon strings in less than a minute. Push the daikon (or onion, potato, etc.) onto the spike next to the blade, push down the disc so the pins dig into the vegetable, and turn the handle. In addition to three widths of julienne strips, this slicer also cuts long corkscrews of cucumbers, carrots, and other vegetables. This model, made of plastic, is 4" wide, 10" high, and 5½" deep.

4.8 LE ROUET TURNING SLICER

Made by the same company as the Bron mandoline, the Le Rouet is the BMW of turning slicers. Like the Benriner, a rotating disc turns the vegetable into the slicing blades; here, however, it is on a sliding carriage that moves horizontally. This easily operated device also leaves a thin core as it transforms vegetables into perfect razor-cut garlands or three widths of strings. Its main uses are for making garnishes, salads, or vegetable spaghetti. The stainless steel and cast aluminum unit is 15" long, 6¼" wide, and 9½" high.

4.9 CHEF'SCHOICE PROFESSIONAL ELECTRIC FOOD SLICER

This handsome model, made of aluminum and stainless steel, cuts everything from a loaf of extra-large thick-crusted country bread to a bushel of cucumbers. Slices range from paper-thin to ¾" thick. The dial for adjusting the thickness of slices is numbered so you can be consistent every time. You'll soon learn that number 1 is perfect for rare roast beef while number 11 yields ½" thick slices of rye bread. Exceptionally quiet operation and a large carriage that can hold a huge block of cheese are among its pluses. But perhaps its best attribute is its multiple safety features: there's an on-off switch that permits operation but doesn't start the 7" diameter blade turning; the blade doesn't rotate until you exert pressure on the back of the food carriage; and if you use your other hand to push the food, there are no idle fingers to accidentally come in contact with the blade. It takes a bit of practice to learn to work with both hands, but you'll find that you approach this machine with less fear than other electric food slicers. The manufacturer includes a small stainless steel tray to catch slices as you work. An optional ham-slicing blade with a nonserrated edge, for which you can also purchase a sharpening attachment, shaves prosciutto into translucent slices. As the unit is 15" long, 12" wide, and 10" high, you'll need to dedicate a fair amount of counterspace to it.

4.10 WESTMARK RADIMAX SPIRAL CUTTER

This simple device is fun and easy to use. The manufacturers call it a radish cutter, but it only works with long daikon-type radishes, potatoes, and firm cucumbers, making it less effective than the turning slicers. You skewer the radish lengthwise with the thin metal rod and slip the blade assembly, screw side down, over the rod. Then you turn the blade so the screw bores into the vegetable, rotating the blade into its flesh and producing a long spiral ribbon. The radish or potato spirals can be used as garnishes (or as an edible necklace). The cutter is stainess steel and should be cleaned by hand.

GRATERS

WITH A GOOD KNIFE you can mince garlic, chop nuts, julienne carrots, and shred cabbage, but five, ten, fifty, or one hundred knives working at once can complete the task faster and more uniformly. A grater, essentially a surface covered with small cutting edges, is precisely that proliferative knife.

Some hand graters are multipurpose tools capable of producing a variety of textures, and others are distinctly single-minded. The grater, operated by rubbing food (and when you get down to the nitty-gritty, your knuckles) over a sharply perforated surface, is the simplest kind. Good rotary graters, mechanical but not electric, are faster, more efficient, and more expensive than hand graters. They operate in the reverse fashion: the cutting surface is rubbed against the food, which is held in place by the pressure of a plate.

Graters are equipped with two types of surfaces. One is made up of punctures, the torn edges of the holes protruding to create a rasplike surface that is characteristic of hand, not rotary, graters. This is the kind of grater that crumbles and abrades the food and is murder to clean. The other type, with holes or slits with raised cutting edges on one side, shreds food into strings, the fineness or thickness of which is determined by the size and placement of the openings. Food that has been processed by a shredding surface will retain more of its integrity and moisture than food that has been grated over ragged punctures. Some graters have slits that will slice, but none of the slicers on a hand grater or rotary grater has the capability of the mandoline. A fine shredder and a medium grater may be used interchangeably on foods like hard cheese, potatoes, and orange peel, and many electric appliances will also grate and shred. Nevertheless, hand graters have their moments of glory even in the most mechanized kitchen—when providing a pinch of fresh nutmeg or a dusting of Parmesan cheese to a dish, for example. And for a quick bit of fresh tomato purée, there's nothing like rubbing half of a ripe tomato over a raspy grater.

WHAT TO LOOK FOR

Graters should be comfortable to use, sturdy, and made of noncorrosive material. Having one that's dishwasher safe may be a plus, though the best way to clean a grater is with a stiff brush. Make sure that rotary graters have a cranking mechanism that provides a smooth roll.

Born to the earth are three kinds of creatures. Some are winged and fly. Some are furred and run. Still others stretch their mouths and talk. All must eat and drink to survive.
—LU YU

4.11 OXO GOOD GRIPS MULTI GRATER

A simple but clever and practical design—incorporating a soft, nonslip rubber handle that reduces pressure on your hands, and nonslip rubber feet that hold steady on any surface—distinguishes this modern grater. There are two grating surfaces attached at the top, one for fine grating, the other for medium-coarse. Both have raised, well-honed cutting edges that transform food into shreds, making short work of carrots, celery root, potatoes, chocolate, or cheese. The OXO grater can rest comfortably on a mixing bowl, one rubber foot holding one side steady on the inside, while the chosen grating surface is fixed on the outside edge by small plastic tabs just above the base. The two surfaces come apart easily from the handle to facilitate cleaning. The OXO Good Grips multi grater is 9" high, 3½" at its widest point, and has white plastic framing the graters with a black rubber handle and feet.

4.12 MICROPLANE CHEESE GRATER-ZESTER

This tool was invented for the wood shop but ended up in the kitchen. Richard and Jeff Grace of Grace Manufacturing in Arkansas designed the Microplane, a thin stainless steel bar perforated by rows of tiny, ultra-sharp blades, as a kind of wood rasp for smoothing out rough edges. Then Lorraine Lee, the wife of a Canadian hardware store owner, discovered that it could effortlessly grate orange zest for cakes. The Lees added it to their Christmas catalogue, and word of this miraculous new zester spread through the cooking world. The long, slim, stainless steel rasp, perforated with hundreds of tiny, razor-sharp, square-edged teeth, shaves hard Parmesan or Romano cheese into a flurry of airy, translucent flakes. The Microplane also works beautifully as a zester. The matte black plastic handle is very comfortable to grip. Since the success of the rasp as a cheese grater-zester, there have been several other graters added to the Microplane line, with larger grating areas, ergonomic handles, and the same sharp teeth. The Microplane cheese grater-zester is 12½" long.

4.13 PROGRESSIVE PROGRIP ULTRA TOWER GRATER

The box grater was around more than one hundred years ago, and will probably still be around one hundred years from now. But as time goes by, this kind of grater, with different grating surfaces on each side, has been improved and refined with imagination and technology. Although many versions of the classic four-sided box grater are still on the market, the Progressive ProGrip Ultra Tower grater is a good example of state-of-the-art design in this category. Handsomely crafted, it's a tall, three-sided pyramid with four grating surfaces cut into it (one side has tandem surfaces). The grater can handle a variety of foods, from nutmeg and cinnamon to chocolate, cheese, and vegetables. On the top is a big, round, ergonomic black rubber handle, while on the base are three nonskid black rubber feet. Perfectly balanced, the grater holds rock steady on a variety of surfaces. It's almost too attractive to hide away in a cabinet. An identical, smaller version with three different grating surfaces is available; together they make a dynamic duo that can handle every grating need.

The Progressive ProGrip Ultra tower grater comes in stainless steel with a black Santoprene rubber handle and feet. The large version is 11½" tall; the small one measures 9".

4.14 MICROPLANE SPICE GRATER

This minirasp, baby brother to the one above, is the perfect little tool for grating nutmeg, cinnamon, and other hard spices. Its curved grating surface, perforated with more than two hundred tiny, eager teeth, transforms the spices' hard exteriors into an aromatic powder, ideal for seasoning a compote, dusting on a custard, or adding to your holiday cookie dough. It also does a nice job of grating chocolate for a quick garnish. The Microplane spice grater is 8" long and comes in stainless steel with a turned wooden handle.

4.15 MOULI DRUM CHEESE GRATER WITH BOWL

This round, large-capacity cheese grater, known as a drum-style grater, is fitted with its own bowl in a sleek, simple design. The roomy stainless steel bowl holds 6 cups of light and powdery grated cheese, and you can clearly see the amount of cheese you have through the airholes that encircle the grater. Resting neatly on the bowl, the grater is quite effective, but the ensemble is somewhat unwieldy to grasp. The stainless steel bowl and grater come apart for easy cleaning. The Mouli drum cheese grater, in stainless steel, is 7¼" in diameter and 3⅛" high.

4.16 ILSA GRATTALO CHEESE SCRAPER

In these days of higher and higher tech, this sleek, stainless steel grater is a beautiful, low-tech tool, a subtly curved swath of metal in a minimalist design vaguely resembling a windshield ice scraper. The gleaming scraper fans out at one end into a set of neat, even teeth, while the other end wraps into a curl that fits comfortably in your palm. Designed for tabletop grating, it scrapes along a chunk of Parmesan or Grana Padano, sending drifts of grated cheese onto your *capellini primavera* or spaghetti and meatballs. With no moving parts and no holes piercing its pristine surface, this grater is as easy to clean as

THE GREATER GRATER, CHOPPER, & GRINDER: HANDS-ON JEWISH COOKING
✣ JOAN NATHAN ✣

Gone are the days when you really labored, maybe suffered, and definitely worked up a sweat in the kitchen. What the food processor now does in seconds the greater grater, chopper, and grinder took hours to do with blood, sweat, and tears. "A good potato latke has to include some blood from bruised knuckles," the venerable Mimi Sheraton once told me. When I have the time, I still find it more satisfying and closer to my culinary roots to grate those potatoes and onions with a hand grater. And what about horseradish for Passover? Who of a certain generation has not shed tears preparing this indispensable accompaniment to gefilte fish on the classic hand grater? Let's not forget the grated beets for those of us who enjoy the intensity of color that makes an appearance at the Seder table (along with the unavoidably stained fingers).

Now, to make the purist's gefilte fish, there are two schools of thought: either you use the hand grinder or the chopper. The chopper has one or two very sharp blades that must meet the wooden bowl with assertiveness. The more you refine your chopping technique, the better your gefilte fish, chopped liver, and *charoset* will be. As for that grinder, what immigrant woman or daughter of an immigrant would trust fish or meat ground in a supermarket? You carefully selected and took home the whole piece of meat or the whole live fish worthy enough to meet your grinder—and to feed your family.

For me today, taking the shiny chopper, aged wooden bowl, sturdy hand grinder, and old-fashioned grater out of the cupboard as I get ready to cook is like calling forth old friends to join me in the warmth of my kitchen.

a knife or fork. The Ilsa Grattalo cheese scraper is 7½" long in top-quality (18/10) stainless steel.

4.17 ZYLISS DELUXE CHEESE GRATER SET

The diminutive but efficient Zyliss Deluxe cheese grater set holds just under 2 ounces of hard cheese, which it quickly transforms into slightly more than ½ cup of grated cheese. Molded of satiny smooth hard plastic, the grater is comfortable to hold in one hand while you grate with the other. The Deluxe grater comes with two grating cylinders, one coarse, one fine, which are easy to change by simply unscrewing the crank arm. With both cylinders, the Zyliss can handle hard cheeses or softer ones like Gruyère—although softer cheeses tend to stick a bit in the cylinder—or chocolate for grating over your cappuccino, bread crumbs for a casserole topping, and nuts to garnish your chocolate tart. A clear cylindrical cheese holder, part of the Deluxe package, attaches to the grater opposite the crank arm and catches the cheese, nuts, or chocolate as you grate. After grating, a blue dispenser cap fits on snugly and offers open and closed settings to seal or shake out its contents. There are measurements marked on the side of the container in ounces, milliliters, and fractions of a cup to let you know how much you've grated. The Zyliss comes apart for easy cleaning. It is 5¾" long, 3¾" high, and comes in white plastic with stainless steel grating cylinders.

4.18 OXO GOOD GRIPS ROTARY CHEESE GRATER

Designed with comfort and ease of use in mind, the Good Grips rotary cheese grater has a smooth, round plastic body that expands when you put a wedge of cheese in its large-capacity chamber. Unlike most rotary graters, which have turning arms on the side, this grater has its turning arm on top, like a pepper grinder. A large nonslip black rubber knob at the tip of the arm facilitates turning. The grater is easy to grasp with just a slightly closed palm, important for those with diminished strength in their hands. An unusual spiral pattern on the grating cylinder makes the grater easy to start, and once started it grinds smoothly and efficiently. A custom-fitted saucer attaches to the bottom of the grater for convenient storage; it also flips over to act as a crumb-catching tray when you use the grater at the table. The grater is 6½" high; it disassembles easily and all parts can be washed in the dishwasher. Cheeses like Parmesan should be measured after grating when the unit of measure called for in the recipe is in volume, e.g., cups. When the unit of measure is weight, e.g., ounces, the measuring should be done before grating.

4.19 KYOCERA GINGER GRATER

A staple of Far Eastern cuisine, particularly in the cooking of Japan, China, India, and Pakistan, ginger can be used fresh, dried, candied, or preserved in sherry, vinegar, or sugar syrup. Its spicy, aromatic qualities enhance meat, fish, vegetables, curries, and tea. Eastern cooks believe that a little ginger in the mix makes stir-fried foods more digestible. Although it is called for much less often in Western cuisine, ginger does play a role in flavoring pastries, cookies, custards, jams, and meats, and it's used with increasing frequency in that blend of East and West called fusion cuisine. Freshly grated, ginger makes a terrific seasoning for meat or poultry marinades. In order to obtain the full flavor of ginger it

GINGERROOT
⚜ SUSANNA FOO ⚜

During my childhood, my mother made a wintertime tonic of gingerroot and brown sugar to give us warmth and energy. In the summer, she steamed gingerroot with pears, which she believed to be good for us.

Fresh gingerroot, the most basic ingredient in Chinese dishes, has gained tremendously in popularity over the past ten years in this country. In the United States, the best gingerroot comes from Hawaii. It is usually about 6" long, but some can be larger than your hand. The skin is smooth and easy to peel and has few small knobs. For dishes where appearance matters, gingerroot should be peeled and julienned.

In the spring and throughout the summer, Chinese markets fill with a real treat: fresh young gingerroot. The skin looks a little like that of a new potato, translucent, with purplish tips. Whereas mature gingerroot is often stringy and pungent and requires peeling, young ginger is tender, with little fiber and a mildly spicy taste.

How to Use Ginger: I use the peel of the gingerroot to flavor stock; the small peeled knobs for braising, sauces, or desserts; and peeled julienned gingerroot for dressings, sauces, sautés, or decoration. The larger pieces are the easiest to handle. To keep gingerroot fresh, I peel and slice it paper thin and julienne it very fine, rinsing the shreds two or three times in cold water. I store the julienned gingerroot in the refrigerator in an open glass jar filled with clean water, changing the water occasionally. That way, it keeps for two to three weeks. Peeled, small gingerroot knobs can be refrigerated in clean cold water for three weeks to one month.

should be finely grated and added with its grating juices. The perfect tool for the process is the Japanese *oroshigane*—a ceramic plate with tiny spikes that break up the plant's fibers and release its juice.

You will find this item from Kyocera in every Japanese chef's kitchen. The Japanese also use it for grating daikon radish. A small, round porcelain dish with a raised grating center and a nonskid bottom, it is an ideal device for grating ginger. The perimeter of the bowl catches the juices as they separate from the grated flesh. (If your recipe doesn't require the juice, reserve it to give a little kick to your next vinaigrette.) The tiny porcelain teeth are quite sharp, grating the fibrous ginger quickly and efficiently. And here's a tip: Freeze chunks of peeled ginger for easier grating. The nonskid coating around the bottom of the bowl grips tenaciously to many surfaces. With its smooth, glazed surface, the Kyocera ginger grater is easy to clean. It's 3½" in diameter, almost 1" high, and comes in white porcelain.

4.20 ROTATING COCONUT GRATER

In India, coconut is eaten primarily in the south of the country and along the west coast. It's also an important ingredient in the cooking of Thailand and other Southeast Asian countries. Many methods have been devised for grating the delectable meat. This tin-plated grater from India clamps onto the edge of a counter or table. A metal rod extends upward, 7½" from the clamp, to support a strong metal bar with a wooden handle at one end and a round, jagged head—shaped something like the interior membranes of an orange—at the other. The coco-nut is efficiently grated by holding a large piece of the meat (in its shell) against the rough edges of the grater and moving the coconut about while turning the handle.

4.21 MOULI GRATER BRUSH

This little tool, with its ultrafine, bent wire bristles, is essential for anyone who frequently grates with "punch-perforated" graters, which have surfaces that are sharp and effective, but a challenge to clean. The wire bristles of the Mouli brush, with their tips bent at a 20° angle, catch the grated residue and lift it away. The brush is also useful for lifting grated ginger off the sharp ceramic grating surface of an *oroshigane* and transferring it to a bowl. This item is 5½" long and comes in white plastic with stainless steel bristles.

PEELERS

SKILLFULLY HANDLED AND SHARP, a good paring knife is the best peeling tool in your kitchen. But there are other tools that can help you remove the skin from fruits or vegetables with greater ease. The simplest is the swivel-action peeler, which lets you remove a paper-thin layer from a potato or a carrot with a natural shucking motion. Then there are other, more specialized tools, like those designed for removing the thick skins from citrus fruits or from asparagus, or the classic hand-cranked gadget for peeling apples and potatoes, which was invented more than one hundred years ago, in the days when farm families baked pies by the dozen. It remains an effective device for removing the skin from an ingredient in a single impressive strip. The following implements easily accomplish the tasks for which they were designed.

4.22 MESSERMEISTER SWIVEL PEELER

You grip this 7¼" long peeler by the comfortable rubber handle. To peel the fruit or vegetable, push away from you the sturdy plastic arch that holds the double-edged stainless steel blade. A good peeler—a must for every kitchen—needs a blade that slices smoothly into the vegetable but removes only the skin, not the flesh. This model wins on both counts, equally effective on delicate and tough-skinned foods. Its sharpened tip doubles as a gouger for scooping out the eyes of potatoes. Though it will fit neatly into a drawer for storage, you could just as easily hang it from the generous hole in its handle.

4.23 ISI PEELZ-IT

Superior sharpness and the ability to hold an edge has made the ceramic blade popular in professional kitchens. This 6½" ceramic-bladed swivel peeler is so sharp it removes the peel with ease and, unfortunately, some of the meat. We use it for large vegetables like eggplant and for cutting strips of vegetables for lasagna or other layered dishes. The Peelz-It only has one blade. If you are left-handed, you can reverse it by bending back the plastic holder, popping out the blade, and then turning it around and replacing it. The streamlined rubber grip is a little small for large hands.

4.24 WÜSTHOF STATIONARY PEELER

Before peelers swiveled, they were fixed, made from a curved blade into which two long slits with sharpened edges were cut. They are not as effortless as the swivel models—you have to turn the blade to follow a fruit's contours—but they do give you more control. The tip is perfect for removing the eyes of potatoes and destemming apples and tomatoes. To use, grasp the plastic handle with four fingers and use the thumb

of the same hand as you would a paring knife to both steady the food and pull the peeler along the surface.

4.25 OXO Y PEELER

This peeler performs the same task as the regular swivel peeler, only with a different motion: you pull the blade toward your body, rather than push it away from you. The OXO was clearly the best item in this category. The two-sided blade makes a smooth, shallow cut, and the patented rubber grip is comfortable for even the longest peeling jobs. It is 5" long and 2" along the cutting front.

4.26 KUHN RIKON SWISS-PEELER

This no-frills harp-shaped peeler has a plastic handle and a single carbon steel blade that bites into the fruit or vegetable without slipping. The cut is smooth and the peel is broad and thin, resulting in little waste. It's great at peeling butternut squash and other thick-skinned vegetables. It is 4½" long with a 2" cutting blade.

CITRUS PEELERS & ZESTERS

Orange, lemon, lime, and grapefruit peels increase in value after they have been removed. Citrus peel has a variety of uses: you can twist it into your martini, grate it into your cookies or cakes, or freeze it for the future—it freezes beautifully. And so we show you a variety of tools designed to help you remove the outer layer of citrus fruits, leaving the bitter white pith behind.

4.27 FRIELING CITRUS KNIFE

This contemporary-looking tool is notable for its design as well as its function. Interesting enough to have been displayed by New York's Museum of Modern Art, it also does its job remarkably well, cutting the peel of an orange or grapefruit cleanly without injury to the fruit's flesh. It is a 4" long curvy piece of heavy, stainless steel with a small cutting edge near one end. To use the knife, score the fruit from the flower to the stem end and pry the peel loose with your fingers, or lift the peel at one end with the cutter and pull off portions of the rind using the knife and your fingers. This piece, both pretty and utilitarian, will serve you well.

4.28 WÜSTHOF LEMON ZESTER

As a flavoring for pies, cookies, stews, and other dishes, lemon zest works best when it is cut as finely as possible, with no white connective tissue attached. Holding the fruit in one hand, you grasp the handle of the zester and pull the short metal cutting head across the peel. Five little metal holes dig into the skin and pull up perfect shreds of zest. This zester, made of stainless steel with a plastic handle, is 5½" long.

4.29 ISI CITRUS PEELER

This tool works on the same principle as a classic lemon zester, only with one hole rather than five. The cutting device is a hole with a sharp outer edge; you grasp the bulb-shaped rubber handle, lay the plastic neck flat side down on the skin, and then pull it backward so the hole cuts

a perfect strip of peel. Reversed, the other side of the neck digs a rind-deep channel through the skin, after which you can peel the fruit more easily. This peeler may not hold up to heavy-duty kitchen use—the plastic cutting edge can crack—but it is perfect for the bar, producing an elegant twist of lemon for your dry martini.

4.30 WÜSTHOF CHANNEL KNIFE

The quickest method for cutting long strands of peel from a lemon, orange, or grapefruit is this simple, effective channel knife. Pull the stainless steel blade across the fruit's skin and it detaches a strip of zest. Most use it as a bar accessory (think gin and tonics with a twist of lime), but you can also use it to make candied

grapefruit peel and as a decorating device for cucumbers, lemons, and other foods. This stainless steel knife (with a plastic handle) is 6" in length.

4.31 MICROPLANE ZESTER

This 12½" long rasp is twin sibling to the Microplane cheese grater-zester (4.12) and performs superlatively when zesting citrus fruit. The lack of handle makes it slightly uncomfortable to grip but it creates more suface area to grate.

SPECIALIZED PEELERS, CUTTERS, & CURLERS

Either you can't live without these highly specialized gadgets—you wonder what you ever did before you discovered them—or you find them totally laughable and a waste of money. Decide for yourself after seeing our miscellany of cutters.

4.32 ZYLISS POTATO CHIPPER

Making great homemade French fries is an art that takes time to master but is worth the effort. The most

tedious part of the task is cutting the potatoes. A number of specialty cutters have appeared to speed the process; many, however, need the strength of a sumo wrestler to push the grid of blades through the potato. Working on the principle of a giant garlic press, the Zyliss potato chipper is the happy exception, easy to operate and clean. You trim the potato to a rough rectangle no more than 3½" long, place it in the bin behind the blades, and push down

the handle, forcing the potato through the blades and making a stack of perfectly uniform raw fries. The Zyliss has two cutting heads, 7 millimeters (¼") and 9 millimeters (⅓"), which slide into the side of the base. The unit is 10" long, 4¾" wide, and 5" high.

4.33 RÖSLE BUTTER CURLER

In traditional white tablecloth restaurants, butter is often served in spreadable little scalloped curls. This

8"-long, shepherd's-crook-shaped device will allow you to do this at home. You scrape its serrated edge along the top of a cold slab of butter and you have an elegant little curl. Unless you are serving them immediately, refrigerate or freeze the curls to keep them from melting.

ROASTED CORN & LOBSTER CHOWDER

1½ quarts chowder

4 ears fresh sweet corn, brushed lightly with butter and grilled until toasted on all sides (about 2 cups cut corn)
2 tablespoons unsalted butter
1 large onion, peeled and diced (about 1 cup)
2 celery stalks, diced
1 leek, split, cleaned, and diced
1 large sweet red pepper, diced
2-3 jalapeno peppers, seeded and diced
2 teaspoons ground cumin
1 teaspoon ground coriander
1 vanilla bean, split and seeds scraped out
1 teaspoon salt
½ teaspoon cayenne pepper
2 quarts hot chicken stock
1 2-pound lobster, tail hacked into sections, claws cracked, body tied in cheesecloth
½ cup crème fraîche

1 Cut the roasted corn kernels off of their cobs, reserving the corn to add later.

2 Melt the butter in a large, heavy-bottom soup pot. Add the corncobs, onion, celery, leek, and peppers, and sauté until the vegetables are soft but not browned.

3 Add the cumin, coriander, vanilla, salt, and cayenne and cook for 2 to 3 minutes to release the flavors.

4 Add the hot chicken stock and bring to a boil. Reduce to a simmer and add the reserved corn along with the lobster body that has been tied in cheesecloth.

5 Cook 40 to 45 minutes; remove the cobs and the lobster body. Add the hacked lobster and simmer for 4 to 5 minutes before stirring in the crème fraîche. Serve immediately.

Michael Lomonaco

4.34 LEE CORN CUTTER & CREAMER

With a firm shove, you push the corncob down the cutter's shallow metal trough; a small curved blade cuts open the kernels, and then a series of short metal spikes tears the juice and soft meat from inside. (Use the corn cutter over a pan to catch the pulp.) You can either cook the sweet creamed corn as is or use it to make corn puddings. To remove the whole kernels, attach the metal cover over the spikes and, using a screwdriver, raise the blade to its high position. Once again, run the cob down the trough, turning it after each push to expose more kernels. (Watch your fingers.) The tool is 17" long, 2¼" wide, and ½" deep.

4.35 WESTMARK RADISH ROSE CUTTER

A radish rose is made by slicing "petals" in the radish and placing it

"We gave them corn last year!"

into ice water until it opens into a "blossom." The 7¼" long Westmark handheld radish rose cutter simplifies the operation. You place the radish on the spoonlike holder and then squeeze the handles to force the blades through it, producing a rose with eight sections and a round core in the center. (You still have to chill it in ice water and wait until it opens.) The tips of this gadget will also cut a zigzag pattern along the rim of hollowed-out citrus fruits.

4.36 HONG KONG VEGETABLE CUTTERS

Asian chefs, particularly those who work in large hotels, have taken the art of the garnish to elaborate heights. Witness the centerpieces of Chinese banquets—dragons, phoenixes, and carp, all painstakingly assembled out of carved carrots, radishes, and other vegetables. Working on the same principle as truffle cutters, this little kit of six stainless steel vegetable cutters produces miniature but intricate garnishes roughly 2" wide, three mythic animals—the dragon, phoenix, and turtle—and three Chinese characters for good luck. They work best on thinly sliced but firm ingredients like carrots, radishes, or apples.

All peoples are made alike.
They are made of bones,
flesh, and dinners.
Only the dinners are different.
—GERTRUDE LOUISE CHENEY

4.37 VILLAWARE BEAN SLICER

Bean slicers became popular in the United States during a time when French haricots verts were not available; they were used to simulate the French beans by slicing regular green beans into thin strips. This little Villaware slicer, designed for that task, clamps onto the side of the table. You take four or five beans, line them up, and feed them into the top of the slicer while turning the handle. Inside are six circular blades turning against a plastic roller that pushes the sliced beans out the bottom. The slicer measures 3¼" high by 3½" long by 6" deep.

4.38 WESTMARK BUTTER SLICER

If you demand precise restaurant-style pats of butter, use this Westmark slicer to turn a bar into eleven perfect slabs. The frame that holds the slicing wires is 5½" long, slightly larger than most American bars of butter. Its width is 4½", which will also accommodate European-style bars. The slicer has a cast-aluminum frame and epoxy-coated stainless steel wires. It is 10" in overall length.

4.39 MATFER PICKLE SLICER

In French bistros, the traditional garnish for charcuterie and pâtés is *cornichons* sliced in a fan pattern. This tool was invented to speed up the preparation. The curved 5¾" plastic handle ends in a row of eight short, sharp, 1¼" blades. Holding the pickle with one hand (this part will become the fan's base), you press the blades into the flesh and then draw the blades downward and backward, cutting the vegetable into a row of precise slices. You can also use it to make garnishes out of cucumbers and small, thin radishes.

4.40 WESTMARK PEEL-STAR ASPARAGUS PEELER

This 7½"-long device is actually two swivel peelers facing each other; they are attached to curved legs that meet at a spring-mounted joint. You can peel any long, thin vegetable (carrots, cucumbers, etc.) in half the time, but it works best on asparagus. Hold the asparagus spear in one hand, and with the other squeeze the Peel-Star's legs so the blades just touch the skin. Then slide the peeler downward to remove the tough, stringy outer layer of the lower spear. Do not squeeze too hard, because you can easily whittle the asparagus down to a point.

4.41 ELAN E-Z-ROLL GARLIC PEELER

This is the gadget that revolutionized garlic peeling. For most cooks, the time-honored method is to smash the clove under the flat of a knife blade and then pick off the skin. This does not work if you want the cloves intact. Enter the E-Z-Roll. You place the clove inside this 5¼"-long rubber tube and roll it briskly back and forth while applying downward pressure with your palm. You will hear the papery skin crackle as it separates from the garlic. The tackiness of the rubber grips the clove, tearing and pulling the skin but leaving the garlic whole (and protecting your hands from garlic odor). Due to the narrowness of the tube (1" in diameter), it does not work with elephant garlic.

4.42 MATFER CHESTNUT PEELER

The shell of a chestnut must be slit before roasting to allow the expanding gases to escape. This is a tricky task: a knife can slip on the hard shell. Designed for precisely this job, the 5¼"-long Matfer peeler makes scoring chestnuts easy. A sturdy plastic handle holds a short, keen-edged blade with a hooked tip, which slices the shell without difficulty. After you cook the chestnut, it is also the best tool for peeling the shell and skin from the meat.

4.43 AMCO AVOCADO SKINNER

The Amco skinner is the best tool for removing the skin of an avocado. Spoons are too curved, and knife blades are too flat; both lose too much of the flesh. The skinner has a 3¾" long metal blade, one side flat,

the other slightly rounded, with a slight curve at the end. To peel an avocado half, insert the blade, round side out, between the skin and the meat and run it all the way around the peel. Then run it around more deeply until the whole lobe of avocado pops out. The manufacturer also recommends this 8"-long tool for removing the pit, but we still prefer the old chef's trick of whacking the pit with the blade of a cook's knife, twisting to loosen, and then flipping it out.

4.44 BACK TO BASICS PEEL-AWAY APPLE & POTATO PEELER

During the nineteenth century, American inventors came up with dozens of competing designs for removing the skin from an apple. This device, which not only peels but slices and cores apples, is the direct descendant of those contraptions; the suction-cup base is its only modern element. You spear the apple (or potato) on the three-tined fork and turn the crank. This spirals the fruit past a little spring-mounted blade that does the peeling. You can also attach the corer-slicer to turn the apple into a perfect spiral with the core removed. The machine works best with symmetrically shaped items, so you should first pare lumpy potatoes to make them as spherical as possible. This peeler is 9" long, 5½" high, and has a 4"-diameter base.

BALLERS

These sharp little scoops extract the pliant flesh of melons and cut raw potatoes into uniform rounds or ovals. They come in an array of sizes; often, two different sized scoops are joined with a single handle. The best are stainless steel, ferociously sharp. They're also surprisingly effective for shaping chilled ganache into chocolate truffles.

4.45 AMCO GARNISH KIT

This set of three stainless steel ballers cuts melons into two kinds of ridged cylinders (the manufacturer calls them "beehive" and "honeycomb") and a little diamond shape. They are not sturdy enough to tackle raw potatoes but work well for cooked vegetables, butter pats, and jelly or aspic garnishes. All three are roughly 7½" long with cutting heads that measure ¾" (diamond), 1" (beehive), and 1¼" (honeycomb).

4.46 RÖSLE BALLERS

These three 6¼"- to 7"-long cutting balls are used on all types of fruits and vegetables, from soft honeydews to hard turnips. The cylindrical stainless steel handles are comfortable and easy to turn (important for bulk jobs), and the rims of the heads are sharp enough to cut into the hardest potatoes. The cutting heads are ⅝", ⅞", and 1⅛" in diameter. Use the smallest to make tiny zucchini balls for garnishing a clear soup, the middle size for hollowing out a new potato to fill later with sour cream and caviar as an hors d'oeuvres, and the largest for seeding a cucumber.

CHERRY TOMATOES FILLED WITH SMOKED SALMON MOUSSE

60 hors d'oeuvres

60 red, firm cherry tomatoes
(about 2 pints)

SMOKED SALMON MOUSSE
8 ounces cream cheese, at
room temperature
2 ounces smoked salmon
few drops of lemon juice
2 to 3 tablespoons heavy cream
white pepper to taste
2 seedless English cucumbers

GARNISH
fresh dill

Wash and dry the cherry tomatoes. With a sharp serrated knife, cut off the round bottom of each tomato. Remove the seeds and pulp with a small melon-ball scoop and put the tomatoes, cut side down, on a rack or on paper towels to drain. Refrigerate until ready to use. (Cutting off the bottom of the tomatoes and standing them on the stem end makes them less apt to roll.)

Combine the mousse ingredients in the bowl of a food processor and blend until the mixture is smooth. Chill at least 30 minutes.

To serve, soften the mousse with a wooden spoon and put it in a pastry bag fitted with a star tip. Pipe the mixture into the cherry tomatoes and garnish with a sprig of fresh dill. Serve on a bed of lettuce leaves, kale greens, parsley, or dill to keep the tomatoes from rolling.

Martha Stewart's Hors d'Oeuvres, by Martha Stewart

4.47 OXO GOOD GRIPS DOUBLE MELON BALLER CUTTER

No wonder that OXO has won awards for its Good Grips kitchen tools. The products are sturdy and well designed and the handles remarkably comfortable, alleviating stress on your hands and making kitchen tasks faster and easier. This 9"-long melon baller is no exception. The two cuplike cutters at the ends are made of heavy stainless steel and attached to rods that are held together in the center by a thick, tapering piece of soft, flexible rubber. The cups (one is ¼" bigger than the other) have a sharp edge, so carving melons takes almost no time or effort. But there are other possibilities here: use these cutters—two sizes give you more options—to cut spheres of potatoes and turnips to accompany a roast, to hollow out cherry tomatoes, to shape ganache for chocolate truffles, or scoop out ice cream for the world's smallest hot fudge sundae.

TRUFFLE SLICERS & CUTTERS

Anyone who goes to the considerable expense of buying truffles, those hard-textured, highly prized, aromatic knobs of fungi, should also invest in a proper cutter designed to handle them. For white truffles, which are shaved raw over fettuccine, risotto, or a baked potato, you need a flat, spadelike implement fitted with an adjustable blade. Black truffles are used to flavor a variety of dishes, from pâté to scrambled eggs, or as garnishes with decorative shapes, cut with tools that are similar to cookie cutters and usually sold in sets. Truffle cutters have edges as sharp as those on knives and are sturdily made, so they will not deform when they are impressed on a resistant slice of truffle. Of course, they are not limited to cutting truffles. You can use them to form tiny spades and diamonds of black olives and pimiento to decorate a canapé, or cut hearts and stars from carrot slices for a salad.

4.48 MOULI CHEESE, CHOCOLATE, & TRUFFLE SHAVER

This device is a razor-sharp serrated 2¼" blade attached to a 6½"-long stainless steel plate. You slide your white truffle over the plate, and the blade shaves off a slice, which, from tissue-thin to about ⅛", is adjusted by a small knob on the bottom. You can either hold the shaver in your hand to perform the ritual or prop it on its feet for better control. It can also be used to shave (chilled) chocolate and hard cheeses like Parmesan. We prefer the stainless steel of this truffle shaver to Mouli's wooden model because it does not absorb the strong truffle odor, which can flavor the cheese or chocolate you slice later.

Truffles thrive in soil near the roots of oak, beech, and hazelnut trees and grow to be anywhere from 3" to 1' in diameter. They are valuable because of their scarcity—they grow only in the wild and have yet to be successfully cultivated.

4.49 J. B. PRINCE TWELVE-PIECE CUTTER SET

In France, black truffles were once relatively cheap and plentiful. Classic chefs used them not only as a flavoring but as a decoration; geometric slices of black truffle were an important design element for elaborate centerpieces or ornate aspic dishes. Though these have almost disappeared, the cutters used to make them are still sold. This twelve-piece set of miniature stainless steel cutters, shaped like stars, diamonds, hearts, clovers, triangles, etc., with an average width of ½", can also be used to cut vegetable garnishes and puff pastry decorations for pies and other desserts. If you do use these cutters for their classic purpose, be sure to save the trimmings. Simply mince the truffles into the sauce.

CORERS & PITTERS

YOU WORK YOUR WAY into some fruits or vegetables by first peeling, then coring or pitting them. A paring knife can do the peeling, but it's less effective for the invasive surgery step. For that, you have available to you an extensive assortment of devices designed for the purpose of removing one specific piece of a fruit or vegetable—the hull from a strawberry, the fibrous central shaft of a pineapple, or the stem cap from a tomato.

Quite often, removing the pit from fruits and vegetables is more a matter of aesthetics and ease of eating than of taste. For example, *clafoutis* are traditionally made with unpitted cherries. However, it's more considerate to pit the fruit before they are put into your desserts, pies, or homemade preserves, and it's a rather simple task to accomplish, so long as you have the proper tools.

4.50 RÖSLE VEGETABLE CORER

Stuffed zucchinis appear in almost every Mediterranean cuisine. The challenge of preparing them is in removing the meat from the zucchini without piercing the skin. This 9½"-long tool makes the task simple. After cutting off the stem end of the vegetable, you insert the pointed end of the curved stainless steel blade into the flesh, turning it so the serrated edges on either side cut the core out of the vegetable. If you want more room for the stuffing, the blade can easily scrape out more of the flesh. You can also use this tool to core cucumbers and small eggplants.

4.51 OXO APPLE CORER

Apple coring takes a strong arm and a steady hand. The problem with many corers is that their grips are slippery and the blades are not wide enough to cut out all of the seeds. With its patented rubber handle and a good, ¾"-wide coring head, the OXO is clearly the best on the market. Center the 8"-long tool over the stem end of the apple, push down firmly, and at the same time twist it so the serrated blade cuts through the meat.

WARM APPLESAUCE WITH CREAM

About 3½ cups

4 cups peeled, cored, and coarsely chopped tart apples
2 cups water
½ cup honey
1½ teaspoons vanilla extract or bourbon
1 cup heavy cream (or more)

Cook the apples in the water in a large saucepan over low heat for about 15 to 20 minutes, or until they are soft. Purée in a food processor and return to the pan. Add honey and vanilla. Simmer for another 30 minutes until liquid is reduced. Serve this warm with cold heavy cream.

The Way I Cook, by Lee Bailey

4.52 MESSERMEISTER TOMATO SHARK

The dense, flavorful meat of juicy, ripe tomatoes fresh from the garden is one of summer's most sensuous rewards. Now the job of cutting out their stems has been made easier by this simple little 6"-long tool. From its black plastic handle extends what resembles a melon baller with short fingers radiating upward. You press in the head of the blade, which is ¾" in diameter, just to the side of the stem, give it a quick twist, and out comes the stem in one easy scoop. You can also use it to scrape out the seeds of a halved tomato.

4.53 VACU VIN PINEAPPLE CORER & SLICER

From its prickly leaves to its leathery exterior, it seems like the pineapple was designed to be difficult to open. All sorts of labor-saving gadgets have been used over the years to extract the sweet flesh, but none work as well as this European device to both core the fruit and remove the meat with as little waste as possible. Depending on the fruit's size, you snap on one of three different sizes of corers. After slicing off the pineapple's top, you center the plastic corer on the flesh and begin turning it clockwise. The Vacu Vin cuts two ways, carving out the cylindrical core and slicing a long spiral out of the meat. When you reach the bottom, simply pull out the corer and with it, the pineapple's juicy flesh in a neat, ready-to-eat stack. You can then cut out the core and use the intact shell to hold a fruit salad or tropical sorbet. Each corer is 9½" high when the handle is attached. They measure 3", 3¼", and 3½" in diameter.

4.54 OXO APPLE DIVIDER

The problem with many apple slicers is that they have too many blades; the resistance makes it difficult to push the slicer all the way through the fruit. This device, measuring 4" in diameter, has only eight blades radiating off a circular corer, widely spaced rubber handles, and a sturdy plastic frame to give you better leverage. Center it over the apple's stem and give a firm downward push: the apple is sliced and cored in one stroke. The divider produces identical slices that make your apple pies and tarts look better and cook more evenly.

4.55 LEIFHEIT CHERRY PITTER

Like apple peelers, cherry pitters challenged the creativity of nineteenth-century inventors. These contraptions sold well because cherry pies ran a close second to apple in popularity on the American table. Despite all the Rube Goldberg–type contraptions you can still find at flea markets, we prefer the simplest cherry pitters. Only 5½" long, the Leifheit fits in your hand and is easy to use and clean. You put a cherry in the circular holder and squeeze the two spring-mounted arms together to push the plunger through the fruit, ejecting its stone out the bottom of the holder. This is the most effective model for all home cherry-pitting jobs, and it also works on medium-sized olives.

4.56 WESTMARK OLIVE PITTER

This 7"-long device works much like the aforementioned cherry pitter, only it uses a pliers mechanism. You place the olive on the holder and squeeze the handles to press the curved metal rod through the olive and push out the stone. Unfortunately, the smallest olives tend to slip through the base of the holder, and the biggest ones do not fit between the holder and the plunger. We use this to pit oil-cured Italian olives for spaghetti *alla puttanesca*.

4.57 LEIFHEIT PLUM PITTER

The French have been making plum jam for centuries. Aside from being delicious on a breakfast brioche, it also is used as the filling for *tarte aux*

prunes, a specialty of Alsace. Stoning the pounds and pounds of plums needed to make a jam can be a time-consuming chore, unless you have this stainless steel gadget. Manufactured by the same company as the cherry pitter, its design is the same except that it is sized for bigger fruit. You place the plum on the plastic-lined holder, squeeze the handles together, and the four pointed blades cut through the fruit and pop the stone out the bottom. The blades cut the plum open along one side but leave the fruit whole, if slightly mangled. As with the olive pitter, plums that are too small or too large may not work. This pitter is 6½" long.

4.58   NORPRO STRAWBERRY HULLER

The pleasure of making fresh strawberry pies and jams from the sweetest, most flavorful strawberries of the season can be dulled by the chore of trying to destem pints of them using just a knife, which is invariably awkward and cuts too much meat. So we recommend this stainless steel huller, a short, wide 2¼"-long tweezer that fits between your thumb and forefinger. Place the rounded ends on either side of the stem of the strawberry; gently push them into the flesh; then squeeze, rotate, and lift. The leaves and the white core below them come out in one quick motion.

SHEARS

SCISSORS ARE MARVELOUS kitchen tools, although that isn't how we tend to think of them. But consider the multitude of uses we have for shears in the kitchen. You use them to cut string for trussing poultry, disjoint the poultry once it has roasted, cut parchment and waxed paper for cake pans, mince chives, and snip off the ends of green beans. All of these functions are performed by common scissors like the ones that you find in a desk drawer or sewing box; all that sets kitchen shears apart is that they must be washable, without too many spaces in which bits of food can hide.

Shears are simply two knives joined in the middle, with the meeting edges similar to the cutting edges of knife blades—a double lever, with the pin serving as fulcrum. Being two knives, they will rust and stain if not made of stainless steel, they must be dried carefully, and they can be sharpened. The thing that sets shears apart from knives is the muscular action that propels them; many people actually find that they are easier to control than a knife. We also show you a variety of egg-cutting tools, including shears designed to cut through eggshell.

4.59   J. A. HENCKELS TWIN LISSI KITCHEN SHEARS

This pair of 8" German high-carbon steel shears is rugged and razor-sharp, with one blade serrated for better cutting. The blades taper to a fine point for easy piercing. Notches just before the handle turn the scissors into a bottle opener. Our only criticism is of the high-style plastic handles, which are designed more for looks than comfort.

4.60   LAMSONSHARP FORGED KITCHEN SHEARS

These forged high-carbon stainless steel blades can cut through anything from parchment paper to small bones. Like all good shears, one blade is finely serrated, and the two blades easily (almost too easily) come apart for cleaning. The shears measure 8¼" in length.

4.61   KRETZER POULTRY SHEARS

These 9¼"-long shears have ergonomic plastic handles, a large and secure safety lock, and keen-edged stainless steel blades. There is a slight curve to the blade that helps to grip curved pieces of chicken when you're cutting them for a fricassée. Like most poultry shears, the lower blade is serrated and has a notch toward the back for holding bones to be cut.

4.62 WÜSTHOF-TRIDENT FISH SHEARS

Stainless steel shears like these are used to trim whole fish. They easily snip protruding fins and can even lop off the head. We also use them to clean crabs, cut off lobster claws, and open lobster tails. The lower blade is heavily serrated for holding slippery ingredients, and the blades unscrew for cleaning. They are 8½" in length.

4.63 PEDRINI DUAL-PURPOSE EGG SLICER

There is not much difference among competing models of egg slicers; they all use a row of fine wires strung across a metal frame over a slotted egg holder, and they all make it easy to cut hard-boiled eggs. This 8½" by 3½" egg slicer stands out, however, because it also holds a second egg upright so that three wires that cross in the middle can slice it into six sections. *Salade Niçoise* has just been added to your lunchtime repertoire.

4.64 ZYLISS EGG TOPPER

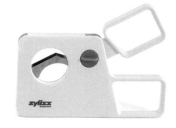

Soft-boiled eggs are the objects of a breakfast cult. Everything must be just so, from the cooking time to the shape of the egg cup and spoon. The most intense moment is the opening of the egg. Will the whack from the spoon cleanly cut off the top, or will the shell break into messy pieces? Egg scissors, such as this 5¼"-long and 3"-wide egg topper, were invented for exactly that moment. You simply place the tip of the egg through the hole and squeeze the handles; an angled, razor-sharp blade cuts into the shell and neatly snips it off, giving you stress-free access to the creamy yolk below.

4.65 ZYLISS EGG PIERCER

To prevent boiled eggs from cracking in the pot, Zyliss has invented this little device that performs one almost invisible task. You place the wider end of the egg in the little depression and push down on the gray button; a short needle clicks up and pokes a tiny hole in the end of the shell. When you bring the egg to a boil, the expanding gases escape out the hole in tiny bubbles rather than force their way out by cracking the shell. Though a pushpin will do the job just as well, with the Zyliss piercer there is no risk of accidentally pricking your finger. The egg piercer is 1¾" wide and 2¾" long.

CHEESE CUTTERS

CHEESE IS FERMENTED MILK. This is like saying that candy is cooked sugar, which scarcely allows for the great variation between a sourball and fudge. And with cheese the spread is even wider, from the rich creamy curds of cottage cheese to the nutty tang of Parmesan, from the chalky bite of a fresh chèvre to that high point of American culture, the individually wrapped slice of processed yellow cheese. Given the fact that cheeses vary, it is only natural that the equipment for dealing with them does too.

4.66 RÖSLE CHEESE PLANE

Scandinavians invented the cheese plane to make thin slices of their firm and often strongly flavored cheeses. The basic design of a handle attached to a spatula-shaped blade with a little cutting slot has not changed for decades; the difference among the various models is in the execution. The 9½"-long Rösle cheese plane has a particularly sharp cutting edge that slices the cheese smoothly and thinly; its trademark cylindrical stainless steel handle is wide and comfortable. We also use it to produce slivers of Parmesan to sprinkle on top of salad.

4.67 MATFER CHEESE WIRE

Piano wire not only makes fine music, but a fine cheese cutter as well. This cheese cutter consists of 29″ of piano wire attached firmly to two 2¾″ handles. It is intended for cutting through large, firm wheels of cheese. To use, make incisions on opposite sides of the top of the cheese, at the point where you want to divide it. Slip the wire under the cheese and into the incisions to give you some grip. Pull the ends of the wire in opposite directions across the top as you cut neatly through the cheese. To shorten the cutting edge for a smaller piece, wind the wire around the handles, then with your hands on either side of the cheese, push the wire down and through it. We have also used this cheese wire to divide layers of cake horizontally to make a towering multilayered chocolate or coconut cake.

4.68 LEIFHEIT CHEESE CUTTER

Some cheeses, like Havarti and Monterey Jack, are too soft to cut with a knife; the slices stick to the blade and end up mashed. The classic cheese wire (a segment of wire with handles on either end) is used to cut these softer varieties, particularly those cheeses sold in rectangular loaves. To use the cutter, you grasp its handle, place the roller on the cheese, and pull it backward as the wire cuts a slice. The pressure from the roller makes the cheese firm enough to cut without sticking to the wire and bunching up. The 5″-wide roller is also adjustable, so you can vary the thickness of the slices. Note that the cheese must be narrower than the width of the roller or it will not cut. This cutter measures 6″ in length.

> A cheese may disappoint. It may be dull, it may be naïve, it may be oversophisticated. Yet it remains cheese, milk's leap toward immortality.
>
> —CLIFTON FADIMAN

"What you want to be holding is a halberd. What you've got there is an adjustable cheese slicer."

STORING CHEESE
❧ STEVEN JENKINS ❧

Those stodgy supermarket cheeses—Brie, Gouda, Havarti, Port Salut—call for no special technique when it comes to storage. Having been manufactured to withstand the abuse endemic to the supermarket industry, these cheeses can be wrapped tightly in plastic wrap, refrigerated, and forgotten about for weeks. Should they grow a little fuzz, scrape it away and do not give it a second thought.

But artisanal cheeses (read: expensive, fragile) from any country deserve some respect as regards storage. Unlike cheeses of factory origin, these cheeses are living and breathing foodstuffs. Their "skin" (rind, crust) is very much like your own. It is *natural*—no paint, paraffin, or plastic covering serving to protect the cheese's luscious interior—and it must be allowed to breathe. Therefore, skip the plastic wrap and opt instead for wax paper or aluminum foil. Your cheese will not suffocate if you wrap it casually, loosely, using just enough material to envelop it. Having ensured that your cheese's exposed surface will not dry out and that it can breathe, your next concern is humidity. In my ripening rooms at the Fairway Markets in New York City the humidity is constantly 85 percent or higher. Your refrigerator is considerably less moist—even at the bottom in the vegetable hamper, where I want you to store your cherished cheeses, whether soft or hard. In order to capture your refrigerator's (and your cheese's) fleeting moisture, place your foil- or wax paper–wrapped cheeses in *unsealed* plastic bags. This will help you extend the freshness factor.

For those of you who keep large hunks of specific cheeses around (Parmigiano-Reggiano, Stilton, aged Gouda, Comté, Gruyère), be aware that they will bring joy indefinitely if shrouded in a damp paper towel or cotton cloth (cheesecloth dries almost immediately), followed by a less casual swath of malleable aluminum foil, and finally ensconced in the vegetable compartment at the bottom of the refrigerator. Know that fresh sheep's and goat's milk cheeses can be deliciously preserved by covering them with extra-virgin olive oil and storing them in the refrigerator.

There are those cheese purists, a stubborn lot, who insist that serious cheeses should never be wrapped or refrigerated. This narrow-minded approach will result in stale, dried-out cheese that has wept out the greater part of its butterfat. Cheese purists also insist that cheese should never be frozen, and I tend to agree in most cases—save that of fresh cheese (*fromage blanc*, ricotta, chèvre *frais*, mascarpone), which freezes and thaws rather well if allowed to return to normal temperature gradually. Let it thaw in its sealed container in the refrigerator, not on your counter. This way it will throw off minimal water, the loss of which would greatly alter its texture.

Perhaps the most valuable advice I can render is to urge you to be stoic. Don't try to fool yourself: if a cheese hasn't withstood the indignity of cold storage, if it smells funny, looks sad, and tastes weird, throw it out. Buy less next time and knock it off in one sitting.

FISH EQUIPMENT

Seafood preparation is easier when you use specialized cutters. There are rough-textured implements that are drawn over fish skin to remove the scales, for example; little nippers can easily lift the shells off shrimp while removing the black vein; and fish pliers can pluck the tiny pin bones from a fillet. Seafood tools made of stainless steel and noncorrosive materials are best. Plastic, if it's sturdy enough, can be used for some high-quality tools. As with utensils dedicated for cheese or truffles, investing in seafood implements presupposes a more than occasional use, but when you do use them, they're a joy to have in hand.

4.69 ZYLISS LOBSTER CRACKER

For most of us, cheap supermarket nutcrackers are the traditional tool for cracking open a lobster's claws. These sturdy all-plastic Zyliss 6¾" crackers are a clear improvement. They are strengthened with fiberglass, making them unbreakable. They do not rust, they are wide enough for you to crack the claw rather than dig into it, and they give you a firm grip on the slippery joints above the claw.

4.70 GOOD COOK SHRIMP TOOL

Some cooking experts advise ignoring the shrimp's "vein" (actually its intestine), cooking it intact. Once you start considering the dark line that runs down the back of the tail, though, you may decide to clean it anyway, and this 10½"-long tool is the simplest and best for the job. You use it on shrimp whose heads have been removed but that still retain the shell. Holding the shrimp in one hand, insert the tip of the tapered plastic wand into the vein hole, at the same time keeping the tail straight. Thread the deveiner down the length of the shrimp until it emerges at the last tail joint, just before the little flipper on the end. Continue pushing the shrimp back on the wand; as it widens it will pop off the shell and most of the vein. Finish the job by washing the tail under cold water.

4.71 J. B. PRINCE FRENCH FISH SCALER

With its attractive heart-shaped blade, we thought this 11" fish scaler would spend more time decorating the wall of our kitchen than scraping the side of a striped bass. Then we touched it to a fish and saw the scales fly off. Unlike most scalers, this is a solid, well-made tool: a steel shaft with a serrated scaling head set into a wooden handle. The teeth dig into the scales and scrape them off with ease. The only drawback to this effective tool is that the flying scales will scatter all over your kitchen. We suggest placing the fish to be scaled in a deep baking dish, covered three-quarters of the way with plastic wrap—the scales will stick to the plastic as you work.

4.72 MESSERMEISTER FISH PLIERS

Large fillets, such as salmon, often have hidden rows of bones. You can find them by gently running your fingers along the fillet, but then you are faced with the problem of how best to remove them. Knives are too crude to extract these bones with finesse, and tweezers do not have the gripping power to cope with large bones. These tapered, finely tooled stainless steel pliers are just right for the job. Strong yet precise, the serrated jaws give you a good grip and enough leverage for a firm yank. The rubber-sheathed handles prevent slipping, and a spring pops the pliers open to attack the next bone. These pliers are 7" long.

A man's palate can, in time, become accustomed to anything.

—NAPOLÉON BONAPARTE

*"Some will love you, son, and some will hate you.
It's always been that way with anchovies."*

LOBSTER ROLLS

6 sandwiches

Because these are made with hamburger buns, they are definitely twentieth century (soft, hamburger-size yeast buns were first manufactured in 1912). This recipe was given to me by a terrific Maine cook named Brownie Schrumpf.

3 cups cubed, cooked lobster meat
2 tablespoons fresh lemon juice
½ cup finely diced celery
2 tablespoons finely grated
   yellow onion
1 teaspoon salt
⅛ teaspoon ground hot red pepper
   (cayenne)

½ cup mayonnaise
6 hamburger buns
6 tablespoons unsalted butter
6 crisp lettuce leaves

1 Mix lobster and lemon juice, cover, and refrigerate overnight.

2 Next day add celery, onion, salt, cayenne, and mayonnaise and toss well to mix; cover and marinate several hours in refrigerator.
3 Spread hamburger buns well with butter, lay lettuce leaves on bottom halves, mound with chilled lobster salad, set bun tops in place, and serve.

The American Century Cookbook, by Jean Anderson

NUTCRACKERS

WE BEGAN THIS CHAPTER with one method of removing skins and shells—peeling—and will end it with another—cracking. Because the shells of nuts are hard and woody, it is quite difficult to open them unless you have the right equipment. However, doing so is well worth it, because nuts taste better and are much cheaper when you buy them unshelled. Once you have cracked the nuts, immediately store any you do not use in the freezer. By the way, did you know that nuts have seasons, like apples or plums? They are best—because they are freshest—in autumn. Also, toasting nuts before using them improves flavor.

4.73 OXO NUT & SEAFOOD CRACKER

Weighing in at ¾ pound, this is the heavyweight of nutcrackers; it crushes everything from large walnuts to skinny almonds. The wide, serrated, and slightly concave nut holders ensure that even irregularly shaped nuts do not slip. The only nut it does not work on is a small hazelnut, which slips through the stainless steel jaws unscathed. The no-slip rubber grips make even the weakest of us feel like Hercules as we crack open a rock-shelled Brazil nut. It measures 6½" in length.

4.74 MOULI LOBSTER-NUTCRACKER

Painted lobster red, this 6" cracker works on both shellfish and nuts. The narrow jaw is designed to split open lobster claws, pecans, hazelnuts, and almonds. The cracker has difficulty with large walnuts, which tend to shoot out the side. Made from strong yet springy steel, it allows you to control the pressure you exert, making it easier to end up with whole meats rather than a pile of shell and nut fragments.

4.75 REED'S ROCKET NUTCRACKER

Working on the same principle as a piston, the Reed's Rocket is the nutcracker for the automobile age. The nut holder is bolted to one end of a short steel beam; this screws forward or back depending on the size of the nut. At the other end, a wood-handled lever pushes the piston forward into the nut and cracks it. You hold the nut in the holder with one hand and operate the 10" lever with the other; once you get the system down, you can open a few pounds of pecans in a matter of minutes. The only drawback is that the holder must be adjusted every time you open a different-sized nut, so a bowl full of mixed nuts cannot be cracked in the same assembly-line fashion. The rocket base is 8" long, 2" wide, and 2½" high.

4.76 BETEL NUT SLICER

Betel nuts are hard, brown, and woody. If you chewed one, your lips and teeth would turn dark red, but your mouth would be refreshed with a cool, clean taste. In India, betel nuts are one of the common ingredients in *paan*, an after-dinner chew made of a betel leaf wrapped around a mixture of exotic ingredients. One popular combination includes sliced betel nuts and a paste of lime, water, coconut, and cardamom. You can buy the nuts already sliced, but if you should find yourself confronted with a whole betel nut, a slicer like this one is ideal. It is made of two curved pieces of nickel-plated steel tapered into handles at one end and joined by a pin at the other. Near the pin, the lower part of the cutter has a blunt, slightly notched

surface to hold the nut, while the upper part is shaped into a curved 2"-long blade that slices down through the nut when the handles are pressed together. The slicer is 6" in overall length.

5

REFINERS, GRINDERS, CRUSHERS, MASHERS, & EXTRACTORS

THE TEXTURES OF THE INGREDIENTS you use contribute as much to the final quality of a dish as do their flavors. Good cooks understand this and can work wonders by manipulating the relationship between these two elements, but novices often forget to consider the importance of texture. It's not just a matter of coarse or fine. Cooking time contributes to texture, but there are other ways to control it.

The tools in this chapter help you transform your ingredients into the necessary textures for whatever dish you are preparing—from the most refined stock to homestyle mashed potatoes—enhancing and intensifying their flavors in the process. Without some of these implements and the textures they produce, it would be difficult, if not impossible, to achieve certain tastes or to prepare certain dishes.

SIEVES

THE BASIC DIFFERENCE BETWEEN strainers and sieves is that while strainers separate liquids from solids, sieves are meant to refine texture. In a sieve, food passes through the holes in a screen of wire, nylon, perforated metal, or a mesh made of horsehair (which was once the most common material for mesh sieves). The ingredients are broken into pieces whose dimensions are determined by the size of the holes.

The sieve called a *chinois* is, in essence, a stable jelly bag; originally it was held by two people, or hooked over a couple of chairs. Named in a fanciful reference to the pointed Chinese hat it resembles, a *chinois* can be made of perforated sheet metal or wire mesh attached to a circular frame that is equipped with a handle and, in the best examples, a bracket for resting the sieve on the rim of a pot, container, or bowl.

When foods are puréed in a metal sieve or *chinois*, a wooden pestle is the most efficient tool for hastening the movement of the ingredients through the mesh. When it is used with a drum sieve, it is called a *champignon,* the French word for mushroom, which describes its shape. With the *chinois*, you use a pointed pestle tailored to fit closely down into the bottom.

A sieve made in a classic drum shape of wood or metal is called a *tamis*—old cookbooks often recommend that fruit jelly be sieved through a "tammy cloth." Wooden *tamis,* used for refining moist ingredients into purées, are being replaced by metal drum sieves; stronger and more sanitary, they are a modern improvement over the wooden classics. Fine sieves do a great job of refining, but also of trapping nearly microscopic bits of food. Rinse sieves immediately after use.

5.1 MOULI *TAMIS* WITH COARSE SCREEN

This generous, professional-weight stainless steel drum sieve, or *tamis,* means business. Pounds of tomatoes or apples for a sauce, mussels to make bisque for a banquet, or tender chickpeas for hummus can pass through the stainless steel mesh stretched across its 12″ diameter. Its wide, flat sieving area allows the food to be spread so that you are pushing it through the sieve with a broad, flat motion that is not tiring. This sieve is strong enough to withstand the pressure of heavy purées and, although relatively expensive initially, is destined for a long and productive life. The wire mesh is sandwiched between the upper and lower frames of the round and locks into place with three lateral clamps. The Mouli drum sieve comes equipped with a coarse-sifting screen, but interchangeable fine- and medium-sifting screens are also available. The size of this sieve, designed for professional kitchens, may make it less practical for your kitchen than the following De Buyer *chinois* would be. The Mouli stainless steel *tamis* is 4½″ high.

5.2 DE BUYER PERFORATED *CHINOIS*

Versatile, well balanced, and attractively crafted, this sturdy *chinois* is molded, but for the handles and the opposing bracket, from a single sheet of stainless steel; from lip to base, there's not a welded seam in sight. Nor are there any narrow rims or crevices to harbor particles of prior purées. The medium perforations in the sieve would be perfect for purée *Bretonne,* the velvety essence of earthy white beans, but not for making seedless raspberry jam— the tiny seeds would slip through the holes. Paired with a large wooden pestle, it did a yeoman job of puréeing a batch of winter squash for a Provençal squash tart. With its handle and the convenient bracket to balance it over the bowl, it is not dependent on a container with a specific diameter, although its shape requires that whatever receptacle used is at least 6″ deep. When not in use it can be hung up with the hole in its handle. The De Buyer perforated *chinois* is 8″ in diameter, 8″ deep, and comes in brushed stainless steel.

5.3 SCI MESH *CHINOIS*

A bit smaller in width and depth than the average mesh *chinois,* which is usually a deep conical utensil, this hefty Italian-made *chinois* does an excellent job straining out the sediment and aromatics from stocks, bouillons, and fruit purées. Since the cone is less deep—7″ instead of the usual 10″ or 11″—you can use it over a larger variety of pots or bowls. The cone is an uninterrupted flow of beautifully woven ultrafine mesh so dense it could filter cloud wisps out of a summer sky. The handle, welded to the frame, is a curved sheet of metal encircling a hollow core, giving you a double layer of metal to hold on to, which is more comfortable to grip than the average *chinois*'s long, thin spatulate handle. The bracket under the rim opposite the handle lets you rest the chinois on a pot or bowl. Because of its fine mesh com-

---

WHAT TO LOOK FOR

Sieves and *chinois* must have the proper mesh or perforations to refine food to the degree required and to prevent seeds, stems, and skins from passing through. The sieve must also be of a size proportionate to the pots, bowls, platters, and baking pans over which it is being used. Perforated *chinois* come in many sizes, from 4″ in diameter to almost 12″ across. For most nonprofessional uses, a 7″ to 8″ perforated *chinois* is ideal.

A drum sieve should be wide, with a flat sieving area that allows the food to be spread and pushed through the mesh with a broad, flat motion that is not tiring. The wire mesh must be strong enough to withstand the pressure of a heavy purée and should fit into the round frame much like the fabric in an embroidery hoop, clamped into place with a metal band held by a sturdy bolt. The clamp makes the most vulnerable part—the mesh—easy to replace.

position and its construction (with seams joining the mesh to the metal frame), you have to be meticulous in cleaning it to prevent traces of food remaining in the mesh and under the seams. In fact, the chore of cleaning this type of *chinois* is a drawback that has led some chefs to opt for using a microperforated metal *chinois* for many, although not all, of the tasks a fine-mesh *chinois* can do. The SCI mesh *chinois* is 8″ in diameter and comes in stainless steel.

5.4 MOULI *CHINOIS* WITH CUSTOM STAND

As fine as a piece of silk, the supple mesh of this French-made *chinois* is tightly woven of ultrathin stainless steel wires to prevent the merest atom of impurity from intruding upon the glorious consommé you strain through it. The mesh cone is fitted smoothly into the stainless steel frame. The delicate filigree of the mesh is protected by a 1″ band of metal that is an extension of the handle. The band descends down around the base of the *chinois*—which allows you to rest the sieve on the bottom of a pot when not using it in its stand—and finishes its journey up on the opposite side of the lid, forming itself into an angled bracket. The Mouli *chinois* comes paired with a made-to-measure tripod stand that will hold the cone steady above any large pot or bowl. Together they

FOND BLANC DE VOLAILLE (CHICKEN STOCK)

Approximately 2 quarts

2 pounds chicken backs and necks (or a 3-pound chicken)
2 leeks, washed and chopped coarse
2 carrots, peeled, washed, and chopped coarse
1 onion, peeled and sliced
2 stalks celery, washed and chopped coarse
2 garlic cloves, unpeeled
1 bouquet garni
½ teaspoon pepper, freshly ground

1 In a pot, cover the chicken parts (or chicken) with 4 quarts of cold water. Add all the other ingredients.

2 Bring to a boil and cook, partially covered, for 2½ to 3 hours. From time to time, skim the fat and foam from the top of the liquid.

3 Strain through a fine sieve. Let the stock cool, and remove all the fat that rises to the surface.

NOTE If you prepare this stock with a whole chicken, you can, if you wish, remove the meat from the bones after the first hour of cooking (return the bones to the pot for the final hour or 2 of cooking). The meat may then be served cold with vinaigrette, or it may be used in a salad.

NOTE This stock may be kept in the refrigerator for several days, or in the freezer for 2 to 3 weeks.

The Lutèce Cookbook, by André Soltner and Seymour Britchkey

offer you a convenient, hands-free way to filter the bouillon from your pot-au-feu or the tiniest seeds from a strawberry coulis. The Mouli *chinois* is 8″ in diameter, 8¾″ deep, and comes in stainless steel. The *chinois* stand, also stainless steel, is 7½″ in diameter and 11″ high.

5.5 MOULI WOODEN PESTLE FOR *CHINOIS*

A graceful, long, tapered hardwood pestle, looking somewhat like a yarn spindle, this pusher fits perfectly into a *chinois*—whether of perforated metal or fine mesh. Wielded with a simple rotating motion around and around the sides of the *chinois*, it

effectively rubs the food through the perforations. Crafted of a single piece of simply turned, unfinished hardwood, its weight and balance are excellent. If you own a *chinois* that did not come with its own pestle, this 10″ tool is essential.

5.6 KÜCHENPROFI *CHAMPIGNON*

This *champignon* looks so much like a mushroom that you would expect it to smell of the damp earth. Made of smooth, unfinished hardwood, it is

8″ long and a good shape for rubbing purées through the screen of a drum sieve. But, with its wide, rounded head, it is at its best coaxing vegetables or fruits—potatoes, tomatoes, avocados, apples, bananas—through a large strainer. Its gently rounded lines negotiate the curves smoothly, sliding up, down, and around as it presses the food against the perforated surface. Though the champignon is a tool with a dedicated use, it can be pressed into service in other ways, for crushing walnuts or peppercorns, for example.

FOOD MILLS

IN A CATEGORY DOMINATED by simple shapes that are clearly expressions of function, the food mill is a baroque obtrusion, all jutting angles, twisted wires, scalloped edges, and curved plates stamped with holes, messages, and designs—it almost looks like a miniature lunar explorer. Yet it is a highly utilitarian example of simple mechanics harnessed for efficiency: a mechanized sieve.

Like a sieve or *chinois*, it separates as it purées, leaving seeds and skins of tomatoes behind, sorting out the peels and cores of your cooked apples as the sauce drops into the bowl beneath. Its ability to separate is its major advantage over the food processor or colander. The degree to which the food is refined is controlled by openings in the disc you select, but your ingredients are never liquefied to death as in a blender. Most food mills come with three interchangeable discs: a fine disc for smooth purées like baby food; a medium disc that permits some texture to pass through, giving character to applesauce and soups; and, finally, a coarse disc for jobs like ricing potatoes or preparing tomatoes for cooking into a sauce. To operate a food mill, you simply turn the crank; the flat curved blade rotates over the perforated disc in the bottom of the mill, forcing the food through the holes. Any jammed particles of food can be freed by simply reversing the direction of the crank.

Fruit and vegetable presses, used for making purées and sauces, go one step beyond the classic food mill in sophistication and efficiency and are close cousins to some electric noncitrus juicers. They look more like manual grain mills with hand cranks on the side. Generally, the presses have two spouts, one where the puréed fruit or vegetable slides out, and another that ejects the waste products—skin, seeds, and core material. The crank turns a spiral rotor like that of a meat grinder, which brings the fruit or vegetable into the pressing cylinder. A finely perforated screen then forces the pulp and juices out through the holes.

WHAT TO LOOK FOR

Your food mill or press should be made of acid-resistant metal like stainless steel, operate smoothly, and have dishwasher-safe parts that remove easily. A 2-quart capacity is adequate for most purposes. For a food mill, interchangeable cutting plates are essential.

5.7 FOLEY FOOD MILL

This earnest food mill is an American classic, a bit frumpy in this era of high-speed food processors, but a stalwart nonetheless, churning out mashed potatoes and applesauce just like Grandma used to make. And the Foley admirably purées tomatoes without the need for peeling, coring, or seeding, something even a state-of-the-art food processor can't claim. It presses the flesh through the perforated holes, leaving seeds, skin, and fiber behind. It's a simple affair—a 2-quart, pot-shaped, stainless steel body 8¼″ in diameter with a hand-cranked blade that forces fruits or vegetables through the convex perforated bottom as you turn the crank. Beneath the base, where a tension spring holds the blade taut, a little pin that extends from the spring revolves around the bottom, scraping off accumulated food as the blade presses it through. There are no interchangeable discs for different textures, but the mill's perforated bottom with its medium-sized holes produces classic applesauce with moderate coarseness and also presses out a nicely textured puréed vegetable soup. A long attached stainless steel handle extends from one side while two riveted brackets on the other side stabilize the mill over a pot or bowl. One small drawback is that you can only use the Foley over a pot or bowl with a circumference just slightly larger than the mill itself, so your choice of receptacles is somewhat limited. The crank assembly is removable for easy cleaning, and the whole thing can be put in the dishwasher. The Foley food mill is produced in stainless steel with a black plastic crank handle. It is 4″ tall.

5.8 VILLAWARE VICTORIO FOOD STRAINER

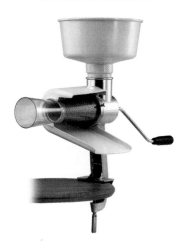

If you frequently make your own tomato sauces, cooking up large batches of a garden-fresh harvest, the Victorio food strainer and sauce maker would be a welcome addition to your kitchen. This is a wonderful, well-made machine that can easily process large quantities of tomatoes as well as other vegetables and fruits. It will also please those who make jams, thick puréed soups, vegetable

sauces, and baby food. You load the food into the large hopper and help its descent with a red plastic plunger. Then you turn the black-handled crank arm that engages the drive shaft, and the spiral rotor forces the tomatoes or other foods through the microperforated screen. The handle may be a little stiff to turn at first, until the food arrives in the pressing chamber. Beautifully puréed pulp comes out of the screen and down the wide squirt guard. At the same time, the residue—seeds, skin, core—is expelled from the long waste funnel on the side. In addition to turning 5 pounds of tomatoes into purée, the strainer did a nice job of processing 2 pounds of kidney beans for a dip, and 3 pounds of unpeeled potatoes for smoothly textured mashed potatoes. To process a wider variety of foods, you can obtain optional attachments like a coarse salsa screen, a medium-coarse pumpkin and squash screen, a grape spiral, and a fine berry screen. The Victorio clamps onto a table or countertop up to 2″ thick, with at least a 1½″ overhang. The strainer disassembles for washing in hot, soapy water. The Villaware Victorio food strainer is 13½″ high. Its body is made of aluminum, the screen of stainless steel, with a white plastic squirt guard and red plastic plunger.

5.9 MOULINEX FOOD MILL

The Moulinex food mill is another kitchen classic, dear to generations

of French housewives and indispensable in the preparation of the classic puréed vegetable soup that the French cookbook author and cooking teacher Lydie Marshall calls "concierge soup." The reason for the name? The aroma of this soup would be the first thing you would smell as you entered the building, emanating from the concierge's lobby-level apartment.

This new generation of the Moulinex mill, with a light and gleaming high-durability plastic body, does a yeoman job of puréeing even the chunkiest vegetables for your own version of a concierge soup. Two interchangeable, acid-resistant tinned steel discs allow you to choose the texture of your purée. The fine disc produces a velvety potage and a nice tomato purée; the coarse one refines apples into sauce and rices potatoes beautifully. The crank handle is topped by an easy-to-grip, bright-red plastic knob and is held in place by a simple tension spring. Although it does not have a revolving pin beneath the perforated disc, as the Foley mill does, to scrape off accumulated purée, you can do this easily enough with a spoon. The arm turns the blade smoothly and easily, rotating with aplomb both forward and back.

The plastic handle is smooth and comfortable to grip, a vast improvement over the hollow-cored metal handle of earlier models. The serrated legs that splay out from the base allow you to set the mill over a variety of pots or bowls from 6½″ to 11″ in diameter. The Moulinex is easy to disassemble and can be washed in the dishwasher. The Moulinex food mill has a white, hard plastic body, a tinned steel handle and blade, and two tinned-steel discs; it is 4″ tall and has a 2-quart capacity. A smaller, 1-quart model is practical for baby food. If properly cared for, this food mill will last for years.

POTATO MASHERS & RICERS

THE TEXTURE OF MASHED potatoes is a matter of personal preference. Some like their potatoes whipped into a silky, buttery purée, a style popularized several years ago by the French chef Joël Robuchon. Others prefer their potatoes smoothly mashed but still retaining a distinct texture, with little bits of potato detectable. Although practical and efficient for so many products, the food processor is not the tool of choice for mashing or whipping potatoes, because the results are too glutinous. (This is because boiling a potato causes its starch granules to swell, and then breaking the cell walls of the granules with the blade of a food processor releases large quantities of this starch, which can quickly give the potato the consistency of wallpaper paste.) What works best for mashing potatoes are two time-honored kitchen utensils: the classic masher, in one of several updated designs, and the ricer.

The old-fashioned wire-loop potato masher with the zigzag presser, still made by several companies, requires many strokes to refine the potato to a smooth consistency, sometimes resulting in potatoes that are gluey yet still lumpy at the same time. This design has recently been superseded by mashers with a round or oval disc at the bottom perforated with small holes or a grid of small rectangles. These mashers do a fine job of crushing boiled potatoes to a fairly smooth, satisfying texture in just a few strokes. They are good for making old-fashioned, though not velvety, mashed potatoes. For many cooks, however, the ideal tool for mashing potatoes is the ricer. With this utensil, the potato goes into a perforated chamber and is forced through the cylinder's holes by a leveraged press—a technique that damages fewer potato cells. The ricing process works well for other root vegetables and for cooked chestnuts, too.

5.10 OXO GOOD GRIPS POTATO MASHER

The Good Grips masher, only 6″ tall, is well balanced with a subtly curved oval disc. In addition to using the traditional up-and-down motion, you can rock it back and forth to crush the potato. The grid of little rectangular openings mashes the potato quickly and efficiently with virtually no lumps. The cushiony black rubber handle, set horizontally rather than vertically, maximizes your strength and makes this tool exceptionally comfortable and easy to work with, confirming the theory that there is no such thing as an OXOmoron. The OXO Good Grips potato masher is 4½″ wide and comes in polished stainless steel with a black rubber handle.

5.11 CALPHALON POTATO MASHER

The tall, sleek Calphalon masher, with its long, vertical handle, is comfortable to grip and offers good leverage for mashing. Produced in durable, matte-black plastic, the masher is 12½″ tall, light, and easy to use. The mashing disc (3½″ by 3¾″) is perforated with twenty-seven long, narrow openings. When you press down, the potato is extruded through the holes in thin, satiny ribbons. As with the OXO masher, the surface of the Calphalon disc is also slightly curved so you can mash with a rocking, back-and-forth motion as well as up and down. With this masher, you can achieve finely textured mashed potatoes with very little effort.

5.12 RÖSLE POTATO MASHER

Fashioned of gleaming, top-of-the-line stainless steel, the Rösle potato masher is an elegant, beautifully made instrument. At the base of the sturdy, round vertical handle is a smooth polished cap where the side of your palm can rest as you mash. The flat, round mashing disc, perforated with a multitude of small, even holes, and seamlessly attached to the graceful arms rising to the handle, quickly refines the potato, leaving no morsel unmashed. The Rösle potato masher, produced in a combination of brushed and polished stainless steel, is 10¼" tall; the disc is 3¼" in diameter.

5.13 OXO GOOD GRIPS POTATO RICER

The Good Grips potato ricer is the only one that made it through our tests and that can also be rested on the top of a pot or bowl as you rice. With handles that are comfortably padded with black rubber, and an oval, rubber-padded extension on the opposite side of the cup, the design makes it easier to squeeze the viselike press, particularly if you have diminished strength in your hands. The press forces the potato through the 3" ricing plate, which is perforated with tiny holes and seamlessly melded to the cylindrical body. The potato emerges in delicate strands. The solid-body construction of sturdy stainless steel makes this ricer easy to clean and store—no misplaced ricing discs lost in the depths of the cabinet. This potato ricer is 11½" long, 4¾" high, holds two medium-size potatoes, and comes padded at three points with black rubber. It is dishwasher safe.

MASHED POTATOES
❧ DANNY MEYER & MICHAEL ROMANO ❧

4 1-cup servings

Who can resist the creamy comfort of perfect mashed potatoes? We've found that even the most persnickety diner can be convinced to try almost any new or unusual dish on our menu—so long as it's accompanied by mashed potatoes. These creamy spuds make everything they come in contact with taste better. We have two tips for making perfect, smooth mashed potatoes. One, use a food mill or ricer; a handheld masher will give you a lumpy result, and a food processor makes them gummy and tough. Two, mashed potatoes are never as good as when freshly made; while this recipe explains how to hold mashed potatoes for up to an hour, they'll change dramatically if you reheat them the next day.

2 pounds Idaho potatoes, peeled and quartered
2 teaspoons kosher salt
8 tablespoons (1 stick) unsalted butter
½ cup heavy cream
½ cup milk
¼ teaspoon freshly ground white pepper

1 Place the potatoes in a 2-quart saucepan with 1 teaspoon of the salt and cold water to cover. Bring to a boil, lower the heat, and simmer, covered, until completely tender, about 30 minutes. Test the potatoes by piercing them with a paring knife—there should be no resistance. Place in a colander and allow to drain well for several minutes.

2 Combine the butter, heavy cream, and milk in another saucepan and heat gently until the butter has melted. Keep warm.

3 Working over the saucepan used to cook the potatoes, pass the potatoes through a food mill or potato ricer. If you have any difficulty, add a little of the hot milk and butter to the potatoes.

4 To serve, place the potatoes over a low flame and begin adding the warm milk mixture. Whip the potatoes with a wooden spoon or spatula while heating. When all the liquid is absorbed, season with the remaining salt and white pepper. Serve piping hot. Mashed potatoes are best served immediately, but if you are unable to do so, or need them for another recipe, keep the potatoes hot for up to 1 hour by placing them in the top of a double boiler, covered and held over barely simmering water.

WHAT TO LOOK FOR

Whichever potato masher you select should be well balanced and easy to move around the pot or bowl as you press your ingredients through. The press itself—the disc on the bottom—should have numerous small openings to refine the potato with every stroke. Because potato ricers work through the exertion of pressure, they need sturdy construction so they do not bend or break. They should have a container capacity of 1 to 2 cups, and must be made of dishwasher-safe, nonreactive metal like stainless steel. Having two interchangeable perforated plates (fine and coarse) is a plus. And, of course, the ricer you choose must be comfortable for your grip.

5.14 VILLAWARE KING POTATO RICER

Two interchangeable 3¼" plates, one perforated with tiny 1/16" holes, the other with 1/8" holes, make this Italian-made ricer practical for refining potatoes into a fine purée for gnocchi dumplings (using the smaller-holed plate), as well as for mashing them as a side dish. The plate with the larger holes also works nicely in pressing tomatoes for a sauce. The Villaware King is made of sturdy, die-cast aluminum, a strong, lightweight material, instead of a heavy, noncorrosive one like stainless steel. The aluminum may discolor over time, especially if you use it on high-acid foods such as tomatoes, but it's a compromise we can accept. The ricer has long, smoothly finished handles and is comfortable to hold even when gripped tightly. The Villaware King potato ricer is 10¼" long and 3½" tall.

GARLIC PRESSES

Certain foods are better, and more efficiently, refined by a viselike press than by a sieve, mortar, or a mill. Garlic is a good example. Some experts object to pressed garlic, claiming that it is stronger than minced or sliced garlic and will overpower a dish, but the garlic press cannot make the garlic "stronger": it simply makes more of the flavor available. Because the output of a garlic press exposes more of the garlic's surface than minced or sliced cloves, a little goes a long way—so be conservative. Although garlic can be easily mashed in a mortar or on a board with coarse salt, no salt is necessary when a garlic press is used.

5.15 ZYLISS SUSI DELUXE GARLIC PRESS

The Susi Deluxe is one of the new generation of garlic presses from Zyliss, a company that pioneered the iconic hinged garlic press of the 1970s. (This was a revolutionary tool with a curved presser section that came up from the bottom and over the garlic, held in the stationary top section, forcing it through the utensil's perforated face as you squeezed.) In this latest model, 6" long and formed in die-cast aluminum with a matte-silver, nonstick coating, it is the bottom section that holds the garlic—two cloves fit cozily in the small cup—while a little plunger flips down from the top portion, neatly and effectively pressing the garlic through the holes in the face.

Thanks to the nonstick coating, this press cleans beautifully; it even comes with a plastic cleaning attachment with tiny prongs that liberate embedded garlic residue from the holes. The Susi Deluxe was designed to press unpeeled cloves of garlic, which it does satisfactorily. Keep in mind that you always need a bit more effort to press unpeeled garlic, and that the yield will be slightly less than a peeled clove since some of the garlic will get mashed into the peel.

WHAT TO LOOK FOR

The best kind of garlic press has a comfortable grip, sturdy construction, and a nonstick surface, which will allow you to press unpeeled cloves and make the tool easier to clean. It should also have a set of reverse pins, which self-clean the pressing surface, or come with an attachment for cleaning the garlic residue out of the holes. Finally, it should be dishwasher safe and hold at least two large cloves.

MAKING GARLIC PASTE BY HAND

The garlic paste that comes out of a mortar and pestle is rewarding, but the work is hard. Adding a few grains of sea or kosher salt at the start of the process greatly reduces the necessary effort.

5.16 OXO GOOD GRIPS GARLIC PRESS

With its sturdy rubber-cushioned handles, its gleaming, hinged metal top and satisfying, well-balanced heft, this state-of-the-art utensil is one of the best garlic presses available. The black rubber handles are pleasingly tactile and comfortable to squeeze. The bottom of the weighted head easily holds two, even three, cloves, which the broad, smooth press on top forces smartly through the little holes in the face. The Good Grips press comes with bright-red reverse pins attached; after you press the garlic through, you can flip the arm in the opposite direction and the cleaning pins push the garlic residue out of the holes and back into the cup, eliminating the tedious task of picking the garlic off. This strikingly designed press should last for many years if its resilience in the wake of relentless "fatigue testing" at the hands of one tester's young son is any indication. The OXO Good Grips garlic press is 6¾" long and comes in chrome-plated die-cast zinc with black rubber-padded handles.

MORTARS & PESTLES

IN THE BEGINNING, there was a rock and a hard place. Not long thereafter came the mortar and pestle. Thousands of years ago, when Neolithic groups figured out how to plant the seeds of wild grains, farming and cultivation were added to hunting and gathering as methods of procuring food. Raw grains, however, are practically indigestible—not only must the grain be separated from the chaff, but it must also be toasted or dried and ground into meal or flour. The first grinder was a tree stump or flat rock and a stone, and it was from these primitive tools that mortars evolved.

After the cutting edge, the mortar is the most basic cooking tool in common use around the world. If the average home in our industrialized societies survives without one, it is because mechanized mills and electric food processors have taken over its ancient tasks. However, as Alice Waters, the talented chef and cookbook author, points out, modern electrical blenders and processors remove you from the sensual aspects of cooking and reduce the information you get from direct contact with the food. A mortar and pestle give you touch and control.

Try using a mortar and pestle to pulverize your own ingredients for a pesto or to crush and amalgamate herbs and spices by hand, and you are in for a treat. In fact, the Italian word *pesto* (or the French *pistou*) means "pounding," related in its meaning and origin with our English word *pestle*. When pesto is made in a mortar, each ingredient is pounded into and builds on the next; a food processor merely chops and tears the ingredients instead of marrying them. Using a mortar also gives you greater flexibility when it comes to quantities—just try grinding half a dozen peppercorns in an electric mill.

5.17 MASON CASH VITRIFIED CERAMIC MORTAR & PESTLE

Made of vitrified ceramic, a hard, non-porous substance that will not stain or absorb flavors, the Mason Cash mortar and pestle exemplify the best of breed in their category. The duo has a distinguished lineage, manufactured in England at a factory once managed by Ralph Wedgwood, nephew of Josiah Wedgwood, who created the first vitrified ceramic mortar and pestle at the end of the eighteenth century. The bowl of the Mason Cash mortar, sturdy and well balanced, is deep and nicely contoured, to keep in what you're grinding. The mortar's matte texture facilitates grinding on the inside of the bowl while providing nonslip handling on the outside. A small pour spout allows you to easily transfer the contents to a pot or bowl. The weighted conical pestle, of the same vitrified ceramic material, is slim on top for a comfortable grip, then gently widens to a broad bottom to maximize grinding ability. Mortar and pestle rapidly transformed both garlic and pine nuts into pastes and efficiently crushed a mixture of fennel seed, cardamom, peppercorns, and cloves to season a pilaf.

The Mason Cash mortar is 5¼" in diameter and comes in green, blue, yellow, or white vitrified ceramic; the 7⅓" pestle comes in white vitrified ceramic. Many other mortar sizes are available, ranging from 2"-high minis to the largest size, 12" in diameter, each accompanied by a correctly proportioned pestle.

5.18 JOYCE CHEN *SURIBACHI*

At first, this looks like an ordinary Japanese bowl, the light-brown interior framed in a rich brown glaze, but look closer and you see sharp ridges in a wedge-shaped pattern with a pouring spout. This is a *suribachi*, an earthenware mortar in which the Japanese mash tofu, grind sesame seeds, or work miso (fermented soybean paste) into a smooth consistency. It is 5½" across the top, 2" deep, and is named after the crater of the extinct volcano on Iwo Jima, which was made famous in the United States by flag-raising Marines during World War II. The mortar's pestle, or *surikogi*, is a 4¾" cylinder of unfinished wood, rounded off at the mashing end. Wood is the material of choice because it won't break the interior ridges. You might be wary of pressing down as hard as you would in a bowl of marble, but the baked-clay mortar is surprisingly substantial. Besides the 1½-cup capacity shown here, the *suribachi* comes in a 3-cup version 6" in diameter with a 7"-long *surikogi*. That model, however, lacks a pouring spout.

5.19 NORPRO MARBLE MORTAR & PESTLE

A nice example of the classic mortar and pestle, this Norpro set is neatly honed from white marble striated with gray. The mortar is sturdy and heavy, polished on the outside, matte within to add resistance and enhance the grinding surface. The slim pestle, slightly wider at the base, is polished except for its grinding tip, which is matte to match the interior of the mortar. The Norpro

WHAT TO LOOK FOR

The best and most expensive mortars are made of marble—a hard, clean, and relatively nonporous material that will prevent the garlic you crush for pesto from reappearing as a living memory in the spices you later grind for a fruitcake. The inside of a marble mortar should be fairly smooth but left unpolished to permit the necessary friction. We think the most practical alternative to marble for a mortar and pestle is ceramic. However, in *The Cuisines of Mexico,* Diana Kennedy recommends native black basalt, and Rick Bayless, the chef-owner of the highly respected Frontera Grill in Chicago, agrees; Alain Ducasse, the famous French chef, opts for granite. Ceramic shares the properties of marble or granite, except perhaps for weight and permanence. Wood, another material commonly used for mortars, is not suited for grinding any ingredients liable to exude moisture, even when it is the most closely grained hardwood. Brass, which is common in India and eastern Europe, is heavy but corrosive and needs polishing. In addition, there are a number of mortars and pestles made of glass—a truly unfortunate choice of material.

When using a mortar, you first press down on the spices with the pestle to crack them open, then you work the pestle in a circular motion, grinding the grains or seeds against the textured walls of the mortar. A mortar with a 4" diameter and sloping sides deep enough to keep in the ingredients is best for most purposes, although a well-equipped kitchen will have several sizes. The mortar should never be filled more than halfway, or it will overflow during the grinding. Be sure your mortar is heavy enough to withstand vigorous pounding, and that the pestle fits both the mortar and your hand comfortably. It is preferable for the mortar and pestle to be of the same material to help equalize pressure and assure even grinding—marble with marble, ceramic with ceramic.

mortar and pestle made quick work of a cup of basil, garlic, and pine nuts for a pesto, as well as almonds, dried thyme, cardamom pods, and juniper berries. The marble stays cool while you work and is easy to clean afterward. The Norpro mortar is 4" in diameter and 2½" high.

5.20 KITCHEN MARKET LAVA STONE MORTAR & PESTLE

The traditional Mexican mortar and pestle shown here look for all the world like pre-Colombian artifacts, and, indeed, are still known by their ancient names: *molcajete* and *tejolote*. Made of porous, rough-textured, dark-gray volcanic stone, these time-honored kitchen tools are still preferred by discerning Mexican cooks for blending and grinding together their sauce ingredients—chilies, herbs, garlic, onions, nuts, and seeds—which would lose much of their texture if puréed in a blender. New *molcajetes* and *tejolotes,* unless fashioned from superior-quality black basalt, a rarity today, are potentially gritty and must be cured before they are used. To cure, first scour the surfaces with a stiff brush and plenty of water. Then, grind a handful of raw rice into the stone. Wash the tools again, and then repeat the operation at least two or three times. At first the rice picks up the stone's gray color, but eventually a batch will remain white. This three-legged *molcajete* stands 4" high, and its shallow

"And when you said that my pesto was the best pesto you ever had and could ever hope to have—was that a lie, too?"

---

bowl is 6" in diameter. The stubby, triangular-shaped *tejolote* is 3½" long and 2" across at the base.

5.21 DANCE OF THE ANCESTORS LAVA STONE CORN GRINDER

A large, rectangular lava stone slab, called a *metate,* and its companion stone roller, known as a *mano* or *metlapil,* are still the oldest and by far the most basic cooking tools used in Mexico. They grind corn, mash softened corn kernels into dough for tortillas, and purée ingredients for sauces. Women can still be seen kneeling before their *metates* in country villages, pressing and scrubbing the roller back and forth across the sloping surface of the stone, just as their ancestors did centuries ago. Our *metate* measures 12" by 9" and

stands 3½" high on three sturdy, triangular legs; the accompanying *mano* is 8" long. Clearly designed for durability, these rough-hewn implements have a pleasant, earthy quality to them, and the heavy, coarse volcanic stone provides a most effective grinding surface. Before using the tools, be sure to cure them using the same method prescribed for the lava stone mortar.

5.22 INDIAN BRASS MORTAR & PESTLE

Few things are as important in Indian cooking as freshly ground spices, and the traditional implements for grinding them are a mortar and pestle. In some areas of India, an upright mortar such as this one is the favored style; in other regions a flat stone tablet and oblong grinding stone are preferred; and often both types are found in the same kitchen. Whatever the shape, a mortar and pestle are so personal and important to an Indian woman that she often takes them with her when she leaves home to marry.

This gleaming mortar is worthy of any dowry. Made of a heavy brass alloy incised with decorative lines, the mortar measures 3" deep and 3" in diameter. The 7"-long, blunt-ended pestle fits the bowl snugly and is heavy enough to easily crush the masala, or spice mixture, for any dish. First dry-toast the spices in a pan over medium heat for a few minutes. Let them cool, then grind them to a powdery consistency. Store the *masala* in an airtight container.

GRILLED BEEF CROSS RIB WITH ANCHOVY BUTTER

2 or 3 servings

Good beef is more popular in the Basque country than it used to be but still falls behind lamb, pork, and veal. A simple grilled steak with perhaps a sprinkling of *piment d'Espelette* is a staple menu item at the *cidreries*, the cider-tasting restaurants. (*Piment d'Espelette* is a small red pepper found in Basque cooking; it is dried and ground to a fine powder, with a sweet, mild spicy taste. One could substitute sweet paprika or mild chili powder.) This recipe is very easy, the flavor coming from the grill and the flavored butter. You can also treat steaks such as porterhouse or sirloin in the same manner.

1 ounce salted anchovy fillets, rinsed and finely diced
4 tablespoons unsalted butter
½ teaspoon minced fresh rosemary
¼ teaspoon *piment d'Espelette*
2 pounds beef cross rib (in one piece)
1 tablespoon olive oil
kosher salt
freshly ground white pepper

1 Preheat a barbecue or grill.
2 In a mortar or small bowl, pound the anchovies into a paste. Add the butter, rosemary, and *piment d'Espelette*. Combine well and set aside.
3 Brush the meat with the olive oil and season generously with salt and pepper. Place the meat on the grill, turning occasionally until cooked according to taste, about 6 minutes for rare, 8 minutes for medium, and 10 minutes for well done.
4 Place the meat on a serving platter and let it rest for 5 minutes before slicing. Spoon the anchovy butter on top of the meat.

The Basque Kitchen: Tempting Food from the Pyrenees, by Gerald Hirigoyen with Cameron Hirigoyen

---

PEPPER MILLS, SALT MILLS, & SPICE GRINDERS

PEPPER IS THE FRUIT of an East Indian plant, a bright-red berry that turns black after harvesting and drying. When the outer layer of dried black pepper has been removed, the remaining part is used as white pepper—actually beige in color—which is somewhat milder in flavor than the black. Chefs choose between black and white pepper based on the intensity of flavor but also on color—in most classic European recipes tiny black spots on a white sauce or surface are considered unattractive.

The Oriental spice routes of the past were paved with peppercorns, and precious pepper, like salt, was used as currency. To this day, pepper is the most widely used seasoning in the world. However, unless it has been freshly ground, pepper may not season at all; it should be dispensed at the source, directly from the pepper mill, the mechanized successor to the mortar and pestle.

Unless you are using a recipe that calls for whole or crushed peppercorns, it is essential that the pepper be ground. The same is not true for salt. Ordinary table salt, however, contains chemical additives that can adversely affect the flavor of food. These days, natural sea salt, fine or coarse, has become widely available in supermarkets, and most people who use it find that it distinctly enhances the flavor of food. We agree and believe that if sea salt is available, there is no reason to use regular table salt. French or English sea salt or kosher salt is a good alternative. Though they usually don't need to be ground finer, some very coarse varieties of sea salt benefit from being brought to a more finely uniform texture.

Salt is born of the purest parents: the sun and the sea.
—PYTHAGORAS

For table use, some people find a salt mill filled with coarse sea salt more convenient than the historic expedient of an open salt dish, especially if they live in a humid climate where salt tends to cake. Those who use sea salt at the table are firmly convinced that their favorite salt tastes better than the packaged grocery-store brands. Top-quality sea salt has an aftertaste that hints at sweetness, and its coarse texture can enrich many a dish, providing a subtle crunch before it melts on the palate. It is so effective that you wind up using less of it than you would regular table salt.

Battery models aside (we do not recommend them), pepper, salt, and some spice mills have four distinct systems for transferring the force of your hand to the grinding mechanism: wing nuts, crank handles, knobs, and squeeze handles. Crank handles allow you to grind continuously without changing your grip, which offers an advantage for someone who needs the help, but otherwise the choice is purely a matter of personal comfort. Most mills utilize a shaft to connect a knob at the top of the mill to a set of grinding heads near the bottom. The upper grinder turns when you turn the knob. The lower grinder is fixed to the mill and does not turn—the pepper is ground between the two. The space around the shaft is used to store the peppercorns, coarse salt, or spice.

5.23 UNICORN MAGNUM PLUS

This tall, contemporary black pepper mill, which many of our authorities thought was the best, may look Italian in design, but only its precision steel grinding heads hail from Italy. The Unicorn Magnum Plus itself was conceived and created on the Massachusetts island of Nantucket, where some of the earliest fortunes in the United States (including the one that funded Yale University) were made by clipper shipowners importing spices to Massachusetts. The mill is the brainchild of the Nantucketer Tom David, who was inspired to create his first pepper mill—the one-handed "Peppergun"—one evening several years back when he couldn't stir his cream sauce and add pepper at the same time. His sleek Magnum Plus, with a smooth, high-

WHAT TO LOOK FOR

This is a category of equipment fraught with disappointment. Some of the most handsome, impressive-looking mills did not perform well in tests, or were awkward or uncomfortable to use. With pepper, salt, and spice mills, you certainly cannot choose by visual appeal or touch alone. A good mill should be comfortable in your hand. It will have a grind that's adjustable in a wide range from fine (white pepper for a white sauce) to coarse (black pepper for a steak au poivre) and hold the setting throughout its use without slipping to the next. The best mills have grinding heads that are made of machine-cut stainless steel, high-carbon steel, or ceramic. These last longer and keep a better edge than those cast of zinc alloy.

The criteria for the selection of a mill to be used in the kitchen are slightly different from those for mills being used at the table. Mills for the kitchen should have a larger storage capacity (at least ½ cup), the mechanism should grind quickly (the larger the diameter of the grinders, the faster the process), and the container should be easy to refill and made of a material that's easily wiped clean. Ideally, the grinding mechanism and the filling arrangement should be independent systems; otherwise every time you fill the mill you need to reset the grind. Speed and capacity are less important for salt and pepper mills being used at the table.

durability plastic body, meets all our criteria. It has a comfortable grip, and the grind is easily adjustable, from very fine to very coarse, with a nut at the base that is independent of the large loading ring in the center of the mill's body—so there's no need to reset the grind after refilling. It holds more than 1 cup of pepper-corns, making it ideal for the kitchen, and it's fast, producing a lot of pepper with just a few grinds. The grinding mechanism—the largest on the market, with a grinding surface almost 1" in diameter—has nickel-plated heads that will maintain their cutting edges and won't rust. The exterior is easy to wipe clean.

The Magnum Plus is 9″ high, comes only in black, and has a lifetime guarantee; you can return it to the manufacturer at any time if dissatisfied. Unicorn also produces two 6″ models, the Magnum pepper mill and the neat Keytop, with a comfortable turnkey on the top; both, in black only, are high performers, perfect for kitchen or table. For travelers, Unicorn offers a beguiling 3″ Minimill, in red, black, or white and packed in a velvet travel pouch, with excellent grind-power for its size.

5.24 WILLIAM BOUNDS MILLENNIUM CHEF'S PEPPER MILL

This hefty, gleaming, stainless steel pepper mill with a clear acrylic center is a state-of-the-art grinder that gives a nostalgic nod to the grinders of yesteryear, with its generous, user-friendly crank-top handle. Designed specifically for cooking rather than table service (although the mill would be an attractive—albeit large—tabletop conversation piece), the Millennium has five distinct grind settings, from extra fine to extra coarse, and each setting produces what it promises. Although you have to peer intently the first time to find the faint raised notch on the plastic that indicates the setting, the settings snap crisply into place. The Millennium holds more than ½ cup of peppercorns and yields a lot of pepper with just a few grinds— almost ½ teaspoon on the medium setting with just five turns of the crank. The mill is easy to load through an opening under the handle. A plastic catch-cup attaches to the bottom of the mill and is handy for gathering and measuring larger quantities of pepper for cooking. An innovative, high-durability ceramic grinding mechanism lets you grind directly over a steaming pot without worrying about oxidizing the grinding heads. This mill also works very nicely with coarse sea salt, although it's best to choose one task or the other for the Millennium to perform.

The Millennium, 6½″ tall, is available in three silver-tone finishes of stainless steel—chrome, satin, or brushed—as well as in two colors—black or white—and comes with a lifetime guarantee.

5.25 PEUGEOT AUBERGE PEPPER MILL

Long before it produced automobiles, the Peugeot company was turning out pepper grinders; the first dates from 1842. The Peugeot Auberge mill, a classic of the genre, is an excellent grinder designed along traditional lines. The peppercorns are loaded into the smooth, gently curved body of turned walnut through a narrow opening at the top of the mill; you must first unscrew and remove the knurled nut that crowns the mill, then lift off the top section. (It is necessary to readjust the grind, controlled by the nut, after refilling, loosening it for coarser, tightening it for fine).

You operate this mill by grasping the body in the middle with one hand and turning the top with the other; this method is somewhat tiring for the wrist if you must produce large quantities of ground pepper, but for most kitchen operations, this mill fits the bill perfectly. As you grind, peppercorns inside the hollow core feed into the precision, case-

---

PEPPERCORNS

India, Indonesia, and China produce the grapelike clusters of berries used to make black, white, and green peppercorns, and the rose plant, cultivated in Madagascar, supplies the berries for pink peppercorns. Black peppercorns are the strongest, picked just before ripening and dried until their skins turn dark. White peppercorns, often used ground in pale sauces where you might not want black specks floating around, are much more mellow, having been allowed to ripen and stripped of their skins before drying. Green peppercorns, picked when soft and underripe, are preserved in brine or freeze-dried and are usually used whole, as are pink peppercorns, adding a colorful accent to sauces and a variety of meat and fish dishes.

hardened steel mill at the bottom, a mechanism justly famed for its durability. Not only is it durable, but unusually large—almost 1" in diameter. A single turn produces a generous flurry of pepper. The Peugeot Auberge pepper mill is 10¾" tall and comes in natural or dark walnut. Peugeot offers a large family of turned-wood pepper and salt mills, all with the company's trademark steel mechanism that comes with a lifetime guarantee.

5.26 OXO GOOD GRIPS PEPPER MILL

Squat and well balanced, like a skilled downhill skier, the Good Grips pepper mill was designed with ease of use in mind. A soft, round rubber knob at the tip of the extended turning arm makes grinding easy, while the smooth, small body fits in the other hand. A clear plastic loading door on the side opens wide to facilitate filling; the mill holds over ⅓ cup of peppercorns. A small wheel on the bottom adjusts the grind from fine to coarse; if you have normal dexterity in your fingers, the delicate wheel will pose no problems, but if your hands, like those that inspired OXO's initial designs, are plagued by arthritis, this mechanism might be a challenge. The stainless steel grinding heads yield a generous amount of pepper with just a few revolutions

"The way you use pepper scares me."

of the arm and would be appropriate for both table and kitchen. A catch-cup on the bottom is practical for measuring small amounts of pepper and prevents bits of pepper dust from falling on the counter or table. The OXO Good Grips pepper mill is 5½" tall and comes in white.

5.27 PERFEX PEPPER & SALT MILLS

Classic in design and excellent in performance for their diminutive size, these cylindrical, crank-top French pepper and salt mills in nickel-plated cast aluminum have been on the market for almost fifty years and have never been outdated or outmoded. Like a classic Chanel suit, a Perfex mill is sleek, elegant, and timeless, with no unnecessary frills. You fill the mills with pepper and salt through an easy-loading chute on the side and adjust the grind, from extra fine for your *pfeffernüsse* to coarse for your tuna au poivre, by twisting a nut on the bottom. The mills each hold 2 tablespoons of coarse sea salt or peppercorns. Both the pepper mill and its mate, the salt mill, work exceptionally well, the stainless steel grinding heads transforming the peppercorns or salt crystals into precisely the texture you expect. The Perfex salt and pepper twins are 4½" tall and come only in satin-finished cast aluminum.

5.28   WMF SALT CERAMILL

One of the true innovations in pepper and salt grinders has been the development of the highly durable ceramic grinding mechanism. The ceramic heads, fired at very high temperatures, are harder and stronger than steel, are noncorroding, and hold their cutting edges longer. The millstones are precision-crafted to fit tightly together and can therefore be finely adjusted to grind a range of textures, from superfine to coarse. The WMF company produces the Ceramill line of salt, pepper, and spice grinders, all using the ceramic grinding mechanism. The best, although not the most beautiful, is this functional, no-frills grinder composed of a clear glass jar to hold the salt and a sturdy, white, ribbed plastic grinder base. The jar unscrews from the base, making refilling through the wide opening very easy. The mill fits comfortably in your hands and in just a few turns yields a generous amount of powdery, superfine salt. It also does well with medium and coarse grinds; a small, serrated gray wheel on the bottom adjusts the settings. Utilitarian and dependable, this grinder seems designed for the kitchen rather than the table but would be fine tableside for casual meals. A slim

cap fits snugly on the bottom to trap tiny crystals of salt that might fall from the grinder when you set it down; it is also convenient as a catch-cup when grinding a teaspoon or two of salt.

Similar Ceramills in a variety of sizes do an excellent job of grinding such spices as caraway seeds, thyme, rosemary, chili peppers, and marjoram in a range of textures. The salt Ceramill is 5½" tall and comes with a clear glass jar atop a white base.

5.29   WILLIAM BOUNDS NUT TWISTER

One of the world's most treasured spices, and one of the most aromatic, nutmeg has been used for centuries as a seasoning. It enhances both sweet and savory dishes, from cakes, cookies, and pies to egg dishes, sausages, and stews, and is a fragrant topping for eggnog, coffees, and teas. Pungent and assertive, a little nutmeg goes a long way, so it makes sense to grate only as much as you need and store the remainder in a cool place. Tinned nutmeg, inferior in flavor and aroma to the freshly grated variety, quickly goes flat since very little is used at a time; with spices, freshly grated is always preferable.

In the past, when nutmeg was called for in a recipe, the traditional method for preparing it was by rubbing the nutmeg against a small, fine grater. Over the last few years an alternative to this system has appeared—the nutmeg grinder. Some work better than others, and one works best of all: the puckishly

---
NUTMEG & MACE

Nutmeg and mace fit hand in glove. Mace is the brilliant scarlet-colored membrane covering the inch-long oval nutmeg seed. After harvesting, both mace and nuts are dried, usually with fire and then sunlight. Though similar in taste to nutmeg, mace is far more pungent. Since it stores better than almost any other spice, the dried mace blades are typically ground before exporting. If you do find them whole, no special equipment is required to pulverize them. The blades are so flaky you could crush them in your hand. Nutmeg, on the other hand, loses its essential oils quickly, so the nuts are exported whole to retain their potency. Before use, nutmeg has to be grated to a powder. Start grating at the smaller end of the seed, only shaving off as much as you need (most graters have a little storage compartment for the unused portion). If you find the grater rough on your fingertips, you should opt for a nutmeg grinder.

---

named Nut Twister from William Bounds. Though technically a grater, its use puts it with other spice mills and grinders. This sturdy, round grater of Lucite and stainless steel, with a pretty crank arm pierced with a heart motif, feels solid and smooth and nestles perfectly in your palm. Neat and well made, it is a fine example of commercial American craftsmanship. Just three turns of the crank yield ¼ teaspoon of finely ground nutmeg. At the base of a powerful spring mechanism (with significantly higher tension than other mills tested), the nutmeg is held in place by six sharp prongs. As you grind, the nutmeg is pressed against the cutting edge at the opening on the bottom of the mill; with each smooth rotation, tiny, airy flakes of nutmeg drift down. For decorative as well as practical purposes, the Lucite top holds seven or eight nutmegs in reserve, which spin round and round as you grind. The Nut Twister is 3½" in diameter and barely 3" tall. It comes in chrome-and-satin-finished stainless steel, as well as in black and white.

5.30 VILLAWARE POPPYSEED GRINDER

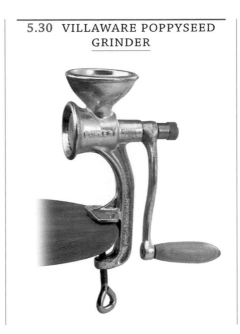

For those cooks who do a great deal of eastern European baking comes this poppyseed grinder from the Czech Republic. Made of tin-coated cast iron, this sturdy, old-fashioned little tool converts the tiny poppyseeds into a granular paste. An adjusting nut lets you set the texture of the grind from fine to coarse. After their turn in the mill, the seeds are ready for mixing into your *hamantaschen*, poppyseed biscuits, Czechoslovakian poppyseed cake, poppyseed crunch squares, or Balkan poppyseed strudel. The grinder disassembles easily for hand-washing. The Villaware poppyseed grinder is 9" high.

GRAIN MILLS

THE GRINDING OF GRAIN goes back more than ten thousand years to the beginning of agriculture, and until a hundred years or so ago a local miller was part of every community. Things began to change during the late 1800s when great industrial roller mills for flour were invented in Hungary and subsequently set up in other countries. They were very efficient and made inexpensive wheat flour available to the world's bakers. In the United States, where gluten-rich wheat had already replaced corn as the common flour for baking, an even lighter, more refined loaf began to emerge. Unfortunately, refinement got out of hand, and the quality of flour and bread declined steadily as the demand for bland, delicate loaves stripped the bran, fiber, and germ from the wheat being milled—bran because the demand was for a white, fine-textured bread; fiber because it interfered with the commercial milling process; and the germ because the oils became rancid in the heat of the mills.

The inevitable reaction set in during the 1960s. A resurgent interest in natural foods and good nutrition had people across the country buying yeast and making their own bread from the best flour they could find. Specialized outlets carried stone-ground grains, and even commercial millers began selling whole wheat and unbleached flours, but many serious home bakers turned to home grinding with more devotion than if they were spinning flax into gold.

If you are a serious bread baker, there are a number of good reasons for grinding your own grain rather than buying flour. As Pillsbury discovered in the 1870s, the oils in protein-rich wheat germ do indeed turn rancid, making stone-ground flours highly perishable. To keep for more than a month or so without spoiling, they must be refrigerated. This is true for both store-bought and mail-order brands. Also, when you buy ready-ground flour you cannot control the type and mixture of the wheat, the texture, or the quantities. Fresh ground flour has more nutrients and fiber than store-bought or commercial-ground flour, and there are no chemicals added. In sum, the ideal is to grind your own. Fine, you say, just as soon as I build a house next to a running stream. Wait—there's an alternative.

> Some people have a foolish way of
> not minding, or pretending not to mind,
> what they eat. For my part, I mind
> my belly studiously, and very carefully;
> for I look upon it, that he who does not mind his
> belly will hardly mind anything else.
> —SAMUEL JOHNSON

5.31 LEHMAN'S OUR BEST GRAIN MILL

Nobody ever said grinding grain into flour by hand was easy. It's basic, back-to-the-earth hard work. In fact, it's a grind. But this hefty, simple yet well-designed grain mill from Lehman's, a venerable company in Ohio's Amish country noted for its well-made, nonelectric tools, renders the task as easy as it's ever going to get. A long, 10″ crank with a comfortable, fist-sized handle gives you very good leverage and a wide-rotation grind. The big hopper holds 5 cups of grain, which yields about 7½ cups of flour.

The grinding mechanism is comprised of two 4″ round stone burrs that crush and refine the grain between them. Stone is the ideal material for manually grinding grain; it can produce a finer, more consistent grind than metal burrs or other mechanisms. The relatively large grinding surface processes the grain at a good pace; about 1 minute of grinding yields 1 cup of finely ground wheat or rye flour. An easily adjusted knob attached to the outside stone burr regulates the grind from fine to very coarse. (The finer the grind, the harder and slower the mill is to turn, but the flour produced by finer grinds is more consistent in texture.)

The Lehman grain mill is made of virtually indestructible cast aluminum and is coated with a white powder glaze that is scratch and chip resistant. The mill clamps to surfaces up to 2″ thick. Two 4″ iron burrs are included to handle any hard-shelled grain, seed, bean, or legume, doing a fine job of milling, for example, rice, corn, and lentils. The stone burrs will tackle hard wheat, soft wheat, and rye. The mill is easy to disassemble and is dishwasher safe. Lehman's Our Best grain mill is 11½″ high.

5.32 GRAIN MASTER WHISPER MILL

Bran is the rough outer hull of the whole wheat berry. Whole-wheat flour is brown because it contains the bran of the wheat; white flour has had the bran removed and is frequently bleached as well.

If you are a serious baker who requires fresh, home-ground flour for your doughs, who places a priority on the nutritional qualities of your flours, and who regularly needs 8 to 15 cups of flour at a pop, then the noisy but fast and efficient Grain Master Whisper Mill is just what you need. *Whisper* is, of course, a misnomer; the powerful motor lets out a banshee of a roar that's louder than a vacuum cleaner, loud enough to annoy everyone in the house. But noise pollution aside, this is a terrific mill. In a matter of seconds, it trans-forms 1 cup of grains into 1½ cups of superfine flour, refined to the texture of dust, if that is your wish. Eight cups of grain are processed into 12 cups of flour in little under a minute.

The Grain Master mill, about the size of a standard food processor, is accompanied by a 12-cup canister that attaches directly to the mill by a short, curved tube. As you grind, the flour exiting from the grind mechanism whooshes through the tube into the canister for instant storage. A "blowhole" in the top of the canister, protected by a flour-dust filter (here called an "air polishing filter"), releases the air forced into it.

The Grain Master did a great job milling all kinds of grains in a variety of textures, including hard and soft whole wheat, corn, barley, red beans, millet, rice, and rye. You control the texture of the flour with a knob in the center of the grinder, turning it all the way to the left for finest, all the way to the right for coarsest. If you had this mill, you would find ways to use it often, not only for bread but for polenta and cornmeal muffins, for barley flour to thicken your winter vegetable soups and stews, for chickpea flour to make Indian pancakes, for bean dips from dried red or black beans, perhaps even for the chocolate-zucchini pound cake made with rye and barley flour, if you follow the recipe offered in the Whisper Mill owner's manual. The Grain Master is easy to maintain: it has a self-cleaning milling chamber, and the white hopper and round white body of the mill can be cleaned with just a few swipes of a damp cloth.

The Grain Master Whisper Mill is 11½″ high and 8″ in diameter; it is backed by a lifetime warranty. The accompanying canister, also white, is 7½″ high and 8½″ in diameter.

MEAT GRINDERS

THERE WAS A TIME when every self-respecting kitchen had a meat grinder bolted or clamped to a table. Grandma, depending on her ethnic persuasion, might use it to produce lutefisk, gefilte fish, *pâté de campagne,* chopped liver, or Italian sausage.

Today, many of the tasks performed by the sturdy meat grinder can quickly and conveniently be done with a food processor, a ubiquitous tool in today's kitchens. Although food processors can do a more than adequate job chopping beef into hamburger, nothing beats a meat grinder for making sausage meat of uniform grind and then stuffing it into a casing. In fact, a meat grinder becomes a necessity if sausage-making is your avocation. A well-designed meat grinder has cutting plates with various hole sizes to produce sausage of varying texture and a funnel-shaped horn that allows you to stuff your flavorful mixture into a casing. The result is glistening, pink links of your own manufacture—both an artful and satisfying task.

All meat grinders work the same way, operating with a rotary movement. A large screw called the "worm" moves chunks or strips of meat toward the propeller-shaped knife blade, which cuts the meat to a particle size dictated by the hole in the plate. The larger the hole, the coarser the texture of the meat. Usually two plates suffice—one with a ⅛" to ³⁄₁₆" hole size and another with a ⅜" to ½" hole size.

When evaluating meat grinders, we gave the amateur sausage maker's needs the highest consideration. A recommended model must be easy to set up, i.e., clamp or bolt to a counter. It must do the job of grinding tough meat and hard fat quickly and efficiently, and it must be effective in turning a ground-meat mixture into sausage links. Don't neglect to compare cost versus efficiency. An electric meat grinder will be the quickest in getting the job done. But the top of the line can cost $500 or more, while other, adequate electric grinders that can easily produce small batches of 20 to 50 pounds can be purchased for under $150. Another less expensive option is the meat-grinder attachment for your home mixer, a fine alternative for infrequent sausage-making. But beware of grinders made of plastic, which can crack and split from frequent use or from the stress of grinding tough, hardback fat.

Hand-powered meat grinders are still made. Little has changed in their design or function since they were first introduced in the nineteenth century. Still made of cast iron, they come in many sizes; smaller ones are more convenient to set up since they are anchored to the working surface with a single clamp, while the larger ones have four feet that must be bolted or fixed to the work surface with extra metal clamps (these must be purchased separately from a hardware store). In general, the larger the hand-powered meat grinder, the more meat per minute it can grind, and the more muscle power it needs to turn the crank. We recommend buying the largest size that will meet your needs and that fits your pocketbook and strength. A cutting plate size of 2" to 3" should be adequate for occasional sausage makers, or for making other forcemeats.

5.33 MAVERICK INDUSTRIES DELUXE FOOD GRINDER

With a peppy 220-watt motor, this grinder can get the job done for most home sausage-makers and even the occasional hunter with a cache of venison. The machine itself is light, compact, and cased in sturdy, easy-to-clean plastic. The business end is all metal except for a 6½" by 4" plastic feed tray that holds the meat. It's equipped with a sturdy 6" plastic sausage-stuffing horn. The medium and coarse grinding plates, both 2" in diameter, are sufficient for most types of sausage, and the blades are of heavy-duty tempered carbon steel and should remain sharp. The machine and its parts come packed in a relatively small storage box where individual parts are easily accessible. The electric grinder strained a bit when grinding hardback fat, but it was easy to mount and kept the meat moving efficiently into the stuffer. The rubber feet held it to the work surface, and it took less than two minutes to grind and stuff a pound of meat. It measures 12¾" high and is 8" long and 5¾" wide at the base.

5.34 MAGIC MILL ASSISTANT
MEAT GRINDER ATTACHMENT

This is a well-designed, sturdy, and powerful machine that can tackle large tasks like turning a successful deer hunt into a pile of sausage links. The meat-grinder attachment is heavy-duty and made to last. All parts except the loading tray are made of metal, and the grinding plates and knife are formed of tempered steel. Only one midsize grind-ing plate comes with the attachment, but additional sizes can be added. The machine also comes with a built-in timer and varying speed control, which adds to its versatility.

Heaven sends us good meat,
but the devil sends cooks.

—DAVID GARRICK

GREAT SAUSAGE MEALS

❧ BRUCE AIDELLS ❧

When it comes to the great sausage meals of the world, it's hard to beat a pink hotdog in a steamed bun, slathered with mustard or perhaps a bit of pickle relish, onion, or sauer-kraut. But the world has provided us with a number of other substantial and special dishes centered around the humble sausage. Not surprisingly, they come from countries where sausage eating is a frequent and important part of the cuisine: Germany, France, Poland, and Italy have all made important contributions to the world of sausage.

In Germany you are likely to see street venders serving up perfectly steamed, grilled, or fried wurst, offered naked on a plate next to a mound of coarse or sweet mustard and a small, chewy roll. One of the best of these street-side banquets can be found in Berlin, where the wurst is flavored with curry, fried, and accompanied with spicy ketchup. Just the aroma of these stands is hypnotically alluring and irresistible. At home and in *Gasthäuser*, sausage is more likely to be served as part of a *Schlachtplatte*. This large mound of braised sauerkraut, smoked meats, and several types of boiled sausages originated during the fall pig slaughter (*schlachten* means slaughter), which was traditionally followed by great feasts of pork. For this gargan-tuan dish, one needs nothing more than a few slabs of rye bread, mustard, and a stein of cold beer.

France, too, has created many fine sausage meals. Alsace, influenced by its German heritage, also has a dish of sauer-kraut, smoked pork meats, and sausage, called *choucroute garnie*. Often simmered in champagne or white wine and a bit of juniper, this dish may have a bit more finesse than the German *Schlachtplatte* but still retains its heartiness. Alsatians would serve *choucroute* with boiled potatoes, mustard, rye bread, and some Alsatian Riesling or *Gewürztraminer*. From Gascogne in southwest France comes the great cassoulet, named for the earthenware casserole in which it's cooked. It is traditionally made with confited goose, stewed lamb, fresh pork sausages such as Toulouse sausage, and white beans. First stewed and then baked in the oven, the best versions of cassoulet are topped with a savory crust of bread crumbs. Like so many sausage dishes, cassoulet is a complete meal in itself and needs only a salad and some red wine. *Boudin blanc*, a delicate white sausage of pork, veal, and black truffle, is an important course in most Christmas Eve meals in France. Served as its own course with *pommes de terres purée* (creamy mashed potatoes), it is much more elegant and delicious than the British version, bangers and mash (*mash* in this case refers to mashed, overcooked peas).

Poland loves its kielbasa, which is eaten as is or used to flavor soups and stews. The most important of these stews is *bigos*, which originated as a "hunter's" stew of fresh game, wild forest mushrooms, cabbage, sauerkraut, and assorted sausages. When the hunt was less than successful, the hun-ter's wife would simply increase the proportion of sausage and maybe add a bit of smoked bacon or ham. Served in large, shallow bowls with dollops of sour cream, *bigos* needs only coarse bread and beer to complete the meal.

Italians long ago learned the importance of using small amounts of pork products such as pancetta, sausage, or pro-sciutto to flavor their recipes. It is not surprising that fresh pork sausage finds its way into the sauces for many pastas. Pasta *con salisicce*, in its simplest form, combines fried sau-sage meat that is moistened with a bit of pasta water and tomato. In more elaborate forms, porcini mushrooms and a bit of cream may be added. But the key to the sauce is relying on the sausage to season and flavor the broth. In cities that have Italian street festivals, sausages are frequently served up with fried onions and peppers and stuffed into Italian rolls. This ultimate shirt stainer is the perfect portable street meal.

5.35 KENWOOD MEAT GRINDER ATTACHMENT

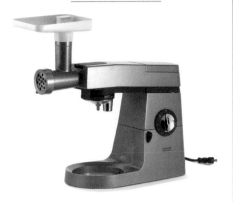

The Kenwood mixer has a powerful motor that makes grinding through tough hardback fat a breeze. The meat-grinder attachment works well and, except for the plastic meat-loading pan, is made of all metal parts. It has two different grinding plates and a sharp knife, all made of tempered steel. A sausage-stuffing horn is included.

5.36 VILLAWARE PORKERT NO. 10 MEAT GRINDER

The design and technology of these heavyweights have hardly changed in a hundred years. Why mess with success? Grinders like these get the job done whether you're grinding raw meat for sausage or cooked meat for hash. They are made of heavy cast iron and are double tin plated to pro-tect against rust and corrosion. Nevertheless, they should be washed and hand-dried immediately after use. The grinding knife and metal plates are made of tempered carbon steel and will rust if not washed and dried immediately.

Made in the Czech Republic, these meat grinders come in five different sizes, with the three smallest ideal for home use, since they come with built-in clamps that allow the grinder to be attached directly to a work surface. The clamps are cush-ioned with rubber pads to stay in place. (Some other brands rocked off the table during the grinding pro-cess.) Since the largest clamped model (no. 10) is not much more expensive than the smallest model, we recommend this one, which will allow you to tackle larger jobs. For the serious sausage-maker, there are two larger-capacity grinders that bolt to the table (no. 22 and no. 32). These require significant muscle power but are sold with a pulley appa-ratus that can be attached to an elec-tric motor (you provide the motor).

Each meat grinder comes equipped with a medium and a coarse cutting plate, as well as a sharp four-winged knife and a somewhat flimsy, easily shattered sausage-stuffing horn. Additional plates of various hole sizes can be purchased

SAUSAGE STUFFERS

Those who are sincere in their sausage-making endeavors will need a sausage stuffer, which is a piston and gear-and-crank system to force the meat out of the cylinder through a nozzle or horn that holds the waiting casing. The best models are easy to clean and made of noncorrosive metal. They usually consist of a removable stainless steel cylinder and a tough plastic piston. The piston must be snug, but not so snug that it traps air and allows air bubbles to form as the meat fills the casing. Good sausage stuffers are not inexpensive but will last a long time and take the hassle out of an arduous task.

5.37 THE SAUSAGE MAKER SAUSAGE STUFFER

This 5-pound sausage stuffer meets all of our selective criteria. The sturdy frame is made of electroplated cold rolled steel. The base and remov-able cylinder are made of stainless steel, and the piston and stuffing tube of strong plastic. The stuffer is quite tall, 16″ (22″ with the handle), and fairly wide at 6″; it is equipped with three plastic stuffing tubes. To use the machine, fill the cylinder with up to 5 pounds of the ground meat and spice mixture, slip a cas-ing over the stuffing tube, and hold it tightly with one hand while you turn the crank with the other. When the casing is filled, twist it around to finish off the completed sausage and release a few more inches for the next kielbasa.

POUNDERS

A FAMOUS MICHELIN THREE-STAR chef stood in the Boucherie Nivernaise, the most respected butcher shop in Paris. He swung his arms in circles, rolled his head from side to side, and jumped up and down shouting, "Tough and tender!" He was making a point to his apprentice: the more a muscle moves, the tougher it is; the less it is used, the greater its tenderness. If you know what part of an animal the meat comes from and how that animal moves, you can predict the meat's balance between tough and tender. In general, muscles that move often (legs, shoulders, neck) have a tougher, more sinewy texture. Muscles that spend most of the time resting (ribs and especially loin) are far more tender.

In certain recipes, however, the flavor and texture of the meat can be enhanced by pounding and tenderizing. *Escalopes* in France, scallopini in Italy, schnitzel in Austria and Germany, and boneless, skinless chicken breasts in the United States all call for pounding. The result is meat (veal, beef, pork, lamb, or chicken) that has been brought to uniform thinness and will cook faster and more evenly. Pounding also tenderizes the meat by breaking up the long muscle fibers, eliminating the grain without pulverizing the meat. While important for some tougher cuts, this is not as essential for chicken breast, turkey breast, veal, and pork scallopini. On the other hand, today's fish carpaccios are often prepared by pounding pieces of salmon, tuna, or bass to near translucency.

After pounding, a typical chicken breast measures about 7" by 9". You can easily turn it into a thin casing waiting to be wrapped around a savory filling: a little prosciutto and cheese, some leaves of sage, fresh goat cheese, or sun-dried tomato and basil. A slice of boneless turkey breast, often sold labeled as *"escalopes"* or "scallopini," also works well after pounding. These small packets have numerous names: *paupiettes* in French, *involtini* and *rollatini* in Italian, and *Rouladen* in German. Pork today is considerably leaner than it once was and has grown to replace veal in many classic

VEAL SCALOPPINE WITH TOMATO, OREGANO, & CAPERS

4 servings

2½ tablespoons vegetable oil

3 garlic cloves, peeled

1 pound veal scaloppine, cut from the top round, and flattened

flour, spread on a plate

salt

black pepper, ground fresh from the mill

⅓ cup dry white wine

½ cup canned imported Italian plum tomatoes, chopped, with their juice

1 tablespoon butter

1 teaspoon fresh oregano, or ½ teaspoon dried

2 tablespoons capers, soaked and rinsed if packed in salt, drained if in vinegar

1 Put the oil and garlic in a skillet, turn on the heat to medium, and cook the garlic until it becomes colored a light nut brown. Remove it from the pan and discard it.

2 Turn up the heat to medium high, dredge the scaloppine in flour, shake off excess flour, and slip the meat into the pan. Brown them quickly on both sides, about half a minute per side if the oil is hot enough. (If the scaloppine don't all fit into the pan at one time without overlapping, do them in batches, but dredge each batch in flour just before slipping the meat into the pan; otherwise the flour will become soggy and make it impossible to achieve a crisp surface.) When done, transfer the meat to a warm plate, using a slotted spoon or spatula, and sprinkle with salt and pepper.

3 Over medium-high heat, add the wine, and while the wine simmers use a wooden spoon to loosen all the cooking residues on the bottom and sides. Add the chopped tomatoes with their juice, stir to coat well, add the butter and any juices the scaloppine may have shed on the plate, stir, and adjust heat to cook at a steady but gentle simmer.

4 In 15 or 20 minutes, when the fat floats free of the tomatoes, add the oregano and capers, stir thoroughly, then return the scaloppine to the pan and turn them in the tomato sauce for about a minute until they are warm again. Turn out the entire contents of the pan onto a warm platter and serve at once.

Essentials of Classic Italian Cooking, by Marcella Hazan

pounded dishes. Slices of pork leg or loin can be pounded for schnitzel or scallopini. Larger slices of pork can be pounded and used to make the aforementioned flavor-filled packages. Pounding can also be used to turn two of the least appealing cuts of beef—the eye of the round and bottom round—into wrappers for such specialties as braciola, *Rouladen,* and *ballotine.* More-over, they are composed of single muscles that make them ideal for pounding and stuffing.

Meat pounders must be heavy—no less than 24 ounces—and must have a comfortable grip, in addition to a head that is at least 3½" in diameter. The surface of the pounder should be smooth and beveled or tapered, without the slightest sharp edge that might damage or tear the meat. Some designs require a slapping arm motion, while others have you punching down on the meat like a border guard with a passport stamp. The punch-down models protect your hands. If you choose the slapping arm design you may prefer an offset handle angled up just behind the head, elevating it above the striking surface and keeping your fingers safely clear of the board.

5.38 MOULI LARGE FLAT POUNDER

Weighing in at 2¼ pounds and with a head surface of 4¾" by 4½", this French heavyweight will get the job done. One side of the pounder is beveled, to make spreading out the meat easier, while the other is flat to finish the job to a uniform thickness. The Mouli pounder easily spread and flattened chicken breasts and pork loin without a tear. Since the handle is at the same angle as the head, you must hold it off the edge of the work surface to avoid crushing your knuckles, but the pounder's 7¾" length makes this a simple adjustment. A hole on the handle makes it easy to store. Made of stainless steel and virtually indestructible, this tool should last you a lifetime.

5.39 MOULI LARGE VERTICAL POUNDER

Of the pounders we tested, weight mattered most with the vertical pounders. With a heavy pounder, the weight of the pounder does the work, while a light one requires an extra stamping motion from the user, which makes control more difficult and the meat more prone to tearing. An advantage to this heavy-duty, one-piece stainless model from Mouli is the long 4¾" handle. Despite its weight (more than 4 pounds), we found this pounder well balanced and very comfortable to use; it accomplished the pounding task efficiently and without tearing. The surface diameter of the pounder is 4".

5.40 NORPRO ROUND POUNDER

Easy to use, with good balance, this 3¾"-diameter stainless steel pounder's reduced surface area and relatively moderate heft of 1⅝ pounds require a little more energy and skill to use. But the offset-angled 7¾" handle provides good leverage, making it safe and comfortable.

USING A POUNDER
❧ MARCELLA HAZAN ❧

Once cut, scallopini must be pounded flat and thin so they will cook quickly and evenly. *Pounding* is an unfortunate word because it makes one think of pummeling or thumping, which is exactly what you must *not* do. If all you do is bring the pounder down hard on the scallopini, you'll just be mashing the meat between the pounder and the cutting board, breaking it up or punching holes in it. What you want to do is to stretch out the meat, thus thinning and evening it. Bring the pounder down on the slice so that it meets it with a flat surface, not with an edge; as it comes down on the meat, slide it in one continuous motion from the center outward. Repeat the operation, stretching the slice in all directions until it is evenly thin throughout.

TENDERIZERS

Professional butchers are never concerned with biting off more than they can chew. Why? They have a machine with waffled rollers that will take a boneless piece of meat and literally masticate it for them. The process breaks up the long fibers and connective tissue of the muscle, making the meat a bit more tender. There are handheld versions of this tool that replace the rolling action with pounding to achieve a similar result. This kind of tenderizing has its downside—honeycombing the meat to tenderize it can dry it out by draining its juices. The best way to tenderize tough meat is to use a slow, moist cooking method like braising, stewing, or pot roasting.

5.41 NORPRO MEAT HAMMER

This dual-purpose hammer from Norpro has both a smooth and a waffled surface; the smooth surface is your pounder, and the side with the waffled texture is a tenderizer. Its weight, 16 ounces, is less than that of most solo pounders but is adequate for a dual-purpose tool. The surface area, about 3″ square, is sufficient to pound and tenderize even large cuts of meat. Made of cast aluminum, the hammer is sturdy, well balanced, and relatively comfortable to use, but we would have preferred a little more weight for more efficient results. It measures 10″ in length.

TENDER BUT TOUGH

Pineapples, papaya, figs, and kiwi contain enzymes that break down muscle and connective proteins in meat and are promoted as natural tenderizers. However, they do not penetrate beyond the surface of the meat, which leaves you with meat that is mushy on the outside and tough on the inside.

CITRUS JUICERS

THE ENGLISH DIARIST Samuel Pepys (1633–1703) made the following entry in his journal: "Here, which I never did before, I drank a pint of the juice of oranges, of whose peel they make comfits; and here they drink the juice as wine, with sugar, which is a very fine drink, it being new, I was doubtful whether it might not do me hurt." Pepys's cautious note is a reminder of how long it has taken for northern Europeans and Americans to accept citrus juice. Orange and grapefruit juices, now ubiquitous as breakfast beverages, have been popular for an extremely short time. They became part of our daily diet in the last half of the twentieth century, only after the development of methods for shipping fresh citrus fruits from southern growing regions.

As is often the case, the acceptance of this new food was followed by the introduction of new equipment for its processing. The tools needed to separate citrus juice from citrus meat and rind can be generally divided into the categories of reamers, leverage presses, and motorized juicers. We show examples of each, as well as a couple of innovative gadgets for the citrus fruits that star in so many recipes: the lemon and the lime.

The reamer has an utterly functional design—a wide cone with ridges that crush the inner flesh of the fruit, releasing its juice. Reamers may be handheld or set into a dish. With no motor to drive the juicing along, you must press down and rotate a citrus half on these implements, so select one with sharp ridges that will make the most of your efforts. Leverage press–style juicers make use of smoother cones to force juice from the citrus flesh, using the weight of metal against metal rather than the friction of a twisting motion. An electric citrus juicer is a reamer set on top of a motor. You press half of a citrus fruit onto the turning reamer, and the juice is released and then separated from most of the pulp by a strainer that surrounds the reamer. Look for a model with either interchangeable reamer cones or one reamer whose tapered shape and size will accommodate the vastly different circumferences of limes, oranges, and grapefruits. You'll also want to make sure it's easy to clean.

You may wish to have a couple different styles of citrus juicers for various purposes. Electric models are more efficient, but unnecessary for obtaining the juice from a single piece of fruit; save these for when you wish to bring a carafe of fresh juice to the breakfast table. For smaller amounts, reach for one of the handheld models, which are often quite powerful and can be quickly rinsed. They possess another advantage in that they offer more control, helping you to avoid juicing the bitter peel.

5.42 BLACK & DECKER CITRUSMATE PLUS

There are those of us who can't quite wake up in the morning without a refreshing glass of freshly squeezed orange or grapefruit juice. If you're one, this compact and user-friendly juicer from Black & Decker is a must-have. A plastic reamer plate and pouring pitcher lock on to the small motorized base, which takes up a mere 6″ on your counter. When you apply gentle pressure with a halved fruit on the reamer, the motor is activated and the reamer begins to spin, alternating direction each time you release and push down again. The motion is effective and gentle. The reamer is perfect for lemons and limes; a separate, larger cone fits over it for juicing oranges and grapefruits. A three-way pulp control switch at the top of the handle creates larger or smaller holes beneath the strainer slots in the reamer plate, resulting in real differences in the texture of the juice. You can squeeze up to four 8-ounce servings at a time. After use, a clear plastic cover keeps the juicer dust-free.

5.43 METROKANE MIGHTY OJ

A downsized version of the tall juice squeezers used in juice bars, this is well proportioned for home use, taking up about 6 square inches of your countertop and requiring little extra headroom. You bring the handle forward and down to lower the steel cap over the orange half sitting on the stainless steel reamer; juice then flows from the bottom of the reamer section into the glass below. This method takes some muscle, but the all-metal construction provides excellent leverage and makes for a satisfying squeeze. Small rubber feet keep the juicer from slipping as you work. You'll need to use a glass that is short enough to fit under the 4″ high-reamer section and slim enough to fit inside the horseshoe base.

5.44 BEST MANUFACTURERS MEXICAN LIME PRESS

Fragrant limes are used constantly in Mexican cuisine, in everything from the tangy base of *sopa de lima* to the vinaigrette for a cactus and jicama salad. So who better to design the definitive lime press? Made in Mexico out of cast aluminum, this handheld leverage 8″-long juicer from Best Manufacturers is lightweight, but its design applies tremendous force to the inside of the fruit. Unlike most juice presses, this tool requires you to place the fruit in cut side down. The metal bowl of the top half does not push into the lime flesh but actually goes against the rind, turning the lime half inside out and pressing both the juice and aromatic oils through the strainer holes in the bottom bowl.

5.45 KOTOBUKI CERAMIC LEMON JUICER

Pragmatists may skip this review; this juicer is for the romantics among us. While the reamer is effective, its 4¼″ diameter bowl is too small to accommodate the juice of even a few lemons. You must either seed your lemon before squeezing it or be obliged to pick out the pits from around the reamer—or pour the juice through a strainer. But this small juicer was sculpted in Japan, coated in a delicate green crackle glaze, and is beautiful and smooth, with sensual contours. It is a little work of art to use when you have the time to cook slowly and enjoy every step.

5.46 WESTMARK LIMONA CITRUS PRESS

Until now, we have been concerned with equipment that renders only the juices from citrus fruits—tools that barely release the fragrant oils in the fruit skins to blend with the clear taste of the juice. However, in certain dishes—Italian *piccata* of veal, Greek *avgolemono*—the oils, in moderation, enhance and intensify the flavor. Here's the tool for the task: a sturdy, cast-aluminum 9½" long handheld press with a yellow plastic reamer and interior cup. Fruit is pressed skin side down as the hinged top and bottom are clamped together; as the reamer pushes into the citrus flesh, juice runs down over the skin into the bottom cup, picking up the oily essences along the way. Pour from the side spout with the press still closed. This is an excellent press for lemons and limes.

5.47 KÜCHENPROFI METAL CITRUS JUICER

Made entirely of nonreactive, heavy-gauge stainless steel, this two-piece

juicer is nicely fitted—the rim of the reamer plate nests onto the bowl with a satisfying click. As you bear down with your half-fruit and twist, the metal cone reams into the fruit. Three rows of round holes circling the reamer effectively hold back the pulp and seeds, allowing only pure, clear juice to flow through. The flat handles on the bowl are easy to grasp. However, the spouts on each side are so small that it's best to remove the upper piece before pouring the juice. When you do, you'll see that the bowl is actually quite handsome and might serve you well on its own as a modern sauceboat. This juicer comes in two widths: 3½" or 5".

5.48 OXO LEMON JUICER

A modern interpretation of a classic, here is a reamer to help you press the flesh. This is a design made with hand comfort in mind, as are all of this company's products. Made of metal, it feels substantial and is beautifully weighted. The soft rubber-padded handle helps you keep your grip, even when it's wet. And the weight of the solid aluminum reamer exerts force so that you don't have to. It is 6½" long.

5.49 SCI WOODEN REAMER

When you need to juice only one lemon or orange, the easiest thing to use is a handheld reamer. Twist it into a half-fruit, and the juice will flow

freely. A traditional wooden reamer is the plainest, least expensive, and lightest option. This 6" one, made of the hard, nonporous wood from the rubber tree, won't absorb juice or develop odors. The ridges are sharp enough to expel juice from the flesh of even the firmest lime, and the pointed, unridged tip is good for removing seeds before you start juicing.

5.50 OXO PLEATED CITRUS REAMER

This 5½" "pleated reamer" departs from the classic model in both shape and material, but it does a fantastic job. Rather than simply pressing a widening hole into your halved fruit, the rippled stainless steel blade rips through the citrus fibers as you twist it, making the fruit softer and much easier for your other hand to squeeze. The juice absolutely gushes forth when you use this tool. Another good idea from OXO.

5.51 FRIELING CITRUS TRUMPET

No matter what array of food processors, mixers, blenders, and other sophisticated utensils you have in your kitchen, you need one of these. This terrific 3" tool provides a few drops of citrus juice to finish a *blanquette de veau* or freshen up your ratatouille. As you insert the sharp bottom end of the stainless steel tube into the end of a lemon (or lime or orange), the metal edge pierces through the rind easily and the tube slides down the center of the fruit, much like a corer. When this small trumpet is fully inside the fruit, gently squeeze the sides of the fruit until juice drains into the metal well. Then, rather than wasting a barely used lemon, store it, trumpet and all, in the refrigerator until you need a drop or two more. Tip: Rolling the lemon or lime back and forth on a hard surface will break up some of the internal fibers and give you more juice.

JUICE EXTRACTORS

UNTIL THE EARLY 1990s, most juice extractors were found in health-food stores. Then one day television infomercials started to appear, telling us that freshly made fruit and vegetable juices preserve health, youth, and vitality (and all for only 3,335 convenient payments of 9¢ each!). Well, someone seems to have believed the hype: at the peak of the promotions, in 1992, more than 3 million extractors were sold.

Juice extractors consist of a motor attached to a cutting disc that grates (noncitrus) fruits and vegetables into juice and pulp and then separates the liquids from the solids using centrifugal force. Though an extractor is not a piece of kitchen equipment that most people use often, it creates fresh juices that have a taste and texture that is delightful and quite different from any processed juice. Combining several kinds of juice—say, carrot, apple, beet, and gingerroot—will give you a truly refreshing elixir, even if you don't believe the health claims. Even haute cuisine has joined the juice craze, following the lead of the French-born chef Jean-Georges Vongerichten, who turned away from traditional meat stocks and glazes and in their place created new taste sensations using the juice of everything from pineapples to radishes.

5.52 CHAMPION JUICER

The Champion Juicer is a slow-speed masticating machine, which means that it chews up the cell walls of fruits and vegetables, producing juices or homogenized purées with large amounts of fiber, vitamins, and trace elements. Made from nylon and stainless steel parts, it is driven by a ⅓ hp, heavy-duty motor that separates juice from pulp in a continuous operation. No intermittent cleaning is required. Fruits and vegetables are sent down the feed tube, juice drains out of the screen holder beneath the cutting shaft, and pulp slides out the tapered end. When the screen is removed and the floating cutter or disc that separates the juice from the pulp is inserted, the juicer is ready to homogenize fruits and vegetables. Our original Champion Juicer came into *The Cooks' Catalogue* test kitchen twenty years ago and has been producing fruit and vegetable juices ever since. Our favorite use of the Champion, however, is to press frozen pieces of banana or melon down the feed tube to make instant all-fruit ice. The Champion comes with a recipe book that explains how to produce juices, fruit and vegetable sauces, sorbets, ice creams, sherbets, nut butters, and baby foods. The manufacturer also offers a grain-mill attachment that handles everything from wheat and rye to corn and coffee. You'll need to devote some countertop space to this 26-pound juicer; it is 18″ in length and 13½″ tall.

THE CHAMPION JUICER
✤ JEAN-GEORGES VONGERICHTEN ✤

I use the Champion juicer all the time—maybe not as often as when I first discovered it, more than ten years ago—but I still think it's the best for wringing the juice out of fennel, ginseng, or any other fruit or vegetable. The juices I make become the vegetable and fruit essences for many of my dishes. And the Champion is the best because you can add back as much or as little of the pulp as you need to thicken the juice. But even if I stopped using the juices in my restaurant kitchens, I would still use the Champion to make the carrot juice I drink every morning.

5.53 OMEGA 4000 JUICE EXTRACTOR

This is a powerful machine, one that will take a load of hard carrots, beets, and apples and issue forth juice without complaint. Everything is sized for large-scale home use: the rectangular feed tube can accommodate generous chunks of produce, and the plastic pulp receptacle is, at about 8 cubic inches, almost as large as the motor unit itself, so you can juice continuously for a while before stopping to discard the pulp. Unlike other extractors of its scale and strength, this one won't vibrate or become unbalanced.

The juice spout is nicely shielded on each side to prevent the colorful liquid from spattering as it falls into your cup; this is important as not only juice but air is forced out of the machine by the centrifugal force. Both the motor unit and the pulp catcher have rubber nonskid feet. You will need your own container to catch the juice. The Omega is roughly 12" tall and 8" in diameter.

5.54 KRUPS OPTIFRUIT

This sleek, shapely 12" by 11" extractor is both attractive and effective. Two lavender-tinted plastic pitchers stack vertically and click into place on top of the motor. As you push produce through the kidney-shaped feed tube, pulp is ejected into the upper pitcher and juice flows into the lower one, which is marked with liter

---

WHAT TO LOOK FOR

In general, it takes about 3 pounds of fresh produce to yield 1 quart of liquid—an expensive way to get juice. As a result, it's important that an extractor have a high yield; you want the machine to give you the most juice possible from each fruit or vegetable. The power of the motor will be an indication of this, so avoid the very low-priced models that house smaller, weaker engines—compare the horsepower and revolutions per minute (RPMs).

A machine with a large feed tube (rectangular or semicircular shapes are generally best) requires less chopping of produce prior to extraction. If the machine does not come with its own container for catching juice, make sure the spout height will accommodate your average glass or cup. And, if you are sensitive to noise, make sure that the baseline sound of the motor (that is, when you're not pushing food through) is not too loud.

Ease of assembly and disassembly is also important. If your extractor takes too long to set up, use, clean, and put away, all your New Year's New Age resolutions about daily juicing for health will get you nowhere fast. And remember, the more parts you have to put together, the more parts you have to wash. Which leads us to the number one reason given for why more people don't use juice extractors regularly: they're a nuisance to clean. It's true; they are. Some, however, are worse than others. Models with internal metal pulp-straining baskets require the most arduous scrubbing. Centrifugal force whips the sticky pulp against the perforated sides of the basket, meaning it must be pried loose. The manufacturers of these models provide filter strips to line the strainer basket for easier cleanup, but these compromise your juice output. For this reason, we recommend the pulp-ejection-style juicers that shoot the pulp out into a smooth plastic receptacle that can be easily and quickly rinsed. Whichever type of juicer you buy, the key is to wash it immediately after use, before you've taken a sip of your fresh beverage—or, at the very least, submerge all the parts in warm water so that the fibrous residue won't harden on the appliance like cement, and a splash of beet or carrot won't give the housing a permanent tie-dyed look.

and ounce measurements and holds a generous 34 ounces of liquid. You'll find that this machine processes the hardest of vegetables smoothly and easily. You may stop the motor and remove the juice pitcher independently, to pour off servings as you work; the unit has a sensor that automatically stops the flow of juice until you replace the pitcher in its housing. The plastic dust cover turns over to become a tray for funneling small berries into the feed tube.

5.55 BACK TO BASICS WHEAT-GRASS JUICER

This looks like an old-fashioned meat grinder, but it's designed to extract wheat-grass juice in your home. Don't be intimidated by the number of parts, or by the fact that this juicer comes with its own tightening wrench. Once you have familiarized yourself with the assembly sequence, it's actually quite simple and quick. With the juicer clamped securely to a counter or tabletop, you feed handfuls of grass into the hopper at the top, cranking the handle with your other hand. Grass is pulled into the spiraling screw-press gears and noiselessly crushed. The deep emerald juice flows out of the round spout beneath the stainless steel body while the grass pulp emerges in rope form from the small end. You need two low containers to catch

CHICKEN & HERB SALAD WITH RED PEPPER OIL

4 servings

An ideal summer lunch or supper dish served throughout the season at JoJo—just filling enough, but light, refreshing, and full of flavor.

1 teaspoon thyme leaves
1 cup mixed coarsely chopped chervil, basil, dill, and parsley
1 tablespoon minced chives
1 tarragon leaf, minced
4 cups mixed salad greens
juice of 2 lemons
3 red bell peppers
5 tablespoons extra-virgin olive oil
salt and freshly ground black pepper
4 boneless, skinless chicken cutlets (about 1 pound)

1 Preheat the oven to 450°F. Mix the herbs together. Place the mixed salad greens on a platter.
2 Marinate about ¾ cup of the herb mixture in the lemon juice while you prepare the peppers and chicken.
3 If you have a juicer, juice the peppers. If not, seed and stem them, then purée them in a food processor, scraping down the mixture occasionally. Squeeze the purée in a cheesecloth to extract all the juice. Cook the juice in a small saucepan over medium-high heat until it is syrupy and reduced to about 2 tablespoons, about 15 minutes. Stir in 3 tablespoons of the olive oil, along with salt and pepper to taste. The mixture will be sweet, with a tiny bit of heat in the finish,
4 Drain the herbs, reserving the lemon juice. Heat the remaining 2 tablespoons olive oil in an ovenproof skillet over medium-high heat, then cook the chicken for 3 minutes on one side; it will barely begin to brown. Turn the chicken over, top with the drained herb mixture, and transfer it to the oven for 5 more minutes, or until it is cooked through.
5 When the chicken is done, drizzle it with the reserved lemon juice. Top the mixed greens with the chicken and its pan juices, then sprinkle all with the remaining herbs. Drizzle the red pepper juice around the edges of the platter and serve.

Jean-Georges: Cooking at Home with a Four-star Chef, by Jean-Georges Vongerichten and Mark Bittman

these respective products. This juicer stands almost 9" tall.

5.56 BRAUN JUICE EXTRACTOR

Here is a well-performing, midsized extractor that liquefies fruits and vegetables with ease and sports some innovative and thoughtful features. The pulp is ejected into a good-sized plastic container on the left side, while juice flows into a cup beneath the spout on the right. Fitted inside the pulp receptacle is an optional second plastic container that acts as a pulp strainer, allowing you to maximize the juice output from foods high in liquid content, like grapes or tomatoes. The juice cup holds 17 ounces and has a built-in foam separator so you pour off only clear juice. The top inverts to become a fruit funnel-tray. There are many parts to wash in this model, but they all rinse off easily. The juice cup, pulp strainer, and pulp container all nest for compact storage. The extractor is nearly 11" tall and 9" wide.

6

COLANDERS, STRAINERS, & SEPARATORS

Colanders and strainers, at the most basic level, are separators that allow you to run water over food or separate one ingredient from another. The colander is a metal or plastic bowl perforated by holes, while a strainer is a bit of air surrounded by thin metal wires. Between them, there are dozens of variations, but all colanders and strainers are similar in that each is a variation on the idea of the net.

COLANDERS

The single most useful tool for washing and draining food is the colander. You should buy the largest one that your sink will hold because you can always drain a few boiled potatoes or gently rinse a few strawberries in a big colander, but you will never be able to rinse three heads of lettuce or drain a couple of pounds of pasta in a tiny one. In short, this is a case where bigger is definitely better. Be sure that you get a colander that sits firmly on its base: some of them, to paraphrase Carl Sandburg, arrive "on little feet": poetic but unstable. Empty a pound of boiled pasta into one of these wobbly tubs and the whole mass can easily tip out and disappear in slippery strands down the drain. A circular metal rim surrounding the base will give you a more secure footing than feet. Handles on the bowl-shaped colander must be comfortable to grip, securely attached, and made of a material that will not heat up even as you pour boiling water through the bowl. The space between handle and colander must be large enough to accommodate your hand while you are wearing cooking mitts.

Some colanders have a long handle on one side and a hook on the other. Both the handle and the hook are used to secure this type of colander to the rim of a pot, allowing the cook to use it as a dipper and then set it over the pot as food drains. Many of these types of colanders are marketed to use for draining pasta, but we prefer emptying all the pasta from the boiling water at once into a sturdy, bowl-shaped colander sitting in the sink; with this technique you ensure that all the pasta has cooked for the same amount of time.

Scoop colanders are useful for retrieving smaller amounts of food from boiling liquid. The most effective models are shaped like miniature lacrosse sticks—their streamlined design sweeps through the water and along the bottom of the pot. Scoops with a hook to rest on the pot for draining are helpful.

The ideal material for a colander does not stain, pit, rust, interact with ingredients, or lose its shape. It is odor resistant, dishwasher safe, and sturdy. Therefore, we recommend that you buy stainless steel. Mesh colanders offer a good, lightweight alternative for washing produce but are best not used for pasta because the wire strands can cause cooked pasta to break. We don't recommend: ceramics, which break; plastics, which bend; wood, which absorbs and stains; or enameled steel, which chips. Copper colanders are decorative but high maintenance and will react with, and gradually release toxic minerals into, hot foods; unless they are lined with stainless steel, they should not be used for cooking. A colander that fits into a big pot with its handles resting on the rim can double as a steamer.

6.1 DANESCO COLANDER

Our first choice, if you have the room for it. This large, stainless steel colander is basic equipment for any family kitchen that cooks for a crowd. It's also good for washing lettuce, draining fruit for canning, or managing a hot, slippery mass of freshly boiled spaghetti. This is a solidly constructed piece of equipment, almost 12" in diameter and standing 7½" high. It holds 8 quarts of food. Its electrostatically welded handles are hollow for lightness, curved for shapely looks, and provide a comfortable grip. Best of all, the base is a heavy-gauge ring that will never allow the colander to tip over. A snow-flake pattern of round holes allows water to drain quickly. If you don't have enough storage space for this helpful giant, consider the 5-quart size (10⅝" diameter) or the 3-quart size (8⅝" diameter). Or, put this out on a counter and fill it with fruit.

> The primary requisite
> for writing well about food
> is a good appetite.
>
> —A. J. LIEBLING

6.2 ALL-CLAD COLANDER

When does an ordinary piece of equipment like a colander become a luxury? When it is made by one of the finer cookware manufacturers in this country and demonstrates attention to design in the smallest details. While this is by far the most expensive colander we are showing you, it is also of the finest quality. Made from a particularly thick gauge of stainless steel, it's exceptionally strong. Its perfectly proportioned 5-quart urn shape and pedestal base proclaim stability. Rows of graduated round drainage holes are larger near the rim and smaller near the base, ensuring that water splashes out quickly through the sides but food does not get caught in the holes at the bottom of the bowl—an important safety feature that minimizes the possibility of boiling water splashing out of the colander if the contents of a pot are poured out too quickly. The solid stainless steel handles are expertly shaped, with a slight curve to follow the contours of the thumb. All in all, this is the finest of its kind and, like all well-made luxuries, should be satisfying every time you use it. It also comes in a 3-quart size.

6.3 RÖSLE COLANDER

Two design features set this colander apart: sunbursts of large round holes and flat, wing-style handles; combined, they give you an effective pasta refresher-steamer insert that will rest neatly in many stock pots. Of course, it will serve you well in the sink, too, holding mussels for scrubbing and keeping steady on its pedestal base as you pour in hot new potatoes. The mirror finish of the stainless steel inside and out makes this colander gleam, and the hanging hole in the rim makes it easy to store.

6.4 METRO MINI COLANDER

In addition to having the largest colander your kitchen—and sink—can accommodate, you may also want to have the smallest. This 1-quart size is nice for tiny jobs—rinsing two servings of blueberries or some fresh snowpeas that you want to keep separate from the rest of the

FANNIE ABZUG'S CHEESECAKE

6 to 8 servings

FOR THE CRUST
1 cup graham cracker crumbs
⅓ cup butter, softened to
   room temperature
¼ cup sugar

FOR THE FILLING
1½ pounds pot cheese
¼ pound cream cheese
6 eggs (separated)
1 teaspoon vanilla
2 tablespoons cornstarch
½ cup butter, softened to
   room temperature
½ pint sour cream
1 cup sugar

1 Preheat oven to 300°F. Combine crust ingredients, and press into the bottom of a greased springform pan.
2 Strain the cheese twice through a colander set over a large bowl; use the bottom of a glass to press it through.
3 Add egg yolks, vanilla, cornstarch, butter, sour cream, and sugar. Beat egg whites until stiff, and fold into the above ingredients. Pour over the graham cracker crust, and bake for 1 hour. Let cool in oven with door closed. *Don't look. Enjoy!*

The Second Avenue Deli Cookbook, by Sharon Lebewohl and Rena Bulkin

---

vegetables you are cooking, for example. Though small, it does not skimp on sensible features: the solid construction, welded handles, and steady ring base that distinguish the better large colanders are found here as well. Alternating rows of round and leaf-shaped holes create an attractive pattern for effective drainage. The hollow stainless steel handles are generous, rather than reduced in proportion to the small bowl. This colander is 7" across and measures a mere 3¾" high so it will easily tuck away for storage inside a larger one.

6.5 NORPRO OVER-THE-SINK COLANDER

We told you that colanders are generally bowl shaped. But this innovative item is an exception, allowing you to work above your sink as well as down in it; you can wash spinach in the sink and drain it there, too. You suspend the oblong mesh basket by pulling out the easily expanding handles until they rest over two opposite edges of the sink. (The handles extend to fit any sink length or width from 14" to 22".) Rubber feet underneath the handles help protect the edge of the sink from scratches and the colander from slipping. It doesn't have the quality construction we would like, but we thought you should see it anyway.

6.6 DANESCO LONG-HANDLED COLANDER

This long-handled colander is an alternative to a standing colander; you dip it in the pot and then lift the food out of the water. Like the standing models, this colander has a sturdy stainless steel bowl perforated with enough round holes for good drainage. It features a long, two-rod stainless steel handle and a curved resting loop that balances the bowl on your pot. Fill the colander with a few ripe tomatoes for quick peeling and submerge the bowl in the hot water. After a few seconds you can simply raise the bowl up out of the water, pause to let the water drain, and you have tomatoes ready to peel. You can then do a second batch without pouring out any of the boiling water or trying to balance the tomatoes on a slotted spoon. You will need to use a mitt because the handle can heat up.

6.7 VOLLRATH SPAGHETTI COLANDER

What a useful implement this is! Designated a spaghetti colander, it is really much more: part colander, serving you well when you want to drain vegetables over the sink, and part strainer—there is a hook on one side that fits onto the rim of a pot or bowl, so you can save the drained liquids. You'll find this handy when you want to reserve pasta cooking water for sauce or when you have to separate the solids and liquids from a homemade stock. It is made of durable stainless steel, and the handle is attached securely, so you can rely on this strainer even for straining beef stock, with its heavy bones. The bowl is fairly large, with a 4"

depth and 8½" diameter, so you'll be able to use it when you're making more than a pound of pasta or a large bunch of broccoli, and its small holes on the bottom and sides ensure that it drains quickly. We found it to be terrific for making steamed clams or mussels in summer. The stainless steel will not discolor or react with any ingredient, which means this strainer will look fresh and clean for years.

6.8 CALPHALON 6-QUART ALL-PURPOSE INSERT

This deep, heavy-duty stainless steel basket is practical and well designed. Use it to cook pasta, lobsters, or corn on the cob inside a soup or stockpot, then simply lift the basket out of the pot and let the water drain out—it's easier and safer than pouring items and their hot cooking liquids into a separate colander. This basket is especially helpful when you are making stock with heavy bones and vegetables. The handles are sturdy and riveted securely and there is ample room to grip even if you're wearing cooking mitts. The bottom of the basket is indented to form five small legs that keep the insert stable within the cooking vessel and steady in the sink. The colander comes in three sizes: the one we show you here fits all of Calphalon's 6½ quart pots. The second size fits all of the 8-quart pots, and the third and largest fits the 12-quart stockpot.

6.9 SITLAX SCOOP COLANDER

There's a reason that the game of lacrosse is played with long-handled baskets; the players—originally Native Americans—discovered that this shape could best catch and retain the ball while advancing and swiveling through the air. You can use a similarly shaped piece of equipment to advantage at the stovetop, swerving not through air but through boiling water to catch and lift anything from a handful of delicate ravioli to a bunch of blanched broccoli flowerets. This scoop colander feels light and well balanced in the hand even when full. The perforated stainless steel "basket" is 6¾" across at its widest and 9½" long—small enough to maneuver, yet large enough to retrieve most of what's in the pot in one swoop. The thin, rolled rim gives this colander a finished look but won't get in the way of your scooping motion. A hook at one end catches onto the edge of a pot so that food can drain. The stainless steel

"Enzo writes that he's getting eighteen thousand lire for a plate of tagliatelle al formaggio on the lower East Side—and that's at <u>lunch</u>!"

handle is welded to the bowl of the scoop in a sandwich of black plastic for a comfortable grip. A hole at the end of the handle is for hanging.

6.10 NORPRO COLANDER-STRAINER

The larger scoop colander we've featured is a smart choice for retrieving and draining all the cooked ingredients from a boiling pot. But when you need to scoop out only one small thing—say, a cinnamon stick floating in mulled cider or the bay leaf you are steeping for a sauce—you'll want a tool small enough to function as an extension of your hand, allowing you to aim precisely.

This glittering little scoop serves that purpose, and beautifully. Consider it for uses for which an especially deep slotted spoon would be perfect—like retrieving maztoh balls from simmering chicken soup. The mirror-finish stainless steel bowl is only 3″ in diameter and is perforated with plenty of round holes. The entire colander is a mere 8″ from the tip of the handle to the tip of the resting loop. We think it deserves a place in the drawer or utensil jar with your other favorite small utensils and gadgets.

SALAD SPINNERS

WHEN PREPARING SALAD GREENS, the difficulty lies not in washing but in drying them. A wet spinach leaf or a damp piece of Boston lettuce will turn limp in the bowl and dilute the dressing. The latter happens because oil and water do not mix: those droplets of extra-virgin olive oil will never cling to wet greens, but instead will pool in the bottom of the bowl, leaving your salad naked rather than properly dressed. There are many ways to accomplish the perfect drying of salad greens. You can wrap them in terrycloth, place them in a plastic bag with sheets of paper towel, or put them in a pillowcase and toss them in the dryer using the no-heat spin cycle. But the most efficient technique is to use a salad spinner. Early salad spinning involved placing wet greens in a wire basket, going outside, and swinging the basket around in a great circle. The method works because of centrifugal force; as the basket spins, the greens and the water are forced out from the center to the sides, so the greens are trapped against the grid while the water shoots out past them. Fortunately, although modern-day salad spinning uses the same principle, it doesn't require quite as much effort or a backyard.

Mechanical salad spinners utilize one of three different methods for producing the necessary centrifugal force: a crank, a cord, or a pump. Each of these spinner styles will provide you with a batch of dry greens in about half a minute, although the crank models require a bit more elbow grease on your part. All three styles have a second bowl outside the spinning basket that catches the flying water as the inner basket spins. When selecting a salad spinner, choose one that will be big enough for the amount of greens you normally use. Make sure the construction is solid and that the lid fits snugly into the basket and outer bowl. Most important, be sure that the spinning mechanism works well.

6.11 ZYLISS SALAD DRIER

Trust the Swiss to make a mechanism that performs like clockwork. This glossy model is the quietest and most stable of the cord-pull spinners, requiring very little bracing. The cord pulls smoothly, rotating the basket in one direction, and retracts quickly, reversing the rotation. The advantage to this action is that instead of pure centrifugal force pressing the lettuce flat against the basket, the greens stay loose and are gently shaken dry by the agitating motion. Woven of sturdy nylon and Perlon, it should withstand years of impatient tugging. The basket is large enough to accommodate a few servings of romaine in each spinning batch. During downtime, the plastic cord handle nestles in a well in the lid. The clear plastic outer bowl is attractive enough for serving. An additional lid turns the bowl into an airtight storage container.

GREEN IN JUDGMENT

❧ ALICE WATERS ❧

I wash my salad greens in quite an obsessive way. I'm very careful about taking off the outer leaves and bottoms. I use cold water in a bowl in the sink, but I don't want the water running while putting the salad in because it could damage the leaves, and I don't like them to soak very long. I'll gently put them into a colander to drain and then do a little bit at a time in my salad spinner, after which I'll lay them out in one layer on a towel, put another towel over it, and roll it up. If I have to wait a couple of hours to serve the salad, I'll put the whole thing into a big plastic bag in the refrigerator.

Depending on what kind of salad it is, I change the dressing around. But my classic way is to put a well-diced shallot into a bowl and add homemade red wine vinegar. Sometimes I'll mix in others—sherry vinegar, a drop or two of balsamic. Then I'll take a pinch of salt, a grind or two of black pepper, maybe some garlic, which I'll smash really finely with the mortar and pestle, and sometimes a bit of mustard, and let it all macerate in the bowl for 10 or 15 minutes. Finally I'll beat in just enough olive oil to taste. I like most salads on the vinegary side. Salads very often are ruined by too much oil.

6.12 OXO SALAD SPINNER

Remember those spinning metal tops you had as a child? This spinner works on the same idea. It wins two prizes—one for innovative design and another for ease of use. You can actually dry your greens with one hand by pushing down on the large rubber-cushioned pump knob that extends up out of the lid. While this sets the inner basket continuously spinning, the downward pressure from your hand, combined with a ring of nonskid rubber on the bottom of the outer bowl, eliminates the need for bracing with your other hand. After several seconds, push the brake button in the lid to bring the basket to a halt. Then spill out the water. The pump knob locks in its down position for a better fit in your cabinet or appliance drawer.

ROMAINE, TOMATO, & AVOCADO SALAD WITH CORNBREAD CROUTONS, WITH CREAMY CHIPOTLE VINAIGRETTE

4 to 6 servings

FOR THE DRESSING

1 cup fresh-squeezed orange juice (about 2 large oranges)
1 cup red wine vinegar
½ cup mayonnaise
2 tablespoons minced chipotle pepper
¼ cup roughly chopped fresh cilantro
2 tablespoons cumin seeds, toasted in a sauté pan over medium heat, shaking, until fragrant, 2 to 3 minutes (or substitute 1 tablespoon ground cumin)
3 tablespoons fresh lime juice (about 1½ medium limes)
salt and freshly cracked black pepper to taste

FOR THE SALAD

1 head romaine lettuce, tough outer leaves removed, inner leaves washed and dried
2 cups cornbread cubes, in ½" pieces, toasted in a 350°F oven until nicely browned, 10 to 12 minutes
2 vine-ripened tomatoes about the size of baseballs, cored and diced medium
1 avocado, peeled, pitted, and diced medium
½ small red onion, diced small

1 In a small saucepan, combine the orange juice and vinegar. Bring the mixture to a boil over high heat, then reduce the heat to medium-low and simmer vigorously until the liquid is reduced by two-thirds, 25 to 30 minutes. Remove from the heat, allow to cool to room temperature, then add the mayonnaise and whisk together until well blended. Add the remaining dressing ingredients and whisk together.

2 Tear the lettuce leaves in thirds and put them in a large bowl along with the cornbread cubes, tomatoes, avocado, and onion. Stir the dressing well, add just enough to moisten the other ingredients (there will be some dressing left over), toss to coat, and serve.

Lettuce in Your Kitchen, by Chris Schlesinger and John Willoughby

The act of putting into your mouth what the earth has grown is perhaps your most direct interaction with the earth.

—FRANCES MOORE LAPPÉ

6.13 COPCO MINI SALAD SPINNER

If you want to prepare a small amount of salad for one or two, or dry a bunch of delicate mint, you'll most likely want to do so without bruising the leaves against the wall of a large and forceful spinner. In such a case, this miniature crank-style model will meet your needs.

A smooth plastic knob serves as crank, turning with ease and spinning the internal basket evenly and without wobbling. Made of molded polypropylene, this spinner is available in white, green, blue, or yellow. A larger version of this model is sold for full-size jobs, but it shook when in motion and proved more difficult to brace. This compact spinnerette is also great for rinsing and storing a handful of berries.

STRAINERS

THE WIRE MESH USED to make strainers comes in many different grades of thickness, from very fine to a gauge nearly that of a chain-link fence. When you buy a strainer, look for strength in the wire construction so that the mesh, no matter how fine it is, will not be easily damaged by a poking spoon.

Very delicate strainers often have shallow bowls, a feature that helps distribute the pressure on the surface and protect the mesh. The rim of the bowl must maintain its shape during use and storage. Look for a hook or ears that are curved enough to firmly clasp the strainer onto the edge of the pot or bowl into which you are straining the ingredients; flat loops look nice but will allow your strainer to slip into the pot. The handle should be comfortable when gripped and securely attached to the wire bowl; optimally, it should be made of a material that is heat resistant.

Fine mesh, although it does a more thorough job of sifting and straining than coarser mesh, is weaker and therefore more easily damaged by the pressure of a spoon or the edge of a pan. Some manufacturers solve this problem by covering the layer of fine mesh with a second, coarser layer that has been stretched as a support over the entire outside of the bowl. This design has its merits, especially if you are using it for sifting flour, but it is difficult to clean because there are many more spaces where food can get trapped. Other double-mesh models contain only one layer of mesh in which fine wires have been double-twisted to create a delicately three-dimensional, "knit-and-purl" texture.

6.14 RÖSLE TEA STRAINER

A fine mesh strainer for tea, this tiny model is most effective at holding back even the smallest particles of sediment. The mesh is exceedingly fine and tightly woven, almost resembling a sheer metallic cloth. It looks delicate, but it's actually quite strong, and it contrasts nicely with the polished stainless steel rim. The double-rod handle stays cool to the touch even when the bowl is resting in hot liquid; a squared loop of the same stainless steel wire keeps the bowl in place.

You can use this 3″ strainer for making infusions, for clarifying a small amount of any other liquid, to strain a few errant seeds from freshly squeezed lemon juice, or for that occasional glass of wine into which a little cork has fallen. Rösle also makes a matching strainer in a larger 6½″ model that is just as attractive and well made and will aid you in finishing a veal stock or draining yogurt to make soft cheese.

6.15 OXO DOUBLE ROD STRAINER

From a kitchenware manufacturer renowned for its attention to comfort, here is a rugged strainer that will complete the most rigorous jobs with ease. The polished stainless steel rim encircles a rigid medium-gauge double-woven mesh. A two-rod handle is welded to the rim on one end, embedded in heatproof rubber in the other. When you pour boiling liquids into the bowl, this handle stays cool and remains easy to grip, even when wet. The resting loop is carefully curved to hook securely onto pots or bowls. This strainer is a workhorse; we don't hesitate to recommend it for everything from straining a sauce to sifting flour. After it's made the rounds, you can toss it in the dishwasher—the rubber on the handle won't disintegrate. In addition to the 6″ diameter model shown here, there is also an 8″ model.

6.16 AMCO SHALLOW STRAINER

This strainer has a shallow bowl, designed as such to protect the fine mesh—the shape ensures even pressure on the wires so they won't break. This mesh is flexible, which means that you can press down on it with your spoon or stuff the strainer into a drawer and the bowl will bend rather than dent. The bowl is rimmed with a ¾″ band of brushed stainless steel; two curved ears welded onto the outside of the rim securely grasp the edges of a pot. It has a long metal handle, attached well with two small rivets. Of course, metal handles can burn your hands when used to drain very hot foods, so make sure and use a towel or pot holder with this one. Use this strainer when you want an ultrasmooth sauce or purée or to strain stock of debris: the tiny holes filter out small particles. You can also put this tool to service for sifting flour, confectioners' sugar, and so on.

The strainer comes in three sizes: 2¾″ (for tea and for dusting confectioners' sugar over dessert), 5½″, and 7″.

6.17 MOULI STRAINER

This strainer's metal handle is formed by one long piece of rolled stainless steel bent and curved to look like two rods. This separation of the metal effectively stops the handle from taking on heat, so there should be little concern when using this strainer with hot food. The bowl is deep and made of medium mesh metal, rimmed with a narrow (½″) band of shiny stainless steel. One gently curved hook at the edge sits nicely on pot rims. You will be able to utilize this strainer for a variety of tasks, from straining the Thanksgiving gravy or breaking up brown sugar to sifting flour. The one here is 6″, a handy size for small quantities of sauce, but it comes in several sizes, from tiny 3″ to 7½″, with 4″, 5″, and 6″, in between; you can stack them for storage.

STRAINER OR SIEVE

You might wonder about the distinction we've made between strainers like these and the sieves—flat and conical—in chapter 5. A strainer separates (tea from the brew, solids from broth); while a sieve refines (soft vegetables to purée and berries to sauce). But uses overlap, like sifting cocoa over a cake or smoothing a gravy.

APRICOT SHERBET

1½ quarts

The flavor of fresh apricots is reinforced by dried apricots, apricot liqueur, and orange juice in this intensely fruity sherbet.

1 pound ripe, fresh apricots (10–12)
6 ounces dried apricots (1½ cups)
½ cup water
3½ cups fresh orange juice (10–12 oranges)
¾ cup apricot liqueur

1 Halve and pit fresh apricots.
2 In a stainless steel saucepan, place the fresh and dried apricots, water, 2½ cups of the orange juice, and ¼ cup of the apricot liqueur.
3 Bring to a boil. Reduce heat and simmer for about 10 minutes, or until the apricots are tender. Purée in a food processor or blender until smooth. Strain through a fine-mesh strainer. There should be about 2½ cups purée.
4 Stir in all or a portion of the remaining 1 cup orange juice to taste and ½ cup apricot liqueur. Chill.
5 Freeze in an ice cream machine according to manufacturer's instructions.

Desserts by Nancy Silverton, by Nancy Silverton

FAT SEPARATORS

ATS FLOAT, allowing you to separate them from the other liquids in soups, sauces, and the pan drippings of roasts. The traditional method for doing so is to skim the fat off the top with a spoon. Another way is to refrigerate the food until the fat floats to the top and hardens, then spoon it off. A third way is to use a fat-separator pitcher. The spout is set into the base of the pitcher, which allows you to pour out the fluids that settle to the bottom as the fats float to the surface. (This also means that the spout fills at the same time that the cup does, so be careful not to fill the cup too quickly or too close to the brim.) A well-designed fat-separator pitcher should be nonbreakable, micro-wave and dishwasher safe, heat resistant, transparent, and large enough to handle a pint of liquid. In addition, the surface should resist scratches and scrapes, and the handle should be comfortable even if you are wearing an oven mitt.

Another option is a fat-skimming ladle, which is lowered into the pot just below the surface of the fat. The fat drains into the ladle, which is lifted above the pot, and the fat is discarded. This process is repeated until all the fat is removed. Shut off the heat under your pot of stock or stew for a few minutes before using a fat-skimming ladle so that the fat rises to the top and the liquid is still.

6.18 CATAMOUNT FAT SEPARATOR

This cup looks like a laboratory beaker and, in fact, is made from borosilicate, or laboratory, glass. White markings along one side provide easy-to-read measurements in cup, liter, and fluid-ounce scales. You may not need that information while you're separating fat from stock, but the scales do come in handy when it's time to measure how much stock you have to make your gravy with. Though the spout has a tendency to drip slightly during pouring, we think this cup is beautiful and versatile enough to warrant inclusion. In addition to the 2-cup size featured here, this separator is available in 6- and 8-cup sizes.

6.19 PEDRINI GRAVY SEPARATOR

Made of clear Lexan, a hard plastic that is likely to survive a fall, this gravy separator has a wide, triangular spout that ensures easy pouring. The cup is indented behind the handle, a good safety feature that keeps your hand away from the surface of the container when it's filled with a hot liquid. Our only criticism of the Pedrini separator concerns the raised plastic liter- and cup-scale measurement markings on one side: they are difficult to read, so this probably shouldn't double as your measuring cup. However, as a good-looking, lightweight, and effective separator, this can't be beat.

6.20 WMF CROMARGAN SKIMMING LADLE

Slot-shaped holes are in one side of the rim, while a curved metal spout forms a small tunnel from the bottom of the cup to the edge of the rim on the opposite side. Lower the ladle cup into the stock, tilting it back slightly to let both broth and fat flow in through the slots. The fat floats on the surface of this small cup, just as it does in the cup-style separators we have shown you. When you tilt the ladle forward, the broth runs out through the spout while the floating fat is trapped against the side of the rim. After you have discarded the collected fat and repeated this process several times, your pot of soup will be rid of much of its fat. For best results, let the simmering soup cool down a bit first.

EGG SEPARATORS

EGGS, like Caesar's Gaul, are divided into three parts—the shell, the white, and the yolk. Sometimes it is necessary to render the edible contents into separate entities. The richest mayonnaise needs only yolks, angel food cake only whites, while soufflés need both but at different times. One way to separate the the whites from the yolks is by cracking the shell in half and pouring the yolk back and forth as the white drips into a bowl. Many chefs simply crack the egg into the palm of their hand and let the white drip through their fingers.

If a little white gets mixed with the yolk, it's not a problem, but as most cooks know, no scrap of egg yolk should be allowed to contaminate the white: the fat will prevent the white from being beaten into an airy froth. To reduce the prospect of human error while separating eggs, there are contraptions that catch the yolks while allowing the whites to slide into a bowl. These egg separators come in stainless steel, aluminum, plastic, and ceramic. Avoid aluminum because it interacts with food, and bear in mind that the ceramic models, often the most attractive, are breakable. Whites have a tendency to adhere to plastic, causing a final stream to hang tenaciously from separators made of this material. Therefore, we like the stainless steel models the best.

6.21 BOJ EGG SEPARATOR

Think of it as the Little Egg Separator That Could. It is decidedly utilitarian, but don't overlook this small tool, as it works like a dream and outperformed some fancier models. Fashioned from sheet stainless steel, this separator traps a yolk in its center cup while the white falls quickly and completely through the curved slots on either side. As the entire contraption measures only 5½" in length, you must prop it over a cup or very small bowl and separate only one egg at a time. It's easy to clean, and a hole in the flat tab handle allows you to hang it up when you're done.

"I'm afraid you have only three minutes to live."

7

HANDHELD UTENSILS FOR BEATING, MIXING, WHISKING, STIRRING, & LIFTING

THE PREPARATION OF FOOD invariably requires some combination of stirring, flipping, mixing, manipulating, and tasting in order to blend the ingredients, keep them from burning, and satisfy the cook's curiosity. Beginners spend a lot of time nervously poking and prodding their food as it cooks, but even a master chef will stick a spoon in a sauce for a taste test. Handheld utensils for beating, mixing, whisking, stirring, and lifting are the most basic of our kitchen tools: they are the spatulas, whisks, cooking spoons and forks, turners, ladles, tongs, and skimmers that have become the cook's sidearms.

A WORD ABOUT WOOD

Kitchen spoons and spatulas are traditionally made out of wood, a material that is both attractive and functional. A poor conductor of heat, it reacts slowly to sudden temperature changes. You can use a wooden utensil at high heat without fear of burning your fingers, and moments later put it in a chilled mixture without transferring heat from the previous dish. Unlike metal implements, those made of wood are unlikely to discolor food or scratch a pan. However, it is only fair to add that most wood is porous, is liable to stain, and absorbs the flavors and odors of foods. Therefore, wooden spoons are not ideal for tasting—who could enjoy a hangover of tomato and oregano in their vanilla ice cream? That is why it's a good idea to own a series of wooden utensils for different purposes as well as spoons and spatulas made of other materials.

Precisely because of the porosity problem, only hardwoods should be used in cooking. Unfortunately, the manufacturers of soft pinewood utensils don't see it that way. We recommend that you avoid buying cheap pine spoons and spatulas: they splinter easily; quickly absorb odors, tastes, and colors; and do not last as long as hardwood implements.

The very closely grained hardwoods, like a beautifully patterned olive or golden boxwood, go into making spoons and spatulas for stirring a risotto or coaxing custard. Beech and cherry are normally fashioned into more workaday tools, like spoons to stir a stew or soup. Delicately finished or lacquered spoons should never be used for cooking. For stir-frying we recommend bamboo, which is even stronger than wood and will not split, swell, or absorb moisture. Be careful to avoid soaking your wooden utensils when cleaning them; they might split or warp. Treated with reasonable care, never torched, soaked, or placed into a dishwasher, good wooden tools will last you a lifetime.

COOKING SPOONS

No MATTER THE MATERIAL used to make a spoon, single-piece construction is superior. Ideally, the head and the core of the handle should be of one piece; at the very minimum the head should be fitted securely and permanently into the handle, because the point where the head joins the handle takes the greatest stress and must be solid. Spoons should be of sturdy construction and should hold their shape during heavy beating, mixing, and lifting. The utensil's balance and handle design must provide a comfortable grip, which you should test before making your purchase.

When selecting spoons, the array of available sizes, shapes, and materials can be dizzying. However, there are a few general considerations that will help guide your choice. If you work with nonstick pots and pans, make sure the material used for the spoon will not damage the surface of the pot or skillet with which it will be used. If the material is metal, it should not interact with your food; stainless steel and anodized aluminum are best in this regard. If the tool is made of wood—the advantage of which is that it does not conduct heat and therefore will not get too hot to handle— the closer the grain of the wood the better. Be sure to wash wooden spoons by hand. In addition to wood, stainless steel, and anodized aluminum, there are utensils made of bamboo, nylon, heat-resistant plastic or rubber and even nonstick-coated stainless steel. With a place for everything and everything in its place, serious cooks treasure their collection of favorites, frequently keeping them in ceramic pots on the countertop, like bunches of flowers, for easy access while cooking.

SOLID SPOONS

These are the most basic kitchen spoons. The ideal shape has a moderately shallow bowl and a flat bottom so the spoon will stay level when put down on the counter. A kitchen needs spoons in wood and stainless steel, at the very least; with experience a cook learns that a wooden spoon feels best when mixing cookie dough, while stainless is preferred for the soup pot.

7.1 H. A. MACK FRENCH MIXING SPOON

A good wooden spoon is as essential to the cook as a baton is to a conductor. This practical, efficient French mixing spoon, constructed by H. A. Mack out of durable beech wood in a single 12″-long piece, is the very definition of a good wooden kitchen spoon. Simple and classic, it can be used for just about anything that needs stirring. The shallow bowl is carved into an oval, and its flat bottom allows the spoon to rest in place on your work surface. The rounded handle is a comfortable ½″ thick. The French mixing spoon comes in several sizes, from 8″ to 18″ in length.

7.2 H. A. MACK ITALIAN COOKING SPOON

Like a matinee idol dressed in a handsome pinstriped suit, this Italian cooking spoon, made of lovely "country cherry," stands out in a crowd. The natural grain, running vertically from the top of the bowl to the tip of the handle, has a warm reddish-gold hue. This spoon is practical as well as beautiful, with a round, wide, moderately deep bowl and an easy-to-grip handle: just right for stirring risotto, thick minestrone, or a pot of Tuscan beans. We like the 12″ size, but it also comes in 14″ and 16″ lengths.

7.3 H. A. MACK SPANISH MIXING SPOON

At first glance, this slender, olive-complexioned hornbeam Spanish mixing spoon looks too delicate for tough kitchen tasks. Don't kid yourself! In the United States, hornbeam is known as ironwood, a tight-grained material so strong it is used for tool handles. Here it takes an elongated shape, with an oblong, rather shallow bowl posed atop a flat, fan-shaped handle that fits snugly into the palm of your hand. Use it to plumb long, narrow jars or pitchers, turn slippery seafood in a marinade, or combine chunks of eggplant and sweet pepper for a salad. In addition to the 12″ length we feature, this spoon is also available in 8″, 10″, and 14″ sizes.

7.4 H. A. MACK PORTUGUESE COOKING SPOON

Made of rough-textured beechwood with an oversized bowl and a relatively thick, stubby handle, this Portuguese cooking spoon is both strong and easy to use. It has a rustic, unfinished appearance but is the kind of spoon that grows on you with use—it's tough and it gets the job done. Long-simmered gumbos, thick soups, and heavy bread doughs have met their match. The paddle-shaped, 3″-wide bowl stirs up chunks of meat or seafood from the bottom of a cast-iron Dutch oven or stovetop casserole in a few quick turns. The spoon is relatively short at 10¾″, but the flat, sturdy handle rests comfortably against the side of a deep skillet during cooking.

7.5 JOYCE CHEN ALL-PURPOSE SPATULA

Although bamboo stalks are hollow and bend in the wind, when bamboo is used for cooking tools it becomes stronger than wood and won't splinter or absorb moisture. This 13″ all-purpose spatula is a good all-around choice to use when stir-frying, pan-frying or sautéing, especially when cooking in deep skillets (like the Western-style wok), including those with nonstick surfaces. Sautéing entails cooking over high heat and stir-

ring with a long, broad-bowled spoon in quick, sure movements, at which this oar-shaped spatula excels. Its tapered flat end pushes food around while scraping up browned bits of onion, ginger, or garlic that may cling to the bottom of your pan.

7.6 PAUL OLIVER SHOVALL

Function meets form and both come out winners in Australia's Paul Oliver handcrafted "Shovall." Thin, yet strong and flexible, this mahogany-colored, gracefully curved, 13″ ironbark tool is equally suited for kitchen chores or serving in the dining room. The tapered flat end is designed to get under and push or lift chunks of seared food, to scrape the bottom of

a skillet (including nonstick) while deglazing, to cook a roux, and to scramble eggs. Sharply angled to a pointed tip, it will reach into the corners of any pan. Wash this beeswax-coated utensil by hand and rub it with vegetable oil to restore its shine.

7.7 J. A. HENCKELS SERVING SPOON

Be it ever so simple, there's no kitchen tool so handy as a sturdy, well-crafted spoon. This 12½″ model is just that—and handsome, too. Made of brushed stainless steel that seems to glow rather than reflect, it has a shallow bowl that's nearly flat and is broad bottomed rather than tapered. The advantage of this wider

---

THE HAND

Whenever your utensil of choice is not available, we suggest you turn to something that's always close at hand. Made of bone and cartilage, the human hand is the most versatile kitchen tool of all—its five flexible moving parts are ideal for gripping, turning, twisting, lifting, and kneading.

Hold your hand up, and spread out your fingers. Doesn't it remind you of a thick wired whisk? Now, close your fingers together with thumb pressed tightly against your forefinger, and then cup fingers in toward your palm ever so slightly. Now it resembles the shallow bowl of a spoon, right? Straighten your fingers in a backward motion, still closed up, to flatten out your hand. There's your spatula. Using both hands (this tool comes in pairs) you can toss a green salad quickly and use thumb and forefinger to portion it. You can mix salt into popcorn, or form a cupped, slotted spoon to lift vegetables or fruit from soaking water. Hands are also excellent for kneading dough or sprinkling spices on a dish. No wonder each pair is priceless.

Be warned that hands do not work well in extremes of hot and cold. The delicate skin covering—which comes in many attractive colors—is subject to nicks, cuts, blisters, and chipped nails.

Easy to clean, the skin benefits from frequent applications of moisturizer. Overall, hands are useful indoors and out. No batteries required.

BOLOGNESE MEAT SAUCE

2 heaping cups, for about 6 servings and 1½ pounds of pasta

1 tablespoon vegetable oil
3 tablespoons butter, plus 1 tablespoon for tossing the pasta
½ cup chopped onion
⅔ cup chopped celery
⅔ cup chopped carrot
¾ cup ground beef chuck
salt
black pepper, ground fresh from the mill
1 cup whole milk
whole nutmeg
1 cup dry white wine
1½ cups canned imported Italian plum tomatoes, cut up, with their juice
1¼ to 1½ pounds pasta
freshly grated Parmigiano-Reggiano cheese at the table

1 Put the oil, butter, and chopped onion in the pot, and turn the heat on to medium. Cook and stir the onion until it has become translucent, then add the chopped celery and carrot. Cook for about two minutes, stirring the vegetables to coat them well.

2 Add the ground beef, a large pinch of salt, and a few grindings of pepper. Crumble the meat with a fork, stir well, and cook until the beef has lost its raw, red color.

3 Add the milk and let it simmer gently, stirring frequently, until it has bubbled away completely. Add a tiny grating—about ⅛ teaspoon—of nutmeg, and stir.

4 Add the wine, let it simmer until it has evaporated, then add the tomatoes and stir thoroughly to coat all the ingredients well. When the tomatoes begin to bubble, turn the heat down so that the sauce cooks at the laziest of simmers, with just an intermittent bubble breaking through to the surface. Cook, uncovered, for 3 hours or more, stirring from time to time. While the sauce is cooking, you are likely to find that it begins to dry out and the fat separates from the meat. To keep it from sticking, continue the cooking, adding ½ cup of water whenever necessary. At the end, however, no water at all must be left, and the fat must separate from the sauce. Taste and correct for salt.

5 Toss with cooked drained pasta, adding the tablespoon of butter, and serve with freshly grated Parmesan on the side.

Essentials of Classic Italian Cooking, by Marcella Hazan

shape and low incline is that when you set your spoon down after stirring or serving, any little bits of food or liquid remaining on the spoon will stay there rather than sliding down and dribbling onto the stovetop. A sleek, tubelike handle balances the weight of the spoon and protects your palm from any heat that might be conducted up the shaft.

7.8 J. A. HENCKELS NYLON KITCHEN SPOON

Though nonstick cookware surfaces are now fairly durable and scratch resistant, it's still smart to use utensils made of softer materials like wood, plastic, or nylon. A nylon spoon such as this 11¾" one has a smooth, forgiving edge that promises not to scratch your favorite skillet or pot. What's more, nylon has some qualities that wood or regular plastic can't offer: it's dishwasher safe and bacteria unfriendly, it won't retain the flavor of yesterday's curry or salsa, and it's practically unbreakable. High-quality nylon beats out cheaper plastic spoons in its ability to withstand heat—up to 400°F. We were also charmed by the Henckels spoon's reluctance to move around on the counter; while other lightweight nylon spoons rock and roll, tipping their contents with just the slightest nudge, this steady gray model sits as still as a rock.

7.9 MATFER KITCHEN SPATULA

Looking more like a small plastic canoe paddle than a spoon, this 13¾" manual mixer is decidedly flat rather

131

than bowl shaped. But as with spoons, its top is rounded and tapers down into a long stiff handle, giving the user both good leverage for stirring and a way to reach into the corners of the pot or pan. It can be scraped clean against the side of a pan or bowl, and like all plastics it's gentle on nonstick surfaces. Be advised that although useful and long-lived, most white plastic utensils do not maintain their clean good looks—over time they generally get scuffed and yellowed.

"What I really hate is knowing that I'm doing this exactly the way my mother did it."

7.10 RÖSLE CLASSIC COOKING SPOON

Perhaps the ultimate marriage of design and practicality, this spoon was created for use in professional kitchens. Made of 18/10 stainless steel, it was designed to replace the all-purpose wooden spoon that had been banished from commercial kitchens in the name of food safety. This spoon is built to get up, down, and around any pot, pan, bowl, or container. Its heavy-duty rounded wires are straight on one side, curved on the other, and zigzag in the center. The flat edge can scrape bottoms and straight sides, the round edge works for bowls and curved pans, and the middle mixes as thoroughly as a whisk. A solid steel button at the neck of the spoon adds balance so that the utensil, if left unattended in shallow cookware, cannot somersault out from the weight of the handle. Free of any sharp edges, this 12½" spoon won't mar nonstick cookware. The only thing it can't do is scoop up the food—you'll have to use another spoon for tasting or serving. It's watertight and dishwasher safe.

PERFORATED & SLOTTED SPOONS

Perforated and slotted spoons are used for separating solids from liquids—eggs out of poaching liquid, for example, or potato chunks out of boiling water. Make sure the handle of whichever spoon you select is long enough to keep your fingers away from the heat.

7.11 H. A. MACK SLOTTED SPOON

Spain is well known for its abundant crop of olives. It is perhaps less known for another product of those fruit trees: wood that makes superior cooking utensils. Olive wood not only possesses deep, rich color and striking appearance, but it is also practical—a hardwood unlikely to split, with a close, smooth-textured grain that is less porous than that of other woods. This 10"-long olive-wood spoon from H. A. Mack has a thick handle that flares at its holding end, and two straight slits centered in its rounded bowl. A flattened bottom allows the spoon to rest on a counter without rolling over. It's also available in a 12" size.

7.12 CALPHALON LARGE SLOTTED SPOON

While all the slotted spoons we tested performed the job of separating liquids from solids, this 14"-long stainless steel slotted spoon from

Calphalon did it best. We found that, in general, slots drain better than holes, especially if you're dealing with such small pieces of food as peas or corn that can easily plug up the round holes. The openings in this model vary in size, but some are as long as an inch and produce a steady stream of liquid. Moreover, the spoon's long, tapered handle, designed with a cozy trough for your thumb, is one of the most ergonomically satisfying utensils we tested.

7.13 BEST MANUFACTURERS BLUNT-END PERFORATED SPOON

This 13¼" spoon's slightly skewed straight end makes close contact with the side of most pots or pans, allowing the cook to trap and easily extract pieces of food—no more chasing peas around the pot. And if there's any scraping to be done in the bottom of your cooking vessel, this stainless steel instrument gives you much more surface area to work with than a traditional pointed spoon. Alas, we only wish that its perforations were slots rather than holes for better drainage and that the blunt handle was more comfortable. But its advantage keeps it on our counter.

7.14 CALPHALON STIR-FRY SCOOP

If you've ever watched a Chinese chef in action you know that stir-frying is like a culinary tap dance, involving lots of different steps executed with speed and dexterity. Often, several utensils are used in the process, which may not be feasible for the home cook. This asymmetrical spoon—a blend of spoon, spatula, and slotted turner—is a practical solution in that it allows you to perform all the stir-fry steps without missing a beat; no need to switch partners, one tool for another, in the middle of a step. Made of sturdy nylon that's heat-resistant up to 400°F and 14" in length, this hybrid invention is dishwasher safe and gentle on nonstick cookware.

7.15 CALPHALON PASTA FORK

To remove pasta from its cooking water most people simply pour the contents of the pot into a colander sitting in the sink, but if you find it difficult to struggle with a heavy pot of boiling water, there is another way to retrieve your noodles: a pasta fork or rake. The Calphalon rake shown here is of excellent quality and design. It's a good 13" long, which means that you can reach deep into the pot without your hand coming near the hot water, and it is crafted of a nylon material that is heat resistant up to 400°F. Its long tines, more than 1" in length, are very effective at grabbing the noodles, and the large hole in the bottom of the basket-shaped head drains the water away quickly from the pasta.

SPECIALTY SPOONS

There are certain spoons designed to tackle specific tasks in the kitchen. Though not essential, they are helpful and make superb gifts for cooks who have, until now, had everything!

7.16 APILCO PORCELAIN TASTING SPOON

Every good chef tastes a sauce before service. The best tool for the job is a tasting spoon made of pure white porcelain, inert, and nonabsorbent. It may be expensive and breakable, but it ensures that the food you taste is not tainted by the flavors from other foods or by the material of the spoon. Porcelain spoons are also the finest utensils for stirring custard or a delicately flavored sauce. (Tasting spoons made out of stainless steel are not as pure as porcelain, but they are less costly and longer lasting). The Apilco spoon is made in France of white porcelain. It comes in three sizes: 6", 7½", and 9". We found the longest to be the most suitable for reaching down into the pot. There is a hole for hanging at one end of the handle.

7.17 H. A. MACK POLISH CHOCOLATE SPOON

Long wooden chocolate spoons, the aristocrats of wooden utensils, were designed for stirring bubbly hot chocolate in tall porcelain pots. This 8"-long spoon is delicately carved from golden, fine-grained beechwood and varnished to protect it from discoloration by the chocolate, one of the most invasive of substances. The bowl is small, thick, and quite shallow, almost paddlelike, and it will not conduct heat or lend any flavor of its own to the brew. The handle is long so your fingers will be kept away from the simmering chocolate. Fine-varnished wood like this should not be subjected to high heat, but then, neither should chocolate.

7.18 H. A. MACK PORTUGUESE EGG SPOON

This charming 13" beechwood spoon is actually an egg lift. Use it to remove soft- or hard-boiled eggs from boiling water; the excess water will drain back into the saucepan through the spoon's generous, 2¼"

tear-shaped hole, and you will be left with a dry egg by the time you reach your egg cup. The spoon's bowl and its hole also serve to steady the egg as you carry it.

7.19 SAVOIR-VIVRE HORN CAVIAR SPOON & SERVER

Caviar is the ultimate gastronomic luxury. It has been a source of inspiration for songwriters and poets, not to mention cooks, and it has stirred the creative juices of artisans who fashioned the proper utensils with which to eat these teeny, sumptuous fish eggs. You could use a plain ceramic or glass bowl and a plastic spoon, but it simply *isn't done*. The czars ate caviar from golden bowls, and the great jeweler Fabergé produced caviar spoons made of malachite and lapis lazuli. In our time, haute manufacturers offer crystal servers; the spoons may be crafted from gold, mother-of-pearl, ivory, or horn, all smooth, nonreactive materials that are also glamorous. Silver is never used because it gives the caviar an off taste. The 5½" spoon we show you here is unadorned horn, with an elongated cup not only for scooping the eggs onto the plate, but for adding a dollop of caviar to a canapé. We also show you a matching horn knife, meant for spreading butter onto toast points before gently dropping the roe from the spoon. It is never right to spread fresh caviar—it breaks the eggs—but you may use the knife as a spreader for pressed caviar.

LADLES

LADLES ARE THE BIG DIPPERS of the kitchen, one of the most commonly used cooking utensils. Because this is an item that will see a lot of action, make sure the one you choose is well made and sturdy. One-piece construction out of stainless steel is the best. Check the manner in which the handle is attached to the bowl (there should be no gaping spaces in which food can collect). Note the angle at which the parts are joined— for plumbing deep into a stockpot, the bowl of the ladle should be attached at a right angle to the handle, but for skimming on the surface, a 45° angle between the head and the handle will work best. Also think of size: a small ladle, like those in most utensil sets, is useful for serving small bowls of soup and for adding liquids during cooking, but a larger one is needed to help deal with the contents of an unmanageably large pot. Ladles with 4-, 6-, and 8-ounce capacities are the most convenient sizes for the home. A curved hook at the back end of the handle is helpful for hanging and prevents the ladle from sliding into the pot. There are also ladles with lips on one or both sides that offer more control when pouring.

7.20 RÖSLE LADLE WITH POURING RIM

A full, generous ladle seems the very emblem of comfort and hospitality. Every kitchen should have one and use it often, filling it to the brim with steaming soup, stock for a risotto, thick stew, warm cereal, or tomato sauce. This rendition from Rösle holds 8 ounces so there'll be no need to go back and forth to the pot for a single serving. The 10" angled handle lets your arm do most of the work (the straight vertical handles found on other ladles can put too much pressure on your wrist). Another plus: This spoon's all-around pouring rim allows for a neat cascade of any liquid contents—there are never any dribbles. This model weighs several ounces less than other stainless steel ladles of the same capacity, so there's less to heft when the ladle is full. It's available in five other sizes—1-, 1½-, 2½-, 3¾-, and 5¼-ounce capacities.

7.21 RÖSLE SCOOP LADLE

Another heirloom-quality stainless steel utensil from Rösle, this ladle was designed by professional cooks for professional cooks. Its flat front end can meet both the bottom and sides of the pot for scraping, scooping, and trapping food, while the deep round bowl at the back of the ladle holds the contents in place. And with a length of 12", it can scoop from the very bottom of the pot, retrieving the last inch of food—something traditional round-bottomed ladles can't get to. A pouring rim on either side is a thoughtful addition. If we had to choose just one ladle to use, this would be it.

7.22 COCONUT COOKERY COCONUT LADLE

The bowl of this exotic-looking ladle from Hawaii is crafted from half a coconut shell and will hold up for years of use. We have concerns, though, about the longevity of the hardware that joins the inside of the bowl to the beautiful, palmwood handle; two small metal studs hold it firmly in place now, but like any spoon of two-piece construction, its future stability is chancy. Certainly, for durability and practicality it can't be compared to a stamped-out stain-

less steel ladle, but then again it has an earthy appeal that cold, hard metal can never give. Since coconuts are like fingerprints—no two are alike—every ladle made from their shells is unique. Those of us who have a Zen mindfulness in the kitchen will appreciate this too. The handle on this ladle is 10½" long. Its bowl is 4½" wide and 1½" deep.

7.23 WMF SAUCE LADLE

Just as a painter reaches for a particular brush to apply color, so does a sauce-maker appreciate a special spoon to put a ribbon of sauce in just the right place. A fine sauce ladle such as this one, with its graceful pouring spout, gives the cook more control, more finesse, when drizzling a red wine sauce or bright-red-pepper purée on the plate than an ordinary spoon would. We can imagine that this 9½" stainless steel implement would be ideal for pouring just the right amount of crepe batter, too.

7.24 RÖSLE EXTRA-DEEP SKIMMER

This stainless steel skimmer has thirty-seven small round perforations in the bottom of its deep 8-ounce bowl, making it perfect for lifting large dumplings, matzoh balls, or even whole poached fruit out of cooking liquid. The pouring rim seems a bit superfluous since the liquid is going out the bottom rather than over the edge. The characteris-

tic Rösle 45°-angled handle, 10" in length, and designed for use in professional kitchens, helps forestall the fatigue that comes from repetitive ladling, while a hook at its top end provides a nice notch for your grip. When not in use, the hook hangs neatly over a wall rack for storage.

7.25 STAINLESS STEEL CHINESE LADLE

Soup is a part of every Chinese meal, making this ladle an essential piece of equipment in the Chinese kitchen.

Ⓑ

RISOTTO MILANESE

4 servings

¼ cup extra-virgin olive oil
1 medium onion, cut into ¼" dice
1 teaspoon saffron threads
2 cups Arborio rice
4 cups chicken stock, hot
4 tablespoons (½ stick) unsalted butter
½ cup freshly grated Parmigiano-
   Reggiano cheese

1 In a 12" to 14" skillet, heat the olive oil over medium heat. Add the onion and cook until softened and translucent but not browned, 8 to 10 minutes. Add the saffron and cook, stirring, for 1 minute. Add the rice and stir with a wooden spoon until toasted and opaque, 3 to 4 minutes.
2 Add a 4- to 6-ounce ladle of the stock and cook, stirring, until it is absorbed. Continue adding stock a ladle at a time, waiting until the liquid is absorbed before adding more. Cook until the rice is tender and creamy and yet still a little al dente, about 15 minutes. Stir in the butter and cheese until well mixed.

Ⓑ

Simple Italian Food, by Mario Batali

The 3¼"-wide bowl is large enough to spoon out wontons with their cooking liquid and deep enough to be used as a small mixing bowl for cornstarch-and-liquid thickeners. It is made of stainless steel—which is better than the more traditional material, iron, because it won't rust. Don't worry about heat conductivity; a short wooden handle fits tightly into the ladle's metal shaft to prevent heat from reaching your fingers. Besides, the ladle should never sit in the wok or the pot: all implements for Chinese cooking should be moving through the wok at speeds that will not allow them to get hot. We also love to use this ladle with a deep stockpot.

SKIMMERS

To Sink or Skim?

A SKIMMER—BASICALLY a large perforated spoon that has been flattened out—is used to remove solids from a liquid. Whether stamped metal, thin woven wires, or mesh, the shape of the bowl and the size of the perforations or spaces between the wires are significant. A deep basket shape is best for deep-frying and for fishing out small foods like dumplings and gnocchi; a less concave form will work better for foods like potato chips and doughnuts. The size of the perforations or thickness of the wires and the spaces between them will also affect the speed and extent of the drainage. The criteria for selecting skimmers are similar to those for ladles: solid construction, particularly at the point where the head meets the handle; a long handle that will allow you to reach foods that have sunk to the bottom of a deep pot and will keep your hand away from hot cooking liquids; and, optionally, a hook at the end of the handle for storing.

SKIMMING IN DEEP FAT

As foods are deep-fried, they rise to the surface of the hot oil. Because each morsel you immerse will differ slightly in size and weight from the others, some pieces will reach the desired golden brown ahead of others. A skimmer is the best tool to turn these pieces when one side is done, and to remove each fried fragment from the fat at the peak of perfection. Why not use a slotted spoon? Simple: A slotted spoon is too bulky and will lower the temperature of the cooking fat too much when you plunge it in to retrieve the food. It will also hold additional oil around the food, as well as remove too much oil with each dip. A wire skimmer, with its network of thin strands, has no such drawbacks. It will slip just beneath the surface of the oil and scoop up the golden-brown fritters or shrimp tempura. Used in conjunction with a deep-fat fryer, it will yield maximum returns for a minimum investment.

7.26 LE CREUSET WIRE SKIMMER

The technique for deep-fat frying hasn't changed for centuries, except now we're doing less of it. But no matter how rarely or regularly you deep-fry, you still need the right tools—namely, a good thermometer and a wire skimmer like this one. Made of coiled stainless steel wire welded to two straight bisecting wires, the basket of this skimmer is only slightly concave, making it ideal for scooping up potato chips, doughnuts, fried calamari, and other foods that need to be quickly extracted from hot oil the moment they're done. This particular model is a manageable 4½" in diameter with a 10"-long handle, but there are bigger sizes available; food service wire skimmers are as large as 8" across with 14"-long handles.

7.27 RÖSLE SKIMMER

Although its manufacturer recommends using this 5"-wide, stainless steel perforated skimmer primarily for retrieving dumplings, wontons, and shellfish from a pot, in a pinch it would work just fine if used to remove French fries from hot oil, or to lift a poached egg or blanched

POACHED SPICED FIGS

6 to 8 servings

1½ cups fruity red wine
½ cup water
6 tablespoons sugar
1" by 3" strip of orange zest

6 peppercorns
1 whole clove
2 allspice berries
½ pound dried Calimyrna figs

Bring all the ingredients but the figs to a simmer in a noncorroding saucepan. Add the figs and cook them at a very slight simmer until they are tender when pierced with the tip of a knife. This will take anywhere from 30 minutes to 1½ hours, depending entirely on the figs. Remove the figs to a container with a slotted spoon, raise the heat, bring the syrup to a boil, and reduce by one-third. Pour it over the figs and chill. They will keep for one to two weeks and will benefit from sitting in their syrup for a few days. Serve with a little of their syrup and some cream to pour over, or with crème fraîche.

Chez Panisse Desserts, by Lindsey Remolif Shere

---

vegetables from their steaming bath. This skimmer is about 13½" in total length and also comes in a slightly smaller 12½" size.

7.28 MOULI FINE MESH SKIMMER

Here is good hybrid implement. Indispensable for some cooks, it combines the functions of a perforated ladle, skimmer, and strainer into one lightweight tool. Use it to lift dumplings out of stew or sweep its fine mesh bowl across the surface of chicken broth to skim off the foam that collects there. Made entirely of stainless steel, its 5"-wide metal netting is flexible yet strong; an 11"-long handle is welded firmly to the rim. Though large enough to remove cannoli shells from their bath of fat, this multipurpose utensil is still small enough to maneuver at the top of a tall, narrow stockpot.

7.29 JOYCE CHEN BRASS STRAINER

Here is the quintessential Chinese strainer for deep-frying. It is made of twisted woven brass wire with a reinforcement of brass—the mark of a good Chinese strainer. It has a long, 11¼" broad bamboo handle that will not conduct heat and will keep your hand a safe distance from hot oil. To hang the strainer, loop a piece of string through the small hole at the end of the handle. Five spokes that extend from the other end of the handle along with a circle of brass wire frame and hold the shape of the basket. The light, wire-mesh construction and slight scoop shape of the basket make this the best type of strainer to use for deep-frying. With this 5"-wide strainer you can pick up

USING A BLOW-DRYER IN THE KITCHEN

DAVID BURKE

Improvisation, vision, and imagination in cooking can be as vital as the recipe, ingredients, and utensils. Of course, being excessively creative can be just as dangerous, but when I combine good instincts with a pinch of logic, the whole experience becomes rewarding, interesting, and amusing.

An example of this is my introduction of the blow-dryer into the kitchen. It may be an eccentric move, but the blow-dryer is a handy and efficient tool for little jobs, like giving duck or chicken a delicious, crispy skin. Sometimes I use it to cook thin slices of meat or fish right on the plate. It can also help with annoying chores like separating eggs—I simply blow the whites away from the yolks—and with enough heat I could even cook the eggs. The blow-dryer won't glaze a crème brûlée like a blowtorch, but it will melt a surface coating of cheese or chocolate. The heat can wilt spinach, remove onion and garlic skins, and can't be beat for softening ice cream to make it scoopable.

Finally, I can fix my hair after a tough day in the kitchen.

a number of deep-fried spring rolls at once, and the excess oil will drain quickly back into the wok. A 7" strainer is also available.

SPATULAS

SPATULAS HAVE MANY USES and come in many forms. Often the word *spatula* is used to describe equipment for lifting or turning food in a pan or on a grill. Here, we use *spatula* to designate those tools that are used for mixing, blending, folding, scraping, and spreading. We call implements for turning and lifting, logically enough, "turners" and "lifters"; we deal with them later in this chapter. For sandwich spatulas or spreaders, see chapter 3. For baking spatulas, turn to chapter 16.

FLEXIBLE SPATULAS

A rubber or plastic spatula is a truly indispensable kitchen tool, so buying the best is a minimal investment considering the generous use you will make of it. Look for flexible spatulas with balanced construction, grip comfort, and ease of cleaning. The handle must be set firmly into the blade, which should be flexible, heat resistant (able to withstand temperatures of 300°F or higher), stain resistant, and dishwasher safe. It is important that the blade repel moisture and grease. Choose a variety of shapes and sizes: spatulas with thin blades will fit into narrow spaces, whereas wider blades are better for folding egg whites. Some spatulas, called scrapers, are notched on one side to make it easier to clean a bowl of batter or a food processor of purée. Flexible spatulas are perfect for scraping mashed potatoes out of a nonstick saucepan: the rubber or plastic won't damage the surface of the pot, and the edge of the spatula will remove every last morsel from the walls. Never leave a rubber or plastic spatula in the cooking pot as it heats—it could easily be deformed.

indestructible (they will not burn or tear). Want flexibility? These spatula blades are so flexible they bend into a U-shape, then snap right back. Made of clear "super" silicone that feels like rubberized putty, they are very useful for scraping food out of any size pan, bowl, cup, or jar. The black, hard plastic handle is firmly set into the blade and has a circular end with a hole for hanging. The set consists of two spatulas. The first is 10¾" long with a 2" wide, gently curved blade; the second is 9½" long with a narrow, straight-edged blade, 1½" wide. Needless to say, these spatulas are dishwasher safe.

7.30 & 7.31 OXO SILICONE SPATULAS

Until recently, cooks have been reluctant to stir a hot, bubbling sauce with a rubber spatula for fear it would melt, crack, or curl. They need fear no longer: spatulas with silicone heads withstand heat up to 600°F and can be used directly in saucepans (though they should not be left sitting in them). The silicone spatula blade also has a pointed edge for getting into pan corners where foods might stick. Making tomato sauce? Reach for OXO's color-coordinated tomato-sauce spatula—the sauce

can't discolor it. The easy-to-grasp, soft handle grip is comfortable. Ridged sides provide a secure thumb rest, while extra length keeps hands away from stovetop heat. These spatulas' sleek black handles contrast with bright white or brilliant red blades. They are nearly 12" long, are dishwasher safe, and have no removable parts.

7.32 REVEREWARE DURA-SPATULA SET

Talk about durability! Here is a spatula set appropriately titled "Dura-Spatula," with heads that are virtually

7.33 & 7.34 LE CREUSET SPOON-SPATULAS

The Spoon-spatula is designed with the shape and carrying capacity of a spoon and the flexibility of a spatula. It folds, scrapes, blends, and—most important—scoops up sauces and batters. Le Creuset offers two sizes, large (11¼") and small (10½"), with sturdy, medical-grade silicone heads that will not scorch (they are heat-proof to 800°F), stain, curl, or absorb food odors. They come in seven colors: flame, yellow, orange, blue, green, red, and white. The Spoon-spatula's one drawback is that the detachable wood handle has to be washed by hand.

7.35 LE CREUSET SUPER SPATULA

Every kitchen should have one extra-large flexible spatula with a handle long enough to keep the cook's hands clean when he or she is folding large amounts of food. Our vote goes to Le Creuset's Super Spatula. With its 9″ wooden handle and 4½″ by 2¾″

heat-resistant silicone blade, this is the tool to have at hand when you need to lift egg whites from a beating bowl or stir the bottom-dwelling ingredients in a stockpot. The flexible, stainproof removable blade has both an angular and a rounded corner, rendering all sorts of nooks and crannies accessible.

7.36 TRUDEAU ALL-PURPOSE SPATULA

Trudeau's wide-handle all-purpose spatula is a boon to home bakers. Its curved, flexible, tapered Santoprene rubber blade is 4¾″ long and 2½″ wide, and cuts through batter or beaten egg whites like an airplane wing through air, providing wide coverage with every stroke. This spatula is easily guided, thanks to grip indentations in the ice blue molded polypropylene handle. There's a notch on one side of the blade for cleaning the edge of a bowl. The spatula is heat resistant to 300°F. This line from Trudeau includes four other models, which range in shape from long and narrow to short and wide.

LIFTERS & TURNERS

THESE TOOLS, often called spatulas, are extensions of your hands that allow you to reach into a pan and lift an ingredient out or turn it over. They flip hamburgers on a griddle, lift a sea bass fillet from a sauté pan, and turn your eggs over easy. A properly designed tool for doing these jobs will have its handle set at an angle to the working blade, so you can use it and still keep your hand a safe distance from the pan's hot surface. The handle should also have a comfortable grip and be heat resistant. The working blade should be made of a material that will not damage the surface of your pots and pans. Like spoons, turners are available in both solid and perforated models. The perforated models will help drain away fat from pan-fried foods like potatoes and onions. A well-designed turner or lifter tapers to a fine edge that easily gets under or around food. You will need a rather rigid one for turning a heavier item like a hamburger, and one with more flexibility for getting underneath delicate foods like pancakes or pralines.

7.37 MATFER SOLID PELTON SPATULA

Though plain-looking, we found this matte gray lifter-turner from France attractive for other than aesthetic reasons. Molded from polyamid plastic and fiberglass, its rigid 3½″-wide surface is sturdy enough to support burgers, fish steaks, eggs, or cutlets without bending and has a heat resis-

tance of up to 430°F. The fiberglass gives the spatula its stiffness and strength, and because it's nonmetallic, it can be used on any cooking surface, including nonstick pots and pans. The handle is set at an angle to the flat blade, which is tapered to a thin edge that will easily slide under food. There's also a cozy trench for your thumb to secure a good grip. The overall size of this tool is generous— 12″ long, with a turning surface 3½″ wide—though not cumbersome inside a standard skillet. This spatula is dishwasher safe.

7.38 GLOBAL SOLID SPATULA

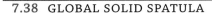

This utensil's small size is its advantage, its paper-thin, flexible stainless steel blade helping it to lift soft and delicate cookies from a baking sheet or get under silver-dollar pancakes. The lifting-turning surface is just 2″ across at the widest point, but the length is a full 5″. Made in Japan of one-piece construction, the blade narrows and thickens into a handle that is angled comfortably at a higher plane. The handle also has an unusual pattern of indentations that make for better gripping. This spatula is 10½" in total length.

7.39 LAMSONSHARP SLOTTED TURNER

Lamson & Goodnow, a 163-year-old Massachusetts-based cutlery company, produces six styles of perforated turners in their LamsonSharp line, all crafted from tempered stainless steel and heat-resistant Delrin handles fastened with nickel silver rivets. We chose to show you this sturdy, slotted turner because it's the most all-purpose item in the group. With a working blade that measures 3" across and 5" long to its tapered front edge, this turner can get under most any food in a skillet or on a griddle. Six 2" slots stamped across the top half of the blade allow cooking fat to drain away, while the remaining solid half gives more rigidity to the turner. An offset handle keeps your fingers farther away from the heat and eases the wrist action. An identical but smaller version of this turner—2" across by 4" long—also makes good sense for the kitchen; not only can it turn and drain smaller items in a smaller skillet, but it also makes for a useful server for pie pieces, brownies, and bar cookies. All models in the LamsonSharp line are dishwasher safe.

7.40 GLOBAL TURNER-SPATULA

"I'm going to ask for a fork. Don't try to stop me."

This ultraperforated turner is a prime example of the maxim "less is more": there's probably as much metal missing as there is metal intact. But that's what so many cooks love about this style of utensil, traditionally known as a "fish spatula." Because of the gaps in its thin, spare metal skeleton, it's extremely flexible, lightweight, and versatile. The upward tilt of its front edge means you can lift and loosen foods from an angle rather than straight on. (Think of the way you scrape paint off a house—if you work the scraper at an angle to the surface, the paint loosens more easily.) The 4½"-long slots in this turner also allow for good drainage, so cooks often use it for lifting fried foods from oil.

Many makers of cooking utensils produce their own version of this classic perforated turner-spatula, but we especially like this one because it's constructed of a single 10¾" piece of stainless steel, so there's no risk of the handle loosening, and the whole thing can go into the dishwasher. A note about the handle: It's imprinted with tiny recessed dots that give the stainless steel a slip-proof grip.

7.41 MATFER SLOTTED PELTON SPATULA

A close relative to the Matfer Solid Pelton Spatula (7.37), this slotted version contains less fiberglass, which makes the blade more flexible and better suited to lifting fish, omelets, and any other sautéed food. Modeled after the traditional stainless steel fish spatula, with its full-length 4½" slots for draining fat and angled front edge for better maneuvering, this is the "next generation" version, made from synthetic materials that won't damage our modern nonstick surfaces. The handle is grooved for a better grip and ends with a wide notch for hanging. Dishwasher safe and matte gray, this tool is 12" long overall.

7.42 AMCO WIDE-BLADE SPATULA

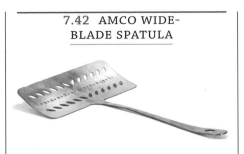

With its oversized, 8½" by 3½" brushed stainless steel blade, transferring whole fish from pan to plate is this tool's true task, but it's also great for lifting long spears of asparagus or stuffed eggplant. The 9¾" handle, tapered and rigid, is made of steel. The blade is slightly concave with three rows of perforations—small and round in the middle, larger ovals on the sides—that allow liquid to drain away from the fish or vegetable. This is a highly specialized piece of equipment that's certainly not for everyone, but it's so helpful for certain tasks that it's well worth making space for it in the kitchen.

CHINESE SPATULA-TURNER

No implement is better suited to the task of stir-frying than the Chinese spatula. Its curved shape matches that of the wok so no ingredients escape its reach, while its leading edge curves outward to scoop up the maximum amount of food. The slight lip around the sides and back of the spatula pushes the food when stir-frying and holds it in place when serving. Iron is the traditional material for a Chinese spatula, but modern stainless steel works just as well and won't rust. Many spatulas have a wooden grip, but it's not strictly necessary to have one—in stir-frying, you should be moving the spatula around quickly enough that it will never become too hot to hold.

7.43 OXO ASIAN TURNER

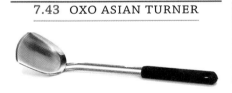

This shovel-like, stainless steel turner from OXO is an excellent tool for wok cookery. Its bowed front edge skims easily along the curvature of the wok, catching any piece of food in its path, while the raised lip around the back and sides helps retain its contents. The tapered front end of this model's blade makes it easier to get under delicate foods or scrape up small bits of garlic and ginger, putting it ahead of its blunt-edged competitors. The 10½" double-rod handle is covered at the grip with OXO's signature rubber sheath, although this one is slim, straight, and long compared to the company's usual round, chunky design. This Asian turner is dishwasher safe. One drawback: The metal blade of this turner will scratch the finish of nonstick woks.

COOKING CHOPSTICKS

CHINESE COOKING CHOPSTICKS are versatile tools. You can use them to stir shrimp with lobster sauce, beat an egg, lift a slice of sweet and sour chicken, turn a dumpling, or retrieve a strand of pasta to test for doneness. Ideally, they should be made of bamboo, which is very strong and does not conduct heat from the pan to your hand. They should be between 12" and 18" long, to keep your hand away from the hot cooking surface, and they are shaped at both ends to make food easier to grasp with either end. Avoid laquerware or varnished surfaces: they are slippery and tend to chip and flake.

7.44 H. A. MACK TAIWAN COOKING CHOPSTICKS

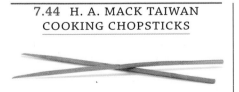

Looking very much like dinner chopsticks for a giant, this 18" bamboo pair is twice as thick as ordinary table chopsticks and twice as strong. Despite their size, you manipulate these chopsticks as you would any pair. Working with cooking chopsticks and discovering all the foods we could stir, beat, turn, and lift with just these simple tapered sticks gave us some cause for reflection—do we really need drawers full of gadgets in our kitchens? Chopsticks are a lesson in simplicity and practicality.

7.45 MUTUAL TRADING COMPANY STAINLESS STEEL–TIPPED CHOPSTICKS

In Japanese restaurant kitchens these chopsticks are an essential implement. As one Japanese chef succinctly explained: "We use them for everything." Any time a piece of food needs to be moved, whether for cooking or serving, the chef uses a pair of these sleek half-metal, half-wooden chopsticks. With their hygienic, needlelike metal points and exquisite smooth taper, they are especially good for picking up and arranging thin slices of sashimi and other delicate sushi items, as well as for positioning garnishes. At 12″ long and easily the sharpest thing we've seen outside a surgeon's kit, these are serious tools for the exacting cook; keep them far from young children, clumsy grown-ups, and any inflatable devices. They should be washed by hand.

HOW TO TEST A FISH FOR DONENESS

ERIC RIPERT

I learned the skewer technique when I was at Robuchon in Paris. It's the only thing that works, that can tell you when a fish is perfectly cooked. Other tests can only tell you if the fish is overcooked.

You slide a thin metal skewer, preferably flat, into the center of the cooked fish at an angle. Then you touch the skewer to your chin, just below the lower lip. For halibut it should just feel warm. Then you know the fish is perfectly done. You also have to be sensitive to the way the skewer feels as you slide it in. There should be no resistance.

But you also have to know your fish. Salmon and tuna should be less well done than other varieties, and the skewer should feel cold. Grouper and monkfish need more thorough cooking than halibut. The skewer should feel hot to the touch.

I avoid all digitized, microchip-driven gadgets.

TONGS

Tongs are the mechanical extension of the opposable thumb. They are a great help when it comes to turning and lifting almost any food; in many cases they offer more control than turners, lifters, and forks, and they won't puncture your food.

There are two types of tongs: those with a spring action and those without. Spring-action tongs contain a device that keeps the tool open until you pinch the two arms closed. These tongs are the most convenient and provide optimum control. They will help you to turn a pork chop, hold an individual piece of meat as you sear it on all sides, or lift corn on the cob from its bubbling water. Make sure that the grip is comfortable. We recommend tongs made of stainless steel because they hold their shape and won't interact with your ingredients. The finer models contain dependable locks that will keep them closed for easy storage.

Tong users are squarely divided in their size preference: some say "bigger is better" and choose long-as-your-arm tongs to work with, while others are more comfortable and capable with the shorter models. We think it's useful to have two pairs, one large and one small. Tongs range in size from 8″ to 18″ so you can take your pick; whichever you choose will undoubtedly become a favorite tool for turning things in a pan or broiler, picking up foods that won't balance on a spatula, and reaching across hot surfaces. They're also a handy household device—great for reaching into hard-to-get-to corners.

7.46 MESSERMEISTER LOCKING TONGS

This well-made stainless steel model would be a practical and versatile addition to your kitchen. Equipped with a spring-action mechanism, it has a lever that pulls in and out for setting or releasing the lock. The tongs are 12″ long, and when fully opened, the arms spread 8″ apart, the widest of the models we tested. The handle feels just right with its implanted rubber sheath for comfort and a no-slip grip. Relying on the Goldilocks principle—not too big, not too small—we think these tongs are a fine all-purpose size for the kitchen, yet also long enough to use for outdoor grilling when we want to be a step back from the heat and smoke.

7.47 CUISINART TONGS

Not as substantial or sturdy as the previously described tongs, this 8¾" flexible nylon pair is nonetheless a good, inexpensive device for grabbing whole items like roasted peppers, baked potatoes, or rolls hot out of the oven. Its clawlike pair of grippers curve inward like fingers, making it possible to gently but securely hang on to pieces of food. There's no spring action or locking device—the arms simply rest apart (2½") until the cook pinches them in. A notched thumb rest in the handle is too sharp to be comfortable, but it worked just fine as a way to hang the tongs on the edge of our thin-lipped salad bowl. Like all things made of heat-resistant nylon, this tool is dishwasher safe and kind to nonstick cookware.

COOKING FORKS

When You Come to a Fork in the Kitchen, Take It

POT FORKS AND KITCHEN FORKS, of construction and materials similar to those used for the manufacture of top-quality knives, are used to lift, maneuver, turn, poke, and push pieces of food. Pot forks, usually 12" long and made of high-carbon stainless steel, have two bowed prongs. A shorter 8" model is known as a "kitchen fork," and a three-pronged version is called a "granny fork." There are also forks designed to hold meat steady for carving or slicing that are commonly (and unsurprisingly) known as "carving forks." Typically 10" to 13" in length, they are forged in carbon or stainless steel. Our only caution for using them: Don't puncture foods that require their internal juices for texture and flavor.

7.48 OXO POT FORK

The basic requirements of a pot fork are that it be long, strong, lightweight, and easy to clean. There are more specialized forks, which we'll get to later, that have other aspects, but for day-to-day use a cooking fork should be like this one. At 12½", it's long enough to keep the cook's knuckles away from hot food; strong enough to securely rotate a big piece of meat; lightweight for comfort; and dishwasher safe for effortless cleaning. This stainless steel product has some extras too, including a non-slip, comfortable rubber handle; a notch in the handle for hanging; and two small indentations at the tip of each prong—rather like a devil's pitchfork—that help prevent the fork from inadvertently slipping out of the meat.

7.49 OXO COOKING FORK

Why invest in a special fork such as this one when an ordinary dinner fork is nearly the same size and shape? First, this 8" model has a thick rubber handle that gives you a better grip than the skinny stem of an ordinary fork. Second, your regular eating fork generally has four tines, and they're dull, while the three tines on this granny fork are sharp and about twice as long. In fact, the pointy, 2" prongs are the reason for the tool's nickname: they're just right for poking the pot roast, brisket, or chunks of homey stews that grannies used to make— by prodding the meat they could judge if it was tender. But they also would've kept this utensil handy for other jobs around the kitchen. Use it to peer into a fish steak to check for doneness, poke holes in a potato before baking, dock a pastry, get a pickle out of the jar, check the apple filling under the pie crust, break up canned tuna for salad, hold flank steaks or small roasts steady for carving, or test vegetables for tenderness.

7.50 WÜSTHOF-TRIDENT CURVED CARVING FORK

Made of fully forged, high-carbon stainless steel brushed to a satin finish, this fork, 11" in overall length, is absolutely first-rate. It will cost you dearly, but as Wolfgang Wüsthof explained, "Your grandchildren will get it for free." Add a sharp knife to go along with it, and you are set for carving any holiday roast. With its curved, tapered 6″ prongs, this fork prevents the meat from slipping and keeps the carver's hand far from the knife. Because it is gently bowed, this tool can also be used like a pot fork to get under and maneuver a piece of meat or neatly move a whole roasted chicken.

7.51 SABATIER BAYONET CHEF'S FORK

With two 6″-long, straight prongs forged into a slender U shape, this implement looks more like a musical tuning fork than a professional meat fork. Of a variety commonly called a "bayonet fork," it's generally used in any cutting procedure where a chef wants to anchor the food and keep his fingers a safe distance away from both the sharp edge of a knife and the surface of hot food. For carving large roasts, a curved-prong fork

would most likely be preferred to this straight variety. However, the smaller, thinner cuts of meat such as flank steak, duck breast, or butterflied lamb are better held with the longer surface area of unbent prongs. Like top-of-the-line knives

in the Sabatier collection, this handsome fork is forged from one piece of high-carbon stainless steel, then fitted with a high-grade polymer handle that is durable, seamless, and balanced. Dishwasher cleaning is not recommended.

CLARITY IN COOKING
 ✤ ALAIN DUCASSE ✤

At its core, my cooking is about clarity of taste, precision in execution, and respect for the product, which for me means retaining its original flavor—at my restaurants a tomato will always taste like a tomato—and, when possible, its original shape. It's actually harder to achieve this faux simplicity—where the essential nature of a product is revealed—than to create a dish where the basic ingredient is hidden by sauces and cream. I use the best ingredients I can find. I use as much of each element as I can—the trimmings, at times the skins, the shells, the baking juices, the pan drippings, the heads, the cooking broth, all the by-products of the process—in order to reveal an ingredient's precise taste. I also incorporate different preparations of the same product in a given dish, each revealing an individual aspect of its flavor. For example, a dish might feature slices of raw artichokes, braised whole artichokes and paper-thin slices of fried artichokes. A dessert might include grated raw pear, sautéed sliced pears, and pureed and then frozen pear. The palate discerns different facets of the artichoke's or the pear's flavor in each incarnation. A chef's ultimate challenge is to respect the natural flavors of foods, and to reveal their truest natures.

WHISKS

LIKE THE SHAMAN AND THE ALCHEMIST, the cook is dependent on the basic elements of fire, water, and air to work his or her magic. Of these three, air is the one that is rarely mentioned in recipes, even though the finished dish may contain more air than anything else. Used to lighten or leaven ingredients, air may be incorporated by chemistry or physics (or both). For example, yeast, baking soda, and baking powder are responsible for chemical reactions that produce bubbles of gas, while the physical motions of beating and whipping trap little pockets of air inside the surrounding mixture. One of the best ways to execute the latter technique is to use a whisk.

The whisk is a concise and graceful design that goes back thousands of years. It consists of little more than a number of wires curved around and gathered into a handle. The wires serve to increase the efficiency of each stroke. A whisk can have as few as two wires or as many as twenty. The shape of the wires, plus their length, thickness, number, and the material they are made of, determine its flexibility and function. In addition to stainless steel, whisks are made of nylon, rattan, and wood.

The lightest and largest balloon whisk is a tracery of tenuous strands, ideal for whipping delicate egg whites. Stiffer, unyielding whisks, large or small, are for blending and beating sturdier sauces and batters. The elegant little "cocktail whisk" that once appeared alongside champagne is only 5″ long, while an industrial egg whisk may be as long as 5′. There is a flat whisk for stirring a roux in a sauté pan and one shaped like a spoon for reaching the bottom edge of a saucepan. Modern technology has brought us whisks with comfortable vinyl-coated handles and nonslip grips to replace the flimsy wrapped wire handles that once were standard on French whisks.

You may even choose to use a manual eggbeater for most purposes. Its classic design remains unchanged. Or you may opt for an electric model. Collect whisks in many sizes and stand them in a countertop jar, as an artist would keep paintbrushes, selecting the proper one for the particular medium in which you are working.

BALLOON WHISKS

These big whisks have a distinct bulbous shape and are designed to whip as much air as possible into egg whites or cream. The bulb shape increases the whisk's contact area and thus the speed of the process. Thin wires work better than thick ones, because they place less pressure on the egg whites or cream and do not press out the air that has been incorporated. The more wires the better. Make sure that the balance and handle are comfortable because whipping air into egg whites can be a tiring process. A 14" balloon whisk is generally the ideal size for home use.

7.52 BEST MANUFACTURERS BALLOON WHISK

Few other whisks can match the performance of this 14" stainless steel balloon whisk from Best Manufacturers. Ten long, high-tensile wires, uniformly spaced, are looped to form an elongated bulbous shape. The wires are securely soldered and sealed into the gleaming handle, which is made of the highest quality stainless steel and has a flat bottom that allows you to stand the whisk upright. The whisk is balanced for maximum whipping action with minimal effort, and the flexible wires are designed so the innermost strand encircles the wires for added sturdiness. This balloon whisk is available in a 12" size as well.

7.53 RÖSLE ROUND BALLOON WHISK

Rösle's round balloon whisk wins our praise for its creative design. At first glance it appears small (10½" long) and delicate (only seven thin stainless steel wires), but the sleek, futuristic design works surprisingly well. Egg whites and cream fluff and mount in record time. The filled 18/8-gauge handle provides the balance needed to keep your arm from tiring; the wires are tightly grouped at the base and firmly attached with a waterproof seal. There is a ring at the end of the handle if you want to hang the whisk for storage.

SAUCE WHISKS

Used for mixing and blending, the sauce whisk has an elongated pear shape and is made of wires that are thicker and more rigid than those of the balloon whisk. Also called a "French whisk," it is good for working with heavier mixtures like pastry cream or a hollandaise sauce. Although sauce whisks come as large as 14", smaller sizes are extremely useful for beating salad dressings or stirring thick sauces in a pot.

7.54 BEST MANUFACTURERS FRENCH WHISK

Slender and elegant, this is a strong, 10-wire beauty that stands out in a crowded utensil jar. We loved the grip and feel of its natural hardwood handle, lacquered to make it germ-resistant and dishwasher-safe. The wood won't become hot, of course, even when the whip is immersed in a broth or sauce for a prolonged period of time. The elongated shape means

To make a good salad is to
be a brilliant diplomatist—
the problem is entirely the
same in both cases.
To know how much oil one
must mix with one's vinegar.

—OSCAR WILDE

that this light, easy-to-control instrument will fit into tall, narrow jugs or pitchers. The firm wires are made of high-strength stainless steel and fastened with an epoxy seal. We are partial to the 12" size, but 10" or 14" versions are also available.

7.55 CHANTAL STANDARD WHISK

If you were forced to choose only one whisk to call your own, we'd recommend Chantal's standard stainless steel whisk. At 12″ long, it's the right size for most jobs. Not only will this all-purpose whisk whip your egg whites as easily as it blends your béchamel sauce, but from a design perspective it is a true work of art. Nine flexible wires are looped on the bias into a classic pear shape. Lightly tap the outermost wires and the whole set shimmers, ready to go into action. The gracefully curved, ergonomically designed handle settles comfortably into the palm of your hand, where it will feel like a custom fit. A watertight seal where the wires meet the handle allows the dishwasher to do the dirty work without harming the whisk. For storage, hang it up by the convenient handle loop.

IN DEFENSE OF HOLLANDAISE
❧ JAMES PETERSON ❧

Why should this great triumph of human ingenuity, perhaps outranked only by penicillin, champagne, and the bed, need defending? How few are the things in this short life that give more pleasure than this warm, buttery foam of egg yolks, lemon, and butter? True, hollandaise has always been a luxury—at one time because only the well-to-do could afford the ingredients, and later because it was considered hopelessly difficult to make—but now that we can finally afford it, and with the slightest effort learn to make it, we think it's bad for us! Have we gone crazy? How is it that we unthinkingly down olive oil–dipped rolls before dinner and wolf down a bowl of ice cream for dessert only to avoid that pinnacle of Western civilization served in the sauceboat next to our grilled fish? I propose a new theory: we're all getting fat because we've forgotten how to enjoy life and because guilt causes more weight-gain and clogged arteries than butter does. Everybody talks about moderation in all things, but what about moderation in moderation? Even during feast days, all I hear is how much time everybody's going to spend punishing themselves at the gym to make up for their enjoyment. My prescription: Put some hollandaise in your life!

JAMES PETERSON'S HOLLANDAISE SAUCE

1½ cups

Even though you can toss it together in 10 minutes and don't have to mix anything in advance, hollandaise makes a lot of people nervous. The only thing you can do wrong is to overheat the sauce at some point, causing the egg yolks to curdle, but hollandaise is so easy to make that it's no big deal to grab another egg and start again. And once you've blown it, you'll have learned to gauge the heat so you won't screw up again.

A common mistake when making hollandaise is to use a double boiler. Double boilers are hard to control and may cause your sauce to curdle. It's easier to make hollandaise in a medium stainless steel mixing bowl held directly on the stove over low to medium heat. Standard saucepans don't work because the egg yolk hides in the corners, where it can't be reached by the whisk, and curdles. If you make hollandaise a lot, you may want to invest in a Windsor pan, which is a saucepan with sloping sides.

2¼ sticks unsalted butter	2 teaspoons fresh lemon juice
3 egg yolks	salt to taste
3 tablespoons cold water	freshly ground white pepper to taste

Heat the butter over medium heat in a small heavy-bottomed saucepan until it melts and froths up. Simmer for about five minutes, until the froth subsides and the butter looks clear. Don't let it brown. Strain the butter through a fine-mesh strainer, a triple layer of cheesecloth, or a coffee filter. Let it cool for 5 minutes—if the butter is too hot it will curdle the egg yolks.

Combine the egg yolks and water in a Windsor pan or medium-size stainless steel mixing bowl and beat off the heat for one minute with a hand whisk until the egg yolk is frothy. Place the pan or bowl directly on the stove over medium heat (hold the bowl with a towel) while whisking. When the egg yolk gets frothy and stiffens slightly—the pan or bowl should feel too hot to touch—take the sauce off the heat and slowly pour in the butter while whisking. Stop whisking as soon as you've added all the butter. Stir in the lemon juice, salt, and pepper.

7.56 AMCO HEAT-RESISTANT WHISK

Nonstick pots and pans, unfortunately, are not non*scratch* pots and pans. So to keep the interior surfaces in pristine condition, arm yourself with a whisk that features "wires" of heat-resistant nylon. We have in mind this heavy-duty model marketed by Amco. There's nothing frail about this 12" workhorse. The four wires, which glide over polished steel and enamel as well as nonstick surfaces, are astonishingly malleable, while the stainless steel barrel handle is thick and sturdy. Use it for blending sauces, thick and thin, or to mix ingredients in mirror-finish bowls. It's dishwasher safe and has a loop for hanging.

7.57 AMCO TWO-WIRE BATTER WHISK

Breakfast cooks and home bakers will come to love this unusual two-wire whisk. It's 13" long and made of high-quality brushed stainless steel, so it's very light, yet surprisingly strong. Its two sturdy loops are spaced so widely apart that batter slides between them without clogging. This efficient tool acts like a whip to aerate and lighten the batter, while cutting through the mixture to smooth out lumps. It's perfect for thick pancake and waffle batters or the dough for batter-style breads such as muffins and teacakes; dessert lovers will find it useful for brownie and cake batters. The light, easy-to-grip handle is watertight, and the whisk is easy to clean. A loop extends beyond the handle for storage purposes.

FLAT WHISKS

This type of whisk is used to incorporate flour into melted butter in the making of a roux. Four or five wires lying flat produce a 3"- to 4"-wide impact area. They are also useful for lightly beating eggs in a shallow bowl.

7.58 OXO FLAT WHISK

All our favorite whisks and knives become extensions of the hand, moving easily and quickly to perform their tasks. As soon as you pick up this 10½" flat whisk and feel its contoured, nonslip handle, you will want to use it. And you will, moving its four flexible, flat wires over the surface and into the corners of saucepans and shallow skillets to make a perfect, lump-free roux, or to loosen browned bits as part of the deglazing process. Away from the heat, use the flat whisk to beat eggs for an omelet or to incorporate oil for a salad dressing in a flat-bottomed bowl. It's light, easy to store, and dishwasher safe.

COILED WHISKS

A semicircular frame covered with coiled wire and attached to a handle, this tool is used for eggs and light batters. More like a whip than a whisk, it has an advantage over sauce whisks in its ability to make contact with the bottom and sides of a pan, but you may find it awkward to use. Be sure your whisk has a heat-resistant handle that angles up from the head to keep your hand away from the cooking surface. Do not use a coiled whisk in any thick mixture, because it will clog up.

7.59 RÖSLE SPIRAL WHISK

This stainless steel spiral whisk has the same design as a coiled whip; each sports a semicircular frame with a thin wire coiled about it. Like flat whisks, spoon-shaped spiral whisks (or coiled whips) are designed to skate over the bottom surface of pans and bowls to blend a roux or thin batter. The whisk head is offset from the frame stem, which disappears into a smooth, round handle. When in use, each coil of the whip is in contact with the pan's surface: guide it by turning it in circles around the sides of the container. This whisk, a compact 8" long with a 3"-wide frame of twenty-five spiraled coils, works well in pans and bowls of all sizes. A hanging loop is attached to the handle for storage.

> The *saucier* is a soloist in the orchestra of a great kitchen.
> —FERNAND POINT

MINIWHISKS

For the 5″ to 8″ miniwhisk, no job is too small. Use it to mix the fruit on the bottom of the container into the yogurt, or to combine a little lemon juice and prepared mustard to start a dressing. Look for a miniwhisk that has a comfortable grip and wires that are closely spaced and not very flexible: the tight spacing and absence of flexibility will create an emulsion but will limit the aeration of your ingredients.

7.60 BEST MANUFACTURERS LIGHT DESIGN WHISK

Bigger is not always better, especially when you're trying to blend ingredients in a small bowl, a task that calls for a miniwhisk. This eight-wire, stainless steel "light" whisk from Best Manufacturers is, at 8″ long, really a maxi-mini, but it possesses the same quality construction as larger models: sturdy, high-quality steel loops are secured to a handle of balanced weight with an epoxy seal. Although smaller versions of the mini-whisk are cute, they can be flimsy; loops tend to separate, and handles are not secured, which is certainly not the case with this model. Its slim design is ideal for mixing marinades and dressings in a measuring cup or narrow container. Little kitchen helpers can use it to blend chocolate syrup into a mug of warm milk.

ROTARY EGGBEATERS

This kitchen classic will tackle almost any whipping and beating job, from egg whites to pancake batter, with respectable efficiency. The range of speeds is, of course, infinite, limited only by the strength of your wrist. On the other hand, this is not the ideal tool for making heavy mixtures like a poundcake batter, and it can't handle large volumes of anything. The primary concerns when selecting a rotary beater are the smoothness of the turning mechanism and the comfort of both grip and turning handle. The best models are made of stainless steel with nylon gears.

7.61 *MOLINILLO*

The Spanish conquistador Hernán Cortés was the first European to taste chocolate when the Aztec emperor Montezuma offered him a cupful. Forbidden to women and reserved for men of superior rank, chocolate was the royal drink of Mexico. According to eyewitness reports, some two thousand jugs of frothy chocolate, sweetened with wild honey and often flavored with vanilla or *achiote* (annatto, a red seed used as a coloring agent), appeared daily at the Aztec court. To make the hot chocolate foamy, the Aztecs used a wooden *molinillo* or chocolate swizzle. *Molinillos* look more like exotic musical instruments than hard-working utensils. Decorated with simple geometric designs, this typical beater is 12½″ long and consists of a stable, rigid knob surrounded by movable rings at the head of a long handle. The head is placed into a pot of chocolate and the handle twirled between the palms of your hand. In

less than a minute a mixture of melted chocolate and boiling water is brought to a froth. It's much more fun than a blender.

7.62 FRIELING HAND BEATER

Here's a kitchen utensil for the anti-technology set. Like an old-fashioned bicycle, it requires some muscle and dexterity to get anywhere. This updated Frieling beater has an upright handle that is comfortable to hold and a turning mechanism with smoothly meshing nylon gears that keep the two interlocking beaters moving in unison. Use it for eggs, cream, and thin batters. The shiny body is made of 18/10 stainless steel and measures 12″ in length.

8

ELECTRIC BLENDERS, MIXERS, & FOOD PROCESSORS

FOR THOUSANDS OF YEARS cooks have performed physically demanding and time-consuming tasks by hand, with only a minimum of technical assistance. A classic whisk, made of a dozen wires, can multiply a single stroke into many—but the cook's arm must still supply the energy.

The invention of the electric motor changed the balance of power in the kichen. The cook had a new source of strength that showed up in the form of stand mixers, hand mixers, countertop blenders, immersion blenders, and food processors. At last, the force was with us.

BISCOTTI ALL' ANICE (ANISE-FLAVORED BISCUITS)

4 to 5 dozen

These are the classic crisp, anise-flavored biscuits so good with a cup of caffè latte or tea. They keep well stored in a tin. I am indebted to Salvatore Maggio of the Pasticceria Maggio in Trapani, for sharing the recipe from which this one is adapted.

3 large eggs

2 teaspoons anise extract

¾ cup sugar

pinch salt

1½ cup all-purpose flour

¼ cup cornstarch

½ teaspoon baking powder

1 Combine the eggs, anise extract, sugar, and salt in a mixing bowl and whip with a hand mixer set at high speed or in a heavy-duty mixer fitted with the whip. Continue whipping until the mixture is very light and increased in volume, 6 or 7 minutes.

2 While the egg mixture is whipping, combine the flour, cornstarch, and baking powder and stir to mix.

3 Remove the whipped eggs from the mixer and sift the flour mixture over them in three additions, folding in after each addition with a rubber spatula. The batter will lose most of its air and become rather stiff.

4 Pipe the batter, using a pastry bag with ¾" opening but no tube, onto a jelly-roll pan lined with parchment or buttered wax paper. Pipe 2 logs about 1½" wide and the length of the pan.

5 Bake the logs at 350°F for about 20 minutes, until they are well risen and golden. Remove the pan from the oven and slide the paper onto a cutting board to cool, about 10 minutes. Slip a knife under the logs to detach them, and, using a sharp, serrated knife, slice the logs diagonally at ½" intervals.

6 Place the *biscotti* cut side down on the pan and return them to the oven for about 10 to 15 minutes, until they color slightly on the cut surfaces.

7 Cool the *biscotti* on the pan and store them in a tin between layers of wax paper.

Great Italian Desserts, by Nick Malgieri

STAND MIXERS

STAND MIXERS are heavy-duty machines that will whip egg whites for a chocolate soufflé, mix butter and sugar for shortbread cookies, beat together the ingredients for banana bread, or knead five cups of dough for a garlic-and-rosemary focaccia. Whipping, mixing, beating, and kneading are the primary functions of the stand mixer; they are also the primary techniques of the devoted baker. These same techniques are often used by the cook, but if you are not serious about baking, the stand mixer is probably not an essential piece of equipment for your kitchen. The attachments available for the various models will perform almost any task.

The best stand mixers operate with "planetary action": the beater rotates around its own axis in the way the earth spins, and at the same time, the beater also orbits the bowl, just as the earth revolves around the sun. Planetary action produces greater contact between the beater and the ingredients; it also results in greater contact between the beater and the inner surface of the bowl, which reduces the need to scrape the ingredients. It will speed up most tasks.

In the more conventional type of stand mixer there are two beaters spinning in a fixed position. Some are designed so the bowl will rotate. Scraping the side of the bowl is essential with this design.

8.1 KITCHENAID HEAVY-DUTY MIXER

KitchenAid is the icon of stand mixers. These American-made legends have been loved by generations of cooks. For serious bakers, this heavy-duty model with a 325-watt motor has ten speeds and a 5-quart stainless steel bowl with handle. Like professional mixers, the head doesn't lift up. Instead, the bowl is raised and lowered by a lever. It uses planetary action, invented by KitchenAid in 1919, for the most thorough mixing. The flat beater, wire whip, and dough hook easily handle every chore, from double batches of cook-ies to egg whites with incredible volume to kneading bread dough with up to 10 cups of flour. Of all-metal construction, this mixer stands firm under the heaviest of loads. It comes with a helpful instruction manual and a pouring shield. For those who care about making a countertop fashion statement, this mixer comes in an array of colors. Many optional attachments are available.

NOTE If the 5-quart mixer isn't large enough for your needs, KitchenAid now makes a 6-quart model. There's also the Classic and the Ultra Power, which have 4½-quart bowls. Excellent options at a lower price, they come in more colors than the 5-quart model. Some cooks find them more convenient when it comes to adding ingredients because the head lifts up, holding the beater away from the bowl. These

---

EXPANDING YOUR CAPABILITIES

The best heavy-duty stand mixers have a dizzying assortment of attachments to expand their capabilities beyond mixing.

KitchenAid: pasta-maker, pasta roller, rotor slicer-shredder, disc slicer-shredder, food grinder, sausage stuffer, fruit-vegetable strainer, grain mill, water jacket, can opener, citrus juicer.

Kenwood: can opener; bean and peel slicer; coffee grinder; cream maker; pasta maker; slow- and high-speed slicer-shredder; standard mincer with attachments for sausage maker, kibbe maker, fine grater, and cookie maker; larger mincer with attachments for sausage maker and kibbe maker; grain mill; citrus juicer; liquidizer (blender); multimill; centrifugal juicer; ice cream maker; potato peeler; colander and sieve.

Magic Mill: citrus fruit press, blender, meat mincer (comes with sausage-stuffing pipe), berry press, grater, pasta attachments (used with mincer), cookie attachment (used with mincer), vegetable slicer-shredder, grain mill, flake mill.

models do not come with a pouring shield, but one can be purchased separately as an accessory.

Height: 17"; weight: 26 pounds. During the first year of ownership, KitchenAid offers a total-replacement full warranty that includes picking up a defective mixer and delivering a new one.

8.2 KENWOOD MAJOR CLASSIC MIXER

All metal, this sleek English workhorse has a 650-watt motor, a 7-quart stainless steel bowl, variable speed settings, and planetary mixing action. It is a great choice if you have a large family, bake in quantity for an organization, or need an extra-capacity machine for catering. The head tilts back and locks in place so there is no danger of it accidentally falling down on your hands as you tend to food in the bowl. The Kenwood Major Classic can tackle four to five 1-pound loaves of bread (about 13 cups of flour) or sixteen egg whites for meringue. Like KitchenAid mixers, it comes with a flat beater, whisk, and dough hook. The splash-guard covers the top of the bowl and has a convenient hinged lid for adding ingredients. The overload protection device automatically stops the mixer and prevents overheating. The three concealed power outlets accommodate a wide range of attachments.

Now for the downside: At higher speeds, this mixer is noisy. In addi-

tion, some attachments—particularly the blender, which is mounted to the top of the mixer head—are at an awkward level.

Height: 14½"; weight: 19 pounds.

WHAT TO LOOK FOR

Weight The machine should be heavy enough to prevent it from creeping along the countertop as it runs. Heavy-duty stand mixers often need to be left out on the counter because they typically weigh too much (between 19 and 26 pounds) to be lifted easily from a cabinet (although cabinets can be fitted with pull-out shelves designed for electric appliances).

Capacity Bowl capacity should be at least 4½ quarts, or large enough to handle a batch of bread dough or the batter for a three-tiered layer cake. The beaters should reach the bottom of the bowl and adjust to the bowl's clearance if necessary. You should be able to beat one egg as well as a double recipe of chocolate-chip cookie dough. In the store, check how easy it is to secure and detach the bowl. A bowl with a handle is convenient to hold when pouring out your mixture. It's also a good idea to purchase a second mixing bowl so you can whip cream, and then egg whites for a mousse without having to wash a bowl between jobs.

Noise Everyone has a different sensitivity to sound; one person's gentle hum is another's deafening blast. Have a store's demonstrator turn on the machine and listen to the sound, remembering that in most cases it will run for several minutes. However, the amount of noise a machine makes should be secondary to how well it functions.

Power A higher wattage doesn't necessarily mean that the stand mixer is more powerful and thus a better choice. The overall design, including the shape of the bowl and how the attachments move, contributes more to performance. As an indication of a model's power, check for the maximum number of cups of flour or pounds of dough it can handle.

Speed Variations A slow speed is essential for adding dry ingredients without sending clouds of them across the kitchen. A fast or high speed is necessary for quickly incorporating air into egg whites or whipping cream. There should be at least five variations between stop and the fastest setting.

Attachments The best machines come equipped with a flat beater or paddle for the most basic tasks like mixing cake batters, a dough hook for mixing and kneading yeast bread dough, and a wire whip for beating air into egg whites or cream. Some machines only have a pair of modified whisk beaters. Having the different shapes tailored for various functions guarantees better performance.

One-year warranty. Heavy-duty stand mixers generally run for decades without needing service, but in case yours does need repair, Kenwood has seven regional service centers. For most consumers this means that if the mixer needs service, it will have to be packed up and shipped.

8.3 HAMILTON BEACH CHEFMIX

If you like the flexibility of a stand mixer but use it mostly for light jobs like making cakes, mashing potatoes, or whipping cream, this model is a fine choice. It has traditional-style double beaters. With a heavy load, the bowl may rotate automatically; otherwise, you must turn and scrape the bowl by hand. It can take 6 to 7 cups of flour and is able to knead bread dough, although the mixer head does bounce slightly. It has a 290-watt motor, fourteen speeds, two dough hooks, and 2- and 4-quart stainless steel bowls. For a modestly priced stand mixer, this has some nice features—quiet operation, a head that locks in the up or down position, and a storage compartment in the base for the cord. With a weight of only 8 pounds, it is light enough to store away in a cabinet when not in use.

Height: 14"; weight: 8 pounds. Two-year limited warranty.

8.4 MAGIC MILL DLX 2000 ASSISTANT

This unit is the ultimate heavy-duty mixer and a bread baker's ideal kneading machine. Manufactured by Electrolux of Sweden, this rugged mixer is an investment that will last a lifetime. Instead of a beater it uses a unique roller and scraper that work beautifully for mixing all types of cakes and cookies as well as for gentle kneading of softer bread dough. For kneading heavier dough, the dough hook can tackle an incredible 20 cups of flour. Since there is no mixer head to block the bowl, adding ingredients while mixing is a breeze. The Magic Mill has a 450-watt motor, an 8-quart stainless steel bowl, variable speed control, and a 12-minute timer that shuts the mixer off automatically. It also comes with a double whisk attachment and a beater bowl designed for whipping cream or from two to twenty egg whites. In order to use the attachments, the base of the Magic Mill has to be turned on its side, which is a rather clumsy setup. The Magic Mill takes a little getting used to, but the superior performance of this machine makes it worthwhile.

Height: 14"; weight: 21 pounds. Three-year limited warranty.

HOUSEHOLD EQUIPMENT IN THE RESTAURANT KITCHEN
✿ THOMAS KELLER ✿

From the six-burner range to the chef's knife, this is the age of industrial-strength kitchen gear. For the most part, it represents an admirable improvement over the flimsy utensils of decades past. But is heavy-duty always necessary?

Thomas Keller, the chef and owner of the French Laundry in Yountville, California, doesn't think so.

We do things in small amounts here so we don't need appliances designed to handle huge quantities. Instead of investing $5,000 in a big Hobart professional mixer we have three regular KitchenAids. They set us back about $230 each, and so what if they have to be replaced every few years. They're more convenient.

I also love my potato ricer, the kind that looks like a giant garlic press. It's great for making mashed Yukon golds and works well when we're making gnocchi. Some kitchens use a Hobart and a *tamis* but our way is easier and the results are more uniform. We have two of them—they cost about fourteen bucks.

And when we do blini we use a regular plug-in electric nonstick griddle, a Presto or some other brand. We can move it around the kitchen, it doesn't take up space on the hot line, and it does a terrific job. For parties we'll pull out two or three of them.

HAND MIXERS

HAND MIXERS WILL MIX, whip, beat, and blend in similar fashion to the stand mixer, but with less power. The best ones can handle a stiff batter without slowing up or stalling. Hand mixers allow you to bring the power to the place where you need it rather than transferring ingredients to the mixer's bowl. They are ideal for tasks like beating eggs over simmering water for a genoise. Hand mixers reduce cleanup and also save counterspace. If you only bake occasionally, a hand mixer makes more sense than a stand mixer.

8.5 CUISINART SMARTPOWER COUNT-UP NINE-SPEED HAND MIXER

This hand mixer has an electronic feedback mechanism to automatically kick in extra power when needed—it tackled heavy oatmeal-raisin cookie dough with no problem. The touch-pad speed control is located in the handle and includes a digital timer that counts up as soon as you start mixing. If you're not sure what "beat until batter forms a ribbon" means and rely more on suggested time to indicate when a batter has reached the proper consistency, this machine takes out the guesswork. Because of the "smooth start" feature, the beaters gradually come up to speed to eliminate spattering. The handle is well balanced and comfortable. The innovative swivel cord can be properly positioned for right- or left-handed cooks. The stainless steel beaters are extra long and wide for faster, more thorough mixing. Also included is a balloon whisk that yielded exceptional volume in egg whites.

Motor: 220 watts. Weight: 2 pounds, 4 ounces. Three-year limited warranty.

WHAT TO LOOK FOR

Design In recent years, many hand mixers have been redesigned. The old beaters, which utilized a thick post down the center, have been replaced with beaters made of thin, curved stainless steel wire. They also work better and are easier to clean. Handles that slant up toward the front of the mixer (as opposed to running parallel to the mixer body) are more comfortable to grip and are designed to reduce the strain on your forearm.

If you are left-handed, a model with a swivel cord will make it easier to maneuver the machine. Check the button for ejecting the beaters. You should be able to activate the button with one finger while holding the handle in the same hand. The beaters should come away quickly and easily without assistance. We don't recommend cordless mixers because they lack the power for anything other than the lightest mixing chores.

Weight A handheld mixer should be heavy enough to feel sturdy and durable but light enough to be held comfortably for 5 to 10 minutes. Around 2 pounds is comfortable for most people. To gauge arm fatigue, hold the mixer at the height it would be at during use.

Noise Turn on a store's demonstration model and see if the sound level is acceptable. Bear in mind that you might be using it for several minutes.

Power As with stand mixers, wattage is not the only indicator of power. The overall design contributes more to performance.

Speeds Like stand mixers, hand mixers need at least six different speeds. The slowest is essential for adding dry ingredients without creating a dust storm. The faster speeds will aerate your egg whites before you lose interest in the idea of baked Alaska. Some hand mixers offer a "soft" or "slow start" feature in which the selected speed is gradually attained (it actually happens in seconds) to reduce spatter. It should be easy to adjust the speed while the machine is running.

Cleaning Mixers without seams on the underside are easier to clean. Look for smooth surfaces with no ingredient-trapping cracks or crevices. Models with touch-pad controls wipe clean easily.

8.6 KITCHENAID SEVEN-SPEED ULTRA POWER PLUS HAND MIXER

KitchenAid is the expert when it comes to mixing, and this hand mixer upholds the family reputation. Strong but lightweight, it is also quiet during operation. The smooth touch controls (which KitchenAid calls "clean touch") are on the handle, and the digital display is large and easy to see. An electronic mixing sensor automatically adjusts power for a steady, consistent speed in any mixture. This little dynamo had no problem mixing stiff chocolate-chip cookie dough. Like the Cuisinart, it also has a soft start feature to eliminate spattering. The ergonomically designed handle is comfortable, and the heel rest is especially wide and stable. The beaters release with a touch of the oversized ejection button and are easy to clean because they have no center post where food could otherwise get caught. Having to use a separate ON-OFF switch positioned on the side of the mixer is a minor inconvenience. KitchenAid's hand mixers come in the same range of colors as its other small appliances. The following accessories are available: blender rod attachment (this functions as a light-duty drink mixer, not an immersion blender), dough hooks, wire whisk.

Motor: 175 watts. Weight: 2 pounds, 1¾ ounces. One-year total-replacement full warranty.

PEAR-WALNUT COFFEE CAKE

6 to 8 servings

3 cups all-purpose flour
1 teaspoon baking soda
1 teaspoon ground cinnamon
¼ teaspoon salt
1½ cups (3 sticks) unsalted butter, softened
2 cups sugar
3 large eggs
2 teaspoons vanilla extract
1 cup chopped walnuts
3 cups canned pears (about two 16-ounce cans), pieces drained and diced

1 Heat the oven to 350°F. Lightly butter a 9" by 13" cake pan

2 In a medium bowl, sift together the flour, baking soda, cinnamon, and salt. Set aside.

3 In the bowl of a stand mixer or with a handheld mixer at low to medium speed, cream the butter and the sugar together, until the mixture is light yellow and holds soft peaks. With the mixer running, add the eggs, one at a time, fully incorporating each egg before adding the next one. Add the vanilla extract and chopped walnuts. Add the dry ingredients and mix at low speed or fold by hand, until just blended into a stiff batter. Do not overbeat the batter.

4 Fold the diced pears into the batter and spread the batter into the prepared cake pan. Smooth the top of the batter in the pan and bake for 50 minutes, or until golden brown and a cake tester or toothpick inserted in the center comes out clean. Cool the cake on a rack for 10 minutes and then unmold. Serve at room temperature.

Bruno Feldeisen, former Pastry Chef, The Four Seasons Hotel, New York, New York

---

COUNTERTOP BLENDERS

In 1937, F. J. Osius registered a patent for a mixer that would "produce fluent substances." Shortly thereafter, he showed his new invention to Fred Waring, a famous bandleader of the time. Fred liked the contraption so much that he formed and funded a company to market the "Waring Blendor." Waring then traveled around the country with his band and a trunk that opened up into a bar at which he demonstrated the use and advantages of the new device. He once used it to make more than four hundred daiquiris at a single cocktail party. Everyone was fascinated with the machine's ability to liquefy fruit. It took about sixty years for the company to give in to popular usage and change the iconoclastic spelling of *blendor* to *blender*.

The modern blender is still an excellent tool for liquefying fruit and blending rum, lime juice, and sugar syrup into a daiquiri, but it will also purée, emulsify, and grind. It will produce a finer textured puréed soup or sauce than a food processor because its blades whirl at much higher speeds. Most models will crush ice. It is not good at aerating egg whites or cream, for which you need a whisk, stand mixer, or hand mixer. And its tall, narrow container prevents it from being able to chop an onion or a cup of nuts as easily as a food processor.

8.7 CUISINART SMARTPOWER DUET BLENDER–FOOD PROCESSOR

Credit Cuisinart for combining a blender with a small food processor without sacrificing the performance or features of either. It's a great space-saving idea. To whip up a banana smoothie, just attach the 40-ounce glass blender jar to the base. There are seven speeds to choose from, including ice-crushing and pulse settings. The lid has an opening, and the bottom of the blender jar is removable for easy cleanup. When a recipe calls for slicing or shredding, simply remove the blender from the base, replace it with the special collar that holds the 3-cup workbowl, cover, and you have a food processor. A chopping blade and reversible slicing-shredding disc are included. An added bonus is having the flexibility to position the food processor with the handle and feed tube facing front, side, or rear. All slicing and shredding tests gave perfect results, and even tough jobs like grinding beef cubes or chunks of Parmesan cheese were no problem. This machine has some extra amenities, like indicator lights on the control-panel pads so you know what functions are operating and hidden cord storage inside the base (not just a cord wrap system). However, the unit is on the noisy side, and you have to remember to activate the ON button before selecting the speed.

Motor: 350 watts. Blender height: 16". Base weighs 2 pounds, 14 ounces, and the total weight of the unit with blender jar is 6 pounds, 13 ounces. Three-year limited warranty.

8.8 KITCHENAID ULTRA POWER BLENDER

KitchenAid's engineers made a good blender even better. The 40-ounce glass jar now has a lip, which makes pouring much easier. The cutting blades operate on four different planes throughout the jar for optimal blending and, like other well-made blenders, the Ultra Power has a "step start" feature that automatically starts the blender at a lower speed for just a second, then quickly increases to the selected speed to prevent spattering. This "clean-touch" model has five speeds plus pulse; a separate ON button activates the unit. Lights tell you at a glance which pads are activated. Crushing ice can be done on any speed, but stirring the crushed ice once or twice with a spatula is necessary to get the best results. This unit is remarkably quiet, even though it has a powerful motor, and because it has a heavy-duty all-metal base, it won't budge an inch during operation. The newly designed lid forms a strong seal but unfortunately was a bit of a struggle to use at times. KitchenAid claims it will become more flexible with use. This blender comes in a choice of colors to match all of the KitchenAid small appliances.

NOTE This version of the blender has the same model number as the

SHRIMP *REMOULADE*

8 servings

½ cup ketchup
½ cup mild prepared mustard
¼ cup Creole mustard (available in specialty food shops and some supermarkets)
½ cup white vinegar
3 eggs
juice of 1 lemon
1 cup finely chopped scallions (including part of green leaves)
½ cup finely chopped celery
½ cup finely chopped parsley
2 garlic cloves, minced
2 tablespoons imported paprika
1 teaspoon cayenne
1 teaspoon salt
dash of Tabasco
1⅓ cups vegetable oil
48 large fresh shrimp
2 lemons, cut in half and seeded
1 head iceberg lettuce, chopped

1 In a blender, combine all but the last four ingredients and blend to a smooth consistency. In a slow and steady stream, add the oil and blend till nicely thickened; transfer the sauce to a bowl, cover with plastic wrap, and chill till ready to use.

2 In a large saucepan, combine the shrimp and enough water to cover, squeeze the lemon halves into the water, and drop in the halves. Bring to the boil, remove from the heat, cover, and let stand for about 3 minutes. Drain the shrimp and, when cool enough to handle, shell and devein them.

3 To serve, make a bed of chopped lettuce on each of 8 salad plates, arrange 6 shrimp on top of each bed, and spoon *remoulade* sauce over the shrimp.

James Villas' Country Cooking, by James Villas

original one. To make sure you are getting the new, improved model, you should check that the blender jar has a pouring spout.

Motor: 500 watts. Height: 15½". Base weighs 6 pounds, 9 ounces, and the total weight with blender jar is 10 pounds, 12 ounces. One-year total-replacement full warranty.

8.9 WARING PROFESSIONAL BAR BLENDER

Pass the salsa and chips—this blender made perfect frozen margaritas. The stainless steel blender jar is indestructible and retains the cold, an advantage when blending and serving iced drinks. Experienced bartenders can tell when a drink is ready by the change in pitch in the sound of the moving blades. If you're a novice, you'll need to remove the lid to see what's going on. It operates with a simple toggle switch and has only two speeds: high and low. The blades are not removable, and the 32-ounce jar capacity, though adequate for a few cocktails, seems meager in comparison to most other blenders. This blender does well at blending any mixture, but its real talent is making drinks.

Motor: 390 watts. Height: 14½". Base weighs 5 pounds, 2 ounces, and the total weight with blender jar is 6 pounds, 9 ounces. Five-year limited motor warranty. One-year limited

---

WHAT TO LOOK FOR

Design It is essential to have a lid that fits tightly on the blender, a jar that sets securely into the base and does not wobble during use, a comfortable grip, and a heat-proof container, either glass, which gives you the ability to see inside, or stainless steel, which offers you less information but will not break. Stainless steel also stays cool. We are less partial to plastic containers; though they are lightweight and hard to shatter, the surface eventually scratches. It's helpful to have a container with easily readable calibrations, a pouring spout, and a cover with an opening for adding ingredients while the machine is running. The opening in the cover also allows steam to escape when blending hot liquids, an important safety feature. The best designs have containers that also open at the bottom to simplify removing what you've blended and to make cleaning easier.

Weight The base should be extra wide, as well as heavy enough to prevent the unit from creeping across your work surface when blending heavy mixtures. Glass containers, because of their weight, also add to the stability of the unit. The minimum weight should be 5 pounds.

Capacity Container capacity ranges from 4 cups to slightly more than 6. Since you can only fill the container about halfway with ingredients for any process, the larger capacity will reduce your refilling chores.

Noise It used to be a given that blenders made a racket, but now designers have found ways to mute the noise level. There is a wide sound range in blenders, so listen to the demo machine in a retail store and discover your tolerance level.

---

appliance warranty. Waring also offers this powerful base with a 40-ounce glass jar.

8.10 KRUPS POWER XTREME BLENDER

One of the quietest models tested, the Power Xtreme blender has six speeds plus automatic pulse and ice-crushing features. It gave especially even results on all tests and crushed ice perfectly, a necessity for making a proper smoothie. The touch-pad controls are easy to use and clean. To start the blender, you simply press the desired speed on the pad, eliminating the extra step of having to press the ON button. With the "soft start" feature the blender begins gradually, to prevent spattering. Its glass blender jar is wide at the base, making it easy to remove ingredients with a spatula. The jar also opens from the bottom for easy cleaning. It has a generous 50-ounce capacity and

Power Today's high-end blenders are powerful and can crush ice without added liquid. The best-performing blenders have wattages between 350 and 500 watts, but as mentioned before, wattage is not the only factor in how a blender performs. Just as important is the shape of the jar, along with the design of the blade.

Speeds Two speeds—high and low—and a pulse button are all the controls you really need. Nonetheless, most high-end blenders have at least five speeds. It's often efficient to start blending at low speed and then switch to high. A wider range of speeds will make the machine a little more versatile, and an ice-crushing speed is a big consideration since one of the most-used blender functions is making drinks. A pulse function is very desirable, as it keeps ingredients moving in the container and makes for more even results. When you are blending basil, pine nuts, and oil into a pesto sauce, for example, the pulse function helps pull the solids from beneath the blades.

Cleaning Blenders with touch-pad controls are much easier to clean (but not always easier to set) than old-fashioned push buttons. If the blade can be removed from the container, not only will cleanup be easier, but you will not have to struggle to scrape out every drop of tomato purée. The blender jar can be cleaned by simply adding hot water and a few drops of dishwashing liquid and running it for a few seconds. Almost all parts of a blender (with the exception of the motor base, of course) are dishwasher safe.

8.11 HAMILTON BEACH CHROME CLASSIC DRINKMASTER DRINK MIXER

It's been more than eighty years since Hamilton Beach introduced the DrinkMaster to the commercial food service business. Now you can bring the same nostalgic look to your kitchen and open a soda fountain whenever the mood strikes. Malts and milkshakes turn out frothy, thick, and caloric, but it will also make a fine yogurt fruit smoothie. In comparison tests the DrinkMaster milkshakes were preferred over ones made in a blender. The unit has a two-speed motor, a tilting head for easy removal of the 28-ounce stainless steel container, and a removable mixing shaft for easy cleaning.

Motor: 70 watts. Height: 14". Two-year limited warranty.

a twist on-off locking lid with an opening—to easily add ingredients—that was a pleasure to use.

Motor: 400 watts. Height: 15¼".

Base weighs 4¼ pounds, and the total weight of the unit with the blender jar is 8 pounds, 2 ounces. One-year limited warranty.

THE UL SYMBOL ON APPLIANCES

The UL symbol on appliances stands for Underwriters Laboratories, and the UL mark has been America's most familiar safety symbol for more than one hundred years. Underwriters Laboratories is an independent, impartial, and not-for-profit organization that does testing for public safety. It acts as a third party between manufacturers and consumers, evaluating thousands of different types of products, components, materials, and systems. Companies bring products to Underwriters Laboratories for evaluation and certification. Product samples are tested and judged according to applicable safety requirements. Manufacturers whose products meet these standards are authorized by Underwriters Laboratories to use the UL mark.

Another symbol you may see on some products is the ETL-listed mark. It means that the safety testing was done by Intertek Testing Services (ITS). The ETL mark is an accredited certification and equally acceptable as UL.

IMMERSION BLENDERS

An immersion blender is a handheld wand with an electric motor at the top and a rotating blade at the bottom. Professional chefs began using them during the 1960s. They were gigantic and heavy—one model was over 4 feet in length and weighed at least 40 pounds—but like Merlin's wand they seemed magical.

Emulsify 5 gallons of mayonnaise in a storage container, purée 20 gallons of pea soup right in the stockpot—no problem. During the late 1980s, scaled-down versions were introduced and gradually became popular with home cooks. The immersion blender (with its attachments) will do almost everything that a counter-top blender will do, and more. Its great benefit is that you get to choose the container. But for the toughest jobs, like crushing ice, you'll need the power of a countertop blender.

You can emulsify yogurt into a sauce simmering on the stove, without risk of curdling, something that's virtually impossible to do otherwise without adding a binder like flour to the yogurt. You'll want an immersion blender the next time you make a hollandaise: consider the convenience of bringing the power to the pot. Beyond blending tasks, a good immersion blender can also whip cream and chop herbs and garlic.

8.12 CUISINART SMARTSTICK EXTENDABLE SHAFT HAND BLENDER & CHOPPER-GRINDER

This is a product that will be out on the counter getting plenty of use. In seconds, it puréed carrots and broth into a silky soup. It operates on four speeds and the shaft extends an extra 2″ so it can reach the bottom of deep pots and tall pitchers, keeping hands and sleeves clean. The shaft also detaches, making it easy to wash by hand or pop in the dishwasher. The SmartStick is much more than just a hand blender; Cuisinart's expertise in food processors is apparent in the miniprep chopper-grinder attachment. It did a perfect job chopping and grinding small amounts of food. With the whipping disc and the ability to work on a lower speed, the SmartStick whipped cream effortlessly. The handgrip and ON-OFF button are made of rubber for comfort and safety. If you have small hands or a weak grip you may find the handle a bit too chunky or the whole unit too heavy—try it before buying. Also

"Phillippe, dice the potatoes."

WHAT TO LOOK FOR

Design Though ergonomically designed, most immersion blenders look awkward. Fortunately, it's not necessary to keep them on display. The cord on an immersion blender should extend away from the wand so it doesn't wander into the pot. Cordless models avoid that problem but may not have the power of plug-ins, and the battery unit must be kept plugged in or on a charging base when not in use. However, the cordless design does offer the cook maximum movement. Make sure the grip and control button are comfortable.

Weight The blender should be heavy enough for control but not so heavy that your arm quickly becomes exhausted.

Speeds Most immersion blenders are manufactured with one speed, but those with a second speed will give the cook more control.

Noise Not so quiet as to hear a pin drop, but mute enough to hear your own thoughts. Be sure to check the noise level on a retail store's demo model.

Cleaning Detachable shafts can go into your dishwasher; they also make storage easier. Otherwise, just run the working head in soapy water and rinse in clear water.

Attachments Some immersion blenders come with a companion container—a useful feature when you are working with smaller quantities. A container with a tapering base is helpful when emulsifying sauces and dressings. Other attachments include a whip for aerating cream or egg whites and a mini-chopper for mincing leafy herbs (but not hard spices). Most provide some kind of stand or housing to store all the parts, a useful feature because the attachments are easily misplaced.

---

included is a mixing beaker and storage stand.

Motor: 100 watts. Weight: 2 pounds. Three-year limited warranty.

8.13 CUISINART CORDLESS RECHARGEABLE HAND BLENDER

Cordless small appliances are notorious for being underpowered, but not this hand blender. It puréed soup and whipped up a smoothie as effectively as the plug-in models, and it can be used at the stove without worrying about the cord getting in the way or being dragged over a hot burner. The unit comes in three pieces: charger handle, motor body, and detachable shaft for easy cleaning. Depending on the food being blended, the normal running time with a full charge is about 15 minutes. That equals quite a bit of use when you consider that typical blending tasks take from 10 seconds to 2 minutes. Recharging time is fairly quick—if fully drained, the batteries regain 60 percent of their full charge in about 3 hours. Cuisinart recommends that the charger be kept plugged into the wall socket to charge so it is always ready for use (an inconvenience if you don't have many outlets). Like its corded sibling this model has a clumsy, awkward-looking (but supposedly ergonomically designed) handle and is a bit heavy. Included is a whipping attachment, beaker, and storage stand.

Charge is on the battery. Weight: 1 pound, 11 ounces. Three-year limited warranty.

8.14 BRAUN MULTIQUICK DELUXE HAND BLENDER & CHOPPER

Don't be deceived by this machine's slender good looks: it may be narrow and lightweight, but it tears through mixtures like a buzz saw. Lumpy split-pea soup was reduced to a smooth texture in seconds. In fact, nothing, from cooked carrots for baby food to fruit drinks, could withstand the powerful blade. The stainless steel whisk attachment did a superior job of whipping cream—

volume and texture were as good as if done by a mixer. The chopper attachment works at high speed—almost too fast in some cases. Finely chopped garlic was a cinch, but coarsely chopped nuts were difficult to achieve. The mixing shaft detaches for easy cleanup. The handle is particularly comfortable and has a soft-touch on-off switch on the side. Also included is a mixing beaker with lid and an easily mountable wall holder for storage.

Motor: 200 watts. Weight: 1 pound, 1 ounce. One-year limited warranty.

FOOD PROCESSORS

FOOD PROCESSORS SHRED cabbage, slice carrots, grate cheese, purée peas, grind stale bread into crumbs, make mayonnaise, and chop parsley in a fraction of the time it takes to do these tasks by hand. They will even cut butter into flour for a pastry crust and are capable of making excellent bread dough.

All food processors come equipped with a clear plastic bowl that locks onto the base (which houses the motor), a lid with a feed tube for adding ingredients to the workbowl while the machine is running, an S-shaped blade for chopping, and an assortment of discs for slicing and shredding. Though a food processor will chop onions and mix pie dough in seconds, it will never purée soup to a silky texture like a blender can, nor will it make mashed potatoes as effectively as a hand ricer. As a matter of fact, food processors will turn cooked potatoes into glue. And though they chop fast, the results are never as uniform as those achieved by a good knife.

Food processors come in three sizes: full-size models are the most versatile, midsize models are fine for the average home cook, and miniprocessors are handy for small chopping jobs like a few cloves of garlic or a handful of parsley.

8.15 CUISINART PRO FOOD PREP CENTER

The pioneers of food processors more than twenty-five years ago continue to make some of the best machines. This 14-cup-capacity workhorse sets the standard by which all other food processors are judged. For serious cooks and bakers who demand a large-capacity food processor that performs flawlessly, this is the ideal model. Powerful enough to knead dough for two large loaves, it also excels at small tasks. It has Cuisinart's signature extra-large feed tube, making it capable of slicing whole potatoes for a gratin or chopping mushroom caps for duxelles. This feed-tube assembly looks complicated and takes some getting used to, but it is well worth the effort. For the times when you are kneading, chopping, or mixing and don't need the feed-tube cover, replace it with the easy-to-handle compact cover that is included. The unit comes with a stainless steel chopping blade, medium slicing and shredding discs, a dough blade, and a whisk attachment for whipping egg whites or cream. The two large control levers for on-off and pulse are easy to operate. An added bonus is the how-to instructional video that is full of useful information and tips.

NOTE If the 14-cup capacity of this model is more than you need, consider the 11-cup version. Cuisinart also makes a 20-cup model that is ideal for catering. All are excellent food processors.

Motor: 720 watts, 6 amps, 1¼ hp. Height: 16"; weight: 13½ pounds. Three-year limited warranty on entire unit with five-year full motor warranty.

8.16 CUISINART POWER PREP PLUS FOOD PROCESSOR

Cuisinart has introduced a completely redesigned 14-cup machine. Both in its appearance and in the scope of

WHAT TO LOOK FOR

Design The most effective, powerful food processors have a bowl and blades that sit directly on top of the motor, not to the side. Some brands have the feed tube in the back of the cover, others place it right up front. The diameter of the feed tube sets the maximum width for the ingredients going into the processor. If you intend to slice a whole tomato, the feed tube must be large enough to make that accommodation. A processor designed with a second, slender inner feed tube will hold narrow foods like carrots. The bases of some feed tubes have pinholes that can be used to drip a steady stream of oil into the bowl—valuable when making a mayonnaise, salad dressing, or aioli. A PULSE switch that quickly turns the machine on and off is helpful—and even necessary for certain tasks, like blending pie dough. As with all small appliances, the machine should carry a UL (Underwriters Laboratories) approval indicating that the model is safe.

Weight The machine should be heavy enough to remain stationary while in operation but light enough to lift easily if you move it for storage. A weight of around 13 pounds is fairly easy to handle.

Capacity Food-processor bowls range in capacity from less than 1 cup to 20 cups. Full-size processors hold at least 9 cups of dry ingredients, but serious cooks prefer 11- to 14-cup bowls. *Dry* is the operative word here; the liquid capacity will be about half that for dry ingredients, because filling the bowl above the level of the blade housing may cause leaking while the machine is running. Mid-size models hold from 4 to 7 cups.

Noise Food processors are generally run for relatively short periods of time, so the noise level is not as crucial as with some other appliances. Still, some brands are quieter than others; these tend to be the more expensive, higher-end models.

Power As with the other appliances, wattage is just one component in how powerful a food processor is, and the motor's efficiency is another. There is really no way you can judge the power of a unit just by looking at it in a store. The more expensive food processors will be the most powerful and will be able to tackle heavy loads without a problem. A good rule of thumb is to rely on the reputation of the manufacturer. Most food processors have a RESET button so the motor will stop and not overheat when performing heavy tasks.

Speeds All full- and midsize food processors come with a single speed and a pulse feature.

Cleaning Touch-pad controls offer ease of cleaning. Look for a base with smooth lines and no crevices that will collect food. Almost all food-processor parts (with the exception of the motor base, of course) are dishwasher safe. The toughest parts to clean are the hollow shafts of the blades, which can become a breeding ground for bacteria. A periodic soak in water with a little bleach added helps keep the parts sanitary.

Attachments Though even a full-size processor can chop a single clove of garlic (just throw it down the feed tube while the machine is running), some models come with a minibowl and miniblade that mount inside the larger bowl for smaller tasks. There is also a shorter stainless steel blade, designed for mixing yeast dough. Circular slicing and shredding discs will produce slices or shreds of varying thickness. Julienne-cutting discs are also available. The attachments for whipping cream and egg whites are good but do not work as effectively as a stand or handheld mixer. Some also have attachments that sit on the motor base and function as juicers and extractors. For a list of available accessories, see the box on page 163.

---

features, the new Power Prep Plus 14-cup machine represents the first major redesign of the Cuisinart since it arrived in 1973. It does everything the previous 14-cup machines do, and it has also broken into new bread-baking territory by adding a redesigned dough mixing blade and a designated DOUGH button.

Aesthetically, the new machine is in keeping with the new aerodynamic style in small appliances. A white oval base, rising slightly higher than previous models, has a solid look and feel. Weighing 1 pound more than the standard 14-cup model, the Power Prep Plus resists crawling across the counter when mixing dough and

GIVE US THE TOOLS & WE WILL FINISH THE JOB

❧ MICHAEL & ARIANE BATTERBERRY ❧

Starting in the late 1960s, a confluence of seemingly unrelated phenomena conspired to spark a revolution in the nation's kitchens, both professional and domestic. Among them, the soaring TV popularity of "The French Chef," Julia Child, heaving vast copper pots about like a duchess turned stevedore. Conversely, a new school of militant feminists, politically intent on setting matches to their bras instead of gas ring burners, started to slam the kitchen door behind them as loudly as Ibsen's Nora.

At the same time, a new breed of self-reliant young men, once territorially relegated to the outdoor grill or barbecue pit, began to make sorties to the stove. Cooking demos staged in such leading department store chains as Bloomingdale's and Ivey's attracted men as well as women, the same males who had been conditioned to respect—and

aspire to—superior tools and equipment by their teachers, fathers, and "men's" magazines like *Popular Mechanics*. When they shopped to equip their own kitchens, more often than not they'd select professional-style cookware, undeterred by price.

The cultural coup de grâce to flimsy flower-sprigged cookware would be delivered not only by newly "serious" Julia-generation home cooks of both sexes, but by the unforeseen ascent of young American chefs to a pop prominence once reserved for tennis champions and radio crooners. As always, hero worship leads to the trappings of the adored becoming objects of desire. Would Emeril or the Too Hot Tamales be caught without a proper chef's knife or, worse, with your grandmother's fake copper-bottomed sauté pan? Unthinkable.

---

dense purées, a common concern when making bread dough in any food processor. A redesigned feed tube sports an angled housing for the mechanics of the lock. This housing, with its very simple lid release, makes it one of the easiest machines on the market to use.

The controls—on, off, pulse, and dough—are smooth touch-pad buttons that you can keep clean with the wipe of a sponge.

The redesigned dough blade and the dough button are great news for home bread bakers. Two stainless steel blades with smooth, sharp cutting edges are attached to a plastic hub. Unlike the plastic dough blade in previous models, which drags through the dough, these 2″ blades cut through the dough and can deal with as much as 1½ pounds of flour at a time. The dough button reduces the RPMs of the machine during the mixing. Because the mixing time is slower, the dough resists overheating during mixing. The steel cutting blade, slicing disc, and grating disc remain as in previous models.

This unit includes a cookbook and instructional videotapes as an added feature, especially useful for the first-time owner of a food processor.

Motor: 720 watts. Height: 15½″; weight: 14½ pounds. Ten-year warranty on the motor, three-year warranty on the body.

8.17 KITCHENAID PROFESSIONAL FOOD PROCESSOR

This sleek food processor combines beauty and brawn. Cooks will love its power, durability, and ease of use.

Every test, from chopping, slicing, and shredding to kneading bread dough, gave very good to excellent results. The feed tube is positioned in the front of the unit so it's easy to see what you're doing when adding ingredients. The workbowl has an 11-cup capacity. It also comes with a small 3-cup bowl and blade that fit inside the larger bowl to do double duty as a mini processor, and there's a 9-cup chef's bowl to let you process larger amounts of food without having to empty and clean the outer bowl. (The chef's bowl is for slicing and shredding only, as the knife blade is not designed to fit inside.) The two bowls nest inside the larger for easy storage. A two-piece food pusher with an insert can be removed to allow a single carrot or other narrow food to be held upright for perfect slicing. The smooth-touch or "clean touch" control pad, as KitchenAid calls it, has large ON-OFF and PULSE pads. There are no seams or crevices on the base to trap ingredients—it easily wipes clean. This model comes with a reversible thin slicing–shredding disc, medium slicing and shredding discs, a dough blade, a spatula, an egg whip, and a Sabatier stainless steel multipurpose blade. The citrus juicer attachment is convenient for juicing large amounts. KitchenAid wisely includes an accessory storage box to hold extra discs for special cuts and attachments. This unit is available only in white.

Motor: 670 watts, 6 amps, ½ hp. Height: 15″; weight: 14 pounds. One-year total-replacement full warranty.

8.18 & 8.19 ROBOT COUPE R2 ULTRA & BLIXER BX3 FOOD PROCESSORS

Think of a food processor on steroids and you have an idea of what these muscle machines are like. They are big, heavy, and not especially user-friendly. On the plus side they are extremely powerful, handle large loads with no problem, and will probably last at least one lifetime. The R2 Ultra works two ways: with a stainless steel bowl and see-through cover to be used when chopping, puréeing, and mixing; and with a separate plastic bowl and continuous feed chute attachment for slicing and shredding. The feed chute cover has two separate feed tubes—a small-diameter one for slender items like carrots, and a wide tube that could take two medium potatoes side

by side. The continuous feed feature means you don't have to stop, remove the cover, and empty the bowl. Instead, the sliced or shredded food comes flying out the chute into a bowl (it is positioned in the rear of the unit, so you can't really see what is happening). The R2 Ultra comes with an S-shaped knife blade and one slicing and one shredding disc; however, eighteen other discs that slice, shred, and julienne are available.

The BX3 model chops, mixes, grinds, and purées, but it does not slice or shred. The see-through cover clamps onto the stainless steel bowl. This unit has a unique built-in

Good living is far from being destructive to good health . . . All things being equal, gourmands live much longer than other folk.

—JEAN-ANTHELME BRILLAT-SAVARIN

"wiper," which is actually a spatula that scrapes down the walls of the bowl and lid during processing. The wiper can be turned manually by rotating the handle in the top of the cover. The bottom line on the Robot Coupe food processors is that they are ruggedly built, work beautifully, and are perfect for high-volume needs. They are designed for commercial use and are the standard in restaurant kitchens. For personal needs, even if you entertain a great deal at home and cook for a crowd, a 14- to 20-cup noncommercial food processor will do the job.

The R2 Ultra is 16″ high and weighs 23 pounds. The feed chute assembly

---

ACCESSORIZING YOUR FOOD PROCESSOR

Food processors have a wide choice of optional slicing and shredding discs and other accessories that help fine-tune numerous food preparation tasks and minimize the effort.

Cuisinart For the 14-cup Pro Food Center Food Processor:
STANDARD DISC SET—thin slicing disc (2 millimeters), thick slicing disc (6 millimeters), fine shredding disc.
SPECIALTY DISC SET—fine-grater disc, French-fry-cut disc (6 by 6 millimeters), extra-thick slicing disc (8 millimeters).
ALSO AVAILABLE: fine square julienne disc (2 by 2 millimeter cross-section), medium square julienne disc (3 by 3 millimeter cross-section), ultrathin slicing disc (1 millimeter), medium slicing disc (3 millimeters), blade and disc holder.

KitchenAid For the 11-cup Professional 670 series:
FIVE DISC SET—shredding disc (6 millimeters), slicing disc (6 millimeters), French-fry cutter, julienne disc, Parmesan- and ice-grating disc.

is 13½" long. The motor is 850 watts, 7 amps. The BX3 is 16½" high and weighs 25 pounds. Its motor is 1200 watts, 10 amps. One-year limited warranty, parts and labor, on both models.

8.20 BLACK & DECKER POWER PRO

If all you'll ever use a food processor for is shredding cabbage for coleslaw or making cookie crumbs for a pie shell, there's no sense in buying a supercharged high-end model. Instead, buy a food processor like this one, which does most jobs well and is affordably priced. It comes with a knife blade for chopping and a reversible slicing-shredding disc that saves space but doesn't always give perfect results—when slicing carrot rounds, tiny chopped bits were left in the bowl. Still, it took on a tough job like processing Parmesan cheese with results equal to the premium models. This is a user-friendly food processor with a bowl and cover that are easy to handle, touch controls, a PULSE button, and "food fingers" to hold food upright in the feed tube. The bowl has a 6-cup capacity, which is adequate for most processing jobs. It also has an on indicator light and cord storage in the back of the base. In a pinch, the food pusher can double as a measuring cup.

BESSARA (FAVA BEAN PURÉE)

6 servings

Bessara is certainly inspired by the Middle East, where they make hummus, a purée of chickpeas, tahini, garlic, and lemon juice. This version is unique because spices are sprinkled on the bread, which is then dipped into the purée. Once you begin eating *bessara*, it is difficult to stop.

1⅓ cup (½ pound) dried fava or kidney beans
3 garlic cloves, minced
¼ cup extra-virgin olive oil
1½ teaspoons cumin
1 teaspoon paprika
¼ teaspoon cayenne
1 tablespoon chopped fresh parsley
2 tablespoons chopped fresh cilantro or coriander leaves
3 or 4 tablespoons lemon juice
1 scallion, white and green, minced
salt and freshly ground pepper

GARNISH
1 tablespoon extra-virgin olive oil
3 lemon wedges
2 tablespoons chopped scallions
1 tablespoon cumin
1 tablespoon paprika
1 small loaf rustic country-style bread

1 Pick over the fava or kidney beans and discard any stones. Cover with water and soak overnight. The next day, if you are using fava beans, remove the skins. Place the beans in a saucepan with enough water to cover by 2". Simmer, uncovered, until the fava beans are tender, 1 to 1½ hours. If kidney beans are substituted, simmer 1 to 1½ hours. Add additional water if necessary. Drain.

2 Place the beans, garlic, and olive oil in a food processor or blender and process until smooth. Remove and place in a bowl with the cumin, paprika, cayenne, parsley, cilantro, lemon juice, and scallions. Mix well and season with salt and pepper.

3 Place the purée on a serving platter and garnish with the olive oil, lemon wedges, and scallions. Serve the cumin and paprika in small bowls or on a separate plate.

4 To serve, sprinkle the bread liberally with cumin and paprika, and then dip the bread into the bean purée or spread with a knife.

From Tapas to Meze: First Courses from the Mediterranean Shores of Spain, France, Italy, Greece, Turkey, the Middle East, and North Africa, by Joanne Weir

Motor: 400 watts. Height: 13½"; weight: 5 pounds, 13½ ounces. One-year warranty.

8.21 CUISINART MINIPREP PROCESSOR

This little chopper looks like it was cloned from a large Cuisinart food processor. It has a 21-ounce capacity workbowl and is great for all those small food-preparation tasks like chopping an onion or a few cloves of garlic. It has high and low speeds for maximum control and a reversible stainless steel blade. The sharp edge is for chopping soft, fragile foods or making purées. The blunt edge is for chopping hard foods and grinding coffee beans or spices. The bowl can go in the dishwasher for cleaning, but the blade should be washed by hand.

Motor: 250 watts. Height: 8½"; weight: 2 pounds, ½ ounce. Eighteen-month limited warranty.

9

POTS & PANS

FROM THE DAWN OF CIVILIZATION, the basic food of mankind has been grain—whether rice kernels, hominy, cracked wheat, whole oats, barley, or millet. But to transform grain and other starches into energy-giving nourishment and palatable food, it must be cooked. Even the toughest raw meat or seafood can be chewed and digested without cooking, but many vegetable foods, especially fibrous roots and dried beans, require heat to become edible. In some cases, cooking is needed not only for digestibility but for safety. Manioc, or cassava, a staple in parts of Asia and South America, is not only indigestibly tough, but also toxic if eaten raw. And acorns, a basic food of Native Americans, are neither wholesome nor palatable unless they are leached and cooked.

The question that naturally follows is: How should these foods be cooked? Barbecuing and oven roasting, which predated stovetop cookery by millennia, do not work for grains, roots, and beans, which are best boiled in water. But it did not take long for innate human genius to come up with the notion of cooking in a container above a heat source, one of the most fundamental human inventions. Finding a satisfactory container, however—one that was waterproof, fireproof, and transmitted heat to its contents without spoiling them—was a challenge, and one that could not be met by a hollow gourd or animal bladder.

The most common primitive solution to the container problem was the earthenware pot. It was fire-

proof, relatively safe, and did not change the taste of the food cooked in it—but it was porous, until it was coated inside and/or out with plant gum that made the vessel waterproof enough to hold thick porridges or stews. Another problem with earthenware was that it did not (and still doesn't) transmit heat very efficiently. Any food cooked in it over the fire required long cooking with much stirring to prevent scorching and to distribute heat evenly.

How to transfer the heat from the fire to the food was a major problem in figuring out how to craft a container to cook food in. One simple answer was to place the pot on the ground next to the fire, which proved workable, but very slow. Another solution was to put the vessel directly into the hot coals or ashes, sometimes using specially shaped containers with pointed, conical bottoms. Other methods called for keeping the pot directly above the heat source; archeologists have identified sites, some tens of thousands of years old, where stacks of rocks surrounding the fire provided a simple stand. There is also evidence that early civilizations would hang a vessel from a tripod stand crafted of wooden poles and set into the ground, or even create containers with built-in legs.

In some places, the heating process was accelerated by dropping hot rocks into the stew. Among the Indian natives of California, even into the twentieth century, food was cooked in tightly woven basketry pots lined with pitch to make them watertight. Water and the food to be cooked—usually stone-ground acorn meal—were placed in the pot, and stones heated in the fire were added to keep the mush simmering.

By about 1500 B.C., the Chinese were firing a silica-based stoneware at high temperatures until the surface vitrified into a moisture-proof barrier. The Chinese also invented porcelain during the T'ang dynasty (A.D. 618–907). Porcelain is a finer type of stoneware with a white finish that lends itself to decorating. The first ornamented "chinaware" made its way to Europe in the seventeenth century. Today, we still speak of tableware as "china"; "porcelain" and "porcelain enamel" are terms often used for cookware.

Though earthenware and stoneware have their virtues, metal is the ideal choice for pots. It is virtually indestructible, can be heated indefinitely, and can be formed into a variety of sizes and shapes. Many metals also transmit heat rapidly and efficiently. Yet even after the developments that ushered in successive ages of bronze and iron, it took a long time for these valuable materials to be used for such mundane purposes as cookery, at least in Europe. Metals were simply too costly and, when available, were put to use for more urgently needed items: tools and weapons.

MY RESTAURANT STOVE
❧ JULIA CHILD ❧

Our first house was in Washington, D.C., where one of our dearest friends, known affectionately as Old Buffalo, was a passionate cook. Whenever you stopped in for a chat you might find long strands of pasta draped over the backs of dining-room chairs, or fat sausages curing as they hung from the rafters. He had the first restaurant stove I had ever seen in a private home. We had to have one, too.

This was back in 1946, and it cost $429. Now, more than fifty years later, I still have that same big old black six-burner restaurant stove, and it is just as good as it ever was. It is simply a wonderful piece of indestructible equipment. It has never needed repairs of any sort, and it is in constant use. Its burners are easy to regulate; its large, well-insulated oven will roast two turkeys, two prime ribs of beef or suckling pigs, or bake one small genoise cake.

I expect to take it with me to my grave eventually—if they can find one large enough for the both of us.

Eventually, however, metal cookware, mostly iron, became common throughout Europe. More costly brass and copper wares were put to everyday use by the European middle and upper classes. However, throughout the Mediterranean region and into Asia, thinner hammered copper and brass pots were the norm. When the colonists arrived in America, they brought plenty of cast-iron pots and pans with them. A short time later (in 1644) the settlers built their own forge—the Saugus Ironworks in Massachusetts. The site has been restored, and among the exhibits is the first object produced: appropriately, a cast-iron cooking pot. There was also a copper foundry in Lynn, Massachusetts, established possibly as early as 1664, which produced handcrafted brass and copper kettles. However, few Americans could afford such luxuries; they continued to make do with iron goods.

Whatever the metal used, as soon as one kind or another became the standard for cookware, a proliferation of sizes and shapes developed, all based on the abundant ancient-clay pot models. Our modern skillets and saucepans, *fait-touts,* and *bains-marie* still acknowledge our ancient ancestors' resourcefulness, at least in an etymological sense, when we speak of all such containers generically as "pots."

Just as cooking containers gradually developed into our contemporary pots and pans, so the heat sources used for cooking slowly evolved toward the modern range. In the process, the ancient Romans came up with a major improvement: they invented a rudimentary stove by enclosing the open hearth in clay, tile, or brick. The walled-in cooking space provided a more concentrated source of heat, could easily accommodate a cooking vessel, and was safer and warmer than an open fire. Over the next several centuries, stoves became popular throughout Europe, although most cooking still took place in an open hearth. The hearth was in the common room, which became the center of activity for the household because of the comforting warmth and light the fire provided. A bar was suspended across the top of the hearth to hold pots for cooking. This was later replaced by an iron crane fastened to a side wall of the fireplace. The cook would swing the free end of the crane out into the room, load it with pots, and then put the crane back into position over the fire.

Cooking vessels for fireplace cookery were almost always made of iron and included long-handled skillets, pots, and tea kettles, as well as vessels standing on three or four built-in legs that mimicked the styles of antiquity. They were placed directly on the hearth close to the fire and tended carefully, their position changed frequently so all sides of the pot came into contact with the heat. The pots and kettles had lids, and, instead of handles, some had a large loop or semicircle of wire attached to the top at opposite sides of the rim so the pot could be suspended. The fireplace remained the chief cooking quarters until the mid-1800s, when coal-burning ranges became available. In terms of human history, real stovetop cooking is a newcomer, one of scores of developments in food and cookery that became commonplace with the onset of the Industrial Revolution and, in America, especially after the Civil War.

How Heat Cooks

Heat changes foods in various ways. Cooking methods and utensils can be used in combination to apply particular types of heat to foods in order to obtain the desired result.

Conduction cooking occurs when heat passes through a solid substance in direct contact with the food. Materials that transmit heat easily are "good conductors." Many metals are good conductors, spreading heat evenly throughout a pot. Heat directed at the bottom of a copper saucepan, for example, will spread rapidly through the walls and cook the food inside. On the other hand, some metals are poor conductors; stainless steel, for example, allows the heat to pass straight through to the food from the heat source but does not spread it around the sides of the pot. Glass and ceramics, which absorb heat well, are poor conductors of it.

Convection cooking involves heat transfer through liquids or gases. As fluids reach higher temperatures, they decrease in weight or density. When you cook stew, for example, the portion of the liquid nearest the heat source reaches a higher temperature first and becomes lighter. The cooler, heavier portions of liquid above it sink to displace the lighter, heated portion, which then rises. This process creates a continual flow of warmed liquid upward and cooler liquid downward; heat is transferred to all portions of the food. When ingredients cook in or over a very small amount of liquid, the fluid becomes steam. The hot steam circulates in currents throughout the closed kettle, heating the food. This natural rotation of currents is the principle behind convection ovens, which have fans that circulate the hot air around the ingredients and help speed up the cooking process (accomplished with radiant heat from the oven walls).

Radiation cooking uses electromagnetic waves to transfer heat and, unlike conduction or convection cooking, does not require direct contact with the food—using hot coals or an oven broiler to cook a steak are examples of this process. *Infrared radiation,* the type used in microwave cooking, heats by means of an electric or ceramic element that emits electromagnetic waves. The waves agitate water molecules inside the food, creating heat and friction (once the water molecules start to move, the ingredients cook by conduction or convection).

Induction cooking is relatively new in the home. It's a technique that operates by means of a magnetic exchange between a coil placed below a flat, ceramic cooktop, and a specially designed iron or other magnetic pot that sits on top. The coil produces a magnetic current that heats the pot and transfers that heat to the ingredients by conduction. The cooktop surface, which may be metal or glass, remains cool.

Virtually all stovetop cookery involves both conduction and convection. Before you choose which pots to buy, it is important to know what the cookware's ability is to transfer heat from the external source to the food inside. Different ingredients and cooking methods have different heat requirements, so it pays to use cookware made of materials that are suitable for specific cooking purposes.

Heat transfer is a significant factor in the types of handles used on cookware. Heat slows down when it goes from one material to another. For this reason, metal handles are usually made of a different material than the pot metal—brass or iron handles will be used on copper pots, for example. Hollowing the metal helps to cut down on heat, which is why some pots and pans have tubular or carved-out handles. Heat doesn't penetrate plastic or wooden handles, so these stay coolest. However, the degree of coolness is not the only point to consider: metal handles may get hot, but they are oven and broiler safe at any temperature, which makes them versatile, whereas phenolic (a plastic that can generally withstand oven temperatures up to 450°F) is not safe for use under the broiler and wooden handles can be used only at moderate oven temperatures, if at all.

Handles are attached to pots in several ways. Riveted metal handles are the most secure and offer still another metal to slow heat transfer. (On the other hand, the rivets are dirt catchers, so you must clean them more carefully.) Some handles are screwed on, but be aware that screws can loosen and become dangerous in the case of flimsy cookware, although superior brands have a good track record. We are also not great fans of spot-welding the handle to the pot because it too has a tendency to loosen.

The Making of a Pot

Today, pottery, stone, and glassware in various forms are still used for specific pieces—like bean pots, pizza stones, casseroles, and griddles—but most of our cooking vessels are metal. There are two regularly used methods for shaping metal utensils: casting and drawing.

In *casting,* molten metal (usually iron or aluminum) is poured into a mold. If there is to be a handle shank, it will be cast in one piece with the pot. After the metal cools and sets, the shaped utensil is removed from the mold, and any surface irregularities are removed by grinding. The utensil is then polished or additional finishes, if any, are applied. A finish or high polish can be important because cast metals are somewhat porous and may contain impurities arising in the casting process that would create a tendency for the surface to pit. If you buy cast-iron pots that have no applied finish (like a nonstick surface), you must season the pan before you first use it.

The manufacture of *drawn* utensils involves a series of two or more stamping (shaping) operations, during which the metal is stretched and formed. The rough shape of the object is cut out of the metal sheet or blank by a machine that acts like an enormous cookie cutter. Brittle metals cannot be stamped or drawn easily because they break, rather than bend and stretch. Such metals must first be heated to improve their tensile strength and flexibility. One of the benefits of using drawn metals is that when they cool, they hold their shape, unlike cast metals, which tend to shrink back or return to their original shape.

Metal utensils may also be formed by *forging,* a method common in North Africa and the Indian subcontinent (where human labor is less costly than technological improvements) but rare in the United States and Europe. Forging involves hammering metal when it is red-hot, as is done with iron, or simply by cold-beating and hammering softer metals like copper and brass.

Welding is an operation used to join two metals. Years ago this technique was done by hand, much like forging—either by hammering together hot hard metals (such as iron) or cold-hammering softer ones (such as silver and gold). Today, welding is usually done with electricity. Sheets of two different metals are pressed together and an electric current is passed through them under pressure, bonding or fusing the metals. This is the way some multilayered pot bottoms are constructed (see "Sandwiches and Other Combinations," below).

All metals expand or contract, or become distorted to some degree, with changes in temperature. This fact becomes important in the design of the bottom of a pot. Single-metal steel or aluminum pot bottoms that are completely flat can become misshapen. The metal expands with heat, causing the center to rise up in a hump—you find that cooking oil or other liquids sit in a ring around the sides of the pot, while the food sits high and dry on a hot spot. Good cookware of a single-metal type is made with a concave bottom so that when heated, it will become flat. Pots made with aluminum as one of two or more layers in their "sandwich" bottoms maintain a perfectly flat plane.

The Stuff of Which Pots & Pans Are Made

There is no such thing as the perfect metal for cookware. Each has its benefits and drawbacks. To choose the best pots for individual requirements, it is important for you to consider the qualities of the metals used to manufacture them.

Iron & Steel

Until the twentieth century, the most common metal for pots and pans in the Western world was iron. Although it is one of the most plentiful elements on earth, iron is nearly always found in ores, combined with other elements. About four thousand years ago people learned how to refine the metal from its ore under very high heat. Molten iron can be poured and cast in a mold, and for centuries this was how pots were made; in some cases, pots are still made this way.

Cast iron is a good conductor—absorbing heat slowly and evenly and retaining it well—and so is excellent

THE NICKEL
BEHIND STAINLESS STEEL

The carbon steel used in the manufacture of pots, pans, and cutlery can rust. It is turned into rust-resistant stainless steel by mixing it with two other metals—chromium and nickel. The quality of stainless steel is determined by the nickel content: the more nickel, the higher the quality. Nickel produces a lustrous, more durable rust-resistant finish.

Stainless steel is usually described in terms of the relationship of chromium to nickel. A pot made of 18/10 stainless steel contains 18 parts chromium and 10 parts nickel. All stainless steel has 18 parts chromium content but its percentage of nickel can vary from 0 to 8 to 10. For culinary purposes, 18/8 and 18/10 are the same. A pan's luster is the result of the finishing process. An 18/8 pan can have a better finish than an 18/10 pan, but an 18/0 pan will always be dull.

for frying and blackening foods and also for braising and stewing. It's less desirable for sauce-making because it does not respond rapidly to changes of temperature, and it isn't good for preparing foods made with reactive ingredients (acids and alkalis) because the metal gives them an "off" taste. Cast iron also rusts easily; it must be properly cared for, seasoned well, and dried thoroughly after being washed. In pots and kettles used for braising and stewing, cast iron is often coated with a hard enamel surface.

Steel is made by combining iron, carbon, and, occasionally, other elements. Steel pans transmit heat well and are useful for searing meats and for cooking foods, such as crepes, that you need to cook quickly over high heat. High-carbon steel is used for traditional woks because it also spreads heat rapidly and works best for high-heat, quickly cooked, classic Chinese stir-frys. Steel pans can corrode, so season them before first use.

Stainless steel was created in 1913 in Sheffield, England, whose steelworking tradition dates back to the Middle Ages. Harry Brearley, a metallurgist, was experimenting with various steel combinations for use in gun barrels. He discarded a number of unsuitable samples but after some months noticed that one of the discarded pieces was still bright and shiny. That discard was a steel containing 14 percent chromium: stainless steel. Brearley patented the combination as well as several others that contained additional elements such as nickel.

Stainless steel is "stainless" because a thin, usually invisible oxide forms on the surface. This film does not combine with any other element or compound and protects the metal underneath. Stainless steel has many virtues: nonporous, it does not pit; nonreactive, it does not combine with acids or alkalis; and it is completely nontoxic. These features give stainless steel great versatility—you can cook any ingredient inside it and the pan will not corrode or discolor or give the food a metallic taste. In addition, the high chromium content not only ensures that the metal will stay bright and shiny, but also gives it considerable tensile strength: this is one metal that resists denting and scratching. It is, of course, also dishwasher safe. This all makes stainless steel sound perfect. Unfortunately, the metal is a very poor conductor of heat. To be effective for cooking, it must be combined with better conductors such as copper or aluminum. The method by which these other metals are combined determines the heat effectiveness and quality of the cookware (see "Sandwiches and Other Combinations," below).

Copper

Copper, like iron, was one of the first metals known to man, and was probably the first to be smelted, or removed from its ore by heat. Despite its long history, it remained an expensive metal until American mines began producing it in quantity in the mid-nineteenth century. Copper cookware has always been favored by chefs and experienced home cooks because the metal is exceptionally responsive to heat. It is an outstanding conductor, spreading heat quickly and evenly through a pan. It also loses heat quickly when temperatures are lowered or the pan is removed from a burner. Recipes that require pots to make quick temperature changes—when a sauce reaches perfect consistency, for example—do best in copper cookware.

Yet copper has its problems. It reacts with moisture in the air to form a greenish film (verdigris) and with salt to form whitish spots (chloride), which you must clean scrupulously as they both can cause food cooked in copper pots to taste metallic. More important, copper

MY FANTASY KITCHEN
❧ CHRISTOPHER STYLER ❧

Brand-new technology shares pride of place with the eons-old in my fantasy kitchen. An open brick fireplace—high enough off the floor to double as a grill and wide enough to accommodate a baby lamb on a spit—sits side by side with a restaurant-width combi-oven. The range sports two large induction cooking hobs and several traditional but powerful 20,000-Btu gas burners. A large refrigerator holds the bulk of the perishables; a smaller one fits under the prep counter and is roomy enough to accommodate setup for dinner or a host of leftovers ready to be reconfigured into lunch.

Cookware runs the gamut, too, from sleek stainless steel sauté pans that heat instantly on the induction hobs to enameled cast-iron stew pots that go from stove to oven. I'll hang on to the jet-black flameproof clay casseroles I bought in Colombia and slow-cook casseroles and stews in them, nestled in the embers on the hearth.

Size matters in my fantasy kitchen. The actual prepara-tion and cooking area isn't colossal, but large enough for a big double sink and a third sink cut into the prep-work surface. There is a spacious butler's pantry for storing seldom-used cookware, platters, and equipment. Off to the side is a large dining table, a couple of floppy chairs, and a compact work station. Because I work as well as entertain from my kitchen, I'll need a wireless headset for making and receiving phone calls and wide-bandwidth-cable access to the Internet, which supplies instant answers to cooking questions, sources for ingredients, and inspiration. Halogen lighting, easily con-trolled from a touchpad located on the side of the cooking island, ranges from bright, eye-friendly levels needed for prep to a more intimate glow for dining. Silent exhaust fans keep the air fresh and haze at a minimum.

Above all, my fantasy kitchen is roomy enough for people to hang around out of the range of sputtering fat and wel-coming enough for them to want to do so.

---

is toxic, and tiny amounts can leach into food. Though the occasional use of pure copper (for sugar confection-ery, zabaglione, or whipping egg whites, for example) won't cause any harm, pure copper is not recommended for daily cooking. Copper pots and pans for regular cooking are always lined with tin, a zinc or nickel alloy, or stainless steel. (There are silver-lined copper pots, too, but they are woefully expensive.)

Aluminum

This element, which has revolutionized the manufac-ture of cooking utensils, was not isolated until the nineteenth century, although compounds had been known and used much earlier. It is the most abundant metal in the earth's crust, but it is found only in combi-nation ores, of which bauxite is the best known and most important. Bauxite is extremely stable, and it took great ingenuity to free large amounts of its alu-minum for commercial purposes. Minute quantities were isolated in 1825 by chemical procedures. At the time, aluminum was considered so precious and rare that honored guests at the court of Napoléon III dined with aluminum flatware, while other guests used ordi-nary gold and silver. About sixty years later, Charles Martin Hall, a young American, removed the element through an electrical process. The major problem he had to surmount in order to extract pure aluminum from its oxide is that the latter has the extremely high melting point of 3,632°F. After much trial and error, working in a woodshed behind his family home in Oberlin, Ohio, with equipment that, for the most part, he himself devised, he was finally successful. Using the current from homemade batteries and carbon-lined containers, and employing cryolite (sodium aluminum fluoride) as a flux to aid melting, he was able to reduce the melting temperature to a manageable 1,832°F and extract the aluminum from its oxide.

Though not as exceptional a conductor as copper, aluminum is remarkably good, spreading heat quickly, evenly, and dependably throughout a vessel. It browns foods well, so it is a good choice for braising and frying. It also holds heat, which is ideal for slow-cooking foods. Aluminum is light in weight, fairly strong, and becomes even harder and stronger when it is alloyed with such substances as magnesium, manganese, tita-nium, nickel, chromium, zinc, iron, and copper. There are many types of aluminum cookware available today, both cast and stamped and drawn.

As with other metals, aluminum has disadvantages too. One is that it reacts with certain ingredients—acids, alkalies, and the hydrogen sulfide in eggs—giving them a peculiar taste and color. Moreover, it corrodes, so the cookware can become pitted if you place acidic or salty items inside. Another unfortunate problem is that thin-gauge aluminum cookware, which is all too plentiful in the market, heats too quickly, creating hot spots that cause food to burn or cook unevenly.

Because aluminum conducts heat so well, cookware manufacturers have tried to correct its problems. One result is *anodized aluminum,* an industrial-looking aluminum-based cookware whose chemical structure has been changed by means of an electrochemical process. The process preserves the metal's heating ability and makes it noncorrosive. It also makes it extremely hard (the cookware is sometimes called "hard-anodized") and durable. As a bonus, the surface is non-reactive and "stick resistant," which means that less fat is needed for cooking. However, anodized aluminum isn't perfect. Although it does have the benefits of regular aluminum, its gray finish makes ingredients more difficult to see, which isn't ideal when preparing dishes that rely on color for their timing.

Coating Cookware

Coating cookware is one way to minimize metal's negative properties while enhancing its positive ones. Some coatings are thin top layers; others form a thicker, more integral part of the pot.

Tin is too soft to be used by itself for pots, but its virtues make it serviceable as a coating for other metals, particularly copper cookware and steel "tin" cans. The benefits of tin are that it is unaffected by moisture, is completely nontoxic, and does not corrode, rust, or pit. It becomes darkened by food acids, but this surface tarnish is actually protective and should not be removed. (The tarnish also helps absorb heat effectively.) Tin is very malleable and can be easily rolled, pressed, or hammered into extremely thin sheets or foil. Items are coated in one of three ways: dipping the base metal into molten tin, applying the tin by an electrolytic method, or spraying it onto the base. A layer only 1/10,000" thick is sufficient to prevent corrosion of the underlying metal. There are, however, a few drawbacks. Because tin is so soft, it wears out easily and is costly to replace. It can also buckle when exposed to high heat. Some cookware is tin-coated on both interior and exterior surfaces. While bakeware that is surrounded by ambient, moderate heat can be tin-coated, it is never practical to use an externally coated tin pan for a dish that must be cooked directly on the stovetop.

Silver is also soft, nontoxic, noncorroding, and nonreactive. A thin layer is applied by electroplating over other metals. It forms a tarnish that is easily removed by polishing. However, it is very seldom used for cooking utensils because it is so costly.

Porcelain-enamel coatings provide moderately thick, nonmetallic surfaces that protect good conducting metals such as cast iron and aluminum. The quality of enamelware depends on the ingredients in the glaze and the number of coats applied. Because it is produced in bright, beautiful colors, enamel cookware is very handsome—many people serve food right from the pan—but its worth goes beyond its visual appeal. Enamel does not interact with food, which gives it tremendous versatility, and it is easy to clean. Because the underlying metals hold heat well, this cookware becomes perfect for long-simmering stews, soups, tomato sauces, pot roasts, and casserole dishes that contain acidic ingredients that would not do as well in the plain metal. Naturally, there are some problems: sometimes the porcelain chips or cracks with extreme temperatures or rapid temperature changes, or if it isn't handled with care. It is subject to scratching by metal utensils and can develop hot spots if the pan contains insufficient liquid. The coating also interferes with heat conduction, so enamel cookware is not ideal for sautéing or browning.

In recent years, several manufacturers have produced copper and aluminum cookware with *stainless steel* linings. Although these cut down slightly on heat responsiveness, they have the advantage of providing stainless steel's durability and versatility.

Years ago, *nonstick* coatings were flimsy plastic surfaces that scratched or wore off quickly. The pans were cheaply made and had to be replaced often. Few good cooks used them. Over the years the coatings have so improved that today cooking authorities and even chefs in fine restaurants use nonstick cookware. As for home cooks, sales figures indicate that nonstick cookware outsells all other types.

All nonstick coatings offer "release" of ingredients—that is, the coating is treated to make the surface slippery, thus reducing the need for fats. But there are different kinds of nonstick surfaces, some slicker than others, some with less release but harder, more heat-retentive surfaces. Today, many cooks rely on this kind of cookware with some fat, not only to prevent the kind of sticking that might occur when pan-frying potatoes, searing meats, or preparing a risotto, but to add flavor.

The quality of nonstick cookware depends on several factors, including the quality of the underlying pan, the quality of the coating (all variations of a plastic known as "PTFE"), and the way it is applied. Many inexpensive nonstick pots and pans begin with thin-gauge aluminum; they don't cook evenly, develop hot spots, and usually come with poor-quality nonstick coatings. Thick-gauge pressure-cast aluminum, hard-anodized aluminum, and high quality stainless steel pans are superior for nonstick cookware, and better brands also come with premium-quality nonstick coatings.

There is no denying the advantages of nonstick pots and pans: less or no fat is needed for cooking, and cleanup, even of sticky foods, is easy. They are perfect for steaming foods, frying eggs, cooking cereal and rice, and all low-fat recipes. Of course, like all other cookware, they have disadvantages. The nonstick coating reduces the surface heat, so foods don't brown as well as they do in regular pans. Nonstick cookware should be washed by hand, and most manufacturers advise against using metal utensils, which can scratch and injure the coating. There are some types of nonstick coating with harder finishes that stand up to metal utensils, but these tend to be less "slick" and require the use of more cooking fat.

Sandwiches & Other Combinations

Sandwich bottoms were invented to take advantage of stainless steel's exceptional qualities—durability, non-reactivity, beauty, and so on—and make up for its poor heating ability by adding a layer of a good conducting metal like aluminum or copper to the bottom of the pan. The process (known as cladding) involves bonding one layer of metal to another. It makes a huge difference, but only if the sandwich is thick enough to add real conductivity. Thinly clad bottoms don't heat well and can make cooking in stainless steel a slow and frustrating chore. The sandwich must also be wide enough to go beyond the flat bottom; otherwise the corners of the pan will be exposed to the heat and develop into hot spots. Even so, because the conductive metal is only on the bottom or, at most, extends a bit up the side, heat does not diffuse well into the pot walls. Heat is not lost rapidly enough by these pans for use in situations where great sensitivity is required.

Some manufacturers, capitalizing on copper's deserved reputation as the cookware metal of choice for many professionals and serious amateurs, include a layer of copper in the sandwich. Unfortunately, it is often thin; outside layers can be just for show. Check before you buy or you'll wind up with a cleaning chore that won't improve your cooking.

Cladding took on new meaning for cookware when manufacturers decided to "sandwich" an entire pan, not just its bottom, by coating highly conductive aluminum or copper pots inside and out with stainless steel, or by lining the inside with stainless steel and the outside with hard-anodized aluminum, copper, or brushed aluminum. These "tri-ply" and "five-ply" pots and pans function with great efficiency, like their core metals, but have stainless steel's versatility. They have satisfying heft, and their outside surfaces are beautiful. This cookware may not have the heat responsiveness of tin-lined copper, but it is difficult to find other negatives. It is expensive but is also designed to give a lifetime of cooking pleasure.

HOME ON THE RANGE
❧ FRED E. CARL JR. ❧

During the late 1970s, I noticed increasing interest in using commercial ranges in residential kitchens. As a fourth-generation homebuilder and developer of custom kitchens, I had many clients requesting restaurant ranges, but I felt that they were totally impractical and dangerous for use in the home. Research confirmed this to be true. Commercial ranges often don't meet building codes for residential installation because of their high heat output, lack of safety features, and excessive energy consumption.

When we were building our own home in 1980, my wife, Margaret, wanted a heavy-duty classic, a restaurant-style range like the Chambers her mother had owned since the mid-1940s. Since the Chambers range was no longer in production, and the commercial products had so many disadvantages, I kept wondering why no one provided an alternative. In 1981, I decided to see what I could do.

The design, engineering, and certification process went on for more than five years because of the tremendous number of refinements and modifications needed. Viking was the first range of its type.

The Care & Cleaning of Cooking Vessels

Good cookware will last you a lifetime if you care for it properly. You should clean pots with mild soap and water, using a sponge or a nylon scrubber or other nonabrasive pad. Don't use strong abrasive cleansers. You can use steel-wool pads to remove crusted-on food, but it is better to let the crust soften with an overnight soak in baking soda and water. Nonstick pans should not require special cleanup, but if foods stick, let these pots soak as well.

Here is a brief care and maintenance guide for specific cookware materials: Iron pans can rust, and the best measures to cope with this are preventive. Season new iron pots before the first use. After washing an iron pan, wipe it immediately and thoroughly so as to prevent rusting. If necessary, turn the pot upside down over a low-burning stove flame to dry it. If you live in a humid seaside climate, cover iron cookware with plastic wrap to avoid pitting by the salty sea air. Should an iron pan rust, use soap and an abrasive pad or commercial rust removers, which are available at hardware stores and marine suppliers; then reseason the pot.

Stainless steel is so maintenance-free that a nonabrasive pad and mild soap should suffice for cleaning. It is also dishwasher safe. Steel-wool pads will scratch a pan's glossy finish but will not affect its performance. Occasionally, if they have been subjected to extreme or repeated overheating, some stainless steel pots develop a blue-gray or brownish tinge from surface oxidation. If this happens, try removing the color with special stainless steel cleaner.

To clean copper, use a specially formulated copper polish. Some are strong enough to strip the metal of its patina and may change its color. Though some people like copper to look newly minted forever, others prefer the warm, mellow look that comes with age. To keep copper softer and more mature looking, clean it with a mixture of coarse (kosher) salt and either lemon juice or vinegar.

Mild detergent and warm water work best for cleaning tin. If necessary, soak tin-lined pans overnight. You should avoid heavy-duty scouring: it will remove the metal.

For silvered presentation pans, snail dishes, and the like, use commercial silver polishes; then wash the item in mild, sudsy water; rinse; and wipe dry.

Aluminum becomes darkened by the alkalies found in some foods and by hard water. Wash it with mild soaps rather than strong alkaline ones, or use a special aluminum cleaner. Discolorations on the inside of the pan can also be removed by filling it with a solution of cream of tartar and water and simmering the mixture a few minutes. For anodized aluminum, use a nonabrasive pad and mild soap. For stubborn stains, make a paste of chlorine bleach powder and water. Rub it on the pan and let it sit for 10 to 15 minutes, then rub the pan with a nonabrasive pad, wash and rinse thoroughly, and let it dry. If food is stuck on, fill the pan with water then boil the water for a few minutes or use a specially made cleaner for anodized aluminum.

Clean porcelain-enamel cookware with a mild soap or detergent. Use baking soda for scouring; harsh powders will destroy the glaze. Soften cooked-on food by soaking the pan overnight in warm water mixed with some mild detergent or a small amount of baking soda. Use ordinary household bleach if necessary to remove stains, then wash and rinse the pan thoroughly.

Form & Function

The shape of a pot or a pan should have a direct relationship to function. Consider, for example, the way a low, wide pan encourages evaporation, as in the reduction of the sauce of a classical sauté, while a tall, narrow stockpot inhibits evaporation as the flavors of many ingredients blend into a broth. A fry pan used for quick searing in dry heat is most efficient when its sides are low, while higher sides are preferable for a braising pan used for long, slow cooking in fluids. Pans heat most efficiently when they fit directly over the burner. Oval pans can be used over two burners or under the broiler, but often are for presentation only—that is, they are not for cooking food, but for keeping it warm and for appearance at tableside.

Contemplate the virtues of different handle styles too. Rangetop pans will be moved, tilted, and otherwise handled, so the handles must be designed to make it easy for you to maneuver. Before purchasing a pot, lift it in the store to see whether the handle is comfortable. Understand that wood and plastic, which stay cool on the stovetop and can be more comfortable, can also be damaged if the pot is left askew over the flame, put under the broiler, or put in the oven at high temperatures. On the other hand, metal handles, which are broiler-proof, can become dangerously hot. In any case, it is always a good idea to keep a pot holder within easy reach.

Cover Story

Cookware lids serve several purposes. They keep bubbling contents from splashing out of the pot. They also control the speed of evaporation, the level of heat, and the amount of moisture within the pot. There is a wide range of variation in lid types, in the way they seal the pan closed or fit on top of it, and in the way the design has been adapted to function. Consider the edges of an earthenware casserole, which are left unglazed so the lid will not slide during cooking, or how the beads of water that collect on the underside of a domed glass lid preserve moisture in a pot roast. Some lids create tight seals with a pan, to preserve the maximum amount of moisture, while others have vents that allow steam to escape. Still others are designed with colander-like straining holes for pouring out water.

Suiting the Pot to the Cook

The goal of cooking is to make delicious food. It needn't be fancy or elaborate, and the simplest recipes can be brilliant. When recipes fail, too many home cooks blame themselves unnecessarily: sometimes the fault has to do with the pots and pans. It takes good cookware to be sure the recipe will come out right. Choosing pots and pans requires some hard thinking. It is a mistake to buy based on eye appeal, on advertising and marketing, or, for that matter, on price. Most important are the real culinary needs of the household.

Your decisions should be informed by knowing what kind of food you are likely to prepare, understanding your lifestyle, and considering the constraints of your kitchen. If you are going to make your own stock on a regular basis, then a high-quality pot is in order, but if you always use canned broth, a lighter, less expensive one will do. If most of your cooking is for two, you won't need a large sauté pan. Are you especially fond of casseroles or tomato sauce? If so, you might want to buy an enamelware pot. And if stir-frys are your forte, you'll need a specially designed pan that works best for this kind of dish. Consider also whether cosmetic appeal is important and whether the cookware you choose must be dishwasher safe.

Whatever these personal considerations turn out to be, it makes good sense to buy the highest-quality cookware you can afford. As with all investments, it is value, not just price, that counts. Cheap pots and pans never save you money—hot spots spoil the dishes you cook, poor-conducting materials make cooking frustratingly slow, and poor design and inferior materials cause the cookware to deteriorate quickly. In the end, flimsy cookware always needs replacing, meaning that you'll save money by buying fewer but better-quality items the first time. These good pots and pans may be costly, but much of the high-end cookware is durable, high-quality equipment, designed for a lifetime of service. Fortunately, the cookware market is so competitive that you can always take advantage of special sales and promotions.

About Electric Pots

Electric pots and skillets are useful in some instances, but they consume lots of electricity, and many of them take up valuable counterspace. They are also more difficult to clean than nonelectric pots. We do mention a few—electric griddles, woks, and slow-cookers, for example—but, given a choice, you are almost always better off using a good pot and the stove rather than an electrical appliance designed for a special and often limited use.

Do You Like Sets?

It's tempting to consider buying multipiece sets of cookware. There aren't so many decisions to make, and there can be unbelievable savings. But there are disadvantages too. For one thing, many contain pieces that are unnecessary or duplicate the function of one of the other pieces. Not many home cooks need three omelet pans in different sizes, for example. More important, all cooking experts agree that there is no culinary rationale for having matching pots and pans. In some kitchens it may be an aesthetic consideration, but no single kind of cookware does the best job for every kind of cooking. A well-equipped kitchen should capitalize on the best features of each kind of cookware, even if the pots and pans don't look alike.

One smart way to build a good collection of cookware is to begin with a small set of all-purpose pots and pans that are suitable for most cooking methods, five to eight pieces, including lids. After you buy the basics, supplement them with assorted pieces made of materials suitable for specific purposes—a wok or copper sauté pan, for example. Which pots and pans are basic? You'll find many opinions, even among experts, on this issue. Much depends on your cooking style, your lifestyle, the size of your family, the size of your kitchen, and so on. Generally, though, the most efficient kitchen includes pots and pans that give you the most use with the least equipment. Must-haves usually include: two saucepans, a 1½- to 2-quart and a 3-quart, with covers; one 7″ to 8″ slope-sided pan (which doubles as an omelet pan); and a 10″ to 12″ straight-sided sauté pan with a lid. The next items on the list might include: a soup or stockpot and lid; a 10″ nonstick frying pan (if you didn't choose nonstick for your basic set); a large enamelware casserole; a large, rounded pan such as a stir-fry pan, wok, or all-purpose *fait-tout* (chef's) pan; a double boiler; a 3½- to 5-quart Dutch oven or braising pan; a cast-iron skillet; and a copper sauté pan.

FRYING PANS

GRIDDLES, which are entirely flat (though some have a low rim), are designed to sear and cook foods quickly. This is the simplest kind of cooking. Fats and liquids are used in small quantities, if at all, and little or no *jus* (pan juice) is produced. Raise the sides of the griddle though, even slightly, and the pan can accommodate a more complex dish—one with a butter enrichment, or pan juices enhanced with wine or stock. After you sear an ingredient over high heat, more sophisticated dishes may require moderate temperatures to finish cooking. For this, you need a frying pan.

Some people call a frying pan a skillet. It makes no difference. What we are talking about is an all-purpose pan with moderately high, slightly flared sides. It is the one you reach for when you want to cook sausage and peppers, hash brown potatoes, or pork chops. We use the word *fry* in a general way, to mean all types of pan frying, as opposed to deep-fat frying, in which food is completely immersed in hot fat. You may also use a frying pan to sauté, which involves rapid cooking in a small amount of fat and, often, the addition of other ingredients to the pan—although a special sauté pan would be more appropriate.

The best frying pans are those made of metals that heat quickly and transmit the heat evenly. However, not every dish requires such precise responsiveness. An expensive copper pan, which cools down quickly, may not be necessary for fried veal chops or home-fried potatoes, which require stable heat. For these kinds of foods, the answer may be a cast-iron pan, such as the Lodge we recommend, because it holds its heat so well. A stainless steel pan with a wide, thick disc at the bottom (see the Farberware model we like) may be all that's necessary when preparing fried onions, mushrooms, and simple fish fillets.

Frying can be messy, so nonstick pans, which clean quickly and easily, can be a real advantage in the kitchen. There is another bonus too: you can significantly cut down the fat needed in a recipe because the surface "releases" food so well. However, only top-quality nonstick frying pans will do. While nonstick surfaces have improved greatly over the years, some are cheap and poorly made and should be avoided. Look for those that show evidence of coating durability. The manufacturer's leaflet may use descriptions such as *grit-blasting* or *arc spraying* to indicate the use of a sophisticated procedure to prepare the pan for the nonstick finish. Pans with several coats will also last longer than those with a thin, single application.

Because nonstick cuts down on the heat that reaches the food, it is particularly important to use a pan with a base metal that conducts heat very well; otherwise, anything you fry will be soggy and never develop the thin, crispy surface characteristic of nicely fried foods. The best choices are pans made with an aluminum core such as the KitchenAid and All-Clad models we show you, or heavy cast-aluminum products such as Berndes Tradition or Scanpan. Most nonstick pans are not dishwasher safe, and metal utensils should not be used with them. Still, nothing beats nonstick for frying eggs or grilling cheese sandwiches, and cleanup is a cinch, so "dishwasherability" should never be an issue. Most burners can accommodate frying pans of several sizes but the largest pan should have a base that's approximately the same circumference as your burner grid.

GRENADINS DE PORC NORMANDE
(PORK CHOPS WITH CREAM AND CALVADOS)

6 servings

6 individual loin pork chops, boned and tied, about 10 ounces each (The chops should be tied if the chop is composed of the loin and tenderloin. After it is boned it separates and should be secured with a string.)

1 package (12-ounce size) large pitted prunes

2 tablespoons sweet butter

1 teaspoon salt

1 teaspoon freshly ground white pepper

2 shallots or green onion bulbs, chopped (1 tablespoon)

2 tablespoons calvados (applejack)

½ cup chicken broth

1 cup heavy cream

1 tablespoon flour

juice of ½ lemon (about 1 tablespoon)

1 Place the prunes in a saucepan. Cover with cold water and bring to a boil. Take off the heat, cover, and allow to cool in the juices.

2 Melt 1 tablespoon of the butter in a large heavy skillet. (Be sure that the skillet is large enough to accommodate the six chops. If not, use two skillets. Be sure the meat cooks slowly or it will be tough and dry.) Sprinkle the chops on both sides with salt and pepper. Cook each chop 10 minutes on each side, on medium to high heat, then place on a warm platter. Keep warm in a 160°F oven.

3 Pour most of the fat from the pan, add the shallots, and cook 1 minute. Add the calvados and the chicken broth. Bring to a boil. Add the cream

and bring to a boil again. Cook for 1 minute. Mix the flour into the remaining butter to make a *beurre manié*. Add to the sauce, bit by bit, whipping hard with a wire whisk. Cook 5 to 6 minutes on low heat. Taste for seasoning and add salt and pepper if needed. Stir in the lemon juice, then strain through a fine sieve.

4 Place 2 prunes on top of each *grenadin* and arrange the remainder around the meat. Coat generously with the sauce and serve at once.

NOTE: If the sauce seems too thick, add a little more chicken broth to thin it. If it is too thin, reduce a few more minutes until it reaches the right consistency.

A French Chef Cooks at Home, by Jacques Pépin

9.1 LODGE CAST-IRON FRYING PAN

Great-grandma used this kind of pan for everything, and if you have a hankering for fried chicken, hash browns, and eggs sunnyside up with bacon, this is still the right pan to grab. Because it heats evenly and holds its heat superbly, it's tops for these and other foods that need quick searing followed by longer, lower heat cooking. We don't recommend it for subtle dishes: the metal can give an off taste and color to certain ingredients, and the pan doesn't cool down quickly enough for delicate sauces. It is heavy, but the handle is well designed to make it

maneuverable enough. It can also go into the oven or under a broiler to finish a fritatta, for example. It can rust, so be sure to dry it thoroughly after washing, and keep it well seasoned. This model has two lips for pouring off pan fat. A domed cover is available. We prefer the 10½" size, but you can buy several sizes, from a miniature 3" skillet to a large 15¼". Any of these should last a lifetime.

9.2 BOURGEAT COPPER FRY PAN WITH STAINLESS STEEL LINING

This beautiful pan's depth, flared sides, and rounded edges give it the

go-ahead as an omelet pan. But it is too expensive to limit it to a single purpose. It is also perfect for searing fillets of sole, chicken breasts, or veal scallops, even a boneless steak—especially if you will be making an accompanying pan sauce. The pan heats and cools down quickly. The thick cast-iron handle is long and high for easy maneuvering. It is sturdy and well riveted to the pan, which comes in two sizes, 9½" and 11".

9.3 DE BUYER COPPER FRY PAN WITH TIN LINING

The tin lining makes this pan fabulously responsive: it spreads heat quickly and evenly and cools down fast when temperatures are lowered or when it is removed from the burner. Everything browns perfectly: scallops of veal, sliced onions, boneless strip steak. When you finish sautéing, you can keep the food warm and make a quick sauce. The simplest way would be to deglaze the pan by adding wine or stock and then scraping the crispy bits and pieces and thickened natural fluids that have accumulated during sautéing. The thick, long, cast-iron handle, which is attached to the pan with three rivets, is helpful, comfortable, and sturdy. The pan comes in several sizes: 7⅞", 9½", 11", and 12½".

9.4 DE BUYER CARBON STEEL FRYING PAN

Carbon steel frying pans, which you'll find in many restaurant kitchens, are not part of the typical home cook's *batterie de cuisine*. Yet the metal picks up heat and distributes it so quickly that these pans are very effective for searing foods at rocket speed—a plus in any busy household. Small or thin foods, such as shrimp, fish fillets, or hanger steak, become beautifully browned but not overcooked. There's a caveat when buying carbon steel pans: cheap and inferior goods are apt to be thin and lightweight, causing them to warp and develop hot spots. The De Buyer model we show you is thick, heavy, and has a sturdy, riveted handle that stays cool. The sides flare, which is helpful when moving food around or flipping it in the pan. Because carbon steel can rust, be sure to dry the pan throughly after washing it and to keep it well

seasoned. De Buyer makes these frying pans in every size imaginable, from the smallest 2-pound, 7⅛"-diameter pan to the hefty 12½-pound, 19⅝"-diameter pan.

9.5 FARBERWARE MILLENNIUM STAINLESS STEEL COVERED FRENCH SKILLET

What a change there's been in Farberware! The old classic has been upgraded and the Millennium line offers especially good performance and value. This 12" pan is 18/10 stainless steel, and it gets its heat from a thick aluminum disc that covers the entire bottom of the pan, assuring even cooking without hot spots. Meats, fish, and vegetables develop a commendably crispy brown surface. The hollowed stainless steel handle stays relatively cool and is well riveted; there's also a helper handle on the opposite side. The pan comes with a gently domed stainless steel cover, so its usefulness goes beyond pan frying to braising and other types of moist-heat cooking.

9.6 KITCHENAID HI✳DENSITY HARD-ANODIZED CLAD SKILLET

Great-grandma may have used cast iron, but she probably would have loved this 12" pan, too. It is large, with a roomy bottom surface for optimum browning space. Although the pan is heavy, which promotes its cooking capabilities, the handle is

thick, large, comfortable, and snugly riveted to the pan. Along with the extra helper handle on the opposite side, you can easily move this skillet as needed. It has a five-ply aluminum core that disperses heat exceptionally well. Cutlets, chops, burgers, and everything else browned beautifully within its confines during our tests. It absorbs heat rapidly, though, so you might want to use a lower heat than you normally would. The stainless steel interior makes it versatile for any ingredients you want to cook. The pan is also available in 8" and 10" sizes (without the helper handle) in both the company's stainless steel and hard-anodized lines; a nonstick coating is also available.

9.7 ALL-CLAD STAINLESS STEEL NONSTICK SKILLET

Nonstick skillets have some obvious benefits: they require little or no cooking fat and they clean easily. However, because the surface cuts down on heat transfer, it is crucial to use a fry pan with a thick, heat-diffusing base metal; otherwise your ingredients won't brown well. The nonstick surface should have several coats, applied well, and should resist peeling and scratching. This wonderful pan meets all our criteria. The underlying material is stainless steel with a thick aluminum core of three layers, which heats well and provides good browning. The handle is riveted securely to the pan. Its arc-sprayed Excalibur surface is of premium quality, with excellent release ability. The 10" size is useful for a variety of fried foods, even a large omelet. Other sizes are 7", 8", and 12".

9.8 SCANPAN CAST ALUMINUM NONSTICK FRYPAN

The company that manufactures this pan uses a proprietary nonstick application process that involves firing molten ceramic-titanium to an aluminum pan at double the speed of sound. The result is a solid pan whose nonstick surface is guaranteed for a lifetime. Its release ability is not as good as most nonstick pans, and it doesn't clean as well—perhaps stick resistant would be a better term. However, the alloy heats better than all other nonstick surfaces, and there is an extra aluminum bottom disc, so foods are nicely browned in this pan. The handle is terrific: it offers a comfortable grip and is made of cool-touch phenolic resin, a plastic formulated especially for Scanpan that can withstand oven temperatures up to 500°F. The size we like is 10¼", but it is also available in 8", 9¼", 11", and 12¼" sizes.

9.9 BERNDES TRADITION SKILLET

Looks can be deceiving. This gray pan appears as if it is going to be heavy, but it is light and easy to maneuver. The thick wooden handle provides a very comfortable grip and will stay cool during use. Despite its light weight, the pan has the thick base needed for proper frying; the walls are appropriately thinner. Because it is made from a cast-aluminum base, there is good heat conduction, sufficient to brown foods well, even with the DuPont nonstick coating. While your foods may not get the richly dark surface they might in a traditional frying pan, and you might not derive as many browned "bits and pieces" to flavor gravy, the tradeoff is its easy cleanup. This is a fine pan for fish, burgers, eggs, chicken breasts, and just about any food you want to fry. High domed glass lids are available. The skillet comes in five sizes: 8", 9", 10¼", 11", and 13".

ELECTRIC SKILLETS

Though electric skillets were once all the rage, their popularity has long since died down; they can't replace a conventional fry pan. Because they heat up and cool down slowly and can't be shaken during use, you don't have control over the cooking process when you're sautéing mushrooms, for example, or deglazing pan juices. Nonetheless, electric skillets can be trusted to maintain a steady heat and are a great convenience when space on the rangetop is limited. Today's best models have detachable heat controls, so the pan itself is completely immersible and can even be cleaned in the dishwasher. Eject buttons on the controls make them easier to remove. Other desirable features to look for are a nonstick finish, a lid that can rest on the base when you need to tend to the food, legs that keep it off the countertop to prevent heat damage, and handles that remain cool to the touch. The value of adjustable vents in the cover is minimal. On all the models we tested, steam escaped between the skillet and the lid.

9.10 FARBERWARE SKILLET WITH DOME COVER

This is the one to choose if you plan to use an electric skillet for formal entertaining. Made of stainless steel, it's exceptionally attractive and would look beautiful on a buffet table. The plastic base doesn't detract from its appearance and stays cool to protect your table. However, we have to admit that its lack of a nonstick interior finish makes it difficult to clean, and we'd be reluctant to bring it out for family meals or even informal get-togethers. Thanks to an aluminum-clad bottom it browns very evenly, but because it has high wattage (1,400) it can begin to burn quickly. It also preheats faster than other models. With a 4-quart capacity and a 12" cooking surface, it measures 15" by 16" with the control in place and stands 9½" tall when covered.

9.11 BLACK & DECKER DEEP DUTCH SKILLET

Because it's 3¼" deep and holds 5½ quarts, this 12"-square skillet can be used for soups, stews, or even deep-frying. Made of cast aluminum, it holds and distributes heat well so it will brown your beef cubes evenly then simmer them in a stew steadily. Expect it to take about 5 minutes to come up to temperature for brown-ing. When you need to stir or turn foods, you can rest the vented lid on the skillet. The plastic base and handles stay cool, there's an eject button in the thermostat, and the nonstick pan as well as the plastic lid can go in the dishwasher. Our only complaint is that the temperatures on the thermostat are printed in small type, making them hard to distinguish. This model takes up 19" by 16" of countertop space, and with the lid on it is 7" tall.

PRESENTATION PANS & OTHER OVALS

Pans are usually round so they can fit precisely on top of a burner. This, however, isn't the ideal shape for many foods. Ingredients such as shell steak and fish fillets clearly fit better in an oval pan than in a round one, and ovals also make sense for cooking—you can cook in them over two burners or place them under a broiler for a few moments to crisp the surfaces of pan-fried foods. With smaller ovals, one burner will do if the heat diffusion in the pan is good enough to spread heat to the ends that don't sit directly over the cooktop. They have another virtue: their graceful lines make them useful as platters for tableside appearance. In fact, many are used as flambé or presentation pans; if so, the food can be cooked in another pan and transferred to the oval either for reheating or for finishing with a sauce, then presented at tableside. All this means is that most oval pans should be at least as attractive as they are sturdy. Our recommendations include three functional but attractive pieces of cookware suitable for tableside service.

9.12 BOURGEAT COPPER OVAL PAN

This beauty is more than a presentation pan. The copper transmits heat so well that even those parts of the pan that don't sit directly above the heat get sufficiently hot for cooking. The stainless steel lining is a bonus too. Not only is it easy to clean, it is appropriate for any kind of sauce, since the metal won't react with any ingredient. The handle is cast iron, securely riveted, and heavy enough to balance the length of the pan. It is also deep, with sloping sides and lovely, curved edges that give it an elegant finish befitting an upscale pan. The 14½" length is suitable for sautéing fish fillets, a couple of steaks, or several chicken breast halves. Cook in it, serve in it; this pan is versatile and attractive, too.

9.13 CALPHALON PROFESSIONAL HARD-ANODIZED OVAL SAUTÉ PAN

This doesn't have the elegance of the copper pan, and yet for casual dinners it is pretty enough to present at the table. It is very functional; the 12" length means you can use it for whole fish, fish fillets, or other long ingredients, or to cook several fish steaks or individual pieces of poultry or meat at a time. Anodized aluminum responds to heat well, so foods can be nicely browned, then finished at lower temperatures. Watch out for the handle on this one: it tends to get hot, so be sure to use a pot holder or mitt.

9.14 ALL-CLAD LTD OVAL PAN

Another good pan—again, not quite as beautiful as the copper model, but pretty enough to use as a serving utensil, and its versatility can't be beat. The aluminum core transmits heat to all parts of the pan efficiently, and the stainless steel lining makes it appropriate for cooking any ingredient. The handle is nicely riveted, provides good balance, and stays cool. The manufacturer calls it an oval omelet pan, and you could certainly cook eggs or omelets in it, but many long foods such as individual steaks or chops or stuffed crepes nestled together all fit nicely inside this 12" pan.

I feel now that gastronomical perfection can be reached in these combinations: one person dining alone, usually upon a couch or a hillside; two people, of no matter what sex or age, dining in a good restaurant; six people, of no matter what sex or age, dining in a good home.
—M. F. K. FISHER

WHAT'S WHAT IN COOKWARE

Three of the major manufacturers of pots and pans produce numerous lines. Following is a chart describing the construction of the individual subbrands.

ALL-CLAD

NOTE: The riveted handles and lids in all the lines are made of 18/10 stainless steel.

LTD LINE

Dark anodized-aluminum exterior; 18/10 stainless steel interior cooking surface; three layers of aluminum sandwiched between the two.

STAINLESS LINE

18/10 stainless steel exterior and interior cooking surface; three layers of aluminum sandwiched between the two.

COP-R-CHEF LINE

Copper exterior; 18/10 stainless interior cooking surface; three layers of aluminum sandwiched between the two.

MASTER CHEF LINE

Brushed aluminum alloy exterior; 18/10 stainless steel interior cooking surface; three layers of aluminum sandwiched between the two.

NONSTICK LINE

Choice of stainless steel, LTD, or brushed aluminum alloy exterior; 18/10 stainless steel and Excalibur nonstick coating interior cooking surface; three layers of aluminum sandwiched between the two.

CALPHALON

COMMERCIAL HARD-ANODIZED LINE

Heavy-gauge hard-anodized aluminum with textured cast stainless steel Cool-V handles and a hard-anodized aluminum lid with Cool-V handle.

COMMERCIAL STAINLESS LINE

Heavy-gauge hard-anodized aluminum exterior; satin-finish 18/10 stainless steel interior cooking surface; cast stainless steel Cool-V handle; tempered glass lid with 18/10 flared stainless steel rim.

PROFESSIONAL HARD-ANODIZED LINE

Heavy-gauge hard-anodized aluminum; nickel-chrome-plated cast-iron handle; and hard-anodized aluminum lid.

COMMERCIAL NONSTICK LINE

Heavy-gauge hard-anodized exterior with nonstick interior and polished cast stainless steel Cool-V handles; domed stainless steel lid.

PROFESSIONAL NONSTICK II LINE

Heavy-gauge hard-anodized aluminum with nonstick interior; handles are satin-finish rolled stainless steel; domed tempered-glass lids with stainless rims.

POTS & PANS LINE

Medium-gauge hard-anodized aluminum with raised-dot-textured nonstick interior; phenolic handles molded to stainless steel shafts.

KITCHENAID

NOTE: The handles in all the lines are made of cast 18/10 stainless steel; the lids are stainless steel.

FIVE-PLY 18/10 STAINLESS STEEL CLAD LINE

18/10 stainless steel exterior and interior cooking surface; three layers of aluminum sandwiched between the two.

HI*DENSITY HARD-ANODIZED CLAD LINE

Hi*Density hard-anodized aluminum (with a high-gloss exterior); 18/10 stainless steel interior cooking surface.

HI*DENSITY HARD-ANODIZED NONSTICK LINE

High-gloss hard-anodized exterior; Dupont Autograph Nonstick coating on the interior cooking surface.

HARD-ANODIZED LINE

Traditional hard-anodized aluminum interior and exterior.

CREPE PANS

MOST PEOPLE DON'T THINK OF crepes as a convenience food. But can you think of another dish so handy, so versatile, and so universally appealing? With a stack of crepes, you can fix a quick entrée by stuffing the delicate pancakes with chicken or seafood, or you can flaunt your flambéing skills with folded dessert pancakes bathed in sizzling, orange-flavored brandy. If all this is too theatrical for you, simply roll the crepes around a filling of applesauce or ice cream or top them with chocolate sauce or cut-up strawberries and whipped cream. Crepes can be the stuff of humble, make-ahead dinners, or the fixings for the most elegant repast. All you have to do is set aside the initial hour or so it takes to make them.

You need a good pan, of course. Although any skillet with sloping sides will do, as long as the pan is made of good heat-conducting materials, a seasoned, French crepe pan makes the task much easier. Classic French crepe pans are heavy and made of materials that absorb, distribute, and retain heat well—typically iron, carbon steel, or aluminum. Smaller-width pans are suitable for dessert crepes, the larger ones for entrée crepes.

Basic crepe batter combines flour, eggs, milk, and cooled, melted butter into a batter as thin as whipping cream. You must be careful not to overmix, because the gluten in the flour will become too active and your crepes will come out tough and rubbery. A wooden spoon, mixing bowl, and strainer are the ideal tools for making crepe batter. Use the smallest amount of butter possible, just enough to create a film of "nonstick" on the surface of the pan (a pastry brush and melted butter come in handy here). Apply more butter only if the crepes stick to the pan. Pour in the minimum amount of batter needed to cover the surface of the pan (about 2 tablespoons in a 7″ pan), and tilt the pan quickly to spread the batter evenly. It takes some practice, but the result will be delicate, tissue-thin crepes. Crepes take about 20 seconds to cook on one side, 10 seconds for the other side. You can turn them by flipping the pan or by using a spatula or your fingers. As they finish, cooked crepes should be stacked between sheets of waxed paper or aluminum foil.

To serve crepes, you may use another type of crepe pan, a more elegant one designed for presentation rather than cooking. For this, consider a beautiful pan that holds its heat and is comfortable and easy to manage, so you can perform your pyrotechnic skills more easily.

9.15 DE BUYER CARBON STEEL CREPE PAN

This pan is a classic and makes perfect, delicately crispy crepes. Made of a heavy-duty carbon steel that holds and distributes heat well, it is still light enough to make swirling the batter to evenly coat the bottom of the pan easy. Its long, flat iron handle is securely attached to the pan and stays cool, even though you are working over relatively high heat. The sides are nicely flared, which helps keep the crepes perfectly round, and the shallow depth allows for easy flipping. The size we show you is 7⅞″ in top diameter, which is a midsize pan suitable for main-course or dessert crepes. There are also 4¾″, 5½″, 6¼″, 7⅛″, 8⅝″, 9½″, and 10¼″ sizes available.

9.16 MAUVIEL CUPRINOX CREPE PAN

You wouldn't want to cook in this beauty, although you could—it is wide (9⅞″), deep, and the sides are slightly flared, making it perfect for preparing seafood crepes for dinner or one large apple pancake for breakfast. But its intended purpose is for serving more luxurious desserts. Its gleaming copper body and long, straight, riveted brass handle single this pan out as one to flaunt at a dinner party. (There's an oval cutout in the handle so you can hang the pan up to admire it in your kitchen.) Use this pan to finish your previously cooked crepes with sauce or to flambé them. The stainless steel lining will stand up to the high temperatures of blazing brandy. The pan is deep enough at 1″ to accommodate plenty of sauce for dessert. You'll make crepes more often if you own this piece of cookware! A larger (11⅞″) size is also available.

9.17 MAUVIEL OVAL FLAMBÉ PAN

This copper pan, lined with tin, is 12" long and 8" wide, large enough to flame a party-sized steak au poivre, a whole fish, or quail flambé. A bright brass handle, as comfortable to the touch as it is beautiful to the eye, extends from one of the ends, and there is a wide lip around the edge to support a lid (separately available). We recommend using an oblong rather than round brazier or burner under this weighty pan in order to ensure even heat distribution. The manufacturer suggests preheating the utensil before use—simply pass both long sides over the flame before setting it flat on the burner to warm. This is the quintessential flambé pan for kitchens that boast nothing but the best.

9.18 MAUVIEL ROUND FLAMBÉ PAN

If your brazier is round rather than rectangular, this flambé pan will be more satisfactory. Again, it is made of copper over tin, and—we repeat ourselves for a purpose—nothing is at once so beautiful and so durable as these pans. The handle, a twin to that of the preceding pan, is equally lovely to look at and delightful to hold. Use the 12" version of this pan for flambéing main courses or preparing desserts for a party; the smaller sizes are for making sauces or for smaller-sized flambéed dishes. Almost a full 2" deep, this pan is deep enough to hold your food plus sauce with no spillover.

OMELET PANS

IT IS A TRIBUTE TO the flavor and to the rich, creamy texture of a good omelet that this dish has survived both the anti-egg outcries of the cholesterol conscious and the frustrations of the many home cooks who try to prepare one. To the first point we can only say that eggs have solid, proven (and inexpensive) nutritional value and may not be as horrific for a moderate diet as once thought. Besides, classic recipes that call for three or four whole eggs may be breached by using a greater proportion of egg whites, and, of course, there are contemporary versions: all-white, no-yolk omelets.

As for those who believe there is some mystery to omelet-making, hear this: you will need a small amount of dexterity and some practice, but success is assured if you follow a few simple steps. First, the eggs must be absolutely fresh and preferably straight from the farm or from organically raised chickens; both have flavor that "industrial" eggs can't match. Two eggs are minimum for an omelet cooked in a 7" pan. The larger the diameter of the pan, the more eggs you will need.

To make an omelet, beat the eggs in a bowl while you heat a lump of butter in the pan over moderate heat. When the butter has melted and the foam begins to separate, pour in the beaten eggs and move the pan around with one hand while you move cooked portions gently from the edges toward the center, so uncooked portions can reach the surface of the pan. When the eggs thicken, lift the pan to a 45° angle and push the omelet away from you so that it falls over on itself. (If you find this intimidating, use a spatula!) Then roll the omelet out onto a plate. If you want a filled omelet, add the ingredients just before you lift the pan to flip the eggs. If you prefer a soufflé omelet, beat the whites separately and fold them into the yolks. Don't miss the opportunity to make an occasional dessert omelet. If this sounds strange, consider that the Romans, who invented omelets, intended the dish as dessert. They whipped the eggs with honey and served the cooked confection as a reward to soldiers returning home from battle.

Omelet pans used to be the pampered darlings of the kitchen: seasoned and left unwashed and unused except for their special purpose. The popularity of nonstick cookware changed all that and, truth to tell, any decent skillet can turn out a good omelet. By decent we mean a pan with some heft and heat conductivity and, of course, with sides sloped properly so you can flip the eggs and slide the omelet out of the pan easily. The pan should also have some depth so that the eggs can set at the bottom but stay moist on top. You can use either a regular or nonstick pan with a smooth surface. Then all you need is a good recipe, a hot fire, and quick hands.

9.19 ALL-CLAD NONSTICK OMELET PAN

This 7″ pan has all the makings of a fine omelet pan. The aluminum core and stainless steel exterior give the pan good weight (but it is not too heavy to maneuver) and assure that heat dispersion will be excellent, despite the nonstick surface. Omelets come out with the desired burnished skin. The pan has good depth, too, so the eggs stay moist and creamy in the center, even as the bottom surface sets. The nonstick coating, made of premium-quality Excalibur, helps in several ways. First, cleanup is a cinch. Next, you'll find you can use much less butter than the amount called for in standard recipes. Finally, the slickness will help you flip the eggs, one part of the omelet-making process that many home cooks find intimidating. The gently curved edges also aid in flipping and in easing the omelet out of the pan. This is the perfect size for a two-egg omelet.

9.20 CALPHALON COMMERCIAL HARD-ANODIZED OMELET PAN

This anodized aluminum 8″ pan heats up quickly and puts a beautiful golden seal on the omelet surface. Depth is good too, so the eggs do not overcook in the center. The riveted handle stays cool and is curved for comfort, which is a help when you flip the pan to turn the omelet over.

The pan's thoughtfully flared sides also make it easy to move the omelet. The material needs no seasoning before use, but the surface is stick resistant, which means you'll need more butter than you might in a nonstick pan, yet not quite as much as for a regular, old-fashioned omelet pan. The 8″ size is appropriate for two- to three-egg omelets.

9.21 FARBERWARE MILLENNIUM STAINLESS STEEL NONSTICK SKILLET

Another capable pan, this one is 8″ and made of 18/10 stainless steel with a thick aluminum disc at the bottom. The disc covers the entire bottom width and provides good, fast, and even heat. It is a deep pan, helpful to beginners trying to flip their first omelets, and also good for keeping eggs moist. The pan has a thick, comfortable, riveted handle, hollowed to stay cool. The DuPont SilverStone Professional nonstick coating is high quality and durable. Although the nonstick gives terrific "release" of ingredients and obviates the need for fats, you'll find that omelets are much tastier if you use a little butter.

9.22 ENDURANCE II TRIPLE-PLY OMELET PAN

This large 10″ pan is a good choice for making a four- to six-egg omelet. It has an aluminum core and a stainless steel exterior; the interior has a superb Excalibur nonstick coating. Heating is quick and even; the eggs set well and develop a lovely golden crust. The sides are nicely flared, to help you flip the omelet and ease it out of the pan for serving. The handle is also well designed; attached with two rivets, it is made of tubular stainless steel, which stays cool. It is long, too, which is comfortable and also helps with flipping.

9.23 JAPANESE *TAMAGO* PAN

This square frying pan is the traditional shape for the Japanese omelet, *tamago dashimaki.* Unlike our scrambled eggs or the French folded *omelette,* the Japanese omelet is a flaky, rolled egg dish cooked by folding successive layers of beaten egg mixed with *dashi* (soup stock) and soy sauce, one around the other. To make this egg package, pour just enough of the batter into an oiled *tamago-yaki nabe* (omelet pan), so that it coats the bottom of the pan lightly. Then, using chopsticks or a wooden spatula, roll up the set eggs and slide the roll to one end of the pan. Next add a touch more oil, pour in more egg batter, and roll the set eggs once again toward the end, enveloping the first roll. Repeat the process, sometimes enfolding a sheet of *nori* (dried seaweed) in each egg layer before it is rolled, to produce a spiraling black filling. Though most *tamago-yaki nabes* are now found in stick-resistant lightweight aluminum, we show you this traditional one made of tin-lined copper with a long wooden handle (9″ long) that is attached by a gold pin. The pan is 8½″ square, 1¼″ deep.

PAELLA PANS

ON SPAIN'S EASTERN COAST, where Mediterranean tides embrace the shore and the earth yields a bounty of rice and oranges, lies the city of Valencia, where paella was created. Some say the dish was the result of the loving tinkerings of a king who wanted to impress his sweetheart with a dish loaded with fresh vegetables and seafood from nearby Iberian waters, and seasoned with saffron, the world's costliest spice, plucked from crocuses that grew nearby. He called the dish *para ella*—"for her." But the more frequently told tale is that paella was named for the two-handled frying pan in which the dish is cooked and served. The word may derive from the Latin *patella,* a wide, flat dish known in Roman times.

The only ingredients needed for paella are vegetable oil, rice, and saffron, but contemporary versions are prepared chock-full of ingredients, from lobsters and shrimp to chorizo sausage, chicken, snails, quail, green beans, tomatoes, and more. Each region in Spain has its own adaptation; the common feature is the pan. A proper paella pan has a wide, flat bottom, so there is plenty of room for the rice to cook in a shallow layer, and two loop handles on the sides, which slope gently to the rim. Classic paella pans are made of carbon steel—but any heat conductive material will do—and usually don't have a lid.

Paella pans come in many widths; many are too big for a conventional cooktop. Classic paella is cooked outdoors over a fire. You can use an outdoor grill, or, to cook inside, straddle the pan over two burners. When it's done, the custom is to let it rest for 10 minutes, then serve the dish from the pan. Like fondue, paella is a dish that inspires conviviality. It's meant to be savored with friends.

9.24 DE BUYER CARBON STEEL PAELLA PAN

This is a classic paella pan: round, wide, shallow, and lidless. The shape lets the rice cook in a thin layer at the bottom, and flares out so you can stuff the dish with clams, chicken, sausage, lobster, or whatever else you choose. Carbon steel conducts the heat well for sautéing the onions and other vegetables. It can rust, however, so be sure to dry the pan well and keep it seasoned. Once the dish cooks initially on the stovetop, put it in the oven. When it's done, serve the paella straight from the pan. Two side loop handles will help you carry the loaded pan to the table. There are many sizes available, from small pans at 7⅛" diameter to large ones 19⅝" across. We chose an 11" size, large enough for dinner for four people.

9.25 BOURGEAT ALUMINUM NONSTICK PAELLA PAN

The 15⁷⁄₁₀"-wide pan can make an especially big paella with 2 or 3 cups of raw rice, chock-full of meats, seafood, and vegetables. It may be too large a pan for most stoves, though you can straddle it between two burners, but why not try it out on an outdoor barbecue? The beauty of this pan is its nonstick surface— hardly authentic, but it does make the cleanup a cinch. The surface doesn't get in the way of sautéing the ingredients properly either. The aluminum is a heavy enough gauge to provide ample heat transfer.

9.26 ALL-CLAD PAELLA PAN WITH DOMED LID

No, it isn't a classic, which might make some purists grimace, but this pan has a lot to commend it. At 13" long and holding 4 quarts, it is large, roomy, and deeper than most. It cooks well on a single burner. The stainless steel–coated aluminum core conducts heat well enough to every part of the pan. Chicken, shrimp, and chorizos sauté perfectly, and the rice has enough room to spread out. The lid comes in handy on occasions when you want to make the dish ahead of time and reheat it; it prevents the rice from drying out. The lid also makes the pan useful for braising and other moist-heat cooking. Together with the glossy stainless steel base, it makes a pan pretty enough for buffet parties.

PAELLA

❧ PENELOPE CASAS ❧

Paella was originally an inland dish prepared with ingredients from both land and sea. It was cooked at midday by field workers in Spain's Valencia region. It was commonly made over an open fire in a wide shallow pan with Valencia's characteristic short-grain rice, olive oil, and whatever other ingredients were at hand, typically fresh-picked vegetables, rabbit, free-range chicken, and land snails.

Rice reached Valencia in the eighth century by way of the invading Moors. In Valencia they found the perfect environment for rice production: moderate climate and vast areas of rich alluvial soil produced by aeons of silting from the rivers. The Moors developed an elaborate system of canals for irrigation that is still in use today, and the rice fields in spring and summer create a sea of green that stretches as far as the eye can see.

Today seafood paella is popular in Valencia, but the paella of meat and seafood—often found in America—is frowned upon by Valencians. In its homeland paella is eaten almost every day. Consequently, it is not one dish but hundreds, as varied as the cooks who prepare them. All paellas, however, rely on similar techniques; on the robust Mediterranean flavors of olive oil, garlic, tomatoes, and peppers; on paprika and saffron for seasoning; and on the paella pans in which they cook.

VALENCIA'S TRADITIONAL PAELLA (*PAELLA A LA VALENCIANA*)

6 to 8 servings

2 cups chicken broth, canned or homemade

4 cups water

6 sprigs rosemary or ½ teaspoon dried rosemary leaves
kosher or sea salt

¼ teaspoon crumbled thread saffron

half of a small chicken

half of a 2–2½ pound rabbit

7 tablespoons olive oil

2 medium green frying ("Italian") peppers or 1 green bell pepper, finely chopped

1 medium onion, finely chopped

8 cloves garlic, minced

2 medium tomatoes, finely chopped

2 tablespoons minced parsley

½ pound green beans, preferably broad flat beans, ends snapped off and cut in halves crosswise

½ pound snap or snow peas

4 cooked or frozen artichoke hearts, in quarters

1 teaspoon paprika, preferably Spanish smoked

3 cups imported Spanish or Arborio short-grain rice

Heat the broth, water, rosemary sprigs, salt, and saffron in a covered pot over the lowest heat for 20 minutes. Remove the rosemary sprigs.

Cut the chicken wing in two parts, discarding the tip. Hack off the bony end of the leg. Hack or cut with kitchen shears the rest of the chicken and the rabbit into 2" pieces. Sprinkle all over with salt. Put aside a few snap or snow peas for garnish. Keep the broth hot over the lowest heat on a back burner. Preheat the oven to 400°F for a gas oven, 450°F for an electric.

Heat the oil in a paella pan measuring 17" to 18" at its widest point (or in a shallow casserole of a similar size), placing over two burners if necessary. Sauté the chicken and rabbit over high heat until browned (it should not be fully cooked). Add the green pepper, onion, and garlic and cook until slightly softened, keeping the heat high. Stir in the green beans, snap peas, and artichokes and cook on high for about 3 minutes. Add the tomato and parsley, cook a minute, then mix in the paprika.

Stir in the rice and coat well with the pan mixture. Pour in all of the hot broth; bring to a boil. Taste for salt and continue to boil about 5 minutes, stirring and rotating the pan occasionally if over two burners, until the rice is no longer soupy but enough liquid remains to continue cooking the rice. Arrange the reserved snap or snow peas over the rice and transfer to the oven. Cook, uncovered, until the rice is almost al dente, about 10 to 12 minutes.

Remove to a warm spot, cover with foil, and let sit 5 to 10 minutes until the rice is cooked to taste. Return the paella to the stove over high heat, until a crust of rice forms at the bottom of the pan (be careful not to burn).

Paella!: Spectacular Rice Dishes from Spain, by Penelope Casas

PANS FOR SAUTÉING

WE BEGAN WITH the frying pan, one step removed from the griddle. Over millennia, as cooking developed into more complicated forms, pans with higher sides became necessary, and so the frying pan evolved in two directions. The first was for quick frying, resulting in pans that heat and cool off quickly and are easy to maneuver. The second kind of pan that emerged is for more prolonged cooking, either of ingredients that take time to cook through or of dishes that require some sauce-making component. In France, it is called a *sauteuse*—a sauté pan.

The French verb *sauter* means "to jump or to leap"—grasshoppers are *sauterelles*—and it's an amusing term that aptly describes the quick, vigorous motions of the cook moving a pan back and forth across the burner over high heat with the ingredients bouncing up and down inside. When sautéing, you cook the food in a small amount of fat and keep things in motion either by tossing or stirring the food or shaking the pan so the ingredients inside won't stick, scorch, or dry out. Picture what it looks like when the motions of your arm cause chunks of vegetables to pop out of the pan and then fall back into place or when you flip a fillet of fish onto the other side—this is sautéing. Sauté pans (in French, a *sauteuse* or *sautoir*) are wide, which gives the inner surface ample room to brown foods well; they are flat, which facilitates quick movement over the burner; and they have straight sides, which are helpful when preparing the pan sauces and embellishments that often accompany the sautéed ingredients.

9.27 MAUVIEL COPPER SAUTÉ PAN

This is the real McCoy. The thick copper exterior, tin lining, and sturdy handle (attached with three copper rivets) combine in a pan that performs perfectly. It heats quickly and cools down when needed; the 10″ diameter gives it room enough to sauté four large chicken breast halves or filet mignons at one time. Its 2¾″ depth provides ample space for sauce. It may be heavy for many home cooks without a helper loop opposite the long cast-iron handle, but the handle is thick and long, adequate to help you move the pan back and forth over the burner. The pan is available in sizes from 7¼″ (1⅜ quarts), to 11⅞″ (6 quarts), in diameter.

9.28 BOURGEAT COPPER *SAUTEUSE*

This elegant pan is as functional as it is pretty. Its graceful, rounded edges give it a soft, luxurious finish, and the shiny copper deepens to a dark, lustrous russet with use. Beauty aside, you will be able to use this pan forever. Unlike the tin linings of classic copper cookware, this pan's stainless steel lining will never wear out. Stainless steel is also noncorrosive and won't react with any ingredient. Yes, it cuts down on heat sensitivity, but only slightly—this pan heats quickly and evenly and cools down almost instantly when removed from the flame. The thick cast-iron handle is attached with three sturdy rivets and is in good balance with the pan.

The lid is slightly domed and sits deeply within the pan while its outer edge rests on the pan's edge. The pan comes in four sizes: 6¼″ (1¹⁄₁₀ quarts), 7¾″ (2 quarts), 9½″ (3⅓ quarts), and 11″ (5⅕ quarts) in diameter.

9.29 KITCHENAID FIVE-PLY STAINLESS STEEL CLAD SAUTÉ PAN WITH HELPER HANDLE

One of KitchenAid's first-rate pans, it, like the others, has three layers of aluminum, which provide excellent, steady, even heat. On the outside and inside surfaces are two layers of bright, shiny 18/10 stainless steel, which optimize the cooking capabilities: you can prepare any dish inside—chicken with balsamic vinegar, beef with red wine—and the pan won't corrode or make the food taste metallic. You can wash the pan in the

WHAT TO LOOK FOR

Material Because sautéing requires intense heat, the best sauté pans are made of heavy-gauge, highly conductive metal that transmits heat well without any spot burning. Copper is the most responsive. Its ability to take up heat rapidly, spread the heat evenly, and cool down quickly is superior to any other metal. Tin linings prevent copper, which is toxic, from leaching into the food, and they enhance the metal's outstanding capabilities. Stainless steel–lined copper is only slightly less heat responsive and has many compensating benefits: the metal won't react with foods, won't wear out, and is easy to clean and less expensive than other linings.

There are excellent sauté pans made of other metals. Aluminum transmits heat well, and it is lighter and less expensive than copper. However, the plain metal interacts with certain foods, affecting their taste and color. For that reason we prefer aluminum-core pans that are sandwiched with stainless steel or sandwiched with an inside layer of stainless and an outside layer of hard-anodized aluminum. Home cooks long ago accustomed themselves to the dark-gray commercial look of solid anodized aluminum—a metal that has been treated electrochemically and will rarely present a problem with acidic or alkaline ingredients. Visual preferences aside, this metal performs well, but bear in mind that sometimes it is difficult to see the color of sauces prepared within the pan.

Stainless steel pans can be suitable for sautéing if they are reinforced adequately with a heat-conducting disc at the bottom of the pan. By adequate we mean that the disc contains a thick layer of aluminum or copper, and that it is wide enough to spread heat completely on the bottom of the pan. Stainless steel pans that have a thin wash of aluminum or copper on the bottom won't heat satisfactorily and can make cooking a chore rather than a pleasure. Discs that don't cover the entire bottom surface often develop hot spots on the areas not protected by the disc.

Nonstick surfaces are less appropriate for sautéing because the materials from which they are made cut down on heat transfer from the base pan. Even in the highest-quality cookware, the responsiveness needed for a well-prepared sauté is lacking. This does not mean you can't prepare sautéed food in a nonstick pan; we simply prefer traditional cookware for this method.

Handles Because you move sauté pans constantly, a good handle is essential. The most comfortable ones are long and slant upward from the edge of the pan. Ergonomically designed handles that are thick, solid, and curved provide a perfect grip for a heavy pan. Most sauté pans have metal handles. Though these never stay absolutely cool (it is always wise to keep a potholder close at hand), they add versatility because they are broiler-proof. Still, some stay cooler than others; look for handles made of metals that are different than the pans (the second metal slows heat conduction). Another design that prevents a handle from becoming too hot is one made of metal that is hollowed or vented in some fashion. Wooden handles never get hot, but shouldn't go into the oven. Phenolic (high heat plastic) can withstand up to 450°F, but can't be placed under the broiler. Riveted handles tend to stay cooler than those that are welded to the pan. It is difficult to lift a heavy pan by a long handle; helper handles opposite the long handle are a real benefit.

Lids Lids are useful for sauté pans because sautéing is often only the first step in a recipe, to be followed by a period of covered cooking. Many of the lids that fit the pans we recommend can be purchased separately and will fit comfortably on either a saucepan or a sauté pan of the same line.

---

dishwasher. The riveted handle is particularly comfortable and well designed. It is long, thick, and curved upward, making it easy to maneuver the pan, which is heavy and would be cumbersome without such a sturdy handle. A helper handle on the opposite side is a bonus. The edges are smooth and rolled, giving a touch of grace and good taste to a remarkably competent pan. The lid is deep and well made. Two size sauté pans are available, a 5-quart and a 3-quart, in all four KitchenAid lines.

9.30 ALL-CLAD LTD SAUTÉ PAN

This is a superb sauté pan with an inner core of thick aluminum, a stainless steel cooking surface, and a lovely matte-finish hard-anodized exterior. Heat is fast, steady, and efficient. Chicken breasts, fish fillets, scallops, and the like brown crisply, quickly, and without scorching. The long hollowed-metal handle is attached to the pan with two rivets and stays relatively cool. There is also an accessory helper handle to help you move and lift the pan. The lid fits snugly inside the pan and has a high loop lifter. All-Clad also manufactures the pan in its other aluminum core lines: Stainless, Master Chef, and Cop-R-Chef, in 2-, 3-, and 5-quart sizes.

9.31 CALPHALON COMMERCIAL HARD-ANODIZED SAUTÉ PAN

This industrial-looking dark gray sauté pan transfers heat quickly, making it a good choice for sautéed chicken, fish, steak, and other dishes that need a golden, caramelized surface. Unlike regular aluminum, hard-anodized pans will not pit or corrode as a result of contact with acidic ingredients, and foods such as tomatoes, rhubarb, wine, and citrus juices won't discolor or taste metallic (some light-hued items such as asparagus or artichokes may darken, though). That means you can sauté some filet mignons, for example, and make a red wine pan sauce, without worrying that the alcohol will ruin the pan or the recipe. Don't put anodized aluminum in the dishwasher, however, or the finish will be damaged. This 5-quart pan has a comfortable, curved metal handle and a side loop handle; the lid is flat, and has a large loop lifter. It also comes in a 3-quart size.

9.32 CALPHALON COMMERCIAL STAINLESS SAUTÉ PAN

Those who appreciate the heating capabilities of anodized aluminum but don't like cooking in dark cookware will love this sauté pan: the interior is lined with stainless steel. The pan browns foods nicely, and the stainless interior makes it easy to see the color of the food being cooked—it's less likely that you'll overcook anything and more likely you will properly judge when a sauce is done. What's more, the surface is nonreactive, so you can use this pan to prepare foods that include acidic ingredients: sautéed chicken with wine sauce or seared fish with a citrus glaze, for instance. The pan edges have a gentle curve, giving it a professional look; these also protect the pan—blows to the pan land on the stainless steel, rather than the seam where the stainless and aluminum meet. The Cool-V handles on this stainless line are the same as those on the other Calphalon Commercial

---

MY IDEAL POT
❧ DANIEL BOULUD ❧

"One day I'd like to design a pot," said Daniel Boulud, a chef who began his professional career in 1969 in Lyon, in a kitchen equipped with only heavy tin-lined copper and well-seasoned cast iron. "It would be something a home cook could use for almost everything."

He would make it about 12" in diameter, 4" deep, and big enough to hold 5 quarts. And though the sides must be straight, they should curve into the bottom, not at a right angle. "It's a shape called a *sauteuse evasée*. You want to be able to use a whisk or a spoon to get to everything. The top edge should be rolled, not squared-off, for better pouring."

"You could pan roast, sauté, or boil pasta in such a pot. I could use it for a big veal chop, to roast a chicken, or cook a piece of fish."

"It would have two handles, one long so the pot could function like a saucepan, and one shorter, to make it easier to manage. The cover should be fairly flat and be ridged concentrically so the vapors can condense evenly back onto the food instead of dripping down the sides."

"Most important, it would have to be made of copper. Maybe for cleaning it should be a copper sandwich with stainless steel inside and outside, but it would have to have twice as much copper as anything made for home cooks today."

Then he wondered whether the outside could be made of chrome. "Then it would be like a Harley-Davidson," he said with a smile.

cookware: large, curved, well balanced, and very comfortable. There's a helper handle, and the tempered glass lid has a moderate dome and a roomy lifter. Its rim is lined with stainless steel to prevent the glass from shattering if dropped. Two sizes of sauté pan are available, 5-quart and 3-quart.

CHICKEN FRYERS

The chicken fryer is a specialized American sauté pan. The French sauté pan has a longer handle that rises diagonally from the side, whereas chicken fryers usually have a short and stubby handle that lies parallel to the stovetop and allows the pan to fit neatly into the oven. Chicken fryers are also likely to have a pouring lip for spilling off pan fat; some have two lips to accommodate left- and right-handers. Chicken fryers are invariably made of materials that hold their heat well—cast iron, heavy aluminum, and enamel over cast iron—so as to maintain the high temperature of the cooking fat. These materials are well suited to prolonged cooking.

Naturally, chicken fryers have uses beyond making fried chicken. They are deep enough for other fried dishes and would be fine for braised foods. Remember, however, that aluminum and cast iron will react with tomatoes and other acidic ingredients. For more versatility in a chicken fryer, consider the Le Creuset enameled cast-iron pan, in which you can cook wine and tomato-laden dishes like chicken cacciatore or osso buco.

9.33 LODGE CAST-IRON CHICKEN FRYER

This pan is deep, which is perfect for deep-fat frying (but also for stewing and braising). It is a bit heavy, but the kind of cooking you do in a fryer doesn't require much moving of the pan, and there is a helper handle at the opposite end. The pan holds the heat well; you needn't worry that the outside will burn before the meat is done. Chicken comes out crisp and brown on the surface, fully cooked within. The heavy, domed lid is dotted on the inside with points that condense steam and help keep your ingredients moist. The cast iron keeps the cooking oil hot, the best assurance that chicken will be as grease free as possible. There is a pouring lip for discarding excess fat. The fryer holds 3 quarts and is 10¼" in diameter.

9.34 LE CREUSET DEEP COVERED SAUTÉ PAN

Though Le Creuset calls this a sauté pan, this 3⅝ quart enameled cast-iron pan is more aptly categorized as a chicken fryer. It comes in several colors (blue, red, flame, green, or white) and the inside is a oatmeal-colored speckled porcelain enamel finish called *glissemail*, which can tolerate steady high temperatures. The 10" pan does its appointed task very well. Because the cast iron holds its

9.35 LE CREUSET SPLATTER GUARD

This is a handy item to have when you're frying. This 11" mesh splatter guard sits on top of the frying pan and stops sizzling fat from splashing out, saving a mess on your stovetop and also helping to prevent possible injury. It comes in black, is framed in lightweight enameled steel, and has a looped handle that stays cool.

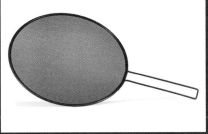

heat so well, it has the same virtues as the pan above—the cooking fat will remain hot, and the chicken or other food will be crisp, not soggy. Unlike uncoated cast iron, which needs to be seasoned and can rust if not properly dried, this pan is easy to clean and maintain. Its short, stubby handle is typical of a chicken fryer, and there is a small ledge on the opposite side to help you lift it. The lid is heavy and fits well within the pan for a tight seal. Two pouring lips on the pan are covered during cooking by corresponding curves on the lid. The lid has a phenolic knob for cool-touch lifting. Just be sure that if you put this pan in the oven with its cover, the temperature does not exceed 450°F.

DEEP-FAT FRYERS & FRYING ACCESSORIES

MOST PEOPLE CLAIM they never eat fried foods—too greasy or filled with cholesterol—but judging by all the French fries and doughnuts that are sold, Americans are eating more fried foods than ever. What few people are doing is making them at home. That's a pity, because the place to have the best fried food *is* at home, where you can make it exactly as you want and as free of grease as possible. The secret to successful frying lies in achieving and maintaining the proper temperature of the fat: it must be hot enough to seal the food's surface quickly so grease will not be absorbed during cooking. This critical point varies with the type of fat used and with the size and type of food you are frying. Most people today rely on vegetable oils for deep-fat frying. In any case, if the fat is overheated or is used too many times, it deteriorates. You will notice an unpleasant odor, and the fat will lose its ability to seize the food properly to form a crispy crust.

You can maintain the proper frying temperature much more easily if you remember to keep your ingredients the same size so they cook evenly. Don't crowd your ingredients in the pan: adding too many of them to the fat lowers the temperature too much. You can recycle cooking fat once, assuming you use it for similar foods, but don't fry doughnuts in the same fat you used for fish. To reuse fat, be sure to strain it through cheesecloth into an airtight jar for storage and refrigerate it if you won't be using it for a while.

Besides maintaining the correct temperature, the other main requirement for proper deep-frying is a pan that is deep enough to prevent spattering and assure that all ingredients will be fully immersed in the fat (which should be at least 3" deep). It helps if the pan has flared sides, wider at the top than the bottom, making it easier to retrieve the cooked ingredients. It also makes sense to use a wire fry basket that holds the ingredients and helps you lift them out when they are finished. Finally, it is a good idea to equip yourself with a special thermometer that tells you the temperature of the fat. You should also consider using your wok for deep-frying. The Chinese do, and use less oil than in a standard deep fryer.

9.36 & 9.37 LODGE CAST-IRON DEEP FRYER & BASKET

This large pot is a 5"-deep, 7-quart Dutch oven that works perfectly for deep-frying. The sides flare out, making room for expanding food to rise to the top. The iron holds heat exceptionally well. You can use the pot by itself; it has a domed cover for use when frying larger items such as chicken. The chrome-and-nickel basket, sold separately, comes in handy when you want to lift out small items. It fits neatly inside and has a long, open handle that stays cool; there is an extra groove in the handle for attaching the basket to the rim of the pan when you want to drain your food.

9.38 MATFER BLACK STEEL FRYING BOWL WITH BASKET

This classic deep fryer is plain and sturdy and perfectly suited to its job: it is 4" deep, with 9" of width at the bottom to accommodate a substantial amount of food, and a 12" diameter at the top. There is room for New Orleans–style beignets to rise, and it is easy to lift them out. The side handles are sturdy and placed high, which keeps your hands away from the heat. The tinned basket follows the contours of the pot. It has curved side handles that latch over the pot handles so you can drain foods before you transfer them to paper towels. The black steel helps keep the fat at a steady temperature.

9.39 *KARHAI*

In India, a deep, round-bottomed pan called a *karhai* is used for deep-frying. The shape of the pan is determined by the burners of traditional Indian stoves: open holes over the fire into which the pan fits. The lower the pan sinks into the hole, the closer it is to the heat, which explains why the *karhai* is so deep and wide at the top. *Karhais* can be made of stainless steel (like this one), cast iron, iron, aluminum, or brass; they all have the typical high-looped handles. Similar in both form and function to the Chinese wok, the *karhai* is more steeply curved than the Chinese pan and provides a perfect well for frying. Three cups of oil will create a generous 2"-deep pool in the bottom of the *karhai*—enough to fry Indian snacks like pakoras or dessert pastries. The pan, made of medium-weight stainless steel, measures little more than 10½" in diameter and is 3¼" deep—just right for making not only fried Indian breads, like *poori*, but also Western treats like chicken wings or Italian zeppole.

9.40 MATFER BIRDS' NEST BASKET

Potato nests are an impressive garnish that require exacting attention to detail in the kitchen. First, the potatoes must be cut into the finest possible julienne strips with a mandoline. (Do not soak the potato slices; it will wash off the starch needed to hold the basket together.) Next, they are pressed into an even layer in

---

9.41 ROSETTE IRON SET

Rosettes are lacy, fried Swedish pastries made from a light lemon-flavored batter; they can be formed and cooked with the equipment in the set shown here. The set consists of an L-shaped, tinned-steel wand with a threaded end, onto which fit any one of these six forms. In this set, the wand is 7¼" long and has a wooden handle. Each of the forms is of heavy cast aluminum, between 2½" and 3" wide, and ½" deep. To make rosettes, put 2" of vegetable oil in a deep fryer and heat to 375°F. Screw in the rosette form of your choice to the threaded end of the handle, and immerse it in oil for a moment. Lift it out, shake off the excess, drain it on a paper towel, and dip it into the batter, which will adhere to the oil-coated metal. Back into the oil again for a quick frying (2 to 3 minutes) until a crisp and delicately brown pastry has been made. Loosen the finished rosette with the tines of a fork and repeat the dipping procedure until the batter is used up. Change forms for variety as you go, but remember that the forms are hot! Only one of them can properly be called a rosette; the others are a fluted heart, circle, and square, and a sectioned circle and star. Rosette-making is not as complicated as it sounds, and the box that holds the set has recipes. The pastries are quickly formed and, when cooled, dusted with confectioners' sugar.

---

the larger of the two wire baskets, which should be lightly oiled. The smaller basket is then brought down over the potatoes, and both baskets are clamped together. The nest is lowered into hot oil and fried until it turns golden brown. The nests can be filled with *pommes de terre soufflées* (puffed, deep-fried potato slices), croquettes, or many other foods. You can also make nests out of other starchy vegetables like sweet potatoes, parsnips, and yucca. The baskets are made of heavy-gauge tinned wire; the larger one is 4½" in diameter, and the smaller one is 4" in diameter. Overall, the implement is 18" long. Both hook and wire loop at the end of the handle permit hanging.

9.42 RIVER LIGHT TEMPURA COOKER

Tempura is any food (but especially shrimp and vegetables) coated in a thin batter and deep-fried: crisp, delicate, and never greasy. Ironically, this dish, which we think of as typically Japanese, is an adaptation of the deep-frying that Portuguese missionaries introduced to Japan in the late sixteenth century. The name supposedly comes from the missionaries' requests for fried shrimp on meatless Ember Days, which they called *Quattuor Tempora* because they came four times a year.

This tempura cooker from River Light is a round, fairly shallow pan of heavy-gauge steel, 11" across with a wide pouring lip. There are two roomy handles on the cooker for easy maneuvering. A handy chromed-steel draining rack, shaped almost like a half-moon, hooks over the pan's rim to provide a shelf on which just-fried food can sit to drain. This cooker also comes with a pair of 15½"-long cooking chopsticks.

ELECTRIC DEEP FRYERS

All of these deep "pots" have electrically controlled thermostats that quickly bring cooking oil to a precise temperature and maintain it throughout the frying process, making it unnecessary to use a thermometer or adjust the heat level on the range to get foods that are perfectly crisp and crunchy on the outside, moist and tender on the inside. Deluxe models come with baskets, have more than one temperature setting, and feature covers with replaceable charcoal filters that stay closed during frying to prevent grease from escaping and spattering kitchen surfaces. Other conveniences to look for include nonstick interior surfaces, removable liners that go in the dishwasher, and built-in timers that beep at the end of cooking.

While there's no arguing with the convenience of having an appliance that brings the oil to a proper frying temperature, electric fryers have downsides. They're large and unwieldy. Are you willing to give them precious storage space if you only make doughnuts once a year? They cook a limited amount of food at one time—for many models it's only about 2 pounds, less than the weight of one chicken, in which case if you're feeding more than two people, the chicken has to be kept warm in the oven or served cold. And forget about serving fried potatoes along with it. On the range, you can have a pair of deep skillets going at the same time and fry up two birds at once.

9.43 PRESTO FRYDADDY ELECTRIC DEEP FRYER

There are no frills on this bucket with a nonstick surface—just a plug-in cord. The bucket can't be immersed in water and wiped out. However, we found that in exactly 10 minutes it heated its capacity of 4 cups of oil to precisely 375°F, an all-purpose frying temperature. When we tasted potatoes and chicken cooked in the FryDaddy we understood why fried foods have such enduring appeal. Along with the fryer, you get a nickel-plated steel scoop to strain and remove foods and a plastic lid so you can store oil in the FryDaddy if you plan to use it a second time. We do suggest straining the oil to remove food particles. We think this basic model that accommodates two legs and two breasts of chicken at a time is a fine size if you're not a frequent fryer. Presto also makes a 2-cup FryBaby that cooks two pieces of chicken at a time, and a 1½-quart GranPappy that holds six pieces.

9.44 DELONGHI ROTOFRYER

This large appliance (12½" in diameter and 9½" high) has a cover equipped with two filters—one is of black charcoal to trap odors, the other helps filter the grease from the steam vapors. The lid stays closed during frying, minimizing, but not eliminating, the escape of vapors that cause odors and grease spots. It brings about a quart of oil to frying temperature—from 300°F to 375°F— in less than 10 minutes, and has a light that goes off signaling the temperature has been reached. Before preheating the oil, you load the basket with food and it sits above the oil as it heats. When the oil's ready, you submerge the basket by lowering an exterior handle, then set the digital cooking timer built into the unit. During frying, the basket moves around in the oil, resulting in evenly cooked food. We found the plastic exterior doesn't get too hot to touch. Our chief gripe with this machine was with its cleaning system. When it's time to filter or discard the oil, you unfurl a drainage pipe, letting the oil flow into the storage container that comes with the unit. (A filter and a cover for the container are also included.) The cooking chamber doesn't have a removable liner, although it has a nonstick coating. To clean the interior and the drainage pipe it's necessary to first pour soapy water, then rinse water into the chamber and allow them to run through, a process we found time-consuming. We'd prefer to be able to remove a liner, pour out the oil, and wash the liner in the sink. There's a small window in top of the fryer, but we found that it steams up so it gives limited visibility into the doings inside. In the back of the unit there's a chamber to hold the cord. The Rotofryer is a good example of a deluxe unit that performs well but still only fries 1 pound of fish fillets or 2 pounds of potatoes at a time.

WOKS

WOKS ARE THE BASIC, all-purpose utensils of Chinese cookery. In recent years they have become staples in the American home kitchen, either the traditional round-bottom style that has been in existence since Chinese cuisine developed or in one of the many modern variations, including flat-bottom woks and stir-fry pans. The traditional wok was designed for the Chinese open brazier-stove. To fit over the heat source, it has a round bottom and good width, to prevent it from falling through the hole into the fire. The pan slopes to the rim so heat at the bottom can radiate evenly to the sides, but also because the shape enables ingredients to fall to the center, where the heat is concentrated. Most traditional woks have two side handles.

For use in most American kitchens, with their flat surface burners, a classic, round-bottom wok may not be stable and should only be used on gas ranges together with a metal ring that mimics the Chinese brazier and supports the wok. On electric stoves the coil touches only a small portion of the metal and can barely provide adequate heat for stir-frying. Thus the flat-bottom wok was developed. Another modern change in the traditional wok is the handle. Americans are accustomed to stovetop cookware with one long handle, rather than two loops, so many flat-bottom woks and stir-fry pans come with a single long handle, or a long handle with a helper handle for added stability and ease of handling.

The Chinese make good use of a wok. In addition to stir-frying foods (which is a technique that's more like sautéing than frying because the food is constantly kept moving), they steam, braise, deep-fry, and stew ingredients inside the pan. Again, American habits are different, and for the most part we prefer to limit the wok to stir-frying and deep-frying. That is why the smaller stir-fry pans were created.

Stir-frying involves cooking small pieces of food quickly over high heat. A good wok or stir-fry pan must be made of conductive materials. In fact, most traditional woks are made from carbon steel. You may also see traditional woks made of cast iron and enameled iron. Although it may seem counterintuitive to apply a nonstick coating to a pan that is designed for high-heat cooking, some nonstick woks are available to help reduce the amount of fat needed. To be at all serviceable, the underlying pan must be made of a heavy, efficient, heat-conductive metal. Also, when using a nonstick wok never preheat it as you would a wok made of carbon steel. Heating it empty will permanently damage the nonstick coating. To cook in a nonstick wok, you should begin with a cold pan and cold oil, then heat. A few dealers may offer copper woks; these are beautiful and do a wonderful job transmitting heat for stir-fried foods, but they are hardly necessary when other, much less expensive metals can do the job well.

Stir-fry pans, a modern cookware term for any rounded woklike pan meant for cooking cut-up ingredients over high heat, are typically smaller than traditional woks. Carbon steel is still the best metal to use. Stir-fry pans made of aluminum and anodized aluminum are available, but do not give you the same amount of control over the heat as a pan made from carbon steel will. Uncoated carbon-steel and iron woks must be seasoned well and dried thoroughly after being washed, to prevent rusting. Other metals don't require special treatment.

Anything that walks, swims, crawls, or flies with its back to heaven is edible.

—EILEEN YIN-FEI LO,
The Chinese Kitchen

193

9.45 ALLIED METAL ROUND-BOTTOM WOK SET

This is a traditional wok, with a rounded bottom and two steel side handles, intended for use only on gas burners. (Not enough of the pan's surface would touch an electric burner, so heat would be inadequate.) A metal ring, which stabilizes the pan and focuses the heat on its bottom, is included, as is a large aluminum cover. The wok is made of cold, rolled steel, which heats very quickly. The smooth, rounded shape helps heat spread evenly throughout the pan. Seasoning is recommended; the pan must also be dried very thoroughly after washing to prevent rust deposits. When properly used for stir-frying, a quick rinse in hot water and a scrub with a brush are all that should be needed. The 14" wok is a good size for most families; however, the set is also available in 12" and 16" sizes.

9.46 JOYCE CHEN PRO CHEF CARBON-STEEL WOK

This 14" wok heats quickly and exceptionally well. It is very roomy: use it for family-size stir-fries as well as for steaming (place the bamboo steamer inside), braising, and deep-frying. The metal can rust, however, so be sure to dry it thoroughly and keep it well seasoned. Though traditional Asian woks have

---

LEMON CHICKEN: THE AUTHENTIC VERSION

4 servings

This version uses oil to cook the chicken briefly, until the flesh is succulent and velvety; hence the term *velveted*. You can use water instead of oil.

1 pound boneless, skinless chicken breasts
1 egg white
1 teaspoon salt
2 teaspoons cornstarch
1 cup peanut oil or 2 cups water (see variation)

SAUCE
½ cup homemade chicken stock or reduced-salt canned broth
2 tablespoons fresh lemon juice
1 tablespoon sugar
1 tablespoon light soy sauce
2 teaspoons Shaoxing rice wine or dry sherry
1 tablespoon finely sliced garlic
2 dried and crushed red chilies
1 tablespoon grated lemon zest
1 teaspoon cornstarch blended with 1 teaspoon water

Cut the chicken breasts into 1½" cubes. Mix the chicken with the egg white, salt, and cornstarch in a bowl and refrigerate for about 20 minutes.

Heat a wok until it is very hot and swirl in the oil. When the oil is very hot, remove the wok from the heat and immediately add the chicken pieces, stirring vigorously to keep them from sticking. As soon as the chicken pieces turn white, in about 2 minutes, quickly drain the chicken and all of the oil in a stainless steel colander set in a bowl. Discard the oil.

Mix together in a saucepan all the ingredients for the sauce except the cornstarch mixture, and bring it to a simmer.

Slowly drizzle in the cornstarch mixture, stirring all the while. When the sauce has slightly thickened, toss in the chicken, coating well with the sauce. Turn onto a platter and serve at once.

VARIATION
If you choose to use water instead of oil, bring it to a boil in a saucepan. Remove the saucepan from the heat and immediately add the chicken pieces, stirring vigorously to keep them from sticking. When the chicken pieces turn white, in about 2 minutes, quickly drain the chicken and all of the water in a stainless steel colander set in a bowl. Discard the water.

Easy Family Recipes from a Chinese-American Childhood, by Ken Hom

round bottoms and two short handles, this one, with its flat bottom and long handle, may be more familiar in concept to American home cooks. The flat bottom can be used on either gas or electric cooktops and makes it more stable than the classic round-bottom pan. There is a small helper handle opposite the long handle, making the pan more manageable. The handles are made of phenolic, which keeps them cool.

9.47 CALPHALON PROFESSIONAL HARD-ANODIZED STIR-FRY PAN

This snug little pan is 10″ wide and 3″ deep, just enough for a bunch of cut-up broccoli florets or spinach or a single order of stir-fried chicken and peanuts. It gets hot quickly, spreading heat evenly for perfect results. It's easy to maneuver this pan, too; it has a well-designed handle that's riveted to the pan and covered with cool-touch phenolic. The bottom is flat, making it useful on any cooktop. Calphalon anodized aluminum is termed *stick resistant,* which means you must use some cooking fat, but you can reduce the amounts called for in recipes.

9.48 JOYCE CHEN PEKING PAN

This pan is the original stir-fry pan invented by Joyce Chen in the late sixties and the company's signature product. Although it is not your tra-

ditional Asian wok, nevertheless it's a great pan for several reasons. The tri-ply metal (carbon steel between two thin layers of aluminum) takes in heat and spreads it well. The cooking surface is arc-sprayed with molten stainless steel—a process known as Excalibur—which helps create a reinforced nonstick surface; it cuts down minimally on heat but makes the pan very easy to use and clean. The outside of the pan has a regular nonstick coating. The pan's bowl-shaped center is deep and capacious; ingredients fall easily from side to bottom. For versatility, the bottom is flat, so you can use it on any type of cooktop. It has one long metal-and-phenolic handle and comes with a large aluminum dome lid for use when steaming foods, particularly firm vegetables like broccoli or cauliflower. The company produces several sizes of Peking pans: 8″, 9½″, 12″, and 14″; dome lids are available separately.

9.49 ALL-CLAD LTD STIR-FRY PAN

This compact pan has a 2-quart capacity, spacious enough for a meal of beef with broccoli or fried rice for four. The pan's core is aluminum, so it heats well; the interior cooking surface is stainless steel, which means that ingredients will not interact with the pan; and the exterior is dark anodized aluminum that will not scratch, chip, or peel. The bottom is flat; you can use it no matter what kind of stove you have. There is one long hollowed handle that stays relatively cool, plus a helper handle on the opposite side. It is available in nonstick in the company's Stainless

Steel and LTD lines, and without the nonstick finish in the Master Chef and Cop-R-Chef lines as well.

9.50 MAXIM HIGH PERFORMANCE ELECTRIC WOK

We are not particularly fond of electric woks. They may hold heat well (this one has 1,600 watts and an accurate thermostat), but you will find that it is difficult to control the heat, and the pan doesn't cool down quickly enough when needed. Nevertheless, if you insist on an electric wok, this one from Maxim comes somewhat close to the real thing. It holds 6½ quarts, so you can cook big meals inside, and you can use the pan to deep-fry, steam, and braise foods as well as stir-fry them. The surface is nonstick, making it easy to clean. It looks attractive, too, with a gray matte finish on a sleek tubular stainless steel base, so it might be a good choice when you have casual company and want to serve right from the pot. It could even go on a buffet table. The wok comes with several additional cooking implements: steamer rack; wooden spoon; spatula; a high, domed aluminum lid; and recipe booklet.

SAUCEPANS

THE SAUCEPAN IS THE WORKHORSE of the kitchen. We use it to make haute cuisine classics like hollandaise and béchamel, but also to cook more rustic fare like tomato sauce and oatmeal. We use a saucepan to put together a few tablespoonfuls of roux, and we reach for the same kind, if not the same size, of pan to cook spaghetti sauce or soup. Because saucepans perform so many different functions, your *batterie de cuisine* should contain several of them in a variety of sizes and materials so that the proper pan can be used for a given quantity of food and the right material will match the needs of the recipe being prepared.

Classic saucepans have straight sides that meet the bottom at right angles. However, there are also a variety of specialty saucepans that have flared sides. This shape, often called a Windsor pan, enhances evaporation; it is a good choice for reducing sauces.

Sauciers are engineered somewhat differently. Not so much a tool for sauce reduction but for convenience, these pans have wider bottoms that are suitable for browning foods before adding liquids for stews and soups. The rounded shape of a saucier makes it easier to stir ingredients (such as the flour mixtures in puddings or gravy or the grains of risotto) that often become stuck in the corners of straight-sided saucepans.

In recent years, Americans have discovered the French *sauteuse evasée*—the *fait-tout* pan. *Fait-tout* means "does everything," and that is precisely what a *fait-tout* pan does—everything. It is a large, flared saucepan with a bottom wide enough for sautéed dishes or pot roast, deep enough for soup or plenty of sauce, and with rounded sides that facilitate preparations such as pudding, risotto, and polenta. Some manufacturers call them "chef's pans"; others name them "multifunction" pans. Whatever their designation, they are so versatile that home cooks would be served well by owning more than one.

A Buying Strategy

Like sauté pans, saucepans must be made of good heat-conducting materials to perform even the most mundane functions. You may wish to have an expensive copper pot for the occasional fine sauce that requires perfect temperature nuance. More reasonably priced pans suffice for everything else. We also counsel you to use nonstick saucepans for certain dishes, such as oatmeal, rice, and other foods that can stick to the pan and make it difficult to clean—these do not require the heat sensitivity that a sophisticated sauce might.

Metals for Saucepans

COPPER Nothing compares to copper's heat responsiveness, which makes it our first choice for sauce-making, even though it is expensive. Copper cookware is always lined because copper molecules, which are poisonous, can leach into the food. Tin linings are traditional, though they can wear out or buckle and must be refinished from time to time. Stainless steel linings diminish conductivity somewhat but are more practical.

ALUMINUM Aluminum conducts heat nearly as well

as copper, and it is light and less expensive. But plain aluminum can be corroded by both acidic and alkaline foods, and an interaction between the metal and ingredients can cause "off" flavors and discoloration. What's more, thin-gauge aluminum cookware may be tempting to buy because it's cheap, but it dents, wobbles, and develops hot spots. If you do wish to purchase a plain aluminum saucepan, be sure it is a sturdy, thick-gauge model (the gauge is represented by numbers in an inverse series—thus, 8-gauge aluminum is thicker than 20-gauge).

We prefer the aluminum-core cookware, made entirely of aluminum with stainless steel linings and stainless steel, hard-anodized or brushed aluminum, or copper outercoats. The aluminum provides heat conductivity; the stainless steel inner lining gives it versatility. We also recommend anodized aluminum for saucepans.

NONSTICK SAUCEPANS Because browning is usually not important in sauce-making or in most other jobs for which a saucepan may be used, it doesn't matter that nonstick cookware cuts down on heat transfer. The slick surfaces provide other benefits: less cooking fat and easy cleanup. Nonstick is suitable particularly when you use a saucepan to cook rice, oatmeal, lentils, and other foods that tend to be sticky or messy. As with frying pans, the value of nonstick cookware depends on the quality of the underlying pan and the quality and durability of the surface. While a saucepan may not take the same kind of utensil-abuse that a frying pan does, the coating must be tough enough to withstand constant stirring. Most manufacturers recommend that you do not stir with metal utensils. Remember that nonstick saucepans are also not dishwasher safe.

STAINLESS STEEL SAUCEPANS Stainless steel is an alloy of steel with nickel, chrome, or other elements. It has an attractive and impervious surface that takes and holds a high polish. It won't rust, pit, or corrode and does not react with any foods, discolor them, or give them a bad taste. Stainless steel is also completely nontoxic, and you can put it in the dishwasher. With all these benefits, stainless steel has one big liability: its relatively poor heat conductivity, which is why we never recommend cookware that is made only of stainless steel. A number of different methods for overcoming the metal's shortcomings have been developed over the years. Most common is combining a sheet of stainless steel with a sheet of another metal that is a good conductor, like copper or aluminum. Inexpensive pans have such a thin layer of these metals applied to the bottom that the heat is never adequate, and cooking can be uneven and slow. Better pans, just like the ones discussed earlier, have a disc of aluminum or copper attached to the bottom of the pan. This can work well, but only if the disc is thick enough to take in and spread the heat, and only if it is wide enough to cover the entire bottom of the pan. In some cases, the disc covers only the inner portion of the pan; this can create hot spots.

The best solution is to wrap an entire pan of a conductive metal such as aluminum or copper with stainless steel. These pans offer the qualities of effective heat transfer and nonreactivity. While not as sensitive as copper, and not as effective in those instances where you want instant heat loss, like a sauce containing eggs, they are appropriate for every type of cooking.

ENAMELED-IRON SAUCEPANS Enameled iron, so useful for skillets and casseroles, is not an ideal material for saucepans because it is heavy; its weight makes it difficult for many people to maneuver on the stovetop. However, this cookware is useful for making sauces that don't require more than an occasional stir. The coating prevents the cast-iron core from rusting and the metal's molecules from leaching into the food, but the conductivity is not as good as aluminum or copper.

9.51 ENDURANCE CRESCENT POT-EDGE STRAINER

Straining vegetables from a steaming saucepan can be frustrating. If you're like many people, you don't want to bother getting out a full-size colander, so you place the pan at a sink edge or hold the lid slightly askew to pour off the water—and lose some peas or cooked beans down the drain. This device will help you. It is made of stainless steel and has a long, looped, comfortable handle. The flat, crescent-shaped portion fits over the edge of pans up to 10" in diameter. It has a narrow lip that holds it on the edge while you are tilting the pan to strain the liquid.

9.52 MAUVIEL HAMMERED COPPER SAUCEPAN

You can't ask for more in a saucepan. This is a flawless performer, solidly made of heavy, tin-lined copper, and beautiful, too. The sides are hammered, which adds strength and good looks, but the bottom is unhammered, which keeps it perfectly flat. Edges of the pan are smooth and nicely finished. The thick, curved cast-iron handle is tightly attached with copper rivets, leaving no dirt-catching spaces, and it provides a good grip for the heavy pan. This tin-lined copper saucepan responds to temperatures exactly the way you would expect: heating and cooling down quickly. It is available in several sizes, from ⅞ quart to 14 quarts.

9.53 DE BUYER HAMMERED COPPER SAUCEPAN

Another winner, this saucepan is made of medium-weight, tin-lined copper. Like the pan described above, it has hammered sides and a flat, smooth copper bottom and does a first-rate job. The cast-iron handle is long and balances the pan; it is

attached with three solid rivets that keep the handle tight to the pot, with no space for dirt or particles of food to accumulate. It comes in several sizes, from a small 4″ diameter, (holding ⁹⁄₁₀ quart), to a substantial 7⅞″ pan holding 3¹⁄₁₀ quarts. Lids are available; sizes include 4″, 4¾″, 5½″, 6¼″, 7⅛″, and 7⅞″.

9.54 BOURGEAT COPPER SAUCEPAN

Another outstanding shiny copper pan lined with stainless steel. Because of the lining, the pan is not quite as quick to respond as the tin-lined model, but it is sufficiently fast for most cooking, and it has a big advantage: stainless steel doesn't wear out, and it is easy to clean. This is a heavy pan too, with a thick, curved, comfortable cast-iron handle that is attached with three heavy rivets. The lid fits snugly inside the pan, its outside rim sitting on the pan's smooth and gently curved edge. The edge gives the pan an elegant, professional finish; this design also improves pouring. The pan we show you is 2.4 liters (2½ quarts). It is available in several sizes, from 0.7 liters (¾ quarts) to 5.4 liters (5½ quarts).

9.55 NORPRO KRONA POT

This little 1½-quart pot has some notable qualities that make it particularly suitable for cooking vegetables and rice. It is a brushed stainless steel pan with a thick, heat-transferring disc at the bottom and two pouring lips that help you drain liquids easily. The tempered-glass, stainless steel–rimmed lid is different from most. First, it is very heavy for its size, and it sits deep within the pan. The rim is pierced on two sides, allowing steam to escape so liquids do not boil over; this feature also comes in handy when you want to spill off liquids. The handles are hollowed and stay cool; the lid loop lifter is high and roomy and also stays cool.

9.56 KITCHENAID FIVE-PLY STAINLESS STEEL CLAD SAUCEPAN

This isn't any old pot. It is a superb saucepan with good, heat-conductive aluminum at its core and a complete coating of 18/10 stainless steel, which provides durability and shine. You must quickly adjust to low to medium cooking temperatures because the pan heats so thoroughly. The pan may be heavy for some home cooks, but its ergonomically designed, thick, curved handle is extremely comfortable and helps with maneuvering. All of KitchenAid's pots and pans, like this one, have snug rivets that prevent bits of food from accumulating between the handle and the pan. The lids are heavy and deep, and they sit tightly inside the pan. The edges of the pan are smooth, rounded, slightly curved, and well finished. This pan has a 2-quart capacity, but it is also available in 2½- and 3-quart sizes.

9.57 ANOLON NOUVELLE STAINLESS SAUCEPAN

This 2-quart pan comes in handy for all types of cooking: preparing vegetables, heating soup, concocting tomato sauce, and so on. The stainless steel materials won't react with or discolor any ingredient, and the metal will never corrode or dent. A thick copper disc stretches completely across the bottom width and provides quick, capable heat for the entire pan. The handle is hollowed in two places, which keeps it cool and comfortable. This is a very practical pot with a distinctive style; the rolled edges give it a finished, attractive look and it has an unusual-looking lid. The lid, inspired by French cookware, has a long handle, which stays cool even after prolonged cooking on the stovetop. The saucepan is also available in 1- and 3-quart capacities.

9.58 ALL-CLAD STAINLESS STEEL NONSTICK SAUCEPAN

This is a terrific all-purpose pot for cooking vegetables, grains, puddings, and dozens of other foods. The pan heats well because of its thick aluminum core, and the nonstick coating does not cut down significantly on heat transfer. The outside of the pan is protected by a layer of shiny stainless steel, and the inside is covered with premier-quality Whitford Excalibur nonstick, which has excellent release ability and cleans easily. The 2-quart pan is a little taller than standard saucepans of this size and therefore has a narrower surface area, which means that you can leave it on the cooktop longer and foods will be less likely to scorch. The handle is riveted to the pan, and the lid has a snug fit. All-Clad nonstick saucepans are available in a 2-quart size shown above, and 3- and 4-quart sizes in the Stainless Steel and LTD lines.

9.59 LE CREUSET PHENOLIC HANDLE SAUCEPAN

This compact pot comes in a variety of warm, comforting colors (with light surfaces inside the pan) that belie the plain cast iron beneath. Like all cast iron cookware, this saucepan retains its heat exceptionally well, making it fine for slow-cooking foods like the morning hot cereal or some polenta. Enamelware also protects ingredients from reacting with metal, so you can use it to simmer acidic foods like tomato sauce or stew rhubarb compote. There is a pouring lip on one side, allowing you to drain off liquids. The thick phenolic handle is comfortable and stays cool. Enameled cast-iron pans can be awkwardly heavy, but the 1½- and 2-quart sizes are fairly easy to maneuver.

9.60 ALL-CLAD STAINLESS STEEL SAUCIER

This pan has a wide base, wider top (12″ in diameter), and flared sides, and although it isn't big enough to be a *fait-tout,* its shape and size offer similar flexibility. You can use it for all sorts of cooking: making sauces, sautéing a small quantity of meat or vegetables, cooking risotto or polenta. The flared design makes it a good choice for reducing liquids. The rounded bottom edges make stirring a cinch. The one shown here is from the Stainless Steel line, but the company also makes it in LTD. Both are well balanced and have the excellent heat conductivity and sturdy design of All-Clad cookware.

9.61 CALPHALON COMMERCIAL HARD-ANODIZED SAUCEPAN

An all-purpose pan; it is heavy and sturdy and has a comfortable, curved cast-steel handle that is riveted securely and balances the vessel. The handle stays relatively cool. The electrochemically treated aluminum has the same excellent heat transfer as regular aluminum and some pluses: it is stick resistant, and it cleans up more easily than standard metal pans. The treatment also protects the aluminum from reacting with acidic or alkaline ingredients. Still, it isn't a good idea to leave such ingredients in the pan for extended periods of time—they can discolor.

9.62 LINCOLN CENTURION BRUSHED STAINLESS STEEL SAUCEPAN

This workable pot is the kind you find yourself using so often that you wonder what you did without it. It is heavy, sturdy, and beautifully balanced. It has a long, thick, tubular handle that stays cool during cooking. The aluminum disc on the bottom heats the pan quickly. You can cook anything inside its stainless steel interior. Given all that, you'd expect this to be a plain, generic-looking pot, but this practical tool is also very attractive, with its brushed stainless exterior, rim trim, and rounded edges. It is narrower and

taller than many saucepans of this size, giving it additional value when you prepare a sauce or other dish that needs to cook longer without reducing. It comes in two sizes, 2¼ quarts and 3¼ quarts.

9.63 BOURGEAT SAUTEUSE EVASÉE

A *fait-tout* pan should, literally, "do everything," and this 4³⁄₁₀-quart one does. The 7½" bottom is ample for sautéing, and the 11" top and 3½" depth give it room for sauce or a small fricassee. The copper heats the pan exceptionally well and causes it to lose heat quickly when necessary—a wonderful feature when your pudding is about to bubble. The stainless steel interior lining doesn't detract

greatly from heat response and gives the pan several advantages: any ingredient can be cooked inside, and clean-up is easy. A sturdy cast-iron handle will help you maneuver the heavy pan, and the edges are smooth and gently curved, which make it easy to pour ingredients. This *sauteuse evasée* is beautiful to boot and comes in other sizes: 6³⁄₁₀" (⁷⁄₁₀ quarts), 7⁹⁄₁₀" (1³⁄₅ quarts), and 9²⁄₅" (2⁷⁄₁₀ quarts).

9.64 CALPHALON COMMERCIAL HARD-ANODIZED CHEF'S PAN

This 4-quart pan is wonderfully adaptable. Heat is delivered quickly via the aluminum, and ingredients brown beautifully. The bottom is broad enough for sautéing a couple of chicken breasts or a few shrimp, and the pan is deep enough for applesauce, pudding, risotto, or soup. Rounded edges prevent food from gobbing up in hard-to-reach corners. The cast steel handle is securely riveted and stays cool during stovetop cooking. It has comfortable curves and, with the helper handle, is easy to manage.

9.65 KITCHENAID HI*DENSITY HARD-ANODIZED ALUMINUM SAUCIER

If you had to choose only one pan for your kitchen, this might be it. The manufacturer calls it a saucier; true enough, but at 2½ quarts, it is large enough to be a *fait-tout,* and in fact, this pan can do everything, and

"Hello? Risotto-crisis hot line?"

superbly. Five layers of aluminum and stainless steel (plus a glossy hard-anodized exterior finish) deliver heat quickly and evenly around the pan, so foods such as chicken breasts and onions brown beautifully. The pan is spacious and deep enough for sauce or several portions of soup. The rounded edges at the bottom make it particularly useful for stirring cereal, polenta, risotto, pudding, and other foods that clump together. As with all KitchenAid pans, the handle is made of cast stainless steel and designed for maximum comfort, and the lid, with an 18/10 mirror-polished interior and exterior, is deep, sturdy, and well made, fitting tightly into the pan. The edges of the pan are smooth and rounded, giving them a professional, finished appearance.

9.66 LE CREUSET *MARMITOUT* (MULTIFUNCTION) PAN

Another knockout, this one in enameled cast iron. There's very little you can't cook in this pan. It holds its heat well, and its surface is nonreactive, making it perfect for such long-simmering items as tomato sauce or chutney. It's a good choice for soup

or creamed spinach—the rounded edges help when you whisk the butter and flour to thicken together in the sauce. You can sauté meatballs—they get lightly crispy—and then add tomatoes, garlic, herbs, and olive oil for an old-fashioned topping for spaghetti. The domed, long-handled lid is multifunctional, too: turn it over and it becomes an omelet pan. Wonderfully versatile, it also is lovely to look at in several colors. We like the 2-quart size, but it is also available in a smaller, 1-quart model.

9.67 CALPHALON PROFESSIONAL HARD-ANODIZED BUTTER WARMER

Why buy a butter warmer? Not simply to enjoy melted butter to accompany lobsters or steamed clams. This tiny pot is terrific for heating brandy or rum before pouring it into a flambé pan for igniting. It has two small pouring lips on either side, making it easy to spill off the liquid. You may also ignite the warmed spirits in the pan and pour the flaming sauce onto pancakes or ice cream. Other uses? Warm maple syrup for waffles, melt jam for glazing tarts,

heat a single cup of milk or stock for mashed potatoes. The metal handle is slim and can become hot, but this pot is not intended for prolonged cooking. It's just a warming device, so the handle stays cool. It has a 2-cup capacity.

9.68 ALL-CLAD LTD WINDSOR PAN

Though rarely used outside restaurant kitchens until recently, this unusual pan, with its flared sides, makes a real difference when you're cooking a sauce that needs reducing. The aluminum core of this model brings ample, even heat to the ingredients, minimizing the risk of scorching. The shape makes it easy for you to stir the contents with a spoon or whisk. More important, the relation of the base to the top shows good engineering: the narrow bottom cooks liquids quickly, sending heat to the top, and the wide top exposes a large surface area that encourages rapid reduction. The one pictured here is 2½ quarts in the company's LTD line; it is available in stainless steel, and a 1½-quart model is available in both lines.

PRESSURE COOKERS

Around since 1939, these stovetop pots continue to fight an uphill battle for acceptance in American kitchens. We can't seem to get the image of Grandma's split-pea soup on the ceiling out of our minds in spite of the fact that models now have multiple safety features, including valves that release excess steam and locking devices that prevent them from being opened

while under pressure. In a pressure cooker, food is cooked in a sealed environment, trapping steam and building up pressure so that the liquids become about 38°F hotter than boiling, 250°F. The higher temperature translates to faster cooking, while the pressure breaks down the fibers in foods, tenderizing them. It's possible to pressure-cook an excellent pot of chicken soup or braised short ribs in less than an hour, although discriminating palates may detect that soups and sauces don't have quite the depth of flavor that they do when cooked for a longer time. Though pressure cookers are fast, keep in mind that it takes anywhere from 5 to 20 minutes to build up pressure and additional minutes to lower it after cooking. Therefore we don't find them appropriate for foods with short cooking times, like vegetables, fish, or chicken breasts.

There's only one feature of a pressure cooker that will affect its performance, and that's the base. It's imperative to purchase a pressure cooker with a thick solid aluminum bottom. Beware of lightweight models.

Having said that, a variety of options will enhance ease of use at the same time that they up the price. Spring-loaded valves give a visual indication of when full pressure's been reached so you may not have to listen for the hissing of escaping steam or the telltale jiggling of a weight resting on the pot. If the cooker has high and low settings, you don't have to control the pressure by aurally gauging the intensity of the hissing and regulating the heat. Particularly useful is a quick release setting that brings down the pressure rapidly—in about 2 minutes as opposed to 20, 30, or more—when you don't want to risk overcooking or simply want to serve dinner quickly.

9.69 PRESTO STAINLESS STEEL PRESSURE COOKER WITH BIMETAL-CLAD BASE

This low-tech 6-quart model doesn't cost a small fortune and will give you results that are just as good as the most expensive model. It has the all-important aluminum base that prevents foods from scorching. While its old-fashioned pressure regulator rocks and hisses, in all honesty we find it comforting to hear it chugging away. To cook at a lower pressure setting, you need to lower the heat; to bring the pressure down altogether, you need to sit the pot under cold running water until you see the safety valve drop. A cooking rack is included that can be used to steam foods as well as to raise big pieces of meat slightly above the pan's bottom away from the heat.

9.70 T-FAL CLIPSO PRESSURE COOKER

Of all the models we tested, this 6⅝-quart stainless steel pressure cooker had the thickest base, was the easiest to use, came up to pressure the quickest, and required the least regulation of heat. We love the unique locking and opening mechanisms that are activated by pressing the knob in the lid and a green button in the knob, respectively. (On other cookers, you need to align the lid and pot and then shift the lid into place to lock it, and shift it back to open it.) It has a spring-valve pressure regulator that is quieter than one that sits on top of the pot, but you do have to listen for steady hissing to determine that it has come up to pressure. Clipso has high and low settings and a very easy-to-use quick-release system, and it comes with a steaming basket. The only drawback is that it takes longer for pressure to drop naturally than on most cookers.

DOUBLE BOILERS & *BAINS-MARIE*

THERE ARE SEVERAL WAYS to mediate between the heat and the food being prepared: aluminum sandwich bottoms on stainless steel cookware and flame tamers, to mention two options. Double boilers and *bains-marie* use water to accomplish this end. Water works well to diffuse heat, which makes it easier to control, so that foods don't burn or cook too quickly. Water mediation is particularly useful when your recipe needs gentle heat or when you want to stop the heating process quickly. This is why we melt chocolate in a double boiler, so it will melt slowly, judiciously. At the exact moment that melting is complete, the top of the boiler is removed from the water pot, eliminating the chance that the chocolate will scorch. Custard preparation also illustrates the benefits of water to mediate and halt cooking.

Though double boilers and *bains-marie* both use water to diffuse heat, they perform different functions. A double boiler is simply two ordinary pots, one made to fit snugly inside the other. The water in the pan below cooks the food—eggs, custard, or chocolate, for example—in the upper pan. A typical *bain-marie* is a shallow pan filled halfway with water; another pan, filled with food, is placed inside. The water in the larger pan surrounds the inner pot and cooks the food within it (or keeps it warm). *Pots de crème* and cream-cheese cakes are good example of foods that finish with perfect textures when cooked this way.

In culinary parlance, the term *bain-marie* also means the pans used to hold prepared sauces or other foods inside a larger pot of water that is already hot and simmering. These *bains-marie* should be straight-sided and tall, to prevent water in the bath from splashing into the contents of the pan. Handles generally are short or emerge upward from the pan so that they will be out of the way of the bottom pan.

9.71 MAUVIEL COPPER *BAIN-MARIE*

This might be a costly device, but it is an interesting piece of equipment, somewhat of a cross between a *bain-marie* and double boiler, and it's beautiful and does the job. There is a ceramic insert, slimmer at the bottom, while the wider portion rests on the pan ledge. Foods to be cooked by the double-boiler method are kept warm in the thick-walled pot that sits above the water in the bottom pan. The bottom pan is made of tin-lined hammered copper; used by itself, this pan functions as a *bain-marie*, that is, it is designed to fit inside a larger pan of water (without the ceramic insert). It has tall (4¾") straight sides so that the water in the bath will not spill into it. The handle is short and looms upward, out of the way of a water-bath edge. Handles are made of brass, attached by copper rivets. The lid is smooth copper with a small brass knob; it fits on both the ceramic insert and the copper pan.

This *bain-marie* holds ⁹⁄₁₀ quart, but it is also available in a 1⅗-quart capacity.

9.72 CATAMOUNT GLASS *BAIN-MARIE*

The company lists this item as a double boiler, but it is actually a *bain-marie* (and is too deep for a double boiler). The two glass parts are flameproof, so you can use the *bain-marie* directly on top of a gas range (for electric-burner cooking, use a flame tamer). Glass is ideal for a *bain-marie*: it lets you see how the water is behaving in the bottom pot—whether it is too close to a boil, and whether it needs replenishing. The looped glass handles stay cool; the inner pot has a long handle and a shorter helper handle on the opposite side. But be careful—this *bain-marie* is fragile! It holds 1 quart, and a ½ quart double boiler is also available.

9.74 ALL-CLAD 3-QUART DOUBLE BOILER INSERT

Many double boilers come with matching bottom pans, but this is an

---

9.73 ILSA HEAT DIFFUSER

A *bain-marie* moderates heat with the use of water. A heat diffuser accomplishes the same goal by creating a layer of material between pot and burner. Like the thick asbestos pads of old, it keeps the pan from the direct heat. Use this device when you want to melt chocolate, keep stock hot for risotto, or cook in an earthenware casserole—or any time you need to diffuse heat and protect the pan from a possibly scorching flame or hot electric element. The one we show you here has a scalloped disc shape and is made of sturdy, heavy-enameled cast iron. It comes with a helpful separate handle that inserts into a hole in the disc.

independent stainless steel insert. It fits into any of All-Clad's 3-quart saucepans, which must be purchased separately. You will reach for this handy tool whenever you wish to melt butter or chocolate; to cook polenta, custard, or cheese sauce; or for that matter, to cook any ingredient or dish that could scorch, curdle, or separate in a regular saucepan without the moderating intervention of water. The insert has a circular ridge that helps it sit snugly inside the base pot. This is a well-made, roomy pan, with a convenient long handle.

STOCKPOTS

STOCKPOTS, like double boilers, cook food by transmitting heat through water, but unlike double boilers, stockpots completely immerse the ingredients in the water so that they impart their own flavor to the liquid. Stockpots are tall and narrow; the relatively limited surface area prevents evaporation, the liquid is preserved longer, and the pot's height forces the liquid to bubble up through layers of ingredients—flavors that begin at the bottom build up through layers of broth, meat, bones, and vegetables, fusing together and enriching one another.

Today, most home cooks don't make stock with great regularity. Even if you take on this task only occasionally, it is worth your while to buy a good stockpot—you can also use it for soup preparation, cooking pasta, or boiling lobsters or crabs. There are stockpots in sizes beginning at about 4 quarts. It is smarter, however, to buy one that is larger. The meat, bones, and other ingredients take up a great deal of room, so a small stockpot won't yield much broth. And if you are the kind of cook who makes homemade *glace de viande* and other such classics, remember that the reduction of broth needed for this recipe requires a large amount of stock at the start. Our advice is to choose a stockpot of at least 8-quart capacity, and larger if you are a serious cook who depends on homemade stock.

Which Metal?

The bottom of a stockpot must be of good quality and thicker than the sides to support heavy bones and other ingredients and to prevent them from sticking or scorching. We don't recommend copper, tin-lined stockpots. They are expensive—and because copper's heat responsiveness has no bearing on stock-making, the money is not well spent. Copper pots are also heavy, and the ingredients and the large quantity of water used for stock add more weight, so copper can become more of a burden than a benefit.

Aluminum is fine because it is light and holds its heat well, but bear in mind that pure aluminum can discolor, and the pot may not look as pretty as it did once—and high-acid foods like wine and tomatoes will interact with the aluminum and may impart a metallic taste. Also be sure to avoid cheap, thin-gauge pots that can warp or cause ingredients to burn. A better choice is either stainless steel–coated aluminum or anodized aluminum. Coated steel holds heat well and is lightweight, making it another good choice for stockpots.

We also recommend stainless steel for stock-making. Well-made pots from reputable manufacturers have either aluminum cores or thick, wide, heat-diffusing discs at the bottom to transmit heat efficiently to the water. Stainless steel does not discolor ingredients, so you can make a perfectly clear stock for soups and sauces. We also show you a marmite, an earthenware pot used to make stock or soup.

Handling Hint

A final word: all stockpots, even those of aluminum, are heavy. A spigot, which is a feature of some professional models, makes it easy to withdraw liquids. Without this feature, you must reach inside the pan to scoop ingredients. Instead of tipping the pot to strain a stock, use a small saucepan (1 or 1½ quarts) as a ladle. A saucepan is steadier than a ladle and usually has a larger capacity.

> The kitchen, reasonably enough, was the scene of my first gastronomic adventure. I was on all fours. I crawled into the vegetable bin, settled on a giant onion and ate it, skin and all. It must have marked me for life, for I have never ceased to love the hearty flavor of raw onions.
> —JAMES BEARD

WINTER SQUASH SOUP WITH RED CHILI & MINT

4 to 6 servings

FOR THE STOCK

seeds and inner fibers of 2½ pounds
   winter squash
2 celery stalks, diced
1 onion, roughly chopped or sliced
1 bay leaf
5 branches parsley
½ teaspoon dried sage leaves
1 teaspoon salt
8 cups cold water

Halve the squash, scrape out the seeds and stringy fibers with a metal spoon, and put them in a pot with the rest of the ingredients. Save the flesh for the soup. Bring to a boil, turn the heat down, and simmer for 25 to 35 minutes; then strain.

FOR THE SOUP

2½ pounds winter squash—butternut,
   perfection, sugar pumpkin, or other
1 red bell pepper or 2 pimentos
1 pound fresh or canned tomatoes, peeled,
   seeded, and chopped; juice reserved
1 ancho chili for chili purée or 1 to 2 tablespoons
   New Mexican chili powder
1 tablespoon butter
1 tablespoon sunflower or olive oil
1 large yellow onion, finely chopped
1 clove garlic, minced
1 to 2 teaspoons nutritional yeast (optional)
1 teaspoon salt
6 to 7 cups stock
1 tablespoon parsley, chopped
1 tablespoon mint, chopped

1 After halving the squash and removing the seeds and fibers for the stock, cut the halves into smaller, more manageable pieces for peeling. Then remove the skins and add them to the remaining stock. (In the case of large, smooth squash, like butternut, the skins can be easily removed with a vegetable peeler.) Cut the peeled squash into pieces, roughly ½" square.

2 To give the peppers a smoky flavor, roast them directly over the flame or in the broiler until the skin is charred, and then set them aside in a covered bowl to steam for 10 minutes or so. Scrape off the charred skin with a knife, remove the seeds, and dice the peppers into ¼" squares.

3 If using an ancho chili, first remove the stem, seeds, and veins. Cover it with boiling water and soak it for 20 minutes; then blend until smooth.

4 Heat the butter and oil in a soup pot; add the onion, garlic, and nutritional yeast, if using; and cook over medium-low heat until the onion is soft, about 10 minutes. Stir in the tomatoes, half the chili, and the salt, and stew for 5 minutes. Add the cubed squash, grilled peppers, reserved tomato juice, and 6 cups of the stock. Simmer until the squash has melted into a purée, about 25 to 40 minutes.

5 Thin with more liquid, if needed; season with salt; and add more chili purée if desired. Serve the soup with the parsley and mint stirred in at the last minute.

NOTE: If the soup sits before serving, the sweet and hot flavors will deepen and merge. This soup, a salad of crisp, tart greens, and cornbread make a satisfying, simple meal. Try a lighter zinfandel with this soup, or if you'd prefer a white, serve a sauvignon blanc.

The Greens Cook Book, by Deborah Madison with Edward Espe Brown

---

9.75 BOURGEAT STOCKPOT WITH SPIGOT

The spigot on this stockpot serves several useful purposes. It provides an opportunity to take a cup or two of stock while the remainder cooks. Because fat rises to the top, if you drain the pot from below, the liquid will be nearly fat free. Withdrawing the liquid also lightens the load, making it easier to carry the pot when cooking is done. This brushed stainless steel stockpot is outstanding in other ways too. It is suitably tall, so flavors fuse slowly with minimal evaporation, and it provides sufficient heat distribution, keeping ingredients at a near simmer. The curved top edge has a professional finish, and the slightly domed lid sits perfectly on top. Thick, rounded loop handles help ease the carrying burden. The handles are hollow so they keep cool on the stovetop. They are also attached by a circular weld, which makes them virtually unbreakable; unlike handles that are spot-welded, there is no place for bacteria to hide. The model we show you is 10⅘ liters (11½ quarts); the pot is also available in 17.2- (18⅕-quart), 25- (26⅖-quart), 36- (38-quart), and 50-liter (52⅘-quart) sizes. A similar aluminum model is available as well.

9.76 KITCHENAID FIVE-PLY STAINLESS STEEL CLAD STOCKPOT

This 8-quart pot is too short to be a proper stockpot, although Kitchen-Aid calls it one. It does, however, have some terrific qualities, making it worth mentioning here. As with all KitchenAid cookware, it is constructed with care and attention: tight rivets; smooth, rounded edges; a heavy, snug-fitting lid that sits deep within the pan. The two riveted loop handles are roomy enough for fingers and sturdy enough to help lift the pan. In addition, the five-ply clad metal assures quick and even heat distribution.

9.77 CERAFLAME MARMITE

This old-fashioned-looking item isn't truly a stockpot, although its bulbous shape and narrow neck serve the same purpose: increasing condensation and preventing evaporation of fluids. You can surely use it for making small quantities of stock,

and it is a marvelous choice for soup. Because it is made of ceramic, it maintains heat exceptionally well, so it can double as a tureen to stay on the table—not only is it attractive enough, but the soup will stay hot for second servings. The side knobs stay relatively cool and are convenient for carrying. It comes in 3-, 4½-, and 7-quart sizes; we like the small one for baked beans.

9.78 CALPHALON COMMERCIAL STAINLESS SAUCEPAN

For those who dislike dark, nonstick, or stick-resistant interiors in cookware, Calphalon offers the home cook another option: this anodized aluminum cookware lined with stainless steel. Although Calphalon calls the pot we show you here a saucepan, we think it has the perfect dimensions for making soup. It is only 6½ quarts, but it is tall and narrow, so while it may not be roomy enough to let you make a huge quantity of stock, it is the right shape. And its handles are particularly well suited to stock-making: they are large, roomy, and attached with four sturdy rivets per handle, making it easy for you to carry the pot even when it's filled with bones, vegetables, and liquid. The tempered glass cover is domed, unlike those on classic stockpots, and the stainless steel rim prevents the glass from shattering if dropped. Leave it askew when

---

THE BEST WAY TO COOK A LOBSTER
⚜ JASPER WHITE ⚜

The briny-sweet flavor of lobster is so special all by itself, with nothing more than a drop of melted butter or a squeeze of lemon, that I often prepare my lobsters in the simplest fashion to make them shine, especially when cooking for friends who don't eat lobster often.

Ideally, I boil or steam them in clean water taken directly from the ocean. If that is not an option, I prefer steaming in only ½" of water in a heavy pot with a tight-fitting lid. Old-fashioned graniteware is fine, but I don't use the double-decker steamer kind. A 1½- to 2-pound lobster takes a 4-quart pot. For two lobsters I figure 8 quarts, and so forth.

I salt the water heavily so it resembles ocean water and when possible use rock weed as the rack to hold the lobster above the water line.

When lobsters are cooked this way, I can enjoy their pure, unadulterated taste. They also provide fully-cooked meat for a variety of dishes.

Alternatively, grilling also produces a terrific, somewhat more complex lobster flavor. I split the lobsters alive and place them shell side down over medium-hot coals. I never turn a lobster over on the grill—it will absorb too much smoke flavor and lose its delicious juices. And I don't worry if the shells get a little charred—it is the forceful cooking of the shells that intensifies the flavor.

you want liquids to evaporate; keep it in place when you use the pot for soups that contain ingredients (such as rice and pasta) that need a closed, moist-heat environment.

9.79 CALPHALON COMMERCIAL HARD-ANODIZED NONSTICK STOCKPOT

This pot's dark, nonstick interior is an advantage and a disadvantage at the same time. The black surface makes it more difficult to see what's cooking inside, but it also makes it so easy to clean up that you may over-

look that particular drawback. It has the right height and heft, and two extra-long, extra-roomy handles help you move the pot, laden with ingredients, from the stovetop. The cover is a stainless steel dome that you can leave askew when you want liquid and solids to gently concentrate flavor over a long simmer. A large insert for making pasta is available. We recommend the 12-quart size, but there is also an 8-quart model.

9.80 CHANTAL ENAMEL STOCKPOT

This enamel-on-steel 9-quart pot holds heat so well that it allows ingredients to cook slowly and decreases the likelihood of overheating or boiling the liquid (which causes debris to collect and make the stock cloudy). It is tall and prettier than most stockpots. The inside is black, and the exterior comes in several colors: red, blue, green, or white. The blue and white exteriors even have matching colored interiors. The lid, which fits inside the pan, is made of stainless steel–rimmed tempered glass, which gives you the opportunity to peek at the ingredients as they cook. There's a bonus, too: a large stainless steel steaming insert is available, giving this stockpot some versatility. The insert, which sits on top of the pot, is roomy enough for steaming lobster or clams as well as vegetables.

9.81 WMF TOPSTAR MULTIPOT

This is an incredibly user-friendly set of tools that will help you prepare stock and dozens of other foods. The parts are top-quality stainless steel; the stockpot is equipped with a thick disc for heat distribution. It has two highly placed, roomy handles and a curved rim that helps with pouring. Two lids are available: a flat one appropriate to stock-making and a heavy one that sits deep within the pan for cooking with little water. The other parts include a *bain-marie*, large vegetable steamer insert, rice steamer, and broth colander. All

"It's Brooklyn clam chowder—you got a problem with that?"

parts are sturdy, dishwasher safe, and—miracle of miracles—they all stack together for convenient storage even though they are all the same diameter. NOTE: Each piece of the multipot is sold separately.

> An idealist is one who,
> on noticing that
> a rose smells better
> than a cabbage,
> concludes that it will also
> make better soup.
>
> —H. L. MENCKEN

9.82 THERMOS HOT POT

This is not exactly a stockpot, but we thought we'd show it to you anyway. If you're going out of the house and have no time to watch the stockpot, or if you are going to a football game or other outdoor event, or if you're simply bringing some food to someone else, this item may come in handy. You boil the ingredients in the stainless steel inner pot, then transfer the pan to the thermos and lock the lid. Several hours later the food is fully cooked and still very hot. We made vegetable stock inside it—it doesn't require the same time or finesse as meat stock—and after five hours we had flavorful broth holding at 160°F. Use it for soups, vegetable or fish stocks, baked beans, or hot cider. Tote it anywhere. It holds 4.5 liters (4½ quarts).

STEAMERS & STEAMING BASKETS

STEAMING IS THE BEST WAY to keep vegetables crisp, brightly colored, and crunchy. What's more, the vegetables taste delicious, with real, earthy flavor, sometimes delicate, sometimes intense, but never bitter. Vegetables—particularly green and yellow ones, which are filled with water-soluble vitamins—retain more nutrients when they are steamed, so they taste good and are good for you. Americans tend to limit steaming to vegetables, but other cultures steam a variety of foods. Many dishes that benefit from moist-heat cooking will do well in a steamer: fish, chicken, shellfish, couscous, and rice among them.

Steamers may be self-contained pieces of cookware or separate pieces—either solid inserts or collapsible baskets—that fit inside cookware. In either case, to function properly, a steamer must have a tight-fitting lid, so vapors build up within the vessel to sufficiently cook the food. But there must also be a means for steam to escape when necessary, so that too much pressure will not be created inside the pot. For optimum steaming, the pot should be deep and wide, so steam can circulate freely around the ingredients.

Any pot can serve as a steamer base; even a large wok will do. As for the insert or basket, stainless steel is the top choice because there is no interaction with the food, it doesn't rust, and it is durable. Bamboo steamers are fine as well. Be careful when lifting the lids after steaming foods. Open the lid at a safe distance and tip it away from your face to avoid the hot steam from burning you.

9.83 NORPRO DOUBLE STEAMER BASKET

This steaming basket has several virtues. It is made of stainless steel, which is durable, never rusts, and cleans easily; the overlapping petals unfold and expand for filling and collapse for convenient storage. In addition, it is two-tiered, to give you more than double the steaming capability. The two baskets can be used separately: they each have three legs to hold the foods to be steamed above the water. One fits inside a 6¼" or larger pot, the other into a 7⅛" or larger pot. They also may be stacked—there is a plastic insert in the center to lock the two baskets together—so you can cook two different vegetables or clams on one layer, vegetables on the other, and so on. The center post is plastic and doesn't get hot, making it easy to lift this basket out of the steaming pot.

9.84 ENDURANCE STEAMER BASKET

Put this basket inside a saucepan and you have an inexpensive steamer. Its eighteen perforated stainless steel leaves expand or close to fit into 6¼" or larger pots, and to hold a small or larger quantity of ingredients. The basket rests on three legs that raise the contents above the water. The leaves never rust, and they fold back into a "bud" for convenient storage. The metal post in the center can be removed to accommodate large vegetables, such as corn on the cob or a whole cauliflower. There is a ring on the center post to lift the basket from the pot. It will be hot inside, so be sure to be careful and to use a pot holder. Steam contains more heat energy, and has the potential to burn you more severely, than boiling water.

9.85 JOYCE CHEN TIERED BAMBOO STEAMERS

Bamboo steamers are typically used for cooking Chinese dim sum, but they have many virtues that make them handy for all types of food. They are especially good for dim sum because of their gently domed lids, which trap steam inside. Bamboo absorbs moisture, so condensed water droplets never fall on the doughy tidbits, which would make

CONSTRUCTING A MAKESHIFT STEAMER
❧ HELEN CHEN ❧

If you don't have a Chinese steamer, you can create a makeshift steamer using a wok, stir-fry pan, or large stockpot. (Many wok sets come with steaming racks.) Be sure the pan is large enough to hold the dish used for steaming. It must have at least 2" of headroom and enough room around it so that it can be easily removed when hot. Remove the top and bottom of an empty tuna fish can to make a stand and place it on the bottom of your pan. Bring water to a boil. Put the plate or bowl containing the food on the stand, cover the wok with a lid, and steam.

them soggy. The bamboo also adds a delicate fragrance to ingredients. To keep the bamboo clean and prevent rancidity, food is never placed directly on the slats inside the basket. The slats are lined with cabbage leaves, parchment paper, or a small plate with a lip to trap juices. These steamers are usually used inside a wok (be sure the wok is about 2" wider than the basket) and can be stacked to accommodate different foods in each basket. The set we show you has two baskets, but you can add more. Caution: foods can stick to the steamer.

9.86 ALL-CLAD STEAMER INSERT

Here is another easy way to transform your pots to steamers: a special accessory insert that fits snugly into the pan. This 3-quart model is made of thick, sturdy, heavy stainless steel. The basket is capacious, with room for two bunches of broccoli or a couple pounds of steamer clams. It has small holes on the bottom to allow

steam to penetrate the food, and it has an outward bulge near the center so it can sit on the rim of the bottom pot, high above the water. The top of the basket has a curved edge, where the lid rests. The long handle stays cool and is riveted to the basket. The length of the handle is particularly convenient for steam cooking. It keeps your hands away from the hot vapors and lets you lift and carry the entire basket to the sink for draining. This insert fits all of All-Clad's 3-, 3½-, and 4-quart saucepans. The company also makes a 12-quart steamer insert, with two side loop handles, to fit larger saucepans.

9.87 CUISINART EVERYDAY STAINLESS STEEL STEAMER

This compact pair of pots have merit, particularly for those with small kitchens. The bottom unit is a 2¾-quart high-quality stainless steel pan. A covered copper disc enhances heating, so you can use it for a number of things: making sauce, poaching vegetables, or even preparing a small quantity of soup or stew. Two side handles make it appropriate for oven use too. The top unit of the set is a spacious basket that works well for steaming. Its bulge fits securely on the gently curved edges of the lower pan so the steam from the water or broth is forced up through the holes in the bottom. Each part in the set is equipped with comfortable, roomy handles to accomodate pot holders or mitts.

9.88 CHARLESTON RICE COOKER

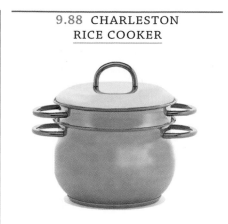

It takes almost no effort for you to make rice in this bulbous, friendly-looking stainless steel pot. All you have to do is place 1 to 3 cups of raw rice in the inner bowl, which is similar to a double boiler but has six cutouts on the sides to allow steam to penetrate the rice kernels. Fill the pot with 10 cups of water, bring it to a boil, and place the inner bowl inside the pot. Cover and cook for about 25 minutes. The thick aluminum disc on the bottom of the pot

COUSCOUS
✤ PAULA WOLFERT ✤

Couscous is usually made from granules of semolina, though barley, millet, corn, and even dried breadcrumbs are also used. The granules or grains are steamed until separate and tender, then doused with herb-scented butter or fragrant olive oil and tossed with a flavorful sauce. When properly cooked, couscous is the great "grain" dish of North Africa. It's also the most misunderstood.

Let me begin by dispelling the myths about couscous.

MYTH 1

Couscous itself is a grain. Yes, couscous is granular, but the substance we normally think of as couscous is made from semolina flour, a product of durum wheat. Thus wheat is the grain. (Of course, if you make a couscous-type dish with barley, corn, or millet, then you actually will be working with a grain.)

MYTH 2

Couscous is dried pasta. Not true! Pasta is made by kneading semolina and water to make a strong dough that can be stretched and cut to specific sizes and then boiled. As food expert Charles Perry wrote in the *Los Angeles Times:* "If you boil couscous (especially handmade couscous), it turns to a porridgy mess. If you steam it, though, it fluffs up into something completely lacking the chewy quality of gluten—something amazingly tender, practically ethereal."

MYTH 3

There's real couscous, sold out of sacks in health food stores, and an inferior product called "instant couscous," sold out of packages at supermarkets ... and never the twain shall meet. Also not true. Nearly all commercially sold couscous, whether labeled instant or not, is virtually the same, since all factory-made couscous is partially precooked. Truly raw couscous, which has been rolled and dried without any steaming, is nearly impossible to find outside of private sources. If you want really good couscous that's fluffy and light, you have two alternatives: make your own, or purchase packaged or loose couscous and steam it properly. If you do this, you will get a yield more than twice—sometimes even triple—what you would get if you followed the instructions on the box. On the other hand, if you *do* follow the box instructions, your couscous will swell up in your stomach rather than in the steamer as it should. Great for people who like to feel full, I suppose, but a disaster for couscous lovers.

MYTH 4

You should line the perforated bottom of your steamer with cheesecloth to keep the couscous from falling into the broth. Not true, because, with steam rising, the grains won't fall though ... except an inconsequential ½ teaspoon's worth before the steam takes over.

You can always tell when couscous is fully cooked. It changes color, turns pale blond, and becomes bouncy and light. That is the moment to turn it out into a large bowl, moisten it, and let it rest, covered, for at least 10 minutes before serving.

Anyone who has ever tried to find coarse semolina in summer will immediately understand why a method was needed to preserve the semolina part of the hard wheat, which quickly goes bad in warm weather from weevils or spoilage. I don't know when couscous was invented (Charles Perry believes it was in the eleventh or twelfth century), but I believe it was created—like pasta—as a way to preserve semolina thoughout the year.

disperses heat well, producing voluminous amounts of steam that cook the rice to perfect fluffiness. But there's more! You can use the bottom pot for soup, sauce, or pasta. You can use the rice steamer insert as a basket for steaming vegetables or shellfish. It is a versatile addition to your cookware collection.

9.89 DE BUYER *COUSSOUSSIÈRE*

A very special kind of steamer, often shaped somewhat like an hourglass, is known as a *couscoussière*. It is used in North Africa to prepare the traditional grain dish couscous, cooked semolina pasta pellets, frequently topped with a meat and vegetable stew. The word *couscous* can refer to the complete dish or to the grain component alone, and the *couscoussière*'s two compartments cook both the couscous and its stew. When the stew in the pot below is almost done, the grain is put to steam in the upper basket, which looks like a colander.

The lower part of the *couscoussière* is called a *gdra*. The upper perforated section, called a *kskas,* fits snugly into the bottom pot. The *kskas,* unlike baskets in other steamers, is perforated only on the bottom and sits high over the *gdra* so that the cooking liquid from the stew will not touch it. Because the couscous must cook in the vapors that rise from the stew, as little steam as possible should be allowed to escape before it can reach the grain. We recommend twisting a dampened and floured length of cheesecloth around the *couscoussière* at the joint between the top and bottom pots to make a perfect steamtight seal.

Though many *couscoussières* come with lids, these should not be used when cooking couscous. In a closed pot the steam would only condense on the lid and drip back on the grain, making it soggy and dense. This is a mortal offense in the eyes of any self-respecting aficionado, since the mark of a good couscous is its lightness, and much preparation time is spent fussing with the grains to keep them separate and fluffy.

The straight-sided *couscoussière* we show here comes from France. It is aluminum, with loop-shaped handles riveted to both the bottom and the top sections. It is 12″ in diameter and stands 13½″ high. The *gdra* of this *couscoussière* holds 11 quarts, but since the stew should not touch the bottom of the *kskas,* its actual capacity is somewhat smaller. While we don't recommend plain aluminum cookware, it's hard to find a *couscoussière* made of anything but.

9.90 AMCO ARTICHOKE COOKER

Cooking artichokes can be a difficult task: they tend to bob up and down in the water (and color unevenly), and their tender leaves cook faster than the stems. Steaming them in a raised contraption like this holder is best for artichokes because it evens out the cooking: the base of the vegetable, which sits nearer the water, cooks faster than the leaves, which are near the top. Steaming the artichokes also preserves their nutrients and flavor. This holder is made of sturdy stainless steel; you simply place the vegetable, stem side down, inside the small circle, then put the holder, still with the stem side down, inside a large pot for steaming.

9.91 AMCO ASPARAGUS COOKER

Like artichokes, asparagus presents a challenge to the cook. The tender tips are done much sooner than the stalks. If you cook the vegetable laying flat in a pan full of simmering water, it is likely that the tips will overcook and become soggy while waiting for the stems to cook through. In order to spare your asparagus from this soggy fate, you can use this device, made of chrome-plated steel, that stands the spears firmly upright. To cook the vegetable, place the holder in a deep pot and put the asparagus in the middle of the holder, thick stem end down. Add about 3″ of water, some salt, and cover the pan before turning on the heat. Only the stems will cook in the water, while the more delicate tips are high above, cooking only by the steam. The asparagus steamer is also useful for cooking a bunch of broccolini so the meaty stalks cook in the water and the tender florets steam.

9.92 MATFER *POMMES VAPEUR* POT

For the kitchen that has everything, here is the fanciest piece of equipment for the simplest recipe: steamed potatoes (*pommes de terre à l'anglaise*). Peeled potatoes, or any other vegetable for that matter, are steamed royally in this copper bucket. First, pour water into the flattened copper ball that forms the bottom of the bucket. Then insert the tinned-steel grate that fits above it. Add the vegetables, cover, and place the steamer on a burner over a low flame. The bucket holds about 6½ cups and is 6″ deep and 6½″ in diameter. Both loop handles on the bucket and the knob on the tight-fitting, domed copper lid are of brass. In restaurants, this piece is sometimes used as a tableside item, once the potatoes are done.

He felt his belly crave for its food.
He hoped there would be stew
for dinner, turnips and
carrots and bruised potatoes
and fat mutton pieces to be
ladled out in thick peppered
flour fattened sauce. Stuff it into
you, his belly counseled him.

—JAMES JOYCE,
Portrait of the Artist as a Young Man

ELECTRIC RICE COOKERS

Walk into any Asian home or restaurant in the United States and you're likely to find an automatic rice cooker at work. It can cook a large portion of rice and keep it at serving temperature for hours, so it makes sense in places where every meal includes rice. We maintain that by measuring and timing carefully, and using a pot with a tight-fitting lid and a low heat setting, you can make perfect rice on the rangetop. If you occasionally serve rice as a side dish at family meals, say once a week, and even less frequently to company, we advise learning to master it on the stove. Electric rice cookers often take as long as an hour, and are relatively large and require storage space you may not want to devote to an infrequently used item.

However, should you decide that it's right for you, don't think using a rice-cooker is fail-safe. Many models are manufactured with people already knowledgeable about rice cookers in mind and come with manuals that are not geared to the average American cook. They give little information about cooking different types of rice and are vague about quantities of rice and water. With the cookers you often get a plastic measuring "cup" that holds 6 ounces rather than a standard 8 ounces. If you lose this accessory you'll find it hard to follow the manufacturer's directions. Virtually all rice cookers call for rinsing rice before steaming, a practice that's standard in Asia but not so here. Just as you would when learning to make stovetop rice, you need to figure out what works for you before perfecting the procedure. By experimenting we found that in some cases we could bypass the instructions that come with the cookers. We followed the directions on the rice package and used standard measuring cups and still got good results.

Select a rice cooker that optimizes ease of use. It's a fact of life that rice is sticky and leaves behind a residue that makes cleaning the pot a chore. You can avoid this by choosing a cooker with a liner that has a nonstick finish. Liners with markings that tell you how much water to add after you've measured out the rice make it unnecessary to memorize proportions or pull out the manual—but, as we said, the measurements are based on the cup that comes with the cooker, so you'll need to be careful not to lose it. Any model worth its salt turns off automatically when the rice is fully steamed and keeps it warm until you're ready to eat.

9.93 ZOJIRUSHI DELUXE RICE COOKER & WARMER

We love this unit because it cooks both white and brown rice perfectly in about the same amount of time it would take on the stovetop—30 minutes for white, 50 for brown. All you have to do is measure out raw rice and water (using either the formula given on the rice package or the cup that comes with the machine and matches the marks in the liner) then press a button. After cooking it automatically switches to a "keep warm" setting and holds the rice hot and moist for up to 12 hours. In addition to the cup, you get a plastic spatula and a holder for it that attaches to the steamer. The cooking chamber has a nonstick finish that rice virtually falls out of, so cleaning it is a breeze. It makes about 6½ cups of cooked rice. There's a built-in carrying handle and room to store the cord in the bottom of this 10¼"-round, 10"-high cooker.

FISH POACHERS

A FISH SPENDS ITS LIFE IN WATER, so it seems only fitting to cook it in its natural liquid environment. This isn't difficult to do, if you use a special poacher. A large poached salmon, Arctic char, or other firm-fleshed fish can make an impressive dinner entrée or buffet item. Barring that, a poacher is also convenient to cook several fish steaks or fillets at a time. Fish poachers come in several lengths; the 16" is a good size for most family meals, but a larger one may be a better choice, though don't expect it to hold a fish bigger than four pounds. They are shaped like long, straight-sided ovals, and you will need to straddle the pan over two burners.

Stainless steel, tinned steel, and anodized aluminum are the best choices for materials because they keep the hot liquid, which cooks the fish, at an even temperature. There are some beautiful tin or stainless steel-lined copper poachers, but they are woefully expensive and don't do a better job. Plain aluminum is not a good choice either, because most poaching fluids are wine or lemon based and can discolor the pan and the food. All fish poachers come with a long rack on which you lay the fish. The rack protects the fish from the direct heat of the burner. Some racks are versatile—you can turn them over, and in that case they sit higher in the pan and are useful for steaming. Otherwise, place small heatproof bowls below the rack to raise it. The rack also helps you to lift the fish out of the pan in one piece.

Fish has delicate flesh and can toughen or dry out if overcooked or cooked too quickly. Remember to keep the liquid below a simmer, as boiling and even simmering can irritate the flesh. Use a mixture of water and white wine plus a judicious amount of fragrant seasonings. The old rules for cooking fish "until it flakes" or for "10 minutes per inch of thickness" are no longer useful. By the time fish flakes, it has dried out, and fish that are more or less than 1" thick may cook to completion in times not exactly proportional using the old formula. Use an instant read thermometer to check: the internal temperature of a cooked fish should be about 145°F. If you are poaching a fish to be served cold, turn off the burner about 10 minutes before the expected completed cooking time and let the fish finish cooking in the liquid as it cools.

Many people wrap fish in a double layer of cheesecloth before poaching. The cloth acts as a mold for the fish, to keep the skin and flesh intact. This procedure may be more important when cooking small fish, which fall apart more easily, but is not absolutely necessary when cooking a large fish.

9.94 DE BUYER FISH POACHER

This pan from De Buyer is almost too pretty to put to such functional service as poaching fish. The bronze side handles and fish-shaped lid lifter are nice decorative touches but serve no culinary purpose. On the other hand, if you are a person whose cooking experience is enhanced by using lovely cookware, this might be the right purchase for your kitchen collection. In addition to its beauty, the stainless steel body has its advantages: you can use wine or lemon and never be concerned that these ingredients will react with the metal. And stainless steel never wears out. The rack on this poacher, also of stainless steel, can be hooked over the edge of the pan, a benefit when you want to drain the fish over the steaming fluids and keep the fish warm while you prepare a sauce. When turned upside down inside the pan, the rack can sit well above the liquid and function as a steaming tray for fish and shellfish. The poacher's dimensions are 23⅝" by 6½" by 4½", large enough for a whole 3-pound salmon. If the head of the fish has been removed, the poacher will hold a larger fish. It will also accomodate two smaller whole fish or several thick fish steaks.

9.95 DE BUYER TURBOT POACHER

Fish, like people, are geographically defined, so the French have the turbot. A virtually scale-free flatfish, the turbot has been described as a fish that's been put through a wringer. The novelist Marcel Proust once described it as a fish that is "all profile." Like its relative, the Atlantic halibut, the turbot's flesh is so delicate that the French accord it special treatment and have named and reserved for it its own particular utensil: the *turbotière*. Diamond shaped and made of aluminum throughout, the *turbotière* measures 20" by 16" and is 4" deep. The inside rack has strong looped handles at either end, and there is a flat handle atop the tightly fitted lid.

9.96 CALPHALON FISH POACHER

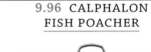

This pot is not as beautiful as the De Buyer fish poacher but it is thoroughly capable. Its 20" length (6½" wide, 5" deep) leaves room to cook a whole 3-pound fish or several fillets or steaks inside, yet it is not too big and bulky for most kitchens. The anodized aluminum keeps the cooking liquid at a steady temperature and, unlike regular aluminum, will not discolor the poaching fluids nor the pan if you use a classic, wine-based court bouillon. Two roomy metal loop side handles are well riveted to the pan. The rack is very sturdy and thick, also with heavy side handles to help you lift the cooked fish out of the liquid. The lid is nearly flat and fits well inside the pan; it has a metal loop lifter in the center.

LIDS

A LID CAN BE ANYTHING from the top crust of a pie, to a heavy iron dome for a pot, to a sheet of buttered parchment paper that gently protects a poaching fish fillet. Lid variables include weight, shape, and the quality of the seal it makes with the underlying cooking utensil. There are many possible combinations of these factors to fit particular cooking needs. There is no single solution to covering a pot; the lid must suit the type of cooking you are doing. A slightly domed lid that forms a sturdy seal with the edge of the pan prevents steam from escaping. As the vapors condense on the lid, droplets fall back into the pan, creating lush moisture for stews and soups. On the other hand, if you are reducing a sauce—tomato sauce for pasta, for example—it is preferable for the moisture to evaporate from the pan. But because bubbling sauce can spatter all over the stove, a flattened or more lightweight lid, placed slightly askew to let steam escape, may be more appropriate.

Most important, a lid helps you to regulate the heat in the pot. Any lid at all—even a pie crust—will raise the heat of the food beneath it (although a glass lid allows heat to radiate off somewhat). When a pot and lid of heavy-gauge, highly conductive metal are used together, they create a tight little oven that surrounds the food and holds temperatures at a high point. This permits the cook to lower the flame significantly, even to shut it off entirely if the intent is simply to keep finished food warm—a real fuel saver. A covered pot should be checked after it has been over the heat for 15 minutes or so; chances are that the heat should be reduced at that point.

Choosing Lids

Some manufacturers of pans make what they call "universal lids," designed to fit all of their pots. A few manufacturers also produce universal lids that are designed to fit pans from other manufacturers. We show you several types of lids from different companies. They may be purchased separately. Remember that, with few exceptions, you need not match a lid to a pan from the same manufacturer—there are enough sizes available to cover all the pots that need a lid.

9.97 KITCHENAID 18/10 STAINLESS STEEL LID

Solid, sensible, and sturdy: this pot topper from KitchenAid is a perfect example of what good lids should be. The lid is heavy, and the raised rim that sits on the edge of the pan is high, so the lid sits deep within the pan, creating a tight seal. This design also cuts down on rattling. The handle is high and roomy and is securely riveted. Both the outside and inside are made of 18/10 mirror-finish stainless steel.

9.98 ANOLON NOUVELLE LONG-HANDLE LID

This American lid, made of stainless steel, was inspired by a classic French design. It has a narrow raised rim that sits on the pan's edge; the middle section is nearly flat. The lid has an unusual feature. The long handle, which is riveted on, stays very cool and eliminates the need for pot holders. The handle is also curved for maximum comfort.

9.99 LE CREUSET ROUND FRENCH OVEN LID

This heavyweight enameled cast-iron lid sits firmly on top of the vessel, preventing steam from escaping. That guarantees a juicy pot roast, stew, or casserole. All lids come in colors that match the underlying pan and have embossed circles on top as a design element. The lid has a wide, easy-to-grip knob made of phenolic. It is oven safe to 450°F.

9.100 BERNDES TRADITION GLASS DOMED LID

This heavy lid is made of glass that resists breakage. The see-through dome collects vapors from the steaming ingredients inside the pan and sends them down in droplets to self-baste the food. It has a large, well-designed phenolic knob that stays cool during cooking. The knob is oven safe to 450°F.

9.101 CHANTAL GLASS LID

This tempered glass lid is shatter-resistant and oven safe to 375°F. It is slightly domed, to help collect moisturizing vapors, and is trimmed on its outer edge with stainless steel to help prevent the glass from cracking if dropped accidentally. The trim is indented underneath so that the lid can sit snugly on the edge of the pan. The lid handle is a roomy and good-looking curved triangle. It is attached to a disc that is hollow inside and screwed onto the center of the lid. The air pocket created inside the disc prevents heat from traveling as quickly from the pan to the knob.

9.102 NORPRO STRAINER LID

This is a tempered glass lid, rimmed with stainless steel. The extra-large and roomy stainless steel lid lifter in the center stays cool during cooking. It doesn't fit snugly inside the pan because it is designed to let steam escape. However, it is heavy, and sits deep inside the pan, so it doesn't rattle during cooking. The inside rim is pierced on two sides, allowing the steam to escape and reducing the chance that liquids will boil over. It also lets you spill off liquids from cooked food.

9.103 CALPHALON FLAT LID

Perfectly flat lids come in handy not only when you're trying to get a sauce to reduce, but also when you want to prevent it from spattering onto the stove by leaving the lid slightly askew on the pot. They are also suitable for stock-making, when it's important to let the ingredients bubble together and infuse flavor without creating too much steam. There are several flat hard-anodized aluminum lids available from Calphalon for just such purposes. They range in size from a small 4½" to 14" for various saucepans, omelet pans, sauté pans, and stockpots, and can conveniently be interchanged from one type of pan to another.

9.104 MAUVIEL FLAT COPPER LID

This is a simple, thin, flat copper disc that comes in many sizes, from 5⅛" to 12¼", made to cover pots from 5" and up. Its lack of rim means that it will sit atop any pan whose circumference is smaller. There is a long, slim, cast-iron handle attached to the top in two places with copper rivets and a hole in the end for hanging. The length of the handle helps it stay cool. The lid design makes it especially useful when you need to partially cover a pan.

9.105 DE BUYER COPPER LID

This copper lid fits snugly within the company's saucepans and stewpans; there are many sizes, and the two largest (8⅝" and 9½") are sold separately. Each lid is lined with tin and has a raised rim that rests securely on the edge of the pot. The loop lifter is made of sturdy cast iron and is riveted securely to the pan; it does get hot, but the loop is roomy enough to fit your fingers and a pot holder. The company makes similar lids that coordinate with its stainless steel–lined copper and brass cookware.

9.106 CALPHALON DOMED LID

Domed lids are useful when you want to retain moisture in a pan for a stew or sauce. These hard-anodized aluminum lids are heavy, medium-high domes. They come in several sizes from 7" to 10" and are designed to fit various pots and pans in the Calphalon line. The lid lifter is a squared loop, made of cast stainless steel that is riveted onto the lid.

9.107 ENDURANCE UNIVERSAL LID

You don't need matching lids for every pot or pan you use. This stainless steel lid will fit any size pan from 9" to 12" in diameter. There are concentric rings on the top that match ridges formed on the underside, which match the pan diameters. This lid also has vents that can be regulated: closed when you use the lid for steaming, and open when you use it for frying. There is a stainless steel loop on top for lifting.

'Tis an ill cook that cannot lick his own fingers.

—WILLIAM SHAKESPEARE

CASSEROLES

Here we make a radical change in the source of the heat, moving away from pots that sit on top of a burner to casseroles that sit in an oven, where heat penetrates the pot from all directions, or mimics the heat of an oven on a stovetop. Casseroles are a step beyond sauté pans: they are low and wide, but the long handle is gone and the lid is designed to provide a tight seal that enhances condensation of moisture that bastes the ingredients. The lids also reflect heat into the pan, making it into a snug oven that envelops the food in moist heat. (Some recipes even specify that you seal the edges of the casserole lid with pastry to enclose the food more completely.) Some casseroles move even further away from the sauté pan and are designed entirely for cooking with moisture. Others allow you to brown foods initially on the stovetop, before their long stay in the oven. Be aware that cate-gories and definitions overlap; one person's Dutch oven is another's stewpot.

The short handles on a casserole (and in some cases, no handles) tell us that the cook need not be actively involved in maneuvering them. They can be made of any material that diffuses and holds heat well, from earthenware, porcelain, and glass to metals such as cast iron, copper, stainless steel, and enameled steel or treated aluminum. Nonstick is appropriate as well, as long as the base pan is substantial. These pots are always covered, trapping evaporating steam within the vessel. The moisture may come from the ingredients—the juices released from a *mirepoix* stewing in butter—or it may be added by the cook (red wine or stock, for example). Moisture serves to blend flavors, soften textures, or create browned pan bits for making sauce and gravy.

9.108 LE CREUSET ROUND FRENCH OVEN

This durable, enameled cast-iron pot is a real honey. The warm colors make it more inviting to cook in than the more typical casserole pan or Dutch oven. These French ovens are available in blue, saffron, red, flame, green, black, and white. The inside is pale tan enamel so you can see what you're cooking. Best of all, the cast iron retains its heat exceptionally well, so foods cook evenly in the oven and stay hot at the table. The tightly fitting lid also helps keep the food suitably moist. The one we show you holds 4½ quarts, but there are many others: 2-, 2⅔-, 3½-, 5½-, 7-, 8¾-, and 13-quart sizes are available for all sorts of pot roasting, braising, and casserole recipes.

9.109 BERNDES TRADITION DUTCH OVEN

It looks heavy, but this Dutch oven is remarkably lightweight and easy to carry: the bottom is sufficiently thick, but the walls are thinner, which is appropriate in a casserole. The pan is made of cast aluminum with a durable, multilayered DuPont nonstick surface. Nonstick has its drawbacks—you won't get as many browned bits for flavor—but if you use a good recipe you might regard that sacrifice as being worth it when it's time to clean up. The metal does brown foods reasonably well, despite the nonstick layers. This is also a deep pan, with room for a whole chicken or beef roast, and it has a tightly fitting glass domed lid with a phenolic knob (ovenproof to 450°F). The side handles get quite hot, but the manufacturer has cleverly included two small mitts that fit neatly over them. This model is 4½ quarts; there are also 1¼-, 2½-, and 7¼-quart sizes.

9.110 SCANPAN DUTCH OVEN

Another deep cooking vessel, this one's top is wider than its base, which can be helpful when you want to reduce pan fluids. Billed as nonstick, this aluminum pan with a sturdy ceramic-titanium finish doesn't release foods as well or clean as easily as most nonstick, but it heats much better, providing crispy brown surfaces that add to flavor. The domed glass lid sits snugly on the pan, making a tight seal that helps collect tasty juices that moisturize ingredients. The side handles and lid lifter are made of a special phenolic resin, which stays cool on the stovetop, and are oven safe to 500°F. The ScanPan Dutch oven comes in six sizes ranging from 8″ (3½ quarts) to 12¼″ (9½ quarts).

9.111 DEMEYERE INCA GOLD MULTIPURPOSE PAN

This pan, with its 24-karat-gold-plated trim, is another that looks too pretty to use as a cooking device, but in fact it has many uses, including a role as a serving piece. Constructed of glossy stainless steel, it has an extra-thick aluminum base that covers the entire cooking surface, helping foods brown well and evenly; there are no hot spots. The cover is a large dome that sits well within the pan. Juices accumulate, assuring moist casseroles, pot roasts, and stews. The lid has a steam vent hidden in the knob (which you turn to keep the vent open or closed). This pan also comes with a steaming rack, for use on top of the stove, and a wire basket, in which you can place small or thin items such as veal scallops or breaded shrimp for deep-frying in the base.

This pan works on all energy sources including induction cooktops and is available in an all-stainless finish.

9.112 ALL-CLAD STAINLESS STEEL DUTCH OVEN

This pan is capacious (5½ quarts) and has good depth: the wide surface area on the bottom gives you room to brown ingredients, and the side walls are high enough to prevent spatter and to help reduce liquids slowly. It can accommodate a whole stewing fowl or large cross rib of beef for pot roasting. The rounded walls make it easy to stir ingredients and to prepare gravy from pan fluids. There's a high, domed lid. Handles are well riveted and sturdy enough to be helpful when lifting a potful of stew. The pan is also available in the LTD line.

9.113 LE CREUSET OVAL FRENCH OVEN

To casserole-cook a whole chicken or duck or a long pork roast or other section of meat, we prefer to use a large oval pot, like this one from Le Creuset, which is made in deep, intriguing colors: flame, saffron, blue, green, and red among them, or the more conservative black or white. This enamel cast-iron pan is an all-

around winner. Its sits flatly and firmly on the cooktop so you can brown foods first over electric, gas, or induction burners. The lid is heavy and fits tightly onto the base, creating a minioven that you can transfer to your regular oven to finish the cooking. It retains heat so well that everything inside stays very hot and it will keep your roast warm for second helpings, even as the pan sits on the table. Two side loop handles will help you transport this hefty pan; the lid has a phenolic knob that is oven safe to 450°F. The size we like is 5 quarts, which is perfect for pot-roasted duck with turnips, or pork and sauerkraut. There are other sizes as well: 3½, 6½, and 9½ quarts.

9.114 DE BUYER COPPER OVAL STEW PAN

No, you don't need an expensive copper pot to make a down-home dish like stew, but this one is stunning, especially when the copper glow burnishes and mellows in the oven heat—you feel that good food is coming. If you choose this pan, cook your food, slice it, and return it to the pan for serving. To tell the truth, it is a wonderful performer too, not just a beauty: you can brown foods quickly because the pan is so heat responsive, then put the lid on top and transfer it to the oven. The interior is lined with stainless steel for safe cooking. The lid is heavy, sealing the moisture in well. Handles are shiny brass loops. It comes in several sizes, from a small 2-quart version to a large 5-quart one, with 3½- and 4-quart sizes in between.

9.115 CHANTAL DINNER-IS-SERVED PAN

The large size (5 quarts, 15″ by 10″) and vibrant colors (blue, green, red, or white) of this enamel-on-steel pan make it an attractive piece for company dinners. It is large enough to hold a leg of lamb, the parts of two whole chickens, or a big brisket of beef. The see-through cover lets you have a look while cooking. The cover is a large dome rimmed with stainless steel (and with a triangular shaped lifting loop) and sits within the flared sides of the pan; these features will help your casserole dishes stay properly moist. Two sleek welded stainless steel side handles help you carry the pan.

9.116 CALPHALON PROFESSIONAL HARD-ANODIZED OVAL BRAISER

The company calls this a braising pan, but its length (a huge 16″ by 11½″ oval) and rounded sides make it more suited to oven-only casserole cooking, where it does very well. If you did want to brown the foods first on the stovetop, you would have to straddle the pan over two burners, letting the pan heat through thoroughly. There's room enough inside this piece for a big brisket or two whole chickens. The bottom pan is secured by two large, roomy riveted stainless steel loop handles. The top is a high dome that creates a good seal and is well designed to collect rising vapors and return them to the food in the form of moisture. It also has a high loop lifter handle.

SAUERBRATEN

Brooklynite Bunny Pollack's stepfather, Leo Nald, was born in Baden-Baden, Germany, and brought the recipe to Brooklyn. The results are most delicious. "For a big party, I make two batches," says Bunny.

6 to 8 servings

4 cups water
2 cups cider vinegar
½ teaspoon freshly ground
    white pepper
2 teaspoons salt
1 large bay leaf

3″ cinnamon stick
1 tablespoon whole
    mustard seeds
1 tablespoon whole allspice
½ cup golden raisins
1 large onion, sliced

1 cup sugar
5- to 6-pound pot roast,
    shoulder or rump
2 tablespoons vegetable oil
2 tablespoons butter
2 tablespoons flour

1 Put the water, vinegar, and all the seasoning ingredients, including raisins, onions, and sugar, into a nonreactive stockpot and bring them to the boil. Stir well and boil for 3 minutes.

2 Put the roast in a large bowl and pour the mixture over it. Ideally, the liquid should cover the roast. If it does not, place a double layer of cheesecloth over the meat; the cheesecloth will "wick up" the liquid, keeping the meat moist. When the liquid is cool, place the bowl in the refrigerator. Leave the meat in the refrigerator for five to six days, turning it daily.

3 When you are ready to cook the sauerbraten, take it from the liquid and wipe it dry. Strain the liquid and discard the solids. Preheat the oven to 325°F.

4 In a large, heavy skillet, heat the oil and brown the sauerbraten on all sides, turning it with wooden spoons. When it is nicely browned put it in a heavy pot with a lid. Add 2 cups of the strained liquid and reserve the rest, as some will be needed for the gravy. Bring the liquid to the boil on top of the stove, then place the roast in the oven. Cook for 3 to 4 hours, until very tender. Check the sauerbraten from time to time, and turn it. If it seems to be cooking too fast, lower the heat.

5 Let the sauerbraten rest on a warm platter before you slice it.

6 Make the gravy: melt the butter in a large skillet or saucepan and stir in the flour. Let cook for 2 minutes, stirring. Pour the degreased juices from the sauerbraten pan, and add enough of the reserved marinating liquid to make 2 cups of gravy. Cook, stirring, for several minutes until the gravy is thickened. Slice the meat, pour a little gravy over the slices, and serve the rest in a sauceboat. Accompany with potato dumplings and braised red cabbage.

The Brooklyn Cookbook, by Lyn Stallworth and Rod Kennedy Jr.

BRAISING: A TRANSITIONAL FORM

Braising pans are something between stovetop frying pans and oven casseroles. Used for both stovetop browning and oven finishing, these pots require thick, sturdy, heat-conducting bottoms. They are less familiar in American kitchens than other casseroles. Their name comes from a French word that translates as "live coals" or "embers." Interestingly, in French cookware parlance, a braising pan is called a *sautoir cylindrique* while the word *braisière* is reserved for what Americans refer to as a *saucepan*. These pans are meant to be used over direct heat—hot coals, a gas flame, or an electric burner. Once the food is seared in hot fat over the fire, it is moistened with liquid and the pan is covered and set over low stovetop or oven heat for prolonged cooking—this is "braising."

Braising pans look like high-sided sauté pans with two short grips in place of the sauté pan's long handle. The shape is wider and shallower than that of a saucepan. Because its width provides a large surface area, it promotes the evaporation of liquids, making it particularly suited for dishes in which you want the sauce to reduce: a chicken sauté, for example, or a vegetable braised in stock. Braising pans are typically constructed of heavy-duty metals and are meant to hold large amounts of food; the two short handles facilitate lifting. The compact handles are also convenient: the pots fit inside an oven or on a crowded rangetop. In fact, to save on cooktop space, many restaurant chefs use braising pans rather than sauté pans for browning or sautéing foods.

9.117 BOURGEAT COPPER BRAISING PAN

This beautiful heavyweight cookware has much to offer. Like all good braising pans, this one transmits heat so well that ingredients get a good initial browning, and it has a tight-fitting, slightly domed lid that keeps moisture within the pan. Braised foods do best when there isn't too much space in the pot: this one is perfect for osso buco for four or a cut-up sautéed fryer-chicken. The two cast-iron side handles are securely riveted and compact enough for the entire pan to fit inside the oven, yet roomy enough to be conve-nient for lifting. Take this 3-quart pan right from stove or oven to tabletop—it's pretty enough to be a serving piece as well as a utilitarian cooking pot. The piece we show is copper with a stainless steel lining and measures 24 cm (9⅖") wide. It is also available in 28 cm (11").

9.118 CUISINART STAINLESS STEEL CASSEROLE

Care must be taken when sautéing in this 3-quart pan; foods brown very quickly, so you might want to keep the heat lower than usual or turn the ingredients more often. Still, it is less expensive than the other braising pans we show you and does have its attributes. This snug pan—10" wide, 3" deep—is a good choice for family dining: it can hold braised lamb shanks or a single cut-up chicken with vegetables. The low, domed, tight-fitting lid helps bring moisture to the ingredients, and the welded-on handles are roomy. Made of shiny stainless steel with a copper disc at the bottom for heat distribution, this pan has a simple design but is pleasing enough to double as a serving vessel.

9.119 ALL-CLAD STAINLESS STEEL BRAISER

This pan is atypical—instead of going straight up, the sides are flared—but it functions well for braising. The 13" width gives ample space to sauté meats and vegetables, and the stainless steel-coated aluminum core assures that the ingredients will be beautifully browned before the pan is transferred to the oven to complete cooking. There's a high, domed lid that collects condensed steam and dispatches it back down to the food, guaranteeing sufficient gravy for luscious dishes like chicken cacciatore. The braiser we show you holds 4 quarts and is made of a high-polish stainless steel, but the bottom portion is also available in a hard-anodized (LTD) finish. Either is attractive enough for table service. The shape of the pan, with its elegant flared edge, makes it suitable to use as a paella pan as well as for braising.

JESSICA B. HARRIS

America's language of food is a vibrant mix of the world's gastronomic terms, from *sauté* to *sushi*. We have borrowed words and techniques from virtually all of the world's continents. Much of Africa's food remains unknown to most of us, but the continent itself lends its vocabulary to the pot in expressions that speak of its rich culinary heritage. The couscous and *tagines* of Northern Africa are common currency, while the *brais* and *sosaties* of the south await discovery. The most-used culinary terms, though, came from West Africa in the memories of the millions of its sons and daughters who arrived in chains. It is from them that we get the Bantu term *nguba*, which gave us our nickname for peanut—goober. The Twi language of Ghana gave us the word *nkruma*, which was corrupted into okra. The word *benne* used in South Carolina to mean sesame changes not one whit and still means sesame among the Wolof of Senegal. *Nyam* remains a verb and means "to eat" in the Gullah of the Sea Islands of South Carolina and Georgia, but becomes *yam*, a noun mistakenly applied to varieties of sweet potatoes, in the rest of the country. The best-known and most-used word that harks back to the African motherland is a variant of the Bantu language's word for okra. It has given us the name of the uniquely American stew—gumbo.

SPECIALTY CASSEROLES

TAGINES

The word *tagine* refers to both a dish and a pot for making it. The dish is a savory stew native to North African countries, particularly Morocco, Tunisia, and Algeria, and it may be any combination of fish, meat, poultry, vegetables, or fruit. As long as it is cooked in a special casserole, it is a *tagine*. The casserole is a flat-bottomed, shallow dish made of earthenware, stoneware, or cast iron with a tall, conical lid. The lid fits snugly inside the dish so that steam (as well as nutrients and flavor) doesn't escape during cooking. Vapors condense on the tall sidewalls and moisten the ingredients below, keeping them juicy and succulent.

To serve a meal from the *tagine*, lift the cover. It is the custom for guests to use fingers (only the first three fingers of the right hand) to lift food from the dish, but you may use serving utensils if you like!

9.120 LE CREUSET *TAGINE*

Tagines have such a fascinating shape that it is no wonder so many of them are used only as serving pieces, while the cooking is done in a different pot. This one is attractive and also fully functional. It is easy on the home cook too. While classic *tagines* are cooked on a brazier over hot charcoal, this one can go on your stovetop or in your oven. The bottom pan is black, heavy cast iron. It holds heat exceptionally well for the long cooking period required and it is large, with plenty of room for a variety of interesting ingredients

TAGINE EL LAHM FELFLA MATISHA
(*TAGINE* OF LAMB WITH GREEN PEPPERS AND TOMATOES)

5 to 6 servings

3 pounds shoulder of lamb, cut into 1½" chunks
2 cloves garlic, peeled and chopped
pinch of pulverized saffron
salt to taste
1 teaspoon ground ginger
1 tablespoon sweet paprika

¼ cup chopped parsley
¼ cup salad oil or less
2½ pounds fresh, ripe tomatoes, peeled, seeded, and chopped
1 pound sweet green peppers, grilled, peeled, seeded, and chopped
juice of one lemon

Trim the lamb of excess fat. Place in the casserole, along with a mixture of garlic, saffron, salt, spices, and parsley pounded to a paste in the mortar. Pour in the oil to make a sauce and toss with the meat. Add 2 cups water, bring to boil, then reduce the heat and simmer 30 minutes. Add the tomatoes and continue simmering for 2 more hours, stirring from time to time while the tomatoes cook down to a thick purée. Add the green peppers 10 minutes before serving. Sprinkle with the lemon juice and serve hot or warm.

Couscous and Other Good Food from Morocco, by Paula Wolfert

(the dimensions are 12″ diameter, 2″ deep, with a 1½-quart capacity). The lid is 9″ tall, glazed lightly on the inside and with a rich, earthy red glaze on the outside surface.

9.121 THE SPANISH TABLE COPPER *CATAPLANA*

From the southern province of Algarve comes the *cataplana*, a large, lightweight metal pan inspired, perhaps, by the humble clam. It has the curved shape of that close-mouthed mollusk—except that its two halves are perfectly round—and the top and bottom are hinged together. This beautiful *cataplana*, made of hammered copper lined with tin, has copper nail heads, hinge, and handles, and two clamps on the sides to anchor the top securely to the bottom. The pan is 9″ across and each half is 3″ deep; the lower half will hold 6 cups. Although the *cataplana* is used for the cooking of a number of Portuguese dishes and brings out the fullest flavor of whatever it cooks—from fish to lamb or pork—we especially like the idea of using it for *amêijoas na cataplana*, a casserole of clams with *chouriço* sausages, *presunto* ham, tomatoes, onions, hot peppers, garlic, and wine. Imagine the effect of throwing open your handsome copper bivalve to a cloud of steam redolent of herbs and shellfish and a splendid array of open clams.

9.122 JAPANESE BLACK-IRON *SUKIYAKI-NABE*

Thin slices of meat (usually beef, but also chicken or pork), various vegetables, noodles, and bean curd, simmered together in a *sake-shoyu* broth, usually at the table over a heat source—that is a brief description of *sukiyaki*. But it cannot begin to convey the succulence of this best known of the *nabemono* (one-pot dishes). The proof is in the tasting—and the cooking is in this heavy, matte black–enameled, cast-iron pan, or *nabe*, which sits on three little feet. It has a broad downward-sloping lip covered with a faint raised design to which two rings are attached. It is 11½″ in diameter, 1″ deep, and it will hold 6 cups of meat, vegetables, and sauce. Use it at the table over a *hibachi* or any tabletop heat source.

9.123 JAPANESE COVERED *NABE*

Nabe is a Japanese word for "pot," and *nabemono* (literally, "pot things") are one-pot dishes cooked at the table. This enameled cast-iron pot (called a *tetsu-nabe*) is 8¼″ in diameter and 3¼″ deep, with a 2-quart capacity—

PIRI-PIRI

❧ DAVID LEITE ❧

Piri-piri is the Swahili word for the incendiary red peppers of Africa—primarily those of Angola and Mozambique, former Portuguese colonies. Because of the seafaring nature of the Portuguese, it didn't take long for these bite-size pods of fire to make their way to Lisbon aboard spice ships returning from the East.

Mainlanders wasted no time in turning the torrid chiles into a versatile sauce. Cooks use it as a marinade, a basting liquid, and a condiment. In fact, take a walk down an esplanade in Lisbon and you'll find bottles of *piri-piri* sauce dotting restaurant tables everywhere. And no wonder: it's perfect with shrimp, chicken, and fish.

PIRI-PIRI SAUCE

Makes 1½ cups

Although *piri-piri* peppers aren't available in this country, you can substitute any hot chiles, such as cayenne, *piquins*, or *santaka*.

3 to 6 hot chiles, depending on the heat
2 garlic cloves, finely minced
juice of 1 lemon
pinch of salt
1 cup extra-virgin olive oil

1 Coarsely chop peppers. Discard stems.
2 Place all ingredients (including seeds) in a small glass jar, cover tightly, and shake well. Let steep for at least 24 hours at room temperature. Sauce will keep in refrigerator for one month.

perfect for a freeform *yosenabe* (a Japanese-style chowder with just a little bit of everything: pork, chicken, shrimps, oysters, white-meat fish, eggs, cabbage, mushrooms, chrysanthemum leaves, ginkgo nuts, and more, simmered in a fish broth). The *nabe* comes with a dark-grained wooden lid that fits down inside the pot and is only used to keep food warm after cooking, since most *nabe-mono* dishes simmer uncovered. A handle arches over the dark brown, baked enamel interior of the pot, the rounded bottom of which sits on three stubby feet. The manufacturer recommends boiling water in the pot before using it the first time and warns that it cannot be placed directly on an electric range. Use it at the table over a hibachi or other tabletop heat source.

OYSTERS IN A POT

6 servings

½ cup (4 ounces/125 grams) red miso
½ cup (4 ounces/125 grams) white miso
1 tablespoon *mirin*
1 quart (1 liter) *dashi*
8″ (20 centimeter) piece *kombu* seaweed
24-30 large oysters, opened
3 *naganegi* onions, sliced
3 stems chrysanthemum leaves; trimmed, rinsed and dried
2 bunches *enokitake* mushrooms, washed and trimmed
3 fresh shiitake mushrooms, wiped
¼ head Napa cabbage, coarsely shredded

Mix misos, *mirin,* and ½ cup *dashi* to a paste and spread inside a *donabe* (earthenware casserole). Score the *kombu* with a sharp knife. Place it in the casserole, gently adding the remaining *dashi.* Bring the *dashi* just to a boil on a portable cooker at the table. Reduce heat. Add all the remaining ingredients, and cook briefly. If desired, the food can be dipped into a beaten raw egg before eating.

The Encyclopedia of Asian Food and Cooking, by Jacki Passmore

SLOW COOKERS

T HE PRINCIPLE EMBODIED in the electric slow-cooker—cooking at a very low heat for a very long time—is as ancient as embers and as modern as the invention of the thermostat. Various consumer surveys report that this appliance was extremely popular at the close of the millennium. While it requires no effort once the ingredients have been combined, the cook still has to assemble and prepare the ingredients. The best we can say for slow-cooking is that it works. Soups that benefit from the extraction of every bit of flavor from meat come out best. Meats emerge sadly overcooked, especially if allowed to simmer for an entire day. Keep in mind that although slow-cooker manuals include recipes for roasts and whole chickens, the U.S. Department of Agriculture advises against cooking large cuts of meat or whole birds because of the risk that they won't get hot enough in the center to prevent bacteria growth.

Look for a slow cooker with a heating element in the sidewall for even cooking and both low and high settings. The cooking vessel or crock is easier to clean if it's removable.

9.124 RIVAL REMOVABLE CROCK POT

An electric slow cooker like this one from Rival will hold dinner for four. If you are reluctant to keep your oven lit for hours on end, but would like to prepare a dish that requires a long cooking period—like a cassoulet, authentic Boston baked beans, or the traditional Jewish Sabbath dish, *cholent* (a savory stew made with beef, beans, and potatoes)—there's no better utensil to use than a slow cooker.

Also called a crock pot, this slow cooker is a versatile size (holding 6 quarts) and has a glass lid that complies with all of our recommendations above. With the lid on it measures 11″ high and is 13½″ wide from handle to handle. Many other models are available from this manufacturer in a variety of sizes in both round and oval shapes. They also come in an array of colors and prints.

FONDUE POTS

FONDUE TAKES ITS NAME from the French word *fondre,* which means "to melt," but it actually encompasses several different dishes. Food historians note that cheese fondue was the first one to develop, perhaps when a shepherd, high in the Swiss Alps, mixed his daily ration of hard cheese and wine together, heated the stuff in a pot, and used it as a dip for his crusty bread. Cheese fondue is still prepared in much the same way.

But there is also fondue *bourguignonne,* in which individual diners dunk chunks of skewered meat into sizzling vegetable oil and then slather the cooked pieces with savory sauces. At one time fondue *bourguignonne* meant a beef dinner. Nowadays it's the concept that counts, as more health-conscious diners use fish, shrimp, chicken, and even vegetables as lower-fat replacements. Italian *bagna cauda,* from the Piedmont, is a similar concept, in which vegetables are dipped in hot, seasoned olive oil.

Chocolate fondue was popularized at the 1964 New York World's Fair. It is melted chocolate with the addition of cream, liqueur, and seasonings. Guests swipe chunks of fresh or dried fruit, cake, brownies, granola bars, and even marshmallows into the velvety brown liquid.

Fondue goes in and out of style, always reemerging because it promotes camaraderie in people. It is quick and doesn't require any cooking skills to prepare. And to top it all, the host has less work to do since individual diners cook their own chunks of food.

Because the vegetable oil must stay hot to cook the meat appropriately, pots for making fondue *bourguignonne* must be constructed of a metal that holds heat well: cast iron, enameled iron, and copper among them. The pot should be deep and should taper at the top or have a splash guard, to prevent hot oil from spattering. For cheese and chocolate fondue use a wide, open-top heatproof ceramic, porcelain, enameled cast-iron, or earthenware pot that diffuses heat well. In addition, for chocolate fondue, you will need a candle warmer to keep the chocolate warm and fluid. The alcohol and Sterno burners that come with other fondue pots are not suitable unless used with a diffuser, because the heat may be too intense for the chocolate.

9.125 CHANTAL CLASSIC FONDUE SET

Fondue *bourguignonne* is a pleasant way to share a meal with friends. Each person skewers pieces of meat on a long-handled fork and dunks dinner into the blistering oil inside the pot. Everyone makes an individual judgment as to when the meat is cooked, then proceeds to dip the food into a savory sauce. A beautiful set like this one makes dinner even more inviting. The 2-quart pot is enameled steel, which retains heat well for a good sizzle. The one we show here is a compelling bright red, although the fondue set is also available in white, green, and blue. The tapered design of the pot prevents oil spatter, as does the scalloped metal spatter shield. The pot sits atop a contemporary-looking, four-legged glass stand; the center holds a burner for solid fuel. In addition, the set comes with six long skewers with from one to six black lines at the handle's bottom, so each diner can distinguish his or her own fork. Because a fondue pot cooks meat quickly, it's important to use a tender cut, like the tenderloin.

9.126 DE BUYER FONDUE *BOURGUIGNONNE* SET

The fondue set we show you here is good-looking and practical, with everything you need for your feast: a well-designed cast-iron pot, a copper fuel burner, six ceramic sauce dishes, and six color-coded forks. The pot holds its heat exceptionally well, and it has a shield to prevent spattering.

The fuel burner contains material that absorbs liquid fuel, and the flame can be adjusted by a movable part on top of the burner. The pot sits on top of a sleek stainless steel base, above the fuel burner; an extension of the burner has grooves so that a black matte metal carousel cover, with six cutouts for the sauce dishes, can fit on top. The cover has three wheels that allow it to move along the burner base so guests can swing the sauce plates to get to the one they want.

9.127 OLD DUTCH COPPER & PORCELAIN FONDUE POT

What a beauty this is: use it when you invite company for cheese or chocolate fondue. The stand, burner, and lid are shiny copper lacquered to resist tarnishing, with brass trim and handles. The deep white porcelain pot sits over a burner that holds small cans of fuel. Bring this set to the table with the lid on for a beautiful presentation, but watch out when you lift the lid—the knob gets hot. If you use it for chocolate fondue, be sure to keep the flame at its lowest.

> What greater restoratives have we poor mortals than a good meal taken in the company of loving friends?
>
> —FLORA THOMPSON,
> *Lark Rise to Candleford*

9.128 SWISSMAR CHEESE FONDUE SET

Imagine how satisfying it can be on a chilly day to gather with friends around a fondue pot, fragrant with melting cheese, dipping in chunks of crusty bread and sharing a bottle of wine! Assuming you can supply the friends, this set will let you do just that. The plump, white ceramic pot (8½" wide, 3½" deep) with its bulbous handle is easy to carry and looks heavy but is actually lightweight. It sits atop a modern-style stainless steel tripod base. The fuel holder, which uses paste fuel, is designed well: the movable part that controls and turns off the flame has a phenolic tip, which helps it stay cool. It also comes with an enamel tray and six plastic-handled forks.

9.129 CUISIPRO CHOCOLATE FONDUE SET

Chocolate can burn easily, so it is really important to make chocolate fondue in a vessel that inhibits scorching, and to use a low, cool flame. This fondue set meets those criteria. It has a simple and unpretentious design. The adorable ceramic pots come in six colors (green, yellow, red, light blue, cobalt blue, and black) and have extensions on both sides for carrying. The pot sits atop a sturdy black metal base that has a candle warmer in the center. Four plastic-handled skewers, color-coded at the tip, are included.

9.130 MONGOLIAN COPPER FIREPOT

This splendid copper firepot exemplifies an ancient utensil first used by the nomadic tribes of the Asian steppes. It is heated by fuel or denatured alcohol that is held in a removable container that sits in the bottom of a decorative stand. A separate cooking pot with large wooden handles rests just above the fuel source and has a central chimney-like tube in its interior. Perforations in the bottom of the chimney let in air to create a draft. The pot stands 11½" high overall, and the tin-lined cooking container is 10" in diameter and holds up to 3 quarts of broth. The chimney in the center, which is just under 7" high, gives the pot its distinctive appearance and carries heat up through the broth. Traditionally, when firepots were heated by charcoal, the chimney also served as a route for smoke to escape. Two sets of handles assist in handling the hot metal firepot: a pair of sturdy brass ones with wooden rollers on the cooking container itself, and two wooden knobs on the cover at opposite sides of the chimney. The cover has a terraced dome shape and a hole in the center so that it can be slipped over the chimney.

Firepot cookery is a kind of do-it-yourself cooking, like Western fondue. Guests pick up raw ingredients with chopsticks and put them in small metal strainers to cook in the bubbling hot broth. Several firepot meals are traditional in China. In the north the Mongolian firepot is made with lamb as the only meat. The Cantonese make a chrysanthemum firepot in which all kinds of meat (except lamb), vegetables, and fish are cooked. There is also a winter specialty of eastern China called "ten varieties hot pot" (the number varies according to how many ingredients you use). It is usually served toward the end of a meal and is made up of ready-cooked foods, such as parboiled cabbage, cellophane noodles, shrimp balls, meatballs, fish balls, star anise beef, and ham. Traditionally, each pot is shaped somewhat differently; but with this single, stunning firepot you can make any fire- or hot-pot dish that strikes your fancy.

SPECIALTY COPPER POTS

WE HAVE ALREADY DISCUSSED the merits of copper cookware: it is durable, beautiful, and conducts heat exceptionally well. We have also mentioned that because the metal can be toxic if ingested in large quantities, most copper pots and pans are lined, usually with tin or stainless steel. But there are some exceptions. Some specialty pots are manufactured without linings. They are all items not put to regular, daily use, so the risk of copper molecules leaching into food is minimal.

One of the categories of unlined copper cookware are pots and pans used to make foods with a high sugar content—spun sugar work, caramel, jellies, preserves, and so on. The primary reason that the lining is omitted is that tin, the traditional covering material, has a lower melting point than the boiling point of sugar. A tin lining would dissolve away before the sugar had reached a temperature appropriate to the recipe. In addition, fruit juices used for jams have a high acid content that could eat away at tin linings too quickly.

Traditional copper zabaglione pans and polenta pots are also unlined, perhaps originally purely as a matter of economics—linings cost more and are not necessary for these dishes (the ingredients do not react with copper). Also, both recipes require constant movement within the pan, a factor that would wear out a lining easily. Using these pans can be tricky; copper heats quickly and you must take care not to let the zabaglione custard curdle or the polenta burn.

Good unlined copper cookware should be thick and heavy, or it will dent too easily. Be sure to clean and dry the pans thoroughly before and after you cook with them to prevent verdigris or other spotting. Use them only for their intended purpose.

9.131 RUFFONI COPPER POLENTA POT

A staple food of the northern Alpine regions of Italy, polenta is eaten as a first course, second course, side dish, bread, and dessert. Made of white cornmeal, it's similar to the cornmeal mush and grits of the American South. But such a description does no justice to a food that, like pasta, has the ability to nourish the body when eaten by itself, or to amplify and make even more delicious a number of sauces that are served with it. Traditionally, polenta is made in an unlined copper pot, called a *paiolo*, that is narrower at the bottom than at the top. The one we show you here is made of copper and looks something like a very large thimble. As it cooks, polenta becomes very thick, with bubbles rising sluggishly through it until they suddenly pop to the surface. The shape of this pot facilitates heat distribution through the mixture. It also facilitates stirring, which should be done every few minutes so the polenta cooks evenly. The pot has an 8"-long brass handle riveted to its side and a small earlike handle on the opposite side to make it easier to lift. This 4½-quart size is quite generous to feed a large family. Because the pot is unlined, it should be used only for polenta and never acidic or highly salted foods. In addition, unless you plan to put this polenta pot to constant use (which would keep its inside corrosion free), be sure to clean it thoroughly before using.

9.132 MAUVIEL ZABAGLIONE POT

A warm velvety custard froth made from beaten egg yolks, sugar, and Marsala wine, zabaglione is considered a great restorative in the Piedmont region where it originated. Whether or not it actually can restore one's health, it most certainly restores one's spirits as a delicious and satisfying end to a meal. This round-bottomed copper pot, 6¼" in diameter and 1.8 liters (1⁹⁄₁₀ quarts), is the classic utensil to use. To make zabaglione, grasp the 6½"-long brass handle, hold the pot over a low flame (an alcohol burner is perfect), and whisk away until the mixture of wine-infused egg yolks and sugar thickens and holds a soft peak. This pot will make enough zabaglione for six to eight servings.

9.133 DE BUYER SUGAR POT

Confectioners and cooks who love to make fabulous desserts know there's nothing like an unlined copper pot to heat sugar or sugar syrups for pralines, buttercream, crème caramel, and dozens of other sweets. Copper transmits heat and loses it perfectly. Its quick reaction to changes in temperature gives you control over sugar-making, specifically at those times when the syrup is just about to reach the necessary stage, and 1 or 2 more seconds will cause it to burn or to turn too dark or too brittle. Don't be concerned about the fact that the pot is unlined. Though it is true that copper is toxic and can penetrate food, the amounts are insignificant when you consider that this specialty pan will be put to very occasional use and should be limited to sugar work. This pan is large and roomy, with a wide bottom area that causes the sugar to melt or dissolve quickly. It is very easy to work with because the riveted stainless steel handle is sturdy and comfortable; its tubular shape and hollow cuts keep it cool. Two lips on either side are helpful for pouring, and the ring around the bottom is handy as a catch-all for sugar drippings that would otherwise fall on food or your counter. Several sizes are available: 1¼, 2, 3, 3½, and 4½ quarts.

EARTHENWARE POTS

THOSE BROUGHT UP ON stainless steel and non-stick may not know about pottery, the world's oldest and most enduring cookware. Clay-based pots are among the earliest man-made objects. They are utensils with prehistoric origins, but with such import that archaeologists date civilizations by the shards found in a given layer of excavation. They inform our cookware to this day, not simply because we still use earthenware to cook in, but because we engineer our pots and pans in shapes and styles that are similar to those used by our ancient forebears. Perhaps we can justly say that although civilization may have begun with the wheel, it was the potter's wheel that transformed human culture.

Pottery is a general term used for utensils or objects made of molded wet clay and fired at high heat to fix their shape. In its more rustic form, pottery is known as earthenware, which is opaque, porous, and often coarse in texture and terra-cotta colored. Earthenware is absorptive if not glazed, and most often it is not vitrified or only partially vitrified. Vitrification involves firing clay to high temperatures that cause its components to fuse together to become glasslike. Unfired clay dissolves partially when mixed with water, but once it has been heated in a kiln to around 1,100°F, its shape is fixed and it no longer dissolves. Clay heated to higher temperatures hardens even more, and at about 2,000°F it becomes vitreous. Vitrification is not the same as glazing; many clay-based products have surfaces that look glasslike, but this has to do with glazing to give the utensil a shiny appearance, rather than firing it to hardness.

Stoneware is similar to earthenware, but it contains silica and is always vitrified, making it harder and less porous. More aristocratic varieties of vitrified pottery use a light clay and are known as porcelain or china-ware. These are hard, nonabsorptive, and white, but translucent. They often cost more than earthenware.

Cooking in Earthenware

Even after millennia, earthenware remains ideal for slow-cooking. It does not heat up quickly, but once it is hot it retains its temperature for a long time, which makes it a good energy saver. It is the opposite of copper, which is so effective for saucepans because it heats and cools quickly.

Pots that are glazed only on the inside, with the outer surface left bare, absorb heat and moisture. For the most part, glazes were developed to seal the clay's surface, thus preventing cooking particles and odors from infiltrating the tiny pores. (Eventually, this practical necessity was transformed into an art form. Almost every society makes its own distinctive glazed pottery, and some—Japan's Imari ware, for example—have earned worldwide recognition.)

A Warning about Clay Pots

Primitive and home-crafted pottery is appealing, and many of us are tempted to purchase such pieces, especially when we travel and visit local markets. But a cheap clay pot may also have a high lead content, which means it could cause lead poisoning if used for cooking. Because there is no easy way to tell which tourist articles are safe without testing them, it is best to reserve these pretty containers for flowers or nuts in the shell, rather than for food.

The Wet-Clay Cooker

Before there were pots, prehistoric peoples in search of a good dinner took their poultry or meat and surrounded it with wet, clay-laden mud. They put the pack into the embers, and when food was cooked, they cracked open the hard shell that formed as the mud dried in the fire. The wet clay and the ingredients' natural fluids kept the food from drying out, and the gently steamed dinner was tender.

Wet-clay cookers were designed to mimic these earliest cooking techniques. All or a portion of the pot and lid are soaked in water and give off steam as the clay heats up in the oven. The food inside the vessel self-bastes in its own juices. Little or no fat is needed for lubrication, and few nutrients escape during cooking. Some wet-clay cookers are made completely unglazed, but in these modern times, manufacturers realize the appeal of easy cleanup and produce some with partially glazed interiors.

9.134 CERAFLAME BEAN POT

This is a typical bean pot, with a bulbous shape and a neck that narrows so the contents bake to tenderness without losing much of the liquid needed for a sauce. The material, a matte-finish black ceramic, holds heat exceptionally well. You can serve from the pot, keeping it at the table, and the beans will stay hot through dinner. The lid is tempered glass so you can see the contents of the pot as they cook. The side knobs and lid lifter stay relatively cool and are convenient for carrying. There's no need to limit this 3-quart vessel to beans; it will also do as a small soup or stew pot or for casseroles.

9.135 CHINESE EARTHENWARE CASSEROLE

In China, this squat-bellied casserole is called a sand pot because of its sandy-textured, off-white, unglazed exterior and rounded shape. It is used for the long, slow cooking of many ingredients that need time to develop and infuse their flavors. The exterior is kept unglazed to absorb more heat while the smooth brown interior is glazed to retain moisture. Sand pots come in several different styles; this one-handle version with a protective wire support is a restaurant staple. It measures 8½" in diameter, 3" deep, and it holds 1½ quarts. The domed lid fits securely into the pot and has a small hole to release steam. Although the casserole is flameproof, it is still important to place a flame tamer under it to prevent cracking. Also be sure to use a wooden spoon to stir the contents of the pot to protect the interior from scratching. There is no need to limit this casserole to Chinese cooking. It will braise a cut-up chicken and can be used to cook mussels or clams in its moist heat.

9.136 RECO INTERNATIONAL *RÖMERTOPF*

Cookers like this one simulate the primitive designs used by our prehistoric ancestors, who molded wet clay around ingredients and cooked them in the campfire. Foods cooked this way are not only tender and succulent, they are nutritious too: there is no need for fats because the ingredients cook in their own juices and nutrients are sealed in. You use little, if any, additional basting fluids because the cooker draws out the water from the vessel, which must be presoaked before use. The inside is unglazed and has a ridged area that lifts the ingredients slightly off the bottom. The heavy lid fits smoothly on top of the bottom. The model we show you holds 3 quarts and is almost oval in shape, with room for a large chicken or rolled meat roast. There are raised decorations on the terra-cotta-colored vessel and the lid. Other sizes are available, including a 17½-pound maxi pot, a vegetable baker, a garlic baker, and a fish baker.

9.137 RESTON LLOYD *SCHLEMMERTOPF*

Reston Lloyd uses a very porous variety of clay for its bakers. This means that the traditional soaking time required for the materials to absorb moisture (about 30 minutes) is shortened: only the lid needs to be soaked, 30 minutes the first time and 10 minutes every time after. We like the contemporary design of this addition to Reston Lloyd's line; it is a sign of modernity for this, the most ancient kind of cooking pot. It has the terra-cotta color of classic clay bakers, but the lines are sleek and there are no traditional pottery decorations on the surface. The cover has a molded-on lid lifter rather than the more typical lid extensions or recessed handles. Despite the new look, the baker functions exactly the way you would expect. No fats and little or no water are needed for recipes—the ingredients' natural juices provide moisture enough, and foods come out tender and juicy. This baker is oval and is very deep, with room for two chickens or even a small turkey. The inside is coated with nonstick materials—modern indeed!—that make it easy to clean.

9.138 MATFER CASSOULET DISH

Cassoulet is the quintessential baked bean stew; a rich, garlicky melange with meats and sausages and, with luck, *confit d'oie* or *de canard* (preserved goose or duck). Some say that a proper cassoulet can only be made in a *cassole d'issel,* an earthenware dish from Issel, in Castelnaudary, a town in southwest France where cassoulet is said to have been invented, and from which the name of the dish is derived. But we believe the dish we show here is perfect for the job: it is made of golden brown stoneware and is wider on top than at the bottom, providing ample room for the top crust of crispy bread crumbs that seal in the moist casserole mixture below. It comes in four sizes; the 8⅝" one is the best for a typical cassoulet. The others are smaller (7⅞", 6⅞", and 5⅞") and can be used for cassoulet or for other, less sumptuous recipes.

9.139 CHEF WALTER *ETRURIA*

This dish copies the designs of ancient Etruscans, who used this variety of clay cookware about three hundred years before the Roman Empire. Chef Walter Potenza, a restaurateur in Rhode Island, is credited with reintroducing terra-cotta ware to the American restaurant kitchen. In 1995, he opened La Locanda del Coccia ("The gathering place of the clay pot") and soon thereafter began selling the terra-cotta ware that he uses in his restaurant. The deep, heavy terra-cotta casserole is solidly crafted and homey-looking. The exterior has a shiny brown glaze, and the inside is left pristine, except for the upper edges. Use it for soup, stew, beans, or casseroles—there is plenty of room (the dish is 10" in diameter, 4" deep). You needn't use much cooking fat when you prepare food in this cookware: soak the casserole in cold water for 15 minutes before using it. The damp surface will help moisturize the food. Serve straight from the vessel, of course. The clay will keep the food warm on the table. Two lips that extend from the rim serve as handles.

9.140 CHEF WALTER
TEGAMACCIO

Another delightful terra-cotta clay casserole from Chef Walter, this one is 12″ in diameter and 2¾″ deep. Its shape and size make it perfect for stew, lasagna, or other layered casseroles and terrines that don't require great depth. Like the dish described above, the exterior is glazed, the inside is left plain, and there are two lips that extend from the top of the pan to use as handles. Soak the casserole for about 15 minutes before using it. Chef Walter clay pots are available in many shapes and sizes for specific foods like pasticcio, *timballo*, and beans.

BEER-BAKED BEANS WITH APPLES & SAUSAGE

A nice flavor variation on an oldtime national favorite. Apples, beer, and sausage, three traditional European foods, combine to make this bean dish rich, dark, and delicious.

6 to 8 servings

1 pound dried pinto beans
6 whole cloves
1 medium onion
8 cups water
1½ cups (12 ounces) beer
1 medium onion, coarsely chopped
2–3 medium apples, peeled, cored, and diced
¼ cup soy sauce
½ cup firmly packed dark brown sugar
4 cloves garlic, crushed
1 teaspoon dry mustard
1 pound smoked sausage (hot, garlic, or Polish), sliced

1 In a large pot soak the beans in 6 to 8 cups cold water for at least 4 hours or overnight. Drain thoroughly. Return beans to pot.
2 Stick the whole cloves into each end of the onion. Add the onion to the beans and pour in 8 cups cold water. Bring to the simmer, then cook, uncovered, over moderate heat for 1½ to 2 hours until the beans are tender.
3 Drain the liquid from the beans and reserve it. Discard the clove-studded onion. Preheat the oven to 300°F.
4 Transfer the beans to a bean pot or large casserole with a cover. Add all the remaining ingredients, plus 2 cups reserved bean liquid. Mix well, cover, then bake for 2 to 2½ hours until the beans are very soft and most of the liquid has been absorbed. Check occasionally while the beans are baking; if the liquid seems to be cooking away too quickly, add more of the reserved bean liquid as necessary. The finished dish should be soft, dark, and moist without being too soupy.

Blue Corn and Chocolate, by Elizabeth Rozin

10

GRIDDLES, GRILL PANS, & IRONS

MAIZE CAKES ARE THE STAPLE of the Zuni Indian diet. They are cooked on stone slabs that have been gradually heated and rubbed with resins. According to Zuni folklore, it is essential that during the process no word be spoken above a whisper, or the stone will crack.

Slabs of rock were some of our earliest cooking utensils: their simple form has endured in the modern griddle. Like the rock slabs, griddles quickly transfer heat to the food without the refinement of liquid and, often, without the intermediary of fat. On a griddle we cook pancakes, scones, and crumpets; we sizzle thin rashers of bacon, strips of meat, fillets of fish, slices of vegetables, and eggs. A griddle can be a flat rock seasoned with salt and laid on the hot coals of a campfire, an aluminum slab, or an iron frying pan without sides placed over the burner of a stove. The cooking method is as simple as the utensil; the only demand is that the surface reach and maintain a high heat in order to "sear" and cook foods quickly and evenly.

10.1 CALPHALON PROFESSIONAL HARD-ANODIZED ROUND GRIDDLE

A handsome griddle, this is made from hard-anodized aluminum, with a flat 10″ cooking surface, high slanted sides, and rolled steel handles. The interior surface is smooth, matte gray, and stick resistant. For best results, wash the griddle and towel dry first, then warm over moderate heat for about 3 minutes, until a hand above it feels warm, then lightly oil. The griddle accommodates five slices of bacon (a tight fit, at first) and beautifully browns and crisps them. The fat spreads evenly across the surface so there aren't any hot (or cold) spots. The handles heat up, so always use pot holders. For perfect, light pancakes, oil the griddle between batches so they release properly.

THE VALUE OF ROASTING SPICES
✤ JULIE SAHNI ✤

Spices are roasted to alter their fragrance. Pan-roasting a spice in an unseasoned skillet lends a distinct caramelized smoky-sweetness, which is quite different from the floral fragrance of raw spices. The decision to use raw or roasted spices is not a question of one being better than another: they're just different techniques. It's a choice based on the requirements of whatever you're making, like deciding whether to poach, braise, or boil. There's a misconception that roasting intensifies the flavor of the spice. Because some of the essential oils are lost in roasting, the intensity of fragrance in raw ground spices is far greater.

Cleanup requires some elbow grease. Once the pan has cooled, soak it, then scour it with dish soap and a nylon scrubbing pad, and towel dry. Lightweight yet hardworking, this 13″ pan produces excellent results. Measure your stove before purchasing; it may be a poor fit on some rangetops. It's also available with a nonstick surface.

10.2 LODGE OLD-STYLE CAST-IRON GRIDDLE

Since McKinley became president, four generations of the Lodge family have produced cast-iron cookware in South Pittsburg, Tennessee. We treasure well-seasoned cast-iron pans, and this homey griddle is no exception. Just the right size for two, it's light with shallow, flared sides. The best care for cast iron is to use it often and never wash it with soap, which strips away seasoning. Simply wipe with a paper towel while the pan is still warm; if it needs a scrub, use boiling water and a stiff nylon brush, then heat it on the stovetop to evaporate any rust-causing moisture. Let the pan cool, then wipe it with vegetable oil or shortening before storing. This griddle is 11″ in diameter but also comes in 8⅜″, 9″, and 10½″ sizes.

10.3 WOODSTOCK SOAPSTONE COMPANY COPPER-BANDED SOAPSTONE GRIDDLE

This lovely piece of cookware boasts a long history in New England. A thick gray slab of naturally nonstick soapstone, it's very comforting and homey, as high-tech coated pans could never be. Rimmed with a thin copper band, the griddle has delicate oval handles so it can hang on the wall. Rinse and dry it before using and oil lightly. Warm on moderate

WHAT TO LOOK FOR

In 1998, Americans spent more than $70 million on griddles and grill pans. Here are the seven criteria for consideration in order to make sure you get your money's worth:

Material Griddles and grill pans can be made of aluminum, anodized aluminum, a sandwich of aluminum and stainless steel, stone, and cast iron. Aluminum is an excellent conductor of heat and is also lightweight, which makes it easier to move the pan about on top of your range, but it will interact with high-acid foods and has a tendency to stain and pit. Anodized aluminum has all the advantages of standard aluminum and will not interact with food, but no matter what the manufacturers would like you to believe, the anodized surface will eventually wear away. A thick sandwich of stainless steel and aluminum produces fast and even heat conductivity and a permanent nonreactive surface. Early New England kitchens had soapstone griddles, which are still manufactured in Vermont. They absorb heat quickly and, because soapstone is nature's nonstick material, they readily give up the flapjacks, eggs, and bacon when they are done. Finally, there is cast iron, which is heavy and has a slow but sure heat conductivity. It needs seasoning, which is easily done and will result in an almost indestructible and reliable utensil. Cast iron can rust, but it is rarely necessary to wash it, and when well seasoned it is relatively nonstick.

In fact, it is rarely necessary to soak or thoroughly wash griddles. Scrape off any residue, wipe it clean, and you're home free. For a more heavy-duty cleaning, a quick scrub with a stiff nylon brush under hot water (no soap), then a thorough drying—with a towel or over a low burner—should suffice. A light oiling after use can't hurt.

Calphalon anodized aluminum cookware is a different story. The Ohio-based Calphalon Corporation began life in 1945 as Commercial Metal Spinning and produced restaurant cookware, among other products. By adapting a process used by aerospace industries to harden aluminum, called "hard anodizing," they developed their now familiar gray cookware line. Made of pure aluminum, it has excellent conductive properties with a surface that is nonreactive and 30 percent harder than stainless steel. In 1975, the first hard-anodized cookware for home use was introduced. Regular Calphalon has to be soaked and scrubbed very well after cooking, or food will stick. The manufacturer states this very plainly. Also, the pans must be towel dried or they may keep a sticky residue. Calphalon or other pans with nonstick coatings only need to be wiped out or, at most, quickly washed in hot, soapy water, then dried. Stiff scrub brushes or cleansers are not recommended for nonstick surfaces.

Shape and Design Griddles and grill pans can be rectangular, circular, or square. Rectangles usually give you a more generous cooking surface, but a circular shape will allow for a more complete and even surface temperature. For a grill pan to produce distinct searing marks, it is important to have troughs between the ridges that are at least ¼" deep.

Size Griddles and grill pans can be made to cover a single burner or two at a time. The double burner size will give you a large enough surface to feed a group of six people at once, but the part of the grill that's over the space between the burners will not be heated as effectively as the portions that are directly above the burners. One way to reduce this problem is to preheat the griddle or grill long enough to heat the space between the burners. Griddles and grills are often put to use for larger groups, but single cooks and couples will treasure grill pans and griddles of modest size that can sear a piece of fish or a chicken breast.

Surface The cooking surface can be made of the material from which the grill or griddle is formed, or it can be coated with a nonstick surface, which will allow you to use less fat and will make cleanup easier. The drawback to nonstick (more accurately described as "an easy-release surface") is that it may not produce the crisp crust that makes proper pancakes, French toast, and hash brown potatoes.

Handles Some grill pans and griddles have no handles; they lie flat on the burner and are kept in place by their weight. If a grill pan or griddle has handles, the handles should be securely attached and made of a material that will not be damaged by extreme heat.

Drainage System Some griddles and grill pans incorporate a drainage system, which collects the cooking fats in a trough or cup. Occasionally you will find a design that requires the griddle or grill pan to be tilted manually in order to move the fat. Others have a slant built into the form. Fat drains in griddles are useful only to a point. If you are cooking batches of bacon (and even the largest griddles only hold about eight slices), you will find that you still must pour off the fat after each batch. Otherwise, it may spill out onto the stovetop. Not a fun job, but to do so, put a bowl in the sink (a can is too small a target) and pour the hot fat from the griddle into the bowl.

Reversible Design Most slab designs cover two burners and are reversible, often offering a smooth surface on one side, grill pan ridges on the other.

er's claims, you need to use some fat when cooking eggs; with a gloss of oil, they released more easily and the bottoms had a baked, brown appearance. For a lacy, bubbly "fried" egg, rub the griddle with oil, and for each egg, slip a sliver of butter onto the griddle and then crack the egg onto the butter. To clean the griddle, avoid using soap; wipe it with a damp cloth. Also available in a 12" round and an 8" by 16" oval.

10.4 CALPHALON COMMERCIAL HARD-ANODIZED SQUARE GRIDDLE

Calphalon's 11" square griddle, made of hard-anodized, heavy-gauge aluminum, sports a well-balanced arched handle that remains cool. It cooks up to five slices of bacon with crisp, quick efficiency. (Drain accumulated fat often, as this griddle is shallow—the sides are just ¼" high—and it has no fat reservoir.) Pancakes will emerge light and high with an old-fashioned speckled finish. Oil the griddle between batches so they don't stick, and try some cornmeal in the batter for a nutty, toasty flavor. Take good care of this griddle and it will reward you with terrific results and wonderful Sunday brunches. To retain its easy-release capabilities, soak, scrub well, and thoroughly dry with a soft towel afterward. It's also available with a nonstick finish.

heat about 8 minutes, until drops of water skitter when sprinkled on the surface. The griddle heats slowly and steadily. The 10" round surface accommodated four small pancakes, which released beautifully and were evenly golden with proper speckled undersides. Despite the manufactur-

I like green eggs and ham!
I do! I like them Sam-I-am!
And I would eat them in a boat.
And I would eat them with
  a goat.
                              —DR. SEUSS

10.5 WISCONSIN ALUMINUM FOUNDRY CHEF'SDESIGN MAXI GRIDDLE

Wisconsin Aluminum was founded by a Russian tinker who immigrated to America. When his horse died in Manitowoc, Wisconsin, he decided to stay on and later started the foundry. A family-owned company as well as one of the largest foundries in the United States, Wisconsin Aluminum has been casting metal since 1908 and making cookware since World War I—doughboys toted Wisconsin Aluminum's cast-aluminum canteens. Before the advent of Teflon, its cookware was highly polished uncoated aluminum, but now nearly all have a tough nonstick coating. Wisconsin Aluminum produces a wide range of griddles, but the extra-large (12¾" by 21") cast-aluminum nonstick griddle is a favorite. Spanning two burners, it is well balanced and heats evenly. The glittery black nonstick coating called "Excalibur" feels rough because of the tiny stainless steel pellets that are sprayed onto the aluminum to help the coating adhere. Prep the griddle with a gloss of oil before heating and keep the heat at medium. The handles, molded from the griddle itself, do get hot when the griddle is heated. Any fat from cooking drains into shallow side wells: a good feature. Despite the griddle's substantial looks, it's light and easy to manage. It cooks beautifully and is a cinch to clean.

10.6 ALL-CLAD LTD NONSTICK GRANDE GRIDDLE

This sleek, roomy 13" by 20" griddle from All-Clad is an excellent heat conductor. Made from an aluminum core that is sandwiched between a dark anodized-aluminum exterior and a nonstick stainless steel interior, it sits comfortably atop two burners and has the benefit of a nonstick surface, so flapjacks and eggs practically jump onto their plates. If you own a bed-and-breakfast or regularly feed a crowd, you'll want this griddle. As with all nonstick sur-

---

HOW TO SEASON CAST IRON

When you purchase cast-iron cookware, it usually comes with directions for seasoning, that is, impregnating the porous surface of the metal with a neutral oil or grease, like vegetable oil, then heating it. This step conditions the metal and helps seal its surface to minimize sticking. Some manufacturers recommend using solid shortening, but it does not do as good a job as oil. This is because solid shortenings contain saturated fat, which does not oxidize and polymerize as readily as oil on the heated metal, and therefore does not create as efficient a seal.

When seasoning a pan, you should apply the oil very lightly and wipe the pan thoroughly with a paper towel before heating it. Place the oiled pan in a cold oven, turn the heat to 300°F, and leave it for 2 hours. Allow the pan to cool thoroughly at room temperature before storing. After that, any time the surface of the pan or griddle is scrubbed, becomes abraded, or shows signs of rusting (from inadequate drying or because of nonuse after being stored in a humid atmosphere) it should be reseasoned.

BRIDGE CREEK HEAVENLY HOTS

50 to 60 dollar-sized pancakes

These are the lightest sour-cream silver-dollar-size hotcakes I've ever had—they seem to hover over the plate. They are heavenly and certainly should be served hot.

4 eggs
½ teaspoon salt
½ teaspoon baking soda
¼ cup cake flour
2 cups sour cream
3 tablespoons sugar

1 Put the eggs in a mixing bowl and stir until well blended. Add the salt, baking soda, flour, sour cream, and sugar. Mix well. This can be done in a blender, if you prefer.
2 Heat a griddle or frying pan until it is good and hot, film with grease, and drop small spoonfuls of batter onto the griddle—just enough to spread to an approximately 2½" round. When a few bubbles appear on top of the pancakes, turn them over and cook briefly.

The Breakfast Book, by Marion Cunningham

THE PERFECT GRILLED CHEESE SANDWICH
❧ JANE & MICHAEL STERN ❧

1 sandwich

The perfect grilled cheese sandwich requires three ingredients (four if you want to add bacon, but that's another story).

THE INGREDIENTS

1 Cheese. Two ¾-ounce slices of pasteurized, processed American cheese is the classic option. If you insist on nonprocessed cheese, aesthetics demand that it be bright orange; melted pale yellow cheese is not appetizing.

2 Sturdy bread. Not handcrafted bread, certainly nothing hand sliced, which could result in a sloping sandwich. (One of the joys of grilled cheese lies in its evenness.) Machine-sliced, high-quality white (or for the adventurer, rye!) is appropriate. Sliced, packaged supermarket white bread is the best.

3 Butter. More than you think you need. A ½ stick, at least.

THE TOOLS

1 A griddle or skillet. Seasoned cast iron is best; it gives a better burnish to the surface of the bread and encourages the use of more butter. In emergencies, a nonstick pan can be used.

2 A spatula.

3 A bacon press or a brick wrapped in a few layers of aluminum foil.

THE METHOD

1 Melt ½ stick of butter in the skillet over medium-high heat.

2 Place the cheese between slices of bread and lay the sandwich in the sizzling butter. Put the bacon press on top of it. (If the cheese protrudes beyond the crust, it may fry when it melts: for some connoisseurs, this is the best part of the sandwich; for other palates, it is anathema.)

3 When the bottom slice of bread turns golden brown, remove the press and lift the sandwich with the spatula.

4 Toss more butter in the pan, and as soon as it has melted, return the sandwich, ungrilled side down.

5 Top with the bacon press. When the cheese has melted and the sandwich is golden brown on both sides and flat, remove it from the pan.

6 Serve immediately, with dill pickle chips as garnish.

---

faces, it produces a somewhat softer crust, which seems a minor issue given the great ease of cleaning and care. Since items tend to slide on this surface, use two spatulas for turning, employing one to steady the food. Lips at opposite corners of the griddle are helpful in draining any fat that collects in the troughs around the pan. It distributes heat evenly, including, unfortunately, to the stainless steel, upright, bolted handles.

10.7 HAWKINS *TAVA* GRIDDLE

When we showed this *tava*, or griddle, to one of our Indian food experts, she smiled. "Ah, yes," she sighed, "a *tava*." Why that pleased recognition? Because on a *tava*, one

cooks chapatis, the daily bread of India. The bread dough is made of a whole-wheat flour and water, and then either rolled out into small, flat circles or flattened between the plates of a chapati press. And this is the griddle that cooks chapatis perfectly. Made of hard-anodized aluminum with a nonstick on Satilon surface (a hard-anodized coating that is twice as hard as steel), the griddle's traditional slightly concave shape, 10″ in diameter, spreads heat evenly and quickly. The well-balanced stainless steel handles are solidly riveted to the griddle and resist heat. Before a meal, the *tava* is laid on an open-fire stove. When it is hot, the chapatis are placed on one by one. The cook keeps moving the bread around constantly until it is lightly browned on one side; she then grasps it with smooth-edged tongs, flips it, and cooks it on the other side. Finally, she holds the chapati with the tongs over a flame for a few seconds until it puffs up, and then serves it immediately.

10.8 EARTHENWARE *COMAL* GRIDDLE

Made of unglazed earthenware, this Mexican griddle is a good example of the traditional type used for cooking tortillas. This 16″ disc is shaped with a slight concave curve that rises 1½″ from the bottom to the outer edge and is capable of holding several tortillas at a time. However, the *comal* has to be cured to seal its pores before being used. The best way to do this is the historic Mexican way— welcome to the fourth century. Start with a thick paste of unslaked lime and water and slather the substance over the entire surface. Place the *comal* over charcoal or gas heat— never on an electric burner—until the coating bakes dry and burns away without blackening. Scrub with plenty of hot water, then start planning your fiesta! If you are using the griddle over charcoal, be sure to place it directly on the coals, not on a grill, because you want quick heat for tortillas. To be truly authentic serve the tortillas in a *chiquihuite*, a square woven basket for tortillas.

ELECTRIC GRIDDLES

THESE SIZABLE APPLIANCES do the work of two large skillets and are especially handy when you want to make a double batch of pancakes or bacon and eggs for a crowd. The work of a griddle is simple—to reach and maintain a high heat—but to do it effectively the griddle must have an accurate thermostat and a cooking surface that distributes heat evenly. If the griddle is coated with a nonstick finish, you'll only need to wipe the surface with butter or oil before cooking, and you'll be faced with a minimal cleanup job. For safety, we recommend that the griddle have feet that keep it off of the countertop and sides that don't get hot to the touch. Because a griddle is often used for frying bacon, it's helpful if it has a grease drain tray.

THE IMPORTANCE OF FAMILY MEALS
✤ PAUL PRUDHOMME ✤

Food has always been important to me, and not just to my taste buds. Growing up on a farm, the youngest of thirteen children, my happiest memories are of all of us gathered around the table. We'd talk about everything from school to life-and-death situations, laugh, and thoroughly enjoy the meal, for Mom was a fantastic cook. We used the time to nourish our spirits as well as our bodies. It was around the kitchen table, where we were not likely to be interrupted, that we learned what it means to be a family. We shared news of the day; we were taught manners; we learned about our brothers and sisters and our parents, about our extended family, and about the give and take of relationships. Eating together was an emotional time, and to this day sharing a meal with a good friend or a loved one is an emotional experience for me.

In the 1960s America began to abandon family meals. In doing so, I think we lost something precious. One person works late, another has a meeting, one has soccer practice, another an early date—no one has time to enjoy a meal together, which means no opportunity to really experience being a family, and that's a shame. I've always said my goal in life is to make your dinner better, and I'm not just talking about the dishes. I like developing interesting recipes to inspire families to cook them together, then enjoy them together. Maybe not every night, but a few times a week. Your taste buds will cheer, and you'll get to know your family better.

Have you ever noticed that when you meet someone you'd like to know better, the first thing you think of is to invite that person to lunch or dinner? Whether it's a young man who wants to impress a date, a businessperson with a new associate, or a couple welcoming a new family to the neighborhood, there's usually a meal involved, either at home or at a restaurant. Of course you want the food to be wonderful, but part of the pleasure is in the conversation, the building of a relationship that seems to grow naturally when you share a meal. Perhaps you'll allow me to give a spin to a traditional saying: "Family and friends who eat together, stay together."

10.9 PRESTO JUMBO COOL TOUCH ELECTRIC GRIDDLE

All of our criteria for performance and convenience were met by this model, which can be set on a countertop or even on a buffet table, and not take over half your stove. It has a solid aluminum nonstick-coated cooking surface that gently slopes to help drain grease away from the food. The thermostat can be set from 150°F to 400°F and reaches 350°F in about 6½ minutes. The drip tray slides out, and the heat control detaches so the entire unit can be thoroughly washed, although you'll probably have to wash the griddle by hand. At 24" by 12" it won't fit in most dishwashers. Because the white plastic frame stays exceptionally cool to the touch and has a contemporary appearance, this griddle would also work as a food warmer with the heat control set at low. Think of it for meals other than breakfast: to keep casseroles warm or a pot of chili warm for a party, alongside baskets of fresh tortillas.

GRILL PANS

GRILLING IS NOT THE SAME as griddling. Grilling is the method of cooking food through the application of intense heat from below. Griddling also involves the application of heat from below, but the heat is less intense and the food lies flat on the griddling surface. In grilling, the food is held above the heat source on strips or ridges of a heatproof material. Originally, it was done outdoors over a flame, with the food held on a metal grill or grid. These days, we grill over charcoal, hardwoods, gas flames, or electric elements, but grilling has also come in from the cold in the form of a grill pan, a type of skillet with raised ridges on its surface, created for home cooks in order to simulate outdoor grilling. Unlike flat griddles, grill pans hold the food up on the ridges, which sear and mark it. However, grill pans will not impart the intensity of flavor that comes from an outdoor grill, because there is no contact with the flame. Best at grilling vegetables, oily fish, and thin cuts of steak, they are not as effective for cooking thicker cuts of meat—the outside of the meat often dries out before the center has cooked.

You might think that a grill pan should be heated to a fairly high temperature, but most manufacturers recommend medium heat, which will not damage the pan and will minimize smoke and spattering fat. Preheating the pans and brushing them with oil are often essential for good results. We found the pans do a good job with firm vegetables, shrimp, pork chops, hamburgers, and hot dogs, and permit a wide range of uses for modest amounts of food.

10.10 LE CREUSET GRILLIT PAN

For many of us, Le Creuset was our first serious cookware—received as a wedding gift or hand-me-down, bought as a splurge or after a move. Even today, a flame-orange Le Creuset pot (produced in Fresnoy le Grand, France, since 1925) proudly adorns many a dedicated cook's stove. This striking enamel-over-cast-iron 12″ griller is sturdy with a solid heft. A thoughtful aid is a flat ledge opposite the handle, which makes the pan easier to lift. The handle is slightly short, and unfortunately the pan's efficient heat distribution extends into it. Lips on opposite sides of the pan are helpful for draining excess fat. It's a spacious pan—it could easily hold halibut steaks for four. The flat-topped grids release food at just the right moment and create nice grill marks. If you oil and preheat the pan first, use it over medium heat, and soak and clean it with a stiff plastic brush and minimal soap after using, it will only improve over time. It's available in blue, white, flame, green, and black, all with black interiors.

10.11 UNIVERSAL CORONA RANGE GRILL

This curious-looking pan resembles a hubcap. It's made in two pieces: a doughnut-shaped drip pan that rings the burner and a round, convex, nonstick-coated grid set atop the drip pan. Fill the drip pan with water, oil the grid, place it on the drip pan, and heat it over a moderate flame for about 5 minutes. Occasionally check the water in the drip pan; it will need replenishing if too much evaporates. This grill does its best work with Korean barbecue (often cooked on tabletop braziers) such as *bool kogi:* very thin slices of tender beef marinated in soy sauce, sugar, garlic, and sesame oil, and quickly seared. The pan performs less well with more ordinary preparations, such as zucchini or onion slices, as you need the marinade and internal moisture to get a crisp, charred exterior. Corona's drip pan is 12″ round, with a cooking grid of 10″.

10.12 KITCHENAID FIVE-PLY CLAD GRILL PAN

Crafted from a sandwich of metals and coated inside and out with mirror-sharp stainless steel, this pan is a fast, excellent heat conductor, and won't stick if cared for properly. Rounded grids impart rich grill marks. The arched handle on this fairly heavy, spacious 12″ pan stays cool, though it's a bit awkward to lift. Before cooking, oil the pan and heat it on low to medium heat (never higher) for 3 minutes. After cooking, cool the pan before you clean it. And now we come to its downfall: it's hard to clean, and afterward, it won't be as beautiful. You can't use chlorine cleanser, steel wool, or harsh detergents; the included directions recommend using lemon juice or vinegar but don't tell you how. Here's how: simmer a solution of 1 tablespoon lemon juice and ½ cup water in the pan for 5 minutes, then scrub it using a nylon scouring pad. It won't be perfect, but most black speckles will be gone. Shine up the exterior with stainless steel polish. Gentle persistence is needed, but even so, the pan's a winner.

10.13 ANOLON PROFESSIONAL GRILL PAN

This square grill pan breaks all the rules: it's nonstick, it has high flared sides, and it's small. But it's wonderful, and the results speak for themselves. Cooking for two? This is a sturdy little 9½" workhorse that you'll use once or twice a week. Three at table? It will comfortably hold three chops, chicken breasts, or salmon steaks, and it works so efficiently that you could cook the food in batches. If chops cool after standing, flip them in the hot pan for a minute; that's how restaurants do it. Especially wonderful at grilling vegetables, this pan's even heat produced respectable grill marks and a tender interior. Light in weight and well balanced, with a riveted tubular steel handle that stays cool, this pan also has the nonstick advantage of easy care and cleanup.

BOOL KOGI (KOREAN SESAME-GRILLED BEEF)

6 servings

FOR THE BEEF & MARINADE

2 pounds beef tenderloin tips, or boneless sirloin
½ cup soy sauce
⅓ cup sugar
3 tablespoons sake, rice wine, or sherry
2 tablespoons Asian (dark) sesame oil
8 cloves garlic, thinly sliced
4 scallions, both white and green parts, trimmed and minced
2 tablespoons sesame seeds, toasted
½ teaspoon freshly ground black pepper

FOR SERVING

Asian Pear Dipping Sauce (see below)
1 head romaine lettuce, separated into leaves, rinsed, and spun dry

1 If using tenderloin tips, butterfly them to obtain broad flat pieces of meat; each should be about 4" long and wide and ¼" thick. If using the sirloin, cut it across the grain into ¼" slices. Whichever cut you use, pound the slices between two sheets of plastic wrap with the side of a cleaver or with a rolling pin to flatten them to a thickness of ⅛". Place the meat in a large nonreactive baking dish and set aside while you prepare the marinade.
2 Combine all the ingredients for the marinade in a small bowl and whisk until the sugar is dissolved. Pour the mixture over the meat in the baking dish and toss thoroughly to coat. Cover and let marinate, in the refrigerator, for 1 to 2 hours.
3 Preheat the grill to high.
4 When ready to cook, oil the grill grate. Arrange the pieces of meat on the grate and grill, turning with tongs, until nicely browned on both sides, 1 to 2 minutes per side. Transfer the meat to a platter when it is done.
5 Pour the dipping sauce into six small bowls, one for each diner. To eat, take a piece of meat and wrap in a lettuce leaf. Dip the leaf in the dipping sauce and eat at once.

ASIAN PEAR DIPPING SAUCE

About 2½ cups

½ cup soy sauce
½ cup sake or dry sherry
¼ cup sugar
1 small Asian pear, peeled, cored, and finely chopped
4 scallions, both white and green parts, trimmed and finely chopped
¼ cup finely chopped onion
2 tablespoons sesame seeds, toasted

Combine all the ingredients in a medium-size bowl and stir until thoroughly mixed and the sugar is dissolved. Divide the sauce among as many bowls as there are people, so each person has his own for dipping and serve immediately.

The Barbecue! Bible, by Steven Raichlen

10.14 CALPHALON COMMERCIAL HARD-ANODIZED SQUARE GRILL PAN

This 11" square grill pan is simple and sleek. Constructed of hard-anodized aluminum with a smooth stick-resistant interior, it sears in well-defined grill marks. By keeping it clean and heating it over a medium-low flame until it's hot, then thinly coating it with oil, you can keep the pan's surface from sticking. Fairly light in hand and nicely balanced, it sits firmly on the range while its handle stays cool. For best results, cut vegetables ¼" thick and choose steaks and chops of a ½" thickness. Toss or brush the food with olive oil and seasonings, heat the pan about 3 minutes, then oil it lightly. At first the food will stick to the hot grids; when vegetables start to crinkle at the edges, or meat begins to change color around its perimeter and releases easily, it's time to turn. The one drawback, as with other Calphalon pans, is cleaning, but the pan also comes in nonstick.

10.15 WISCONSIN ALUMINUM FOUNDRY CHEF'SDESIGN RIBBED GRIDDLE

Though called a griddle by its manufacturer, this well-balanced, roomy, and surprisingly lightweight pan is a grill pan. It measures 10⅜" by 18⅞" and spans two burners. The grids are well spaced, running on the diagonal instead of straight across, and sear in deep, rich grill marks, which add a pleasant charred accent to vegetables and meat. Cure it first with a quick wipe of oil. It will accommodate six chops, fish steaks, or burgers, which will cook in short order. While the meat is resting, grill peppers and mushrooms to accompany it. Cleanup is a snap.

10.16 & 10.17 LE CREUSET MINI & GIANT REVERSIBLE GRILL-GRIDDLE

The larger pan measures 9" by 18" and spans two burners, while the mini grill is 10" square, fitting over a single burner. Produced in France, and crafted from a cast-iron base, the pans are coated on both sides with slightly textured black enamel, which won't react to acidic foods. Over time they'll develop a fine stick-resistant surface. Oil them before use, heat slowly, and maintain moderate temperatures; use a gentle hand when cleaning. Avoid cooking bacon or sausage patties on the griddle side—there's nowhere for fat to flow—but pancakes, French toast, or griddled sandwiches emerge crisp and well browned. The grill side is better still, especially on the larger pan, which perches more firmly on the stove. Rounded grilling grids, set close together at an angle, produce excellent grill marks. Whichever you choose, both pans cook rapidly and evenly. The mini grill is a fine choice for a small kitchen with limited storage space because it performs two jobs.

> You can find
> your way across
> this country
> using burger
> joints the way
> a navigator
> uses stars.
>
> —CHARLES KURALT

THE TRUTH WILL SET YOU FREE . . . BUT NOT FAT FREE

The stovetop grill pan has become one of the most popular pieces of cooking equipment in the United States. Some manufacturers assert that a grill pan reduces a food's fat content. They claim that the ridges hold your steak, hamburger, or chicken breast above the surface of the pan while the fat drips away into the grooves. It sounds good, but it may not be true. A series of laboratory tests at the Good Housekeeping Institute and *Consumer Reports* found that there was no significant difference in the fat content of hamburgers cooked on a flat surface and those cooked in a grill pan. Just as surprising, the burgers cooked on a cast-iron skillet had more of a "backyard grill" taste than those prepared in the grill pan. What the pans do is allow you to cook with little *added* fat, which may make the end result more healthful.

ELECTRIC INDOOR GRILLS

UNTIL RECENTLY, grilling was reserved for the backyard in warm weather, but because it imparts flavor without adding fat, it's becoming increasingly popular all year round, indoors and out. There are two types of countertop grills, "open" and "contact." Open grills have a cooking surface above an electric element. We recommend models with elements that are either embedded or nestled into channels in a ridged cooking surface. They provide superior browning, which translates into better flavor. Grills with a rack positioned several inches above the heat source are less successful. Also on the market are contact grills, which close like a waffle iron and heat from two sides at once, significantly speeding up the cooking time. Smaller than open grills, they hold less food.

When you're shopping for an electric grill, the same rules apply for both types. A higher wattage will result in better browning and faster cooking. Look for an indicator to let you know when the grill is hot enough to start cooking. Virtually all grills have nonstick finishes, which our tests showed did not hinder browning in any way. Just be sure to treat them kindly—use wooden or plastic tools, and if the grill can't go in the dishwasher, clean it with plastic scrubbing pads.

10.18 DELONGHI ALFREDO HEALTHY GRILL

With 1,500 watts, this grill takes less than 10 minutes to preheat and sears food quickly. The heating coils are embedded in the nonstick-finished, cast-aluminum cooking surface, which rests on a plastic base. A small metal cup in the middle of the base beneath the surface can be filled with water and seasonings to flavor foods, but we found the results barely discernible. The Alfredo is 18½" long, 11½" wide, and 6" high.

10.19 T-FAL DELUXE HEALTH GRILL

With a wattage rating of 1,600, one of the highest of any grill, this contact model browns exceptionally evenly, as beautifully as an outdoor barbecue, yet without the charring that comes from flare-ups or the clouds of smoke. It has a drip tray beneath the surface that not only collects grease during the cooking process, but holds water, which helps to minimize the smoking without steaming the food. This 15" wide by 12" long by 6" high grill has three temperature settings and can be used in an open position as well. It's a versatile unit, large enough to cook fish steaks for four people or beef steaks for two. The cast-aluminum, nonstick-coated grids detach from the grill for thorough cleaning by hand or in the dishwasher.

"Take your time. Breakfast is the most important meal of the day."

10.20 SALTON-MAXIM GEORGE FOREMAN'S LEAN MEAN FAT-REDUCING GRILLING MACHINE

The prizefighter who lent his name to this appliance and appears in television infomercials to promote it has single-handedly turned it into a national phenomenon. In spite of our skepticism, we have to admit that this uncomplicated contact 820-watt grill is handy. Its only special feature is a signal light that turns off, alerting you that the surface is hot enough to begin cooking. Four burgers are done in a mere 4 to 5 minutes, boneless skinless chicken breasts in 6 to 9, and they emerge with characteristic grill marks (if not deep browning) and remain moist and juicy. Perhaps our favorite use for this machine is quickly turning out grilled cheese sandwiches that are properly crunchy on the outside, gooey on the inside. We don't advise using the grill for cooking thick steaks or chops, as the sides remain raw unless you cook them to well done. During cooking, the grill smokes just a little. The grids don't detach for cleaning, but the nonstick surface and the plastic exterior wipe off easily. When not in use, the 13″ long by 10″ wide by 6″ high unit stands on end to minimize the amount of space it occupies on your countertop. Just don't be fooled into thinking that you're reducing your fat intake significantly by cooking on the Foreman. The surface is slanted so that fats and cooking juices run out—a small tray sits underneath the grill to catch the drippings—but only a small part of what drips out is fat, so little that it won't make much of a difference in your diet. This item is also available in smaller (two-burger) and larger (six-burger) sizes. This particular grill comes with four extra plastic feet to increase the machine's height when making fajitas or taco fillers. The taco shell sits in the tray with its opening at the lip of the grill. When the filling is cooked, it is pushed directly into the taco shell using a spatula. We don't consider the feet a huge asset and suspect that they will wind up in a drawer and be difficult to find when you need them.

RACLETTE-MAKERS

HUNDREDS OF YEARS AGO, cow herders in the Swiss Alps carried supplies of potatoes and pickled gherkins to eat along with cheese from the milk of their cows. At night, they baked potatoes in their campfire and placed a hunk of cheese on a rock near the fire. As the cheese melted it was scraped onto the potatoes and pickles. In fact, the name *raclette* derives from the French word *racler,* which means "to scrape." Today in Switzerland this simple meal is still served, although rarely is it cooked over a fire. Contraptions that hold a half wheel of raclette cheese under a heating element are used in restaurants, while at home small grills are placed in the middle of the table to serve as surrogate campfires. Traditional Swiss cheeses made from whole cow's milk in mountain villages like Bagnes, Conches, Gomser, and Orsieres are still used. You can find the place-names in the dark beige rinds of these strong-flavored cheeses.

10.21 SWISSMAR RACLETTE WITH GRILL

Unless you have a cooking hearth, this is your best choice for making raclette at home. Imported from Switzerland, this 18″-long tabletop grill is 5½″ high and 19″ wide. It comes with eight small enamel-coated pans that you fill with cheese slices, then insert beneath the heating element until the cheese is bubbling. Wooden spatulas are included for scraping the cheese onto the potatoes. Though you can use the nonstick-coated surface above the heat source for cooking other foods, it's not our top choice for indoor grilling. The element is not embedded in the cooking surface, and it only has 1,100 watts of heating power, which means it will take longer and not brown as well as many others on the market; it has a variable heat control without specific temperature readings; and the use and care instructions that are included with this product provide only minimal information. In other words, this piece of equipment is for those who are sure they love raclette and will serve it often.

WAFFLE IRONS

THESE ARE SPECIALIZED PIECES of equipment for which there are no alternatives. While you may not fire up a waffle iron weekly, or even monthly, it's a relatively small item to stash away. You can choose from machines that make classic thin waffles in squares, circles, or hearts, or puffy Belgian waffles that bake up crunchy on the outside and cakelike on the inside.

In spite of their limited function, we found that relatively few waffle irons did what they're supposed to do—deliver waffle after waffle evenly browned and crispy on the outside, cooked through yet not dry on the inside. Some machines have surfaces that remove for cleaning and reverse to a flat griddle side for grilling cheese sandwiches. We prefer those with a single surface—almost all are nonstick and easy enough to wipe clean, and we don't like the fuss of removing and replacing the grids. Plus, we found that removable surfaces sometimes pop off during baking. We love audible tones that tell us when the surface is hot enough to add the batter and when the waffle is done.

10.22 CHEF'SCHOICE WAFFLEPRO

The manufacturer of this model established a reputation for excellence in knife-sharpening machines and maintains it in every product it brings to market. This machine makes traditional thin 7"-wide waffles that you can customize to your personal preference. By flicking a switch, you can instruct the Wafflepro to bake waffles with a crisp exterior and moist interior or ones that are crunchy throughout. You also have a choice of six settings for crust color. Trust us, whatever selections you make, this machine delivers. In addition to a nonstick cooking surface, and a chime that lets you know when it's preheated and then when your waffle's done, it has a place to wrap the cord in the base and can stand on its end for storage. Don't limit your waffle repertoire to the familiar plain favorites. Try baking up the crunchy cornmeal or fudgy brownie varieties from the owner's manual.

10.23 VILLAWARE UNO BELGIAN WAFFLER

It takes more work to prepare the batter for Belgian waffles than for traditional ones, but once the batter is mixed it's almost effortless to bake the waffles in this handsome chrome iron. It has a nonstick coating so there is no need to use grease, the waffle pops right out, and cleanup is minimal. When the waffler is done preheating, which takes about 5 minutes, a tone sounds. Roughly 2 minutes later, when two perfect 1¼" thick waffles are ready, it chimes again. There are seven doneness settings. The cord wraps around the bottom, and the machine stands up for storage. This 4"-high beauty is 11" wide and 9½" long from the back to the tip of the stay-cool plastic handle.

10.24 NORDIC WARE BELGIAN WAFFLER

This stovetop, cast-aluminum waffler requires more work than an electric model, but it rewards you with a thick 7"-square waffle with a moist cakelike center that you can break into four smaller squares. It takes about the same amount of time to heat as a plugged-in one, but you need to turn this long-handled (5½") model over once during preheating. It takes longer to bake, and you need to flip it at least once during this process too. Also be aware that you can't expect even browning and consistency from waffle to waffle. Cleanup is minimal as the cooking surface has a nonstick coating.

WAFFLES

About 16 to 18 waffles

There are any number of different kinds of waffles in Belgium. The one that is most characteristic is a thick waffle, at least twice as thick as our native waffles, which is crusty on the outside and soft inside. The following recipe has the taste of a Belgian waffle, though not the consistency since the waffles have to be baked on our native irons.

2 cups water	2 cups milk
1 ounce fresh yeast or 1½ envelopes granulated yeast	10 tablespoons (½ cup plus 2 tablespoons) butter, melted
4 cups sifted flour	½ teaspoon salt
4 eggs, separated	1 tablespoon salad oil
½ cup sugar	1 teaspoon vanilla flavoring

Heat ½ cup of the water to lukewarm. Dissolve the yeast in the water. Put the flour in a large bowl. Stir in the egg yolks, the sugar, and the yeast. Beat in the remaining water, the milk, butter, salt, salad oil, and vanilla. Beat until the mixture is smooth. Beat the egg whites until they stand in stiff peaks. Fold them into the batter. Let the batter stand for 1 hour, stirring it 4 times. Bake the waffles in a waffle iron as usual. Serve with whipped cream, fruit, jam, or sugar.

The Belgian Cook Book, by Nika Hazelton

SCANDINAVIAN SPECIALTY GRIDDLES & IRONS

IN SCANDINAVIA THERE IS a class of food, neither bread nor cake, neither breakfast nor dessert, that falls into all these categories. They are the many pancakes and waffles that are cooked in special iron pans on top of the stove and are meant to be eaten as soon as they are cooked, fresh from their sizzling hot pans.

10.25 SCI SWEDISH *PLÄTT* PAN

Plättar are small Swedish pancakes, customarily served with lingonberries or fruit preserves as dessert. This heavy, cast-iron griddle (called a *plättlagg*) has circular depressions, each 3" in diameter and ¼" deep, allowing seven pancakes—one hearty serving—to cook at a time. Lightly grease the pan and heat it over a medium-high flame. When the pan is hot, drop a tablespoon of batter into each depression. When the edges begin to brown, after about 2 minutes, turn the pancakes with a narrow spatula and cook another two minutes to brown the other side. The griddle is 9¼" in diameter and has a 5"-long handle.

10.26 LODGE DANISH *AEBLESKIVE* PAN

Each of the Scandinavian countries has its favorite iron-baked batter specialty. From Denmark comes this *aebleskive* pan, which cooks seven puffy little ball-shaped *aebleskiver* at a time. *Aebleskive* is a favorite national dish that is served with spiced red wine during the long winter months. These apple pancakes are either made of a batter containing bits of apple or they are served with applesauce. The cast-iron pan is 12" long overall and 8" in diameter. Each *aebleskive* cooks in a small, bowl-shaped depression 2¼" in diameter and 1" deep. As with other cast-iron pans, be sure to season this before you use it.

10.27 SKEPPSHULT SCANDINAVIAN WAFFLE IRON

Fløtevafler, the crisp heart-shaped waffles that are eaten with cold lingonberries and fresh butter in Scandinavia, are tender in both design and texture. This iron is the traditional equipment for making *fløtevafler.* You place the iron over a burner on top of the stove and heat it until a drop of cold water flung on its surface sizzles, then pour the ginger-flavored sour-cream batter into the center. Close the top, and cook for 5 minutes on each side. This cast-iron pan is 8" in diameter and contains five heart-shaped sections. The long cast-iron handles are 7" in length.

10.28 BETHANY NORWEGIAN *GORO* IRON

A *goro* is a unique Norwegian cookie made from a butter dough containing brandy and whipped cream. It is rolled out to fit into and bake in this iron, which consists of two 4½"-square cast-aluminum plates. They are hinged together at one end, and have 7"-long handles on the opposite end. Each handle has a 4"-long wooden grip. The plates are subdivided into two smaller rectangles with stylized floral designs that transfer to the finished cookies when the dough is compressed between the plates. The iron rests in its niche on a circular cast-aluminum stand, which sits over a burner on top of the stove. The hinge fits into a socket in the stand. Roll out the dough and cut it into rectangles the size of the *goro* iron plate. Lift the dough carefully and place it in the open, preheated but ungreased iron. Close the iron and bake until the cookie is golden around the edges; turn the iron over in its stand and continue baking until done. Turn out and cut into individual *goros.*

10.29 NORDIC WARE NORWEGIAN *KRUMKAKE* IRON

Thin, sweet, golden cones filled with fruit, whipped cream, or ice cream, *krumkaker* are traditionally served at a Norwegian Christmas. To imprint *krumkaker* with their typical seasonal or floral patterns, use this heavy cast-aluminum *krumkake* iron. The iron itself has two patterned plates hinged together; a ball joint at the hinge rests in the socket of a ring that holds the iron over a stove burner. To make the cookies, both sides of the iron are heated, and a teaspoon or so of the sweet batter is placed in the center of the iron. The top is lowered, and the two sides squeezed together. The *krumkake* is baked for a few minutes on both sides, then removed and rolled into a cone with a *krumkake* roller. The cone can then be filled with a flavored cream or stored in an airtight container for future consumption. The *krumkake* iron is 5" in diameter with two 5 ½"-long handles. The ring it sits in measures 8½" in diameter with a 4½" handle.

10.30 SCI *KRUMKAKE* ROLLER

When the finished *krumkake* comes out of the iron, it will be a fragrant disc, brown at the edges and imprinted with whatever design was carved into the face of the iron. Then quickly, before it has time to cool, it should be rolled around a *krumkake* roller like this one. Within a few minutes it will have cooled and hardened into a cone-shaped cookie. It may be eaten just as it is, or filled with whipped cream. This 8"-long roller is made of pale unfinished wood, with a softly curved handle and an end shaped like an elongated Christmas tree. Although designed for rolling Norwegian *krumkaker,* its shape is perfect for forming a similar confection called *fyllda strutar,* Swedish pancake cookies filled with whipped cream and lingonberries.

PIZZELLE MAKERS

O**NE STORY HAS IT** that these thin round wafers with fancy designs originated in a small Italian village to celebrate the end of a plague. Today, it's not Christmas in some Italian American households without anise-flavored *pizzelles,* often tinted pink and green. Like waffles, they are prepared in an iron that cooks both sides at once. In the case of *pizzelles,* the irons have flat surfaces with engraved patterns. The original *pizzelle* irons were placed directly over a heat source, required turning, and had long handles and patterns that included family crests or initials; they are now heirlooms handed down from generation to generation.

Though nonelectric models can still be found, we prefer the convenience of an electrified maker that bakes both sides at once, has a thermostat to maintain a consistent baking temperature, and turns out cookies in less than a minute. We recommend one with a non-stick finish that makes it effortless to remove cookies and wipe the surface clean.

10.31 VILLAWARE PRIMA *PIZZELLE* BAKER

Following the recipe for Italian *Pizzelles* provided with this model, we turned out vanilla-flavored goodies that are nothing short of addictive. It bakes two 5″ cookies at once with a flower on one side and a crosshatch design on the other. Featuring an indicator light that lets you know when it's preheated, nonstick-coated grids, and stay-cool plastic handles that clip together during baking, it's very easy to use. The 3¾″-high iron measures 13½″ from the back to the end of the handle and 10½″ in width, and it stands on end for storage.

10.32 SCI *PIZZELLE* IRON

A handheld *pizzelle* iron like this one will produce a traditional result when used over a modern stove burner. This iron consists of two 5½″-diameter, cast-aluminum grids hinged together. Two 11¾″-long handles end in lightly varnished wood grips. *Pizzelle* irons and their many patterns—including this waffle grid and rosette combination—are also used to make similar wafer cookies called *cialde.*

It is customary today to think of the Christmas holidays as December 25 and New Year's Eve or Day. But traditionally in Italy and for the early Italian-Americans, the feast of the Natale spanned the twelve days from Christ's birthday to the feast of the Epiphany, January 6, when the Three Wise Men arrived in Bethlehem. It was a more celebratory time, filled with special foods, required visits to relatives, and tradition.

—NANCY VERDE BARR,
We Called It Macaroni

11

TOASTERS & TOASTER OVENS

TOASTERS

AMONG THE FIRST APPLIANCES to be "electrified," a toaster is still a staple in most households. Its task is a basic one—to heat, brown and crisp bread without drying it out completely—but it is, to judge by our testing, not so easy to accomplish. A good toaster should produce toast that's evenly colored on both sides and should be able to do so at each of its settings, whether the desired result is uncolored but crisp or almost charred, and regardless of whether you're toasting one or more slices. It should turn out evenly browned toast batch after batch.

We found that toasters with electronic controls that sense moisture in the item being toasted, and adjust cooking times accordingly, give better results than those with timers that toast for a specific amount of time at each setting regardless of the size, variety, or freshness of the bread. Another desirable feature is a self-centering mechanism that adjusts to the thickness of the slices so that each side is kept the same distance from the heating elements. Given the popularity of bagels today, any toaster worth the dough should be able to accommodate half of a thick "New York" bagel, even if its cut is slightly uneven. Unless otherwise noted, all of the toasters shown here perform these functions.

Other helpful but not essential features include controls for raising toast before it pops up, cords that wrap around "legs" in the base to keep the countertop neat, and removable, as opposed to hinged, crumb trays. Special settings for bagels, English muffins, defrosting, and reheating are useful when they work well.

11.1 T-FAL AVANTE DELUXE ELECTRONIC TOASTER

While this two-slice model will appeal to anyone with an eye for the unusual, we found the angled design did serve its promised purpose, which is to give easy access to the slots for both putting in and removing bread. It was among the best performers we tested, with electronic controls that allowed for a range of toast shades, from pale to almost burnt, that were fairly consistent from batch to batch. The cord can be wrapped around the bottom of the toaster, and there's a recessed handle that makes it easy to carry. We found it slightly inconvenient to have the crumb tray on a hinge. The stainless steel sides remain extremely cool to the touch even at the longest toasting times. In addition to six toast

246

settings, there's one for defrosting then toasting frozen items, a reheat button, and a lever to raise bread before it pops up. It measures 7¼" long, 11" wide, and 8½" at its highest point. It's also available with a white plastic housing.

11.2 DUALIT TWO-SLICE TOASTER

This good-looking, hand-assembled toaster, imported from England, is the darling of prop stylists and appears frequently in magazine layouts. It comes with a high price tag, and there's no question that it's well made and should prove exceptionally durable. However, it has an old-fashioned mechanical timer that at each of its three settings will always toast for a fixed amount of time regardless of the type, thickness, or condition of the bread. This means that results are extremely inconsistent. Moreover, there's no mechanism to keep bread evenly centered between the heating elements, and therefore the Dualit toasts unevenly as well. To lower and raise bread, you use a lever that we found very unintuitive, because you have to raise it to lower the bread and lower it to raise the bread. On the plus side, since the toast doesn't pop up until you activate the lever, it stays warm inside the cavity if you don't retrieve it right away. A thick bagel half barely fits in the slots. During toasting the stainless steel housing gets quite hot to the touch, especially on the top near the openings. It takes up a bit of space at 10¼" in length, 7¾" in depth, and 8½" in height. We tested the all stainless steel model; it also comes in versions with yellow or white accents.

11.3 HAMILTON BEACH TWO-SLICE INTELLITOAST TOASTER

Looking for an inexpensive no-frills model that is reliable and stays cool to the touch? Here's your toaster. It browns evenly and consistently, although it's weak at producing very pale or very dark shades. The IntelliToast has six color selections and a bagel setting, a removable crumb tray, a stop button, and a wrap-around cord. It is 10½" wide, 6" deep, and 8" high.

11.4 SUNBEAM TWO-SLICE TOASTER WITH TOAST LOGIC

The Sunbeam toaster was among the most consistent, even, and quickest performers we tested. With three main color choices and a pullout crumb tray, this is an uncomplicated choice. We love the classic design that's reminiscent of older kitchens but found the stainless steel housing gets too hot to touch. It measures 10½" in length, 6½" in depth, and stands 7½" high.

> The smell of buttered toast simply talked to Toad, and with no uncertain voice: talked of warm kitchens, of breakfasts on bright frosty mornings, of cozy parlor firesides on winter evenings.
>
> —KENNETH GRAHAME, *The Wind in the Willows*

11.5 CUISINART CUSTOM CONTROL TOTAL TOUCH FOUR-SLICE ELECTRONIC TOASTER

Among the relatively few toasters that can toast four slices at once, this model from Cuisinart has seven color settings that consistently provide a good range of doneness. It does, however, have a tendency to make striped toast. There's an easy-to-clean electronic control panel with touchpads for the toast, bagel, defrost, reheat, and stop settings; a pullout crumb tray; and a wrap-around cord. The lever can be boosted above its up position to raise small, hard-to-retrieve items. The plastic housing gets slightly warm to the touch. In spite of its large capacity, it's fairly compact at 14½" in width, 7¾" in depth, and 7½" high.

11.6 KITCHENAID DIGITAL ULTRA POWER PLUS TOASTER

If you prefer a sleek design that toasts two slices in one long slot, this toaster is the one for you. It's 20" wide but only 4½" deep and 7½" high. We found that although it was quite consistent when used for consecutive batches, it didn't toast as evenly as some other models. There are nine toast settings, but if you like your toast almost burnt you may find that even the highest one doesn't satisfy you. Noteworthy features include a smooth control panel with a lighted digital display for toast shades; bagel, frozen, reheat, and cancel settings; a removable crumb tray; and a wraparound cord. To remove small items like English muffins, you can raise the lever a little higher than its pop-up position. The black plastic housing stays very cool to the touch, and the toaster also comes in white, cream, empire green, cobalt blue, red, and yellow.

TOASTER OVENS

A TOASTER OVEN IS INDISPENSABLE for quickly reheating pizza slices and preparing tuna melts and other open-face cheese sandwiches. These small ovens also do quite a nice job of baking potatoes or meat loaf, broiling burgers or chicken. However, unless you have the luxury of enough counterspace to accommodate a toaster as well, you may compromise on both the speed and quality of bread toasting. The models we prefer do a decent job of toasting as well as serving as a countertop oven, but as a rule toaster ovens take longer than toasters to toast and almost always produce toast with stripes on the bottom side. If you plan to use your toaster oven primarily for toasting, look for one with toast controls that can be operated independently of the baking settings, so you don't have to reselect the toast color with every use. As with toasters, toaster ovens that sense moisture in the bread and then determine the toasting time are preferable to ones with mechanical timers that always toast for the same amount of time at a particular setting.

11.7 HAMILTON BEACH INTELLITOAST TOASTER OVEN BROILER

This is the one to choose if you're looking for a bread toaster and you frequently warm up pastries or melt cheese on a sandwich. To toast, you merely have to press the toast lever, and the oven browns up to four slices of bread in 2 or 3 minutes, as opposed to some others that can take as long as 7. It does a fairly good job at each of its three color settings. In a pinch you can use it to bake a cake or a meat loaf, but it won't hold a whole chicken and takes a full hour to broil chicken parts. We find it's easy to forget to turn off the oven feature on a toaster oven and love the fact that this one will automatically shut itself off after 2 hours. With a crumb tray that pulls out from the front and a nonstick interior finish, it's easy to clean. It's only 15½" wide, 10½" deep, and 8" high and has a wraparound cord, making it minimally obtrusive on the countertop.

11.8 CUISINART CONVECTION OVEN TOASTER-BROILER

With chrome housing and touch controls for all functions, as well as sensors for toasting and maintaining an even oven temperature, this is state of the art in the toaster oven category. A four-slice capacity, a good range of toasting shades, and special settings for bagels and frozen bread mean this unit will serve you well in the mornings—as long as you don't mind waiting a minute or two longer for it to deliver your toast than you would if you used a dedicated toaster. But it's the oven function in this model, with both conventional and convection baking, that really shines. Like a full-size oven, it beeps when it's preheated. Cakes, biscuits, cookies, and potatoes baked without the convection fan browned just as quickly and evenly as if baked in the oven. Using convection bake, a roast chicken and meat loaf were ready in less than an hour. We broiled chicken in just 17 minutes, although we have to point out that only three chicken quarters fit on the broiler pan at once, a definite disadvantage if you're feeding a family of four. However, there are no conveniences we could think of that this model doesn't have: after 4 hours it turns itself off, and it has a slide-out crumb tray, nonstick interior finish, built-in kitchen timer, and cord wrap. How much room does it take up? In

length, 17¾"; in width, 14¼"; and in height, 9¹³⁄₁₆".

11.9 BLACK & DECKER DINING-IN CONVECTION COUNTERTOP OVEN-BROILER

This is our recommendation if you're looking for a second oven that can double as a toaster. You'll need to give it some space: It's 20" wide, 14½" deep, and 10½" high. However, the convection-cooking feature produces a golden brown roast chicken in just 1 hour and a beautiful 13" by 9" by 2" cake in only 20 minutes. The Dining-In broils as quickly and as well as a broiler in a full-size oven. The large window gives excellent visibility during cooking. Because you can set the timer on this model to bake or broil for a specific amount of time, you don't have to worry about forgetting to shut the oven off. You can toast without adjusting the oven dials to a toast setting (though the oven dial does need to be in the off position), and the unit comfortably holds up to six slices of bread. Though it gives even results at three color settings, it can take longer than 6 minutes to make dark toast. This appliance is low maintenance thanks to a crumb tray that pulls out from the front and a nonstick finish on the interior.

CINNAMON TOAST

1, 2, or 4 servings

In my house, cinnamon toast was a daily after-school indulgence. It is a perfect sweet pacifier, easy to make, and nothing in the world is quite like it. Mix 1 cup of sugar with 1 tablespoon plus 1 teaspoon of ground cinnamon. Stir to mix well, and store it in a plastic bag, having it ready so you can make cinnamon toast in a minute.

> 4 slices fresh white bread
> 4 tablespoons butter
> 4 tablespoons sugar
> 1 teaspoon ground cinnamon

PREPARING THE CINNAMON TOAST

1 Toast the bread. Spread each slice of bread generously with butter, about 1 tablespoon.
2 Mix the sugar and cinnamon in a small bowl until the mixture looks tan-colored. Using a spoon, sprinkle the toast from edge to edge, so each slice is completely covered with the sugar mixture.
3 Put the toasts in a single layer on a baking sheet.

BROILING THE TOAST

1 Put the oven rack about 3" below the broiling element.
2 As soon as the broiler element heats and turns red, slide the baking sheet under the broiler. Stand right there and keep an eye on the toasts. It will take a minute or two for the sugar to melt and begin to bubble a little. When the sugar bubbles, remove the toasts and eat immediately.

Learning to Cook with Marion Cunningham, by Marion Cunningham

12

ROASTING EQUIPMENT

IN 1959, James Beard, one of America's leading food authorities, was on the management team searching for the chef who would open the Four Seasons restaurant in New York. Beard devised a test. He required each candidate to perform the single most challenging culinary task the judges could think of—roasting a chicken perfectly. It sounds simple, but it is actually extremely difficult. The dark meat must remain moist but be fully cooked to an internal temperature of at least 160° to 165°F. At the same time, if the breast meat reaches an internal temperature of more than 150°F it will become dry, begin to toughen, and lose its flavor. Food scientists have analyzed the problem, and books by such masters of the art of roasting as Barbara Kafka, Shirley Corriher, and Harold McGee teach various techniques. However, we think they would all agree that reliable roasting equipment is an important key to success.

Sources of Heat

Originally, roasting was defined as exposing a food to direct heat from one side—with no pot, pan, liquid, or fat between the food and the fire. Placing a piece of freshly caught meat on the end of a stick and holding it above a flame was probably the earliest cooking technique. It worked, but fat would drip into the fire and flare up, and the delicious drippings would be lost. At some point a good cook realized that applying heat

from the side might be a better solution. The fat self-basted the food turning on the spit, then dripped into a pan where it could be used to cook other foods.

For millennia, roasting spits were made of wood, but when English metalworkers perfected the art of casting iron during the middle of the seventeenth century, pit dogs, firedogs, gridirons, andirons, and creepers became essential kitchen tools. In Tudor England, cooks in great houses spit-roasted their meat, often using trained dogs (encouraged by live coals) to turn the mechanism. There are even records of geese being trained as turnspits. Upon seeing a goose turning a turkey on a spit, one observer remarked: "Alas! We are all turnspits in this world: and when we roast a friend let us be aware that many stand ready to return the compliment."

A Note on the Language of Roasting

Heat applied to food from beneath is called *grilling;* if the source of direct heat comes from above, it is considered to be *broiling;* and when heat surrounds the food in a pan, it is called *roasting.* The accepted definition of *baking* is also to surround a food or mixture of ingredients, like breads, cookies, or lasagna, with dry heat. How, then, do roasting and baking differ? After the introduction of the home stove in the late nineteenth century, meats that were previously spit-roasted were often cooked in the oven. Although this was technically baking, the word *roasting* continued to be used, with some exceptions (like baked ham or baked meat loaf), largely as a matter of custom. Mary Ronald addressed this point in her *Century Cookbook*, published in 1895, explaining that the old practice of spit-roasting in the fireplace had given way to our modern method of bake-roasting. "To roast beef on a spit before a fire is unquestionably the best method of cooking it; but as few kitchens are equipped for roasting meats, baking them in the oven is generally practiced and has come to be called roasting."

HOW TO PERFECTLY ROAST A CHICKEN
❧ ANDRÉ SOLTNER ❧

Nothing is simpler or more delicious than a perfectly roasted chicken. To me, when executed with perfection, it is the ultimate dish, whether in a restaurant or at home. Unfortunately, it's a rare thing to find in a restaurant. Because it is so simple, chefs take it for granted and don't pay enough attention to the details. A chef should be judged by a roasted chicken. It requires technique, attention, patience, and a lot of love.

1 fresh chicken about 3½ pounds, preferably free range
coarse salt
½ teaspoon freshly grated black pepper
1 small onion, peeled, cut in 4 pieces
2 sprigs fresh thyme (or ½ teaspoon dried)
1 sprig oregano (optional)
1 sprig rosemary (optional)
1½ tablespoons unsalted butter
2 tablespoons peanut oil
1 medium carrot, peeled, washed, and cut in ½" pieces
2 cloves garlic, peeled
½ cup dry white wine (or water)

1 Preheat the oven to 450°F.

2 Remove the giblets from the cavity of the chicken, rinse them under cold water, and set aside. Rinse the chicken under cold water inside and outside. Pat dry with paper towels.

3 Cut off the wingtips.

4 Salt the chicken with coarse salt and black pepper inside and outside.

5 Into the cavity of the chicken, insert ½ of the onion, the chicken liver (salted), 1 sprig of thyme, the oregano and rosemary if used, and ½ tablespoon of the butter.

6 Truss the chicken with a string. This is important to keep the chicken in a good shape.

7 Rub the chicken with 1 tablespoon of oil.

8 Add the remaining oil into a roasting pan and place the pan in the preheated oven until the oil is very hot, about 4 minutes.

9 Carefully remove the pan from the oven and add the chicken, lying on its side, then add the neck, gizzard, and wing tips.

10 Place the pan back into the oven for 15 minutes.

11 Turn the chicken on its other side, basting with the pan juices, and continue roasting for another 15 minutes.

12 Turn the chicken on its back, basting again with the pan juices, and continue roasting for 10 minutes.

13 Remove the pan from the oven and reduce the heat to 375°F.

14 Carefully discard all the fat from the pan and replace with 1 tablespoon of the butter. Add the remaining onion, carrot, garlic, and 1 sprig of thyme and put the pan back into the oven. After 5 minutes, baste the chicken with the pan juices and add 1 tablespoon of water to the pan. Repeat this process every 5 minutes four more times.

15 The chicken is roasted in about 1 hour and 10 minutes. The outside should be crisp and golden brown, and the inside should be very moist and juicy. If you use a meat thermometer it should read between 175° and 180°F for well done.

16 Remove the chicken from the oven. Lift the chicken up so the cavity's juices flow into the pan. Remove the contents of the chicken's cavity into the roasting pan. Let the chicken rest on a serving platter and keep warm. Put the pan over medium heat on top of the stove and add the wine or water and scrape the pan thoroughly with a wooden spoon. Simmer for 2 minutes and then pass this liquid through a fine sieve. Serve with the chicken.

ROASTING PANS

THE TURKEY IS TRUSSED, the roast is tied, the leg of lamb is studded with garlic slivers, the ham is ready to be glazed with port wine: in short, it is time to cook the meat you have just so carefully prepared. These days most roasting takes place in an oven and involves a less direct exposure of the food to the heat than broiling or grilling. However, the fact that a pan stands between the fire and the bird or the beef is of little consequence—a beautifully browned roast will still result as the dry heat of the oven reflects back onto the food.

12.1 CALPHALON "POTS & PANS" ROASTER

This 13" by 9" by 2½" pan breaks several of our "rules-of-the-roast," and caused considerable controversy among our experts, but came out a winner. A 3-pound chicken roasted perfectly at high heat, even though the space between it and the sides of the pan was only 1½", not the recommended 2". The interior is dark, but it produced a satisfying amount of caramelized browned bits, which were easy enough to see developing. Though the material is nonstick, it did not prevent browning and allowed the delicious residue to slip out with ease and not remain stuck to the pan waiting for an attack by a nonmetal spoon or spatula. (It's best to retrieve the drippings by straining them through a sieve after the cooked food is removed and then returning the bits to the pan for gravy-making.) Another advantage to this small, relatively lightweight anodized aluminum roaster is that it can easily be moved to the top of the stove for basting or for finishing the gravy. The side-set handles are easy to use and radiated no heat through oven mitts. Cleanup is, of course, a snap.

12.2 ALL-CLAD STAINLESS ROTI PAN

Beautiful to look at as well as to use, this 16½" by 14" by 3½" heavy-gauge stainless steel pan is an excellent performer. The upright, riveted, solid-cast stainless steel handles are comfortable to grasp, even with hands encased in oven mitts, and they cool rapidly. A 7½-pound roasting chicken cooked at fairly high heat browned evenly and well. The pan produced a nice amount of tasty, caramelized morsels; with most of the fat removed, and the remaining solids deglazed with vermouth and chicken broth, the resulting gravy was delicious. The Roti pan, though heavy, is not too heavy to lift with a large bird in place. Cleanup is easy, too—nothing stuck to the pan when we used it—but avoid steel wool! Another good feature: The pan comes with All-Clad's lifetime warranty.

WHAT TO LOOK FOR

Material Roasting pans can be made of stainless steel, stainless steel with an aluminum core, aluminum alloy, anodized aluminum, lined copper, blue steel, and enameled steel, each available with and without nonstick coatings. Enamel over sheet steel, stainless steel, and aluminum alloys are all effective. Copper is a great conductor of heat, and beautiful as well. Nonstick surfaces can be problematic because some, but not all, can prevent the pan drippings from browning. And a dark surface, nonstick or not, makes it more difficult for a cook to see how the pan sauce is developing. We did not select any pans made of heatproof glass, ceramic, or earthenware because they may crack when subjected to direct heat during deglazing, and in most cases their handles were not designed for heavy roasts.

Weight Roasting pans are meant to carry heavy ingredients and so must be sturdy enough to handle the weight without buckling, but they also must not add unnecessary pounds to the total you have to lift—a 20-pound turkey in a 10-pound pan is an unreasonably heavy load. Test the pan with some weight in it before you make a purchase to see if you can handle it easily.

12.3 CIRCULON RECTANGULAR ROASTER

12.4 MAUVIEL CUPRINOX *PLAT À ROTIR* ROASTING PAN

This roaster is constructed of hard-anodized aluminum, which is twice as hard as stainless steel. It's called *Circulon* because of the concentric pattern of raised grooves on the interior surface. The combination of the grooves and the nonstick coating makes this pan stickproof. The pan is heavy enough to perform beautifully but not too heavy to lift, even when it held a 14-pound turkey, which browned perfectly. The stainless steel upright riveted handles are comfortable and cool quickly. This handsome 19" by 12" by 3" roaster can withstand high oven heat and is guaranteed for ten years.

You can get from here to there in a budget compact or a Rolls-Royce, but all things considered, which would you choose? With this roaster, it was easy to abandon some practical considerations and be seduced by its high-quality copper exterior, stainless steel lining, and capacious 14" by 10" by 2" dimensions. It is a luxurious pleasure to use. It's heavy, but not too heavy to lift easily. A 4½-pound chicken, with just a drop of oil under the bird, roasted at 400°F to a browned and juicy perfection, with lots of caramelized bits for a delicious gravy. The riveted bronze handles radiated little heat through oven

mitts. Marvelous, but like a high-end car, this pan needs maintenance. The steel lining needs polishing with a good soft cleanser. The copper exterior also needs care, preferably with a good quality copper polish.

COVERED HIGHS & OPEN LOWS

The high covered roaster cooks with steam, making your meat more or less a pot roast whether you want one or not. These roasters are the subject of much controversy. James Beard liked to roast in a heavy low open pan with a V-shaped rack, which holds the meat out of the fat and permits the circulation of hot air all around it. Others claim that nothing in the world can equal the moisture and tenderness of a large turkey roasted in a high-sided pan. Those who have taken the high (covered) road believe that the word *roaster* should only be applied to deep-sided pans—they maintain that the function of a roaster is to create a second, smaller oven inside the oven that greatly magnifies the heat as it bounces off the hot walls of the pan. Furthermore, with a high-sided pan you can cut the cooking time in half, because of the intensified heat. (However, make sure to adjust recommended temperatures and cooking times accordingly.) The high-sided experts suggest covering poultry for most of the roasting time, then removing the top at the end to brown and crisp the skin.

Size When it comes to size, consider the dimensions of the foods you roast most often, and bear in mind that pan drippings from a small roast in a large pan will burn. You may end up buying a smaller pan for pork tenderloins and a larger pan for your turkeys. Make sure that there will be about 2" of space between the meat and sides of the pan and 2" between the pan and the oven walls. (When planning to buy a large roasting pan it's important to measure the inside of your oven first.) Roasting pans should be about 2" deep; any deeper and the food may steam.

Disposable roasting pans are flimsy, hard to grip, and almost impossible to deglaze. We disposed of them permanently after testing.

Handles The final consideration is the handles. We were disappointed by many attractive and sturdy pans that did not have handles that were rigid. We feel strongly about this, since hot fat, like hot steam, is a real danger in the kitchen. Balancing an oddly shaped piece of meat, often suspended on a rack over a pan full of hot fat, requires secure handles. The best design, known as a French roaster, has roomy upright handles that are riveted to the sides of the pan. Loop handles that swing up from the sides of the pan can be difficult to grip and are not reliable. Avoid pans with inset handles or with no handles at all.

AN ANCIENT ROASTING METHOD
✤ LARRY FORGIONE ✤

Old doesn't always mean obsolete. I find old methods to be inspirational. I've found that forgotten cooking methods just need someone to rediscover them, lighten them up, and make them fun and interesting. The joy about cooking this dish is that it leads us back to our own traditions, our culinary heritage. With cedar-planked salmon, I have utilized a forgotten, Indian-style cooking technique. *Planking* is a method of roasting that originated in the Pacific Northwest; Indians would tie sides of salmon to cedar logs and stand them up at the base of an open fire to cook and enhance the flavor of fish.

My interpretation of this age-old approach began when I took a plank from my neighbor's house to cook salmon. Now, I buy plain, untreated cedar planks at a lumberyard, place fresh salmon or other fish fillets on top, then put the plank under the broiler and let it smolder; then I finish off the dish in the oven.

Accenting the planked salmon recipe is my old-fashioned egg sauce, inspired by a traditional sauce from the eastern part of the United States. New England Fourth of July celebrations customarily include poached salmon with a rich sauce similar to this one. The salmon can be served hot or cold. If you want to serve it cold, as a change from poached fish on a buffet table, for example, stir some mayonnaise and lemon juice into the cooled egg sauce.

CEDAR-PLANKED SALMON

4 servings

1 teaspoon salt
¼ teaspoon freshly ground black pepper
¼ teaspoon dry mustard
1 tablespoon unsalted butter, at room temperature
four 8-ounce salmon fillets, skinned
Old-Fashioned Egg Sauce (recipe follows)
2 untreated cedar shingles or shims (available from lumber yards), 4" to 5" wide and about 12" long

1 Mix together the salt, pepper, and mustard. Brush the top of the salmon fillets with a little butter and then sprinkle both sides with the mustard mixture.

2 Preheat the broiler. Soak the shingles in cold water for 5 to 10 minutes.

3 Put the soaked shingles under the hot broiler 4" to 5" from the heat source for 2 to 3 minutes, until the wood is browned on the top. Carefully take the shingles from the broiler.

4 Immediately, so that the shingles do not cool, lay two salmon fillets on the browned side of each shingle. Return the shingles to a 450°F oven and cook the fish for about 5 to 7 minutes, until firm but not dry. Lift the salmon from the shingles, or serve it on the shingles if you like, with the egg sauce.

OLD-FASHIONED EGG SAUCE

¼ cup dry white wine
¼ cup fish stock or chicken stock or canned chicken broth
1 teaspoon minced shallots or scallions
2 tablespoons fresh lemon juice
¼ cup heavy cream
8 tablespoons unsalted butter, cut into 8 pieces
½ teaspoon Tabasco
salt and freshly ground black pepper
2 hard-cooked eggs, coarsely grated
3 tablespoons chopped flat-leaf parsley
1 tablespoon salmon caviar (optional)

1 Combine the wine, stock, shallots or scallions, and 1 tablespoon of the lemon juice in a small nonreactive saucepan. Bring to a simmer over medium heat and cook for 3 to 4 minutes until reduced to about 2 tablespoons.

2 Stir in the cream and simmer for about 3 minutes until the cream thickens slightly. Lower the heat and stir in the butter a tablespoon at a time: do not add another tablespoon until the one before it has been thoroughly incorporated.

3 Remove the sauce from the heat and stir in the remaining 1 tablespoon lemon juice and ½ teaspoon Tabasco. Season to taste with salt and pepper. Strain the sauce into a bowl. Cover to keep warm until ready to serve.

4 Just before serving, mix the grated eggs with the parsley and caviar. Stir the mixture into the warm sauce and serve with the salmon.

12.5 CIRCULON OVAL COVERED ROASTER

Made of durable hard-anodized aluminum, this versatile 16½" by 10" by 9½" covered roaster is good-looking enough to be presented at the table. It comes with its own shallow rack, which allows juices to accumulate while keeping the meat elevated.

This roaster works equally well as a Dutch oven, fine for stews and braised dishes. The raised concentric grooves of the aptly named Circulon ensure a nonstick surface and an easy cleanup. The wide-set, riveted stainless steel handles are comfortable to grip with oven mitts.

12.6 GRANITE WARE COVERED ROASTER

It's a pretty safe bet that your mother—and your grandmother—owned a covered roasting pan like this one, and it's not a bad idea for you to own one, too. This same U.S. company, Granite Ware, has been making these black porcelain-on-steel roasters, specked with white flecks, since 1871. The generously proportioned 19" by 13½" by 8⅜" roaster has a "tree" embossed pattern on the bottom, to partially lift food off the surface; nevertheless, it's best to rub the bottom with a drop of oil to prevent any sticking. To store the pan, just invert the lid. The Granite Ware roaster is a practical, economical, time-honored choice.

ROASTING RACKS

A NUMBER OF LEADING chefs prefer their roasts to be in direct contact with the pan, which they believe produces superior drippings for their pan sauces. Others feel that true roasting requires that air circulate completely around the food for consistent browning. You can accomplish this by using a spit, but it will probably be easier to use a roasting rack. Roasting racks sit in roasting pans and hold the meat away from the bottom of the pan, which allows the hot air to move beneath the meat and the fat to drip away.

Not counting the usually flimsy rack that sometimes comes with the purchase of a roasting pan (and can be discarded with the shipping container), there are five types of roasting racks: vertical poultry roasters, basket racks, nonadjustable V racks, adjustable V racks, and flat racks. Whichever design you choose, the rack must be well constructed and sturdy, fit easily into your pan, and, with whole poultry or a large roast positioned on it, allow for at least 2" clearance at the top of the oven. The handles must be securely attached and easy to grip, even when your hands are in bulky mitts. Stainless steel is a good material, and a black nonstick coating helps with cleaning; the following racks (except for the Spanek) are all nonstick.

12.7 ADAMS INDUSTRIES NON-STICK ROAST RACK

This slightly curved rack, 10¼" by 8¼", is very easy to clean. It can be placed in an oven bag, which is a great advantage for those who use them, as it prevents the food from stewing in its own juices. It is also shallow, elevating a roast less than ½" from the floor of a pan, an ideal choice for those who usually prefer to roast without a rack—you get the advantage of the deep heat which radiates from the pan without the danger of sticking. The rack can be easily lifted from pan to cutting board, with the roast still on it, to allow for proper resting before carving.

12.8 AMCO ADJUSTABLE ROAST RACK

This rack from Amco is wonderfully versatile. Adjustable to six positions, it measures 11½" wide by 7⅝" long by 5⅝" high at its most upright position, and 11½" by 10⅝" by 1" when used flat. It's also fine to use as a broiling rack. Made of nonstick-covered wire, it conducts heat quickly and it comes apart for cleaning.

12.9 CALPHALON LARGE ROAST RACK

Never has roasting a turkey—placed in this large nonstick roast rack—been easier! The basket rack is 15" long, but the 14" width, including handles, means that you must use a large roasting pan. The rack is heat-safe to 425°F, fairly light in weight, and no trouble to clean. Its identical (except for size) little brother, the small roast rack, measures 12" by 12" and is equally as efficient. We suggest storing the rack in its cardboard coverings to prevent any scratching of the nonstick surface.

12.10 AMCO CRADLE ROAST RACK

This nonstick rack, which looks like it should be holding logs for the fireplace, easily accommodates a 3- to 4-pound chicken, a pork tenderloin, or other roast. The compact

12.11 DE BUYER CHESTNUT PAN

Paris in the fall: Can you ever forget the slightly sweet smell of roasting chestnuts that emanates from the carts of countless vendors? To bring the memory home, use a pan like this 11"-diameter (across the top), perforated blue steel skillet made especially for roasting those delicately flavored nuts. Cover the bottom of the pan with chestnuts and hold it over a low to moderate flame, shaking it occasionally to keep the nuts from burning. (The iron handle is 9" long so you can even reach safely into a fireplace.) Before using, be sure to wash off the protective coating on the pan and to season it with oil. Remember to score the chestnuts with an X for easy peeling.

dimensions, 10⅝" by 6¾" by 3¾", mean that it fits easily into a relatively small roasting pan. Food browns well in the cradle, and caramelized bits as well as fat drip through the perforations. In a covered roaster it can even be used for steaming fish. The nonstick finish ensures an easy cleanup.

12.12 SPANEK VERTICAL POULTRY ROASTER

Until we tried the Spanek, we found vertical roasters to be little more than gimmicks. But this 8"-high, tempered-steel chicken roaster did a grand job. The Spanek really does what it claims: sears the inner cavity of the bird, cooks all the meat thoroughly, drains the fat, and crisps the skin. Cooking time is faster, too. You position the bird, legs down and untrussed, over the Eiffel Tower–shaped frame that Denis Spanek's mother, a professional cook, invented, and that his father, an engineer, crafted. The Spaneks, of Czech origin, lived in France before moving to the United States; Mrs. Spanek, nostalgic for the ducks of her homeland, got the idea for vertical cooking from the dripping ducks she saw hanging in Chinese restaurant windows. Get rid of the fat the easy way!

Besides the 8-ribbed chicken/duck roaster, there are the 10-ribbed turkey roaster (you can roast two turkeys, side by side, at the same time), the 6-ribbed game hen roaster, and a 4-ribbed small roaster for quail. Before you invest in one of the larger sizes, make sure your oven is big enough to hold it. You can also use the Spanek vertical roasters on the barbecue; just follow the instructions that come with them.

BASTING

BULB BASTERS, which look and act like large eye-droppers, are used to suction up the fat and liquids from the bottom of the roasting pan and pour them back over the meat, keeping it moist, adding flavor, and creating a glaze as it cooks. A large spoon will do a similar job, but bulb basters hold more liquid, can distribute the juices more evenly, and are easier to use.

The bulb of the baster should be firm enough so it won't collapse and stick together when squeezed. Heat-resistant rubber is ideal. Plastic bulbs will eventually split and can be difficult to maneuver. The baster's tubular shaft, particularly the tip, should be wide enough to avoid being clogged with large drippings. They come in four materials: stainless steel, glass, Lexan, and nylon. Stainless steel is strong and easy to clean but makes it difficult to judge how much liquid you are taking up. Glass does not present that problem and is equally easy to clean, but it can shatter. Lexan is transparent, heat resistant, and strong. Nylon, though strong and semitransparent, is our least favorite—it can melt at high pan temperatures and tends to retain traces of every fluid it slurps.

Some basters come with an attachable needle that screws into the tip, turning your oversized eyedropper into a hypodermic syringe. It is used for injecting a marinade of melted fat, oil, or herb-infused wine into the meat to tenderize and flavor it. Be aware, however, that the injected liquids can create steam inside the meat, turning your roast into a pot roast.

An alternative to the bulb baster is the basting brush. Its long bristles soak up drippings that you can brush over your bird as it roasts. Choose a brush made of pure natural bristles with a long handle (at least 12"); the length keeps your arms away from the heat.

12.13 FOX RUN STAINLESS STEEL BULB BASTER

With a 10¼" steel body and a yellow rubber "nonroll" bulb, this workmanlike baster does the job. The tube is sturdy, and the bulb draws efficiently. It comes with a cleaning brush, which unfortunately does not work well; it might be useful, though, if a piece of food got stuck and needed a push to dislodge. The injector needle is effective: we used it to inject juice into the flesh and under the skin of a chicken. To clean the baster, put the bulb in the top part of the dishwasher and the tube in the silverware basket.

"I try to eat right, but huge chunks of raw meat are all you can find these days."

12.14 FOX RUN HEAT-RESISTANT GLASS BASTER

This 10¾" glass baster with rubberized bulb has good "pull." The shaft slips easily into the bulb and has ½-ounce to 2-ounce markings, which you might find helpful. The glass tip touched the bottom of a roasting pan in a 450°F oven and passed the test by not shattering. Still, if you are at all wary about possible breakage, stainless steel or sturdy plastic might be a better choice.

12.15 PEDRINI SPIRIDOSO

The 11"-long baster, including the big-capacity white rubber bulb, has the good looks we expect of Italian design. The shaft is made of clear polycarbonate Lexan and has markings in both ounces (¼, ½, ¾, and 1) and milliliters (7, 14, 21, and 28). It is heat resistant and dishwasher safe. A great choice for basting chicken, turkey, duck, or other fatty meats.

12.16 LAMSONSHARP BASTING BRUSH

This 12"-long basting brush has a plastic handle, a sturdy metal shaft, and a head made of pure boar's bristles that will last for years. The bristle head is also removable, which lets you buy two heads, one for heavy barbecue sauces and one for pan juices. The metal flange between the shaft and the bristles allows the brush to rest on the counter with the bristles elevated—no mess. The entire tool is easy to clean with detergent and warm water, or you can just pop it into the dishwasher.

LACING

THE EASIEST TECHNIQUE for closing the cavity of a stuffed bird is to use poultry lacers—small skewers, pinned through the skin of the fowl, around which twine is laced as though you were hooking up ice skates. The lacers should always have a blunt end that has been turned into a ring, so that the cook, confronted with these hot needles in a freshly roasted chicken, can slip the tines of a fork through the rings and pull out the lacers. Stainless steel is the ideal material for poultry lacers, and the length should be more than 4".

TRUSSING WITH A BUTCHER'S NEEDLE

Victorians, confronted by the indelicate end of a chicken, stuffed it and then sewed it up with heavy twine and a darning needle—a perfectly good technique for a roast that is stuffed or needs a compact shape. Today we use a trussing or butcher's needle, a sharp needle with a large eye in the tip that is threaded with butcher's twine; just be careful not to use nylon thread, which might melt, or waxed cotton, which might add an unpleasant taste to your bird. If butcher's twine is not available, a heavy white button or carpet thread or unwaxed dental floss is a fine substitute. Trussing needles should be made of stainless steel and measure at least 8". The needles come curved or straight; the curved ones allow you to stitch around corners that are too difficult for a straight needle and are better at navigating around bones.

12.17 MATFER TURKEY LACERS

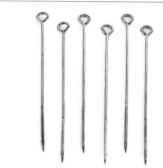

Six sturdy, 4½" rods, constructed of rigid stainless steel with rounded ends for easy removal, these lacers should never bend and will last for years. A sketch on the back of the package shows you just how to use them, but don't forget that you'll need a ball of butcher's string. By the way, keep the lacers in their storage tube: loose lacers in a kitchen drawer, like socks in a dryer, tend to vanish mysteriously .

12.18 WÜSTHOF TRUSSING NEEDLE

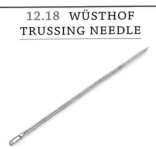

The slender, straight stainless steel needle, 8" long, has a flattened, spearlike tip and a flattened eye. Thread it with a sufficient length of butcher's or kite twine, make a knot, and you can sew up a chicken or turkey cavity with ease.

ROASTING BELL PEPPERS & CHILIES

❧ DOUGLAS RODRIGUEZ ❧

This cooking technique results in tender peppers or chilies with an intensely smoky flavor and also enables you to remove the tough, bitter skins with ease. You can prepare roasted peppers and chilies ahead of time and store them by covering them with vegetable oil (mixed with a small amount of finely minced garlic, if desired). They will keep in the refrigerator for up to two months.

Prepare the grill, preferably using wood chips that have been soaked in water. Leaving the stems on, lightly brush the peppers or chilies with olive oil and place them on the hot grill. If you don't have a grill, a stovetop gas burner can be used: pierce the pepper with a fork and hold it over the open flame. (Be sure to wear an oven mitt; the metal fork can heat up fast.) Let the flame char the skin, rotating until it's evenly blackened.

Transfer the peppers or chilies to a large paper or plastic bag and seal the top. Let them steam for 10 to 12 minutes, or until cooled, then remove them from the bag and peel off their skins. Cut off the stems, and remove and discard the seeds.

LARDING

LARDING INVOLVES THREADING fat through a piece of meat that is about to be cooked. To a nation obsessed with low-fat foods, the French practice of larding lean meats seems almost suicidal. Yet the fact remains that some cuts, such as veal roasts, venison, or bottom round of beef, are greatly improved by being threaded with ribbons of seasoned fat. This bastes the meat from the inside as it cooks, adding both flavor and tenderness and in the end producing a lower fat content than a prime rib roast, heavily marbled with its own built-in larding.

Larding is done with strips—lardons or lardoons—of blanched salt pork, fresh pork fatback, or suet. A strip of fat is placed in a *lardoir,* or larding needle, and pushed into the meat, usually parallel to the grain. The meat is larded at regular intervals, with special attention to the design that will result when the meat is carved against the grain and across the lardoons. For hundreds of years chefs prided themselves on their ability to produce elaborate larding patterns. Fat is not the only ingredient that can be threaded into a roast: raisins, slivers of dates, and sticks of carrots add color, flavor, and a change of texture. For a dazzling effect, lard monkfish fillets with a pattern of blanched carrot, the dark skin of zucchini, and red pepper strips.

Larding needles should be made of stainless steel and be long enough to go completely through the food you are about to cook.

12.19 WÜSTHOF LARDING NEEDLE

This little 7½" steel larding needle has a pointed tip to glide through meat easily. The hinged end, when open, resembles an alligator's jaw. Cut the lardoons a little longer than the piece of meat you wish to lard. Slide the strip of fat about 2" along the bottom of the open hinge and snap it shut so that the teeth grasp the end of the strip. Then push the needle through the meat—the lardoon will be drawn after it—until the hinge appears on the other side. Open the hinge and gently pull out

259

the needle. Continue using the larding needle, preferably making a decorative pattern of strips that will be seen (and appreciated!) when the meat is sliced. After you have finished larding, trim off the ends of the lardoons flush with the meat.

12.20 MATFER LARDING NEEDLE

This slender, 9½"-long stainless steel needle is hollow, so that strips of seasoned fat, cut into very narrow ribbons, can easily be tucked into it. After cutting the strips, freeze them until they stiffen, then insert them, one at a time, into the needle. Be sure that you cut the strips long enough so that a portion hangs out for you to hold on to as you push the needle through the meat. When the tip of the needle exits the far side of your roast, gently pull it out until you see an inch or so of fat. Continue loading and larding, then trim off overhanging fat.

ROAST SHOULDER OF LAMB WITH PANCETTA

Rather than stud a lamb roast with the usual garlic (which not everyone adores), try larding it with good, fatty pancetta as they used to do in the Middle Ages. It adds flavor and succulence to the meat.

shoulder of lamb, about 3¼ pounds
6 ounces pancetta, sliced about ¼" thick
salt

Preheat oven to 425°F. Cut the pancetta into small strips and, using a paring knife to pierce the meat, insert them into the lamb. Sprinkle the lamb with salt, and roast for about 1¼ hours, either on a rack in a roasting pan or skewered on a rotisserie. When it is done, turn off the oven and leave the door ajar; let the meat rest for about 15 minutes before serving. Serve with green sauce, to which you have added the meat juices from the roasting pan.

The Medieval Kitchen, by Odile Redon, Françoise Sabbon, and Silvano Serventi

---

TURKEY LIFTERS

LIFTING AN 18-POUND turkey out of a roasting pan and onto a carving platter is not an easy task. Barbara Kafka suggests in her book *Roasting: A Simple Art* to "move the bird by placing a large wooden spoon into the tail end and balancing the bird with a kitchen spoon at the other end." You might also sacrifice a clean pair of oven mitts or pot holders to the task, immediately consigning them to a bowl of warm, soapy water afterward. Another alternative is to use a commercially made turkey lifter. There are three styles: a series of chains that slide under the bird and act as a cradle, with handles on the side to assist you in lifting the bird (they are not particularly helpful when turning a roast); a set of hefty forks, each with four tines, that are designed to scoop up a turkey (they pierce the flesh, letting the juices escape, and are awkward to use); and a hook.

12.21 OXO GOOD GRIPS TURKEY LIFTER

The OXO Good Grips turkey lifter is a beautifully engineered piece of equipment. Using just one hand you can lift a 4-pound chicken or a 20-pound turkey with the same ease, and tilt it so that interior juices (if the bird is unstuffed) pour into the roasting pan. The bulbous, Santoprene handle offers a secure and comfortable grip, which does not slip even when wet. The curved steel prong ends in two sharp tines, to get a fast hold on the interior. You'll never have to worry again about dropping the bird between pan and carving board. Even if you roast only one turkey a year, you'll still be glad you invested in the OXO lifter.

12.22 NORPRO TURKEY-ROASTER LIFTER CHAIN

This stainless steel lifter is 20½" long, so be sure to use a roasting pan that is not too wide, unless you want to fish the handles out of hot juices. In order to use the lifter, you position the chains across the narrower part of the pan and place your turkey or roast on top. Drape the handles over the sides. When the roast is done and ready to be lifted out, it will balance perfectly as you transfer it to a carving board. Be sure to use oven mitts. The lifter is very easy to clean: just pop it in the dishwasher.

ELECTRIC ROTISSERIES

AS ROTISSERIE CHICKENS have proliferated in take-out stores and restaurants, so have electric devices for making them at home. These large countertop appliances cook chickens and other foods either in a horizontal or vertical position as they turn on spits. We find them perfectly adequate for roasting but unnecessary. They don't turn out foods that are any crisper or any moister than if you prepared them in an appliance you probably already own—a gas or electric oven. Nor, in most instances, do they cook any more quickly. The task of cleaning them varies from easy to almost impossible.

12.23 RONCO SHOWTIME ROTISSERIE & BBQ

If you want to rotisserie your own chickens *often,* you may want to consider this versatile model from Ron Popeil, the man who invented the Veg-O-Matic and the Pocket Fisherman. He claims this may be the best product he's ever invented, and he may be right. It does a good job of roasting food on a horizontal spit. We single it out not only for performance but because of all the rotisseries we tested it was the easiest to clean—all the parts that get dirty go in the dishwasher. Therefore, if you don't have a self-cleaning oven and hate the way roasting chickens spatter, you may find this a useful appliance. The Showtime comes with a basket, similar to the ones used for cooking hamburgers on an outdoor grill, that also turns on the spit, making it possible to spit-roast smaller items—from vegetables to hamburgers. The machine is 12¼" deep and 13¼" high, measuring 17" at its widest point.

During the fifteenth century, France divided the food-vending business into a series of guilds, each responsible for a specific type of preparation. If you wanted to buy something that was roasted on a spit you went to a *rôtisseur;* chicken came from the *poulailler.* If it involved bread, the vendor was a *boulanger.*

"I bit someone once. It tasted like chicken."

ELECTRIC ROASTERS

ALTHOUGH THESE APPLIANCES are never one's first choice as a cooking method, we wouldn't discount them altogether; they make acceptable pinch hitters when there's no oven available. They range in capacity from 4 quarts, or Cornish hen–size, up to 18 quarts, big enough to hold a 22-pound turkey. The temperature in these deep "pots" can be varied, so you can use them for keeping foods warm, slow-cooking, and braising, as well as for roasting a whole bird or a large cut of meat. However, the term *roasting* should be taken loosely; because the cover must stay on during cooking, large cuts of meat or whole birds emerge with spotty browning and a moist, steamed character. Expect a roaster to preheat and cook in roughly the same amount of time as your oven. The best ones have coils in their sidewall, not just on the bottom, for better heat distribution. On roasters, as with other heat-producing appliances, we prize "feet" that raise the appliance from the countertop and removable cooking chambers with nonstick interiors to simplify cleaning.

12.24 NESCO COOL SIDE 5 ROASTER OVEN

Because this 5-quart electric roaster is modestly sized—16" long, 11½" wide, and 9½" high—it won't require a big area on the countertop and can be stashed in a cabinet or closet rather than up in the attic. This makes it ideal for apartment dwellers with limited space or anyone who wants a small model to use often rather than a giant one to pull out for church suppers or family reunions. It can accommodate a chicken or roast up to about 4½ pounds. What makes this Nesco unique is that its exterior is made of heat-resistant plastic, so that while it won't quite stay "cool" to the touch, its external temperature is reduced. As well as all the features we recommend in any electric roaster, this model has a light that signals when it's properly preheated, an adjustable steam vent in the plastic lid, a nonstick roasting rack, supports on the rear to rest the cover when you're checking on food, and hooks on the underside to wrap the cord.

"Wanna do lunch?"

13

BAKING DISHES & MOLDS

BAKING DISHES

BAKING DISHES MAY HAVE EVOLVED from the days when cooks roasted meats on a spit over an open fire. Shallow pans were placed beneath the turning roasts to catch the rendering fat as it melted away from the meat. One day, we assume, some clever cook put a handful of onions or parsnips into the pan and savored the delicious result: caramelized vegetables enriched by the drippings. Yorkshire pudding, a simple combination of eggs, milk, and flour, was originally baked this way under a roasting mutton, the batter gaining its flavor from the melting fat.

In colonial New England, where the family fireplace was needed as much for heat as it was for cooking, fireproof earthenware baking dishes were used as containers for dinner. They were placed into small hollows built into the wall—forerunners of today's ovens—where they could take in heat slowly throughout the day. Today's baking dishes, whether contemporary styled or old-fashioned looking, are descendants of these original pans and still function perfectly for foods that need lengthy, gentle cooking.

Baking dishes are exceptionally serviceable, all-purpose vessels. Use them to make noodle casseroles, lasagna, moussaka, family-sized custards, corn breads, and other foods that do well cooked slowly in an oven and that gain appeal from a crusty, browned top. They are also good surrogates for a great many other kinds of cooking paraphernalia. Once they join your *batterie de cuisine*, they may become your most-used dishes. They may even be the most important containers for cooked food in a noncook's kitchen.

For the best results, baking dishes should be shallow and open to allow the oven heat to circulate around the ingredients. There are so many choices in materials, shapes, and sizes that you may decide to purchase several types for your kitchen. Whatever your personal style and taste, whether you prefer stark white cookware or something colorful, old-fashioned items or pieces that are sleekly modern, be sure to choose dishes designed specifically for baking. Bakeware is usually made of porcelain, enameled cast iron, or glass, but porous materials, like glazed or unglazed earthenware, are also effective. The dishes must diffuse heat evenly and be safe for oven use. Some are suitable for microwave cooking. Practical handles are helpful, since filled dishes can be heavy and awkward to lift. Because baking dishes vary in shape and size, knowing the capacity will help when adapting a recipe.

13.1 LE CREUSET OVAL BAKING DISH

This straight-sided 11½"-long, 1½-quart oval baking dish looks like Le Creuset's hallmark enameled cast iron, but it isn't. It's part of the company's Poterie line, which consists of several shapes and varieties of enamel-coated stoneware. The items in the Poterie line are easy to clean and have all the benefits of clay cookware, holding heat and distributing it evenly. This bakeware is also safe for freezer storage. The oval dish is 2" deep, a fine choice for a small pork tenderloin as well as for roasted vegetables or Indian pudding. The outside is lightly ridged for a decorative effect, and the top flares out gently to aid in evaporation or to leave room for bubbly overflow. The ridged handles provide a comfortable thumb grip. Like all Le Creuset cookware, this dish comes in a variety of bright colors to coordinate with kitchen decor: flame, green, citrus, red, blue, jade, and white. It also comes in 9½" (1⅛ quarts) and 14" lengths (3¼ quarts).

13.2 MATFER BAKING DISH

The simple beauty of this oval porcelain baking dish belies its versatility: it is a workhorse, fit for fish fillets garnished with bread crumbs, scalloped potatoes, or fruit cobbler. Use it for baked noodles or for chicken breasts cloaked with mushrooms and cheese. The one we show you here is blue on the outside with an off-white interior; it is also available in yellow. A lip finishes off the top interior edge. A rim on the outside tapers at the long ends to form a groove for fingertip gripping. The dish is 10¼" by 7" by 1⅝" but comes in larger 12⅞" and 15" lengths, and is handy for a main dish casserole for two or a side dish for more.

13.3 CERAMIKA ARTYSTYCZNA BOLESLAWIEC BAKING DISH

This stoneware dish is hand painted in Poland by artists who follow the traditional forms of Polish and German folk art that have prevailed for the last two hundred years. Both inside and outside are covered with a pattern reminiscent of peacock feathers in tones of rich cobalt blue, egg-yolk yellow, and terra-cotta rust. It is 2" deep, making it useful for layered casseroles, a small roast, fruit crisps, and bread pudding. It may look too fragile and too pretty to be functional, but the dish is sturdy, fired for microwave or regular oven use, and dishwasher safe. It is 13¾" long and 9½" wide and can hold between 2 and 2½ quarts depending on what you are baking.

13.4 EMILE HENRY RECTANGULAR BAKING DISH

Another striking dish, for those with less than minimalist tastes, this one is a simple rectangle with rounded edges, with a lush cobalt blue exterior and vivid white interior. Like so many of the other baking dishes, it is utilitarian. It holds 2⁹⁄₁₀ quarts and measures 12¾" long, 10" wide, and 2¼" deep, making it spacious enough to accommodate a dozen stuffed tomatoes or a quartet of Cornish game hens, and it conducts, diffuses, and retains heat extremely well—you can take it from refrigerator or freezer to microwave or standard oven without risking cracks or breaks. The pan's heavy glaze resists scratches from metal cutlery and utensils. The sides of the pan are sloped, so cooking liquids such as sauce or natural juices fall to the bottom instead of bubbling out all over your oven; it also makes slipping a spatula in and under the food easier. When you remove the dish from the oven, the heavily ridged outer edge serves as a grip. This rectangular dish comes in three other sizes: 14" by 11½" (3½ quarts), 10¼" by 7¾" (1³⁄₁₀ quarts), and 7½" by 5½" (⅗ quarts). Other shapes include ovals and a square. All are offered in an array of colors: red, white, green, blue, saffron, and sable.

13.5 PILLIVUYT DISH

This plain, pristine white, no-nonsense, deep (almost 3") rectangular baker is a classic for layered dishes like lasagna. Its functionality suggests dozens of uses. A rim around the perimeter extends to form useful handles that make it easy to carry the dish, even when hot and filled with bubbling lasagna. You can take it from the freezer (cover with aluminum foil) straight to a microwave or conventional oven. It is available in two sizes, 13¼" by 9¾" (6 quarts) and 11½" by 9½" (5 quarts).

13.6 SPANISH TABLE *CAZUELA*

The Spanish Table sells a number of gorgeous, rustic-looking terra-cotta casserole dishes used in Spanish, Mexican, and Latin American cooking. Beauty aside, like all good earthenware, this *cazuela* is superb for long, slow cooking, holding its temperature and cooking ingredients evenly. It has been left unglazed on the outside, so it can absorb both moisture and heat better, but it has a smooth, glazed interior that is semiporous. You must soak the dish for 6 hours before the first use (and then occasionally) to rehydrate the clay. After that, you can use it for cooking directly on the stovetop or in the oven or microwave, and it is dishwasher safe. The smaller *cazuelas* come in handy for serving tapas, like tiny shrimp sizzling in olive oil and garlic, or as little containers for guacamole, salsa, or nacho condiments, or to bake *crema Catalana,* the Spanish crème brûlée. Sizes range from a tiny 3" (¼ cup) to a supersized 18" (8 quarts). Those up to 6" in diameter have straight sides and flat bottoms; the larger ones have slightly rounded sides and rounded bottoms (and come with two loop handles). The company also offers a variety of lidded *cazuelas.*

13.7 LE CREUSET QUICHE/PIZZA DISH

This Le Creuset quiche and pizza dish is part of the company's Poterie line of enameled stoneware. It is a superb choice for both baking and serving. The dish, like all earthenware, offers steady heat for even baking. Don't expect crispy crusts—it produces tender, bready, deep-dish pies. You can make good use of this versatile dish in many ways: for vegetable tarts, shallow flans, gratins, or any other thin or flat food that needs reheating or crisping in the oven or broiler. The quiche/pizza dish is 9½" in diameter, holds ⅞ quart, and comes in white, green, flame, red, citrus, jade, and blue.

SCALLOP SHELLS

A SCALLOP SHELL WIDENS OUT, fanlike, with grooves radiating from the center of one hinged edge. The great painter Botticelli was inspired to set his *Venus* inside one, and pilgrims would carry scallop shells to pay homage to Saint James, their patron saint, giving rise to the French name for sea scallops: *coquilles St-Jacques.* Today cooks use the shells as baking and serving dishes for *coquilles St-Jacques* and other seafood specialties. The shells also come in handy as molds for pastry or chocolate. Some cooks like to use natural scallop shells, because the color and the thin, brittle texture lend authenticity to the recipe. Porcelain shells may not be the real thing, but they are more stable and easier to clean.

13.8 NATURAL SCALLOP SHELL

French cooks use natural shells to make the classic *coquilles St-Jacques,* a Breton recipe featuring chopped sea scallops bathed in cream sauce. The mixture is placed inside individual scallop shells, then dotted with butter and topped with bread crumbs before being baked. Of course, you could serve this seafood gratin in any baking container, but the shells add a touch of grace and elegance. To keep the shells from tipping over, recipes often recommend setting them in a bed of rock salt or crumpled foil on a jelly-roll pan before baking. Natural scallop shells are inexpensive and fragile but will last if you're careful. Although no two shells are alike, they all are roughly 4½" long and 5" wide and come in sets of four.

Medieval pilgrims to the Spanish city Santiago de Compostela (one of Catholicism's three holy cities) pinned scallop shells, the symbol of St. James, patron saint of Santiago, to their cloaks to show they had been there.

13.9 BROWNE & COMPANY PORCELAIN SCALLOP SHELL

This white porcelain scallop shell from Browne & Company does an honest job of imitating nature. Although it is nearly ½" longer than the real thing, it is fanned and grooved like a natural scallop, and it offers a bonus—a circular projection on the bottom to keep it firmly in place. The shells are perfect not only for scallops but for gratinéed seafood dishes of all sorts, seafood risotto, seafood salads, and cold, poached crab, mussels, or lobster. Think of using them the next time you serve ceviche, a marinated seafood dish that's delicious when made with scallops. These shells also work for desserts like mousse, and you can use them to hold nuts, mints, or other small nibbles. Three sizes are available: 5⅜", 6", and 7".

BAY SCALLOP AND TOMATO GRATIN

6 servings

¾ cup fresh bread crumbs
6 sprigs Italian parsley, leaves only, finely chopped
3 sprigs thyme, leaves only, finely chopped
3 sprigs basil, leaves only, finely chopped
6 cloves garlic, peeled, split, germ removed, and finely chopped
salt
freshly ground white pepper
9 tablespoons extra-virgin olive oil
2¼ pounds bay scallops
3 large ripe tomatoes, peeled, seeded, and cut into ½" dice

1 Toss together the bread crumbs, half the parsley, the thyme, basil, and three-quarters of the garlic; season with salt and pepper; and set aside.

2 Preheat the broiler. Butter six shallow gratin dishes. (The dishes should be only 1" deep and about 6" in diameter.)

3 Heat 3 tablespoons of the olive oil in a large sauté pan or skillet over high heat until it is very hot. Pat the scallops dry, then season them with salt and pepper and slip them into the pan. (Do this in batches if necessary.) Cook, turning the scallops as needed, until they're golden brown on both sides, 2 minutes. Toss in the diced tomatoes along with the remaining parsley and garlic and cook, stirring, for 1 minute more, to cook off some of the tomato juice.

4 Divide the scallop mixture evenly among the gratin dishes and sprinkle an equal amount of the seasoned bread crumbs over each dish. Drizzle 1 tablespoon of olive oil over each gratin and slide the dishes under the broiler for 2 minutes—watch them closely—or until the tops are golden brown. Immediately pull the dishes from under the broiler.

TO SERVE
The herb-crusted scallops should be served in their gratin dishes, so place the hot dishes on heatproof dinner plates and rush the gratins to the table. (If you've prepared this in a single dish, divide the scallops among heated dinner plates and serve immediately.)

Daniel Boulud's Cafe Boulud Cookbook, by Daniel Boulud

SNAIL-SERVING EQUIPMENT

THE ANCIENT ROMANS WERE the first to fatten snails and savor them at the table, and the tradition has been maintained by both the French and Italians, who consider these gastropods to be exquisite delicacies. Americans were always more reluctant to dine on an animal considered little more than a garden pest, although these days, many Francophiles enjoy snails in garlic butter.

The variety of snails raised for restaurant dining, and for canning and sale in food shops, are traditionally a specialty of Burgundy—harvested from the moist vineyards, damp orchards, and stone walls, though Taiwan is often the source of less delicious ones (read the label on the can). There are now snails being raised in America for sale to restaurants and shops; they're good, but don't quite compare to the French imports. Classic *escargots à la bourguignonne* are dressed with garlic butter and parsley and baked in their shells. It's even possible to buy the snails at fancy food shops already stuffed with garlic butter and ready for the oven. However, anyone who has seen Julia Roberts in the movie *Pretty Woman* trying to lift out a snail without the proper equipment can tell you how difficult that can be. Fortunately, some smart people invented special tools that make baking and eating escargots effortless.

13.10 BROWNE & COMPANY ESCARGOT DISH

This heavy, toast-brown, ceramic escargot dish is the perfect vessel for baked snails and butter. You don't need to use the shells. The center of the glazed 5" dish is indented with six generously deep bowls to fit both snail and plenty of garlic butter to soak up with your baguette. To catch and keep the inevitable bubbly butter overflow, there is a ¼" lip around the edge. Unlike many escargot dishes, this one has a gently curved handle that protrudes from one side, making it easier to remove from the oven. The outside has a few decorative ridges, and the bottom is slightly hollowed. The Browne & Company dish is also available in white.

13.11 HAROLD'S KITCHEN ESCARGOT FORK & TONGS

"When you're on their flowers, you're a snail. When they want to eat you, suddenly you're an escargot."

If you've ever tried to muscle a snail out of its shell, you know it requires some skill and dexterity, but there are a couple of tools that work in tandem to help you extract the creature. The first are 6¼" stainless steel tongs that hold the shell in place while you pick out the juicy meat. The tongs, which resemble 1950s eyelash curlers, are made from a single piece of stainless steel and bent to provide tension. The ends are molded into the spoonlike shapes to grasp the shell securely. The second item is a 6" cocktail-size, two-pronged stainless steel fork that you can use to pick the snail either out of its shell or from an escargot dish.

GRATIN PANS

GRATIN IS A FRENCH WORD FOR food that is browned in a hot oven or under the broiler to form a crispy, bronze-colored crust, classically with a topping of crumbs, or *grattons*. The traditional steps to prepare one involve cooking the food first, then placing it into a shallow pan, topping the dish with sauce, and then sprinkling it with buttered bread crumbs and perhaps grated cheese. For these classic gratins, the pan used during this final step of browning is mainly for presentation. As a result, old-fashioned gratin pans tend to be attractive. Today's home cooks may not want the fuss and bother of using two pieces of cookware, so many gratin pans are made for cooking as well as browning and serving.

In either case, gratin pans must be shallow and wide, to ensure that the largest area possible will become brown and crispy. The crust makes a satisfying counterpoint to the creamy, tender, or moist ingredients beneath it. Gratin pans require fireproof materials that attract heat, like earthenware, cast iron, porcelain, stainless steel, and copper. When little actual cooking will take place, the metal ones need not be the heaviest gauge. Good handles to move the dish in and out of the oven or broiler quickly are a plus.

13.12 OLD DUTCH COPPER GRATIN PAN

This 8" round pan is made of bright, heavy-gauge copper, fine enough for cooking and handsome enough for serving. It is lined with nickel and lacquered to resist tarnishing. A pair of securely riveted cast brass handles stand straight out from the sides. With use, the copper takes on a lovely low-gloss glow, making this dish a good-looking addition to a dinner or buffet table. It holds up to 1 quart.

13.13 ALL-CLAD STAINLESS STEEL GRATIN PAN

This 12" by 9" by 2" oval gratin pan is one of the items in All-Clad's aluminum core, stainless steel Tri-Ply cookware line. Purists may balk at using modern, commercial-looking stainless steel for so homey and old-fashioned a dish as a gratin, but this pan has several advantages: it is deeper than most classic gratin dishes, so it can be put to service not merely for a creamy potato gratin but also for casseroles, and, because the underlying materials are sturdy and heat conductive, you can use this pan for stovetop cooking as well as for baking and presentation. Fine, riveted handles are roomy and easy to grasp with oven mitts.

13.14 LE CREUSET OVAL AU GRATIN

Made of heavy enameled cast iron, this cozy-looking oval pan is 11" by 8", giving it sufficient room for vegetable or potato gratins, and deep enough (1¾" or 1½ quarts) to layer thick slices of eggplant or portobello mushrooms for a casserole. It can also be used to bake fish in a wine sauce or with tomatoes—these acidic ingredients will not react with the porcelain interior. The sides slope gently to help you ease out the cooked food, and ridged handles provide a good grip to take the pan securely and safely from the oven. You can do stovetop cooking in this pan too; because the bottom is uncoated, it takes heat as well as any cast-iron pan and it won't chip. The heat-retaining properties of cast iron will keep the gratin piping hot even after it is removed from the oven. The pan comes in five colors: white, flame, green, red, and blue, and in one other size, 14" (2⅞ quarts), which is only available in white, green, and blue.

13.15 MATFER SALAMANDER

In mythological tradition the salamander was a lizard-like creature believed to inhabit fire as that element's guardian, and philosophers as far back as Aristotle and Pliny touted its power to vanquish flame. It is not surprising, then, that some French epicure thought to name this metal tool after the salamander. If you want to gratinate a dish with a delicate sauce or other ingredients that might suffer from overheating, a salamander will quickly brown the top without damaging the food. It will also save you from having to use the broiler, which is very handy if you need the oven for something else. Just put the metal end of the salamander on your stovetop burner for a few minutes until it becomes red-hot, then pass it over a custard or gratin and you will see the surface of the food turn golden brown before your eyes. Our 17"-long salamander has a comfortable wooden handle that is held by a brass collar to a heavy steel rod. The other end of the rod curves to hold a 2"-diameter steel disc.

13.16 APILCO PORCELAIN GRATIN DISH

Apilco produces round and oval gratin pans in several sizes, all of fine, elegant, pure-white porcelain, with sides that flare out to form two delicate embossed handles. Surfaces are smooth, glossy, and nonporous; the bottoms have been left unglazed. The porcelain holds heat well, keeping cooked foods hot at the table. The 8" dish we show you here is superb for foods as diverse as macaroni and cheese, ratatouille, and apple crisp. Consider buying several sizes, as these dishes will come in handy for a variety of uses. You can take the plates from the freezer to oven to table. Other sizes include round: 2¾", 5¼", 5½", 6¼", 7", and 14"; and oval: 6¾", 8", 8¾", 10", 11", 13¾", 15¾", 17", and 18".

13.17 MAUVIEL *POMMES ANNA* PAN

Among the more inventive French potato dishes is *pommes Anna,* a glorified potato cake made in a special pan that conducts heat effectively, like this one. Potatoes are trimmed into cylinders and then cut into fine round slices that are sautéed lightly in clarified butter. Next, the slices are placed in overlapping concentric rings around the bottom and sides of a buttered *pommes Anna* pan. The pan is filled, until slightly heaping, with layers of potatoes added more casually, sprinkled with lots of clarified butter. The potatoes may be cooked on top of the stove, covered; in the oven, uncovered; or started on top of the stove, covered, and finished in the oven, uncovered. Take your choice, but if you use the oven it should be hot (about 425°F), so the potatoes will turn golden brown. (If you use the oven alone to cook the potatoes, either the top or the bottom of the pan can be filled.) Always let the *pommes Anna* sit for about 5 minutes after they are taken from the heat to let them shrink a bit in the pan to prevent sticking. Then turn the decorative potato cake onto a platter or onto the top portion of the pan and serve. Although the bottom of the tin-lined, copper pan we show here has a diameter of only 6½", the top is 7" in diameter with a depth of 1¼" and will make enough *pommes Anna* to feed four people; the 2¾"-deep bottom should hold enough for six to eight people. The matching pair of handles on top and bottom are made of solid bronze. And just who was Anna? Anna Deslions was a Second Empire fashion plate. Adolphe Dugléré, the chef of Café Anglais, the illustrious nineteenth-century Parisian restaurant, created the dish in her honor. With potatoes cut in julienne strips, the dish becomes *pommes annette.*

OVEN DISHES FOR EGGS

Eggs CONTRIBUTE nutrients, flavor, chemistry, and physical properties to innumerable dishes, but they also can stand gloriously on their own. One of the simplest egg classics is shirred eggs (known in France as *oeufs sur le plat*), a sorely neglected meal from the good old days, comprised of eggs that are broiled in low, round dishes closely related to gratin pans. To make *oeufs sur le plat,* add some melted butter to the dish, then crack in an egg or two and broil the ingredients until the whites have set but the yolks are still runny. They make a lovely breakfast alternative to the expected scrambled eggs or eggs over easy. You might want to fancy them up a bit for brunch, lunch, or dinner by bedding the eggs onto some creamed spinach, sautéed mushrooms, slices of ham, or steamed asparagus. Baked eggs, another option, require a deep dish such as a ramekin (or cocotte), which looks like a tiny soufflé dish and accommodates a single egg, though some have room for two, plus garnishes.

There are also soufflé dishes and custard cups to be included in the home cook's kitchen. Porcelain, stoneware, and glassware are ideal because of their smooth, nonporous surfaces and ability to diffuse heat and maintain even temperatures. All are dishwasher safe and can go from freezer to oven to table, but some cannot go directly on a stovetop.

Probably one of the most private things in the world is an egg until it is broken.
—M. F. K. FISHER

13.18 PILLIVUYT ROUND-EARED EGG DISH

This simple white fireproof porcelain plate is the classic shape for *oeufs en cocotte,* a round, shallow, gratin-type dish big enough for one or two eggs. Its sloped sides extend to two daintily fluted handles that angle up, making it easy to hold from underneath. The bottom is left unglazed for better heat distribution. Several of these will come in handy not only for egg cookery but also for individual servings of side dishes including quick vegetable gratins and baked tomatoes, or for desserts like crumbles and crisps. The 5″ dish can be used for cooking on top of a gas flame if a diffuser is used and on an electric range if there is liquid in the dish.

13.19 PILLIVUYT EGG COCOTTE WITH EARS

This small white porcelain cocotte has elegant lines; unlike many such dishes, the sides are vaguely curved and the top flares out gently. Two tiny ears on either side serve as small handles. This simple dish is perfect when you want to serve plain baked eggs, and roomy enough for additional ingredients, even a sprinkling of black truffle. Try filling the bottom with buttered toast before plopping in the egg, and cover the egg with cream and grated cheese. Take this dish from oven to table. We show you the 4″ size, which holds 5 ounces, but Pillivuyt also sells a smaller 3¼″ (3-ounce) size. You'll probably want to own four or six.

13.20 EGG CODDLERS

To coddle an egg you break it into one of these charming little cups with some cream, seasonings, and fresh herbs, then screw the lid on tightly and simmer the cup in boiling water until the contents are done to your taste. The old name for a coddler is a pipkin. Our clear-glazed stoneware pipkins are the color of clotted cream. Though coddled eggs are almost always a breakfast item, an English devotee might have his or hers at high tea. Our coddlers stand 3¾″ high with flat lids that have small loop handles in the center. Though many English manufacturers of fine bone China make coddlers, we prefer these country coddlers for the simple breakfast meal.

RAMEKINS

Ramekins look like small soufflé dishes. The classic shape is a straight-sided vessel with tall sides, a smooth interior, and a ridged exterior. They are usually made of porcelain, earthenware, or stoneware and typically are plain, though some may be adorned with flowers, birds, and other decorative additions. Most ramekins hold from 2 to 5 liquid ounces.

Though they do have a specific culinary purpose, these little containers are so versatile that you will call upon them for a variety of tasks—individual servings of mousse or soufflé, baked custard, or even for meal preparation; use them to hold the chopped parsley, shredded cheese, and grated lemon zest you will be adding to a recipe.

13.21 PILLIVUYT RAMEKIN

Pillivuyt, a French company that has produced outstanding porcelain since 1818, sells several different-sized ramekins, both standard height and extra deep; the former can be bought individually or in packages of six. They come only in white in 2-, 3-, and 5-ounce capacities (standard) and 4-, 5-, and 7-ounce capacities (deep). The smooth surfaces are glazed except for the topmost part of the rim; the exterior is decorated with the traditional fluting. These containers are perfect as mini soufflé dishes or for individual servings of potpie or custard. We like to keep one filled with kosher salt by our stove, making it easy to grab a pinch or two when seasoning a dish. We recommend the 5-ounce ramekin (3½″ in diameter) for the most versatility, but you may want to equip your kitchen with several sizes in multiple quantities.

13.22 EMILE HENRY RAMEKINS

These ramekins, with their rich, rough-looking, cherry-red glaze, look luscious in an all-American way that belies their French origin. The interiors have a smooth white glaze, the sides of the dishes are thick, and the top rims are scalloped to resemble a pie crust. Their 4″ width and 2″ depth make them adequate for two large baked eggs. In addition to red, the ramekins, part of the company's Patisserie line, are available in other primary colors: cobalt blue and saffron yellow. They have a capacity of 1 cup.

CUSTARD CUPS

Soft, caramel-cloaked flan; creamy, brittle-topped crème brûlée; densely rich *pot de crème:* All are variations on the simple custard. All of these desserts are a harmony of eggs, milk, and sugar, plus any number of flavorings, including chocolate, vanilla, orange, mint, almond, and even some new-wave variations like ginger, saffron, and chai, a spiced milk tea from India.

Some custards are cooked completely on top of the stove, like crème anglaise, the opulent sauce used for innumerable desserts; some are baked, like crème caramel, the French variation of the Spanish flan; and some, like crème brûlée, are finished by broiling briefly or firing with a handheld torch, to glaze with a sugar crust.

There are special dishes designed to cook and serve custard. For crème brûlée you must use either a shallow ramekin or, preferably, a shallow gratin or other dish that has a wide surface area, for a better sugar crust. Custards to which gelatin has been added, like Bavarian creams, are meant to be chilled in fancy molds, then freed from the container for serving on a platter. The traditional custard cup may evoke Proustian memories of childhood or less romantic images of old-fashioned cafeteria or diner meals. It is similar to a ramekin but deeper, narrower, and with rounded sides. The shape helps prevent "skin" from developing on top of the custard while producing a creamy interior.

13.23 MESSERMEISTER CHEFLAMME BUTANE CULINARY TORCH

It is difficult enough to make a lush, creamy crème brûlée custard; but it is the fragile, brittle sugary top that most home cooks consider the more daunting task. Here's help. This culinary torch, which operates with butane fuel, has an adjustable flame that makes it easy to melt the sugar within the confines of the custard dish. The flame heats to 2,700°F—far hotter and more efficient than a home broiler or salamander. In just seconds you'll achieve the hallmark thin-ice crust of first-rate crème brûlée while the custard and the serving dish stay properly cool. The torch is lightweight and easy to store. It will come in handy for a multitude of other tasks, too, from browning meringues for baked Alaska to roasting bell peppers to thawing frozen pipes during the winter.

THE MINITORCH
❦ JACQUES TORRES ❦

When I buy a minitorch, I make sure it has a porcelain top. That makes it stronger. I also prefer stainless steel to plastic in the body. If it is cheaply constructed, it won't hold up to the wear and tear. I like a body that holds a fair amount of fuel so I don't have to stop and refill it. A flame regulator and stand are also very important. Here are some of the uses I've found for the minitorch: Flambé a dessert or a cocktail easily and elegantly. Remove fingerprints and give a nice shine to a cake with a chocolate glaze. Light a lot of birthday candles all at once. Use it to light a gas burner or the pilot light of the stove. This tool is essential when working with sugar and making sugar presentations. I especially appreciate that it has a stand so I can set it on the counter while I am working. If I'm really in a pinch, I can use it to finish a crème brûlée or two. It is a handy gadget and I'm glad to have one.

13.24 B.I.A. CORDON BLEU CUSTARD CUP

This is the classic custard cup of babyhoods gone by: heavy, glazed white porcelain with a faintly ribbed exterior. It holds a generous 7 ounces, and its rounded body flares outward toward the top. The rim has a lip, which is helpful when you want to remove the dish from its hot *bain-marie*. Use these for all sorts of custards, from savories seasoned with garlic and herbs (to accompany roasts) to the more traditional dessert treats, like the classic crème caramel.

13.25 PYREX CUSTARD CUPS

How many people remember their moms serving them Jell-O or junket in these Pyrex dishes? Or perhaps these remind you of dinners at dormitory dining halls? In any case, these homey glass cups are certainly familiar, and they are also versatile enough to hold a variety of foods, including custard. The cups are 3¾" wide at the top (the dish narrows toward the bottom) and 2" deep. There is a three-dimensional petal design inside the rim that will imprint Bavarian creams and other unmolded custards. Three ridged lines encircle the outside of the dishes. You might find them at yard sales, but they are also sold brand-new, in four-packs, in 6- or 10-ounce sizes.

HOW TO CRACK AN EGG
❧ SHIRLEY CORRIHER ❧

I sometimes feel I've spent a good part of my life looking for an edge to crack eggs on. Now, alas, I find I was wrong all along. Experts tell us that the best way to crack an egg is on a hard flat surface. There is less shell shatter if you do not crack an egg on an edge, so you will be less likely to have bits of shell in your eggs.

Crack an egg onto a plate. Hit the egg firmly but not forcefully on the side and pull the shell apart with your thumbs. If the white is thick and does not spread widely, the egg is fresh. A fresh egg's white is nearly all thick. As the egg ages, this part of the white deteriorates into runny white. Notice the two chalazae (the cords at each end of the yolk); prominent chalazae are another sign of a fresh egg. Membranes in the egg also change with age. The yolk membrane becomes weaker and eventually breaks. Look at the yolk. If it stands up, the yolk membrane is strong and the egg is very fresh. If the yolk is flat and spread out, you have an older egg. If you've cracked an egg carefully but the yolk broke anyway, the egg could have been so old that the yolk sac was broken even before you cracked the shell.

13.26 JAPANESE CUSTARD CUP

And now for *chawan-mushi*, a marvelous Japanese custard made of eggs, broth, and tiny pieces of chicken, fish, shrimp, or mushrooms. Unlike Western custard—the Spanish flan or the French crème caramel—it is not a dessert dish but a main course, one of the *mushimono*, or steamed dishes. To make *chawan-mushi*, combine beaten eggs with *dashi*—a soup stock made from kelp (*kombu*) and flaked dried bonito (*katsuobushi*)—a dash of soy sauce, sweet rice wine (*mirin*), and selected diced ingredients. Our richly glazed earthenware cup is really just a teacup, called a *chawan*, with a lid to keep the surface of the custard smooth. It sits on a 4"-square wooden base, indented to hold the cup securely. The cup is 3" deep, 3" in diameter, and holds 1 cup. It is ovenproof, so instead of steaming the custard, the cup could be placed in a water bath in the oven.

13.27 APILCO *POTS DE CRÈME* SET

Graceful little porcelain pots like these, although sometimes used to serve chocolate mousse, are ovenproof and really meant for cooking rich custards in a water bath (*bain-marie*). The custards are then served either at room temperature or chilled. Each pot holds 2 ounces, has a curved handle for easy maneuvering, and has a lid to prevent a thick skin from forming on the custard. The cups are 2½" in diameter and stand 3" high with lid.

CRÈME BRÛLÉE

8 servings

FOR THE TOPPING

1 cup (135 grams) firmly packed light brown sugar

FOR THE CUSTARD

4 cups heavy cream
1 vanilla bean
1 large egg
6 large egg yolks
¾ cup plus 2 tablespoons (175 grams) granulated sugar

PREPARE THE TOPPING

The brown sugar will be used to finish the dessert, and it needs time to air-dry to remove the moisture it contains. To do this, spread the sugar on a large plate or baking sheet and let dry, uncovered, for about 3 hours. When it is properly dried, it will feel dry and sandy. Set aside.

PREPARE THE CUSTARD

Pour the heavy cream into a nonreactive 1½-quart heavy-bottomed saucepan and place over medium heat. While the cream is heating, slice the vanilla bean in half lengthwise, using a sharp paring knife. Separate the seeds from the skin by scraping the bean with the knife. Place the skin and seeds in the heating cream. Scald the cream by heating it until bubbles start to form around the edge of the pan. Remove from the heat.

In a large mixing bowl, whisk together the whole egg, egg yolks, and sugar until well blended. Continue to whisk while slowly pouring the hot cream into the egg mixture and whisk until the mixture is smooth and homogenous in color. Pour the mixture through a fine-mesh sieve to remove the vanilla bean pieces and any overcooked eggs. Your next step will be made easier if you strain the mixture into a large measuring cup with a spout.

Preheat the oven to 320°F (160°C). Place the molds on a baking sheet with 1"-high sides. Fill the molds half full with the custard and set the sheet in the oven (it's much easier to transfer the sheet with the molds only half full). Now, finish filling the molds to the top. It is important to fill the molds to the top, as the custard will lose volume as it bakes. Traditionally, crème brûlée is baked in a hot water bath to insulate the custard from the direct heat of the oven and to keep the eggs from cooking too fast, which would cause them to separate. Using hot water from the tap, pour enough water into the baking sheet to reach halfway up the sides of the molds. If you are using a convection oven, however, a water bath is not needed because the even circulation of the air insulates the custard from the direct heat.

In either case, baking time is approximately the same, about 30 minutes. When baked correctly, the custard should tremble slightly when gently shaken. If you detect any liquid under the skin, the custard is underbaked. Put the molds back in the oven and shake them every 5 minutes or so until they are ready.

Remove the molds from the water bath and place on a cooling rack for 30 minutes, then refrigerate for 2 hours (or for up to 3 days) before serving; the custards will finish setting in the refrigerator. Let the water bath cool before removing it from the oven.

To finish the crème brûlée, preheat the broiler. Pass the dried brown sugar through a sieve to remove any lumps. Immediately before serving, spread a thin layer of the brown sugar over the tops of the custards. You have spread enough sugar when the custard is no longer visible, about 2 tablespoons. It is important to spread the sugar evenly; if it is too thick or too thin in places, the caramelization will not be even across the top. Place the molds on a clean baking sheet. When the broiler is hot, place the sheet about 4" under the broiler and broil until the sugar is caramelized. Keep a close eye on the crème brûlée during broiling. It is finished when it is light brown. Place each mold on a small dessert plate and serve immediately.

NOTE

When working with sugar and egg yolks, it is important to mix them together quickly and evenly. When sugar comes in contact with egg yolks, a chemical reaction occurs, heat is produced, and the eggs begin to scramble. The scrambled egg will cause lumps in the final product.

Dessert Circus: Extraordinary Desserts You Can Make at Home, by Jacques Torres

13.28 APILCO CRÈME BRÛLÉE DISH

Crème brûlée has replaced chocolate mousse on the popularity charts. Basically, it is a chilled custard that is given a sprinkling of sugar and broiled or otherwise "burnt" to form a crackling, glasslike, amber surface. These baking dishes are perfect for crème brûlée: shallow and 4½" wide to balance the tender and brittle textures of custard and crust. Scalloped sides add some gracefulness to the pure white, exceedingly plain porcelain. Each dish holds 4 ounces and can be useful for many other culinary preparations, including gratins; they ensure well-crisped surfaces for side dishes like sliced tomatoes scattered with buttered bread crumbs or sautéed vegetables capped with grated cheese.

SOUFFLÉ DISHES

Many people think of the soufflé as a restaurant dish, too daunting a recipe to cook at home because of its reputation for deflating like a punctured balloon in minutes. Actually, a well-made soufflé, one for which the essential egg whites are not overbeaten, is more resilient than you might think.

Be sure to whip the egg whites until they hold peaks but are still glossy looking and smooth. If they are overbeaten, the egg bubbles will break and you won't be able to adequately fold them into the base ingredients of a white sauce, sweet or savory custard, or pastry cream. A soufflé can even be made just with egg whites and fruit. At Taillevant, among the most famous Michelin three-star restaurants in Paris, one traditional dessert is a pear soufflé made simply with Italian meringue (egg whites beaten with simple syrup) with fresh finely diced pears folded in. A copper bowl and balloon whisk come in handy for beating the whites, but if you have a good electric mixer that will be fine, too. Chefs today have many techniques to simplify soufflé-making, like preparing the base in advance.

The oven must be preheated so that the soufflé can immediately begin its ascent. Be sure the temperature is steady. The French cook their soufflés at high temperatures (about 425°F) for a short period of time to produce soufflés that are moist, rise high, and are more fragile than the drier and more substantial soufflés in American cookbooks. These are baked at lower temperatures (about 375°F) for a longer time.

For perfectly textured soufflés with the highest rise, you'll need a traditional soufflé dish; there can be no substitutes. Soufflé dishes have straight sides and flat bottoms. A dish whose sides or bottom are rounded in any way may inhibit rising. In general, a standard four- to five-egg recipe will need a 1½-quart dish, but your recipe will specify the required size. The most important thing is not to use a dish that's too big. For the most spectacular presentation, or if the dish you have is too small, tie a doubled strip of aluminum foil or parchment paper around its circumference to form a collar that increases the height. The collar should be at least 3" above the rim of the soufflé dish; cut the paper about 8" wide and several inches longer than the dish's circumference. Fold it in half lengthwise, butter it and sprinkle with sugar or bread crumbs, and tape it in place until you can tie it securely around the dish with twine. Remove the collar quickly after the soufflé is cooked. This technique is just as effective with frozen soufflés and mousses.

13.29 B.I.A. CORDON BLEU INDIVIDUAL & MULTIQUART SOUFFLÉ DISHES

These are basic, no-nonsense soufflé dishes suitable for everything from savory individual goat cheese soufflés to start a dinner to a dramatic raspberry beauty to end it. Made of milky white porcelain and bearing the standard vertical ridges, they are among the heaviest soufflé dishes available. They can stand up to freezer storage, regular or microwave oven use, and dishwasher cleaning. They have a wide base and low rise, allowing the eggs to spread out, grab the sides, and puff up over the lip on the inside. The outer bottoms have been left unglazed to provide better heat absorption. Several sizes are available, from the smaller individual soufflés (10 ounces), to medium sizes (1 quart and 1½ quarts) that serve four to six people, to the large, 2-quart model (shown here) that can feed a family. The individual dish pictured is 4" in diameter, 1¾" high, and holds 10 ounces. The 2-quart dish is 8½" in diameter and 3½" high.

13.30 APILCO EXTRA-HIGH INDIVIDUAL & MULTIQUART SOUFFLÉ DISHES

These exquisite porcelain dishes are taller than most soufflé containers, and they are slim, with sides that slope ever so slightly inward down to the bottom. All surfaces except for the bottoms have a highly polished, extra-smooth, white glaze. These features assure that your soufflé will be strikingly high and stately looking. The stark white exterior is decorated with the traditional, narrow pleats and the usual lip around the top edge. The individual dish is 4" in diameter and 2¾" high; it holds 9 ounces. The larger model, 7½" in diameter, 4¼" high, holding 2¼ quarts (9 cups), will easily feed six to eight people. Though intended for soufflés, these vessels, like all soufflé dishes, are sure to come in handy for moussaka and other casseroles.

13.31 CATAMOUNT GLASS SOUFFLÉ DISH

This simple, pristine, 2-quart container never brings attention to itself but it is a real culinary star. It lets you see what's being cooked inside, giving the food more visual importance. Imagine the sight of the crusty sugar-browned sides of a soufflé Grand Marnier or the entire petal-pink fluff of a cold strawberry mousse! For that matter, you can use this tempered-laboratory-glass vessel to serve gazpacho in its glorious colors of red and green, or for layered confections like English trifle. It is practical to boot: you can use it on the stovetop or in a regular or microwave oven, and you can clean it in the dishwasher. Remember, however, that when baking in glass, you must lower the oven heat about 10°— it heats up faster than porcelain or earthenware. It measures 4" high and 6½" in diameter.

CHEESE SOUFFLÉ

4 servings

The basic cheese soufflé is a white sauce—béchamel—enriched with egg yolks and cheese, into which beaten egg whites are folded. You will undoubtedly feel safer hovering over your oven during your first soufflé experiments. After two or three you'll have the confidence to set the timer and take yourself off until it summons you back into the kitchen.

2 tablespoons finely grated Parmesan or other hard cheese
2½ tablespoons butter
3 tablespoons flour
1 cup hot milk
SEASONINGS: ½ teaspoon paprika, speck of nutmeg,
½ teaspoon salt, and 3 grinds of white pepper
4 egg yolks
5 egg whites (⅔ cup)
1 cup (3½ ounces) coarsely grated Swiss cheese

1 PRELIMINARIES: Butter a 1-quart baking dish, 8" across. Roll the grated cheese in the buttered baking dish to cover the bottom and side, and fasten on the aluminum collar. Preheat the oven to 400°F, and set the rack in the lower third level. Measure out all the ingredients listed.

2 THE WHITE SAUCE—BÉCHAMEL: Stir and cook the butter and flour together in the saucepan over moderate heat for 2 minutes without coloring. Remove from heat, let cool a moment, then pour in all the hot milk and whisk vigorously to blend. Return to heat, stirring with a wooden spoon, and boil slowly for 3 minutes. The sauce will be very thick. Whisk in the seasonings, and remove from heat.

3 FINISHING THE SAUCE BASE: One by one, whisk the egg yolks into the hot sauce.

4 THE EGG WHITES: In a clean separate bowl with clean beaters, beat the egg whites to stiff shining peaks.

5 FINISHING THE SOUFFLÉ MIXTURE: Scoop a quarter of the egg whites on top of the sauce and stir them in with a wooden spoon. Turn the rest of the egg whites on top; rapidly and delicately fold them in, alternating scoops of the spatula with sprinkles of the coarsely grated cheese—adding the cheese now makes for a light soufflé.

6 AHEAD-OF-TIME NOTE: You may complete the soufflé to this point ½ hour or so in advance; cover loosely with a sheet of foil and set away from drafts.

7 BAKING: 25 to 30 minutes at 400°F and 375°F. Set in the preheated oven, turn the thermostat down to 375°F, and bake until the soufflé has puffed 2" to 3" over the rim of the baking dish into the collar, and the top has browned nicely.

8 SERVING: As soon as it is done, remove the collar, then bring the soufflé to the table. To keep the puff standing, hold your serving spoon and fork upright and back to back; plunge them into the crust and tear it apart.

The Way to Cook, by Julia Child

275

MOLDS

MOLDS ARE THE TOOLS that transform a mound of shapeless, everyday food into stunning dishes suitable for a party. All kinds of delicacies, from ice cream to sweet or savory mousses and puddings, can become pyramids or crowns, footballs or fish, all to create a culinary trompe l'oeil that delights guests and cooks.

There is nothing new about molded food art; it has been going on for hundreds of years, particularly in France, where those who created the original *haute cuisine* insisted on beautiful, ornate food. Today we rely on molds not merely because they make food attractive but because they offer convenience: the dish can be made well ahead of serving. There are dozens of shapes and sizes to choose from and an endless assortment of recipes to consider.

Some molded foods are meant to be served cold. The molds used to make these are generally made of metal, which keeps the ingredients well chilled. Hot molded foods are often cooked in ovenproof porcelain dishes, though a metal container is typically the choice for a lush, crusty apple charlotte. There are also molds that can withstand both heat and cold—enameled cast-iron terrines, for example, in which you cook the loaf before putting it into the refrigerator to chill. Smaller items (chocolates, for example) can be molded in flexible rubber or plastic forms, and there are wooden molds for making designs in butter. You may use some molds for more than one purpose—a terrine for a ladyfinger-lined cold charlotte, or a pudding mold for a cold aspic. However, you won't be successful steaming a thick pudding in a thin, elaborately designed metal mold meant for gelatin, so be sure you know the capabilities of the mold you choose.

The simpler the shape of the mold, the easier it will be to dislodge the contents. Resist the urge to buy one with intricate designs—a Spanish castle for instance, all

CLASSIC TERRINE OF FOIE GRAS

One of life's greatest pleasures is a whole foie gras, grade A, of course, slowly cooked in a terrine with Sauternes, the wonderful sweet white wine from France. Serve chilled with slices of peasant bread and drink a glass of Sauternes, late-harvest Jurançon, or Côtes de Gascogne.

10 servings

1 whole Grade A foie gras, about 1½ pounds, at room temperature, cleaned and deveined
salt and freshly ground white pepper to taste
⅔ cup Sauternes

1 Preheat oven to 200°F.

2 Season liver generously all over with salt and pepper. Place the large lobe smooth side down in a rectangular or oval porcelain terrine mold about the same size as the foie gras. Pour a little of the Sauternes over it. Add the small broken pieces of liver, a little more Sauternes, and finally the smaller lobe, smooth side up, and the rest of the wine. Cover the terrine with its lid or, since cooking at such a low temperature, use microwavable plastic wrap.

3 Put a folded kitchen towel or 6 paper towels layered together in the bottom of a pan large enough to hold the terrine, and set the terrine on top. Fill the pan halfway up the sides of the terrine with hot, not boiling, water, transfer to oven, and cook until internal temperature measures 120°F on an instant-read thermometer, about 1 hour, depending on the thickness of the terrine or mold.

4 Remove the terrine from the water bath and place in a deep dish. Invert the lid to exert a light pressure on liver; this will force rendered fat to the surface. If the terrine does not have a lid, or the lid has a handle, cut a piece of cardboard slightly smaller than the mold and wrap it in several layers of plastic wrap. Place the inverted lid (or cardboard) on liver and weigh it down with a full bottle of Armagnac (or two 1-pound cans from your pantry) for 20 minutes at room temperature. Then remove the weights and cover the terrine with the fat that was forced out.

5 When the foie gras is entirely covered by its fat, wrap the terrine tightly, and refrigerate for at least three days before serving. To serve, unmold by dipping the terrine briefly in hot water and, using a hot knife, cut into serving slices.

D'Artagnan's Glorious Game Cookbook, by Ariane Daguin, George Faison, and Joanna Pruess

battlements and turrets—because part of your mousse will surely get stuck inside one of the tiny crevices, spoiling the intended result. To release your aspic, charlotte, or other food with ease, run a knife around the inside of the mold, then wrap a warm, moist towel around it. Alternatively, put some lukewarm water in the kitchen sink and dip the mold in it up to the top edge for a few seconds. Remove the mold from the water, cover it with a serving platter, invert the two, and the food should come free. Repeat the procedure if it doesn't. It helps if you brush or wipe the inside of the mold with unflavored vegetable oil before you fill it.

TERRINES & PÂTÉ MOLDS

Many a sophisticated food lover would be hard pressed to tell you the difference between a terrine and a pâté. The two terms are often used interchangeably, but there are historic distinctions, and the tools used to prepare these dishes are different as well.

The word *terrine* comes from the French word for "earth," *terre*. By definition, most terrines are made of earthenware, though you can find many that are fashioned from porcelain, glass, and enameled cast iron. Typically they are rectangular or oval in shape and have straight sides. They often come with a vented lid; the tiny opening allows steam to escape, preventing the contents of the dish from exploding. Sometimes the tops are decorated with the figure of an animal, to indicate the type of meat within.

At some point in culinary history, the word *terrine* came to describe not only the cookware, but the food within it: a glorified meat loaf, if you will, made with seasoned, ground meat. Sometimes one kind of meat predominates, but often a terrine mixes several—liver, pork, veal, pheasant, venison, and often game meats—and it may be wrapped in strips of moisturizing bacon or fresh pork fat. Today the category has been greatly expanded to include colorful layered vegetable creations, or nuggets of seafood interlaced with a fish mousse. Before it is served, the terrine may be encased in a clear, golden aspic. Pistachio nuts, chopped truffles, green or black peppercorns, and other aromatic and texture-enhancing ingredients may be strewn throughout the mixture. Whether composed of meat, vegetables, or seafood, the loaf may be unmolded, served on a platter, and garnished beautifully, but just as often it is presented as rustic fare, sliced and served from the vessel itself.

Pâté's beginnings are slightly different. Originally it referred to a terrine that was wrapped in a crust. The word *pâté* comes from the French word *pâte*, or "paste," the flour-and-water mixture used to make dough for foods such as pie crust and pasta.

Nowadays, though, no one pays much attention to such literal distinctions. In culinary parlance we use the word *pâté* for those sinfully rich, smooth, silken concoctions of fattened goose foie gras and also for coarser "country pâtés," which are the same as terrines but served unmolded, on platters. But the term *pâté en croûte* is reserved for meat mixtures encased in crust. Because of the encasing pastry, *pâté en croûte* needs a special dish. The crust is fragile and may crumble if unmolded from a terrine. It's better to use a metal mold with sides that dismantle, so the crust will remain intact. Some molds have patterns etched into the sides, imprinting a lovely design onto the pastry as it bakes.

13.32 MATFER OCTAGONAL TERRINE

This elegant, unusually shaped dish dignifies whatever is cooked within it. It is made of white porcelain, holds 10 fluid ounces, and has mitred corners and flared edges. The domed lid fits neatly inside; it has a steam-release hole, and in the center is an oval depression across which there is a narrow molded handle. This mold is 7⅞" long and 6⅛" wide. Its 4⅜" height makes it deeper than most. As with any terrine, you may serve straight from the dish, but when unmolded, the octagon of, say, ground pork or pheasant studded with coarsely cut liver and a scattering of pistachio nuts would be a stunning presentation for a first course at a special dinner.

13.33 APILCO OVAL TERRINE

This stark white 10-ounce oval porcelain dish is perfect for classic terrines and pâtés, both plain and surrounded by aspic, but its shape and depth make it a candidate for newer versions, too: a salmon mousse layered with scallop slices and spinach, soft goat cheese alternating with sliced morels and the first fava beans of spring, or julienne vegetables in a spongelike jelly. Made in Chauvigny, France, just north of Limoges, this dish, like all Apilco porcelain, is fired at 2,600°F, to ensure a totally non-porous surface. Its loose-fitting lid and knob handle are both attractive and practical. The terrine we show you is 5" long and 3½" wide. It comes in two smaller 6- and 4-ounce sizes.

13.34 LE CREUSET
PÂTÉ TERRINE

This Le Creuset mold, made of enameled cast iron rather than earthenware, is rustic-looking and traditional, the stuff of country cooking. It comes in earthy red, flame, and blue, as well as white. The top is fitted with a snug lid complete with hole for escaping steam. The base is straight-sided and has two pretty, protruding handles that make the dish easy to grasp. Its high sides leave room for the accumulated cooking juices to keep the pâté moist as it ripens. The 4" by 12½" rectangular shape produces classic loaf-sized slices and holds 1½ quarts.

13.35 J. B. PRINCE
GALANTINE MOLD

REFLECTIONS ON FOIE GRAS
❧ ARIANE DAGUIN ❧

Foie gras—which literally means "fat liver" in French—has been a delicacy since the days of the pharaohs in ancient Egypt. There are even remnants of hieroglyphics showing flocks of geese being force-fed by Egyptian slaves so they would grow large, fattened livers. But it wasn't until the late eighteenth century that foie gras became widely known and appreciated among the French and the European aristocracy. In 1778 a foie gras–loving French chef from Alsace named Jean-Pierre Clause created a pâté de foie gras, then wrote down the recipe and proceeded to popularize the dish in Paris. The seductive pleasures of foie gras—the rich, luscious, delicate flavor so pleasing to the palate, the satiny, unctuous texture on the tongue—have been sought after for celebrations and special dinners ever since.

There are two distinct kinds of foie gras available: goose foie gras and duck foie gras. Goose liver, the more expensive of the two, with a more delicate flavor, comes mainly from France. The livers are larger than duck livers and take longer to produce. For a prime goose liver you must feed the adult goose five times a day for thirty days; the same person must always do the feeding or the goose won't cooperate. For a duck liver you must feed the adult duck three times a day for fifteen days. Goose liver is used mainly in terrines or in a pâté. You rarely see it served hot since it melts too quickly when it's heated. Duck foie gras, on the other hand, is much more versatile, as well as more widely available; it's produced from moulard ducks in America, France, Canada, parts of Eastern Europe, and Israel. The flavor of duck foie gras is still delicate, but fuller and a bit heartier than goose foie gras, and you can use it in many ways—baked in a terrine, cubed in a soup such as chestnut or pumpkin, as stuffing for a quail or a guinea hen, scattered in a lobster salad, or seared and served with sautéed apples or grapes, complementing the richness of the foie gras perfectly with a sweet and acidic balance of flavors. For years foie gras has been an essential component of French gastronomy, but now its pleasures are experienced in cuisines around the world.

Galantines are among the more challenging of recipes, but they are also so visually stunning that if you present one, you can be sure of rave reviews. First you must prepare a seasoned forcemeat, typically made with poultry, game, or pork, and stuff it inside a whole boned chicken, duck, pheasant, capon, or other bird. The stuffing may contain aromatic garnishes such as truffles, or other ingredients like chunks of ham, cut-up cooked vegetables, tiny fatback dice, or pistachio nuts. Once that's done, the filled poultry must be wrapped in cheesecloth, then poached in an appropriate broth, and cooled in the cooking liquid. (Some home cooks use a fish poacher to accomplish this.) Once cooled, a galantine can be served freestanding, but for the most elegant versions, producing uniform slices, a mold is required. The ingredients are weighted in the mold to shape it properly. After being chilled, the contents of the mold are removed and are ready to serve (or to decorate prior to serving). This heavy, ovenproof, white china mold does its job well, turning out a perfectly formed galantine. It is decorated with ridges and has awning-style handles that are easy to grip. Two sizes are available: 10" by 3½" by 3½" that holds 1 liter (1 quart) and a larger, 2-liter (roughly 2 quarts) mold that is 11½" by 4" by 4".

13.36 MATFER
PÂTÉ EN CROÛTE MOLD

Made of shiny tinplate, this mold is engineered to give you a classic-looking *pâté en croûte* with as little fuss as possible. It consists of two L-shaped sidepieces that slide onto a rectangular base and are fastened together with two pins. Remove the pins and peel off the sides; your pâté unmolds easily, without damage to the pastry. The mold can be ordered either plain or with a herringbone design stamped in the interior; the design makes an attractive pattern on the pastry as it bakes. This pan is solidly built, with thick, rolled edges. It is dishwasher safe and collapses for easy storage. It is available in several versions: plain in 11¾" and 13¾" lengths; with herringbone pattern in 9⅞", 13¾", and 19⅝" lengths.

13.37 MATFER NONSTICK
PÂTÉ MOLD

It can be frustrating to take the time and trouble to prepare an intricate *pâté en croûte*, only to witness the crust crumble upon unmolding. Here's something to make it easier on the home cook: a nonstick mold. It isn't authentically old school, but you won't care. This oval-shaped steel mold has been coated with a proprietary nonstick coating. Open the hinged sides and there's your pâté, lovely to look at and in one piece. The sidewalls are vertically grooved to provide a pretty pattern on the dough. You can tote this mold, filled with country pâté, to a picnic (along with a bottle of good wine) and end up with a most impressive lunch. As with other nonstick coated products, metal tools will scratch the surface, but foods release so easily from the sides that it should never be a problem. What's more, cleanup is a cinch; any particles of caught-on crust come off easily with a swish in soap and water. We like the 5½" by 3⅛" by 2½" size, but it also comes in three larger sizes, ranging from 7" to 9½" long.

13.38 MATFER ROUND
FLUTED PÂTÉ RING

Here is a tool that will help you prepare perfect and pretty individual *pâtés en croûte* for picnics, buffet tables, and first courses at special dinners. This mold is made of nonstick aluminum, which heats up well enough to brown the surfaces of the pastry properly and then to release the food easily; you need never be concerned that the pâté's fragile crust will crumble. Held together on one side with a clip, the mold springs open when the clip is removed. Consider it for savories, as well as sweets like a frangipane tartlet. It comes in three sizes; the one we show you is 3¾" diameter, and the others are smaller: 3⅛" and 2½".

ON A DESERT ISLAND
✤ JACQUES PÉPIN ✤

Years ago Jacques put together a list of the five ingredients he would like in unlimited supply if he were stuck on a desert island. Assuming that fresh water was available, sufficient wood for cooking, and a good selection of wild herbs, Jacques wanted

- chickens (for the eggs, meat, and fat)
- salad
- potatoes
- flour (to make bread)
- onions

We recently asked him for his cooking equipment list, which follows:

- 8" chef's knife
- stainless steel tongs
- a *fait-tout* or Windsor saucepan (tri-ply aluminum core with a stainless steel interior, 3 quart)
- 10" skillet with lid
- kitchen spoon (stainless steel)

FISH MOLDS

Some animals are so enchanting or interesting to look at that they warrant molds contoured to their own intrinsic shape. You wouldn't say this for, say, chicken liver or pork loin; pâtés made with those ingredients work best when shaped into rectangles or ovals in classic terrines. But fish, lobsters, and chickens are another story. Fish in particular, with their long, slender bodies, swishy tails, and glistening scales, are visually interesting. And so, when fish mousse is on your menu, it deserves its own mold. Fish molds are usually made of tin-lined copper, stainless steel, or aluminum. The most intriguing ones are hand-hammered, complete with scales, fins, and tail. Some are straightforward figures, but many are in a curved form, as if the fish was frozen in midleap.

Fish is held out to be one of the greatest luxuries of the table and not only necessary, but even indispensable at all dinners where there is any pretense to excellence or fashion.

—MRS. ISABELLA BEETON

13.39 COPPER PRODUCTS OF ITALY FISH MOLD

This mold has the curved shape of a fish leaping in and out of the water and it is perfectly shaped to fit on a large, round serving platter. It is made of heavy, tin-lined gleaming copper that has been hand chiseled to create the proper scales, fins, eye, mouth, and tail. The fish mousse you prepare in this mold will be finely detailed and visually exquisite. It is suitable for both cold and hot foods, such as jellied trout salad or hot baked salmon mousse. When you are not using this for a recipe, you may hang it in your kitchen as a decoration: there is a hook on top for just such a purpose. The company makes two versions of this mold: one facing left, the other, right, so you can prepare twin salmon mousses or even an ornate dessert mousse for a buffet lunchon or dinner. Both hold 2½ cups and are 11" in diameter.

PUDDING MOLDS

It was during the reign of Henry VIII, king of England, that Christmas feasting began. His Majesty loved the suckling pigs, the roasted deer, and the stuffed geese of a normal royal holiday dinner, but he had a particular craving for plum pudding—the same sticky, gooey confection so cherished by Tiny Tim. Puddings, both sweet and savory, were the rage then, not just at Christmas, but throughout the year, and continue to be favorites in England. The ingredients used to make them were combined and stuffed inside a muslin sack and boiled or steamed for hours.

Today health- and diet-conscious cooks reject these typically heavy, cholesterol-laden, suet-based concoctions. Though some still pay homage to the past by baking a figgy pudding once a year, most prefer more contemporary recipes. Puddings now are lighter blends of sugar, eggs, and milk plus fruit or other flavorings. To make them, you mix the ingredients, pour them into a greased and floured pudding mold, cover it tightly, and place it on a rack above boiling water in a large pot with a tight lid. When the pudding is done, unmold it onto a platter and serve it, accompanied by fresh, sweet cream, whipped cream, ice cream, or crème anglaise.

If you plan to serve steamed pudding even occasionally, you'll need a good pudding mold, though a sturdy glazed pottery mixing bowl can also double as a pudding basin (see chapter 2). Pudding molds aren't expensive, and you can use them for Bavarian creams as well. They come in a variety of shapes and sizes, in both ceramic and metal.

13.40 A. METALÚRGICA PUDDING MOLD

This 5"- tall, tin-plated pudding mold has the traditional bucket shape and is centered with a narrow, hollow tube that tapers as it rises to the top. The elegant-looking puddings, aspics, and frozen desserts that emerge from this vessel look like small angel food cakes. Elaborate flutes and scallops, stamped onto the bottom and sides of the mold, provide a decorative effect. The base has two metal

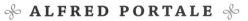

COMPOSING A DISH
❧ ALFRED PORTALE ❧

Composition—assembling a group of complementary elements that balance and highlight each other on a plate—is one of the most important and challenging aspects of creating a dish or a menu. You must keep in mind the variety of flavors, texture, color, and even the cultural appropriateness of one item juxtaposed with another when planning your meal.

For the home cook, one of the easiest ways to go about composing a successful dish is to start with one featured ingredient—say salmon fillets that you'd like to sauté—then build up a supporting cast around it: perhaps mashed potatoes with butter and sour cream, fresh peas tossed with olive oil and lemon juice, and an herbed butter sauce. Let the market and the season be your guide, and pick something fresh and beautiful that catches your eye.

It can also be helpful to choose a cuisine as a theme (Italian, French, New England) so that the pieces fall more naturally into place. You might, for example, find a great porterhouse steak at the butcher that you'd like to serve at a dinner for friends. You love cooking Italian, so that's going to be your dinner's theme. It's easy now to decide on the menu: you pick a recipe for beefsteak *Fiorentina*—a double-thick porterhouse grilled, then drizzled with a little extra-virgin olive oil—add a mushroom polenta and broccoli rabe with garlic as garnishes, and finish with a dessert of roasted peaches with sweetened mascarpone. Serve it with a nice Chianti Classico or a Barolo and you have an extremely pleasing, coherent, and successful meal.

For contrast, it's a good rule of thumb to use two or three colors, and a couple of different textures on a plate. Be mindful of the season—no rich, heavy dishes on a hot day in August—and follow your whim if inspiration strikes. In the midst of a gray and icy winter, I might do a spicy Caribbean meal: exotic rum cocktails, then a spice-rubbed prime rib served with sweet-potato purée and some sautéed greens, capped by a passion-fruit granità with tropical fruits or a tropical fruit tart. On a dark February evening, this is a meal of culinary sunshine.

---

clips hinged to the outside; these hold the gently domed lid securely in place. The lid is well designed; it overhangs the base so that condensation that accumulates on its edge will fall back down, instead of seeping into the batter. You steam a pudding upside down in this mold. There is a small, metal, rectangular handle on the lid, but be sure to use a pot holder when lifting the pudding from its steam bath; the metal will be very hot.

CHARLOTTE MOLDS

The legendary chef Antonin Carême created the lovely dessert we call charlotte for Princess Charlotte, the only daughter of King George IV of England. The dish was a sweet purée of apples surrounded by a golden brown butter-rich crust. Years later when Carême moved to Moscow, he reinterpreted the dish as a cold Bavarian cream encased in ladyfingers, which he called charlotte Russe. Today charlottes are virtually the same: either hot, crusty, and filled with baked apple or other fruit, or cold and based on flavored jellied creams surrounded by strips of cake or ladyfingers. In either case, the dessert can be made in a soufflé dish, but a metal charlotte mold will be an improvement for both hot and cold versions. The classic mold is a simple, undecorated tin-plated cylinder that flares toward the top and has a pair of heart-shaped handles. Because of the metal's heat- and cold-conducting qualities, Bavarian creams chill thoroughly and slip out easily when warm towels are pressed to the mold's sides, and the casing of toasted bread surrounding hot fruit charlottes browns beautifully as well.

13.41 DE BUYER CHARLOTTE MOLD

Pure and simple, this is the quintessential charlotte mold: a plain case of tinned steel and high sides that splay gradually toward the top. The flared sides allow for easy unmolding of some of the most fabulous hot or cold confections. Two flat, heart-shaped handles near the top of the container are intrinsic to the design and help you ease the dessert out of the mold. A matching lid is also available for storing chilled custards and puddings. The lid is flat and sits within the mold; it has a roomy looped lifter on top. This charlotte mold is safe for oven and freezer use but not for the dishwasher or microwave oven. It comes in seven sizes, including a tiny ½-cup model and a large one that's 3 quarts. We show you the 3⅛"-high mold with a 5½" diameter that holds 1 quart; others hold 13 ounces, 3 cups, 1½ quarts, and 2 quarts.

OPEN MOLDS

Open molds are ideal for forming aspics and other jellies. Aspics are savory jellies. They are used for several purposes: for molded salads of meat, seafood, poultry, or vegetables; for glazing cold foods; and for garnishing (the gelatin is chopped or cut into decorative shapes). In all cases, the jelly must be crystal clear, which requires preparing stock, defatting, and ridding it of any debris, then incorporating flavorings and packaged gelatin (unless it was made with a natural gelatinous ingredient like calves' knuckle). For molded aspics, the hot liquid is poured into a pretty container and refrigerated; the fluids chill into sumptuous shapes that please both eye and palate.

With a mold, you can also transform plain ice cream into something extravagant; you can even dress up a commercial product to look magnificent. You have a choice that includes rounds or squares, fluted patterns, regal crowns, stars, flowers, butterflies, fanciful designs, and cute containers in shapes that coordinate with almost every occasion. There are large molds that hold enough ice cream for a party of ten, and smaller ones for individual servings.

Because metal cools quickly and thoroughly, it is the material of choice for most cold dishes. You are likely to find them made of tin or copper. Some have convenient nonstick coatings. Release food as you would from any mold: by wrapping the outside with a moist, warm towel or by dipping the mold in lukewarm water.

copper lined with tin, it is hardly necessary for the preparation of aspics or molded ice cream because copper's heat-conducting qualities, so ideal when cooking, don't come into play. And copper molds are expensive. But they are also pretty, and many people keep them on display in their kitchens—there's a hook on this one for hanging. This 1½-quart mold is 7" in diameter and has thick flutes on the side and a large flower pattern at the base (it becomes the top of the dessert). There are no narrow little crevices, so you can be sure the food will slip out easily. You can also use this mold for baking. Try it for plum pudding, *Bundt*-style cakes, and sweet breads.

13.44 PIAZZA TIMBALE

Timbale is a French word that means "kettledrum," which this mold is said to resemble, though it actually looks more like a short tumbler with flared sides. It is also known as a *dariole*. Both the mold and the dish cooked within it are called a *timbale*. The mold shown here is made of heavy stainless steel, suitable for cold foods, ice creams, and mousses, or baked savory mousses, vegetable cus-

13.42 SCI ASPIC MOLD

This handy little oval mold, the traditional shape for making *oeuf en gelée* (poached egg in aspic), has several advantages. Its nonstick surface makes it a cinch to unmold the food. The simple flower design on the bottom is decoration enough for the most lovely of gelatin salads. And its 4-ounce capacity makes it perfect for individual servings that look sensa-

tional on a dinner plate or buffet platter. It can also be used for ice cream. We suggest buying several of these 3" molds for use when you will be entertaining.

13.43 COPPER PRODUCTS OF ITALY MOLD

Here is a utilitarian kitchen tool that is also beautiful. Made of hammered

tards, and even small, individual yeast breads, cakes, or quick breads. It comes in 2-, 4-, 5-, and 6-ounce sizes, ranging from 2" to 2¾" high.

13.45 MATFER PYRAMID ICE CREAM MOLD

The ice cream that emerges from this stainless steel mold may make you dream of visiting Egypt or going through the crystal pyramid that stands before the Louvre in Paris. This graceful, geometric design has been a universal shape in art through the ages. The mold will make a splendid ice cream presentation to serve on your best dessert plates, in a pool of sauce or garnished with berries. We suggest you buy several of the pyramid molds; they come in four sizes. The large (4"-high) mold holds 3¾ fluid ounces and will serve two people. Use the smallest one (1½" high, 1⅝ fluid ounces) for miniservings of three different flavors. The two other sizes are 2⅜" (2½ fluid ounces) and 3⅛" (3 fluid ounces). You needn't limit the molds to ice cream; they will also work for Bavarian creams, mousses, and aspics, or even for a vegetable terrine.

13.46 A. METALÚRGICA BOMBE

What a horrible name, bombe! It's called that because the elliptical

13.47 FALAFEL SHAPING KIT

Falafel (or *ta'amia*, as the dish is called in Egypt) are fried patties of ground beans, garlic, onions, and spices. *Ta'amia* patties are made with fava beans (*ful nabed*), but in Israel, where falafel is sold by street vendors, chickpeas replace the *ful nabed*. For centuries falafel has been shaped between the palms with a few brisk and efficient pats. But the old way evidently was not good enough for the anonymous Syrian who invented this falafel shaper, the Middle Eastern equivalent of the hamburger press. It consists of a stainless steel spatula and a circular mold—2¼" in diameter and ½" deep—at the end of a brass cylinder. To shape falafel, depress the lever on the mold's cylinder, spread a dollop of paste inside the mold using the spatula, then release the plunger lodged inside the cylinder. A falafel patty the shape of a mini-hamburger is formed and ready to cook.

TIMBALLO ALLE MELANZANE (EGGPLANT AND PASTA TIMBALE)

When Naples was ruled by a Spanish branch of the French Bourbons, the French cooks who came with them put pasta dishes into molds for a more elegant presentation.

6 to 8 servings

1½ pounds eggplant	1 teaspoon sugar
salt	½ cup chopped basil leaves
olive oil for frying	14 ounces penne, ziti, and other
2 cloves garlic, crushed	short macaroni
1½ pounds tomatoes, peeled	1 pound mozzarella, diced
and chopped	6 tablespoons grated Parmesan
pepper	1¼ cups ricotta

1 Slice the eggplant lengthwise into about ⅓" slices; sprinkle with salt and leave for 1 hour; rinse and dry. Fry in hot oil, turning over once until browned.
2 MAKE A SAUCE: fry the garlic in 2 tablespoons oil, add the tomatoes, salt, pepper, and sugar, and simmer 15 minutes. Then add the basil.
3 Boil the macaroni in salted water until half cooked; drain.

Line an ovenproof bowl about 6" deep and 9" in diameter with overlapping eggplant slices. Fill with alternate layers of pasta, tomato sauce, and the three cheeses.

4 Cover with foil, gently press down, and bake at 400°F for 45 minutes. Unmold by turning the bowl upside down on a serving platter. Serve very hot.

The Good Food of Italy, by Claudia Roden

shape resembles the bombs used at the time the dish was created, but the name belies the food's elegance and beauty. A bombe is a festive, exquisite dessert, suitable for parties and special dinners. Typically it consists of two or more layers of different ice creams, sorbets, or mousses with contrasting textures and flavors to please both eye and palate. The layers are formed in concentric circles inside the mold. It takes some time to prepare one, but the work is done in stages. This tinned mold is the perfect container in which to make a bombe. The metal gets cold quickly and thoroughly, and the fluted ridges make deep, smooth patterns in the ice cream; even if the mold melts slightly when releasing, it won't show. The bowl is fairly flexible, which will help you ease out the contents. The lid fits tightly, keeping out air, and has a small but sturdy ring handle that will help you pry it off. Unmold your bombe by wrapping it for several seconds with a warm, damp kitchen towel and complete the presentation by piping some whipped cream rosettes around the base. This mold holds 1.5 liters (1⅗ quarts) .

13.48 A. METALÚRGICA NONSTICK FLUTED MOLD

This lightweight but sturdy metal mold will serve you well whether you wish to make a hot pudding or a cold mousse, a jellied salad or a statuesque ice cream sculpture. It is sim-ply designed with indented arches around the sides and circles at the top. There are no tiny food-catching nooks and crannies, so unmolding is fairly easy. To make the job even more effortless, the pan has a non-stick coating, which makes cleanup a cinch, but you can also purchase this mold in a tinplate version. Both hold 1.5 liters (1⅗ quarts) and are 4¼" high and 7¼" in diameter.

13.49 J. B. PRINCE INDIVIDUAL TURK'S HEAD MOLD

One legend has it that the *Kugelhopf* mold, shaped like the Sultan's turban, was invented to commemorate the defeat of the Turkish armies which besieged Vienna in 1683. Large *Kugelhopf* molds always have a metal post in the center in order to send heat to the middle of the cake.

The piece we show you here is used to make individual 4½-ounce servings of the rich, raisiny coffee cake and is small enough (3¾" in diameter) for the pastry to bake through without the help of the post. It is heavy for its size and is coated with a non-stick surface, so you'll never have a problem unmolding the mini confection or cleaning the mold after use. The classic, fluted design will produce a lovely, traditional-looking *Kugelhopf,* but don't stop there. You can use this versatile form for individual portions of ice cream, mousse, or jellied salads, all of which will create an air of festivity. However, be sure to thoroughly dry the mold after use, or it will rust.

13.50 ENDURANCE STACKS THE KIT

Those who enjoy the look of tall, vertical food on a plate will revel in these molds. There are six in the package, two each of 4"-high triangles, squares, and rounds. They are made of sturdy stainless steel and are bottomless, resembling tall cookie cutters. To make towers of food, you set the molds on top of a cookie sheet; pack in layers of ingredients such as chopped chicken, tomatoes, pasta, and cheese, or dessert items like pound cake, poached fruit, and mascarpone cheese; then tamp down the ingredients. The kit comes with a tamping rod plus three flat discs for each shape. Chill or bake the stacks, place one on each plate, and lift off the mold.

13.51 MATFER ROUND BOTTOMLESS FORMS

These versatile rounds are serviceable for a variety of culinary tasks. You can use them to shape cooked foods like a rice pilaf, or to present a serving of tuna tartare. But because they are stainless steel, you may also put them in the oven to bake foods, as you would use a flan ring. Place the rings on a cookie sheet and when cooking is complete, unmold each onto a serving plate. Or use them to mold and freeze layers of different flavors and colors of ice cream or mousse. They come in three sizes: 2⅜" diameter (1¼" high), 2⁷⁄₁₆" diameter (1³⁄₁₆" high), and 2½" diameter (1½" high). They also come in handy as cookie and biscuit cutters.

13.52 DE BUYER HEMISPHERE MOLD

Molds often have elaborate designs or interesting shapes that make food look fanciful or stylish. This hemisphere mold is quite the opposite. Its very simplicity is starkly stunning: picture perfectly rounded domes of salmon mousse, chocolate Bavarian cream, or even cherry Jell-O. The food can make a statement as is but also works beautifully with garnish; if you like, circle the bottom of the salmon spheres with feathery dill-weed, or surround the Bavarian cream or Jell-O mounds with tiny whipped cream rosettes, or give ice cream rounds a brittle chocolate coat. This mold is 3½" in diameter and holds 5½ fluid ounces. It is made of stainless steel, which means you can use it for baking single servings of cake. It is also useful for shaping cooked foods such as rice or mashed potatoes. The mold comes in twelve sizes, from a tiny 1⅛" diameter (⅜ fluid ounces) size, perfect for ice cream bonbons, to a large 7⅞" (67⅞ fluid ounces) mold suitable for an ice cream bombe.

13.53 APILCO *COEUR À LA CRÈME* MOLD

Coeur à la crème, sweetened fresh white cheese molded in the shape of a heart, is an exception to the French practice of almost always accompanying cheese with bread. Often served with fresh wild strawberries, *fraises des bois,* it combines both the fruit and cheese courses into the dessert course. The cheese, *fromage blanc,* is made from whole milk that is allowed to curdle; then the curds are drained in heart-shaped molds or baskets. It can be full fat, low fat, or skim. Often the cheese is mixed with cream and sprinkled with sugar before draining. This heart of pure white porcelain is pierced on the bottom with tiny holes to allow excess liquid in the sweetened cheese to run off as it chills. Line the container with dampened cheesecloth, fill it with cheese, and set it on a plate in the refrigerator to chill. Raised above the plate on three little feet, the mold will be clear of any liquid that drains out. To serve, unmold and unwrap the heart and accompany it with berries, a colorful fruit sauce, or thick, fresh cream. The mold measures 7" in diameter and will serve six.

BUTTER MOLDS

Serving little butter pats imprinted with pretty designs tells your guests that you are the kind of host for whom every particular counts and that you take entertaining seriously enough to put in a little extra effort for their benefit. Actually, once you have allowed your butter to soften up, making molded butter takes only a few minutes with old-fashioned wood molds or the more modern and practical rubber molds on sheets. In either case, you'll have the loveliest butter imaginable. But if you go to the trouble of using a butter mold, be sure the butter that goes into it is top quality.

13.54 SCI BUTTER PADDLE

If you wish to create the small grooved balls of butter you may have seen in restaurants, you'll need these wooden butter paddles. Soak the paddles in ice water for about 10 minutes. Place a small piece of cold butter on the ribs of one paddle, and set the other paddle, rib side down, on top of the butter. Move the paddles back and forth to roll the butter in the grooves, until the ball is indented.

13.55 TABLE ART BUTTER MOLD

These soft, pliable rubber molds do a terrific job of changing spreadable foods into edible art. Use them not simply to make beautiful pats of butter, but also to make chocolates or cheese nibbles or tiny servings of mousse or pâté. The molds have six indentations per sheet and come in a dozen different designs, from whimsical piglets to elegant fleurs-de-lis to romantic wedding bells. The work is easy: fill each indentation with softened food, level it off with a knife, and refrigerate the sheets until the ingredients are firm. Then, simply press the back of the mold to pop the food out. The molds should be washed by hand with soap and water.

13.56 SCI BUTTER MOLD

This old-fashioned tool is used to create butter rounds imprinted with a pretty design on top. Made of unvarnished wood, it is comprised of a bulbous cup through which runs a plunger; at the bottom of the plunger is a thick disc carved with pears hanging from a tree branch. To make the fancy pats, place hard butter on a work board on your kitchen counter, then plunge the pole down over it. The disc cuts out a coin-shaped round with the pear engraving. Soap and water are all that is needed to keep the wood clean.

PRESENTING A MEAL
✤ ROCCO DISPIRITO ✤

Whether you're a home cook or a restaurant chef, your job is not just to prepare food but to present it attractively. Vision is one of the first senses to receive information about the food and to respond, ideally, by stimulating the appetite, so naturally you want the food to look appealing. When entertaining at home, you might want to serve the first course on individual plates, the second course family style at the table, and then plate the dessert. This provides a bit of variety at the table. There's a tendency at home to prepare too many things and to put too much on the plate; I think three or four carefully considered items is the limit.

Before you think about the visually pleasing composition of a plate, however, you have to think about the composition of a meal. In my restaurant I try to create excitement and tension on the palate using harmonious combinations of the four elemental flavors—sweet, salty, sour, and bitter—that the tongue can perceive. Just as all colors derive from the three primary colors, red, blue and yellow, all flavors are created from these four primary flavors. If you keep in mind the concept of using these four elements in combination, it will help you create a well-composed meal that is naturally attractive on the plate as well. For example, I have wild salmon in the kitchen today; very rich, subtly sweet and almost gamy, it needs to be moderated with something acidic. I have beautiful squash blossoms, just in season, so I might pickle them to be the acidic element, and, adding one more flavor, I might make a sauce of red bell peppers to give the dish a slight bitter edge. When you combine these components on a plate—the delicate pink salmon, the bright yellow and orange squash blossom, the red of the bell pepper sauce—you have a presentation that will be as stimulating to the eye as it is to the palate.

Another mistake that I think home cooks make is in unnecessarily garnishing a plate, or garnishing it with things that have nothing to do with what is being served. Let beautiful food speak for itself. If you're serving a platter of perfect roast chicken with green beans and a tomato salad, that's all you need; the color each item provides is enough in itself.

When you're planning a menu for a dinner party, remember that there are very attractive serving vessels, baking dishes, and molds that can help you make a striking presentation; you might want to compose your menu to take advantage of them. Soup tureens are wonderful for table presentation. I love them, love the drama of ladling a soup out of a beautiful vessel in front of my guests. Molds are another tool that can help you make a dramatic presentation. One of my favorites is the savarin mold, originally intended for a baba-like cake soaked with rum-flavored syrup. The molds come in all sizes and lend themselves to many uses: cakes, of course; rice salads; warm rice pilaf; vegetable or fish mousses; and aspics. The large ones are ideal for a buffet presentation while the small ones are just right for an individual serving. And the hole in the middle is perfect for holding a colorful garnish, such as a bright assortment of fresh fruit to accompany the savarin cake.

Finally, as important as it is for the food to look attractive and to be presented well, it is still more important that it taste good than that it look good. This is always the bottom line. I am much happier with a dish that tastes better than it looks than with a dish that looks better than it tastes.

SUSHI EQUIPMENT

ONE OF THE GREAT DELIGHTS of Japanese cuisine is sushi—vinegared rice molded into different forms and garnished with any number of ingredients, from raw fish or vegetables to omelet strips or seaweed. The sushi rice itself is simply boiled rice with *kombu* (kelp), mixed with a vinegar dressing that also includes sugar and salt. There are several ways to shape the sushi rice and fish or vegetables: roll them in seaweed to make *makizushi,* pat them into oblong individual forms topped with raw or cooked fish for *nigirizushi,* or top them with seafood and vegetables on a bed of rice for *chirashi-zushi.*

13.57 WOOD *BATTERA* SUSHI MOLD

Made of pale blond, unfinished wood with beautifully mortised joints, this elegant oblong box appears at first glance far more suitable for storing jewelry than for mundane kitchen chores. But—unsurprisingly, when one reckons with the Japanese taste for purity of design—its form and function are beautifully matched. The 8"-long, 4½"-wide box, called an *oshiwaku* (or "push frame"), has a removable top and bottom. It is used to press sushi rice and its garnishes of fish, omelet strips, or vegetables into a firm cake that can then be sliced into individual servings to make *battera* sushi, one of the oldest sushi styles. *Battera* comes from the Portuguese word for "ship," *bateira.* The pressed sushi was said to resemble a ship. The vinegared rice is spread over the bottom of the box (the interior area is 5½" long by 2¼" wide by 1½" deep), topped with your garnish of choice, and pressed down with the inset top. When the top and the frame are removed, the rice cake remains on the base.

13.58 *MAKIZUSHI* MAT

Uniquely Japanese are the delicacies called *makizushi,* in which vinegar-seasoned rice is spread over a thin sheet of toasted black seaweed called *nori* and then rolled around a center of raw fish or crisp vegetables. This gadget, which resembles a small bamboo roll-up window shade, is known as a *sudare* and is helpful in rolling up the whole assembly—it's used in the same way as a linen towel or napkin is used to roll up a jelly roll. In a pinch, you can roll *makizushi* with a damp linen napkin, but this 9½"-square bamboo mat is the authentic way to do it, and it works very well. The round slats are held together by five rows of twisted string, knotted together with short ends left hanging at opposite sides of the mat. After rolling, be sure to leave the *makizushi* resting in the *sudare* for 5 minutes until it "sets." Then unroll, and cut the *nori*-wrapped

"From right to left, you have your tekkamaki, your futomaki, and then your yamaimo roll. The little pile of pink stuff is ginger, the green one's wasabi. And, of course, you already recognize your vodka martini."

cylinder into 1" lengths. Serve as an hors d'oeuvre or as a first course, preferably on round bamboo or lacquer trays.

13.59 *HANGIRI* TUB WITH PADDLE

Making good sushi rice is an art: you must begin with a suitable variety of rice, cook it properly, and season it correctly. But that's not all. You must also cool the rice quickly and toss it carefully, without breaking the grains. The best utensils for these tasks are a *hangiri* tub and wooden paddle. *Hangiri* tubs are made of wood because wood absorbs the excess moisture from the cooked rice; nonporous materials like metal or porcelain would make the rice gummy by trapping the steam. The bowl should be damp before you use it so the rice won't stick. *Hangiri* bowls are always very wide and relatively short, giving plenty of surface area for quick cooling and for additional evaporation of moisture. The one we chose is also beautiful, holds 1½ quarts of rice, and is 17½" in diameter and 4" high, with two copper strips that encircle the sides. The 19" wooden paddle (*kijakushi*) lets you mix the rice and seasonings gently.

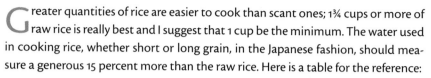

HOW TO MAKE PERFECT RICE
❧ ELIZABETH ANDOH ❧

Greater quantities of rice are easier to cook than scant ones; 1¾ cups or more of raw rice is really best and I suggest that 1 cup be the minimum. The water used in cooking rice, whether short or long grain, in the Japanese fashion, should measure a generous 15 percent more than the raw rice. Here is a table for the reference:

For 1 cup raw rice, use 1 cup plus 2 tablespoons water
For 1¼ cups raw rice, use 1½ cups water
For 1½ cups raw rice, use 1¾ cups water
For 1¾ cups raw rice, use 2 cups plus 2 tablespoons water
For 2 cups raw rice, use 2⅓ cups water

To the uninitiated, the timing of rice cooking may seem tricky at first. But be assured that with several attempts you most certainly can produce lovely pearly grains of cooked rice. There is an old Japanese nursery rhyme that tells how. It goes like this:

Hajimé choro choro	At first it bubbles
Naka pa ppa	And then it hisses
Akago naité mo	Even if the baby is crying [from hunger]
Futa toru na.	Don't remove the lid.

This chant melodically describes the basic rule: never remove the lid to see what is happening. You should know from the sound the pot makes (bubbling or hissing) just how the rice is doing. Peeking inside allows precious moisture to escape and it also reduces the valuable cooking pressure within the pot.

14

PASTA-MAKING EQUIPMENT

I T IS QUITE POSSIBLE that no food is as firmly associated with a nation as pasta is with Italy. Whether it is the delicate egg ribbons that are the specialty of Emilia-Romagna, or the hardy semolina rigatoni of Naples, pasta is the staple of Italy. Italians consume more than 60 pounds of pasta per person a year; Americans eat half that much.

Scholars still debate the exact origins of pasta, and especially of *pasta secca,* or dried pasta. There is some evidence—linguistic, anecdotal, and scientific—that it might have been of Arab origin and later taken root in Sicily. Or it might have been made in Sicily in the first place, where it was well known by the twelfth century. At any rate, what is clear is that Italy is the only country where pasta is universal, enjoyed by every class of society and in every region.

Nonetheless, the world seems to have embraced pasta. In January 1999, the *Chicago Tribune* reported that 62 percent of Americans cook pasta at home at least once a week. This wasn't always the case. Although it had enjoyed more than six hundred years of Italian devotion, pasta did not find its way to the New World until 1786, when Thomas Jefferson discovered spaghetti, along with ice cream and French wines, during his stay in Europe as minister to France. Upon his return to America, he sent to Italy for a spaghetti die so his cooks could duplicate the dish. Though noodles were part of the German and Pennsylvania Dutch culinary repertoire, it was not until 1848 that spaghetti was

produced commercially in the United States, and not until the beginning of the twentieth century, when large waves of immigrants began to arrive from southern Italy, that Italian pasta became popular.

There are hundreds of forms of pasta and, unfortunately, almost as many misconceptions about it. The saddest is that dried pasta is inferior to fresh pasta (*pasta fresca*). In reality, they are different products, and Italians do not substitute one for the other; they appreciate the difference. Dried pasta is factory made from hard semolina or durum wheat flour and water. It is sold in boxes or bags and comes in numerous shapes, from elongated strands of spaghetti, linguine, and perciatelli to the hollow macaroni shapes of rigatoni, ziti, and penne to the tiny shapes used in soup known collectively as pastine. Dried, factory-made pasta is the perfect choice for bold and chunky sauces, for soups in which long cooking would disintegrate a more delicate product, and for baked pasta dishes (*pasta al forno*). It was always the preferred staple of southern Italy, where the wheat grows strong and the air blows warm for perfect drying.

When, in the late 1800s, southern Italians were migrating to America, many others moved to northern Italy to work in factories. They brought their pasta preferences with them, and it was at that point that northern Italians found room in their kitchens for dried pasta alongside their fresh, homemade, soft, flour-and-egg pasta (*pasta all'uovo*). Since egg pasta is most often made at home, Italians also refer to it as *fato in casa* (made in house). They seldom say *pasta fresca*, which is an unfortunate name anyway, since many consumers assume that if the product says "fresh" it will be the best they can buy—and this is simply not the case. To enjoy pasta as the Italians do, buy dried pasta imported from Italy when the sauce demands that choice, and when you want the toothsome delicacy of homemade pasta, make your own or purchase it from a good retailer.

MAKING PASTA BY HAND

MAKING *PASTA ALL'UOVO* BY HAND involves four separate steps: mixing, kneading, rolling, and cutting the dough. With practice, you can become adept at doing all four at home. Pasta dough likes to be warm, so many Italians insist that it must be mixed and kneaded by hand; we find it easy and rewarding to do so, but not compulsory. Many food processors and heavy mixers generate enough warmth to make the dough, though the result may be firmer and not as delicate as handmade. Either way, make sure your ingredients are at room temperature and that you work on a warm surface, such as wood, not on cold marble or granite.

14.1 J. K. ADAMS BUTCHER BLOCK COUNTER BOARD

Here is one of the most practical boards to own, not just for rolling and cutting noodles but for all tasks, from making pie dough to mincing onions. Handsome enough to leave permanently in place on a counter, it will also convert any table into an efficient work surface. Made in Vermont of laminated sugar maple, it differs from other rolling boards in having two wooden bars that attach to the long sides, one projecting ¾" above the upper surface, the other projecting ¾" below the lower surface. (It is necessary to attach these bars yourself; the well-designed fittings and plastic top screws go together in a snap with a screwdriver.)

To use, place the board on the counter or on a table so the bar that projects downward overlaps the edge nearest you. As you roll the dough, this bar will keep the board from shifting, and the bar projecting upward at the far end of the board will keep the flour from spilling over. This board is available in three sizes: 16" by 20", 20" by 24", and 24" by 29". All are ¾" thick. Buy the largest one for which you have room; it will become your favorite work area. Use one side for dough (pasta, bread, and pastry) and turn the board over for chopping. This way, strong flavors such as garlic and onions won't influence the taste of the dough. Wash the board with warm water and a little soap after each use and it will serve you for years.

14.2 H. A. MACK ROLLING PIN

Hand rolling pasta takes patient practice. Those who do it often are able to produce large (36" in diameter or more), even sheets of silky dough. To create something worthy of your best ragú, you must work with a proper pasta rolling pin like this smooth beechwood pin available in lengths of 20" and 23". If you are optimistic about your skills, buy the longer one. What makes pasta rolling tricky is that the dough must be stretched under and over the pin at the same time, a skill not unlike patting your head and rubbing your stomach while standing on one foot. This pin is 1½" in diameter and shaped to give you the control you need. According to Italian purists, your reward will be pasta with tiny nooks and crannies that hold the sauce. After use, the pin should be wiped clean with a damp cloth.

14.3 BARTELT DRYING SCREEN

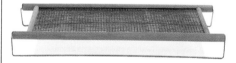

Once pasta has been cut and shaped either into nested noodles or stuffed pieces, it is usually placed on a towel to await cooking or to be dried for longer storage. Because the dough is still slightly moist, there is the possibility of it sticking to the towel, sometimes tearing open the bottom of the stuffed pieces when you attempt to remove them. Most cooks flour the towel to prevent this, but

HANDMADE PASTA VS. MACHINE PASTA
❧ GIULIANO BUGIALLI ❧

Whether preparing fresh pasta at home or in a restaurant there is no short cut. The real thing must be kneaded by hand and stretched with a rolling pin or with a manual pasta machine. The key to making excellent fresh pasta is keeping tactile contact with the dough. Only the sense of touch can alert you to the subtle adjustments that must be made as you work along. You must compensate for variation of humidity in the air, the season, the temperature, and the difference in the ingredients. You can do this by making the dough manually, kneading with your hands and later with the rollers of a manual pasta machine, and stretching with that machine or with a rolling pin. The result we are aiming for is a sheet of pasta that is silky and elastic, soft and smooth, yet resistant and not easily broken. Fresh pasta should cook quickly and be tender. It should never be "al dente": that is appropriate only for commercial dried pasta (which, by the way, is wonderful for a variety of dishes).

Using an electric mixer to knead the dough does not produce a first-class pasta—the proportions of ingredients necessary to withstand the strength of the mixer produce a rather tough dough and overexpand the gluten in the flour. All manual pasta machines are built in a similar way—with two rollers to help with the later stages of kneading and finally to stretch the layer to the thickness you require—but the quality of the machines varies a great deal. You should look for a solidly built machine with rollers that close evenly at each setting. And make sure that the machine has enough settings so you can make several different sizes of pasta, from thick to paper thin.

The original extrusion pasta machine was the Venetian *bigolo*, producing a kind of extremely long fresh spaghetti for which the dough had first been kneaded by hand. The recent electric extrusion pasta machines, whether for home or restaurant use, produce a rather tough product not recognizable as fresh pasta. It is too bad that many restaurants present this type of pasta as "fresh" pasta. An in-between type, neither dried nor fresh, it rarely gives satisfaction to a true pasta lover.

then there is the threat of a raw flour taste remaining when the pasta is cooked. Instead, you can use a piece of equipment specifically designed for drying pasta. We looked at a number of wooden pasta-drying racks but found their capacity too small and their construction flimsy. This Bartelt drying screen is clearly the best tool for the task. The pasta does not stick to or fall through the 12″ by 16″ galvanized steel mesh screen. Air circulates freely above and below the pasta.

Although a simple design, the rack is sturdy and well constructed. The metal braces, which elevate the birch frame, snap off or fold down so the screen can be stored flat with trays or cookie sheets. If you usually make your pasta in large batches, buy two because you will fill the screen capacity quickly. Also, in a pinch, you might use the screen as a cooling rack for your *biscotti*.

STRAPS

SPAGHETTI   FETTUCCINE   LASAGNA

crawford

SHAPING & CUTTING PASTA

If you are making stuffed pasta like ravioli or cappelletti, you should work with the dough immediately, while it is still slightly moist and flexible. Your filling should be mixed and ready to use. The shapes can be completely free-form, or you can select from a number of stamps and molds. Your main concern is to be sure that the filled shapes are firmly sealed, or the pasta will split apart while it boils, leaving you with "filling soup."

If you are making noodles, you should allow the sheets of dough to dry, uncovered, on a towel for at least 15 minutes and up to 1 hour, until they feel a bit like soft leather. This will prevent them from sticking together as they are cut. Then either roll the sheets up and cut them into the desired width, or attach the cutting blades of the pasta machine and feed the dough through the blades. In one side goes an amorphous sheet of dough; out the other side comes tagliatelle or fettuccine.

PASTA SHAPES & DRIED VS. FRESH PASTA

❧ EDWARD GIOBBI ❧

Although there are always exceptions, there are general rules that match certain types of pasta with certain sauces: thin pasta with fish and seafood sauces, cut pasta with meats and vegetables, egg pasta with meat sauces and cream sauces. But be flexible and use the rules only as a guide. The marriage should be one in which the pasta complements the sauce and the sauce does not overwhelm the pasta. For example, linguine is considered the right thing for a white clam sauce because its thin, flat shape enables it to absorb more of the liquid in that particular sauce than a thicker pasta would. But should you want to use a cut pasta like *farfalle* with a thin sauce, a good solution is to cook the pasta until it is almost done and then finish cooking it with the clam sauce (without the clams in it, and adding a little more liquid, such as white wine); that way the pasta will become saturated with the sauce, and you have solved the problem.

Perhaps the biggest rip-off in the food industry today is what is touted as "fresh" pasta. It's impossible to cook it properly because it has not been allowed to dry as it should, and the result is a tangled, gluey mess. When homemade pasta is prepared, it should be dried at least an hour before it is cut and at least another hour before it is cooked; actually, the longer the pasta dries, the better it will cook. Soft pasta will not separate properly in the boiling water, and it cannot be cooked al dente because it cooks unevenly and too quickly.

So why is the pasta not properly dried? The answer is obviously economic: drying requires space and additional labor. If you have any doubts on the subject, buy a package of dried fettuccine (egg noodles) imported from Italy and cook them according to instructions. At the same time cook "fresh" fettuccine, and then compare. Anyone who has a taste for pasta will agree that this is one of the rare instances when fresh is not best.

14.4, 14.5, & 14.6
SCI SQUARE PASTA STAMP
FOX RUN ROUND PASTA STAMP
SCI ROUND PASTA STAMP

These three cookie cutter–like devices are used for making *pasta ripiena* (stuffed pasta) such as *tortelloni* and ravioli. One of the stamps forms 2½" squares, which may be filled and then folded into triangles to form *pansoti*. The Fox Run 2½"-diameter circle forms rounds that may be filled and folded into the half-moon *agnolotti*, which, deep-fried, becomes *panzarotti* ("little bellies"). SCI's small, 2"-diameter cutter is used to make tortellini. Unlike regular cookie cutters, the bottoms of pasta stamps have tightly zigzagged edges, which cut and firmly seal two layers of dough around a filling. The cutting end is solidly attached to a lacquered, natural wood knob, which is easy to grasp and use.

14.7 VILLAWARE PASTA JAGGER

This fluted wheel jagger is used to make the familiar ruffled edges of lasagne, ravioli, and *farfalle* (butterfly-shaped pasta) or to spruce up the lattice strips on top of a *crostata di ricotta* (cheese tart). Known in Italian as a *rotella pasta*, the jagger's 1½"-diameter stainless steel wheel is held firmly in a nickel-steel frame set into a polished wood handle, and is of top quality.

14.8 CHITARRA

A modern version of an old provincial device, this rectangular, cast-aluminum-and-wood frame strung with steel wires—called a *chitarra*, or "guitar," for its resemblance to that instrument—is still used to make spaghetti. A thin sheet of rolled-out pasta dough is placed across the *chitarra* wires and then gently pressed through with your hand or a rolling pin. The spaghetti thus formed will fall neatly onto a sliding Masonite tray beneath. This *chitarra*, unlike some of the old, hand-fashioned ones, is strung with wires on both sides, ⅛" apart on one side and ¹/₁₆" apart on the other, to produce two different widths of noodles. The frame is 19" long, 8½" wide, and 4½" high, with the wires attached to aluminum terminals at each end. Should the wires slacken, they can be tightened by turning the thick aluminum nuts on one end of the frame.

14.9 FUSILLI PIN

This instrument looks so much like a double-pointed knitting needle that one might very well ask, what's it doing in the kitchen? This simple, handy gadget of heavy-gauge steel, 12¼" long, is for shaping the curly fusilli noodles. To make fusilli, take a long, thin strip of fresh pasta and wrap it around this pin like the stripes on an old-fashioned barber pole. Then push it down and off and you have one fusilli as twisty as Shirley Temple's long-gone curls.

TORTELLINI WITH NAVY BEAN SAUCE

6 to 8 servings

½ pound uncooked navy or white beans
2 tablespoons olive oil
1 cup finely chopped onion
1 tablespoon finely chopped garlic
1 cup chopped fresh tomato
2 tablespoons tomato paste
7 cups chicken broth
¼ teaspoon fresh ground white pepper
1 pound tortellini, with the filling of your choice, cooked
2 tablespoons chopped fresh basil

1 Cover the beans with water and soak for at least 8 hours, or, if you are in a hurry, boil the water-covered beans for 2 minutes, then set aside for 1 hour to soak. Drain the beans of the soaking water.

2 In a 3-quart saucepan, heat the olive oil over medium heat. Add the onion and cook for 1 minute. Stir often. Mix in the garlic and cook for 30 seconds. Add the tomato and tomato paste, stir, and cook for a moment. Add the beans, chicken broth, and pepper; bring to a boil; reduce the heat, and simmer, uncovered, for 1½ hours.

3 Pour the bean mixture into the bowl of a blender or food processor and process into a purée. Adjust the consistency with more stock if necessary. The sauce should be the thickness of a rich tomato sauce. Return to the saucepan and keep warm.

4 Add the cooked tortellini and the basil to the sauce and toss to combine. Serve.

John Doherty, Executive Chef of The Waldorf-Astoria, New York City

After drying, fusilli can be used with an array of sauces, especially those with rich or creamy mixtures of meat and vegetables.

14.10, 14.11, & 14.12
VILLAWARE 2½" SQUARE RAVIOLI MOLD
VILLAWARE 2" ROUND RAVIOLI MOLD
VILLAWARE 2" SQUARE RAVIOLI MOLD

These high-quality molds consist of two rectangular plates: one of cast aluminum with a raised zigzag pattern, and the other, which resembles an egg carton, of plastic. To use them, cut a sheet of pasta dough into two rectangles, each slightly larger than the ravioli plates. Sprinkle the top of the metal plate and the bottom of the plastic plate with flour, and tap off the excess. Place one rectangle of dough over the zigzag plate and gently press the plastic plate into it to stretch the dough and form pockets. Remove the top plate, fill the pockets with your favorite ravioli stuffing, and then, using a small pastry brush dipped in water, moisten the dough along the zigzag lines before topping it with the other rectangle of dough. Run a rolling pin back and forth over the dough until all the ravioli are cut and tightly sealed. Turn the plate upside down and tap it on the counter to release the pasta.

The ravioli plate is available in three styles. One will make twelve 2" square ravioli, and the second makes ten 2½" square ravioli; both come packaged with small rolling pins that are easy to maneuver over the forms. The third style makes twelve 2" round, fluted ravioli, and does not have a rolling pin included.

RAVIOLI

Ravioli appears to have been invented by thrifty sailors of Genoa who saved leftovers while at sea to be stuffed into pasta for another meal. The Genoese claim the name even comes from a word in their dialect—*rabiole,* meaning "something of little value." If indeed ravioli originated with Genoese nautical orts, they have nonetheless evolved into one of the more sophisticated forms of pasta, yet one of the easiest to make. Although they can be made free-form with a sheet of pasta and a cutting tool, special molds will give your ravioli a more uniform, professional result. You will be amazed at the quantity of ravioli you can turn out quickly. Moreover, once made, ravioli may be frozen.

14.13 SCI RAVIOLI MOLD

It was love at first sight when we saw this ravioli mold, and, after numerous *piatti de ravioli,* we are still smitten. Given all the attractive qualities of this particular ravioli maker, it's hardly surprising. The top and bottom plates are molded of a high-quality but lightweight plastic and are connected to each other. That means that you can toss it into a drawer or cupboard to store without worry of losing a part or damaging other kitchen tools. Used in the same manner as the traditional molds, its zigzag cutting edges are particularly sharp and well defined so you will need very little effort to cut and seal the ravioli. The end of the top plate is curved upward and grooved, which makes it easy to grasp for lifting and lowering, even with hands that are floured or sticky with stuffing. This model comes in white and makes twelve 2" square ravioli.

14.14 VILLAWARE GNOCCHI PADDLE

Although the making and cooking of gnocchi have more in common with dumplings than with pasta, the Italians treat gnocchi like pasta; that is, as a first course served with a sauce. The people of Tuscany, in fact, refer to their spinach gnocchi as *ravioli nudi* ("nude ravioli"), meaning the filling is naked of its pasta. *Gnocco* is a colloquial term for a person whose personality is that of a "lump." There are many forms of gnocchi, and the starch used to make them varies by region. They may be made of cornmeal, of potatoes, or of semolina, milk, and eggs, for example; some are dropped by 2 teaspoons into boiling broth or water, while others are baked. This 8" long by 2½" wide beechwood paddle is traditionally used for potato gnocchi, which are made of flour and cooked potato dough rolled into ropes and then cut into about 1"-long pieces. The dumplings could be cooked at that point, but rolling them on the board makes them ridged to capture more sauce than if they had a smooth surface. The dumplings are then boiled in salted water, sauced, and served. The paddle can also be used to make *garganelli,* a pasta specialty of Bologna made by wrapping 1½" squares of fresh dough point-first around a small wooden dowel or a pencil, and then rolling them over the board to form ridges. The results look like ridged penne.

MAKING PASTA BY MACHINE

At the outset, we should make it clear that by "pasta machine" we mean the type that rolls and stretches the dough, not the type that mixes and extrudes it. To use the former type of machine, take a piece of dough the size of a large lemon and feed it through the rollers, which should be adjusted to the widest setting. When you have done this five or six times, folding the dough in halves or thirds after each passage, it will become uniform and smooth. Then, set the rollers a notch closer together and begin to stretch the dough. Instead of folding it, pass the elongating shape through the rollers over and over again, moving the rollers closer together every few times, until the dough is the thinness you desire. After ten trips through the machine, it will become a long strip of well-kneaded, perfectly stretched pasta dough.

WHAT TO LOOK FOR

Good machines are available in hand-crank varieties and in versions with motorized rollers and cutters (again, not extrusion machines). Whether manually operated or electric, the machines work in the same way and produce equally good pasta. At a cursory glance, most pasta machines look alike, but there are some important details to consider.

Stability The machine should have some heft to it. The better ones are made entirely from steel in one form or another and will feel compact and slightly weighty. However, none of them should be too heavy to be easily lifted. (Those with inner plastic parts are too lightweight.) They should include a set of sturdy clamps that firmly affix the machine to the counter.

Construction The rollers and cutting blades should be made of a nonreactive material like stainless steel. The handle or the motor that turns the rollers should fit firmly into the machine so that they do not slip out during use. Test the store's demo model to be sure. Check to see how many width adjustments the rollers accommodate. Since the dough should be stretched gradually, all the way to paper thin if desired, nine gradations are ideal. Turn the knob that adjusts the settings to make sure it gives you a definite feel or clear marking of the change from one setting to another. There should also be cutters in at least two widths. If the rollers or the cutting blades are separate from the base of the machine, make sure that they attach firmly to the base.

Noise Keep in mind that even the most expensive motors that drive the machines are made in a country that believes that the sound of a Ferrari engine is music to the ear. They will be noisy, but, like the car, they get you where you're going so quickly that you hardly have time to notice.

14.15 TRATTORINA PASTA MACHINE

Trattorina translates to "little restaurant," and that is what your kitchen will feel like when you set up this very professional, but home-scale, hand-crank pasta machine. This sturdy, intelligently designed, and well-constructed machine stands 8" high on an 11" by 9½" base and weighs 13 pounds. The front of the machine has a smooth, rounded steel protrusion below the rollers (a bit like a potbelly) that supports the pasta as it is stretched into longer and longer pieces. The workings of this sleek machine are made from one piece of nonrusting chrome-plated steel; hence, there are no small parts to break or fall off. The rollers and cutters are stainless steel with a coating of nickel on the underside, which prevents the pasta from sticking or breaking. Indeed, the dough and the noodles flow smoothly and effortlessly from this machine. The rollers have nine settings for thickness, which are easily adjusted with a smooth-action knob marked with easy-to-see numbers. The rollers are 7⅘" wide as opposed to the average 5½" of most machines. This means not only that you can turn out more pasta at one time but also that you will have wider strips for making lasagne or for cutting into rounds or squares to make special shapes. The cutting blades, permanently attached to the machine above the rollers, make fettuccine and *tagliolini* (somewhat narrower noodles). The machine comes with two strong clamps that firmly secure the base to the counter. It has a well-balanced, detachable crank that fits securely into the machine. Use a soft brush or, as the manufacturer suggests, an old toothbrush, to clean the rollers and cutters after use. An instructional video and a ravioli attachment are available, although both are sold separately.

14.16 KITCHENAID PASTA ROLLER SET

If you own a KitchenAid stand mixer and love to make pasta, your prayers are answered. Although this three-piece attachment is not made directly by KitchenAid, it has the same quality of design and construction that we

THE NATIONAL MUSEUM OF PASTA FOODS, ROME, ITALY

The National Museum of Pasta Foods, housed in a fourteenth-century palace, has eleven rooms devoted to the history, folklore, manufacture, cooking, and eating of pasta.

Italians have been justifiably sensitive about the myth of Marco Polo discovering pasta in Asia; pasta had been part of the Italian diet for at least three hundred years prior to Polo's travels. Posted on the first display panel in the museum is a document, dated 1154—a century before Polo's birth—clearly stating that a traveler from Arabia observed Sicilians producing pasta for export to all Christian and Muslim countries. Other documents confirm that Genoa was making pasta in 1244, Naples in 1295, and Bologna in 1338.

The remaining rooms contain displays that illustrate how Italians developed a simple mixture of flour and water into a craft, a major business, and an international passion. You will discover how pasta was born, how it evolved, and how Italy's creation of dry semolina pasta allowed it to be preserved in perfect condition for months or even years. You will even learn why pasta cooked al dente is more easily digested. There are exhibits of antique pasta-making devices, machinery, taped cooking lessons, and numerous rare prints.

The National Museum of Pasta Foods
Piazza Scanderbeg, 114-120
00187 Rome, Italy
Telephone: 39-06-699119
Fax: 39-06-6991109

FLAVORED PASTAS

❧ MARIO BATALI ❧

Pastas flavored with anything from black squid ink to roasted beets are served all over Italy in both traditional and creative kitchens. My favorite variations include puréed blanched chives, lemon thyme, golden or purple beets, roasted red peppers, and red wine. In this country, pasta producers have taken the concept to unfortunate extremes with such variations as licorice, strawberry, and chocolate.

To infuse basic pasta with herbs or cooked vegetables, first chop or purée your intended addition—2 to 3 tablespoons per pound of pasta—to the texture of fine flour. Incorporate the flavoring agent by stirring or blending it into the eggs and carefully kneading it into the pasta as usual. The ball formed may be too wet, in which case extended kneading with a little extra flour may be necessary. From this point, proceed as you would with the basic pasta recipe, being especially gentle in the rolling machine because flavored pastas tear more easily.

expect from the company. The pasta roller set is, in fact, made by Marcato, the Italian company that also makes the Atlas machine. It has the same well-designed rollers with nine setting adjustments for thickness. The set has a good weight and a compact feel and comes with a roller attachment and two cutting blades, one for fettuccine and the other for a thinner noodle, *linguine fini*. A cleaning brush is also included. The set is chrome plated and features tempered steel gears. The rollers have a layer of copper on the underside, which prevents the dough from sticking and breaking so the pasta flows through easily. To use the attachment, you remove the hub above the Kitchen-Aid logo (where the meat grinder fits on the stand mixer), insert the attachment, and turn on the machine. After rolling the dough, remove the rollers and insert either of the cutters. Because the mixer stands high, there is a longer distance from the rollers to the counter and you will find that you can handle longer pieces of dough, cutting down on the time it takes to feed what you have made through the machine.

14.17 ATLAS PASTA MACHINE

This *macchina per pasta* will make child's play of rolling out dough. It is a sturdy, well-made machine with a 7½" by 5¼" chromed steel base and nickel-steel kneading and cutting rollers. The sheets of pasta are on the narrow side, but are easy to cut and, if desired, fill for ravioli. The detachable cutting head that comes

PASUTICE, FUZI, PAPPARDELLE

6 servings

Pasutice and *fuzi* are unique to Istria and are always made fresh at home. As legend goes, a young man courting a woman would go to her house, and after having had *fuzi* for the Sunday dinner would reach for the wooden board the dough had been rolled on. If he found traces of the old dough on the board, that was the end of the courtship. The Istrian pastas known as *pasutice* and *fuzi* represent two stages of a single process. *Fuzi*, served mostly with game and meat sauce, is simply *pasutice* (best with seafood sauces) carried one step further.

4 cups unbleached flour
2 eggs, beaten
½ teaspoon salt
1 teaspoon olive oil
½ cup warm water

1 On a marble or wooden surface, make a mound of 3½ cups of the flour, reserving ½ cup, and form a well at the mound's center. Place the eggs, salt, and olive oil in the well and, while beating with a fork to incorporate all the ingredients, add the water slowly, in a thin stream.
2 Sprinkle your hands liberally with the reserved flour, rubbing them together to remove any scraps of dough from your skin. With a knife, loosen any dough attached to the work surface and knead the mass for 20 minutes, or use a mixer to process it, until smooth and satiny. Allow

the dough to rest 2 hours in a covered bowl, refrigerated, before rolling it out.
3 Cut the rested dough into four parts and roll them out one at a time on a lightly floured surface until very thin, or feed the dough through the rollers of a pasta machine at successively narrower settings, stopping short of the narrowest opening. With a knife, cut the dough into 1½" strips. Flour them lightly and lay them atop one another, forming three stacks, then cut the strips crosswise at a slight angle at 2" intervals, forming lozenges. At this point you have *pasutice*.
4 To convert *pasutice* to *fuzi*, roll the pasta lozenges around the tip of the left index finger (assuming right-handedness) or the tip of a wooden dowel, pressing ends lightly as they meet and overlap, to form quill shapes. Line them up on a

floured clean kitchen towel or a cornmeal-dusted baking sheet until they are to be cooked.
5 To cook, bring 6 quarts of water to a boil with 1 tablespoon of coarse salt. Drop in the pasta a handful at a time, stirring it as it drops into the boiling water. Mix well and cook until the water reaches a full boil and pasta rises to the top, approximately 3 to 5 minutes. Drain well and coat with the sauce of your choice.

To make *pappardelle* use the same recipe and procedures as for *pasutice*. When you have cut the dough into 1½" strips and have formed the stacks, cut the stacks at 5" intervals. At this point you will have ribbonlike pasta, *pappardelle*. Set them on a clean kitchen towel dusted with flour and cook.

La Cucina di Lidia, by Lidia Bastianich

---

with the machine has two settings: one will cut fettuccine, and the other, *tagliolini*. Optional cutting heads sold separately will turn your kitchen into a veritable pasta factory—we enjoyed using the linguine, spaghetti, *pappardelle, capelli d'angelo, trenette,* and a narrow, wavy-edged *lasagne ricce*. The machine stands 5¼" high, has nine roller widths, comes with a detachable handle, and has a C-clamp that secures it to the work surface. To clean stray bits of dry dough, use a small brush; do not wash in water.

No man is alone while eating spaghetti—it requires so much attention.

—CHRISTOPHER MORLEY

14.18 PASTADRIVE MOTOR FOR ATLAS PASTA MACHINE

When you are kneading and cutting dough in a pasta machine, one hand turns the crank while the other feeds the dough into one side of the rollers and then quickly moves to the other side to catch the dough or noodles as they emerge from the other side. It is not a difficult action, but if you find it so, this electric motor will simplify the operation. It replaces the crank so that the rollers and cutters turn

electrically, freeing up both hands to feed and catch the pasta. It definitely speeds up the process and makes for a more uniform product, especially in the initial kneading stage. Approximately 7" by 5½", it is surprisingly lightweight and easy to attach and detach, which you will need to do when switching it from the rollers to the cutters. It comes with a detachable polarized plug.

14.19 TRATTORINA *RAVIOLERA*

In general, we are not fans of machine ravioli makers. They never

COOKING PASTA

Now that your pasta is made, you must cook it. Keep in mind that in Italy, pasta is usually served as a first course, to be followed by a second course, so it is a modest-size portion. Together, both courses should equal one normal American-size main dish. A total of 2 to 4 ounces per person, depending on the sauce, should be your guide.

Homemade pasta cooks in a very short time and requires much less boiling than dry pasta. Using 5 to 7 quarts of water per pound of pasta will keep the starch from building up and making the pasta gluey. Add salt to the water as it comes to a boil—not before—and then add the pasta (all at the same time so it cooks evenly), pushing it down gently until it is all submerged. To keep the pasta separate, stir it frequently until the water returns to the boil. Some cooks add a tablespoon of olive oil, but this is not a common Italian practice. (Italians may do it with stuffed pasta so the pieces will slide against each other and not break apart, or with very fine pasta such as *capellini* so the strands won't stick together.) Do not cook filled pasta at a roiling boil—they may break.

To test the doneness of pasta, take out a piece and bite it. Italians cook dry pasta to a point where there is still some resistance, and fresh pasta until it is tender completely through.

"I love it. Who did it?"

seem to seal the pasta as well as the trays, which are also easy to use. This 5½-pound stainless steel, chromium-plated attachment is an exception. The rollers, which stamp and seal the pasta, are designed so that they firmly press the pasta sheets together while discouraging the filling from entering the sealed area. The sealing-cutting rollers are made of heavy-duty plastic with well-defined zigzags. There are two wooden dowels, which support the pasta sheets, and the underside of the attachment is lined with nickel to prevent sticking or breaking. To use the *raviolera*, fold a long sheet of pasta dough in half and place the folded end into the rollers, giving them a quarter turn. Open the sheet up, like a book, and place a few spoonfuls of filling into the opening. As you turn the handle the rollers pull the filling between the pasta sheets and the plastic blade seals and cuts the sheet into 2"-square ravioli. There will be four pieces across; the number lengthwise will depend on the length of your pasta. The attachment fits firmly onto the base and uses the same handle that turns the rollers of the machine.

14.20 BEEBO *CAVATELLI* MAKER

This machine is for those who are mad for *cavatelli*, those short, curled noodles whose shell-like ridged surface captures and holds the flavors of a sauce. A specialty of the *Puglia* (Apulia) region of Italy (the heel of the boot) and known regionally as *cavatieddi, cavatelli* may be made from simple egg pasta dough or one with ricotta cheese added. To make *cavatelli* with this *cavatelliatore,* feed a strip of very stiff pasta dough that has been rolled to a thickness of ⅜" into the machine, working it slowly and steadily with one hand while turning the handle with the other. The texture and thickness of the dough are important, so do follow the directions enclosed in the box. The machine does the rest, and the

The simplest ingredients achieve harmony and beauty when brought together in classic proportions. If too much sauce has been added, the dish becomes a soupy mess. Too much cheese in the correct amount of sauce dries it out and glues the spaghetti so that you cannot twirl it. Most importantly, it overpowers the flavor of the sauce and ruins the dish.

—FRED PLOTKIN,
The Authentic Pasta Book

fun is all yours. The rollers send the dough past a drum set with two tiny blades, which cut the dough into small pieces and press them against the drum's ridged lining; the charmingly seashell-patterned pasta will fall from the other side. This *cavatelli* maker is made of cast aluminum, stands 9½" high, and has a C-clamp attached to it. The machine also makes a firm potato *cavatelli,* a variation that is akin to gnocci.

MAKING & COOKING SPAETZLE

THE WORD *Spätzle* (English *spaetzle*) means "little sparrows" in German, but in culinary terms it refers to tiny morsels of dough that are best defined as something between fresh pasta and dumplings. Some cookbooks describe the size of the dumplings to be that of "small walnuts"; others think they should be "not much larger than oversized rice." The wide range of these descriptions testifies to the popularity of spaetzle in the regional food cultures of central Europe. They are common on the dinner tables of the southwestern parts of Germany as well as in Hungary, Austria, and the Alsace region of France. There is also an Italian first cousin served in soups, *passatelli,* which like spaetzle are made from a simple batter pushed through a colander or food mill into boiling liquid. Easy and quick to make, these little nuggets are a delicate but comforting side dish to a variety of roasts, especially those with rich, thick sauces and gravies. Toasted in butter with bread crumbs, spaetzle are the traditional and delicious accompaniment to sauerbraten. They are also added to soups and stews and served alongside goulash.

Spaetzle are made from flour, eggs, and milk or water, and are seasoned with salt and nutmeg or paprika. The resulting mixture should be between a stiff pancake batter and a very loose bread dough. There are a number of ways to transform the batter into dump-

lings. Stiffer dough may be pinched into small pieces by hand or snipped with scissors and dropped into boiling water or soup. Looser dough can be worked with a wooden spoon through a colander or scraped from a board. The simplest way is to use a special device that forms, cuts, and drops the spaetzle into the water.

Spaetzle are not difficult to make, but a few pointers will ensure your success. Cook small batches in lots of well-salted, boiling water: the dumplings need space between them in order to cook properly. To avoid the possibility of burning yourself with steam, be sure that the water is not too high in the pot and that the boil is not too rapid. Once the dumplings float to the surface, let them cook another 30 seconds to a minute longer, or until they lose their floury taste, then drain them immediately. Since they cook so fast, make only enough for one round of servings. If people want seconds (they probably will), return to the batter, which will hold for a couple of hours, and make another batch. Spaetzle makers vary in size and shape according to the regional cuisine in which the dumpling originated. Choose your maker by determining what shape spaetzle you wish to make. Whichever one you choose, remember to wash (or soak) it immediately after use or the dough will harden and become difficult to dislodge. And dry it immediately, too.

14.21 BRASS NOODLE PRESS

At first glance, this lovely brass object appears to be an exotic grinder or mill of some kind, but it's actually an Indian noodle press. Indian-spiced noodles, or *saive*, are deep-fried and eaten as snacks, usually around eleven in the morning or at midafternoon. *Saive* made of chickpea-flour dough are the most popular of all, and they may be flavored with a single spice like anise or caraway seeds, or with a mixture of spices. Once cooked, *saive* can be stored in an airtight container for up to a month. This *saive* maker has six parts: a central cylinder, open at both ends; four interchangeable discs—perforated with small holes, medium holes, thin slots, and a large single star—that fit on the bottom of the cylinder; and a flat disc-shaped press attached to a spiral shaft with a top and handle that drive the dough downward inside the cylinder. The unit is 6" high and 2¾" in diameter. To make *saive*, drop the disc of your choice into the cylinder, place some dough on top of it, and attach the press. Turn the handle while moving the press slowly over a pan of hot oil. In just a few minutes the golden, curled noodles will be done and ready to serve.

EGG SPAETZLE

4 servings

1 cup plus 2 tablespoons sifted all-purpose flour
⅛ teaspoon freshly grated nutmeg
½ teaspoon salt
1 extra-large egg
6 tablespoons milk
3 tablespoons unsalted butter or margarine, melted

1 Combine the flour, nutmeg, and salt in a small bowl and make a well in the center.

2 Whisk the egg with the milk in a measuring cup, pour into the well in the dry ingredients, and beat hard with a wooden spoon until the batter is bubbly and elastic (or mix the batter in a food processor, then give it 3 to 4 one-minute pulses until smooth and elastic).

3 Push the batter through a spaetzle maker into a large kettle of rapidly boiling salted water. Cook the spaetzle, uncovered, for 8 minutes, stirring occasionally. With a slotted spoon, lift the

spaetzle to a large bowl of ice water and let stand until ready to serve—but no longer than 1 to 2 hours.

4 Drain the spaetzle well in a colander, then warm for 4 to 5 minutes in the melted butter in a large sauté pan over moderately low heat, stirring now and then. Serve at once.

If the flour in your area contains a high proportion of hard wheat, as it does in much of the West and Midwest, you may need to reduce the amount of flour in this recipe by about ¼ cup to achieve a workable spaetzle batter.

The New German Cookbook, by Jean Anderson and Hedy Würz

14.22 KULL SWABIAN SPAETZLE PRESS

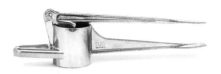

From Swabia in southwestern Germany comes this extremely sturdy cast-aluminum gadget for making thin, rather long strands of spaetzle, which are much more like noodles than dumplings. Measuring 16" long, with a 3" diameter and a 3½"-deep container, this spaetzle maker works like a potato ricer: the hinged upper handle with its attached circular press forces dough through the perforations in the bottom of the container. Since the holes are less than ⅛" in diameter, the noodles produced are very thin and elegant. To make short noodles, rest the dough-filled press above the boiling water and squeeze the handles together; for longer noodles hold it about 5" above the water. The press works best if rinsed with cold water before filling or refilling. The dough should not be too stiff. Cooked potatoes, vegetables, and fruits could also be puréed with this press, but it is not as effective as a ricer for making mashed potatoes. Wash and dry it immediately after using.

14.23 VILLAWARE AUSTRIAN SPAETZLE-MAKER

This spaetzle maker is made of tinned steel with a handle of shellacked wood. It has two parts: a perforated tray—13" long and 4½" wide—and a 3"-deep, cone-shaped hopper that is almost 5" across at the top and 3" at the bottom. To make spaetzle, rest the tray across a pot of boiling water so the small hook on its bottom catches on the side of the pot. Put some dough in the hopper, press it lightly, and slide the hopper across the tray. The dough is forced through the perforations and then cut as you press and slide the hopper again. This maker produced tiny spaetzle, just a bit larger than cooked grains of rice.

14.24 SCI SPAETZLE MAKER

This item from SCI is similar in construction to the Austrian maker

above. The perforated tray is 10" long and 4" wide, and has a plastic handle on one end. The 3"-wide hopper is square and about 2" deep; it fits well into the tracks of the tray, moving back and forth smoothly and easily. The spaetzle produced are small, satisfying, teardrop-shaped dumplings, almost like bits of thick noodles.

14.25 ZENKER SPAETZLE MAKER

Resembling nothing so much as a food mill, this sturdy spaetzle maker is constructed of tinned steel and wood. Its bowl is a generous 2½" deep and 7" in diameter, with ¼"-wide perforated holes. The implement has two feet that grip one side of the pan to stabilize it and a 7"-long wire handle on the other. The wooden handle on top turns a disc that forces the dough through the mill and forms the spaetzle, dropping them into the water below. Depending on the consistency of your batter, a reverse action may be required to release dumplings, which will be round morsels about the size of a raisin, from the grates. The maker comes apart for easy cleaning.

THE DIFFERENCE BETWEEN
COOKING FOR A FAMILY & A RESTAURANT
❧ LIDIA MATTICCHIO BASTIANICH ❧

In a restaurant, people are dining on different items at different times, unlike the home setting, where you plan a meal, cook it, and serve it to everybody at the same time. You need much more planning and programmed prep work in a restaurant because the timing required for the dishes served is so different from that required at home. As a result, you do not have a one-man band but need orchestration and teamwork. Like a conductor, the chef needs to direct so that the right notes come out at the same time to create perfect harmony; it's a delicious challenge indeed.

Another difference between home cooking and professional cooking is in the quantity. How do you handle 20 pounds of spinach, 30 pounds of onion, 40 heads of garlic, or 100 servings of sauce? You need bigger pots, pans, ovens, and ranges. Cooking professionally also requires bringing professional expertise to the marketplace. The chef's ability to find the best products is the first step. Then comes one of the most important aspects: the chef's creativity when using these products. The chef must be able to apply different techniques and have equipment that delivers the best results—high-heat griddles, convection ovens, brick wood ovens, copious steamers, and so on. Even the chef's knife skills will give a different edge to the end result.

Restaurant dining has often been likened to theater. To me it's more like a concert filling a dining room with chords of flavor worthy of applause.

15

BREAD- & PIZZA-MAKING EQUIPMENT

THE BEAUTY OF BREAD-MAKING is in the simplicity of its basic ingredients: flour, salt, water, and leavening. An experienced baker innately understands the chemistry of these ingredients and uses this knowledge to transform a batch of dough into a fragrant loaf of bread. It can be done with no special tools: just your hands, a flat surface, and an oven. But today, in a modern home kitchen, the use of proper equipment can help your baking and ensure that you make delicious bread.

Measuring

Before you begin you must measure your ingredients. Where dry ingredients are concerned, using volume measures invites disaster. For example, a cup of flour can weigh between 3 and 5 ounces depending on how it is scooped. Serious cooks know that a proper scale is an essential piece of equipment, and rely on it to measure all ingredients in a recipe, including the liquid. In fact, commercial bread recipes are written in a type of code; each ingredient is expressed as a percentage of the total weight of the flour in the recipe. This way, any recipe may be easily scaled up or down to make two or two hundred loaves.

A good thermometer is also important for the bread-making process. Yeast is a living organism that thrives at temperatures between 70°F and 120°F; outside of that range it may stay dormant or die. The baker needs to control the temperature in order to know when to push the dough or let it rise more slowly. Instant-read thermometers measure the temperature of ingredients and dough at all stages—from the flour and water going into the dough to the temperature of the final baked loaf. Select a thermometer with a temperature range of at least 40°F to 220°F.

Kneading & Mixing Devices

The magic of bread-making begins once you start to mix your dough. In this process, the protein in wheat flour comes into contact with water and a strong elastic bond called *gluten* is created. As the dough is kneaded, a marriage takes place between the flour, water, salt, and leaven so that a living, active dough mass is created. The proper development of the gluten bond contributes to the quality of the bread dough, so that it bakes into a flavorful and fully risen loaf.

Kneading is a critical part of bread-making, and the equipment you use and the way you use it will greatly enhance the quality of the bread you produce. For the true artisan, all the equipment necessary to knead dough is a pair of strong arms. However, you'll find that a wide-mouthed ceramic bowl and a wire bread whisk simplify the initial step of blending the first few cups of flour into the water.

Even though everyone should experience kneading bread by hand, it won't take many batches to comprehend the French expression *être dans le pétrin,* which means "to be in the dough-kneading trough," i.e., to be in trouble or in a fix. This refers to the obstacles faced by the baker before mechanical mixers were invented to help cope with 60 or 70 pounds (27 or 32 kilos) of flour at a time. Despite the Roman invention of horse-drawn rotating kneaders in the fifth century B.C., mechanical kneaders did not become widespread until the nineteenth century.

Fortunately, the home baker today has more options when it comes to kneading, including the use of the versatile stand mixer. The two main criteria for selecting a stand mixer for making bread dough are the power of the motor and the capacity of the bowl. Select the most powerful machine you can afford, one with at least a 450-watt motor, multiple speeds, a dough hook, and a bowl that holds at least 5 quarts. The mixer itself should have a heavy base for stability. Mixing bread dough strains even the most rugged machines; when mixing a heavy, wet dough like brioche dough, the motor casing on the machine may heat up.

The food processor, once thought of as a tool used exclusively for cutting, chopping, and puréeing, can also mix bread dough when properly used. The machine should have a capacity of at least 11 to 14 cups; although it has a smaller capacity than a stand mixer, it can make the same amount of dough or more because the mixing time is much shorter—only 45 seconds. In 5 to 10 minutes of mixing successive batches of dough in a food processor, you can knead as much as 10 pounds of dough, more than double the amount it would take most stand mixers to knead in the same amount of time. The brief mixing time and the fact that the processor blends with a swift cutting motion exposes bread dough to less oxygen than the stand mixer. As a result, bread baked from dough mixed in a food processor retains more of the golden color of the wheat and may retain more vitamin E than bread dough mixed by other methods. For making most types of bread, the metal cutting blade outperforms the plastic dough blade included with some models. Typically, this blunt dough blade drags through the dough, heating it excessively and exposing it to more damaging oxygen.

Bowls for Fermenting

Bread dough and wine share a common ingredient—yeast—and like wine, bread dough ferments. As the yeast enzymes in the dough feed on starches and sugars in the flour, alcohol and carbon dioxide gas are released. As these gases build up, air bubbles form and are caught in the elastic web of the bread dough; miraculously, the bread rises. Some of the simplest breads benefit from a prolonged, cool rising, which gives the dough a chance to extract the maximum flavor from the ingredients. The heat conductivity of metal makes stainless steel bowls poor containers for rising dough. Use a heavy ceramic, glass, or plastic bowl instead. Select a bowl or container just large enough to accommodate the dough when it has tripled in volume. Anything larger will leave too much headroom where cool air could accumulate and suppress rising. In a smaller container, the dough will rise and stick to its covering. Dough rapidly forms a crust when exposed to air, so a container with its own lid is helpful, as is a roll of heavy plastic.

Other Equipment

Most breads benefit from a burst of steam when placed in the oven, and hearth breads must be steamed or the intense heat will seal the crust and prevent it from fully expanding. Steam energizes the yeast, protects the surface of the dough so that the bread rises fully while baking, and gelatinizes surface starch, giving the baked bread a shiny crust. You can introduce steam in a home oven by placing an empty cast-iron pan on the lowest rack or the bottom of your oven as it preheats, then adding hot water to create steam once the bread is placed in the oven.

KNEADING DOUGH BY A BREAD MACHINE VS. OTHER METHODS

According to P. J. Hamel, senior editor at the King Arthur Flour catalogue, tests at the company have found that bread dough kneaded in a bread machine is kneaded more thoroughly and effectively than dough mixed by a stand mixer or by hand. Tests there also showed that bread kneaded in a food processor rose slightly less than bread kneaded in a bread machine, though the food processor produced a creamier-looking loaf.

Metal and plastic dough scrapers are useful. Metal scrapers or a wide-blade knife help divide dough for forming into loaves A razor-sharp blade, or *lame*, is needed to score the dough. For an attractive, rustic appearance, use a fine-mesh sifter to sprinkle flour on your loaves before scoring and baking.

COUCHES & BANNETONS

WHEN MAKING HEARTH BREADS, a specialized set of tools is needed to ensure that the carefully hand-rolled dough retains its shape in order to rise properly without drying out before being baked. Because of the increasing interest in baking a wide variety of breads at home, much of the well-designed, durable equipment used by professional European bakers has been adapted for home use.

To create the toothsome crust on bread baked in a hearth oven, the entire surface of the dough is exposed directly to the heat. Bakers proof what will become crusty long breads, such as the French baguette and *ficelle* or Italian loaves, in the folds of floured linen known as a *couche*, or "bed." This cloth nest prevents the surface of the dough from drying out while it's proofing. The dough lies topside down in the folds of the *couche*. This way, what will become the upper crust of the bread is kept moist so that after being slashed and placed in the oven, the baking bread may expand freely. Heavy linen, similar to artist's canvas, makes the best *couche* material. It is less absorbent than cotton or muslin, so the bread resists sticking to it. Look for professional baker's linen manufactured in Belgium or France. *Couche* fabric comes in rolls of varying widths sold by the meter. A 26"-wide piece fits the length of a baking sheet. Linen dish towels also work well, but their small size is a limitation. It may take some time for you to perfect your skills at rolling baguettes to place in the *couche*, but once you do, the *couche* will help insure that your loaves bloom in the oven.

As delicate as a soufflé, a fully proofed baguette must be transferred from the *couche* onto a peel for placing in the oven. The fully risen dough is so fragile that it stretches and punctures easily in your bare hands. A thin piece of wood about 6" wide and the length of a baking stone, called a *planchette*, helps the baker move the fully proofed breads without destroying them in the process. The bread is rolled from the *couche* onto the wooden board, then transferred onto a baking sheet or peel to be placed in the oven. Use a long, broad metal spatula or fashion a *planchette* from a shingle to serve the same purpose.

For round and oval loaves, hearth bread bakers also use *bannetons* or *Brotformen*, reed or cloth-lined willow baskets, to help hold the shape of some of their distinctive country breads. In France, before there was central heating, a *banneton* full of bread dough might be placed to rise under the warm folds of a down comforter. Rugged construction is the main criteria when selecting these baskets. Choose a basket that is firm and does

THE ECOLOGICAL BAKER
 DANIEL LEADER

At the bakery, we hardly ever use plastic wrap. Our rising breads are covered with canvas sheets that have been well impregnated with flour, so if the dough touches the fabric, it won't stick. At home, you may find it more convenient to use plastic wrap to cover your doughs and starters. If you use a damp kitchen towel, be sure to wet it occasionally with water so it doesn't dry out. If your towel dries out, so will your dough! However, don't use plastic wrap like there's no tomorrow because, ecologically speaking, there *is* a tomorrow. Use the same piece of plastic wrap for all stages of rising and proofing. If it's relatively clean, set it aside to recycle for your next batch of bread.

not flex easily. Make certain that the ends of the willow or reed are firmly attached to the surrounding coils and that they are well tucked in. The last coil in a reed *banneton* must be securely affixed to the top edge with a heavy staple. The shape and texture of the baskets contribute to the aesthetics of the finished loaf. You must heavily coat the interior of these forms with flour, cracked grain, or seeds to keep the dough from sticking. The best reed baskets are made in Germany, Austria, and France from ¼"-thick coils. The same French artisans who make fine willow trays and picnic baskets make most of the linen-lined *bannetons* sold today.

15.1 KING ARTHUR FLOUR HALF-SHEET LOAF-RISING COVER

Have you ever watched a loaf of beautifully formed bread dough self-destruct when it got stuck to its plastic wrap covering? Avert this disaster by using a clear, acrylic cover. Measuring 14" by 19" by 5¼", it is cleverly designed to completely cover a baking sheet, sealing out air and its drying effects. A square 12" model, 7½" tall, covers two plump loaf pans full of dough.

15.2 CAMWEAR CAMSQUARE DOUGH-RISING CONTAINER

As recently as the 1920s, commercial bakers mixed and stored rising bread dough in wooden troughs. A relatively inert material, the wood protected the rising dough from drafts and temperature shifts. Plastic, which does not readily conduct heat or cold, is today's sanitary substitute. Made from crystal-clear polycarbonate, this 6-quart container has bright-orange markings so you can easily monitor the dough's rising. With a snap-tight lid to keep the natural moisture in the dough, this container holds 1 to 5 pounds of dough with plenty of headroom for expansion. Its square shape takes up less space, making this container ideal for retarding dough or storing sourdough starter in your refrigerator.

15.3 KING ARTHUR FLOUR ADJUSTABLE BREAD *COUCHE*–MULTILOAF *BANNETON*

This clever device sets up into a cloth cradle for rising loaves. It comes with two wooden brackets and five dowels (two metal and three wooden). You slide the dowels into channels sewn in the canvas, then push them into holes in the sides of the brackets. Dust the canvas with flour and place formed loaves in the slings. Voilà! A bread hammock measuring 12" by 19". Reposition the dowels in several combinations to make a variety of shapes—four thin baguettes, three plump loaves, two country loaves, or one large loaf, or put three or four small rolls in each channel. When you're ready to bake, place a peel or baking sheet over the rack then invert it to easily transfer the delicate bread dough to the oven.

15.4 FBM *COUCHE* LINEN CANVAS

Less absorbent than cotton because it is made from 100 percent natural flax, this hefty *couche* should be lightly floured to create a stiff, nonstick surface on which to proof formed loaves of bread before baking them in a hearth oven. Buy this 26"-wide fabric by the meter; 1 meter, which is roughly 1 yard, will hold about ten thin loaves or six fat Italian loaves.

15.5 FBM DOUGH PROOFING BASKET

This tightly woven willow basket, 8¼" in diameter and 4" deep and lined with thick Belgian linen, holds up to 2 pounds of dough. It is perfect to use when making a *pain de campagne,* the sort of dense country loaf that benefits from a long, slow proof. For the final rising, shape the dough into a tight ball and place it in the heavily floured basket. When it has doubled in bulk, turn the dough out upside down onto a peel or baking sheet lightly sprinkled with cornmeal, then score and bake.

15.6 FBM REED BREAD FORM

Made in Germany, this coiled bread form leaves its distinctive ribbed impression on the country breads proofed in it. The mold is generously floured, and then a plump ball of bread dough is placed inside. The dough releases easily from the form onto a baking sheet or peel to be transferred directly onto a heated baking stone. This form measures 11½" long, 4⅓" wide, and 3" deep, and can hold about 1½ pounds of bread dough. To get a bread with a distinctive aromatic coating, sprinkle the form with a combination of cracked rye, caraway, and coriander seeds, as the Germans do, before placing rye bread dough inside. This item is also available in a round shape 8½" in diameter and 2½" deep.

THE BEST BREAD EVER: EPIS

2 epis, 14" loaves

500 grams (1 pound or 3⅓ to 4 cups) unbleached bread flour
2 teaspoons fine sea salt
1 teaspoon instant yeast
1¼ cups water
cornmeal for the baking sheet

1 Place the flour, salt, and yeast in a food processor fitted with the metal blade. Using an instant-read thermometer, adjust the water temperature so that the combined temperatures of the water and the flour give a base temperature of between 130° F and 150°F for most food processors. With the machine running, pour in all of the water and process a total of 45 seconds.

2 Place dough in a large ungreased bowl, covered with plastic wrap. Ferment the dough 1½ to 2 hours at room temperature.

3 Scrape dough onto a lightly floured work surface. Divide the dough into two equal pieces. Shape the dough into rough balls and let the dough rest, covered, for 15 to 20 minutes.

4 In preparation for the final proofing, spread a sheet of canvas or a heavy linen cloth on a counter or tabletop and sprinkle it lightly with flour.

5 Roll each piece of dough into a long log about 3" in diameter. Place the loaves on a cornmeal-dusted baking sheet. Cover with plastic and let rise for 30 to 45 minutes, until dough increases by half its size. It should feel soft but still spring back slightly when poked with your finger.

6 One hour before baking, put the oven rack on the second shelf from the bottom of the oven and place the baking stone on the rack. Place a small pan for water on the floor or lower shelf of the oven. Preheat the oven to 475°F.

7 Just before baking, dust the top of each loaf with flour. Holding a pair of scissors at a 45° angle over the top of the loaf, cut about 2" into the dough. Lift this piece of dough and twist and turn it over to one side. Make another cut about 2" farther down the loaf. Lift this knob of dough and twist and turn it over to the opposite side. Continue cutting and twisting each piece in opposite directions for the entire length of the loaf.

8 Carefully pour about 1 cup of warm water into the pan on the oven floor. Slide the baking sheet directly on the baking stone. Reduce the heat to 450°F.

9 Bake the loaves for 25 to 30 minutes until the crust is golden brown. (Halfway through the baking you may transfer the partially baked loaves directly onto the baking stone to develop a crisper crust.) Tap the bottom of the loaves: a hollow sound means they're done.

10 Remove the bread from the oven and immediately place the loaves on a wire rack to cool completely before serving or storing.

The Best Bread Ever: Great Homemade Bread Using Your Food Processor, by Charles Van Over

---

SPECIALTY BREAD PANS

MOST CRUSTY, ARTISAN BREADS are baked without a bread pan. Some loaves, however, call for a specific shape, at which point a bread pan is needed. The use of space-saving convection ovens has made bread forms for baguettes and country loaves more common in commercial bakeries, even in Europe. Made from steel, aluminum, or fiberglass, such forms are useful for baking crusty, hearth-style bread in a conventional or convection oven without a baking stone. The criteria for selecting the pans are solid construction, heat conductivity, and proper shape. The most common pans are made from sheets of solid or perforated metal bent to form smooth channels in which the dough will rise. Look for shallow pans whose edges do not curve inward, which would restrict the way your loaves rise. A well-constructed steel pan has rolled edges and, often, a steel frame to help the pan keep its shape.

Traditional bread doughs made with little or no shortening and sugar bake better in dark-coated or steel pans. Black steel pans also work very well in a standard oven without convection capabilities because steel absorbs heat evenly and conveys it quickly to the bread. Shiny, reflective metal pans like those made from aluminum are better to produce a golden brown crust on a rich loaf. Enriched bread dough baked in a black steel pan may develop a thick and darkened crust.

Although perforated aluminum pans were designed for use in a convection oven, they also work well in a standard oven. The best perforated metal pans are made from nonstick coated aluminum; the darker color adds to the pan's ability to conduct heat and brown the bread. The heavier a perforated pan is, the more it will resist warping. The latest development in bread-baking equipment is flexible bakeware made from silicon-coated fiberglass, in designs for everything from tart shells to baguettes. It is lightweight yet durable, designed to withstand the rigors of the commercial kitchen. We find that such pans produce a pale, crisp crust, and are best suited for making rolls with a soft crust and crumb.

Traditionally in France, only tender, even-grain sandwich bread, called *pain de mie,* is made in what an American would recognize as a "loaf" pan. The same is true in Italy, where such a pan is used to make sandwich bread and bread for *tramezzini*—those triangular grilled sandwiches served with *aperitivi* (cocktails) in bars. You will have the best results with a loaf pan made from single sheets of steel, textured and then folded into a perfect 4″ square. A sliding lid fits snugly over the pan so that the bread is totally enclosed during baking. Blackened steel rusts easily, so your best bet is a pan that is coated with a nonstick finish. If you want a larger slice of perfectly square sandwich bread, look for what we call a "Pullman pan," which produces an enormous (like so many things American) 14″ loaf with a 5″ face.

15.7 CHICAGO METALLIC PROFESSIONAL NONSTICK FRENCH BREAD PAN

Whether you want a 16″ loaf of soft bread for an all-American style hero, or two stout baguettes, this pleated 16″ by 8″ by 3″ sheet of perforated metal will do the job. A center ridge rises ½″ higher than the 2″ sides, a real advantage when it comes to keeping the two loaves from sticking together as they swell and bake. A glaze of SilverStone nonstick coating helps the breads release from the pan. If you use a wet dough, fill each section slightly below the outside edges to keep the dough from overflowing. Bread develops a thin, crunchy crust when baked in this pan.

15.8 CHICAGO METALLIC PROFESSIONAL NONSTICK BAGUETTE PAN

The dough for a fine baguette is relatively moist and sticky. Using a pan specifically designed to bake baguettes makes it easier to handle the dough and ensures that the dough, once baked, forms a pleasing, uniform shape. This is one of the more solid baguette pans available for the home oven. Each channel measures 3″ by 17″, to create long baguettes. Two aluminum braces support the long sides of the pan, keeping it from bending or warping over time. The slightly darker SilverStone nonstick finish on this aluminum pan makes it conduct heat better, which helps the bread form a good crust and also keeps it from sticking to the pan after baking.

15.9 MATFER TWO-CHANNEL METAL BAGUETTE PAN

Any number of hotels in Paris still include a breakfast of café au lait accompanied by a portion of *ficelle,* a skinny baguette served warm with unsalted butter and chunky apricot jam. This blackened steel pan makes crunchy, thin *ficelles,* for those who really prefer crust to crumb. A hefty pan, manufactured by one of the finest professional companies in Europe, it measures 17¾″ by 5½″. A center ridge separating the two 2⅜″ channels is perforated, and it lets

"I just dialled 1-800-BAGUETTE."

keeps the air from touching the dough and forming a tough crust on the surfaces and also forces the rising dough to swell uniformly into a flat top instead of a bulging one. Our *pain de mie* pan, made for use in commercial bakeries, is heavy-gauge sheet steel with a dark, preoxidized surface that simplifies removal of the bread. The construction is solid throughout, with welded corners and a rim beaded around a wire rod. It is somewhat longer than a traditional American loaf pan, measuring 15¾" by 4" by 4", and will bake a 2-pound loaf of sandwich bread. It's also useful for making molded desserts and icebox cakes as long as you line the pan with plastic wrap before using. NOTE This steel pan is prone to rust when the coating wears or if left in contact with water for a long time. Dry thoroughly if you wet the pan. Or simply wipe out with a paper towel after each use.

heat from the bottom of the oven circulate through the pan and up over the baking loaves. The dark metal absorbs more heat, guaranteeing a well-browned crackling crust.

15.10 DEMARLE SILFORM BAGUETTE MOLD

Think of this as a nonstick *banneton* that goes directly into the oven. This Silform baguette mold is made from fiberglass impregnated with silicone, woven wide enough so that air can circulate over the bread for even browning. Form your loaves, then let them proof in this flexible form. When ready to bake, the Silform baguette mold slides onto a baking sheet that is then placed on a rack in your preheated oven. Loaves baked in the Silform mold develop a thin, crisp crust (as long as you steam the oven). Every day, fifteen thousand Subway sandwich shops worldwide bake their bread in similar pans, which are ideal for baking plump hero rolls. The form measures 11⅞" by 16½", and the diameter of each channel is 3". Each channel will hold about 12 ounces of dough.

15.11 MATFER *PAIN DE MIE* PAN

For canapés, for toast, even for peanut-butter sandwiches, nothing is better than *pain de mie*, a long rectangular loaf of firm, close-grained, nearly crustless white bread. It can best be produced in a loaf pan that has right-angled corners and a removable flat sliding lid. The cover

15.12 & 15.13 MATFER BRIOCHE MOLD & INDIVIDUAL BRIOCHE MOLD

In French slang, to make a mistake or act foolishly is to *faire une brioche*. The phrase originated long ago when members of the French Opera were fined for playing out of tune. The money collected was spent on brioches, which the whole orchestra then shared at a gathering; but all those fined had to wear an emblem representing a brioche. There is no mistaking a brioche or its particular

PÂTE À BRIOCHE SURFINE (BRIOCHE DOUGH)

This dough should be made the night before intended use. If preferred, it can be frozen and used at a later time. Brioche dough may be mixed with an electric mixer equipped with a dough hook, but it is best to knead small quantities by hand.

PREPARATION: 30 minutes   RISING TIME: 3½ to 5½ hours   RESTING TIME: 12 hours

FOR APPROXIMATELY 2 POUNDS, 10 OUNCES (1,200 GRAMS) DOUGH

1 pound (450 grams) butter
1 cake (15 grams) compressed baker's yeast
2 teaspoons warm water
2 teaspoons (15 grams) salt

2 tablespoons (30 grams) granulated sugar
1½ tablespoons milk
3¾ cups (500 grams) flour
6 eggs

FOR APPROXIMATELY 1 POUND, 5 OUNCES (600 GRAMS) DOUGH

½ pound (225 grams) butter
½ cake (8 grams) compressed baker's yeast
1 teaspoon warm water
1 teaspoon (8 grams) salt

1 tablespoon (15 grams) granulated sugar
2¼ teapoons milk
1¾ cups (250 grams) flour
3 eggs

FOR APPROXIMATELY 12½ OUNCES (360 GRAMS) DOUGH

½ cup, generous (135 grams), butter
⅓ cake (5 grams) compressed baker's yeast
¾ teaspoon warm water
¾ teaspoon (5 grams) salt

2 teaspoons (10 grams) granulated sugar
1½ teaspoons milk
1 cup, generous (150 grams), flour
2 eggs

NOTE: This dough works best if made in large quantities. The following instructions are for making 2 pounds, 10 ounces (1,200 grams) of dough. The same method applies for making smaller amounts, but the amount of egg added at the various steps must be reduced according to the total number of eggs used.

1 MAKING THE DOUGH Take the butter out of the refrigerator 1 hour before making the dough. Dissolve the yeast in the warm water. In another bowl, dissolve the salt and sugar in the milk. Never bring yeast into direct contact with salt or sugar.
USING AN ELECTRIC MIXER In the mixing bowl, place the salt-milk-sugar mixture. Add the flour, then add the yeast solution. Beat for 1 minutes at low speed, then all at once add 4 eggs and continue to beat until the dough is firm, homogenous, and smooth. Add the remaining 2 eggs one at a time, then beat at medium speed for 10 to 15 more minutes or until the dough is light and silky and no longer sticks to your fingers. Place the butter between two sheets of waxed paper or plastic wrap and tap it a few times with a rolling pin to flatten it. Break the butter into pieces the size of an egg. With the mixer on low speed, quickly add the butter to the dough—this should take no more than 2 minutes.
KNEADING BY HAND Have all the ingredients measured and ready for use. Place the flour on the table in a mound and make a well in the center. Put the yeast solution in the well and mix it with a little flour, then add 3 eggs. Incorporate about half the flour, then add the salt-milk-sugar mixture and 1 more egg, working with your fingers to mix all the ingredients together.

When all the flour has been mixed in, knead the dough for 15 minutes, stretching it and slapping it back onto the table as you do so. When the time is up, add the remaining 2 eggs and keep working the dough until it becomes elastic and stretches easily without breaking. Now add the softened butter, prepared as described above for using an electric mixer, to ⅓ of the dough, half of it at a time, using a plastic scraper to cut and mix the dough together. Try not to use your hands too much because the butter will melt too quickly.
2 RISING Place the dough in a large bowl, cover the bowl with a cloth, and let it stand for 1½ to 2½ hours at room temperature. When the dough has risen to twice its original bulk, punch it down and stretch it twice. Let the dough rise again in the refrigerator for 2 to 3 hours—it should be rounded on top like a ball. Punch the dough down as before and keep it refrigerated overnight. The next day, place the dough on a floured board and flatten it quickly by hand, then place it in the molds that will be used for baking.
3 TO FREEZE The dough will keep for one month if wrapped tightly in plastic or aluminum foil. If you are making a large quantity, divide it into two or three pieces before freezing. Let the dough thaw for 24 hours in the refrigerator before using.

Lenôtre's Desserts and Pastries, by Gaston Lenôtre

shape: fluted sides (as you can see by the pan's shape), and a round cap made by anchoring a small ball of the yeast dough in the center of the brioche before it is baked. It is called a *brioche à tête* (brioche with a head). A brioche is golden colored, buttery but lightly textured, and is wonderful for breakfast with unsalted butter and homemade jam, especially when it is still a little warm from the oven. For variation, you can add some Gruyère cheese to the dough and serve the brioche as a luncheon bread. The dough should always be made a day in advance and left to rise in the refrigerator to develop the best flavor. The larger coated-steel mold holds 6 cups and is 7" in diameter across the top and 3" deep. If you prefer individual brioches, a 4-ounce mold, 3½" in diameter, is also available. It pays to own six.

15.14 *BRIOCHE MOUSSELINE* MOLD

Brioche mousseline is the soufflé of the bread world. It is baked with a brioche dough modified to include more butter for a richer taste and an ethereal texture. The mold for baking this column-shaped bread is a tinned-steel cylinder, 5" in diameter and 5½" deep. Not content to make a bread nearly 6" high, the French usually fill the 6-cup mold ⅔ full and tie a paper collar around the top so that by the time the bread has finished rising and baking it stands a majestic 8" to 10" high. This same pan works well to make *pannetone*, the delicate

Italian holiday bread studded with raisins and nuts.

15.16 MATFER
BABAS AU RHUM MOLDS

Legend has it that in the seventeenth century, while King Stanisław Leszczyński of Poland was exiled in France, he found the *kugelhopf* too dry; he tried soaking it in rum, and so pleased was he with his creation that he named it after the hero of his favorite book, Ali Baba.

Today *babas au rhum* are made from a rich yeast-and-butter dough studded with raisins and baked in diminutive molds like these here. Measuring 2½" tall and 2½" wide, these coated steel molds hold 6 ounces. While it is baking, the dough blooms over the top of the molds, forming a mushroom-shaped dome. Before serving, the *baba* is brushed with a simple syrup (equal parts sugar and water) and rum. These same pans make individual *brioches mousselines* or tiny cork-shaped yeast cakes called *bouchons*.

15.15 WOOLEY VIENNA ROLL STAMP

Almost five hundred years ago a Viennese baker made round rolls stamped with a likeness of Emperor Frederick V for his children. In the modern Republic of Austria, these soft, round airy rolls are no longer marked with the emperor's picture, but they are still called "emperor's rolls" (*Kaiser-semmein*). Today, they are also impressed with a pinwheel-like stamp that makes it easy to break the rolls into sections. This solid, cast-aluminum stamp will make the traditional swirled design on your rolls. Roll the bread into fist-size balls and, just before baking, press the stamp almost all the way through the dough. Each of the arms is 2" long, and the stamp measures 4" in overall length.

PIZZA PANS

There is no disputing that a great pizza begins with great crust, full of the wheat flavor of good bread dough, chewy yet so firm it can stand up on its own without bending. Whether you like your pizza with a thin or a thick crust, you'll get the best results if you bake your pizza dough directly on the searing hearth of a baking stone. Lacking one, you will need a pan that delivers as much heat as possible to sear the bottom crust.

The criteria for selecting a pizza pan are the same as for bread pans. You want solid construction, heat conductivity, and proper shape. Pizza pans are made from blackened steel, brushed aluminum, anodized aluminum, perforated metal, wire mesh, or clay. This is one instance when an insulated baking pan is not desirable. The pans that perform the best are made from blackened steel or heavy, 18-gauge anodized aluminum; some pizza shops serve their pies on these wide-rimmed anodized-aluminum pizza trays. A heavy, 18-gauge professional-style half-baking sheet or rimless cookie sheet also works well, especially for baking several individual pizzas. Choose a pan without a nonstick finish—sprinkling cornmeal on the bottom of the pizza will prevent it from sticking—because you will end up scratching the finish when you cut the pizza directly on the pan. Perforated metal pizza pans combine the fast-heating characteristics of aluminum with the maximum crust exposure of a pizza rack. We find that perforated pans made from heavy-gauge aluminum with large holes, ¼" in diameter, perform better than those with numerous smaller holes.

Wire pizza racks, which look like discs made from radiator grills edged in curved aluminum, do an excellent job of cooking pizza in an oven heated to 500°F. You place the pizza dough (or precooked frozen pizza for that matter) directly on the rack, then put the rack on a shelf in your oven. It can also be put on top of a pizza stone for those who feel uncomfortable wielding a peel. The racks, whether square or round, come in several sizes, but those that measure 14" in diameter or less are best. If you have a heavy hand with the toppings, choose a wire pizza rack that is rigid and does not bend easily when twisted.

Deep-dish pizza breaks all the rules. You're basically looking for a soft, white-bread type crust, more suited to eating with a knife and fork than with your fingers. A hefty baking sheet works well, as does an unglazed clay baking pan. Chicago-style deep-dish pizza is a breed unto itself, requiring a heavy, round cake pan to hold its bulging filling. Such pans come in sizes from 6" across (for a "personal" pie) to 12". Stick with a smaller size, 10" or less, to get the most heat to penetrate through the crust and weighty fillings. A blackened steel or aluminum pan will produce the best crust.

The moment a pizza is removed from the oven, it should go directly to a cooling rack for a few minutes before serving; otherwise, escaping steam will soften the crisp crust. Any large wire cake rack works well for this purpose.

We tested many perforated pizza pans and liked this one best. The ¼"-wide holes allow oven heat to baste the bottom crust while the lightly darkened metal conducts heat directly onto the bottom surface of the pizza dough. Made from a medium-gauge aluminized steel, this pan resists warping. Its generous 14" size will accommodate a fully loaded pizza and is ample enough to feed four.

We suspect that this pizza crisper may have been designed as a pizza cooling rack. It looks like a round radiator grill or an air filter. The base of the pan is a screen of aluminum rimmed with a narrow band of aluminum for safety and to give the pan some tensile strength. You form the crust, place it on the crisper, and add the toppings before placing it in the oven. The heat from the oven comes in direct contact with the bottom crust of the pizza. You can bake the pizza on an oven rack or on a pizza stone with good results. Just be parsimonious with the toppings; the pan is somewhat flexible and can bend under too much weight.

When you don't have a pizza stone or haven't set aside the time to preheat one in your oven, this 12" pizza tray is all that you will need to make professional-quality pizza at home. The same model used in commercial pizzerias, this sturdy pan is made of anodized aluminum. The dark surface yields a nice brown crust. Although the pan itself is strong and will stand up to a lot of use, the surface is not so durable: it will scratch should you use a sharp serving implement or cut your pizza directly in the pan. When your pizza is finished baking, slide it off the pan onto a serving platter or cutting board and then slice it.

SCORING & SLICING

MOMENTS BEFORE A LOAF is placed in the oven, you need to cut the top of the dough with a sharp knife or razor to make an escape hatch for the expanding dough. This is because a last burst of activity from the yeast causes the loaf to swell when the intense oven heat hits it. If you bake your bread on a heated hearth you'll see the bread rising from the hearth in what is called a moment of "oven spring." The cuts in the top of the loaf allow it to enlarge uniformly and create an interesting and rustic textural surface when baked. You need a sharp blade or lame to make swift, smooth strokes through the moist dough. A serrated paring knife also works very well. Professionals use specially forged steel blades or razor blades to slash their loaves. Some skill is required to master the use of the lame, for the slightest change in angle will effect the appearance of the baked crust. The angle with which you hold the blade will also make a difference. A slash placed on the edge of a loaf, angled to the right, allows the dough to burst up and out. A deep slash straight down the middle of the loaf causes it to burst open almost in two.

15.20 VICTORINOX TWINE KNIFE

With this serrated twine knife, you'll always be prepared for scoring bread with a *coup de lame* ("slash of the blade") before baking. The 2½" serrated blade is made from stainless steel, safely retractable in a 3½" red-brushed aluminum sheath. The curved point easily pierces the surface of the dough and works equally well as a pocket bread knife.

15.21 FBM RAZOR BLADE HOLDER

The simplicity of this slender piece of steel belies its usefulness. This 5" wand is a holder for double-edged razor blades that can be used to score bread before baking. A razor blade slips securely over the arched end of the holder, and, once in place, the blade maintains its curve. When the blade dulls, remove it—carefully—and replace with a new one.

15.22 MATFER LAME WITH PLASTIC COVER

The *maître boulanger,* "master baker," teaches his apprentice to judge a well-scored loaf by the ridge, which rises along the top of the loaf once it bakes. The ridge should be sharp enough to cut. This handy 5" lame with its own blade cover is made from sturdy acrylic; the supersharp blade should last through hundreds of loaves.

15.23 BRON BREAD CUTTER

In a restaurant or brasserie, where long baguettes are consumed in large quantities, slices are often lopped off into 2" lengths with a special bread cutter similar to this one. It works like a paper cutter and looks like one too. Lift the stainless steel knife by its handle, press the baguette against the guide, and push the blade down through the bread. The width of the slices may be adjusted by loosening a bolt affixed to the stand and sliding the curved metal guard in or out for thinner or thicker slices. The knife blade, a 10" scimitar with a serrated edge, is a fearsome weapon, fixed, fortunately, to a stainless steel stand that is screwed securely into a 9" square wooden base. Rubber suction cups attached to stout legs keep the cutter from moving while in use. A curved plastic strip, a required safety feature, makes it difficult for your fingers or hands to get near the blade as it cuts.

15.24 MOUNTAIN WOODS CRUMB TRAY

For a household where crusty bread is part of the daily menu, here is a cutting board that really makes sense. It consists of a shallow tray with hardwood slats nesting on a fitted box. When bread is sliced on top of the tray, crumbs drop through the slats and collect inside. Made from cherry wood, it is 6½" by 9½" and 1½" high. The sturdy top resists cutting and doubles as a bread server or trivet.

BAKING & PIZZA STONES

HEARTH BREADS, of which European country breads, pizza, and authentic German rye are just a few, are those baked directly on the heated floor of a stone oven. Stone has tremendous heat-retaining capabilities, and the bread is placed directly on the surface of the stone hearth, enabling the loaves to expand to their full volume and develop a brittle, crackling crust.

The temperature in a home oven can fluctuate by as much as 75°F while baking (the thermostat switches the heating element off and on to maintain temperature), with electric ovens baking more evenly than gas ones. We also prefer electric ovens for hearth baking at home because they do not require extensive exhaust systems, which quickly remove the steam from the oven. In a home oven, we use a baking stone to replicate the effects of a true hearth oven, which stays hot longer with greater efficiency. Place the stone in your oven during preheating to charge it with heat. During baking, the stone releases the heat into the foods being baked in a constant manner quite unmatched by any other baking method. A thick, broad baking stone also balances the heat in the oven, effectively insulating your pizza and breads from heat swings and allowing them to be baked at high temperatures without burning.

There are three materials used to make baking stones: cordierite, clay, or terra cotta. Cordierite is a natural mineral mixed into clay that, fired at temperatures over 2,000°F, creates a hard, nearly unbreakable baking surface—it's used to make the shelving in ceramic kilns. Unglazed clay and terra-cotta stones are thin, breakable, and retain less heat than those made from cordierite. But since clay and terra cotta are more malleable, they can be shaped into individual containers for loaves of bread or rolls. Covered clay bakers capture the moisture in the dough and release it back onto the bread, eliminating the need to add steam in your oven. Look for the thickest baking stone you can find. The thickness of the stone is indicative of its ability to retain heat; greater heat retention will let the stone recover temperature quickly on successive bakes.

There is a misconception that baking stones should be placed near the bottom of the oven. The opposite is true. The stone-lined decks of a commercial oven measure between 6½" and 9" high. In that confined chamber, the conductive heat of the hearth penetrates the dough while the radiant heat from the oven's metal ceiling reflects directly onto the bread or pizza. To maximize the performance of your oven, place the baking or pizza stone on the middle or top shelf, keeping in mind the dimensions above, to emulate the effects of the baking chamber in a true hearth oven. The heat reflected from the top of the oven onto a pizza baked at this height will be stronger, so the topping will cook at the same rate as the crust.

One more word of baking advice: a deeply darkened crust signals a flavorful loaf of bread. Do not be afraid to bake your bread at a high temperature—425°F to 465°F—when baking on a hearthstone, and bake it long enough so that the crust darkens thoroughly. *Pizzaioli* in Naples bake their thin-crusted pizzas at 700°F or higher. Preheat your oven to its highest temperature (500°F or above) for at least 30 minutes with the stone in place for the best results.

Baking stones also absorb moisture and oils from whatever doughs are placed on them, smoking and burning readily. Bake enriched doughs on a sheet of parchment on your baking stone or on a baking sheet placed on the stone. Cleaning a baking or pizza stone is simple but often frustrates the home cook. Between successive bakes, you simply brush any flour, cornmeal, or crumbs from the stone into a dustpan using a brush with natural bristles that resist burning. Continual use in the high heat required to bake bread and pizza essentially keeps these stones sanitary. Baking stones darken naturally with age, never appearing to be as clean as when first purchased. This patina is desirable because dark surfaces encourage browning. Scrape off any drips of cheese and pizza toppings with a metal spatula. If your baking stone becomes heavily stained or if thick ridges of flour and crumbs develop, wash the cooled stone under warm water without soap.

15.25 HEARTHKIT OVEN INSERT

By far the heaviest and most sophisticated of the baking stones for the home oven, this three-piece cordierite device converts any home oven into a professional hearth oven. With this insert you can bake artisan breads, bake pizzas, or roast meats and vegetables with equal ease. It weighs more than 30 pounds, consisting of a hearthstone and two side plates. The base plate, tapering from 1¼" in the back to 1" in the front, slides onto one of your oven racks. Measuring 15" deep by 21" long, it practically covers the entire oven rack in a standard 30" oven. You then position each side plate, curved side facing inward, in one of the channels routed in the base. The sides help project heat back onto bread baking inside. The roof of your oven completes the chamber.

Five 14" baguettes or a large 16" pizza can be baked on its surface, and the slight slope makes it easier to remove the bread. The Hearthkit is designed with a cavity in each side channel to house an oven thermometer so you can gauge exactly when the stone is sufficiently heated.

15.26 SASSAFRAS SUPERSTONE LA CLOCHE

One of the earliest ways to bake bread was underneath a curved cover or cooking pot placed over an open hearth. La Cloche is such a cooking

PIZZA DOUGH

4 7" to 8" pizzas

3 cups all-purpose flour
1 teaspoon salt
1 tablespoon honey
2 tablespoons olive oil
¾ cup cool water
1 package fresh or dry yeast
¼ cup warm water

1 Place the flour in a food processor.
2 Combine the salt, honey, olive oil, and the ¾ cup cool water in a small bowl or measuring cup. Mix well.
3 Dissolve the yeast in the ¼ cup warm water and let proof for 10 minutes.
4 With the motor running, slowly pour the salt and honey liquid through the feed tube. Then pour in the dissolved yeast. Process until the dough forms a ball on the blade. If it is sticky, add sprinklings of flour.
5 Transfer the dough to a lightly floured surface and knead until it is smooth. Place in a buttered bowl and allow the dough to rest, covered, for 30 minutes.
6 Divide the dough into 4 equal parts. Roll each piece into a smooth, tight ball. Place on a flat sheet or dish, cover with a damp towel, and refrigerate.
7 One hour before baking, remove the dough from the refrigerator and let it come to room temperature.
8 Lightly flour a work surface. Using the fleshy part of your fingertips, flatten each ball of dough into a circle, about 6" in diameter, making the outer edge thicker than the center. Turn the dough over and repeat. Lift the dough from the work surface and gently stretch the edges, working clockwise to form a 7" to 8" circle. Repeat with the other 3 pieces. Place the circles on a wooden peel or on baking sheets, and build the pizzas as desired.

NOTES To make the dough in an electric mixer fitted with a dough hook, place the flour in the bowl and add the ingredients in the same order as when using a food processor. Knead the dough in the machine until it forms a smooth ball. Place the dough in a buttered bowl and allow it to rest, covered, for 30 minutes.

To prepare by hand, place the flour on a work surface and make a well in the center. Add the wet ingredients and proofed yeast. Slowly incorporate the flour into the wet ingredients working from the center outward. When a dough forms, knead it on a floured surface until smooth. Place in a buttered bowl and allow the dough to rest, covered, for 30 minutes.

You can also roll out the pizzas with a rolling pin, then inch up the edges with your fingers to form a little ridge.

The Wolfgang Puck Cookbook, by Wolfgang Puck

bell made from hard-fired clay that nests on a lipped baking stone 10″ in diameter. Place your bread dough on the pie-shaped base, cover it with the bell, then put it in a preheated oven. A 2-pound loaf fits under the 8½″ high dome. The lid traps moisture escaping from the bread to create the steam needed to produce a light, brittle crust. During the last few minutes, remove the cover to lightly brown the crust.

15.27 SASSAFRAS SUPERSTONE DEEP-DISH BAKING STONE

This deep-dish pizza baking stone is made by one of the oldest potteries operating in the United States. Made from natural clay, it measures 11½″ by 14½″ by 1″ deep. It evenly distributes the oven heat and absorbs moisture released from the pizza crust when baking. Though its form might tempt you to make a deep-dish pizza inside it, it's best to place the stone in the oven and preheat it for 20 minutes before sliding your pizza onto the stone.

15.28 KITCHEN SUPPLY COMPANY BAKING STONE

This firebrick baking stone is ideal for pizza- and bread-baking. It is ample in size, 16″ by 14″, yet able to fit in most home ovens. The ¾″ thickness of cordierite retains heat well. Kitchen Supply, among other companies, makes a metal rack on which the baking stone rests; the rack makes it easier to move the stone in and out of the oven. The raised "feet" underneath the stone help keep the rack in place when moving the stone and also allow the stone to cool off more quickly when removed from the oven, because air can reach underneath.

> You better cut
> the pizza in four
> pieces because
> I'm not hungry
> enough to eat six.
>
> —YOGI BERRA

PIZZA CUTTERS

WHAT IS THE BEST WAY to cut a pizza? In pizzerias, you'll see two types of knives in use: the rolling pizza wheel and the rocking, two-handled pizza knife. The best pizza wheels have the simplest form, consisting of a molded, one-piece, slip-resistant handle that fits comfortably in the palm of your hand, and a solid 4″ blade attached with a large screw and nut. The wheel should sit close to the handle for safe and steady cutting. The wide blade, sharp and tapered at the edges, will easily cut through all of the toppings on a thick pizza, and a built-in finger guard will prevent slipping. The wheel should feel evenly balanced between blade and grip when held loosely in your hand.

The double-handled rocking pizza knife resembles an elongated mezzaluna, the Italian half-moon-shaped cutter. Two handles are riveted to the top edge of a 16″ to 20″ blade. You position the knife over the pizza, then rock back and forth, alternating the pressure you exert through the palms of each hand. This is a great addition to any kitchen where pizza is served regularly. It is also a safe and functional knife for cutting large wedges of hard cheese.

15.29 OXO GOOD GRIPS PIZZA WHEEL

There are not many pizza wheels that meet our rigorous standards. We look for a combination of weight, balance, and safe design before we judge the cutting blade itself. Manufactured by a company recognized for its slip-resistant Good Grips handles, this 4″ pizza wheel meets all our criteria. Weighing more than 9 ounces, this pizza cutter has a 4″ wheel mounted close to the 5″ handle for balance and rigidity. A generous 2″ chrome-plated scabbard protects your fingers while the blade sails through the toughest pizza crust or rustic fruit *crostata*. Although it's dishwasher safe, we recommend carefully washing the pizza wheel by hand to keep the blade sharp—so sharp it's best not used on a nonstick surface.

15.30 ALLIED METAL PIZZA CUTTER

We have yet to find a better way to cut pizza than with this professional rolling knife. A generous 4″ stainless steel blade is attached to a rod mounted in a molded plastic grip. The flanged edges of the 5″ handle protect the fingers while you apply forward and downward pressure on the blade. Rocking back and forth a few times helps separate the slices. Replacement blades are available, providing this cutter with a long life.

GODZILLA MEETS MOZZARELLA

PEELS

BREAD AND PIZZA DERIVE their satisfying crust from direct contact with a heated hearth stone. Positioning a pizza or a free-form bread on a baking stone in a 500°F oven is not an easy matter. You need a peel, a flat wooden or metal shovel used to slide breads and pizzas into and out of the oven. A rimless cookie sheet or the back of a baking sheet can serve the same purpose, but a thin peel with a long wooden handle is more maneuverable, especially when chasing a stray dinner roll deep in a searing oven.

Peels come in a range of sizes and materials. Select the largest peel that will fit into your oven, and remember, when forming a pizza on the peel, do not exceed the dimensions of your baking stone or you'll end up with a surrealist sculpture dripping down the oven rack. Peels are made from wood, aluminum with a wooden handle, or solid aluminum. If the peel is not one piece like most wooden ones, the handle shaft should be firmly soldered on in at least three places on each side for best adhesion, and it should feel solid and strong enough to help lift a 3-pound casserole from the oven. A peel with an aluminum blade and a hardwood handle is the most versatile and may be used for all sorts of baking, such as placing bread or pizza on a baking stone or moving a hot casserole into and out of the oven. The handle is virtually heatproof, and the thin metal blade slips under any size loaf. While quite handsome, a wooden peel can be more difficult to slide under a baked loaf of bread or pizza—you often end up pushing your bread back, deep into the oven. A slight tapering along the edge of the blade helps make a wooden peel more useful. Most wooden peels are made from pine for lightness, but those made from oak will last longer.

Just remember, wooden peels can warp, so never let them soak in water. To restore a warped peel, wet it, then place it under a baking tray loaded with weights until it dries. Aluminum peels with metal blades and handles are generally designed for moving a hot casserole out from under the broiler. As such, they tend to be smaller, with blades rarely larger than 10″ by 8″.

Blues is to jazz what yeast is to bread—without it, it's flat.

—CARMEN McRAE

15.31 ALLIED METAL ALUMINUM PEEL

The usefulness of this professional metal peel with hardwood handle will surprise you. Its 14″-wide blade, tapering to a sturdy 21″ wooden handle, slides under as many as five loaves of crusty bread or a family-sized pizza. The peel is well balanced and supports even the weight of a bubbling fruit crumble wedged in a hard-to-reach spot in the oven. Three solid rivets attach the blade to the tubular handle holder, assuring that this rigid peel will last through a lifetime of home baking and heavy-duty cooking.

15.32 ALLIED METAL BAKER'S PEEL

An elite group of twenty-six Italian pizzerias has come together to form the Associazione Vera Pizze Napoletana, the defenders of the true Neapolitan pizza. All members vow to make their pizza in time-honored ways, which means the pizza must be thin-crusted, baked in a wood-fired oven, and made with classic toppings, not the newfangled likes of Peking duck. Their symbol is Pulcinella, Italy's masked clown, carrying the large wooden peel necessary to place their masterpieces into the oven. This diminutive version sports a 12″ by 14″ rectangular blade ideal for use in a home oven. The overall length of this peel is 22″, long enough to be useful but not so long as to be unwieldy. One end of the blade is sharpened slightly so it slips easily under the bread.

TORTILLA & CHAPATI PRESSES

LONG BEFORE THE EARL of Sandwich lent his name to a classic portable food, flat pieces of cooked bread dough were used to wrap and transport any number of savory foods—the Mexican tortilla, the Indian chapati and *paratha,* and the Turkish *pide* are just a few. Simply patting a ball of sticky dough between flattened palms or rolling it with a wooden pin will transform it into a smooth, uniform circle, but there are also specialized tools to assist with the process. Most presses operate on a simple mechanism—when pressure is exerted on the handle, the two flat plates of the press force the dough out into a flat disc. The main criteria for selecting a tortilla or chapati press are the same: proper construction, whether made from wood, cast iron, or aluminum, and a secure and comfortable handle, which acts as a lever to exert pressure on the plates. The plates must sit evenly on top of each other.

15.33 VILLAWARE METAL TORTILLA PRESS

For centuries the sound of gentle hand clapping was heard throughout Mexico as women prepared each meal's tortillas from scratch. Sadly, the ancient and difficult art of the *torteando*—slapping a small ball of corn dough into the paper-thin flatness of a tortilla—is dying out. Nearly everyone in Mexican cities buys ready-made tortillas.

For those of us who still prefer to make our own, a simple heavy-duty tortilla press like this one is essential. It consists of two round, flat, cast-aluminum plates 6″ in diameter with a hinge at one end and a 7″-long handle at the other end. To use the press, lay a piece of plastic wrap—a sandwich bag is ideal—on the bottom plate, then place a walnut-sized ball of dough made from *masa harina* corn flour on top. Cover the dough with another layer of plastic wrap, close the press, and push the handle down firmly. Open the press and lift off the top section of plastic. You should have a flat, round tortilla ready for the griddle. This same press is an excellent tool to use to flatten

CORN TORTILLAS
❧ RICK BAYLESS ❧

With powdered *masa harina* so widely distributed these days, more of us have learned how wonderful a fresh-baked tortilla is. And with the fresh-ground dough (*masa*) becoming available from *tortillerias* in so many communities, it won't be long until the freshest-tasting home-baked tortillas are part of many of our lives. Though tortillas take some time to prepare, it's time well spent—at least on special occasions. Other times, store-bought, factory-made tortillas can be served as the authentic accompaniment.

15 tortillas

1 pound fresh *masa* for tortillas, store-bought or homemade

or

1¾ cups *masa harina* mixed with 1 cup plus 2 tablespoons hot tap water

1 THE DOUGH If using *masa harina*, mix it with the hot water, then knead until smooth, adding more water or more *masa harina* to achieve a very soft (but not sticky) consistency; cover with plastic and let rest 30 minutes. When you're ready to bake the tortillas, readjust the consistency of the fresh or reconstituted *masa* (see Cook's Notes, below), then divide into 15 balls and cover with plastic.

2 HEATING THE GRIDDLE Heat a large, ungreased, heavy griddle or two heavy skillets: one end of the griddle (or one skillet) over medium-low, the other end (or other skillet) over medium to medium-high.

3 PRESSING THE TORTILLAS Cut two squares of heavy plastic to fit the plates of your tortilla press. With the press open, place a square of plastic over the bottom plate, set a ball of dough in the center, cover with the second square of plastic, and gently flatten the dough between. Close the top plate and press down gently but firmly with the handle. Open, turn the tortilla 180°, close, and gently press again, to an even 1⁄16″ thickness.

4 UNMOLDING Open the press and peel off the top sheet of plastic. Flip the tortilla onto one hand, *dough-side down*, then, starting at one corner, gently peel off the remaining sheet of plastic.

5 GRIDDLE BAKING Lay the tortilla onto the cooler end of the griddle (or the cooler skillet). In about 20 seconds, when the tortilla loosens itself from the griddle (but the edges have not yet dried or curled), flip it over onto the hotter end of the griddle (or onto the hotter skillet). When lightly browned in spots underneath, 20 to 30 seconds more, flip a second time, back onto the side that was originally down. If the fire is properly hot, the tortilla will balloon up like pita bread. When lightly browned, another 20 or 30 seconds, remove from the griddle (it will completely deflate) and wrap in a towel. Press, unmold, and bake the remaining balls of *masa*, placing each hot tortilla on top of the last and keeping the stack well wrapped.

6 RESTING Let the wrapped stack of tortillas rest for about 15 minutes to finish their cooking, soften, and become pliable.

COOK'S NOTES

TECHNIQUES

ADJUSTING THE CONSISTENCY OF THE DOUGH You want the dough to be softer than shortbread dough (or Play-Doh, if that rings a louder bell), about like a soft cookie dough (though it isn't sticky). Reconstituted *masa harina* should be as soft as possible, while still having enough body to be unmolded; it should feel a little softer than perfectly adjusted fresh *masa*. *Masa* is not elastic like bread dough, but fresh *masa* will have a little more body than a dough made from *masa harina*. Because the dough dries out readily, it is necessary to add water from time to time; tortillas made from dry dough usually won't puff much, and they'll be heavy and somewhat crumbly.

UNMOLDING If the tortilla breaks when you peel off the plastic, the dough is too dry. If the tortilla refuses to come free from the plastic, either you've pressed it too thin or the dough is too soft.

GRIDDLE BAKING If the lower heat isn't low enough, the tortilla will bubble and blister immediately and the result will be heavy. If the higher heat isn't high enough, the tortilla will not puff, which also means it will be somewhat heavy. Don't leave the tortilla for too long before flipping it the first time; it will dry out and then not puff.

GETTING TORTILLAS TO PUFF After you flip the baking tortillas the second time, pressing on them lightly with your fingertips or the back of your spatula will encourage the two layers to separate.

INGREDIENTS

MASA VS. MASA HARINA Though fresh *masa* is unsurpassed for taste and texture, *masa harina* makes good tortillas, ones with a certain toasted flavor and a slight graininess.

TIMING & ADVANCE PREPARATION

Masa harina dough should be made at least ½ hour ahead (though it will keep for several hours at room temperature). Allow 15 to 30 minutes to press and bake the tortillas, depending on your proficiency and amount of griddle room. The hot tortillas can be wrapped in foil—towel and all—and kept warm in a *low* oven for an hour or so.

dough for Chinese dumplings or scallion pancakes.

15.34 CHAPATI PRESS

It is not easy to roll thin, evenly shaped chapatis or *pooris* out of damp and sticky whole-wheat dough. As a matter of fact, if you don't have an Indian grandmother, a press like this is probably the best way to make proper Indian breads. Even in India, many urban families have taken to using presses for their bread-making. The device resembles a tortilla press and works on the same principle. A ball of dough, placed in the center of the press, is quickly and smoothly flattened into a perfect circle when the press is closed over it. This press is made of two hexagonal pieces of enameled cast aluminum that are joined by a large, barrel-shaped hinge. Circles of pale blue plastic, 5" in diameter, are fastened to the inner surfaces of the press to prevent the dough from sticking. With an implement like this in your kitchen you should have no hesitation about making a variety of Indian breads.

MY SOURDOUGH STARTER
❧ NANCY SILVERTON ❧

When I decided to open a sourdough bakery in 1988, I didn't know much about wild yeast starters. But I knew what I didn't have, which was the one-hundred-year head start of the Poilâne bakery in Paris. If I was going to make a quality bread, I needed to get my century going *tout de suite*. Certain information about starters had trickled down to me: I knew that flour and water were all you needed and that the natural yeast that lives on the skin of grapes is what kick-starts the process. But how many grapes? And what proportion of flour to water? "Eureka!" was achieved in a rented refrigerator that stood in the middle of what would be the dining room of Campanile, containing three white plastic buckets of fragile experimental slurry that I prayed wasn't being corrupted by sawdust and grit. Two batches were abject failures: 5 gallons of papier-mâché paste. But the container that bubbled ever so slightly is the mother to not only 15,000 pounds of white starter used daily at La Brea Bakery, but of loaves produced all over the country by protégés and consultees. What I discovered along the way is that wild yeast starter and an old Bordeaux have nothing in common but grapes. Age has little to do with a starter's success. It's all about daily monitoring and constant care.

BREAD MACHINES

INVENTED IN JAPAN, the bread machine came to the United States in 1987, where it was initially viewed as a novelty that would never fly. To the astonishment of the appliance industry and food professionals, however, the American consumer embraced bread machines. Never mind that most of the loaves they produced were not as good as the store-bought kind. They enabled unskilled, time-pressed cooks to bake the most basic, yet most complex, demanding, and exacting food by themselves without doing much more than measuring ingredients, dumping them in, and pressing a button. For many, the aroma of a loaf in the "oven" was a new but divine experience. Modern folklore is full of stories of how homes have been sold thanks to the smell wafting in the air of bread baking in an electric machine. On a more serious note, for those who do not have ready access to a good bakery, a bread machine will provide loaves made without chemical additives and with nutritional boosters like wheat germ and nonfat dry milk.

There are wide discrepancies between the performances of various models. The best ones turn out a credible loaf that can compete with many in the supermarket, if not in the artisanal bakery. While bread machines come with a laundry list of special features—everything from beeps indicating it's time to add raisins and nuts, to crust-color settings, to jam and cake cycles—your most important consideration should be the quality of the finished product, and that's hard to tell from reading the box. For the most part, we've found that those with pans in a traditional horizontal shape bake loaves with a better texture, not to mention that they're easier to slice. You may be tempted to choose one that's speedy—some machines now have programs that make a loaf in one hour from start to finish—but the longer the cycle, the better the bread is likely to be. All have timers, which can be set to work while you sleep, and dough cycles, so the machine can do the mixing, kneading, and first rise, after which you shape the dough and bake it in a conventional oven. Many excellent time-pressed bakers take advantage of the dough cycle; if a good recipe is followed and the bread is baked in a traditional pan and oven, few would be able to tell that the lion's share of the work was done by a bread machine. One note of caution: avoid whole-wheat bread-machine recipes that call for a dose of vital wheat gluten. Many manufacturers and cookbook authors include it to ensure a good rise, but a bite of bread made with gluten has all the taste of a mouthful of cotton.

15.35 WEST BEND AUTOMATIC BREAD- & DOUGH-MAKER

Looking for a relatively low-priced machine that turns out decent 1½- to 2-pound loaves of everything from old-fashioned white to 100 percent whole wheat to banana bread? Here's a reliable choice with a horizontally shaped aluminum pan coated with a nonstick finish. It has six settings: basic, whole wheat, sweet, quick bread, and dough, plus "One-Hour Bread Express"—that in this case turns out quite an acceptable loaf exactly an hour after you've pressed the start pad. If you don't remove the loaf immediately after baking, it will stay warm for up to 3 hours. Other features include a choice of light, medium, and dark crust and a beep signaling it's time to add ingredients like raisins, nuts, or chips. The bread maker, which measures 16½" by 10" by 12", has a window in the lid so you can check the status of your loaf without opening it. Built-in handles in the sides, a cover that comes off for cleaning, and cord storage add to its ease of use.

15.36 PANASONIC BREAD BAKERY

The first, and still the best, brand on the market. The secret? It doesn't rush. The basic cycle is 4 hours—an hour longer than average on most other machines. The long cycle allows the dough to rise slowly and naturally, and the recipes that come with the bread bakery call for less yeast than most bread-machine recipes, so the finished products have a less pronounced yeasty taste and aroma. Every loaf made from the recipes in the manual that comes with the bakery is a winner, including the 100 percent whole wheat, which takes 5 hours from start to completion and doesn't need a boost from vital wheat gluten. The cast-aluminum loaf pan makes up to a 2-pound loaf. This company has an exclusive patent on an automatic yeast dispenser, a small compartment in the lid of the machine that opens and drops the yeast into the pan at the beginning of the kneading cycle. What this means for you is that you can set the bread bakery to delay baking without having to worry that the yeast will combine with the liquids and activate early. It also has a beeper to let you know when to add ingredients like raisins or nuts. The machine is 13⅓" wide, 9" deep, and 14" high.

16

BAKING & PASTRY EQUIPMENT

T O *BAKE* IS TO COOK IN an oven by means of dry heat that surrounds the entire pan as opposed to other types of oven cooking—broiling, for example—where the method involves heat applied from above. In this chapter, we talk about the tools required for baking cakes, cookies, pies, tarts, and pastries. Baking is more precise and scientific than any other type of cooking, with recipes that must be followed as carefully as chemical formulas. In baking, we recommend that you read the recipe twice and have all your ingredients measured before getting started, then follow the recipe exactly the first couple of times you make it. Once you feel you have mastered the recipe, you can begin to vary the ingredients or change the pan size, making adjustments according to your previous results.

The Baker's Reasons

There are many good reasons for baking at home: the things you make yourself may taste better and cost you less than those you buy commercially, and you have control over the kinds and quality of the ingredients you use. Homemade cakes, cookies, and breads can be free of preservatives and made with your favorite ingredients. Best of all, home-baked sweets and breads give the baker a great sense of accomplishment and, when shared, a great sense of pleasure. Of course, baking is a science, so to make certain that everything you

bake at home is successful, you should have the right equipment to do the job.

Bakeware Standards

Pans used in the oven are subject to a different form of heat than those produced for use on a stovetop burner. Oven heat is indirect; a pan for oven use, therefore, can be tinned or enameled on all surfaces without danger of the tin melting or the enamel cracking at a hot spot caused by the application of direct heat. Oven heat is general and even: the pan simply transfers the heat to the contents from all sides, rather than transmitting it intensely and directly through the pan's bottom. This makes glass a better material for a baking dish than for a saucepan.

In baking pans we often prefer weightiness and solidity of construction, but there are whisper-light pastries like *langues de chat* (cat's tongues) that are best baked on a lightweight pan that heats and cools rapidly enough to avoid overcooking the tender cakes. Bakeware should not encourage foods to stick; you want a surface that gracefully loosens its hold when required. Metal surfaces release cakes easily when they are properly greased or buttered and floured, and most nonstick surfaces are quick-release artists whether they are buttered or not. We are partial to standard finishes for baking sheets and cake pans, but today's high-tech nonstick finishes are almost irresistible when used for certain pans. Dark finishes encourage browning. Where we found one surface to be clearly better than the other for a particular item, we tell you so, but when several do a fine job, we give you a choice.

Using Baking Pans

A few words of caution: when we mention the capacity of a baking pan, such as "½ cup" or "1 quart," this refers to the amount of batter that it will hold if filled to the brim. That's how baking pans are measured and often identified in recipes. Of course, this leaves no room for rising, which is what you hope your batter will do; to allow room for rising, you generally should use only two-thirds as much batter as the pan will hold.

Shapes

Many cakes and breads have a unique shape: consider the brioche, the madeleine, or the muffin. In baking, the pan and the product often seem to have evolved together, the pan becoming an integral part of the recipe. Can you imagine trying to cook brownies in brioche tins, or a lemon pie in a loaf pan? Ridiculous as these prospects are, they illustrate the enormous importance of using the right pan when baking.

BAKING SHEETS

THIS IS THE PAN to use for baking any kind of cookie, from chunky oatmeal to fragile Florentine. It's the lack of sides that make a baking sheet a baking sheet and not a jelly-roll pan. A baking sheet must have at least one side without a rim of any kind and may have as many as three rimless sides. The open sides ease the task of removing baked products from the sheet.

A nonstick finish is a blessing when it comes to cleaning up, and it may be what you'll want to use for certain kinds of tuiles and lace cookies, but a nonstick baking sheet often will bake faster than a regular one and, if the finish is dark—and most nonstick finishes are—you may find that the bottoms of your cookies are too well done and the cookies themselves too hard. Of course, you can get all the advantages of a nonstick baking sheet without the accompanying problems by lining a traditional baking sheet with parchment paper, reusable parchment sheets, or one of the rubberized silicone baking mats from France.

What size should you choose? In general, you should try to buy the largest baking sheets your oven can accommodate—obviously, the larger the baking sheet, the fewer batches of cookies you'll have to bake—but remember to allow at least 2" of air space between the pan's sides and the oven's walls. However, you'll need at least one smaller baking sheet in your cupboard. There are times, for example, when you will have to chill a dough on a sheet before baking it so, depending on the size of your refrigerator and freezer, a small sheet may be necessary.

How many should you have? Two baking sheets is the baker's minimum and four is the ideal. Having four sheets will help you in two ways: first, it will save time because you can shape cookies on one pair of sheets while another batch bakes on the other pair; and second, you can be more certain of your cookies' quality because you're putting dough on a cool baking sheet, an absolute necessity for success. But no matter how many sheets you have and no matter what their finishes, it is important to remember that when you bake with two sheets at the same time, if you can't fit both sheets on the same oven rack you should rotate the sheets top to bottom and front to back halfway through the baking period. This helps eliminate the risk of having the cookies on the bottom sheet brown too much from the heat reflected off the top baking sheet.

16.1 MAGIC LINE COOKIE SHEET

Here is the best-of-class in baking sheets. Even if you stock up on sheets with nonstick finishes or purchase an insulated baking sheet, you should have at least two of the Magic Line sheets because they are made of shiny aluminum, the standard among bakers and, more important for the home baker, the standard among most recipe developers and cookbook authors. The shine on the finish is important because it reflects rather than absorbs heat, so cookies and biscuits don't overbake, and the aluminum heats quickly and evenly. Use this baking sheet and, all other factors being equal, the baking time for any of your cookies should match the baking time given in your recipe, a condition that does not always hold true with sheets that have darker finishes. This sheet, rimless on two sides, is 18" long by 12" wide and made of one seamless piece of heavy-duty aluminum that rises on the two rimmed sides to a height of 1" and finishes with ½"-wide flanges that are handy to grab. The sheet is strong, durable, and unlikely to warp under normal baking temperatures, which is important since a buckled sheet will not heat evenly.

16.2 FARBERWARE MILLENNIUM COOKIE SHEET

As nonstick baking sheets go, this one best approximates the baking conditions of a standard-finish sheet, and it has the added convenience of an easy-release surface. It's 18" long by 13" wide, with long sides that flare slightly to create 1"-wide raised rims with nicely rounded corners. The nonstick dishwasher-safe finish, which the manufacturer guarantees for a lifetime, is a medium gray color with a slight sheen to it, which is part of the reason it bakes so well. However, even with its lighter-color finish, the manufacturer wisely recommends that you check for doneness at the shortest baking time—we recommend that you check even earlier than that—or reduce the oven temperature by 25°F. This sheet is sturdier than it appears, and will not warp under normal cookie-baking heat.

16.3 MATFER OVEN BAKING SHEET

Neither a true baking sheet nor a jelly-roll pan, the Matfer sheet is a hybrid with heft. Weighing in at 3¼ pounds, it's about 14½" long by 10¼" wide with ½" wide flaring sides and rounded corners. The four slightly rimmed sides keep this from being a traditional baking sheet, while the low and flaring construction of the rims keeps it from being a jelly-roll pan. Whatever you want to call it, this baking sheet, fashioned from gunmetal-colored black steel, is fine for cookies and breads, and strong enough to support the heaviest tarts, tortes, or soufflés. With its extra-heavy weight and all-around rims, there's no risk of buckling, no matter the temperature. However, because of its color, we recommend that you check the doneness of anything you bake, particularly cookies, very early and often.

16.4 KAISER EXTRAORDINAIRE COOKIE SHEET

This 16" by 14" baking sheet with three open sides is constructed of two layers of nonstick steel joined only at the perimeter, a design that creates a layer of insulating air under the baking surface. The bottom sheet is pressed into several X patterns that add strength to the sheet's structure and keep it from warping. When insulated sheets first came out, their gentler heat meant that cookies took longer to bake than

---

A PASSION FOR PASTRY
✤ FRANÇOIS PAYARD ✤

For as long as I can remember, I've had a passion for pastry—a gift from my parents, who had a pastry shop in Nice on the French Riviera. The passion grew significantly when I was thirteen, when they arranged a summer job for me with an amazing 65-year-old pâtissier, Monsieur Ghinone. The hours were long, the work was hard, but in the end I had such a wonderful sense of accomplishment. "Look!" he would say. "Look what you did! Look what you can create!" His passion and enthusiasm were contagious and they inspire me to this day. Pastry-making is so much more than just following a recipe. It is an art before it is anything else, and it is a science. You have to be able to draw, to sculpt, to have a refined dexterity with chocolate. Then you need the scientist's control of temperature, leavening, and crystallization, and you need to know the chemistry of the ingredients—butter, flour, chocolate, eggs. You can only improvise and break new ground when you understand the ingredients, but once you do, there are almost no limits. For me there's tremendous excitement in creating something different every day, of finding new ways to combine flavors. There's also real pleasure and deep satisfaction in working with the dough and mastering it. The passion for pastry is as obsessive as any great love in one's life. It keeps you coming back, every day, renewed and ready to begin again.

most recipes indicated. Now, with sheets like this one, the darker nonstick surfaces neutralize the effects of the air cushion—the heat is still gentle, but the baking times come closer to the norm. Still, to be sure the manufacturer suggests that you check for doneness early. As with all insulated bakeware, cleaning can be a little tricky. It's best to wash this sheet by hand and not to immerse it in a sink full of water, since immersion can allow water to seep between the layers. Just to be on the safe side, it's good to evaporate any water that may have absorbed into the interior by drying the sheet in a warm oven for a few minutes. This pan should not be your only baking sheet, but it's a good addition for anyone who bakes cookies and biscuits frequently.

JELLY-ROLL PANS

A jelly-roll pan is a baking sheet with inch-high sides all around. In a pinch, it could be used to bake cookies, especially if used upside-down, but because of its sides, it's much better suited to the cakes that gave it its name, as well as to sheet cakes, rolls, or breads, and to supporting tartlet tins that might slide off a baking sheet. The criteria for choosing a jelly-roll pan are the same as those for selecting a baking sheet: an even heating capacity, sturdy construction, and a size that's compatible with your oven and your refrigerator. Jelly-roll pans come with uncoated and nonstick finishes. There's even a jelly-roll pan with a perforated base, a neat tool for getting the bottoms of your rolls toasty brown.

16.5 & 16.6 CHICAGO METALLIC COMMERCIAL STANDARD & NONSTICK JELLY-ROLL PANS

Jelly-roll pans are useful items for doing everything from baking a *genoise* sheet cake to roasting peppers. These Chicago Metallic pans measure 18" by 13" and have a rim that's 1" high, rolled at the top and gently rounded at the corners. They are strong, well constructed and available in models roughly half their size (that is, 12¼" by 9"). Made of steel, they come with a matte uncoated aluminum finish or a Silverstone nonstick surface. If you plan to use the pan for baking, the standard matte finish is your best choice, since most cakes bake better in an uncoated pan and, if you're making sheet cakes, in all likelihood you'll be lining the pan with parchment anyway. However, if roasting vegetables and fish or toasting croutons is what you've got in mind, the nonstick jelly-roll pan may be better for you; certainly you'll be happy with it when cleanup time rolls around.

16.7 CHICAGO METALLIC PERFORATED BAKING PAN

This pan looks like an 18" by 13" nonstick jelly-roll pan, but don't try to make a sheet cake in it: its baking surface is covered with tiny holes, hundreds of them. The pan, used primarily by professionals, allows the oven's heat to come in direct contact with the bottom of whatever you're baking, making it just right for formed doughs, such as buns and rolls. It's especially good for use in a convection oven, where foods are cooked by hot air that is circulated around the food.

LARGE & SMALL CAKES

In France distinction is usually made between individual cakes, *gâteaux à la pièce* (éclairs, mirlitons, *salammbôs*, conversations, *puits d'amour*, etc.) and large cakes (Genoese sponge cakes, *croquembouches*, *vacherins*, etc.). Both sometimes bear the name of the person who created them (*quillet*, *beauvilliers*, etc.) or the person to whom they were dedicated (such as *savarin*), or the name of their place of origin (pithiviers, Paris-Brest, breton, etc.). However, cakes are most often given a fanciful name or a name that describes their method of preparation (manqué, *quatre-quarts*, mille-feuille, etc.).

The name *gâteaux secs* is given in France to plain petits fours, biscuits (cookies), etc., served with tea or ice cream.

Finally, the name *gâteau* is given to culinary preparations made with vegetable purée or various hashes molded and cooked in a *bain-marie* and served as an entrée or a garnish.

—*Larousse Gastronomique*, edited by Jenifer Lang

LINERS & BAKING MATS

IN ADDITION TO standard parchment paper, baking liners and mats are new tools that can give any pan a quick-release surface. The most popular materials for these high-tech wonders are rubberized silicone and reusuable parchment (a nonstick-coated fiberglass); both are excellent, able to withstand temperatures up to 500°F, reusable hundreds (and some thousands) of times, and easy to clean.

16.8, 16.9, & 16.10
KATCHALL COOK-EZE
REUSABLE ROUND, SQUARE,
& RECTANGULAR PAN LINERS

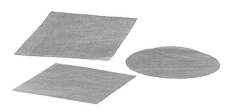

These nonstick-coated fiberglass liners are as thin as parchment paper and as slick as waxed paper. They may look like a fine silk-and-linen fabric that a designer would turn into an evening dress, but they are kitchen workhorses, tough, durable, and dependable—just drop them into a baking pan (there's no right or wrong side) and you have an instant nonstick surface. These reusable baking pan liners come in all different sizes: an 8" or 9" round, a 7½" or 8½" square, a 12½" by 8½" rectangle, or a 17" by 11½" rectangle made for a baking sheet or jelly-roll pan. Two liners of the same size come packed in a clear plastic tube for easy storage. Like their more expensive French relative, the Silpat, Cook-Eze pan liners can be reused (the manufacturer says hundreds of times per side). They easily wipe clean and withstand an oven temperature of 600°F.

16.11 DEMARLE HALF-SIZE
SILPAT LINER

At first, this baking mat was available only in France, and then, when it arrived in the United States, only to professionals. Recently it has become available to home bakers throughout North America. It gives any baking sheet or jelly-roll pan a perfect nonstick surface. The mat is about ⅛" thick and made of flexible glass fiber and food-grade silicone. It measures 16½" by 11⅞" and is smooth on top and a little nubby underneath. With one of these mats lining your baking sheet, you can make anything from the most delicate cookies to the stickiest sticky buns. Nothing will adhere to the surface, and cleaning will be a breeze—just wipe it dry with a sponge. The mats can withstand oven temperatures of 500°F, and according to the manufacturer, can be used more than two thousand times. Never store your liners by folding them in half: they will split in two. Instead, keep them stored flat in a baking sheet. The liners also come in three other sizes: 24½" by 16½", 11" by 17", and 11" by 8¼".

BAKING PANS

WITH THESE PANS, we enter the realm of brownies and bar cookies, cornbread squares, sweet marble cake swirled with dark chocolate, tea cakes, quick breads, and yeast-raised loaves. The pans for making these goodies are available in earthenware (see chapter 13), metal with a choice of uncoated or nonstick finishes, and glass. What you are baking will determine whether you want a glass pan or a metal pan (the preferred pan for the sweet things), and whether that pan will be nonstick or not. Since glass and dark metal pans bake their contents darker and faster and often produce a thicker crust than other metal pans, they are a better choice for breads, including quick breads without too much butter or sugar, than for cakes. Similarly, when it comes to loaf pans, glass pans and the darker metal ones are better for breads and meat loaves, while uncoated metal pans are the best choice for baking cakes, especially chocolate cakes and cakes with a lot of sugar, both of which have a tendency to burn under too much heat.

There's no firm rule about which kind of pan to use for which kind of food, but in general, square and rectangular pans are used for cakes, brownies, bar cookies, and quick breads. The most common sizes are 8″ by 8″, 9″ by 9″, and 9″ by 13″. The most common sizes for loaf pans are 9″ by 5″ by 2¾″ and 8½″ by 4½″ by 2¾″, but the 7½″ by 3¾″ by 2¼″ pan is nice for tea cakes, while the not-often-seen 1½-pound, 10″ by 5″ by 2¾″ pan is good for sandwich breads, pâtés, and meat loaves.

Now, there's a third alternative for baking pans, besides metal and glass ones: flexible molds made from silicon-coated fiberglass. They come in all different sizes and shapes. Though the material is lightweight, resilient, and easy to clean, the pans tend to produce a pale, crisp crust, not our preferred golden, moist crust for cakes and quick breads.

16.12 MAGIC LINE SQUARE BAKING PAN

This heavy-duty aluminum 8″ by 8″ pan, with its straight 2″ high sides and crisply mitered corners, is ideal for brownies and gingerbread, homey coffee cakes, and simple butter cakes. Its weight, shiny finish, and aluminum construction work together to provide even heat and produce cakes with thin, supple crusts. The manufacturer's hallmark, a ½″ flange, finishes each side and makes it easier to grip the pan when sliding it, full of batter, into the oven or checking on a cake's progress at the midway point. Unfortunately, although the flanges are rounded at the corners, they were not finished as smoothly as we might like—a problem that has since been corrected. Magic Line also makes rectangular pans ranging in size from 8″ by 11″ by 2″ to the commercial 16″ by 24″ by 2″. We suggest both a square and a rectangular pan if you're an enthusiastic baker.

The wedding cake ritual took hold in the 1930s, when dense British cakes were encased in extra-hard white icing to hold up pillared layers. The groom "helped" the bride to cut the cake with a beribboned knife or sword. Now the pair perform as a team.

—MARGARET VISSER,
The Rituals of Dinner

this 9″ by 13″ pan will serve you well (it's also available in an 8″ square). This German import is made of commercial-weight steel and coated inside and out with a medium-gray nonstick finish that is not affected by acidic foods. While the manufacturer says that the finish will remain unharmed if you cut against it, we recommend that you treat this pan as you would all other bakeware—gently. Cuts and nicks on any pan can affect its performance and make the removal of your baked goods difficult. The pan has 2″-high sides, two of which extend for easy handling. It is ideal for corn breads and other quick breads and fine for cakes, provided you pay close attention to the baking times and check for doneness at the shortest baking time given in the recipe. This pan holds up to 12 cups.

around for decades (actually since 1919)—Pyrex. Originally called "fire glass" because it could withstand heat, Pyrex has proven to be an excellent material for bakeware—the best, in fact, for pies, and very good for quick breads, custardy cakes, and fruit desserts, not to mention countless savory dishes. This 3-quart oblong pan measures 13″ by 9″ by 2″. Pyrex also makes a smaller 2-quart version and larger 4-quart one, along with an 8″ square cake dish. Although these pans are not technically nonstick, few things stick to them and those that do clean away quickly and easily after the pan has been soaked in hot water. Because Pyrex pans attract and retain heat so efficiently, it is recommended that you reduce the oven temperature specified in your recipe by 25°F.

16.13 KAISER LA FORME RECTANGULAR PAN

When a delicate color or lighter side and bottom crust is not paramount,

16.14 PYREX OBLONG BAKING PAN

With all the high-tech equipment in the marketplace these days, it's easy to overlook something that's been

16.15 MAGIC LINE LOAF PAN

This aluminum loaf pan has straight sides, well-joined corners, and the manufacturer's characteristic flanged edges for an easy grip. The pan is a

BAKING PANS: STANDARD VS. NONSTICK

One of the greatest changes in bakeware over the past few decades has been the proliferation of nonstick finishes. Once found primarily on cookware, today just about every size, shape, and kind of baking pan can be purchased with some type of nonstick finish, and almost all of the finishes are effective, releasing cakes, cookies, muffins, or tartlets with no resistance and simplifying the clean-up. However, convenient as these finishes are, they are not the answer to every prayer for every type of baked good. Since nonstick surfaces are dark and usually not shiny, they have properties that differ from standard finishes and you need to take these differences into account when you're working on a recipe.

The trouble has to do with the fact that recipes rarely tell you the kind of bakeware, standard or nonstick, that the recipe's creator used to develop the recipe. As a rule of thumb, unless a recipe specifies a nonstick pan, you should assume that the recipe was developed, tested, and written for standard pans. Since most nonstick finishes will often shorten the baking time, darken the color of your baked good's crust, and possibly affect the texture of whatever you're baking—cookies baked on nonstick baking sheets are often overdone on the bottom and sometimes hard all around—it's best to follow the instructions provided by the bakeware manufacturer. Many manufacturers of nonstick bakeware suggest that you lower the oven's temperature by 25°F to compensate for the tendency of a nonstick finish to retain heat, and check the doneness of whatever you're baking at the shortest time specified in the recipe, maybe even a few minutes earlier. Do this and you should end up with a result that comes close to what you would have got had you used a standard pan and, of course, you'll have the conveniences that come with nonstick finishes.

---

petite 7½" by 3¾", a nice size for tea and pound cakes, though it's also available in a larger 12½" by 4⅝" by 2¾" size. With this pan's shiny finish and aluminum construction, your cakes and quick breads will bake and brown evenly. While it is adequate for breads, it is definitely not the pan you should choose for meat loaves or pâtés, in part because such loaves are traditionally not unmolded and you wouldn't want to cut in this pan, and in part because the aluminum might react unpleasantly with any acidic ingredients.

16.16 PYREX LOAF PAN

Since it was first patented at the Corning Glass Works in 1919, Pyrex has consistently been a useful and economical material for kitchen equipment. Plain as it is, it has acquired a certain classic attractiveness. The glass conducts heat efficiently and, because it is colorless, it permits the baker to watch the dough as it forms that nice crust characteristic of loaves baked in glass. This 1½-quart loaf pan, 8½" by 4½" by 2½", is good for yeast breads and quick breads and, because you can cut in it without marring the surface, usable for savory terrines. This pan's popularity will endure for generations to come.

16.17 CHICAGO METALLIC PROFESSIONAL LOAF PAN

This is the loaf pan you'll turn to when you want to produce a yeast bread with a deeply browned crust, and it's also the one for baking quick breads or loaf cakes with a firm crust and moist interior. The pan's Silverstone nonstick coating provides the deep browning capability. The pan is constructed from a single piece of steel that is pressed into shape, with the fold lines visible on the outside of the short ends. It is a useful 8½" by 4½" by 2¾", with rolled top edges, straight corners, and ever-so-slightly flaring short sides, a nice shape for breads and a traditional one for certain kinds of very simple European nut and pound cakes. We recommend that you lower your oven's temperature by 25°F when using this pan and check for doneness early. It's best if you unmold any cake, meat loaves, or terrines before serving; a sharp knife or spatula could damage the finish of the pan.

16.18 KAISER LA FORME NON-STICK MINI-LOAF PAN SET

Perfect for turning out loaves of bread destined to be used for tea sandwiches, cakes to be wrapped for gift giving, or savory terrines to be served as dinner-party starters, these non-stick loaf pans come packaged in sets of four. Measuring 6" by 3" by 2" deep, each is constructed of a single piece of steel folded into shape, rolled at the top, and coated with an effective medium-gray nonstick finish. Each pan holds 2 cups.

16.19 CHICAGO METALLIC MINI-LOAF STRAPPED SET

This set of four mini-loaf pans (each 6" by 3" by 2" deep, wih a capacity of 2 cups) is built for the long haul. Each

"Who could have imagined that such a wonderful recipe for brownies would be hidden in the Dead Sea Scrolls?"

pan is constructed from a single sheet of aluminized steel, folded into shape at the sides, rolled at the top, and secured to inch-wide steel bands so that they line up with an inch of space between them. Because the pans are made of aluminized steel, combining the excellent heat-conducting properties of aluminum and the strength of steel, they are particularly good for cakes, quick breads, and sweet, rich yeast breads like brioches.

CAKE PANS

WITH FEW EXCEPTIONS, cakes, from the plainest to the most elaborate, depend on pans to give them form. Since the batters are most often raised by air trapped in beaten eggs or by gas formed by baking powder or by baking soda plus acid, they are fragile, and need pans that will heat evenly and help them rise to their fullest potential. In this section we cover only round cake pans—what many bakers think of as layer-cake pans—but within this seemingly limited purview, there are variations in materials and even more variations in kind.

How do you choose the right kind of cake pan? Most cakes are baked in round cake pans that are 9" across and at least 1½" high. Once considered an item only for professionals, there are now several pans available to the home cook with 2" high sides, a depth we recommend. Even if you are a once-a-year birthday-cake baker you'll appreciate their versatility. Today, there are also round cake pans with decoratively patterned bottoms—bake a plain cake, invert it, and you'll have to do nothing but dust it with sugar. Then there are springform pans, pans with removable sides, which are often used to make cheesecakes but fine for any kind of cake that is too fragile to be turned out of a conventional pan. Finally, there are cake rings, the preferred baking pan for French pastry chefs. Cake rings are bottomless and depend on a parchment-lined baking sheet for support and a base; they turn out beautifully straight-sided cakes and double as forms for layering cakes.

How do you choose a material? For the most part, round cake pans come in aluminum and steel, with or without nonstick finishes. Aluminum remains the traditional first choice, as it does for most baking pans, since it heats most evenly. As you'll see, however, today's nonstick pans, and pans made of combined materials, particularly a combination of steel and aluminum (a favorite among commercial bakers), are worthy rivals to the aluminum standard.

How many pans should you buy? It is best to have at least two, preferably three, round cake pans of the same diameter. Most American cake recipes call for a 9″ round pan, but 8″ pans are also popular. The most practical pans are at least 2″ deep because they allow you to cut two American-style or three European-style layers from one cake. You may only need one springform, but when you see the varieties available, you may have a problem deciding on just one. As for cake rings, the number you will need will depend on the kind of baking you do. Usually, one ring is enough to bake a cake and then assemble it, but you might want to have rings in more than one size.

LAYER CAKE PANS

These are the pans that produce the classics, the cakes that you stack one layer on top of another with lots of frosting or whipped cream in between, or cut into thinner slices to spread with jams or ganaches. Because symmetry is important in a layered cake, the pan's ability to heat evenly and thereby produce an even cake is paramount. Straight-sided pans are also important in keeping the cake's shape uniform. Any of the choices below will give you the even heat you need, but some, notably the pans with nonstick finishes, will give you a slightly darker crust. For most people, the slight deepening of color is a fair trade for the convenience of easy release and easy cleanup.

16.20 MAGIC LINE CAKE PAN

This is the kind of pan pastry chefs prefer and most cookbook authors use when they are developing recipes, and it is the pan we recommend you buy and use as your standard. It is a simple 9″ diameter pan constructed of one piece of heavy-duty aluminum that heats quickly and, most important, evenly. Its sides are straight, 2″ high, and rolled at the rim. Because the sides are high and straight, the pan is perfect for American layer cakes, just as good for any European recipes, fine for quick breads (an Irish soda bread would turn out well in this pan), sticky buns, and even *tarte tatin*. This pan is available in diameters from 2″ to 24″.

16.21 CHICAGO METALLIC PROFESSIONAL CAKE PAN

Fashioned in heavy-gauge steel and finished inside with an excellent Silverstone nonstick coating, this 9″ diameter cake pan has 2″-high straight sides that are rolled at the rim. It will turn in a fine performance if you follow the manufacturer's direction and set the oven temperature 25°F below the temperature specified in your recipe and check the degree of doneness at the beginning of the time period given in your recipe. This is a well-made pan that should be long-lasting if you take proper care of the nonstick finish. This means avoid cleaning it with a scouring pad, use wood, nylon, rubber, or plastic tools, and do not cut in the pan, a restriction that shouldn't be a problem since the nonstick finish should eliminate the need to run a knife around the sides of the pan to release a cake.

16.22 ALL-CLAD CAKE PAN

You know a pan attracts and retains heat well when, like this one, it's almost too hot to handle when you wash it. What makes this pan problematic in the sink is what makes it stellar in the oven: five-ply construction. The outer layer is stainless steel, which is bonded to alloy aluminum, which in turn is bonded to pure aluminum, then another layer of alloy, and finally another of stainless steel. This last layer is given a gold-color stick-resistant finish that forms the inner surface of the pan. The manufacturer, All-Clad, has earned a fine reputation in cookware and you can see why with this 9″ round cake pan with 2″-high sides, a shallow rim, and two generous grips. The pan has the look and heft of high-caliber cookware. While it bakes remarkably evenly and cleans easily, you'll be just as satisfied using it for macaroni and cheese as for molten chocolate cake. Given that the pan's cost is at least five times that of most other cake pans, double duty is doubly appreciated.

16.23 EKCO BAKER'S SECRET ROUND CAKE PAN

Surprising is the best word to describe this simple pan from EKCO: it performs surprisingly well. Made of steel coated with a shiny medium-gray nonstick finish, it is 9″ across with sides that are 1½″ high. The sides are not quite straight, which presents a structural problem when you need to stack two cakes. However, what the pan lacks in straightness it makes up for in utility. It is a fine pan for American cakes, quick breads, and even yeasted rolls. Because its nonstick finish is light and shiny, there is little risk of overbrowning a cake, although the manufacturer does suggest that you set the oven temperature to 25°F below the recipe's

---

TRADITIONAL VANILLA BIRTHDAY CAKE

1 three-layer 9″ cake or 24 cupcakes

1 cup (2 sticks) unsalted butter, softened
2 cups sugar
4 large eggs, at room temperature

1½ cups self-rising flour
1¼ cups all-purpose flour
1 cup milk
1 teaspoon vanilla extract

PREHEAT OVEN TO 350°F.
Grease and lightly flour three 9″ by 2″ round cake pans, then line the bottoms with waxed paper.

TO MAKE THE CAKE
In a large bowl, on the medium speed of an electric mixer, cream the butter until smooth. Add the sugar gradually and beat until fluffy, about 3 minutes. Add the eggs one at a time, beating well after each addition. Combine the flours and add in four parts, alternating with the milk and the vanilla extract, beating well after each addition. Divide the batter among the cake pans. Bake for 20 to 25 minutes, or until a cake tester inserted into center of cake comes out clean. Let cakes cool in pans for ten minutes. Remove from pans and cool completely on wire rack.

If you're making cupcakes, line two 12-cup muffin tins with cupcake papers. Spoon the batter into the cups about three-quarters full. Bake until the tops spring back when lightly touched, about 20 to 22 minutes. Remove cupcakes from pans and cool completely on a rack before icing.

When cake has cooled, ice between the layers, then ice top and sides of cake.

TRADITIONAL VANILLA BUTTERCREAM

Icing for 1 two- or three-layer 9″ cake or 24 cupcakes

1 cup (2 sticks) unsalted butter, very soft
8 cups confectioners' sugar

½ cup milk
2 teaspoons vanilla extract

Place the butter in a large mixing bowl. Add 4 cups of the sugar and then the milk and the vanilla extract. Beat until smooth and creamy. Gradually add the remaining sugar, 1 cup at a time, until icing is thick enough to be of good spreading consistency (you may very well not need all of the sugar). If desired, add a few drops of food coloring and mix thoroughly. Use and store icing at room temperature, as icing will set if chilled. Can store in airtight container up to three days.

The Magnolia Bakery, by Jennifer Appel and Allysa Torey

recommended temperature or check the cake for doneness at the shortest specified time.

16.24 J. B. PRINCE MINI ROUND CAKE/FLAN PAN

While this looks like just the kind of cake pan you might give to the kids to mold mud pies, this little pan is the one professionals reach for when they are making individual-size desserts. It is 4" across with 1¼"-high straight sides and constructed of steel, its outside a brown enamel and its interior a lighter brown nonstick finish that is matte with a slight sheen. The pan is ideal for one-to-a-person plain cakes (use your favorite butter-cake recipe) and even better for any kind of upside-down cake, since its nonstick finish removes the risk of breaking the cake when turning it out. We suggest that you buy at least six.

16.25 MAGI-CAKE STRIPS

When a loaf cake crowns and cracks, it looks homey and inviting. But when a layer cake domes, it's a problem—the dome must be sliced off before the cake is frosted, which can be a tricky business. Cakes dome primarily because the sides that come in contact with the metal pan bake more quickly than the interior. Magi-Cake Strips, aluminized fabric strips that are wrapped around an 8" or 9" round cake pan, are designed to level layer cakes. The strips, which are sold in pairs, are moistened, then pinned into place shiny side out, so that they reflect heat away from the pan. The reflection and moisture slow down the rate at which the sides bake, and the cake emerges from the oven without a high-rise center or cracked top.

CAKE RINGS

European cake rings are hard to find in nonprofessional American kitchens, but should be considered by home bakers who want to turn out cakes with professional polish. Like tart and flan rings, cake rings (or *entremet* rings as they are known in France) are bottomless rings that must be used in conjunction with a lined baking sheet. Since a cake baked in a ring is not unmolded—it's the ring that's removed, not the cake—the ring is ideal for baking delicate cakes. Here's how it works: the batter is spooned into the ring and baked on a lined baking sheet; the resulting cake is then cut into layers and the ring, washed and dried, is used to assemble the finished cake, a nifty way to construct a multilayered cake with sides as straight as an arrow. The ring is placed on a parchment-lined baking sheet and the first layer of cake is slipped into it. Using a pastry brush, the cake is soaked with a flavored simple syrup. A layer of frosting, whipped cream, ganache, or mousse is then added, followed by the next cake layer, which is slipped into place. The process is continued until the cake is assembled, at which point the cake is refrigerated or frozen until the layers are set. Then comes the neatest trick, one we learned from the renowned Parisian pastry chef, Pierre Hermé: you use a hairdryer to warm the metal ring so you can easily lift it off the cake. Do so and you'll find a clean, straight-sided cake that's ready for its final icing or finish. Once you learn to use cake rings—and adapt your recipes accordingly—it's easy to become a convert to this different way of baking.

16.26 J. B. PRINCE ENTREMET RING

Nothing more than a 1⅓"-high band of stainless steel, this cake ring can be used to bake the fanciest French confections or the simplest American layer cakes. It is 9½" across, a common size, but the rings are available in diameters from 2¾" to 12". The single piece of heavy-gauge steel, unfinished at the top and bottom, is perfectly flat—a characteristic that should also hold true for the baking sheet you'll use to provide the ring's bottom and support. Since the same ring can be used for baking and assembling, and since most European layer cakes are cut from one cake, it is not imperative that you start your ring collection with more than one ring of one size. You can also use the smallest sizes for assembling cylinders of chopped vegetable salads. This cake ring is available with 2⅓"-high sides as well.

16.27 J. B. PRINCE QUADRANT CAKE FORM

This is an unusually fanciful cake ring—more a form than a ring—that would make a stunning chocolate cake finished with shiny chocolate glaze. It is almost a square, but its corners are gently rounded and the middle of each side is slightly curved. The form is about 7½" across and the sides are a little over 1½" high, to make a small and elegant cake.

16.28 MATFER ADJUSTABLE TART RING

If you're not certain that baking a cake in a ring will be right for you, you might want to start with this adjustable blued-steel ring imported from France. Although Matfer calls this a tart ring, we think it works well for cakes. It is constructed of a 2"-high band of steel that can be expanded by adjusting two metal bands that move easily around the ring. At full size, the ring measures 14" across; pulled tight, it is a petite 7¼" in diameter. Unfortunately, the metal bands that adjust the ring can leave their mark on the sides of a cake, but this seems a small price to pay for the convenience and versatility of this ring. The band is extremely well made and will last through years of baking if you take care to butter the ring before filling it with batter and, most important, be certain to dry the ring immediately; otherwise it will rust. For best results, put the washed ring back in the hot oven until it is dry.

CAKE PANS WITH DESIGNS

Like *Bundt* and *Kugelhopf* tube pans, whose shapes become part of the cake's decoration, round cake pans also can be decorative. Obviously, cake pans with designs have the designs on the bottom of the pan, so that what is normally the top of a cake becomes the bottom. In choosing a cake pan with a design, it is important to choose a pan with the same heat conducting properties you value in your other baking pans.

16.29 KAISER LA FORME *GÂTEAU* PAN

Here is a large pan that can turn your plainest cake into a special-occasion treat. It is 10½" in diameter and a full 3" high, made of commercial-weight steel with a matte, medium-gray nonstick finish. The bottom of the pan is embossed in a daisy pattern, with raised petals, narrow at the center and broad at the edge, radiating from a center circle. If you do nothing more than dust the cake with sugar or cocoa, it will be attractive. However, the pattern lends itself so readily to elaboration that you may want to glaze the cake and accentuate its lines with icing.

16.30 DR. OETKER *OBSTTORTE* PAN

The Germans are fanatics about the health-giving properties of fruit, but they also have a weakness for *Kuchen* (cakes). *Obsttorte* (fruit torte) provides the happy solution for someone torn between eating healthful food and indulging his sweet tooth, and *Obsttorten* of all kinds are understandably popular in most areas of Central Europe. The depressed center area of the baked cake is spread with fresh fruit according to the season. In the fall, a flurry of canning ensures that *Obsttorten* will still grace the winter *Kaffeetisch* (coffee table). Often a variety of fruits are used: bananas, pears, cherries, and peaches may be arranged in colorful patterns. The fruit may be glazed with gelatin and the torte is often served with generous mounds of whipped cream. This form for making *Obsttorten* is stamped out of a single sheet of metal. The waffled bottom is scratch resistant and gives the metal added strength and the fluted sides provide a decorative finish to the rich, cakelike pastry that will hold the fruit. The pan is 11"

in diameter and 1½" deep—large enough to hold a quart of batter.

The German word *Rehrücken* is literally translated as "roe's (deer's) back," and means "saddle of venison." In fact it is also the name of a delicious chocolate log cake with crosswise ribbing, richly iced and studded with almonds, made in a mold like this one. It is an Austrian delicacy of long standing. After feasting on a genuine saddle of venison, visibly and generously larded with fat to add succulence to the meat, a successful and contented hunter could enjoy the joke of a look-alike dessert; for the unsuccessful hunter, the *Rehrücken* could conceivably offer consolation.

A flat "backbone" runs the length of this 12" gray steel nonstick pan to balance it, and the nineteen "ribs" make it easy to divide the cake into uniform slices. The classic cake, made with ground almonds instead of flour, is so rich that the portions should be small. You can use the pan for baking other cakes, too, or for bread.

SPRINGFORM PANS

A springform pan is a superb solution to the problem of removing a delicate cake like torte or cheesecake without damaging it. It is the unique construction of the springform that makes this possible: the sides of the pan are separate from the bottom and spring free automatically when a clamp is released, so the cake can be removed without having to invert it.

It is not an exaggeration to call this pan revolutionary. A fairly standard 9½" by 2¾" size, it has three unusual features. First, its sides, which like all springform pans release at the flick of the clamp, have a nonstick coating, so there is usually no need to run a knife between the pan and the cake, a process that often results in the cake having ragged edges. Second, its base is heatproof glass. Since most cakes made in a springform pan must be served on the pan's base, it is nice to have a base that, once the first slice is removed, reveals your serving plate rather than a crumb-covered piece of metal. Also, since you must slice on the base, it is comforting to know that your knife won't mar the glass. Finally, the pan has two handles large enough to grip, even when you're wearing oven mitts. The handles are firmly bolted into the pan's sides, and a blessing when the pan is filled with batter and needs to go from counter to oven.

If this were a traditional springform pan, we would still recommend it for its fine baking qualities and its excellent nonstick finish, but it has a few innovative features that make it exceptional. The pan is 9" in diameter and almost 3" high. Its sides release, as do all springforms, when you open a clamp, but because the side piece is symmetrical—there is no right-side-up—you can flip it so that both right- and left-handed users can easily maneuver the clamp. The base has the usual groove for the side piece to rest in, but it also has a trough that circles the side, which is what gives the pan its "leakproof" name. While the trough is more drip-than leakproof, it is effective. As anyone who has baked a buttery cake in a springform pan knows, a drip here and there is inevitable; with this pan, it may still be inevitable, but it won't be as messy. Best of all, the pan is coated with a nonstick finish that is resistant to cuts, solving the problem of how to cut a creamy cheesecake without damaging the base.

TUBE PANS

Tube pans come in many shapes and patterns, but whether the pans are fluted, as they are in the *Kugelhopf* and *Bundt* versions, or plain, the function of the central tube is the same. The tube conducts heat into the center of the batter, an area which otherwise might still be uncooked by the time the outside of the cake is beginning to overbrown. For this reason, the tube pan is especially suited for baking heavy batters, like nut and pound cakes, or for those that need quick heating, like angel food cake.

Standard tube pans, without flutes or flourishes, are called tube pans or angel food pans and can be made from either one piece of metal or two. If the pan is of two pieces, the base and tube comprise one piece, the sides the other. The tube conducts the heat from the center out, while the sides conduct the heat from the edges in, ensuring even baking. In addition, the sides of the tube give batters for angel food, sponge, and chiffon cakes a second surface to cling to as they climb. These pans have another virtue: cakes of tender crumb, once unmolded from the tube pan, can be cut more neatly because there is no need to worry about a fragile center point. Additionally, you can put a sweet filling in the cavity, a simple act that can turn a plain cake into an elegant dessert.

16.34 CHICAGO METALLIC NONSTICK TWO-PIECE TUBE PAN

A dark-colored nonstick pan may seem inappropriate when you're thinking about baking delicate angel food or chiffon cakes, but this pan actually works well. It is 9½" across the top and 4" high, the size most commonly called for, and composed of two pieces—a good construction for cakes with a fragile crumb structure. Typically, recipes for cakes like angel food and chiffon call for inverting the pan over a bottle, the tube resting over the neck of the bottle, until the cake is cooled, to prevent it from deflating, then turning the pan right-side up and, working gingerly, running a knife between the cake and the sides of the pan. This is where you can run into trouble with a nonstick pan: when running the knife around the cake, you must be extra careful not to nick the nonstick finish.

16.35 J. B. PRINCE ANGEL FOOD CAKE PAN

Here's the pan you need if you are making a nut, marble, or pound cake, a bubble loaf, or monkey bread (a sweet yeast bread made by placing balls of dough in overlapping layers in a pan—when baked, the bread forms a solid loaf). It is made from one piece of commercial-grade spun aluminum, and is 9½" in diameter and a generous 5" high. While you can make angel food or chiffon cakes in this one-piece pan, it is better used for heavier cakes, and works best when you line the bottom with a piece of parchment paper or even a round of super parchment.

16.36 MATFER TIN-PLATE *KUGLOF* MOLD

A German *Kugelhopf*, Austrian *Gugelhupf*, or Hungarian *Kuglof* (like the one made in the pictured pan) is an elegant, fluted coffee cake dusted with powdered sugar. It is usually prepared with a yeast or sponge-cake dough enriched with dark raisins and almonds and flavored with vanilla and rum, and sometimes a hint of citron or orange peel. To achieve its characteristic swirled fluting, you must bake the cake in a special pan. This one from Matfer, made of smooth-seamed, heavy-gauge tinned steel, is excellent. As in all *Kugelhopf* pans, the center tube extends above the sides—so that, when inverted, the tube provides a base on which the pan can rest while the cake cools. This pan is 8" in diameter and 4" deep and holds 40 ounces, approximately 5 cups of cake. It is also available in diameters of 6¼" and 9½". If the traditional *Kugelhopf* doesn't tempt you, try a marbled version or a chocolate sponge.

Wouldst thou both eat thy cake and have it?
—GEORGE HERBERT

16.37 KAVALIER SIMAX GLASS *KUGELHOPF* MOLD

Unlike the thick, heavy glassware we usually think of as ovenproof, this a *Kugelhopf* mold of borosilicate glass is light and graceful. One imagines using it for a gelatin dessert with layers of fruit or for an elegant Bavarian cream, but it too is intended for the tall, sugar-dusted coffee cake called a *Kugelhopf*. With its handsome, fluting and narrow center tube (which is high enough above the mold's edge to let air circulate under the inverted cake while it cools), this 2¼-quart mold is suited to not only the raisin-and-almond-studded *Kugelhopf*, but also other heavy batters, such as those of nut cakes and pound cakes. The tube allows heat to reach the center of the batter and provides a cavity that can be filled with fruit or whipped cream when the cake is unmolded. The mold is 8" in diameter and 4" deep. It is also available in a much larger 3½-quart capacity.

16.38 & 16.39 NORDIC WARE ALUMINUM & CAST-ALUMINUM BUNDT PANS

A *Bundt* is a German coffee cake of a denser texture and different form than a *Kugelhopf*, although they are related confections. These *Bundt* pans are made by the same manufacturer, with the traditional central tube. They are attractive and well made. The larger, 10¼" by 4", 12-cup pan has been stamped out of a single piece of seamless aluminum; the thickness of the aluminum, combined with the strength provided by fluting, makes the pan rigid and durable. The smaller 6-cup pan is 8" by 3" and made of cast aluminum of exceptional strength, and is also available in formed aluminum like the larger pan. Both pans are lined with nonstick Teflon and have a baked-on enamel exterior in a choice of colors: blue, green, or red. (Remember that if a light color is chosen, baking time will have to be extended by about 5 minutes.) The smaller cast-aluminum pan is available without the enamel finish, too. You could also plan to use these pans as molds for cold foods, since the space provided in the center of the tubed molds can be filled with fruit, a sauce, or other goodies.

KUGELHOPF LENÔTRE

This cake is prepared with a brioche dough, and it is richer than the Alsatian *Kugelhopf*. It is a good idea to bake two at the same time and freeze one for later use.

8 servings

3 tablespoons rum
½ cup, scant (100 g), granulated sugar
6½ tablespoons (1 dl) water
½ cup (100 g) raisins
1 cup, generous (100 g), slivered almonds
12½ ounces (360 g) brioche dough
1 whole egg, beaten
confectioners' sugar (to decorate)
melted butter to brush the top of the cake

SHAPING THE DOUGH

Prepare a syrup by mixing the rum, sugar, and water in a saucepan. Bring this mixture to a boil, then remove from the heat. Soak the raisins for about 1 hour in this syrup (the syrup can be kept for several weeks in the refrigerator if placed in a tightly sealed container). Butter the mold and sprinkle all over with slivered almonds. On a lightly floured board, roll the chilled brioche dough into a long rectangle. Drain the raisins, place them on top of the dough and roll the dough tightly in a long roll; bring the ends together to form a circle and stick them together with some beaten egg. Place the dough in a 9½" (24 cm) *Kugelhopf* mold; let the dough rise at a temperature of about 80°F (25°C) for 2 hours or until the dough fills ¾ of the mold.

BAKING

Preheat the oven to 400°F (200°C). Bake the cake for 30 minutes; check the color after 20 minutes. If the *Kugelhopf* is already brown on top, finish the baking after covering it with aluminum foil. To find out if the *Kugelhopf* is done, insert a knife; if the blade comes out dry, it is cooked. Turn out the *Kugelhopf* while it is still warm. Brush the surface of the cake with melted butter and dust with confectioners' sugar just before serving.

TO FREEZE

You can freeze the *Kugelhopf* while it is still lukewarm, but do not brush on the butter or dust with confectioners' sugar. When you take the cake out of the freezer, let it thaw for 2 hours at room temperature and then bake at 325°F (150°C) for 10 minutes to warm the cake. Brush the surface of the cake as indicated above and serve.

Lenôtre's Desserts and Pastries, by Gaston Lenôtre

16.40 MATFER *SAVARIN* MOLD

The *savarin,* a yeast cake, was born around the mid-nineteenth century from the same dough as the baba, but it was given a different shape, a different flavor, and a new name: *brillat-savarin,* in honor of the famous gastronome, Jean-Anthelme Brillat-Savarin. It was created by the famous Parisian pastry chef Julien, who omitted raisins from the cake, baked it in a hexagonal mold, and soaked it in kirsch instead of rum-flavored syrup. Between then and now, the name of the cake has been shortened and the shape of the *savarin* has been changed to a distinctive round ring baked in a pan of the same name. Usually a *savarin* is brushed with apricot glaze, then decorated with almonds, glacéed fruits, or fresh berries. The center of the cake is filled with whipped cream or pastry cream, and/or berries or mixed fruits that have been soaked in kirsch with sugar. This *savarin* mold of tinned steel holds 34 ounces and is 9½" in diameter and 2" deep, with a 4"-diameter center hole. Small, individual *savarin* molds are also available from Matfer.

MUFFIN TINS

UNTIL THE LATE nineteenth century, breadstuffs were leavened either with yeast (a time-consuming process), by air trapped in well-beaten eggs, with saleratus (baking soda), or with pearl ash (potassium carbonate). Cream of tartar was also sometimes used, often in conjunction with baking soda. Then in 1892, a German pharmacist named August Oetker introduced the first successful version of baking powder; it was foolproof, while the other leaveners were not, and quick, unlike yeast—hence the name "quick breads" for the confections that depended on baking powder for rising. And *quick* is the operative word where muffins are concerned: the batter is mixed lightly and quickly to ensure maximum tenderness and baked in small cups in a fraction of the time required for other breads or batters in large pans.

When buying a muffin pan, choose one with rounded corners, seamless cups, and a nonstick surface. If your muffin pan is not nonstick, you may want to line the cups with papers made especially for muffins—they will help the muffins rise more evenly and aid you in getting the muffins out of the tin intact. If you plan to bake muffins in large quantities, it's best to use two pans that can sit side by side on one oven shelf with ample air space around them, not touching each other or the walls of the oven. However, if you must put the pans one above the other on two oven racks, stagger them and make certain to rotate the pans, front to back and top to bottom, when the muffins are half-baked. A standard muffin pan will hold roughly ½ cup (4 ounces), a mini 2 tablespoons, a jumbo 1 cup (8 ounces), and the tops-only pan 4 tablespoons.

16.41 CHICAGO METALLIC SILVERSTONE TWELVE-CUP MUFFIN TIN

Here's a simply made nonstick pan that will work well whether you're making muffins, cupcakes, or rolls. Its dozen seamless cups are bonded securely to the frame; each one is almost 3" across and holds nearly 4 ounces, just right for regular-size muffins. The pan measures 13½" by 10½"; in most ovens you should be able to fit two pans side by side on one rack. Even though the pan's medium-gray nonstick finish is effective, you might want to line the cups with muffin papers. Nonstick muffin tins like this one from Chicago Metallic can also be used to bake a dozen garlic flans to serve with roast lamb or to chill twelve panna cottas for dessert.

16.42 CHICAGO METALLIC MINI MUFFIN TIN

Each little cup in this twelve-cup muffin pan holds a mere 2 tablespoons of batter, just enough to make a one-bite muffin, tea cake, cupcake, or micro sweet bun. The cups are 2″ across and ½″ deep and, like the pan, coated with a medium-gray nonstick finish. Because the muffin pan itself is less than ¾″ high, getting a grip on it, especially if you're wearing oven mitts, can be tricky. We recommend that you place the pan on a baking sheet—a sure way to avoid jabbing your thumb into a muffin while pulling the pan from the oven.

16.43 LODGE SIX-HOLE FLUTED MUFFIN PAN

American pioneers baked small breads (they didn't have muffins) in cast-iron pans like this 3-pound one. A compact 5″ by 8″, it has six small fluted cups, each 2½″ across and 1″ high, perfect for hearty muffins and crusty corn bread. Cast iron is prized for its capacity to heat evenly and retain its heat. However, the

benefits of a cast-iron pan come with a price: this is not a low-maintenance item. Before you bake your first batch of muffins you must season the pan by scrubbing it, rubbing it with vegetable oil, and then heating it upside-down for an hour in the oven. (Seasoning helps the pan develop a nonstick surface.) After each use, you must wash and dry it carefully, spray it with cooking spray, then wipe it dry again. It may seem like a lot to do, but the seasoning is a one-time operation while the pan is a lifetime tool.

16.44 NORPRO SIX-HOLE GIANT MUFFIN TIN

When these pans were first marketed they were called "Texas" muffin tins, and with good reason—it takes an appetite the size of Texas to down a muffin from this pan. The steel pan

has six cups and each produces a muffin that's three times the size of a regular one. The cups are 4″ across, 2″ deep, and hold 1 cup of batter to the rim.

16.45 NORPRO SIX-CUP PUFFY CROWN PAN

For those muffin lovers who enjoy eating the crown of the muffin more than the base, here's the pan of your dreams—it produces nothing but muffin tops. The pan has six cups that are coated with a black nonstick finish, each as wide as a jumbo muffin (4″ in diameter) and shallow as a mini muffin (¾″ deep). Spoon in a little batter and you'll end up with a muffin that resembles a mushroom—all crown and just a bit of base. Because this pan is so shallow, you'll find it easier to transfer it in and out of the oven if you put it on a baking sheet first.

SPECIALTY BAKING FRAMES & FORMS

THERE ARE CERTAIN small cakes, cookies, and breads that we recognize as much by their shape as their taste. Chief among them are the French *cannelé,* made only in small fluted molds; the Scottish shortbread cookies, recognized as authentic when pressed into a triangular mold; and the distinctive, scallop-shaped golden sponge cakes known as madeleines. Here we have a variety of baking forms and frames, each well made, each attractive in its own way, and each indispensable for making the product it was created for.

16.46 LODGE "EAR OF CORN" PAN

Here is a set of joined miniature pans, shaped to make the traditional "ears of corn" baked in cast iron come out

crusty on the bottom and golden brown on the top. The thick cast iron holds the heat and prevents the crust from burning before the interior is cooked, while the individual size assures more crust—and crunch—per portion than is offered by corn bread baked in a conventional pan or skillet. You may have seen pans like this hanging in kitchens and antique

shops; like early American examples, this pan has seven ear-of-corn molds lined up in a heavy cast-iron rectangle with handles on both ends. It is ready for immediate baking after you season, grease, and preheat it. If you aren't used to cast iron, the 5-pound weight may surprise you, but this pan is as much a classic as any muffin pan or soufflé dish.

16.47 LODGE CORN BREAD SKILLET

Here we have a modification of yet another traditional device for baking corn bread. Early Americans baked the bread in hot ashes, on stones, on boards, on the flat blades of hoes, or in three-legged "spiders" and other types of skillets; then they broke or cut the flat bread into individual portions. It must have been someone who loved the crusty surfaces of the corn-bread slices who invented this skillet with partitions, so that the unique corn-bread crust is on all sides of each slice. This skillet is made by Lodge, founded in 1896, one of the oldest existing brand names in American cookware. The pan is covered with an FDA-approved wax that protects the skillet from moisture and humidity during shipping, but like all cast-iron pans, it should be seasoned, greased and preheated before it is filled. Attractive to look at, the 9″ skillet weighs a hefty 5½ pounds and has a hole in the handle for hanging.

16.48 LODGE CAST-IRON POPOVER PAN

Popovers, like corn bread, are traditionally baked in a cast-iron pan. The only leavening agent in these feather-light, hollow, crusty quick breads is very hot steam; tradition says that only a heavy iron pan which is sizzling hot when the batter is poured in will retain enough heat to create sufficient steam within the batter. As standards change, many cooks swear that ceramic custard cups or even aluminum cupcake tins will do just as well; some maintain that popover pans need not in fact be preheated, and the popovers can be started in a cold oven set at 425°F. Be that as it may, this heavy, cast-iron, eleven-hole pan from Lodge remains a classic. Like all Lodge cast-iron products, it has been covered with a food-grade wax at the factory to protect it from moisture and humidity during shipping and is ready for baking after seasoning the cups. The pan performs best when it is preheated and the cups are greased before pouring in the batter. To help you cope with the impressive 6½ pounds the pan weighs, there are finger holes added on either end. Peek through the window of your oven while the batter rises rapidly to a chef's cap, and you are likely to agree that this is still the best way to bake popovers.

16.49 J. B. PRINCE MADELEINE TIN

One wintry day Proust's mother sent out for "one of those short, plump little cakes called *petites madeleines,* which looked as though they had been molded in the fluted scallop of a pilgrim's shell." With the madeleines she served tea, into which Proust dipped the small cake that was to trigger the famous experience he described so memorably. "I raised to my lips a spoonful of the tea in which I had soaked a morsel of the cake. No sooner had the warm liquid, and the crumbs with it, touched my palate than a shudder ran through my whole body . . . an exquisite pleasure had invaded my senses." Thus, he began to recall the experiences and feelings of his childhood, associated with the madeleine. Although you might not remember things past when you bite into a moist, spongy madeleine, the experience is worth remembering. They are beautiful, golden cakes made simply of sugar, butter, eggs, flour, and a touch of lemon or vanilla and then baked in shell-shaped tins like this one. This 14″ by 7″ pan is stamped from a single sheet of tinned steel, with the edges folded over, and holds twelve madeleines, 2¾″ long each.

16.50 J. B. PRINCE LADYFINGER TIN

Ladyfingers, or *biscuits à cuillère,* are an elegant accompaniment to champagne, tea, ice cream, or a fruit dessert. They are wonderful sandwiched around buttercream or a bit of jam, and they are perfect for lining a charlotte (a cake- or bread-covered dessert) mold that can be filled with a number of delicious mixtures. Stamped out of a single sheet of tinned steel with rolled edges, this pan is 12″ long and 4¾″ wide. It has ten shallow, 3¾″-long depressions into which the ladyfingers batter is spooned or piped with a pastry bag.

16.51 DEMARLE SILPAT FLEXIPAN MADELEINE MOLD

This unusual baking mold looks like thin rubber and has rubber's flexibility, but it is made of fiberglass and food grade silicone. It is able to withstand oven temperatures of up to 560°F. Madeleines bake properly puffy, tender, and evenly colored. The materials are nonstick so that even without the use of butter, vegetable oil, or baking spray, the small cakes release easily when the mold is inverted. You'll find many other uses for this pan as well. It is refrigerator- and freezer-proof, making it handy for mousse or ice cream molded into lovely fan-like shapes, to serve with fruit or cookies. It is microwave safe as well. You can also use the mold for sugar confections and homemade chocolates. When baking madeleines, follow Demarle's suggestion: freeze the batter-filled mold for 5 to 10 minutes prior to putting the pan in the oven. This step helps assure the cakes will be moist and thoroughly cooked without becoming crispy and browned at the edges. There are several sizes. The one shown here bakes eight madeleines at a time.

16.52 & 16.53
J. B. PRINCE SMALL & LARGE *CANNELÉ* MOLDS

Like *Bundt* and *Kugelhopf, cannelé* is the name of both the mold and the sweet that is made in it. A specialty from the Bordeaux region of France, *cannelé* means "fluted" or "crenulated" and, indeed, a *cannelé* mold is tightly fluted. In fact, it looks like a miniature *Bundt* pan, only narrower and without a tube. Traditional *cannelé* molds were made of copper and lined with tin. Today, the molds are still copper, but can be lined in either tin or stainless steel. These molds are lined with tin. The smaller model is 1½" in diameter and comes in two sizes, 1½" high, like the one we show you here, or 1" high. The larger mold is 2" high and 2" in diameter. The molds are beautifully made—beautiful enough to display—and very expensive, but if you are a devotee of these soft crepe-like cakes with their firm caramelized crust, there is nothing to do but splurge; you cannot be successful baking a *cannelé* batter in anything but a *cannelé* mold.

16.54 GEFU
CHRISTSTOLLEN PAN

Stollen is a rich, delicious, sugar-dusted yeast cake filled with almonds, raisins, currants, and candied fruits that have been steeped in rum. It is a traditional part of every German Christmas. The *Stollen* is usually folded into loaves whose tops are higher than their sides, which are slightly ridged. The dough may also be baked under a tin-plated mold, like this one, which will give the cake its traditional shape, but create a softer crust. This mold, 12¼" long and 5½" wide at the bottom, has a flat lip around the edge that rests on the baking sheet. Form the dough with your hands into an oblong shape that fills the mold a little less than halfway. Place a baking sheet over the inverted mold and quickly turn the mold and baking sheet over together. Then leave the dough in place to rise again before baking. Dredged in powdered sugar, this simple, fruit-filled cake is lovely with morning or afternoon coffee, and it improves with age.

16.55 BROWN BAG COOKIE ART
CERAMIC SHORTBREAD PAN

Shortbread is the quintessential butter cookie, a nearly univeral favorite, and one of Great Britain's most delicious gifts to the world of baking. The classic recipe calls for a mere three ingredients—butter, sugar, and flour—but few foods are as sumptuously rich. This mold bakes the cookies perfectly and will help make your versions as attractive as they are tasty. It is an 8" octagonal ceramic pan with grooves that separate the cookies into eight wedges with a thistle design on each. There are handles, but be sure to use potholders; the stoneware will be hot. The pan comes in an attractive box, making this a neat gift for friends who enjoy baking.

PIE PANS

P IES, more than almost any other dish, are identified with America, forever linked with those holidays that are especially patriotic. Besides the all-American apple, there's pumpkin for Thanksgiving, cherry and blueberry for the Fourth of July, and, of course, good old-fashioned Southern pecan.

American slope-sided pie pans come in 8″, 9″, and 10″ sizes, standardized not for the sake of the pastry—you need just about the same amount of dough for any of these sizes—but so that the recipes for filling will make the right amount. (Pie pans are measured from the inside top of the rim to the opposite side.) Pie recipes are usually given for the 9″ size. We suggest you buy two pans of whatever size you find most useful—while you're in the kitchen rolling dough or peeling apples, making two pies seems just as easy as putting together one. Also consider a deep-dish pan. "Deep" is usually defined as 3″, in contrast to the regular 1½″. It's just what you'll need for sweet or savory biscuit-topped pies, or pot pies. A deep-dish pie usually has only a top crust.

American pies come in three versions: open-faced, double crusted, and top-crusted. American pie pans are commonly made of three materials: glass, an ideal substance for pie pans; metal, with standard and nonstick finishes; and earthenware. With the exception of earthenware pans, most pie pans are functional rather than attractive; this is unfortunate, since pies, unlike tarts, always come to the table in their pans. However, as American pie makers have known for centuries, if you make a good pie, no one will ever notice the pan.

A word on materials. For reasons that range from even heating to easy cutting, glass pans are best for pies, followed by ceramic. Yet there are bakers who enjoy using metal pans, and for them, aluminum is a good option. For cake pans, aluminum is the metal of choice, with nonstick finishes second because they demand special attention in terms of oven temperature and baking times. For pie pans, aluminum is still a good choice, but nonstick finishes, with their darker colors and greater heat-retaining properties, are more desirable because pie crusts, especially those that are not baked before they are filled, need extra help in the browning department. Nonstick pans have one important drawback: the finishes are easily scarred by cutting, and the nature of pies calls for them to be cut in their pans.

16.56 PYREX TRADITIONAL PIE PAN

This simple, homey Pyrex glass pan is the perfect American pie pan. Measuring 9″ across its top and a standard 1½″ high, it has sloping sides and a ½″ rim. Heatproof glass is efficient—so efficient that recipes suggest you lower the oven temperature by 25°F when you use a glass pan. It absorbs and retains heat evenly, qualities you need to obtain an appealingly golden crust, and, because it is transparent, you can check your crust's progress at every stage. All this and you can cut the pie in the pan without ever worrying about damaging the glass. The foregoing, along with superior performance and a low price, are an unbeatable combination.

Pyrex also makes a 2″-high deep-dish pie pan with gently rounded (rather than sloping) sides and two small but useful handles. It enjoys all the same admirable qualities as the traditional Pyrex pie pan.

"If I told you the secret of making light, flaky piecrust, it wouldn't be much of a secret anymore, now would it?"

16.57 EKCO COVERED PIE PAN

This steel pan is coated with a slightly shiny, medium-gray nonstick finish. The standard 9″ in diameter and 1½″ high, it has two handles and comes with a plastic carrying lid that clips onto the handles, a convenient feature if you're bringing a pie to friends. The pan does a fine job of browning crusts, a benefit of its darker nonstick coating; in fact, it does such a good job that you'll want to lower the oven temperature by 25°F and keep an eye on your pie's progress. If you're blind-baking a crust, you may want to remove it a few minutes earlier than the specified time. Like almost all nonstick pans, this one cannot tolerate nicks and cuts, both of which are inevitable with pies. To save the pan, try cutting your pies with a plastic or nylon pie cutter.

16.58 FASMODEA PIE PARTNERS

Made of one seamless piece of spun aluminum, this 9″ diameter pan has typical sloped sides 1¼″ high and a ½″ rim. It comes with an ingenious companion piece: a perforated pan, its rim higher and rounder than the pie pan's rim, that fits neatly over the pie pan. The manufacturer calls this the "pie partner" and it is meant to be used when you are blind-baking a pie crust. Because the partner weighs down the pie crust, it elimi-nates the need for parchment paper filled with pie weights or beans, the usual materials bakers use to keep crusts from puffing or slipping when baked unfilled. The partner also encourages browning, since it too is made of heat-absorbing aluminum You can leave it in place until the crust is fully baked.

16.59 EMILE HENRY PIE DISH

An exception to the ugly pie pan rule, this French import possesses both rustic charm and modern utility. Made of prized Burgundy clay, beautifully glazed in "Lavender" blue, the pan is smooth, straight-sided (not sloped), always cream-colored on the inside, textured with softly raised rings around the outside (which give the glaze variation and depth), and finished with a generous ¾″ rim that is ruffled like the edge of a farm maiden's bonnet. The pan's shape and dimensions (9″ across and 2″ deep) make it more suitable for deep-dish recipes than for standard pies, but if you adjust your favorite recipes to this pan, the effort will be rewarded, not only when you bring this beauty to the table, but when you cut into your pie. Clay heats evenly, retains heat well, and produces nicely browned crusts. This pan is also durable: it can be put in the freezer, can be used in the microwave, handles temperatures up to 500°F, and can be cleaned in the dishwasher. Think of it for quichelike savory pies as well as desserts. It is also available in olive green, piedmont red, cream, and "cognac" yellow and comes in an individual 5″ size and a large 12″ size.

ACCIDENTS WILL HAPPEN
❧ SARABETH LEVINE ❧

One day, the dough for our apple crumb pies had been overmixed. When it's overmixed it becomes very fragile, and when you bake the little individual crumb pies in ramekins lined with the overmixed dough, the dough cracks. So there I am sitting with two large sheet trays of broken miniature apple crumb pies. We're talking about ten pounds of filling and dough. So I made a pound cake batter and I chopped up the pies and folded them into the batter. They were the most fabulous little apple pie pound cakes. I don't know that they'll become a regular part of our menu, but the result of another accident did. I had asked someone to double a chocolate chip cookie recipe and they doubled the sugar but forgot to double the flour and the butter, so we wound up with what we call "clouds," now one of our very famous cookies.

The tomato soup also came about through an accident—two, actually. I sent someone shopping for onions, and instead, he bought shallots and prepped them. I made the soup and said, "Something's not right here." Then, when the soup was being ladled on the line, a container of cheddar cheese used for the omelets tipped over into it. We couldn't serve the soup and put it aside. One of the waiters later decided to eat it, and he said to me, "Sara, taste this." I tasted it, and that's how the cheddar cheese wound up in the tomato soup!

16.60 MASON CASH CERAMIC PIE PAN SET

It would be easy to mistake these pie pans for serving dishes, soup bowls or the most cheerful cereal bowls in your cupboard. Available in sets of three, complete with a pie funnel shaped like a small oval bottle, these pie pans are made in England from vitrified ceramic, an excellent baking material for pie pans. The largest pan, a standard 9" across and 1½" deep, is French blue; the middle pan, 7½" across, is sea-foam green; and the smallest pan, 5½" across, is a yellow somewhere between maize and mustard. Both are also 1½" deep. All the pans are matte-finished on the outsides, shiny on the off-white insides, and finished with 1"-wide rims that are the same colors as the outsides of the pans and etched with two off-white concentric circles. The etched rims are attractive and useful—they give you a good hold on the pan when you're slipping it in or out of the oven. They also provide just the support needed for a crust's edges. The pie pans nest for easy storage.

TART PANS

IT'S THE WARM, inviting nature of a pie that makes it so appealing. But a tart—a tart's another story altogether. It may be the American open-faced pie's first cousin, or even its grandmother, but it never looks homey. Take every ingredient you use to make a pie and construct a tart instead and you'll have a dessert that looks polished and, if you've put in a little extra effort, professional. The trick is in the pan: tarts, which are most often unmolded, are constructed in pans that leave none of their finishing touches to the baker. There's no crimping, pinching, or turning the edges of the crust into designs that may or may not keep their shape in the oven. A tart's crust is most often cut level with the top of the pan, and it's the pan's sides, fluted or straight, that give the crust its elegant finish.

STANDARD & LOOSE-BOTTOMED TART PANS

Unlike an American pie, a tart is never served in its baking pan, so the look of the pan is not important. What counts in a tart pan is its ability to heat evenly and quickly enough for the dough to "seize" or set. Tart pans come in two versions: one with a fixed bottom and the other with a loose bottom. Both types of pans come in traditional shiny steel or blued steel, as well as nonstick finishes. Professionals rarely use nonstick tart pans, since every tart dough has enough butter in it to prevent it from sticking. However, there is always the risk that your filling may bubble over and stick to the pan, which is reason enough to choose a nonstick model. As with all baking pans, whether the finish is nonstick or traditional, you need to take care when cleaning tart pans and make certain not to scrub them with harsh cleaning pads or detergents. If the finish is tinned steel or blued steel, make certain to dry the pans well and immediately so they don't rust. Finally, if you are serving the tart on the bottom of the pan (something we don't recommend), you must take care not to scratch the pan's bottom when you cut the tart—scratches and abrasions can create sticking spots on any pan. Loose-bottomed tart pans simplify removing the contents. Allow the tart to cool on a rack. Then place the pan on a smaller cylinder— a tuna fish can will do. Let the sides of the ring drop down, then put your tart on a perfectly flat plate and with a spatula, carefully nudge the bottom of the pan out from under the tart.

16.61 MATFER FLUTED TART MOLD

This Teflon-coated nonstick pan, made from a single piece of aluminum, has a flat 9½" base and fluted 1"-high sides. The construction is solid, the sides strong, and the combination of Teflon and aluminum ideal for producing well-browned crusts. This is not, however, the pan we'd recommend if you're just starting your collection of tart pans or if you're new to tarts. Since this pan has a fixed bottom, you will have a hard time turning out whatever you make in it—and you certainly wouldn't want to cut the tart in its pan and damage

LEMON TART

Most lemon tart recipes are made with lemon curd, which involves a lot of cooking, but this is a streamlined version. The tart shell can be made the day before, and so can the filling, but they should be stored separately.

6 to 8 servings

grated zest and juice of 3 lemons
3 large eggs
½ cup plus 1 tablespoon (112 grams) sugar
3 tablespoons (43 grams) unsalted butter, cut into ½" pieces
one 9½" tart shell made from Sweet Tart Dough, prebaked (see page 351)

GARNISH
1 lemon
¼ cup (60 grams) apricot glaze
mint leaves

1 Preheat the oven to 325°F.

2 Fill a medium saucepan one-third full with water and bring to a simmer. Put the zest and lemon juice in a medium bowl and whisk in the eggs. Add the sugar and butter and place the bowl over the simmering water; the water must not touch the bottom of the bowl. Cook, whisking constantly, until the butter is completely melted and the mixture is smooth. Remove the bowl from the pan of hot water and allow the mixture to cool for 15 minutes.

3 Place the prebaked tart shell on a baking sheet. Pour the filling into the shell and bake the tart for 8 to 10 minutes, or until the center is just set. Cool the tart completely on a wire rack.

4 Make the garnish: Using a channel knife, cut 6 lengthwise grooves in the lemon, removing 6 strips of rind. Cut a crosswise slice from the center of the lemon and place it in the center of the tart. Slice the remaining lemon halves lengthwise in half and then cut the sections into half-moons. Arrange the slices around the edge of the tart with the cut sides out.

5 If necessary, rewarm the apricot glaze over low heat or in the microwave. Using a pastry brush, lightly brush the top of the tart with the warm apricot glaze. Garnish with a few mint leaves.

Simply Sensational Desserts, by François Payard

---

the finish. This pan is best used to blind-bake crusts that will be unmolded and then filled, but it must be handled with great care. It also comes in diameters of 7⅞" and 11".

16.62, 16.63, & 16.64
MATFER TINNED-STEEL, BLUED-STEEL, & NONSTICK STEEL TART MOLDS

If you are a tart maker, you will want to have a selection of these traditional loose-bottomed tart pans ranging in size from tartlet to grand and, perhaps, in an assortment of finishes. The pans have removable bottom discs and fluted 1"-high sides and come in three versions: shiny tinned steel, the classic option; blued steel, considered by many professionals to be the material of choice for producing deeply and evenly browned crusts; and nonstick steel, with a finish that is medium gray on the outside and a darker gray on the inside. All three versions produce even and well-browned crusts.

The joy of a loose-bottomed tart pan is the ease with which it is released. Fit the dough into the pan—the pan guarantees beautifully fluted sides—then bake the crust blind or put the filling in first and then bake it. In either case, it's best to place the tart pan on a baking sheet, not only because this will provide more even heat to the bottom of the pan, but because it will make transferring the pan from oven to counter easier. When the tart is ready to be unmolded, place the tart pan on top of a jar that is smaller in diameter than the pan's bottom, and let the fluted side drop to the counter. Next, gently slide the tart off the bottom disc onto a serving platter or cooling rack. This last step isn't hard, but doing it the first time takes a little courage. Matfer's tart pans come in diameters ranging from 6¼" to 12½".

16.65 & 16.66 J. B. PRINCE RECTANGULAR & SQUARE TART MOLDS

A rectangular or square-shaped tart is as easy to make as a circular one, yet there is something about the angular shapes that make them special and festive, perhaps because the shapes are associated with professional bakers. These pans will give you pastry shop results at home. Both are constructed of shiny tinned steel (although the rectangular pan is available with a nonstick finish), and both are loose-bottomed. The rectangular pan is 14¾" long and 4½" wide, and the square pan measures 9" on a side; both have fluted 1" high sides that rise straight up from the base. Traditionally, the rectangular pan is used to make classic fruit tarts with sweet crusts, a base of thick pastry cream, and a topping of glazed fruits, but there's nothing that says they can't be used to turn out any other type of tart, from a golden-brown pear frangipane to a quiche.

16.67 MATFER *TARTE TATIN* PAN

Who were the *demoiselles* Tatin whose names are immortalized in the upside-down apple tart, one of the best French desserts, that bears their name? It is said they were joint owners of a hotel but, aside from that, the circumstances of how the dessert originated are shrouded in the mists of history.

At first, the tart was baked over a charcoal fire in a heavy buttered and sugared pan. The sugar caramelized during the baking, so that when the tart was unmolded, its top was amber-colored. Most modern recipes call for caramelizing the mold before filling it with apples and topping it with pastry. That is a safe method, but with this tin-lined, hammered-copper pan, it is not necessary. Simply follow the traditional recipe and the 2"-deep pan, with its flaring sides, will make an 11" tart that is especially beautiful. A 9½"-diameter pan is also available.

TARTLET MOLDS

Pans for individual tarts or tartlets, in their various shapes and sizes, are as useful as they are decorative. Use them to bake tartlet shells of sweetened pastry dough to be filled with fruit, cream, or custard, or of unsweetened dough to make savory hors d'oeuvres. (Placing the molds on a baking sheet, by the way, is an essential step when dealing with a large number of such small items.) When buying tartlet molds, keep in mind that it is better to have twelve of one sort than two each of six kinds; in fact, you should buy no fewer than four of each shape.

16.68 & 16.69 MATFER PLAIN & FLUTED BARQUETTE MOLDS

Called "barquettes" because they resemble French flat-bottomed sailing barks, these molds are 1½" wide and just a breath over 3" long. Both the smooth-sided and fluted versions are made of tinned metal and come in packages of twenty-five, a quantity that sounds high until you start making perfect little sweet pastries or hors d'oeuvres, twenty-five of which will disappear in no time.

16.70 J. B. PRINCE REMOVABLE BOTTOM TARTLET

A tart pan brought down to a small size, this shiny stainless steel tartlet pan, with its 4¾" removable base and fluted ¾" high sides, is perfect for individual servings of anything you'd make in a larger pan. The question in buying tartlet pans is always how many to get. One is never enough, two might be just right for dessert tête-à-tête; four is a safe number, but six is better yet. More than that might be the ticket if you have a large family, entertain often, or like to keep tart shells in your freezer, fitted into their tins and ready to bake. This pan is also available with a nonstick finish.

16.71 MATFER PETITS FOURS PASTRY SET

These miniature tart-pastry molds are housed in a colorful tin box depicting a luscious-looking selection of glazed and decorated petits fours. The set consists of five each of ten molds in different shapes—oval, square, round, triangular, and so on. Each tin-plated mold makes a crust that will hold only a teaspoonful or so of filling, just enough for one sugary bite. And although they look as if they belong in a doll's kitchen, the molds are surprisingly sturdy. Think of them for making pastry shells to fill with cheese or a spiced fish concoction for a cocktail party, or place a single, perfect glazed strawberry in each for a sweet delight.

FLAN OR TART RINGS

First of all, a flan ring is not used to make the sweet custard served in Spanish-speaking lands. A flan or tart ring is one of the simplest devices used in pastry making; it is nothing more than a round of stainless steel used to form the shell of what will become a free-standing tart. The ring is placed on a parchment paper-lined baking sheet, which becomes the pan's bottom; rolled-out dough is fitted into the ring and then baked. The pastry will shrink somewhat during baking, so it is easy to remove the ring once it is cool. Flans are usually made with fruit fillings, but savory fillings can be used as well.

16.72 MATFER PLAIN TART RING

Made of stainless steel, this classic ring is 9½" in diameter, but it is also available in diameters from 4" to 13⅜". It is ¾" high, straight-sided, securely spot-welded at the joining, and smoothly rolled at both the top and bottom edges. The sides of the tart ring are slightly lower than those of the standard loose-bottomed tart pan, reducing its capacity; you may have to make some adjustments if you are making a tart-pan recipe with a tart ring.

16.73 MATFER FLOWER TART RING

Made in the same fashion as the classic circular flan or tart ring, this 9¼" diameter, ¾" high ring is bent into six gently rounded petals. When fitted with dough, it produces a flower-shaped tart. The ring is made of stainless steel, rolled top and bottom around a copper tube. Any tart that you would make in a round ring can be made in this petal-shaped ring.

QUICHE PANS

Quiches are savory egg tarts traditionally baked and served in porcelain, pottery, or glass pans with fluted sides specifically designed for the purpose. That said, there is no reason not to bake a quiche in either a tart pan or ring, removing the pan or ring and serving it on a platter.

16.74 APILCO ROUND QUICHE PAN

This is the pan that comes to mind when you think of making a quiche. It is the most traditional mold, made from white porcelain. The pan is 10" in diameter with softly fluted sides that are 1½" high. Both the inside of the pan and the sides are glazed, while the bottom is left matte, which increases its heat absorption. The pan can withstand very high heat, can be used in a microwave oven, and is dishwasher safe.

16.75 EMILE HENRY *TOURTIÈRE*

Here is a quiche pan that is as attractive as it is effective. Handcrafted of Burgundy clay, a legendary material for bakeware in France, the pan is 11" in diameter, 1½" high, and beautifully glazed. The fluted sides of the pan we show are an elegant cobalt blue, although it is available in green, red, white, saffron, country blue and sable. The interior sides are glazed white, the bottom matte white for better heat absorption; indeed, crusts baked in this beauty were perfectly and evenly browned. All this, and the pan is also sturdy and fuss-free—it can go from freezer to oven or microwave oven to dishwasher. It's perfect for a quiche with 6 cups of filling, but you may find that you'll use it for other purposes: baking a potato gratin or macaroni and cheese.

SPECIALTY PASTRY FORMS

Here are the molds for shaping those hollow pastry forms that are filled with whipped cream, custard, or pastry cream: cornucopias, cornets, cannolis, and lady locks. In any shape, they are made by forming pastry dough around the greased molds, and then baking them on a baking sheet. When the pastries have cooled, the molds slip out easily and you can pipe in the fillings.

16.76 J. B. PRINCE CORNET MOLD (FRENCH CORNUCOPIA FORM)

Originally, pastry cornucopias were formed over simple dowels, but this metal mold, sealed at the pointed end and slanted at the open end for a true horn-of-plenty shape, is now the standard. It is 2" across at the top and 5½" long (a 3½" long model is also available), so it can be filled generously with cream. The form is molded of tin-coated sheet steel, sturdily soldered along its seam. To keep it from rusting or discoloring, it should be washed and thoroughly dried immediately after each use.

16.77 J. B. PRINCE LADY LOCK FORM

The shape of this pastry mold resembles the cornucopia, but its tapered end is not sealed and its open end is not slanted. Available in two lengths—one almost 6½" long, and the other almost 4½"—this lady lock form is made of tinned steel and point-soldered along its seam. They're called lady locks because the long strip of pastry curling downward from the tip has the look of a corkscrew curl. In Germany, lady locks are sometimes called *Schillerlocken,* or "Schiller's locks," in honor of the style in which the romantic poet wore his hair. These forms are also ideal for shaping puff pastry cones that can later be filled with whipped cream, ice cream, fruit, or a combination of all three, and either would serve as a good mold for shaping tuiles or lace cookies.

16.78 MATFER *CROQUEMBOUCHE* FORM

In French, *croquembouche* means what it sounds like: "crunch in the mouth." That is what your guests will do to the confection constructed around this 13¾"-high, stainless steel form that resembles a party hat. Only for a party, in fact, would you go to the trouble of making a *croquembouche,* traditionally a towering cone of cream puffs dipped in, and then cemented together with, caramelized sugar. The crunch comes from the thin shell of sugar around each cream puff. (Actually a *croquembouche* can be any kind of sweet or piece of fruit that is glazed with hardened sugar.) Before using the mold, make sure to butter it, then start building your tower, layer upon layer until you reach the top. When the sugar has completely cooled, slip the form out and admire your free-standing masterpiece.

16.79 ATECO CANNOLI FORMS

When we see cannoli, we are reminded of long afternoons spent talking about the meaning of life over espresso and these delicious fried tubes of pastry filled with sweetened ricotta. To make these Sicilian sweets yourself is not too intricate a task, but you will need this inexpensive set of four tinned-steel forms for shaping and frying the pastry tubes. Solidly constructed, they are 5⅝" long, ⅞" in diameter, with a double-folded seam running their length—identical to the forms used in every *pasticceria*.

BASIC PASTRY TOOLS

THE BATTERS FOR SOME CAKES, pies, cookies, or small pastries can be beaten in a mixing bowl and then go directly into a baking pan without the intervention of more than a big spoon—but such recipes are rare. Most require specialized tasks—sifting the dry ingredients, scraping the batter out of the bowl, rolling out the dough, and transferring these amalgamated ingredients into the proper baking pan—that call for specialized tools made to do them with the greatest efficiency. The work goes with the territory in baking, and adds to the satisfaction of producing a great-looking and tasty result.

Many of these tools are small and seemingly miscellaneous. It pays to obtain only those which you are likely to use with some regularity—even once a year—and store them where you'll find them easily. Those that have multiple uses, like dough scrapers and pastry brushes, are best kept close at hand, ready and waiting.

SCRAPERS

Although the most common kind of scraper, the rubber spatula, can be pressed into bowl-scraping duty, the work goes more smoothly when you've got a bowl scraper, a piece of strong but flexible plastic specifically designed to run around the sides of a bowl. It should have enough flexibility to skim a bowl and enough tension to hold its shape as you transfer the batter from the bowl into a pan. When it comes to bench or dough scrapers, the key is strength and comfort. The scraping blade should be a rectangle of strong stainless steel with some flexibility, so you can get under the dough at an angle, particularly when you're kneading. For the sake of cleanliness, we recommend scrapers made of metal, rubber, or polypropylene.

16.80 J. B. PRINCE BOWL SCRAPER

Nothing more than a D-shaped piece of hard but flexible plastic, straight on the holding edge and lightly beveled on most of the curve, this bowl scraper gets the last of any sticky dough out of a mixing bowl, jiggles loose small pieces of dough from a counter, and gently pries delicate cookies (including tuiles) from a baking sheet. A cinch to clean, it's 4½" long on its straight edge and 3" wide. Consider owning several.

16.81 J. B. PRINCE BENCH SCRAPER

Designed to scrape dough off a baker's bench (the professional's name for a bread baker's work counter), this tool is useful whether you're working with bread, cookie, or pastry dough, and just about indispensable if the dough is soft and sticky. The scraper is a 6" by 3" straight-edge rectangle of stainless steel topped by a gently rounded, comfortably gripped polypropylene bar that is an ample 1½" in length. The metal edge is blunt enough to be safe on just about any kind of counter, but thin and sharp enough to be used to cut bread dough. The scraper can be used for kneading—keep it in one hand and use it to pick the dough off the work surface and fold it over on itself so you can push and knead it with the other hand—and also for cleaning away the crackly flour and water crust that is the inevitable by-product of kneading and rolling.

The fine arts are five in number, namely: painting, sculpture, poetry, music, and architecture, the principal branch of the latter being pastry.

—MARIE-ANTONIN CARÊME

347

SIFTERS

Sifting seems like a thing of the past when so many recipes now suggest just whisking the dry ingredients together, and flour companies tell us their products are presifted. However, there are some ingredients, such as confectioner's sugar, cake flour, and cocoa powder, that tend to clump and must be sifted before being blended into a batter. Sifting also helps combine and aerate your ingredients, ensuring that you have a uniform mixture to work with.

Because they are always working with large quantities, professional bakers use large strainers instead of sifters. We think you should follow their lead; when you've got more than 4 cups of dry ingredients to sift, we suggest you turn the ingredients into a fine-mesh strainer and stir them through the mesh. When you're working on a smaller recipe, however, reach for a hand sifter. Sifters come with different kinds of mechanisms—some call for squeezing the handle of a metal spider that agitates the ingredients through one or more layers of mesh, others work by turning a crank, which spins a wheel to send the flour through the mesh. We recommend a simple old-style shaking sifter because it is efficient and worry-free. No matter which kind of sifter you choose, you want to keep it away from moisture while you're working. Never wash your sifter, just shake or brush it out thoroughly after each use and store it in a plastic bag.

> The black stove, stoked with coal and firewood, glows like a lighted pumpkin. Eggbeaters whirl, spoon spin round in bowls of butter and sugar, vanilla sweetens the air, ginger spices it; melting, nose-tingling odors saturate the kitchen, suffuse the house, drift out to the world on puffs of chimney smoke. In four days our work is done. Thirty-one cakes, dampened with whiskey, bask on windowsills and shelves.
>
> —TRUMAN CAPOTE,
> *A Christmas Memory* (1956)

PASTRY BLENDERS

After the dry ingredients are combined, the next step in making pastry dough is to cut in the fat, a process which culminates in each tiny piece of butter or fat being coated with flour while remaining separate. If you're an experienced pastry hand, you can "cut in" the fat with two knives or you can "rub in" the fat by hand, briskly flaking it and the flour together with your fingertips and palms until the mixture resembles coarse meal. The French call this preparation *sabler* ("to sand") because the mixture should look like sand when it's done. But if, like so many first-timers, you're intimidated by pastry, these methods might not suit you—in which case, you should turn to your food processor, which is excellent for this task, pulsing flour and cold pieces of butter together in a matter of seconds, or try using either a pastry blender or pastry fork.

16.82 OXO FLOUR SIFTER

Appearing at once old-fashioned and modernly minimalist, this stainless steel sifter with its wide, comfortable plastic handle is both simple and effective. Marked inside and out with 1- and 2-cup measures as well as 125- and 250-gram notations, the sifter works by being gently shaken back and forth. Attached to the black plastic handle is a stainless steel extension that descends along the inside wall of the sifter; when it reaches the sifting screen at the bottom, it splays to become a flat, forklike agitator resting on the screen. As you shake the sifter from side to side, the agitator also moves from side to side, encouraging the flour to pass through the screen. The sifter comes with top and bottom plastic lids to seal it for storage, a much neater solution than a plastic bag.

16.83 BROWNE & CO. PASTRY BLENDER

Sturdier, broader, and slightly longer than most of the pastry blenders we've seen, this model has a classic oval shape fashioned from six rolled steel wires that will get to the bottom of the deepest mixing bowls and quickly incorporate the butter into the flour for a pastry dough. The handle is made of brushed stainless steel and finished on the ends in hard plastic. The grip is a round-edged rectangle that is comfortable whether you're grabbing it around the center with all your fingers gripping the underside, or working sidesaddle with your thumb stretched across the top, a grip many prefer for the added control.

16.84 NORPRO BLENDING FORK

You can get through life without this small implement, but when you've got a big batch of biscuit dough that needs a few sticks of butter cut into it, you'll be glad to reach for this unusual fork. Made of cast aluminum, it's larger than your average table fork and its tines are longer; each measures almost 2½". But it's

the back-of-the-fork construction that sets it apart: the tines are arched, their tips bordering on lethal, and their backs are sharply angled, almost pointed in fact, so that they're perfect for incorporating fat into flour. Once the fat is in, use the fork to toss the dough as you slowly spoon in the liquid. The fork, which was a favorite in James Beard's kitchen, can also be used to mash vegetables and fruits; it's ideal for crushing boiled potatoes for a homey mash. The blending fork is 8½" long.

PASTRY BOARDS & CLOTH

There are bakers who can roll out dough perfectly with nothing more than a wine bottle on a wobbly table, but most of us do better when we get a little help from well-made equipment and an ample, smooth surface for rolling. Your countertop is probably good enough for kneading bread dough or rolling out a simple pastry shell, but counters are often plagued by residual moisture, and dampness is death to a well-rolled pastry. To be safe, buy a wooden or marble pastry board and always keep it dry and ready for use. Wood makes a fine board for pasta, bread, or simple pastry, especially since the grain picks up and holds onto a little of the flour you sprinkle on it, minimizing sticking. Marble is the finest rolling surface because it remains cool, an important condition for butter-rich doughs like puff pastry and brioche, and has the additional benefit of being easy and quick to clean. Or, you can go the old-fashioned route and choose a canvas pastry cloth to put on top of your kitchen counter; some bakers swear by it.

uneven; to store, just wrap it around a rolling pin.

16.86 SCI MARBLE PASTRY BOARD

Marble is the ultimate pastry-making surface. It's perfectly smooth, it never absorbs fat or moisture, and it is always cool and dry. This beautiful slab is 18" by 12" by ½" thick, weighs about 11 pounds, and has smoothly finished edges. Because it is so large and heavy, you might want to consider keeping it out at all times, but if you've got the storage space and the muscles, you can stow it between sessions and, when necessary, chill it. Many bakers slide the slab into the refrigerator before rolling a finicky dough like puff pastry, and then put the slab and the pastry back in the fridge the instant the dough softens or needs a rest. The marble will always be ready for its next roll-out if you just wipe it down with a damp cloth, never put acidic substances in contact with it, and dry it well. This board is available in both white and green marble.

16.85 NORPRO ROLLING PIN COVER & PASTRY CLOTH SET

Short of rolling out dough on your counter, this is the simplest and least expensive aid to rolling pastry. Made of heavyweight cotton, the canvas pastry cloth provides a generous 20" by 24" rolling surface, and the cotton knit rolling pin cover—which resembles a sock—is 14" long and stretchy enough to fit over the widest two-handled pin. (The sock is too short

for a standard straight or tapered French pin.) To get the most out of this duo, place the cloth on a nonskid surface or, for extra stability, tuck one end of it under a wooden pastry board. Rub a few tablespoons of flour into the weave of the cloth and sprinkle some on the surface, then lightly flour the pin cover. While some bakers insist a pastry cloth should never be washed, we suggest you give it a good soap-and-water scrubbing between uses; rinse it well and lay it flat to dry. You can machine-wash it, but don't put it in the dryer. Never fold the cloth, since crease marks will make rolling dough

ROLLING PINS

To transform a lump of dough into a thin disk of pastry ready to be baked there's only one kitchen tool to use: a good rolling pin. Whether the pin has handles or not, is straight or tapered, it should always have a smooth finish that will prevent sticking and resist the absorption of fats and moisture. It should have enough heft so that it, not you, provides the flattening force, and good balance, so you're not working against the pin in order to roll a sheet of dough to an even thickness.

Rolling pins were once made exclusively of hardwood, but today's wooden pins now share shelf space with those fashioned from stainless steel, porcelain, marble, nylon, or polypropylene. Among our experts, the standard is still wood. We recommend that you steer clear of hollow pins that can be filled with ice cubes; they tend to sweat from condensation and dampen your dough. As for beautiful porcelain and marble pins, they are too fragile for real work. And the stainless steel pin? A fine idea, but it's no more effective than a heavy wood pin and, if it doesn't have ball bearings, it's less comfortable because the handles are secured to the pin. As for the bearings, nylon is as good as steel—neither will wear out.

Rolling pins come with or without handles. The classic American pin has two handles with a heavy wooden cylinder that turns independently between them on ball bearings. The pin has a smooth action and requires little pressure; because of its weight, it is ideal for rolling heavy doughs. A rolling pin without handles is called a French pin, and is typically longer and lighter than the American kind. French pin cylinders can be straight or tapered, and are perfectly suited to rolling out cookie and pastry doughs. Their advocates appreciate the pin's maneuverability and claim that, since the baker's hands are closer to the dough than they are with an American pin, they get a better feel for the dough. Given their different attributes, we recommend that if you're an avid baker, you buy one rolling pin of each type. Whether French or American, all wood pins should be wiped clean with a damp cloth after each use and then dried immediately.

16.87 & 16.88 MATFER WOODEN & NYLON FRENCH ROLLING PINS

The French rolling pin is the sports car of the pin world. Long (19⅝"), slim (1⅛" in diameter), sleek, and gently rounded on the edges, it handles like a Ferrari—quick, graceful, and easy to manuever. French pin users like its weight—at 2 to 3 pounds, it's heavy enough to do the job without much pressure—but they like its responsiveness even more. Because your hands are in direct contact with the pin, you can, with experience, actually feel the thickness of the dough, detect thick and thin spots, monitor the dough's progress, and make adjustments quickly and accurately. The classic French pin is made of beechwood, but this new nylon pin has all the benefits of its wooden cousin with the additional hygienic advantage of being able to take a good scrubbing or even a dishwasher bath. Sensualists may go for the wood, pragmatists for the nylon; the choice is yours.

16.89 J. K. ADAMS TAPERED ROLLING PIN

This well-made pin is a pleasure to hold and behold. It is made of smoothly finished New England maple and comes with its own wall mount, a handsome wood backing with a stainless steel retaining ring. (The mount can also be used to hold the pin on a counter.) The pin itself is a French-style pin: it has no handles and is gently tapered from its midsection to its ends, 22½" long and a plump 2¾" in diameter at its center. Using a tapered pin takes a little practice, since its balance is different from pins with straight cylinders. Its best use, the one that takes full advantage of its shape, is rolling dough into a circle.

16.90 THORPE ROLLING PIN

A tool for heavy-duty rolling, this maple pin, a favorite among profes-

---

SWEET TART DOUGH

2 9½" tart shells

In addition to its use as the pastry shell for tarts and tartlets, this rich, sweet short dough (also known as *pâte sucrée*) is frequently used in petits fours, for filled cookies, and as a thin crust under mousse desserts.

> 1 cup plus 1 tablespoon (122 grams) confectioners' sugar
> 1¾ cups (254 grams) all-purpose flour
> Pinch of salt
> 9 tablespoons (127 grams) unsalted butter, softened
> 1 large egg

1 Sift together the confectioners' sugar, flour, and salt into a bowl.
2 Place the butter in a food processor and process until smooth, about 15 seconds. Scatter the flour mixture over the butter, add the egg, and process just until the dough forms a mass; do not overmix. Turn the dough out onto the counter and divide it in two. Shape each half into a disc, wrap in plastic wrap, and refrigerate for at least 2 hours or up to 24 hours. Half of the dough may be well wrapped and frozen for up to one month.
3 Let the dough stand at room temperature for 30 minutes to soften. Lightly butter two 9½" fluted tart pans with removable bottoms.
4 Dust a work surface lightly with flour. Dust one of the discs lightly with flour and, using a floured rolling pin, roll it out into a rough 12" circle. Lift the dough often, making sure that the work surface and dough are lightly floured at all times. Roll the dough up onto the rolling pin and gently unroll it over one of the prepared tart pans. Press the dough into the pan and roll the pin over the top of the pan to remove the excess dough. Repeat with the remaining dough and tart pan. Prick the bottom of the tart shells all over with a fork. Chill the tart shells for 20 minutes. (The tart shells can be refrigerated for up to 24 hours.)

TO PARTIALLY BAKE THE TART SHELLS:
Preheat the oven to 325°F. Lightly butter two pieces of aluminum foil large enough to generously line each tart pan. Line the tart shells with the foil, buttered side down, and fill with dried beans, rice, or pie weights. Bake the tart shells for 15 minutes. Remove the foil and beans and continue baking for 5 minutes, until just set: the tart shells should have little or no color. Cool completely on a wire rack.

TO PREBAKE THE TART SHELLS
Preheat the oven to 325°F. Lightly butter two pieces of aluminum foil large enough to generously line each tart pan. Line the tart shells with the foil, buttered side down, and fill with dried beans, rice, or pie weights. Bake the tart shells for 15 minutes. Remove the foil and beans and continue baking for 8 to 10 minutes longer, until evenly golden brown. Cool completely on a wire rack.

Simply Sensational Desserts, by François Payard

---

sionals, weighs in at 4 pounds, 5 ounces. It has comfortable handles, 5" long with metal tip caps and nylon bearings. A steel rod is threaded through its barrel, which measures a generous 15" with a 3" diameter—long enough for wide laminate doughs like puff pastry or croissant. Couple the pin's easy movement with its weight and you won't need much muscle to roll elastic yeast dough into submission—the pin will do the lion's share of the work for you. Though this pin is availabe in six other lengths, ranging from 10½" to 18", we think this 15" is the most versatile.

16.91 MATFER FLUTED PUFF PASTRY ROLLING PIN

In the loose amalgam that is pastry dough, the fat must, by one means or another, always remain separate— it must never soak into the flour. When a flour-and-water dough is stacked in hundreds of layers separated by layers of butter—that is, when it is being transformed into puff pastry—the segregation is even more essential. Although any good-quality plain rolling pin can be used to make puff pastry, the ultimate instrument for this purpose is the French grooved rolling pin. The ⅛″ grooves run lengthwise on the plastic roller. The rounded ribs separating the grooves distribute the butter evenly between the layers as the dough is rolled and as the layers become thinner and thinner and multiply in number with subsequent folding and rollings. The bite of the grooved pin is also effective when beating and softening the dough

"Do you love the margarine story, or what?"

after it has been chilled between workings. This is an expensive piece of equipment, but worth the price if you intend to make puff pastry for croissants, vol-au-vents, napoleons, crust for beef wellington, or any number of sweet and savory fillings. It is 15¾″ in length.

DREDGERS

Today's dredgers, used mainly in the kitchen, are descended from much fancier shakers made for use at the table. In eighteenth-century England, the dredger was made of perforated silver and held cinnamon to be sprinkled on food at the table. Our dredgers are halfway between canisters and shakers and meant to be used while cooking, for sprinkling powdered sugar on pastry, cinnamon sugar on cookies, or flour on a pastry board. Dredgers come in metal and plastic, with mesh screens or perforations. In general, fine holes or mesh are preferable for sugar and cocoa, while larger holes are best for flour.

16.92 BEST MANUFACTURERS FLOUR WAND

If Tinkerbell were a baker, this would be her magic wand. At the end of a stainless steel handle with a squeeze mechanism is a spiraled ball that is pointed at either end. Composed of round bands of stainless steel, this coiled top gives little hint of what it can do. Give the simple wire handle a gentle squeeze (there are finger molds to show you just where to do so) and the spiraled ball opens. Dip the open ball into your flour, take the pressure off the handle, and the ball closes, trapping a few spoonfuls of flour in its spiral. That done, you have only to wave the wand over your dough and counter and you're ready to roll: the simple, oddly elegant wand produces a fairy-light dusting of flour. Since it does the same thing with confectioners' sugar and cocoa, think of it the next time you want to decorate a cake top in the simplest way. The wand fits easily into a sealed canister for convenient storage.

16.93 ENDURANCE FINE MESH SHAKER

Here's a solidly made dredger fashioned of stainless steel that feels good in your hand. Even though it has no handles, it is easy to control because it is 2¾" across, a good size even for people with small hands. The shaker top is fitted with a fine mesh screen that is just right for dusting the top of a cake with confectioners' sugar or cocoa powder. (A dredger with a coarsely perforated top, suitable for dusting a counter with flour or sprinkling a cake with finely chopped nuts, is also available.) To use, hold the dredger horizontally and shake it gently while tilting it forward. The top fits snugly onto the canister so there is no risk of its loosening while you're working and, when you're ready to store the dredger, there's an airtight plastic top that caps the mesh.

ON INSPIRATION
❧ PIERRE HERMÉ ❧

Inspiration can come from anywhere at any time, there are no rules. The idea for one of my favorite flans came to me when I was shopping in a New York City supermarket and I spotted a container of dried cherries. I had never seen these before—France doesn't have the variety of dried fruits you find in America—and I had to taste them. I loved their acidity and intense flavor and thought they would be great paired in a flan with the sweet creaminess of coconut. Another idea came to me after I had puréed some fresh pineapple in the food processor. The top was all foamy with tiny bubbles and it occurred to me that sprinkling sugar on the top would be interesting, changing the texture. Then I added a bit of salt and pepper and it made a very thin crust. It made a wonderful topping for very thin slices of pineapple. And the idea of embellishing a walnut cake with Chinese ginger and coffee cream came to me at the end of a dinner at a Chinese restaurant. I had ordered coffee and it was served with a piece of crystallized ginger on the side. The flavors complemented each other beautifully. You never know where inspiration will strike; you just have to have an open mind.

BAKING SPATULAS

A BAKING SPATULA RESEMBLES a rounded, blunt-edged knife with a spatulate shape. The blade, thinner than the metal used in knives, is tapered at the point where it connects with the handle, which can be made of wood or polypropylene. These spatulas come in lengths that range from about 4" to 14", and are offered in two versions, straight or offset. The straight spatula is the more traditional kind, but the offset one, with its blade angled so that it is about ½" below the handle, is the more useful: it can do everything a straight-blade spatula does, but also serves admirably as a lifter. We recommend that you have both a long offset and a long straight spatula, as well as a few short, thinner ones for finishing pastries.

16.94 & 16.95 ATECO LONG BAKING SPATULAS WITH PLASTIC & WOODEN HANDLES

For assembling, glazing, frosting, and icing layer cakes, or smoothing on a luscious layer of whipped cream, you need a spatula that's just a little longer than the cake's diameter or width. Since most American cakes are 8" or 9" across, we suggest you buy at least one spatula that's 9½" to 12" long and the standard 1¼" to 1½" wide. Whether you choose the spatula with a dishwasher-safe polypropylene handle or the one with a wooden grip, and whether you opt for the straight or the offset blade, is a matter of personal preference. Both handles are comfortable and sturdy and both styles have stainless steel blades with enough flexibility to glide gracefully over the soft surface of a cake and enough strength to support the cake or its layers when necessary. When used as lifters, these spatulas are great for removing cookies from parchment or a pan, or for turning silver dollar pancakes or blini as they brown on a griddle or in a skillet. We show you two spatulas here, one with a 10" by 1½" straight blade with a wooden handle and a 9¾" by 1½" offset blade with polypropylene handle.

16.96, 16.97, & 16.98 ATECO SMALL STRAIGHT-BLADE, OFFSET, & TROWEL-SHAPED ICING SPATULAS

If you are a miniaturist, you'll find myriad uses for this trio of baby baking spatulas. Each 4" to 5" stainless steel blade is about ¾" wide and set into a wooden handle with two brass rivets. For the task of glazing and frosting cookies, petits fours, tartlets, and cupcakes, we suggest you have a straight-blade spatula, an offset spatula, and a trowel-shaped offset spatula whose rounded tip is a mere ¼" wide and delicate enough to put the tiniest swirl of frosting atop the tiniest tea cake.

BAKING KNIVES

If you are a serious cake maker, then you might want to consider having a serious knife—or set of knives—dedicated to cutting cakes. Ideally, you should have two kinds of cake knives, or one knife with two kinds of blades: a smooth blade for cutting firm cakes with dense crumbs, and a serrated blade for cutting cakes that have a more open, delicate crumb. A cake knife should be long—you'll want to be able to cut through large layer cakes in a smooth motion—and as well-made as all the other knives in your collection. As tempting as it might be to use your baking knife to slice ham or cut off a hunk of bread, it's best if you set it aside for cakes only, sparing the blade from bumping into bones or any other foodstuffs tougher than your favorite fruitcake.

16.99 WÜSTHOF BAKER'S KNIFE

Trust this baker's knife to slice through even the softest freshly made cake without damaging the delicate crumb. The smooth, composite handle is comfortably narrow and it is well-shaped for control. It's the semi-flexible spatula-like blade however, that makes this knife so unusual—1¼" wide, saw-edged on one side and smooth and sharp on the other, it is almost a foot long, so you can cut through most cakes in one seamless pass. The saw-edged side has a series of extremely tight serrations that are interspersed with a wider tooth at about 1" intervals. In addition, the blade is slightly rounded, a feature that reduces resistance as the knife moves through the cake, consequently reducing the possibility of tearing the cake's crumb. With the serrated side of the blade to handle spongy, open-crumbed cakes and the smooth, sharp side for dense pound-cake confections, you should be able to cut through any cake in your repertoire.

MINOR PASTRY TOOLS

Each of these tools—including pastry brushes, a cake tester, a docker, a crimper, a pie bird, and baking weights—does a job that you might be able to do with other kitchen implements, but that you'd do less well. In most cases, these are single-purpose tools, but they are inexpensive and, when you've got that particular job to do, they will become your right hand, making your baking a little easier and more efficient.

16.100 J. B. PRINCE ROLLER DOCKER

It's easy to mistake this odd-looking gadget for an instrument of torture. The business end is a 5"-long heavy-duty plastic cylinder embedded with evenly spaced spikes. Grab the handle, roll the cylinder over sheets of pastry, then stand back and admire the rows of deep pricks that will allow the dough to bake evenly. You could make these pricks with the tines of a fork, but the rows would never be as elegant. The docker, used by professionals and particularly well-suited for puff pastry, is easier to use with large sheets of pastry, or even when making focaccia or crackers, than with average-size tart shells.

16.101 MATFER FLAT PASTRY BRUSH

What sets pastry brushes apart from paint brushes is the bristles: pastry brushes are made from nylon or from unbleached hog bristles that have been sterilized. This pastry brush, designed to smooth jam over a cake, egg glaze over a bread, or even pan *jus* over a chicken, is of the hog-bristle variety. Its handle is 6½″ long and made of a washable composite material. Its ferrule, the band that binds the bristles to the handle, is plastic and also easy to keep clean. The bristles on this brush are blunt-cut, 2½″ long and 1½″ wide. You can find similar brushes with wider and narrower bristles to do bigger or daintier jobs, but we think this size is the golden mean and recommend that you have at least two of them: one for basting and one for butter, jams, and glazes. Wash and air-dry a pastry brush after each use.

16.102 ATECO NATURAL WHITE BRISTLE GREASE BRUSH

Professional bakers have a bowl of softened butter and a brush like this one close at hand to make fast work of buttering pans and baking sheets. The job can be done with a wad of paper towels, or even with the wrapper you may have peeled off a stick of butter, but once you butter your first batch of pans with this king-size brush, you'll understand why the

pros like it; it's a time-saver, for sure, but it also does a more thorough job. This 11″-long brush can get into the corners of a brownie pan or the curves of a *Bundt* pan and, despite its size, is even effective with tartlet and muffin tins. Because its natural hog bristles are 2½″ long and are gathered into a 1½″ wide round, they cover a lot of surface quickly and well. The handle is a composite material, the ferrule stainless steel, and the entire brush a boon when you're on a baking binge, to say nothing of when you've got a turkey to baste. The brush will be long-lasting if you wash and air-dry it after each use.

16.103 MATFER BAKING BEANS

Crusts that have no-bake fillings and those that you want to keep crisp and dry are prebaked, or blind baked, without their fillings. For a blind bake, the crust is covered with parchment paper or foil and filled with weights that prevent it from bubbling and buckling from the heat. For years, bakers weighted their pies efficiently with reusable, inexpensive rice or dried beans. They did a good job of weighting the crusts, but they had two drawbacks: they might become rancid and, more often, they'd have you dreaming about pie but smelling hot pinto beans. There are no such problems with these aluminum pellets. Packed in 2¼-pound bags, they can be used sparingly for weighting *pâte brisée* and heavily when you're trying to keep down a puff pastry crust. They have the added advantage of attracting and

maintaining the oven's heat, so crusts brown better and faster. They're washable, too.

16.104 N.Y. CAKE & BAKING PASTRY CRIMPER

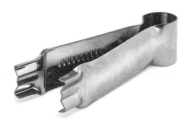

All filled pastries—pies included—require a tight seal between the top and bottom crusts. You can pinch them together between your fingers, press them with the tines of a fork, or use a crimper. This one, made of stainless steel, is 3½″ long; its serrated gripping edges need little pressure to squeeze closed. And when it's not being used in the service of pastry, it doubles as a strawberry huller.

16.105 BOSTON WAREHOUSE TRADING CO. PIE BIRD

We show you a single blackbird, not four-and-twenty, to bake in a pie. He looks as though he's singing, but he's really providing a vent so that steam doesn't accumulate beneath the pie crust and make it soggy. This charming little fellow is of blue shiny-glazed ceramic, and stands 4″ tall. Set him on the bottom of a pie pan, put in the filling, and lay the top crust (with a hole cut out for the bird) over him. His beak should protrude through the unbaked top crust, making it unnecessary for you to slash any other vents in the top of the pie.

16.106 ATECO CAKE TESTER

At times, finding the right cake tester can resemble the story of Goldilocks and the Three Bears. A toothpick can be too short, a thin-bladed knife too long and invasive, but this specialized tool is just right. It's a 6"-long, thin metal skewer with a ring hold on top. Slide it into the cake, pull it out, and if it's free of crumbs or clinging batter your cake is done. It's hardly a necessary tool, but it won't put a dent in your budget or in the top of your cake.

> If writers were
> bakers, this sentence
> would be exactly
> a dozen words long.
> —DOUGLAS R. HOFSTADTER

CUTTERS

IT'S NOT UNTIL cookie dough is cut into a Christmas angel, a piece of puff pastry shaped into a scallop-edged shell, or a rectangle of *pâte brisée* cut into strips for a lattice crust that the range of a dough's personality can be appreciated. For each form and function, there is a specially designed cutter.

Whether the cutting tool is a knife, a wheel, or a template, its edge must be sharp enough to part dough neatly, never tearing, stretching, or in any other way distorting it. The cutter must also be sturdy and easily gripped. It should require little pressure to use. With few exceptions, exoglass chief among them, the most effective cutters are made of metal, which takes and keeps a sharp edge.

There's no rule that says you can't use a biscuit cutter to form cookies, a cookie cutter to shape fanciful tea sandwiches, or a doughnut cutter to make peek-a-boo cookies, but there are some cutters that work better with some doughs than they do with others, as you will see when you look at the following tools.

16.107 J. B. PRINCE PLAIN PASTRY WHEEL

"A knife made round" defines this simple cutting tool, a honed and beveled steel wheel set on an axle and attached to a comfortable wooden handle that keeps your hand a safe 5" or so from the rotating business end. If you're accustomed to cutting dough with a knife, you'll be delighted the first time you cut with this wheel; the motion is fluid and clean, so the dough is never pulled or stretched, as it can be with even the sharpest knife. Run the wheel alongside a ruler and you'll have perfect pastry strips for lattice crusts or cheese straws, squares for pinwheel pastries, or triangles for turnovers. This wheel, the smallest in a family that also includes pizza cutters, is a petite 2" across.

16.108 J. B. PRINCE FLUTED PASTRY WHEEL

Paging through books of antique cookware, you're bound to find collections of fluted pastry wheels forged from iron, carved from wood, or crafted from copper. Called "jaggers" in eighteenth-century English and American books, these cutters work on the same principle as their less decorative sibling, the plain pastry wheel. The jagged cutting edge of this 2"-diameter wheel, set on an axle and attached to a wooden handle, makes any pastry look as though it has been cut with pinking shears. The rippled edge is appealing on lattice pastry strips, thin crackers, or pasta for lasagna and ravioli.

16.109 ATECO TWELVE-PIECE PASTRY CUTTER SET

If you plan to buy only one set of pastry cutters, make it this set. Comprised of twelve round tinned-steel cutters neatly nested in a metal storage tin, this set has rolled tops and cutting edges sharp enough to tackle the most delicate puff pastry requiring the sharpest, cleanest cuts. Because the cutters range from about 1" to 4½" in diameter, you'll use them for myriad jobs. Reach for the smallest cutter when you want to punch a steam hole in the center of a pie's top crust, the largest when you want to cut dough to fit into tartlet pans, and any of the in-between sizes when you're making cookies, crostini, pizzettes, biscuits, or even tea sandwiches. A set with fluted cutting edges is also available.

16.110 MATFER PUFF PASTRY CUTTERS

This nesting set of seven fluted cutters is almost identical in shape to French sets of more than a century ago, but no nineteeth-century French baker accustomed to working with tinned-steel cutters would know what to make of this set's lightweight, ivory translucence and cool matte finish. These antique-style fluted cutters are molded of a high-tech composite plastic called exoglass, and while they are fine for cutting cookies, they are really meant to cut puff pastry. With puff pastry and an ordinary cutter, you run the risk of producing a cut that seals the top layer of pastry to the bottom and prevents the dough from rising in the oven. With cutters made for the job, you get a whistle-clean cut, so sharp it might seem you can riffle through the pastry's layers as you would the pages of a book. The seven cutters range in diameter from 1¼" to 3¾" and come packed in a plastic storage container. They should be

---

GRANNY'S OLD-FASHIONED SUGAR COOKIES

These are crisp, large, thin plain cookies with a divine lemon and cinnamon flavor. Everyone raves about them and asks for the recipe. It is best to refrigerate this dough overnight before rolling it out and cutting it with a cookie cutter.

18 to 24 large cookies

1¾ cups unsifted all-purpose flour
2 teaspoons double-acting baking powder
¼ teaspoon salt
4 ounces (1 stick) unsalted butter
Finely grated rind of 2 lemons
1 tablespoon lemon juice
1 cup granulated sugar
1 egg graded "large"
2 tablespoons whipping cream

1 Sift together the flour, baking powder, and salt and set aside. In the large bowl of an electric mixer beat the butter until it is soft. Beat in the lemon rind and juice, and then add the sugar. Beat in the egg and the whipping cream. Then, on low speed, gradually add the sifted dry ingredients and beat until smoothly mixed. Remove from the mixer.
2 Turn the dough out onto a length of wax paper or plastic wrap, wrap it, and refrigerate overnight. (In a hurry, I have used the freezer instead of the refrigerator—only until the dough was cold and firm but not frozen.)
3 When you are ready to bake, adjust two racks to divide the oven into thirds and preheat the oven to 375°F. Line cookie sheets with baking pan liner paper or with foil shiny side up. Set aside.
4 Spread out a pastry cloth, flour it well, and flour a rolling pin. Unwrap the dough, cut it into thirds, and place one piece on the floured cloth. If it was refrigerated overnight, it will be too stiff to roll out; pound it firmly with the floured rolling pin, turning the dough over occasionally until it is soft enough to be rolled. Roll it out until it is quite thin, about ⅛" to ³⁄₁₆" thick.
5 Use a large round cookie cutter about 3½" in diameter (more or less). Start to cut the cookies at the outside edge of the dough and cut them so close to each other that they are touching. With a wide metal spatula transfer the cookies to the lined sheets, placing them ½" apart.

It is best not to reroll the scraps if possible because they would absorb additional flour and become a bit tougher than otherwise. Here's a hint: Do not press the scraps together but, with smaller cutters, cut out as many smaller cookies as you can. Or use a knife and cut squares or triangles. There will be some leftover scraps, but much less than otherwise. Reserve the scraps. Roll and cut the remaining dough. Then press all the scraps together, refrigerate if necessary (it probably will not be), roll it out, and cut with a knife or with cutters.

CINNAMON-SUGAR

1 tablespoon granulated sugar
⅓ teaspoon cinnamon
Pinch of nutmeg

1 Mix the above ingredients and, with your fingertips, sprinkle over the cookies.
2 Bake for 10 to 13 minutes, reversing the sheets top to bottom and front to back as necessary to ensure even browning. When done, the cookies will be only sandy colored, slightly darker on the rims.
3 With a wide metal spatula transfer the cookies to racks to cool. Store airtight. These last well if you stay away from them.

Maida Heatter's Book of Great American Desserts, by Maida Heatter

washed with warm soapy water. Matfer also makes a set with straight edges—effective, but less decorative.

16.111 J. B. PRINCE LATTICE DOUGH CUTTER

Once you get the hang of it, this ingenious tool produces perfect lattice tops. It's composed of two pieces: a plastic disk, 11½" in diameter with ½"-deep diamond-shaped cutters, and another flat diamond-shaped plastic disk that slips snugly into the cutter circle. To use it, fit the pieces together and place them, cutter side up, on your counter. Roll out your pastry dough and lay it over the cutter. Once the dough is in place, run your pin against it so the cutters can do their job. Use your finger to poke out the pieces of dough that inevitably stick to the cutters and, if you've got the time, pop the cutter and dough into the freezer for 5 to 10 minutes—a quick chill will make handling the dough much easier. Once the dough is chilled, you've got a choice: you can lift off the plastic disk and turn the dough onto a parchment-lined baking sheet, where it can then be kept covered and chilled until needed; or you can turn the dough over directly onto its intended pie. Either way, you're guaranteed a sleek, professional-looking lattice top for your pastry.

16.112 J. B. PRINCE LATTICE DOUGH ROLLER

More compact than the lattice dough cutter but a bit more complicated to use, this roller is made of heavy-duty plastic. Its handle is angled, like a paint roller, and its cutting edge is a 5"-long cylinder that resembles a miniaturized rotary tiller. Run it across a piece of rolled-out dough and it will produce a pattern of long and short linear cuts that look like a television screen experiencing transmission problems. But pull the dough gently along the cuts and it opens to reveal an impressive honeycomb lattice, provided you've got the right kind of dough. Puff pastry is the ideal dough to lattice with this tool, but you can be successful with other sturdy elastic doughs, like brioche. There is one drawback: by the time you've rolled out the dough, run the lattice maker over it, and then separated the lattices, the dough is likely to be soft, warm, or both. We suggest rolling and cutting the dough on parchment paper or a nonstick liner, so if it goes soft you can slide it onto a baking sheet and give it a quick chill between operations.

16.113 & 16.114 ATECO STAR & HEART CUTTERS

These sets of six pastry or cookie cutters nest neatly in their own metal storage containers and offer the baker a variety of sizes with a consistency of shape. Both the star and heart cutters are formed from single strips of metal that are bent into shape, with sharp cutting edges and rolled tops. Because these cutters, which range in diameter from 1¾" to 3½", are more than

1" deep, you could also use them as mini cake rings.

16.115 ATECO TRICK OR TREAT CUTTER SET

It's all treat and no trick with this Halloween cutter set. The six metal cutters cover the roster of spooky icons: a bat, an owl, a cat that cries out for a shiny black glaze, a jack-o'-lantern, a broom, and, of course, a witch. The cutters, which are between 1½" and 4" in diameter, are strong enough for the once-a-year workout they'll get and whimsical enough to send you to your oven when All Saints' Day rolls around.

16.116 NORPRO ROLLING COOKIE CUTTER

This cheery red-and-white plastic rolling cutter looks more like an infant's playpen toy than a piece of kitchen equipment. The roller's handle secures a wheel with slots for six 2"-diameter plastic cutters. In fact, the kit comes with eighteen interchangeable cutters that easily slide in and out of the wheel. Most of the shapes are geometrical, but there's also a snowman, a plump gingerbread boy, and an even plumper angel. Fit the wheel with your selection, press one of the cutters against your rolled-out dough, move the wheel along the dough until you've come full circle and you'll have six cookies and barely a wasted scrap of dough between them. But because the dough has a tendency to attach to the cutters, you must stop after each rotation, knock or pry out the cut dough, and then continue.

16.117 SUR LA TABLE EIFFEL TOWER CUTTER

Anyone with a polished sweet tooth and a soft spot for the City of Lights will appreciate this Eiffel Tower cutter, hand-crafted in copper. The cutter is long—a full 11″ from base to what would be the tower's flagpole—broad and sturdy: press it into dough and it won't wiggle or wobble, a potential hazard with cutters this large. The handle is strong and wide, with enough room to allow mitts as big as the Cookie Monster's to get a good grip, and the cutting edge is sharp and a full ½″ deep. Whether you're working with dough that's sugar cookie–thin or gingerbread-thick, the cut is always clean and complete. Unfortunately, the beautiful pattern of latticework

and arches that has been pressed into the copper won't press into your dough, but the large smooth cookie the cutter produces is an ideal canvas for decorations.

16.118 J. B. PRINCE CROISSANT CUTTER

The flaky, crescent-shaped rolls known as croissants, so sacred to the French breakfast, are coveted by foreigners as well. With a large cup of café au lait and some jam, a croissant or two are rich enough to tide one through a morning. This croissant cutter of stainless steel will trim enough croissants out of a sheet of dough to last you for days. With a minimum of waste, it cuts a continuous strip of triangular dough pieces that must then be rolled and curved into the shape of a quarter moon before baking. Some professionals feel the cutter is unnecessary for small amounts of dough, but it is efficient. The cutter is 16″ long overall, with wooden handles and a blade that is 6¼″ long and 5″ in diameter.

16.119 ENDURANCE BISCUIT CUTTERS

Biscuit cutters haven't changed much since Colonial times, but new

materials and a tweak here and there on construction have made modern-day cutters, like this handsome set, more efficient and more practical. This set of four cutters, ranging in diameter from 1½″ to 2¾″, is not called "Endurance" for naught—it's made of heavy-gauge polished stainless steel and is likely to last a lifetime. The cutters themselves are a generous 1½″ deep—it's the depth that sets a biscuit cutter apart from a shallower cookie cutter—and their cutting edges are nicely beveled on the outside while the top edges are smooth. The handles are a pleasure to hold; constructed of two rounded bands of stainless steel, they arch 1½″ above their cutters, so there's plenty of grip room.

16.120 NORPRO ENGLISH MUFFIN RINGS

Contrary to what their name would lead you to believe, English muffins as we know them in America aren't exactly English; the famous Thomas's English Muffins were first made in New York on Ninth Avenue. In addition, they are not really muffins, and they are not baked in muffin tins. In fact, they're not even baked. The yeast batter—and it is more batter than dough—is cooked on a griddle, making the English muffin actually a type of Americanized crumpet, a cross between a pancake and a flatbread. The rings, 3¾″ diameter, 1″ high bands of metal rolled on top and bottom, give the muffins their characteristic shape. The rings are often preheated with the griddle, then the batter is spooned into them and the muffins are cooked on one side before the rings are removed and the muffins flipped over to finish cooking. Packaged four to a box, the rings can be used to make perfectly round pancakes and sunny-side up eggs, they can double as biscuit cutters and even shape portions of rice.

16.121 SQUARE VOL-AU-VENT CUTTER

The legendary nineteenth-century French chef Antonin Carême said of vol-au-vents, "This entrée is pretty and good." That was an understatement. Few things are more appetizing than a golden case of puff pastry filled with an exquisite dish like sweetbreads *à la financière,* in truffle-flavored Madeira sauce with green olives, mushrooms, truffles, and veal mousse dumplings. As they have for almost every special culinary preparation, the French have devised timesaving professional tools for shaping vol-au-vents.

For making vol-au-vents, these cutters turn out rectangular cases rather than the round ones. Somehow we see them as destined to be filled with strawberries in whipped cream. Imagine a shiny square doughnut cutter 4¼" on each side, with its inner cutter ⅝" inside the outer one and with a reasonably sturdy handle spanning the entire construction. The inner cutter doesn't cut entirely through the dough at two of its corners, and thus the center square is anchored only lightly at those corners to the outer border of pastry.

After cutting the pastry, you form the case by a procedure much easier to do than describe. Beginning at an outer corner where the inner square is unanchored, you lift the border of dough and fold it diagonally, placing its point precisely over the opposite corner of the inner square. Then you lift the outer corner opposite to your beginning point and fold it in turn to lie over *its* opposite corner of the center square. The remaining two corners are twisted into points by these maneuvers—they look somewhat like arrowheads. The case, when it has been baked, will be approximately square, with twisted knobs at two corners—decorative and effective. The top of the central square can be pried out to form a lid. The extra-sharp blades of the cutter pass cleanly through puff pastry without sealing the edges together, which would prevent it from rising.

16.122 ATECO DOUGHNUT CUTTER

In a pinch, you could use two cookie cutters to cut a doughnut, but having a well-made doughnut cutter at the ready makes the process much easier. This doughnut cutter is properly proportioned to produce more cake than hole: the cake cutter is 3½" in diameter while the center hole cutter is just 1⅛". The top of the cutter is rolled and the cutting edge is particularly sharp, so the cut is clean even when the dough is raised with yeast. Indeed, the 1¾" depth of the cutter makes it a good tool for working with puffy yeast doughs. The cutter does not have a handle, but its rolled edge, and the four spokes that attach the hole cutter to the larger cutter, stabilize the tool and keep it rock steady during cuts. The cutter also comes in a smaller, 2½" diameter, with the same 1⅛" center hole. Don't forget to fry the cut-out "holes" as well; they make great bite-size treats.

16.123 THE HOUSE ON THE HILL *SPRINGERLE* ROLLING PIN

Nothing heralds Christmas more delightfully than *Springerle,* pale, cream-colored cookies embossed with familiar images and flavored with lemon and anise. An alternative to the *Springerle* board (below) is this powdered-wood-and-resin rolling pin, 14¼" long with sturdy, finished handles. The rolling surface alone is

---

WHO INVENTED THE DOUGHNUT?

In 1941 The Great Doughnut Debate was held in New York to determine who invented the small fried cake with the hold in its center. At the meeting, it was determined that Captain Hanson Crockett Gregory had invented the doughnut in 1847, but how he created it is still in dispute. Our favorite legend is that he stuck the fried cake onto the spoke of the wheel to free his hands as a storm approached his ship.

6" long and has twelve designs that include birds, flowers, and peasants. It is sometimes helpful to chill the pin for several hours in the refrigerator before rolling the dough to prevent it from sticking. Cut along the ridges between the cookies with a large, sharp knife to separate them neatly. If you haven't already thought of it, *Springerle* make irresistible ornaments on Christmas trees and packages.

16.124 THE HOUSE ON THE HILL *SPRINGERLE* COOKIE ROLLER

With this diminutive cookie roller, you or your offspring can make a twining vine of pineapple, flower, and strawberry-figured *Springerle* for Christmas. The vine is carved into the powdered wood and resin wheel, which is 3¼" wide and 3½" across. Turning the wheel with the 10"-long handle is child's play—and what nicer way to get assistance for the pastry chef? The resulting cookies

can be cut to the size of your choice. It's also good for gingerbread cookies.

16.125 THE HOUSE ON THE HILL *SPRINGERLE* BOARD

Springerle are among the most beautiful cookies in the world, and they are an old tradition in both Germany and Switzerland. In Switzerland, they are known as *Anisbrötli* or *Anisli* because of their distinctive anise flavor. The stiff dough is made with eggs, sugar, and flour, and flavored with anise and lemon. The cookies are imprinted with designs by a press like this one, which is a replica of old presses. Carved in clay, wood, and

metal, presses have been created for hundreds of years to celebrate marriages, births, and to record the daily goings-on of life.

This press is made of powdered wood and resin and measures 8" by 5" by ½". To use it, first dust it with flour, then press it firmly but evenly down onto a ¼" to ½" thick sheet of rolled-out cookie dough. Gently lift the board off, and then cut the dough into rectangles or squares, each with an embossed design in the center. All of the incisions in this *Springerle* board are sharp and imprint a clear image, and the cuts slope outward toward the top to permit free release of the dough. The designs—birds, a flower, a turkey, two sheep, a knight, and a hunter—are charming, and separated by the double incised lines that frame them. Air-dry the cookies for 24 hours and then bake them for only about 15 minutes until they are the palest gold color, never brown. The cookies keep a long time and soften after a few weeks in a cookie jar. *Springerle* are traditionally baked about a month before Christmas. For the rest of the year when the press is not in use, hang it by its hook in your kitchen as a decoration.

COOLING RACKS

Cooling, like everything else in baking, is a procedure that must be done properly for your baked goods to turn out well. With very few exceptions, cakes, cookies, and individual pastries need to be removed from their baking pans or sheets and set on racks that lift them above the counter and allow air to circulate around them. Leave them in or on their pans, or transfer them directly to a platter, and you'll trap the steam under them and end up with soggy sweets. There are some cakes that are too fragile to be removed from their pans while hot. In these cases, the cakes should be left in their pans and the pans should be placed on a wire rack to speed cooling. Once your cake or cookie is set enough to be removed from its pan, unmold or lift it onto a metal cooling rack with feet that raise the rack at least ½" above the counter. Look for racks that have tightly spaced grids—you certainly don't want your petits fours falling between the supports—and buy several. You'll want two large rectangular racks for cooling batches of cookies (you might want even more) and at least three round racks, the minimum number you'll need to invert and then cool two cake layers. Why three for two layers? The extra one is for the job of inverting.

16.126 WILTON INDUSTRIES STACKABLE COOLING RACKS

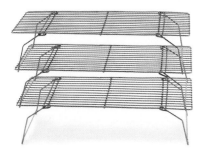

If counterspace is a problem, consider these stackable cooling racks. This three-in-the-space-of-one cooling system offers a trio of racks, each 9¾" by 13½" with collapsible 3"-high cooling legs. The chrome-plated steel racks feature horizontal cooling wires that are spaced ¾" apart and stabilized in three places with strong vertical wires. Of course, each rack can be used individually, but they are easily stacked—just move the legs into standing position and nest the small rounded feet inside the lower rack's grid area. When stacked, they are miserly on space but generous on cooling area; the 3" between racks allows even the tallest cakes to have good air circulation, the key to proper cooling.

16.127 & 16.128 WILTON INDUSTRIES NONSTICK & CHROME-PLATED COOLING GRIDS

Whether you've got a heavy *Bundt* cake laden with fruits and nuts or a few paper-thin wafers, an airy angel food cake or loaves of bread, these sturdy cooling racks will keep your baked treats high and dry. Available in heavy-gauge, chrome-plated or nonstick steel, these racks are constructed with tightly spaced grids that provide even support, and have four little feet to keep them—and your baked goods—at least ½" above the counter so that air can easily circulate underneath. Because the feet are softly rounded, there's no danger of their scratching polished countertops. The round rack, 13" in diameter, can be used to cool baked items of almost any variety, but its size and shape make it most efficient for cooling cake rounds and loaves. (If you're going to cool two rounds, then you'll need three racks; the leftover rack will be the one you'll use to invert the cakes.) The well-constructed rectangular rack comes in two sizes, 10" by 16" and 14½" by 24". The larger size is a blessing when you've got batch after batch of cookies coming out of the oven, but storage can be a problem. Try tucking them in with your baking sheets.

DECORATING TOOLS

IF, AS THE OLD SAYING GOES, we eat with our eyes before we eat with our mouths, then it is not surprising that we decorate almost every cake we bake, whether with a simple dusting of confectioners' sugar, a layer of rich frosting or shimmering glaze, or a cascade of buttercream flowers. From the most basic decorating combs and stencils to the most elaborate piping tips for forming intricate frosting flowers, the chef's kit is a treasure trove, and one that hasn't changed substantially since Antonin Carême created his intricate pastry and sugar confections in the early nineteenth century. Peek into a pastry chef's tool box and you'll find decorating syringes, pastry bags of varying sizes, and tens, if not hundreds, of decorating tips, as well as parchment paper for forming small cones perfect for writing in chocolate or icing. Nearby will be a turntable on which to steady the creation being embellished. To this collection we've added cookie presses and a scoop—not really decorating tools, but certain to turn out decorative, beautifully shaped sweets—and an almost-automatic whipped-cream maker for those times when you want to do something special but have only a minute.

You can make a plain cake look fancier with nothing more than a shaking of confectioners' sugar over a stencil, or you can frost the cake and give it a fussed-over look by running a decorating comb against the frosting, but if you want to do some serious decorating, you'll have to choose your weapon: a syringe, a pastry bag, or a parchment cone. Beginners may opt for the syringe because it is the least complicated to use. However, what you gain in control you lose in sensitivity. The syringe is like a student's violin; the pastry bag is a Stradivarius. When you graduate to a pastry bag, you'll be using the tool the professionals choose. As for the parchment cone, it is best used for piping small dots and delicate squiggles to decorate a dessert plate or for writing gracefully across a cake. The trick is in constructing the cone, a skill you can master in five minutes.

16.129 J. B. PRINCE CAKE STENCILS

If you want to dress up the top of a plain cake or give an extra flourish to an iced or glazed cake, these stencils will produce good looks without much effort. They are made of food-safe white plastic and include a tab so you can easily place the stencils on a cake and just as easily remove them. The package of four stencils, which range from 5½" to 7¼" in diameter, includes two geometric patterns and two floral. All of the stencils can be used for templates when you want to dust a cake with confectioners' sugar or cocoa, and they are perfect if you want to finish an already iced cake with a different-colored icing—simply smooth the icing evenly over the stencil with a metal baking spatula, then lift off the stencil.

16.130 ATECO CAKE & PASTRY DECORATING SET

It is unlikely that this decorating syringe with its six dainty metal tips will replace the pastry bag in the affections of professionals, but this syringe is an easy and effective substitute for the many home bakers who haven't gotten the knack of filling, twisting, and wielding a bag. The barrel of the syringe, which is easily filled with anything from meringue to buttercream, is made of gold-tinted aluminum and capped with sturdy white plastic couplings. The bottom coupler secures the decorating tip while the top coupler has two winged finger grips that are well-placed and comfortable. The plunger, topped by a thumb hole, moves easily within the barrel, giving you the control you need for decorating. The kit's six tips should see you through most small cake and cookie decorating jobs, but should the task at hand call for more options, the syringe is compatible with any of the tips included in the 55-piece decorating set from the same manufacturer.

16.131 KUHN RIKON COOKIE PRESS

While there are many kinds of cookies that can be shaped with a press, most people turn to these devices when they want to make spritz cookies for Christmas. If you're a fan of these rich butter cookies, or even if you want to give ready-made packaged cookie dough a different look, then you're a good candidate for this press, a well-made tool. Constructed of dishwasher-safe plastic and stainless steel, the cookie press has a clear barrel—that's where the dough goes—and an easy-to-squeeze press-ing mechanism. With each squeeze of the handle, the ratcheted rod pushes out one cookie. The pattern of the cookie depends on which of the twenty different disks you insert in the press. In addition to the disks, the kit comes with six small piping tips in assorted shapes. The tips are useful for very basic decorations, but if you've got tiny pansies or fluted curlicues on your mind, better to reach for a pastry bag.

16.132 ISI EASY WHIP

It is not surprising that this ingenious whipped cream maker comes from Austria, the land of *shlag,* or whipped cream. Austrians put whipped cream on everything, from their first cup of coffee in the morning to their last slice of torte before bed and, as you'd expect, they're fussy about it. With this whipped cream maker they, or anyone else, won't have much to fuss about. The metal siphon, which holds up to two cups of cream, is made to be fitted with a single-use nitrous oxide cartridge. Pour in well-chilled fresh cream, insert the cartridge, shake the canister a few times, and then press the nozzle to pipe out fluted swirls of whipped cream. Like all whipped cream, it is better served soon after it has been whipped, but the filled canister can remain in the refrigerator for up to two weeks. The siphon comes with one cartridge;

MAKING A PARCHMENT PAPER CONE

A parchment cone, the ideal tool for piping delicate chocolate curlicues or writing "Happy Birthday" in jam across a cake, is made from a triangle of parchment paper. You can either buy ready-cut triangles or cut a piece of parchment paper in half on the diagonal to form two triangles. To fold the cone, place the parchment triangle on a counter, keeping the longest side of the triangle at the top of the counter edge opposite you. Fold the left-hand point down so that it meets the point at the bottom. There's no need to fold the paper down into a crease; better to just have it curve and anchor the two points in your left hand. (If you're left-handed, you might be more comfortable grasping the points in your right hand.) Now, take the upper right-hand point in your right hand and draw it completely around the points in your left hand. Keep wrapping until the three points of the triangle meet. They won't meet in perfect symmetry, but they should come close. Grab the three points and fold down the parchment just enough to secure the points and seal the cone. (If you're not sure you've done a perfect job, you can finish the cone with a small piece of tape.) If you want to use a decorating tube with the parchment cone, slip the tube into the cone, cut the tip of the cone just enough to have the tip exposed as it would be if you were using a pastry bag, then fill the cone. Fill it about half to two-thirds full. If you are not using a decorating tube, just snip off the tip of the cone to create an opening that's the right size for your job. When you are ready to pipe, fold down the top of the cone.

---

additional cartridges are available in packages of ten.

16.133 ATECO DECORATING STAND

This cake-decorating turntable, built like a potter's wheel, adds steadiness to the delicate job of finishing a cake. Put your cake on the thick aluminum top, which is 12″ in diameter, then spin it slowly with one hand while you frost the cake with the other. The precision machining allows the turntable to rotate smoothly and evenly above the heavy cast-iron base. As the wheel turns, you can press ground almonds into the sides of a cake, run decorating combs across the frosting, or scallop butter-cream shells around the edge. The turntable and stand are heavy—heavy enough to support even a monumental wedding cake—well-made, easy to take apart, just as easy to clean and, if you're a passionate baker, worth every penny you plunk down: buy one and you'll have it for a lifetime.

16.134 ZEROLL UNIVERSAL EZ DISHER

It's a baking basic: spoon out an equal amount of dough for each cookie and, unless your oven has serious hot spots, every batch of cookies will bake in exactly the same number of minutes, and the cookies will all be the same size. Symmetry is easy with a cookie scoop that assures that each dollop of dough is exactly the same as its neighbor. This stainless steel and heavy-gauge plastic scoop lets you scoop a perfect, and perfectly round, tablespoonful of dough each time. Scoop the dough as you would ice cream, then press the scoop's handle (which takes a little pressure), and the geared wheel and ratcheted bar will slide a wire around the dough and push it gently out of the scoop. Because there are no springs, the scoop, made in England and labeled a disher, should be nearly indestructible.

16.135 J. B. PRINCE DECORATING COMBS

For decorating a cake without fuss, nothing beats a decorating comb. These combs, which create various lines and ridges when they are run across a frosted cake, are bright orange heavyweight plastic and almost 3″ square. Each has a hole for hanging and all have three straight sides for easy handling and precision; keep a straight edge against the base of a revolving decorating stand or the counter and you'll skim a steady course along the cake frosting. The decorating edge of each comb is sharply cut and, provided you keep it clean, produces a well-defined line whether you're working on a thick frosting or a thin glaze. The quartet includes decorative edges with pointy zigzags; softly rounded, undulating curves; zigzags with sharp tops and rounded bottoms (this comb has a flat space in the middle so the decoration can be applied to the edges of a cake); and similarly, a combination of sharp zigzags and a flat space. A quick rinse and the combs are clean.

16.136 NORPRO CAKE DECORATING SET

This compact set provides you with tools that do much the same work as those in the decorating syringe kit, but here the syringe is replaced by a 9"-long pastry bag. The cloth bag, with its interior plastic lining, is fitted with a plastic coupling that holds the pastry tips. The kit comes with six rust-proof tips in shapes that will produce flowers and leaves, ruffles, rosettes, and fluted ridges, as well as writing. Because the pastry bag is small and the tips delicate, this set is best used for cakes, cookies, cupcakes, and petits fours. Any decorating you might want to do with such heavy foodstuffs as mashed potatoes or deviled eggs is best left to larger bags with bigger decorating tips.

PASTRY BAGS & TUBES

Pastry chefs use pastry bags with as much efficiency and ease as most people use spoons—and often for the same jobs. In addition to piping perfect wedding-cake decorations out of a pastry bag fitted with a decorative tip, chefs use pastry bags for jobs that home cooks might normally do with spoons, jobs like piping batter into a cake pan, filling into a tart shell, potatoes over shepherd's pie, or purées to stuff vegetables. Of course, with the exception of icing flowers and leaves, rosettes, scallops, and shells, you can get by doing most jobs with a spoon or a Ziploc plastic bag with a corner cut off, but you can't do the jobs as beautifully, a fact pastry chefs have known for a long time; cookbooks from the nineteenth century show pastry bags and their tips looking just as they do today.

The first pastry bags were made from canvas. These are still available, still hard to clean, and still very good for piping out heavy mixtures. Today, you can find pastry bags in sizes that range from 7" to 24" long, and in materials both natural and man-made. Among the bags which are popular today are those made from plastic-lined fabric, those constructed from super pliable nylon, and those that are made of clear plastic and are meant to be tossed away after a single use. Of course, only the disposable bags do not require cleaning. Scrub your bag inside and out with hot soapy water and rinse it well after each job. To dry—and the bag must be thoroughly dry before you store it—either hang it by its loop or reinforced hole, or turn it upside down on a rack or over a long-necked bottle.

The material you decide to buy will depend on the job you have to do and, just as important, how comfortable you are with the feel of the bag's fabric and the manner in which it handles. As for size, that too depends on the way you plan to use the bag. For making delicate designs on pastry, you will want a smaller size of bag than one used for piping *choux* paste to form cream puffs, or making scalloped borders on a grand scale.

16.137, 16.138, & 16.139 ATECO DURA CLOTH, SURE-GRIP PLASTIC-COATED, & FLEX NYLON PASTRY BAGS

When it comes to pastry bags, function will determine the fabric used. Canvas bags were the standard for generations, and they are still just right for jobs of almost every description, from making lacy icing decorations and shaping plump meringue shells, to piping out cookies from a heavy batter or scalloped rows from creamy mashed potatoes. This particular canvas bag, made from double-seamed duck, is supple to begin with and will soften even more with use and cleaning. Needless to say, cleaning is an issue here. Pastry bags demand scrupulous cleaning, and cleaning canvas is not as easy as cleaning the sleeker plasticized and nylon bags. However, if you like the feel of the canvas bag—

and feel is of utmost importance when you're doing delicate decorating work—the hassles of cleaning will seem relatively minor.

Easier to clean and, for many, more comfortable to handle, is the plastic-coated pastry bag. The bag is made from a fabric that has been plastic-coated on the inside. You get the strength and the grip of a canvas-type fabric—the outside of this bag will never get slippery—and the convenience of plastic. The plastic inside makes this bag less supple than a canvas or nylon bag, which may be a problem if you are decorating and a blessing if you are piping larger, rougher shapes or dealing with a heavy batter. And it will never leak.

Finally, for pliability, nothing compares to the nylon pastry bag. Best for piping out lighter-weight batters or doing dainty decorations, this is the bag that beginners are bound to find most comfortable. It is easy to use and easy to clean, but it does have a tendency to get slippery. Each of these bags is available in lengths from about 7" to 24".

16.140 ATECO BISMARCK TUBE

"Bismarck" is the name given by Germans long ago to jelly dough-nuts, in honor of that favorite Prussian statesman. They are also known more commonly as *Berliner Pfannkuchen*. Made of a nickel-silver alloy, this tube is 2⅝" long and ⅝" in diameter at the widest end. With its slanted opening—measuring only 3⁄16" at the small end—it is designed to make the narrowest possible hole in the surface of a cooked doughnut. After frying the yeast-raised dough-nuts and allowing them to cool, fit a pastry bag on the tube and fill it with thinned jam, jelly, or custard. Inject the filling into the centers of the doughnuts, dust the doughnuts with powdered or granulated sugar, and watch them disappear.

16.141 ATECO FIFTY-FIVE-PIECE DECORATING SET

With this set and either a decorating syringe or a pastry bag, you will have almost unlimited possibilities for decorating. The set includes forty-eight nickel-plated decorative tips, also called tubes, for producing delicate

CLASSIC CREAM PUFF PASTRY

This is the basic recipe for cream puff pastry but with a slightly
higher amount of egg than usual, to insure lightness.

*About 4 dozen 2 by 1½" high puffs, or
about sixteen 5 by 1¾" high éclairs*

1 cup water (236 grams)
8 tablespoons unsalted butter (113 grams)
1 teaspoon sugar (4 grams)

½ teaspoon salt (3 grams)
1 cup bleached all-purpose flour (142 grams)
5 large eggs (250 grams)

OVEN TEMPERATURE: 400°F
BAKING TIME: 30 minutes (plus 1 hour 40 minutes in the turned-off oven)

EQUIPMENT
Cookie sheet(s) or inverted half-size sheet pan(s); for puffs
or éclairs, a pastry bag and a number 6 (½") plain round
tube plus a second pastry bag and a Bismarck tube for puffs.

In a medium saucepan, combine the water, butter, sugar,
and salt and bring to a full rolling boil. Immediately remove
the saucepan from the heat and add the flour all at once.
Stir with a wooden spoon until the mixture forms a ball,
leaves the sides of the pan, and clings slightly to the spoon.
Return the pan to low heat and cook, stirring and mashing
continuously, for about 3 minutes to cook the flour.

FOOD PROCESSOR METHOD
Without scraping the pan, transfer the mixture to the bowl
of a food processor fitted with the metal blade. With the
feed tube open to allow steam to escape, process for 15 seconds. With the motor running, pour in eggs all at once and
continue processing for 30 seconds.

HAND METHOD
Without scraping the pan, empty the mixture into a bowl.
Add the eggs one at a time, beating vigorously with a wooden
spoon after each addition.

FOR BOTH METHODS
The mixture will be smooth and shiny and it should be too
soft to hold peaks when lifted with a spoon. If it is too stiff,
add a little extra water. (The dough can be stored in an airtight container and refrigerated overnight. Beat it lightly
with a wooden spoon before piping.)

SHAPE THE PUFFS
Dab a small dot of the dough in each corner of the baking
sheet and line the sheet with parchment or a Teflon-
type liner, pressing lightly to make it adhere; or use foil.
Alternatively, you can grease and flour the baking sheet.
(Do not use Baker's Joy, as it makes piping the puffs
too slippery.)

Preheat the oven to 400°F at least 20 minutes before baking.
Set an oven rack in the middle of the oven before preheating.

FOR CREAM PUFFS AND ÉCLAIRS
Fill a pastry bag fitted with a ½" diameter tube with
the dough.
FOR CREAM PUFFS Pipe puffs about 1½" in diameter and ½" to
¾" high about 1" apart onto the prepared sheet. (By hand,
you can use two greased teaspoons instead of piping. Use
one to scoop out the dough and the other, or your fingertip,
to push it off onto the baking sheet. If necessary, use your
fingertip, dipped first in a little water, to smooth the shape.)
FOR ÉCLAIRS Pipe 4 by 1½" lengths, ½" to ¼" high, about 3"
apart onto the sheet. (If you are using a spoon, use a damp
metal spatula to spread them into shape, making the ends
slightly wider that the centers.) Run the tines of a fork down
the length of the tops to encourage the éclairs to crack
evenly when they bake.

TO FILL THE PUFFS
FOR CREAM PUFFS Use a pastry bag fitted with a Bismarck
tube to pipe the filling through the slit or hole into the hollow center of each cream puff. Then dip the tops of the puffs
into chocolate glaze.
FOR PROFITEROLES Use a serrated knife to split them horizontally in half. Fill with small scoops of ice cream and pour hot
glaze on top.
FOR ÉCLAIRS Use a serrated knife to split them horizontally in
half. Remove some of the soft dough from the inside. Use a
pastry bag fitted with a number 6 (½") round tube (or a teaspoon) to fill each one with a scant ¼ cup of filling.

STORE
Unfilled puffs, in reclosable freezer bags or airtight containers, refrigerated, up to 1 week; frozen, up to 6 months.

UNDERSTANDING
The small amount of sugar in the dough adds flavor and
helps in browning.

The Pie and Pastry Bible, by Rose Levy Beranbaum

flowers, lines, writing, and shapes both fluted and plain, four larger tips for forming leaves, two flower nails on which you can construct many-petaled blossoms for later transfer to special occasion cakes or confections, and a plastic coupler to secure any of the tips to any pastry bag. It all works very easily and can be stowed neatly, thanks to the fitted see-through plastic storage case.

16.142 ATECO TWELVE-PIECE PASTRY TUBE SET

Once you have a pastry bag, you'll need a set of basic tips, or tubes, to give decorative shapes to what is pushed through the bag. This set of assorted tips is designed to produce large-size designs; they're perfect for shaping savory food, like potatoes or purées, as well as frostings and icings. Use them not just for decorating but for piping cream puff pastry onto a baking sheet for fluted mini éclairs or stiff meringue onto your lemon pie or baked Alaska. The tips do not need a coupler to be used with a pastry bag; simply drop the tube in through the bag's wide end and the narrowness of the opening at the other end will prevent it from falling through. The dozen seamless, nickel-plated tubes have openings of various sizes and shapes—some round, some jagged, some like stars, and some slitlike to make ribbon shapes. The kit comes in a clear plastic storage box and includes a miniature Christmas tree–shaped brush for getting the tips clean.

16.143 ATECO DISPOSABLE BAGS

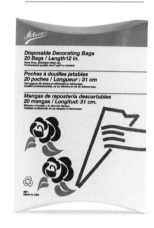

Here's a tool that nineteenth-century pastry chefs couldn't have dreamed of: toss-away pastry bags fabricated from strong but supple clear plastic. Sold in packs of twenty, the bags are 18″ long and easily cut down, if necessary, with household scissors. To use the bag, snip off just enough of the bottom so that when a decorating tube or coupler is inserted only its small opening is exposed. Fill the bag with whatever you're working with—it's flexible enough to handle whipped cream and strong enough to control thick doughs and batters—twist the top closed, then pipe away. The see-through plastic lets you see exactly how much is in the bag. When you're finished, there's no washing-up to do.

16.144 ATECO PARCHMENT TRIANGLES

If you've ever seen pastry chefs putting dots of icing on a cake or writing "Happy Birthday" in chocolate or jelly, then you've probably seen them working with a small cone made of parchment paper. When the decorations need to be minuscule or the calligraphy must resemble script from a pen's fine nib, a parchment decorating cone is the tool of choice, since you construct it yourself and can control the width of the bottom opening. To fashion a cone, you can cut a large sheet of parchment on the diagonal to make a triangle—the shape from which a cone begins—or you can purchase a pack of one hundred pre-cut triangles, each 15″ by 15″ by 21″. The ready-made triangles can be folded to produce tiny openings just right for writing with melted chocolate, or constructed so that the opening is large enough to accommodate a decorating tip. Either way, the cones are quick to put together and, of course, disposable.

17

ICE CREAM MAKERS, SCOOPS, & A YOGURT MACHINE

ICE CREAM MAKERS

ITALIANS WERE MAKING ICE CREAM in the mid–sixteenth century after developing a technique to freeze liquid using ice and salt, a combination that still generates the freezing power of many ice cream machines. In our own country, frozen custard was a favorite with a number of presidents in the White House; Thomas Jefferson brought a recipe for it back from Paris, where he served as ambassador, and offered it at his renowned table in Monticello. Advertisements for public ice cream parlors appeared in major U.S. cities as early as the mid-1700s, though it was clearly a special treat not available every day.

When the modern ice cream churn was patented in the 1830s, frozen sweets became much more popular. The old-fashioned wooden bucket filled with ice and salt surrounding a sealed churn became a fixture in many homes and commercial establishments. That same type of ice cream maker, in both hand-cranked and electric models, is still marketed today, and it still makes excellent ice cream.

The argument for making your own ice cream, aside from the fun of it, is that you can include exactly what you wish, both in terms of fat content and flavoring. Once you've tried it, you'll see that just like freshly baked bread or just-brewed coffee, there is absolutely no substitute for fresh ice cream. Given the infinite variety of flavors you can produce and the way you can tailor the product to suit your preferences, homemade ice cream is outstanding no matter which machine you use. The fresh product, still quite soft, does exhibit subtle but marked differences in smoothness, airiness, and texture among the many models, but once the sweet has been frozen for longer than an hour or so, those differences become much less noticeable. At any rate, since there are many choices of equipment, here are a few observations that may help you decide.

In general, the least expensive model is a nonelectric, hand-turned, double-insulated canister. When this device first appeared on the market, it seemed miraculous. Small and inexpensive, it made a pint of passable ice cream in only 20 minutes with a few turns of a handle—all you had to do was remember to put the container in the freezer a day before you wanted to make ice cream. Now, however, this simple appliance is available only in a 1-quart size, which produces results that are much less consistent than its smaller predecessors. Hand-turned models are not much cheaper than electric machines and the electric ones work better, providing a major step up in quality. They have a motor either on the bottom, the top, or sometimes the side of the container that either turns a paddle or rotates a bowl around the paddle. Like the manual machines, all of these require freezing the canister first. For the best results, don't even think about making ice cream until the canister has been in the freezer for 24 hours. It may be easy to remember to store the canister permanently in your freezer instead of in a kitchen cabinet, and to replace it there after each use, but even so you must wait 12 hours or more for the canister to refreeze before you contemplate a second batch. Whether you opt for a nonelectric or a motorized ice cream maker, you must have room in your freezer for a container that ranges in diameter from 6" to 9" and may be up to 6½" tall.

With the consumer equivalents of commercial ice cream makers on the market, you don't need to put canisters in your freezer. The highest in both price and performance, these models have refrigerator units built in and only need to be switched on to use. They are extremely convenient, up and ready to go whenever a craving for chocolate chip takes hold, and they produce an excellent product that is denser than the ice cream made in a frozen canister. But they are heavy, command a good deal of counterspace, and are expensive.

The last type of ice cream maker is the old-fashioned canister in a wooden bucket. Chilled to the proper temperature with ice and salt, it requires no prefreezing and is churned either electrically or by hand. It can produce more ice cream—up to a gallon and a half—than any other device. Though it's fun for parties, especially where there are a lot of young volunteers to turn the crank, this method does take a bit of doing—you have to fill the bucket with the proper proportions of crushed ice and salt and deal with the drain-off when you're through. There is a certain charm to making ice cream in exactly the same way it was made in the first part of the nineteenth century, but given the hassle involved, if you have electricity in your house, we suggest that you go for an insulated model and forgo the ice and salt.

All that said, following are our top picks from among the many ice cream makers on the market. Most models not listed either produced very uneven results or had motors that were not strong enough to churn the ice cream base to anything even close to the proper consistency. Any machines that began "walking" across the counter when in use were eliminated. A final note: All ice cream is best made with chilled ingredients, so a certain amount of preparation may be needed even with high-end electric models.

17.1 SIMAC IL GELATAIO MAGNUM II

This machine is the Armani of ice cream makers. The sleek modern style for which Italian designers are so famous has been applied to this compact, clean-looking machine. Given its relatively small footprint—11½" by 16"—and its unobtrusive tailored appearance, if you have room, you might opt to leave this designer ice cream machine out on the counter in full view, like a Ferrari in the driveway. It produces 1⅓ quarts of excellent, satiny ice cream in 45 to 50 minutes. The "II" in its name identifies it as a second-generation machine; the original Simacs, which were introduced in the early 1980s, were wildly popular. They used Freon (the same chemical used in air conditioners and refrigerators), however, and after the ban on fluorocarbons in 1992, it took some time for engineers to come up with a design that would accommodate the substitute coolant, which is not as efficient and consequently requires a larger compressor. Hence the extra weight of the newer machine: a hard-to-heft 35 pounds.

A big improvement in this new model is its removable bowl, which makes cleaning effortless. If you purchase an extra bowl, you can make one batch after another. Though the ice cream is smooth-textured and creamy right out of the machine, it is really softer than you'll want for most purposes, so we recommend packing it in a covered container and freezing it for about 30 to 60 minutes before serving.

On the downside, this model has an annoying, constant, loud whir that makes you breathe a sigh of relief when it is turned off. We also worry about the durability of the release arm on the workbowl. The Simac II comes with a 1-year limited warranty.

17.2 MUSSO LUSSINO PRO

BUTTERMILK SORBET

About 3 cups

2 cups buttermilk
¾ cup white corn syrup
¼ cup fresh lemon juice
3 teaspoons freshly grated lemon zest
2 sprigs fresh lemon verbena, chopped

Combine all of the ingredients in a medium saucepan over low heat. Cook for about 2 minutes, or until just barely warm. Do not overheat or buttermilk will separate. Remove from heat and strain through a fine sieve into a nonreactive bowl. Cover and refrigerate until cool. Place in an electric ice cream maker and freeze according to manufacturer's directions.

Great American Food,
by Charlie Palmer with Judith Choate

If Simac is an Armani, Musso's Lussino Pro, an eccentric postmodern machine, is a Versace: sexy, iconoclastic, and futuristic. In truth, some think it resembles R2D2, with its little rubber feet and domed plastic bubble covering its workbowl. You could almost imagine the Lussino a pet, or an ice cream robot. Whatever your take, the high-profile, perforated stainless steel oval (10½" by 18") is a guaranteed conversation piece. The most important thing of all is that it makes superb ice cream, of the exceptionally smooth and creamy sort you might have thought you'd never enjoy outside Italy.

The Lussino Pro is durable—it has all-metal castings with little that can break—and faster than the competition. It chills 1½ quarts of ice cream in 25 to 35 minutes; 15 to 25 minutes quicker than the Simac. Another plus: The resulting dessert is firm enough to serve right out of the machine, though we still prefer 15 to 30 minutes "ripening" time in the freezer. This model is also relatively quiet, with a low-pitched chug not unlike a dishwasher. It is sturdy enough to produce quart after quart of ice cream with no worry of overheating. Weighing in at 38 pounds, a tad heavier than the Simac, it is nonetheless easier to lift and stow away. But given its looks, why would you?

One big drawback to the Lussino Pro is that the workbowl is stationary and nonremovable, so it must be sponged out and wiped clean between batches. Such dubious sanitary practices are particularly worrisome with egg-based French ice creams and frozen custards. Also, the Lussino Pro will make a substantial dent in your budget. If you're planning to go into the gelato business, Musso makes an even larger, heavier (74 pounds), and more expensive version, the Pola, which is popular with chefs, especially in small restaurants. Both machines come with a 1-year limited warranty.

17.3 THE PACOJET

A brushed chrome box roughly 24" tall by 6" wide, the Pacojet looks something like a restaurant coffee machine. It's actually an innovative new device used in professional kitchens that combines the functions of a mixer, a blender, and an ice cream maker at the price of a subzero refrigerator.

PACOTIZING FOR FUN & PROFIT
❧ GRAY KUNZ ❧

I did not trust the new Pacojet machine that was being demonstrated. How can you freeze a food and then whip it up in seconds, I wondered. But it didn't take long for me to become a total believer in Pacotizing.

The first time I saw it in action there was a frozen mixture of whole peas, cream, pieces of bread, and bacon. Zap, zap! and you had two portions of mousse. Quail bones, egg whites, and vegetables, frozen, were zapped and then briefly reheated—and like magic they became quail consommé to order.

Now I can't live without the Pacojet. I keep dozen of canisters of frozen mixtures in the restaurant freezer, ready to be made into ice creams and sorbets. Chocolate? Zap, zap, and it's ready to eat, a perfectly textured, scoopable serving or two (or six or more). I'm lucky enough to also have one at home, to make treats for my kids.

Pacotizing is the exact reverse of what you usually do. Instead of mixing your ice cream ingredients and gradually freezing them, you freeze them first and then make the ice cream. And because you keep the ingredients frozen, it's safer, and there's no danger of contamination. The process goes so fast you can use almost anything. I even froze a whole lobster, cooked and cut up, along with a *mirepoix*, butter, and tomatoes—one zap and it was mousse, shells and all. We're still trying to find out all the things the Pacojet can do.

GINGER ICE CREAM

About 1 quart

1½ cups milk
½ cup heavy sweet cream
3 tablespoons minced fresh ginger
¾ cup sugar
6 egg yolks

1 Combine milk and cream in a saucepan. Add ginger and half the sugar. Stir and bring to a boil. Remove from heat and strain.

2 Combine remaining sugar and egg yolks. Beat for about 2 minutes, or until ingredients are thoroughly combined.

3 Gradually add the milk mixture to the egg-yolk mixture. Stir to combine and return to the saucepan. Cook over low heat, stirring constantly, until mixture coats the back of a spoon. Be careful not to allow mixture to boil.

4 Cool and pour into an ice cream machine. Follow manufacturer's directions.

Cooking with David Burke, by David Burke and Carmel Berman Reingold

---

A SHORT GLOSSARY OF ICE CREAMS & FROZEN DESSERTS

Bombe A molded, usually melon-shaped dessert made of layers of ice cream or sorbet.

Frozen custard Ice cream with an egg custard base, also called French ice cream.

Frozen yogurt An ice cream–style frozen confection with a yogurt base.

Gelato Italian ice cream, usually fairly soft and creamy-textured.

Glace French for ice cream.

Granità Coarsely shaved Italian ices.

Ice A frozen confection made of sugar, water, and flavoring, usually fruit juice.

Ice cream A milk- or cream-based frozen confection in any of scores of flavors, often with fruit, nuts, and other additions. American standards require ice cream to have at least 10 percent butterfat. Premium ice cream usually has around 16 percent.

Ice milk Ice cream with less than 10 percent butterfat.

Kulfi A dense Indian ice cream often flavored with mango or pistachio.

Parfait A layered ice cream dessert, often made with whipped cream.

Semifreddo A frozen Italian dessert made with whipped cream, Italian meringue, and flavorings.

Sherbet A frozen fruit-based confection made with some milk.

Sorbet A French frozen confection made just with fruit or other flavorings, and no milk.

Sorbetto Italian for sherbet and sorbet.

The Pacojet reverses the way a sorbet or frozen mousse is usually made: instead of churning and gradually freezing a liquid or purée, it emulsifies hard frozen ingredients into the perfect consistency. The food to be "Pacotized" (as the company likes to say) must be frozen in one of the special containers that come with the machine. When ready, the cook simply attaches the container with its frozen contents to the machine, selects the number of portions (from one to ten), and presses start. The Pacojet's high-speed, rotating blades descend into the frozen mixture, finely shaving off the desired amount of the contents.

The resulting concoction can be the makings not only of sorbet or ice cream, but also of various soups or sauces that can be heated after processing. The unused remainder of ingredients, still deep-frozen, can be put back in the freezer for later use. The Pacojet has a 1-year warranty.

17.4 KRUPS LA GLACIÈRE

This machine boasts a very smart design: all white, with a big dark green dot adorning the unobtrusive motor on top. Surprisingly powerful and quiet for its size, its sturdy plastic combination bowl-and-canister and easy-access feed tube all add up to a good value indeed. When assembled, the machine looks almost diminutive, though it can churn out 1½ quarts of ice cream at a fast clip.

Part of the La Glacière's handsome appearance is due to Krups's modern "form follows function" design, which allows no extraneous features. There's not even an on-off switch—one less part to break—you just plug it in. Contributing to this compact efficiency is the fact that the canister and outside bowl, which are two separate pieces in many machines, here are incorporated in one for better insulation and a neater look. But the unit, which must be stored in the freezer for at least 24 hours before use, takes up a fair amount of space at 6″ high and 9″ in diameter. It comes with a 1-year limited warranty.

17.5 SALTON-MAXIM BIG CHILL

Form most decidedly does not follow function in this rococo design, an asymmetric (the motor is on the side), scalloped, plastic contraption evidently meant to look something like an ice palace. Whimsical is about the kindest thing you could say about the design, but the quality of the ice cream this machine produces is surprisingly good, and it takes just 20 minutes to make 1 quart, faster than many higher-priced models. Its efficiency and the even quality of its product are due to the flat, wide, Teflon-coated freezer disc, which is much easier to store in the freezer than a tall, wide bowl. Though it whips more air into the ice cream than either the Simac II or the Lussino Pro, the Big Chill's results are creamy and uniform. It has a 1-year warranty.

"Surprise! High-fibre ice cream!"

17.6 & 17.7 WHITE MOUNTAIN HAND-CRANK & ELECTRIC ICE CREAM FREEZERS

If you want to try an old-fashioned wooden bucket ice cream maker, White Mountain still makes the best. This classic is now available only in two sizes, 4 quarts and 6 quarts, but is still distinguished by fine workmanship. The electric version boasts a 12,000-rpm commercial-grade universal motor. Both the electric and hand-cranked models contain a heavy cast-iron dasher (the paddle that stirs the ice cream mixture), designed never to warp. A double layer of self-adjusting beechwood blades scrape the sides of the stainless steel internal canister clean. And the tongue-and-groove maple-stained pine bucket is constructed of staves that are more than ½″ thick. The stainless steel canister resists the rust-encouraging onslaughts of the freezing brine that surrounds it. Choosing between the hand-cranked and electric versions of this reliable ice cream maker depends largely upon whether you have an outdoor electric outlet, or helpers who will delight in turning the crank for you. As far as a warranty goes, the stainless steel canister has a 5-year guarantee against manufacturing defects. All other parts have a 1-year limited warranty.

SCOOPS

DESPITE THE SURPRISING variety of ice cream scoops on the market, it's not hard to choose the best ones. With the exception of specialized sizes and shapes, the most important factors in determining how well a scoop works are its heft and ease of leveraging the handle and, secondly, the size and shape of the bowl.

17.8 & 17.9 ZEROLL SCOOP ZEROLL SPADE

Zeroll makes a selection of ice cream scoops that are handsomely designed and work exceptionally well. Their distinguishing feature is the defrosting liquid sealed inside them. The liquid is supposed to warm up in response to the heat of your hand (we found a brief run under warm, not hot, water helps), making it easier to cut through a frozen dessert. We particularly like the 7¼" black Teflon scoop, which carved out a nice, round ball of ice cream. At 8¾", the polished metal Zeroll spade is handy for anyone who consumes large amounts of frozen desserts. Its sturdy blade will slice through half a gallon or more of the hardest ice cream, sorbet, or gelato, or even scrape out a granità. One caveat for this excellent line: Do not put the utensils in the dishwasher, or they will lose their defrosting properties.

17.10 & 17.11 OXO SCOOP & OXO NONSTICK SCOOP

OXO manufactures an assortment of scoops. All have easy-to-grip handles and are nicely weighted. The 8" squarish scoop, when used properly, cuts easily through the hardest ice cream. Another model, one of our

NEW YORK SUPER FUDGE CHUNK

1 generous quart

New York Super Fudge Chunk was developed as a regional flavor for the sophisticated New York palate. After coming up with several variations in our lab in Burlington, Vermont, we packed the samples in dry ice and shipped them by bus to our New York consultants, a group of musicians on Manhattan's Upper West Side. Following several weeks of refinement and discussion, we agreed upon this final recipe—a chocolate lover's dream.

¼ cup coarsely chopped white chocolate
¼ cup coarsely chopped semisweet chocolate
¼ cup chopped pecan halves
¼ cup coarsely chopped walnuts
¼ cup halved chocolate-covered almonds
4 ounces unsweetened chocolate
1 cup milk
2 large eggs
1 cup sugar
1 cup heavy or whipping cream
1 teaspoon vanilla extract
1 pinch salt

1 Combine the coarsely chopped chocolates, pecans, walnuts, and chocolate-covered almonds in a bowl, cover, and refrigerate.
2 Melt the unsweetened chocolate in the top of a double boiler over hot, not boiling, water. Whisk in the milk, a little at a time, and heat, stirring constantly, until smooth. Remove from the heat and let cool.
3 Whisk the eggs in a mixing bowl until light and fluffy, 1 to 2 minutes. Whisk in the sugar, a little at a time, then continue whisking until completely blended,

about 1 minute more. Add the cream, vanilla, and salt, and whisk to blend.
4 Pour the chocolate mixture into the cream mixture and blend. Cover and refrigerate until cold, about 1 to 3 hours, depending on your refrigerator.
5 Transfer the cream mixture to an ice cream maker and freeze following the manufacturer's instructions.
6 After the ice cream stiffens (about 2 minutes before it is done), add the chocolates and nuts, then continue freezing until the ice cream is ready.

Ben and Jerry's Homemade Ice Cream and Dessert Book, by Ben Cohen and Jerry Greenfield with Nancy J. Stevens

favorites, is the 7½" pointed non-stick scoop that digs into the ice cream and removes a neat, egg-shaped oval serving.

17.12 NORPRO SCOOP

Norpro's 18/8 stainless steel scoop operates on the action of a coiled spring attached to the grip. Though the scoop comes in two larger versions, 2" (5 centimeters) and 2¼" (5.6 centimeters), they were too long to get leverage and difficult for a small hand to squeeze. We preferred the 1½" (3.9 centimeters) scoop, which is easy to use and forms perfect little rounds. These rather charming miniature balls are especially nice for an assortment of flavors or for sorbet. They are also perfect for filling profiteroles. This small 8"-long scoop can carve out close to fifty balls from a quart of ice cream and is useful for making cookies. The scoop is also available in 1" and 1¼" sizes.

17.13 J. A. HENCKELS SCOOP

Designed with a thinner handle than many scoops, this 8" model might be hard to use for people with large hands. The Henkel's is a heavy scoop, bearing more of the weight up front, making it effective for carving out small ice cream curls. The design is utilitarian and includes a handy slot for hanging.

YOGURT MAKERS

THOUGH AMERICANS WERE LATE to discover the virtues of yogurt, in the last thirty years it has become a staple in supermarkets and is available in what seems to be an infinite variety, ranging from artificially sweetened coconut cream pie to plain organic goat's milk. However, yogurt, like almost every other food, seems to taste better when it's made at home and completely from scratch. This can be done without any special equipment: all that's required is to gently heat milk to just below the boiling point, cool it until it's lukewarm, add a little commercial unflavored yogurt or dried yogurt culture as a starter, and let it stand until it thickens. However, the mixture must be kept constantly at the correct temperature if the culture is to grow properly. Electric yogurt makers take the guesswork out of temperature control.

17.14 SALTON-MAXIM YOGURT MAKER

We like this small, 9"-high, 6½"-round, simple, plastic appliance because it yields a single 1-quart container of yogurt. Others on the market make several small 6-ounce containers that require slightly more effort to fill and to measure out a quantity of the finished product for a recipe. This yogurt maker has a signal light that glows when the unit is on. It doesn't turn off automatically, but we don't consider this an inconvenience, as you need to be present when the yogurt's done anyway, in order to refrigerate it promptly. After 4 hours the machine produces wonderfully thick and creamy yogurt. It will taste rather mild, but for more tartness, you can increase the heating time to up to 10 hours. The flavor and texture of the yogurt also depend on the type of milk and culture you use; yogurt made from sheep's, goat's, or even water buffalo's milk is a staple of the Middle Eastern diet and has a creamier, thicker texture than yogurt made from cow's milk, as it is in the United States. The Salton-Maxim Yogurt Maker is covered by a 1-year warranty.

18

WINE TOOLS

THE COOK IS OFTEN OBLIGED to open a bottle of wine for the saucepan, for guests as an accompaniment to dinner, or even for an inspirational glass while preparing the meal. In this chapter you will find products designed to help you open, serve, and store wine. They have been chosen not only because they perform well but also because they are beautiful, useful, and life-enhancing, like wine itself.

18.1 NOW WE SEE THROUGH A GLASS, FACE TO FACE

Wineglasses come in dozens of shapes and sizes that are meant to match the character of individual wines. Long narrow champagne flutes keep the bubbles bubbling longer than would a widemouthed balloon glass designed to maximize the nose of an important Bordeaux. The most sophisticated glasses are specifically designed to complement wines made from particular grapes. The glasses we show here are the brainchild of Georg Riedel, an Austrian whose family has been making wineglasses for generations.

Riedel glasses are laboriously calibrated to enhance the wine they are to be drunk with. For example, a flared-rim glass directs wine to the tip of the tongue, thereby highlighting fruit and sweetness while minimizing acidity—an ideal shape for high-acid Burgundies. Conversely, the Riedel Sauternes glass has a broader bowl and a tapered top, which directs wine to the sides of the mouth, favoring acidity and balancing the wine's obvious sweetness. Fully tapered glasses send the wine to the center of the tongue, focusing fruit through the tip of the tongue and acidity from its sides—just what you want for moderately acid wines such as Rieslings.

Riedel glasses are luxury glasses. But they will pay for themselves again and again, by dramatically improving the taste and flavor of the wines drunk from them. This has been proven many times over in professional "glass tastings," where the wine stays the same but is put through a comparative tasting in many types of glasses. At such events, Riedel glasses have impressed professional and amateur wine bibbers alike.

WINE FUNNELS

RED WINE, as it ages, can throw off sediment. If this happens, the wine will look murky and unattractive, but it may still be drinkable. To keep the sediment from ending up in their glasses, oenophiles carry out an elaborate and anxious ritual. First, they stand the bottle upright for several days to let the sediment settle to the bottom. Then, after gingerly pulling the cork, they slowly pour the wine out of the bottle into a clear glass decanter, scrutinizing the bottle—which is held over a candle or electric light—so they can stop pouring when the first wisps of sediment appear. One important point is worth making, however: just because a wine is old does not mean it should be decanted. A *very* old wine in good condition is best opened and consumed with as little aeration as possible, so the fruit and body don't dissipate before they can be enjoyed. On the other hand, young red wines benefit from being allowed to "breathe" for an hour or so before serving, to develop their bouquet and soften their taste; decanting aids this process.

18.2 "CHÂTEAUNEUF" BOTTLE FUNNEL WITH REMOVABLE SCREEN

Since most people don't decant wine often, they lack the skill of a seasoned sommelier: they carry out the process without finesse and inevitably waste valuable wine. The "Châteauneuf" bottle funnel, 6½" long and formed in the classic bell shape, solves these problems. All you do is place it in the mouth of the decanter and pour the wine into the goblet end, which is 3½" in diameter, of the attractive, highly polished pewter funnel. The removable fine-mesh screen at the bottom will catch sediment but permits the cleansed wine to flow through the thin spout, whose curved end directs the flow against the side of the decanter, gently aerating the wine and saving it from a long fall that ends in the shock of a splash. To clean the funnel, simply rinse it with water and towel dry. For a more thorough cleaning, use a commercial pewter polish.

CORKSCREWS

THIS IS THE ONLY PIECE of wine equipment you can't do without. The corkscrew is a device familiar to everyone—a metal helix or "worm," pointed at one end and fitted with a handle that turns the worm into the cork. Once the worm is all the way in, you use the handle to pull it, and thereby the cork, out of the neck of the bottle. There are other ways to do the job, and inventors have come up with a great many, most of which are no improvement on the worm.

A worm is normally the shape of a helix—a continuous curve advancing at a constant angle around an axis. You can think of it as a line wrapping around a cylinder, like a candy cane or a barbershop pole. Better worms have five instead of four turns and are covered with Teflon to make them easier to insert into corks. We think the helical type works best, but there are spiral worms that do a good job. A spiral, you may recall from solid geometry, is a continuous curve turning at a constant angle around an axis while steadily increasing its distance from the axis. If we think of a helix as a line wrapping around a cylinder, we can think of a spiral as a line wrapping around a cone. Good spiral worms, which look something like wood screws, have extremely sharp edges.

The most widespread version of the corkscrew is called the waiter's corkscrew. In its proper form, it has a short knife blade at one end, a foldaway worm in the center, and a short hinged lever at the other end that enables the waiter, or anybody else, to jack up the cork from the bottleneck. However, because this force is applied at an angle, waiter's corkscrews frequently break the cork as it emerges. Yet they are still an improvement over absolutely plain corkscrews that offer no mechanical advantage during the pulling stage, forcing the user to hold the bottle between his or her knees or brace it on the table, relying on brute force to extract the cork.

Then there are the continuous-turning corkscrews that, as the name implies, continue to turn even after the worm is all the way in the cork. Because the worm can't move any farther down, the pressure applied by the user as he or she turns the handle forces the cork up out of the bottle. The most convenient models of this type of corkscrew are engineered so that they first remove the cork from the bottle, and then, as they keep rotating, from their worm.

Better corkscrews of all shapes and sizes make life easier and safer for the wine and you. Screw-on metal caps would eliminate the need for any kind of corkscrew—and would seal wine bottles just as well as corks, possibly better over the long haul, since they wouldn't deteriorate—but until quality wines stop coming to market with corks, we will all need corkscrews. Here are some of the best.

18.3 BOJ KEA CORKSCREW

The problems with the traditional waiter's corkscrew have been triumphantly solved by the innovative Spanish firm of B. Olaneta y Juarista (BOJ). Its Kea corkscrew, made of plastic and stainless steel, is curved to fit the hand, and comes in such arresting colors as canary yellow: it's a dandy machine overall. The beauty of its function is due to the hinged lever that presses against the bottle lip during extraction. After the cork is halfway out—the point at which it is subject to breakage by an ordinary waiter's corkscrew because the rocking angle has increased—the Kea's arm can be extended to twice its length and locked to permit a vertical pull with the flexibly mounted worm until the cork is out. The Kea's foil-cutting blade is angled to follow the curve of the bottleneck. A handsome bottle opener is mounted at the business end. It is 5″ in length.

WHAT TO POUR WITH SALMON
❧ MARCUS SAMUELSSON ❧

Coming from a restaurant with a focus on salmon, I'm always looking for new ways to serve it, and for interesting pairings with wine, beer, Aquavit, and other beverages. For me, salmon, so versatile and so widely available, is the king of fish. It is almost unequaled in the variety of ways you can prepare it: raw as sushi, seared and rare, tenderly poached, and grilled or broiled as a steak.

The way you prepare the salmon determines what you'll serve with it. With gravlax—one of the greatest Swedish dishes, in which the salmon is cured using salt, sugar, and dill to create a beautiful velvety texture—I think a chilled Aquavit, the Swedish caraway-flavored spirit, is wonderful, but you can also pair the gravlax with sake or beer. For a citrus-marinated salmon and arugula salad, I would pour a white Alsatian or German riesling. For a poached salmon, you could serve a dry, clean New Zealand Sauvignon Blanc as a counterpoint to the salmon's fattiness. For dishes with smoked salmon, I would go to the reds, perhaps a pinot noir or a South African pinotage. And for a heavier, richer main-course salmon dish, such as a marriage of balsamic-poached salmon and seared foie gras, you should go for a bold, full-bodied red such as a cabernet sauvignon or even a Spanish Rioja. Each of these wines highlights a different facet of the salmon's complex flavor.

18.4 CORKPOPS II WINE OPENER

The Corkpops II is actually the third stage of the only truly successful new corkscrew innovation in the two hundred years since the Reverend Samuel Henshall invented the corkscrew in Oxford, England. It's the clever friend of the Corkette, a small

---

PORK MARINATED TO TASTE LIKE WILD BOAR

6 to 8 servings, with leftovers

Wild pig is very tasty if cooked properly. This recipe can also be applied to any good-size piece of domestic pork, however, and is especially good with Boston butt and fresh pork leg. The marinade will give most cuts of pork a little of the gamy flavors of the wild meat. This is a version of the French recipe called *à la façon de sanglier*, in which pork is marinated to taste like *sanglier*, or wild boar. Serve with mashed potatoes and turnips with maple-glazed carrots.

"WILD BOAR" MARINADE:

2 cups full-bodied red wine

¼ cup red wine vinegar

¼ cup port wine

1 medium onion, thinly sliced

1 cup chopped carrots

4 garlic cloves, chopped

1 tablespoon chopped fresh thyme or 1½ teaspoons dried

1 tablespoon chopped fresh marjoram or 1½ teaspoons dried

3 bay leaves

8 crushed juniper berries or 2 tablespoons gin

6 crushed peppercorns

1 teaspoon salt

1 4- to 6-pound rump end or center cut of fresh pork leg or whole Boston butt, skin removed and trimmed of excess fat

1 cup beef, chicken, or pork stock

salt

freshly ground black pepper

1 Combine the marinade ingredients. Put the pork in a large bowl, and pour the marinade over it. Pierce the meat with a carving fork or skewer all over to help the marinade penetrate. Cover and refrigerate for at least a day and up to 2 days, turning every so often.

2 Let the meat rest at room temperature for an hour or so before cooking. Preheat the oven to 325°F.

3 Remove the pork from the marinade and place in a roasting pan. Pour the marinade into the bottom of the pan. Roast the pork for about 2 hours, basting often with the marinade. Add a little water, stock, or wine to the pan if necessary. Test the roast at its thickest part with an instant-read meat thermometer—it should register 150° to 155°F. When it's done, remove the roast from the oven and cover it loosely with foil. The temperature should rise about 10°F while it rests.

4 To make a sauce, strain and degrease the pan drippings. In a small saucepan, mix with the stock. Bring to a boil and reduce until just syrupy. Taste for salt and pepper. Slice the meat and pour the sauce over and serve.

The Complete Meat Cookbook, by Bruce Aidells and Denis Kelly

---

plastic hand pump attached to a perforated needle: you insert the needle through the cork and pump until the compressed air forces the cork out of the bottle. The Corkpops people took this idea and eliminated its defects. First, for the Corkpops I, they fitted a small tank of compressed, inert propellant onto the needle; you pressed on the tank, and the inert propellant forced out the cork. For the Corkpops II, they put around the needle a cylindrical cage with an adjustable, foil-cutting circle at the bottom that rests on the bottleneck during extraction. The cage also has a sliding disc at the top that, when pulled down, forces the cork off the needle. The Corkpops II measures 7" tall.

18.5 LE CREUSET SCREWPULL LEVER MODEL

When oil engineer Herbert Allen applied what he knew from petroleum drilling to the mechanics of the corkscrew, the Screwpull was born. The worm was covered with a nonstick coating and was a bit longer than the normal corkscrew for extra lever-

age. The device was a sensation in the 1980s, but wine drinkers soon sobered up about it as they found that its coating wore off: friction increased, as did the risk of cork breakage, and corks became even more difficult to twist off. Now Le Creuset has taken over Screwpull and added the lever model. It has two 5½"-long black handles that clamp it on the bottle and a 7½"-long geared lever that pulls the cork out of the bottle and off the worm. The worm is coated with a durable proprietary nonstick finish that can handle more wear and tear than the 1980s model. The lever model comes in several versions, but the simplest is also the most attractive; all black, it comes boxed with a Screwpull foil cutter.

18.6 BOJ WALL-MOUNTED CORKSCREW

For the wine bibber who has everything, there are a couple of megacorkscrews on the market. Some attach to walls, others clamp onto tables; some are garish, some are elegant; but they all give you maximum control of cork penetration, because they are solidly mounted. This can make all the difference with dubious corks, and for someone opening many bottles in rapid order, mounted corkscrews are the obvious answer. BOJ makes an extremely attractive "coppered" machine that mounts on the wall and holds the bottleneck in a spring housing while you pull the slot-machine-style handle. The lethal-looking spiral worm goes through corks like butter, then retracts and, when pulled completely upward, drops the cork. There are three easily changed positions that predetermine the depth of penetration of the worm, so not a crumb of cork will drop into your Chateau d'Yquem.

18.7 AH SO CORK PULLER

If in your caves you have stashed a few rare bottles of antique vintage— a St. Estephe '27 or a Romanée-Conti '37—you must necessarily approach the cork with reverence. And caution. Remember that cork is a natural product that suffers from the ravages of age, and take the safest route.

WINE STUFF

❧ KEVIN ZRALY ❧

If you've seen George Carlin perform, you know how he makes fun of people collecting things they don't need. He uses the word *stuff* to describe these unnecessary items. Over the last twenty years there has been a tremendous increase in the consumption of wine, and entrepreneurs have tried to capitalize on this growing market with the introduction of wine stuff.

In the old days, "A glass of wine, a loaf of bread, and thou" fulfilled a wine lover's needs. In today's wine world, the all-purpose wineglass has been taken over by a glass specifically designed for your oak-aged Chardonnay or your young, tannic Cabernet Sauvignon. Glassmakers have introduced more than a hundred different glasses, each designed for a specific wine or spirit.

When I began my wine journey almost thirty years ago, I used 99¢ jumping-jack corkscrews to open my wine. Last month in the mail I received a catalog that offered more than three hundred different styles of corkscrews. I'm not saying it's all bad—some of the stuff has been useful. Other stuff borders on the absurd. I have carefully considered all the stuff that has crossed my path, and the following is a list of my top five picks for the worst:

1 VINTAGE ENHANCER Why wait until 2015 to drink your 1995 Château Lafitte Rothschild? Designed for those who fear the world will soon end, this device has a special chip that "actually helps to enhance the flavor of alcoholic beverages to make them taste as if they have been 'cellared' or 'aged' for years in only minutes." Personally, I'd rather wait until 2015.

2 CHAMPAGNE SWIRLER Supposedly designed for women in the "Dark Ages," this item takes the carbon dioxide bubbles out of champagne so that lady drinkers may refrain from belching.

3 WINE-FLAVORED FOOD ITEMS I don't know about you, but I can certainly do without Merlot cookies and Cabernet chocolate fudge and Chardonnay toothpaste.

4 WINE CDS A few marketers have come out with these "indispensable companions" to drinking wine under the premise that a Chardonnay should be consumed with Mozart and a Bordeaux with Brahms. Frankly, after the third glass, I'd rather listen to the Rolling Stones.

5 POP-UP BOOKS ON WINE I actually enjoy pop-up stories with my children. I don't believe they have a place in the literature of wine.

When you are opening an aged treasure, do not pierce the cork; pry it. The Ah So cork puller, despite its smarty-pants name, does this most efficiently. Two flat, flexible blades are sturdily attached to a wide oblong handle. The longer of these pieces is inserted between the cork and the bottle and wiggled gently downward until the shorter piece enters the other side. Gentle tugging while rocking the cork back and forth extricates it "ah so" easily from the bottle. But no method is foolproof—it can happen that the cork will enter the wine instead of leaving the bottle when you use the Ah So. Don't despair—you can use the handy-dandy cork retriever (see 18.8 below). Be sure to dry the dark-steel blades of the Ah So carefully before sheathing it in its metal scabbard, or you'll ruin it with rust. If, by some miracle, a portion of your rare Burgundy remains after dinner, the Ah So recorks as well. Just place the cork between the blades, insert them into the bottle, and force the cork back in. At 4½", the Ah So may be pocket sized, but it's powerful.

CORK RETRIEVERS

THE MOST CAREFUL wine drinker, even when stone sober, will from time to time force a cork into a bottle. Then it becomes difficult to pour the wine, because the cork floats into the neck when the bottle is tilted and interferes unpredictably with the flow, sometimes stopping it, other times letting it splash out at an unexpected angle. Serving a bottle of wine with a fallen cork in it is always an embarrassment; if you keep a cork retriever on hand your wine will be safe and your reputation intact.

18.8 CORK LIFT CORK RETRIEVER

This 10½" item looks like all the other cork lifts, but it is better made. It has three sturdy, flat, stainless steel wires attached to a plastic handle. The wires are bent into little catching hooks at the end. You hold the wires close together and insert the ends into the bottle. Then, using a cheerful red plastic cylinder that slides up and down the wires, squeeze the wires tight around the cork and pull it out.

"And in this climate-controlled cabinet I keep my collection of vintage Good & Plentys, Black Crows, Dots, Jujyfruits, Raisinets, and Goldenberg's Peanut Chews."

WINE COOLERS

ALL WHITE WINE, and some light red wines, should be chilled. Experts disagree about the exact temperature, but like most things people disagree about, there is an accepted range. White wines should be somewhere between 40°F and 50°F, Beaujolais and other light reds belong in the mid-50°s, and the low-to-mid-60°s are ideal for heavier reds. In practice, life is not so precise. Traditionalists put room-temperature

PLANNING THE WINES FOR A MENU
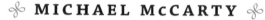
❧ MICHAEL McCARTY ❧

First, the basics: How much wine to serve and what kind of glasses to serve it in. A standard fifth-size (that is, ⅕ of a gallon) wine bottle holds 24 ounces of wine—six glasses, or five if you're pouring a little more generously. I generally figure on a glass to a glass-and-a-half per person for each course. For a dinner of more than one course, you can count on pouring at least half a bottle of wine—three glasses—per person. A really long, multicourse dinner lasting 4 or 5 hours will call for up to a full bottle's worth of wine for each person present. And if I'm serving dessert wines, I pour only half or a third as much of it per person as the other wines, since these sweet wines are meant more for sipping and savoring.

Of course, you should change wineglasses for each different wine you pour. Long, narrow flutes are a must for champagne, since they hold the bubbles in longer; whatever you do, don't pour champagne into those wide, shallow glasses, which will make it go flat in no time. I'm not a real stickler on the shape of glasses you use for the rest of the wines in a meal, just as long as they have bowls that are bigger in the middle than at the top, so that the wine has room to develop its bouquet, which the narrower top holds in. Wineglasses should be large enough so that you fill them by no more than a third to a half, again so that the wine has a large surface area from which its bouquet can develop. Finally, they should be clear, so you'll be able to appreciate the wine's color. I don't use different glasses for whites and reds, but I do tend to serve lighter or sweeter wines in smaller glasses, and bigger wines, whether white or red, in bigger glasses.

Just as the courses of a meal progress from simpler, lighter tastes and textures to more robust and complex dishes, the wines you choose to serve should generally follow the same pattern as your menu: from champagnes and light, white wines; to heavier, more serious whites; to light red wines; to heavier, more complex reds; and finally to sweet dessert wines. But there's a lot of flexibility in that pattern, just as

there's a lot of flexibility in how you go about choosing the foods you want to serve. The important thing to remember is that, one way or another, you can bend the rules. There's nothing in the world stopping you from serving red wines before white, if there's a good reason. There's logic, for example, in serving a light young Beaujolais—a red wine—with your appetizers, and then moving on to a robust Chardonnay. Your own taste buds and experience will suggest endless other possibilities. When you have enough guests to make it practical, it's also very interesting to serve more than one wine—a white *and* a red—with the same course, using the principles I've discussed for finding the common denominator that matches both wines with the food.

One course of the menu for which I don't suggest wines is soup. As a general rule, people aren't sipping their wine while they're sipping their soup; they've already got enough liquid to deal with in the bowl. People who want wine with their soup will usually be finishing what was poured for the course before. And while the soup is being served is a good time to pour the wine that will accompany the next course, to give it a little more time to breathe and develop its flavor and aroma in the glass.

To conclude, let me add a note here on drinking temperatures. Wine can't get colder in your glass; it can only get warmer. I like my white wines, and particularly champagnes, well iced in an ice bucket—colder than most wine connoisseurs do. Generally, the lighter the wine, the colder it should be. Even red wines should be served cooler than most people think. The often-repeated rule that reds should be at room temperature came from an era before central heating. *Cool room temperature*—that is, a proper wine cellar temperature in the low 60°s—is best for red wines, even the biggest ones. I'd suggest placing a red wine that's been at warm room temperature in the refrigerator for 20 to 30 minutes before you open and pour it.

white wines, and some reds, in ice buckets to chill them. Modern drinkers keep whites in the fridge and try to keep the fridge at 45°F. But refrigerated bottles can warm quickly in a kitchen or at today's "room temperature" (which is a great deal warmer than that of the past), so some method of keeping them chilled at the table is necessary. The ice bucket is not the only solution: hard to use without getting everything around it wet, and stuffily reminiscent of formal service in cabin class on the North German Lloyd Line, the ice bucket is a cold blast from the past. Here are a couple of modern alternatives.

18.9 OENOPHILIA CHAMPAGNE CHILLER

Oenophilia's champagne chiller is a handsome green marble cylinder (7″ tall and 5″ in diameter) that absorbs cold from an already chilled bottle and maintains the bottle at that temperature. It requires no ice and no preparatory chilling: no muss, no fuss. Restaurants should definitely use them instead of ice buckets, since they put the wine in reach of the customer, not miles away, languishing for the attention of a busy waiter. And because there's no ice in it, there's no water to run off the bottle when you lift it out of the cooler to pour. At home, the marble chillers take up less space, don't waste ice, and are as handy on the kitchen counter as on the dining table. The champagne chiller also works with ordinary wine bottles, though Oenophilia does sell a narrower version for wine. Both styles are available in black marble. (These marble cylinders also make great cooking utensil holders.)

18.10 SIERRA HOUSEWARES QUICK CHILL WINE & BEVERAGE WRAP

It isn't always possible to have cold white wine on hand just when you need it. Until recently, last-minute solutions came down to either using the dreaded ice bucket or putting the bottle in the freezer, where it could be forgotten and left to freeze and crack. Now, you can leave Sierra Housewares's Quick Chill Wrap in the freezer, and when that emergency comes, just slip the cold-retaining thermal ceramic band around the bottle and fasten it in place with its Velcro closure. After a few minutes, the wine is chilled and will stay that way for hours. The fabric's pattern of purple grape clusters might not be everybody's idea of beauty, but the Quick Chill does its job well, chilling the wine and keeping it cool. You can also use it to chill juices and other beverages. It needs at least 15 to 20 minutes in the freezer before it can be reused. It is 6″ wide and 15″ long.

THE COOKS' WINE & SPIRITS CELLAR

These are the basic items you should keep on hand for cooking use:

Wines
White wine
Red wine
Riesling
Sweet wine (like Muscat-de-Beaumes-de-Venise)
Champagne

Fortified Wines
Dry sherry
Dry vermouth
Marsala
Ruby port

Spirits
Light rum
Dark rum
Brandy or cognac

Liqueurs
Grand Marnier
Pernod or Ricard
Triple Sec or Cointreau
Eaux de vie:
poire, framboise and cassis

Bronze is the mirror of the form; wine, of the heart.
—AESCHYLUS

CHAMPAGNE OPENERS

Popping a champagne cork can be an act as flamboyant as that of a caped magician pulling a rabbit out of a top hat, but it's much more dangerous. Flying champagne corks regularly send people to the emergency room with serious eye injuries. The duc de Nonancourt, whose family owns and operates the champagne house of Laurent-Perrier, showed us a sound method for opening a bottle of champagne (see page 386). However, now there are easier ways to remove a champagne cork, and all they require is a modest splurge on one of these official champagne cork pullers.

18.11 LE CREUSET SCREWPULL CHAMPAGNE STAR

The Screwpull champagne star is a clever device. Matte black composite metal, lightweight, and about the size of a demitasse cup, it resembles the bottom of a rocket with its four sharp fins joined at the top. The fins slide into the thin creases left in the cork by the pressure of the wire cage. Grasp the star, press it down on the cork, twist, and pull: the cork comes away trapped in the fins.

18.12 MOULI CHAMPAGNE KEY

The Mouli champagne key looks something like a pair of chic chrome pliers from outer space. The two short, 4″ handles, set on a spring hinge, have three teeth on their inside surfaces. Squeeze the handles and the teeth sink into the cork, which, with a twist, you remove.

SALADE DE FRUITS AU SABAYON DE CHAMPAGNE
(FRUIT SALAD WITH CHAMPAGNE SABAYON SAUCE)

4 servings

We stayed at the Royal Champagne hotel between Epernay and Reims, a stately place fronting the road but whose rear looks out across the verdant countryside. The name is that of a famous regiment that used the building as a stopover when this was a major military area standing between Paris and France's enemies to the east. In those days, the officers would not bother to pull the corks from the champagne bottles; in traditional military fashion, they would cleanly decapitate the bottles at the neck with their sabers. Today there are still antique pistols and sabers all around the place. One of the dishes we prepared there was a dessert, using demi-sec champagne, the sweetest of these wines. Although specific fruits are called for in the ingredient list, seasonal fruits can be substituted.

1 cup kiwi, peeled and cut into ¼″ cubes
1 cup figs, peeled and cut into ¼″ cubes
1 cup grapes, sliced in half
1 cup fresh strawberries, sliced in half
1 cup fresh raspberries
2 egg yolks
⅓ cup granulated sugar
1 cup demi-sec champagne

1 Heat broiler to its highest setting.
2 Divide the cut fruits into four soup plates, arranging them decoratively in each.
3 Make the sabayon sauce by combining the egg yolks and sugar in a large mixing bowl. Whisk together briskly until the yolks begin to turn a light lemony color. Add the champagne a little bit at a time, whisking constantly until well blended.
4 Place the mixing bowl in a pot or pan and pour about 1″ of water around it. Bring the water to a simmer and continue to whisk vigorously until the mixture becomes light and foamy. Once the mixture starts to thicken, remove the bowl from the heat. Do not overcook. Continue to whisk for 10 seconds.
5 Pour equal amounts of the sabayon sauce over each portion of fruit salad. Place the plates under the broiler about 3″ from the source of heat and allow them to cook just until they are lightly browned on the surface. Rotate them from time to time to assure even browning.
6 Serve immediately, with a glass of champagne to accompany the dessert if desired.

Pierre Franey's Cooking in France, by Pierre Franey

18.13 MUNINI BOTT CHAMPAGNE CORK REMOVER

Munini's Bott champagne cork remover is an elegant, rounded, 5½"-tall acrylic tube made to look like polished cherry wood. At one end it has an opening with hard black plastic teeth. Push this end over the cork and twist the lower portion closest to the cork to tighten the grip of the teeth. Next twist the top of the acrylic tube to extract the cork, and then twist the bottom to release the teeth. Remove the cork from the tube. It's that simple.

18.14 MONOPOL NUTCRACKER & CHAMPAGNE OPENER

Monopol's nutcracker and champagne opener is a handsome, black enameled marvel of simplicity. It has two 5¾"-long handles that end in a hinged, truncated, 2¼"-tall cone with concentric toothed ridges inside. Place the wide end of the cone over the cork, squeeze, and twist. When you're done opening champagne, try this device on nuts of any size. It offers remarkable control and precision for that task as well.

18.15 CHAMPAGNE SABER

"*Sabrer le Champagne!*" was the victory cry of Napoleon's officers, who were rewarded by their commander with bottles of champagne. They would decapitate the bottle with a swaggering blow of their saber and drink directly from the open neck, an impressive but potentially dangerous method of opening a bottle of champagne. The tradition is still very popular in France, where champagne is sabered at important gatherings and celebrations. In recent years it has begun to show up in the United States.

A 30" military sword is the standard tool for sabering champagne, but the task is also performed with replicas half that size and even very sharp kitchen knives. It takes one brisk swoop of the blade along the seam just under the lip of the bottle. The wire cage with the cork and a ring of glass should come shooting off like a missile, leaving a clean cut from which the champagne can be poured. Of course, the bottle doesn't like to be treated in this fashion—and can take its revenge by exploding. Chilling the bottle and making sure not to shake it helps reduce pressure and the odds of an explosion, but some experienced grandstanders do just the opposite to create a crowd-pleasing geyser effect after the top blows. Don't try this yourself—it is work for a gifted professional.

BOTTLE STOPPERS

Suppose, after you've opened the champagne or the wine, you don't finish the bottle and want to keep it for later, or even for the next day? You can: with a proper stopper, your champagne's effervescence will not be evanescent, and your wine will keep for days.

18.16 MUNINI ELMO WINE STOPPER

To reseal an opened wine bottle using Munini's stopper, simply place it over the bottle opening and push down. The spring-loaded teeth firmly fasten it to the bottleneck, and its internal rubber seal assures a tight fit. To release the stopper, push down on the two side knobs with your thumb and forefinger, then pull them up slightly—the cap should spring off. The stopper measures 2½" in height and 1¾" wide.

18.17 LE CREUSET SCREWPULL CHAMPAGNE CROWN RESEALER

Le Creuset offers this Screwpull bottle resealer that matches its champagne star. A matte black composite metal device, its cap is channeled at the bottom so that the resealer slides directly onto the ridge at the top of the bottleneck. Once the cap is on the bottle, you pull down the 2" lever on top, which lowers a rubber stopper into the opening of the bottle and locks the stopper in place. With this device a good champagne will keep its fizz. To release the resealer, you simply pull the lever up. The crown resealer is 2¼" in height.

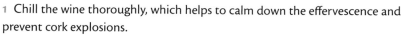

BREAK OUT THE CHAMPAGNE
❧ DUC DE NONANCOURT ❧

1 Chill the wine thoroughly, which helps to calm down the effervescence and prevent cork explosions.

2 Remove the foil, peeling it off with your fingers or a small knife. (As yet, there is no official champagne foil remover.)

3 Twist open the wire cage that prevents a spontaneously exited cork from flying off.

4 Place a cloth over the wire cage and the cork and grip the cage and the cork securely.

5 Slant the bottle away from any inappropriate target. The slant also spreads out the surface of the wine and reduces the concentration of the pressure inside the bottle.

6 Holding the cork firmly inside the cloth, grasp the neck of the bottle. With your other hand, slowly twist the bottle, not the cork. Twisting the cork can easily crack off the mushroom top.

7 When the cork has cleared the rim of the bottle, bring the bottle to an upright position. Use the cloth (still over the top of the bottle) to catch any froth that bubbles up. Holding the wire cage and the cork beneath it, lift the cloth and begin to pour.

18.18 BOJ CHAMPAGNE BOTTLE STOPPER

BOJ makes a highly practical stopper. Made of stainless steel and fitted with a rubber O-ring, it snaps into the bottle's neck and seals it closed. Using this 4½" long stopper requires no strength at all, and it is easy to remove.

WINE PRESERVATION EQUIPMENT

WINE, like many fine things in life, is perishable. Some wines lose their soul in the course of a meal, but most wine can be saved if oxidation can be prevented. A cork won't do a good job, but it will prevent off flavors in the refrigerator from penetrating the wine. We found that vacuum pumps are essentially no more effective than plain corks. The only way to preserve the quality of wine after the bottle has been opened is with nitrogen, which does not react chemically with wine and acts as a protective barrier against oxygen.

Restaurants have all sorts of equipment for preserving the wines they serve by the glass, but increasingly, they are doing away with it; if they gauge consumption properly, they rarely have to store an open bottle until the next day. Similarly, at home you might enjoy sipping the remainder of a fine wine after dinner so as not to waste its magic. If truth be told, for anything but a rare and fragile bottle, a night in the refrigerator is unlikely to destroy it. Just allow the wine to warm up a bit before pouring it again.

I love everything that's old: old friends, old times, old manners, old books, old wines.
—OLIVER GOLDSMITH, *She Stoops to Conquer*

18.19 OENOPHILIA PRIVATE PRESERVE WINE PRESERVER

Until Oenophilia came along with its Private Preserve wine preserver, only wine bars and plutocrats could afford nitrogen preservation. Now, it is democratically available to the ordinary wine drinker. The wine preserver comes in a pressurized metal container so light it feels empty even when it's full. Actually, it contains a blend of nitrogen, carbon dioxide, and argon—inert, nontoxic, non-flammable, flavorless gases. All it takes is just a few blasts into the neck of the bottle: then you recork the bottle and leave it standing up until the next time you're ready to imbibe. Oenophilia's wine preserver will preserve wine for a week. One canister is good for 120 wine bottles.

POIRES AU VIN ROUGE
(PEARS BRAISED IN RED WINE)

6 servings

Pears cooked in red wine are served in all the different wine-growing regions of France. The dish is most successful, in my opinion, when made with a strong, robust wine that sustains hours of cooking and still retains some of its excellent flavor. An earthy Beaujolais is excellent. The best pears are the hard species, such as the Bosc (which is the brown, long tapered-neck variety); the Anjou (speckled with red and green); and the Comice (usually large and potbellied with green markings). The Bartlett will fall apart too easily for this recipe, so it should be avoided or the cooking time should be adjusted accordingly.

6 large pears
½ cup sugar
1 quart good dry red wine
the skin (yellow part only) of 1 lemon

Peel the pears, trying not to sever the stem (the reason is aesthetic). You need a kettle in which the pears can stand up, tightly pressed against each other. Add the sugar, the wine, and the lemon peel. The liquid should just cover the pears. (The pears are poached standing up so that they retain their shape.) Bring to a boil and place in a 350°F oven for 3½ hours. *Be sure to place the kettle on a metal tray to have a uniform transfer of heat. Cover the pears so that they do not dry, but leave a little space open for the steam to escape and for the juices to reduce.* Let the pears cool off slowly in their juices. When done, they should be a nice mahogany color. At serving time, place them standing up on a large platter. You will have approximately 1 to 1½ cups of liquid left. You may add 2 to 3 tablespoons of liqueur (such as cognac or kirsch) to the liquid if you wish. Pour over the pears. Excellent with a rice pudding or fresh slices of brioche.

A French Chef Cooks at Home, by Jacques Pépin

OTHER HANDY WINE EQUIPMENT

THE FOLLOWING ITEMS may not be strictly necessary, but we think you'll find that they are quite useful for specific tasks. At the very least, they may make wine drinking easier or even more fun.

18.20 BOJ ANTI-DRIP RING

BOJ, that estimable Basque company, wants to keep your tablecloth clean. It makes a silver-plated ring (1½″ in diameter) that slips over the neck of a wine bottle and catches drips in its absorbent green felt lining. The only other way to prevent dripping is to remember to twist the bottle every time you pour from it.

> During one of my treks through Afghanistan, we lost our corkscrew. We were compelled to live on food and water for several days.
>
> —W. C. FIELDS,
> *My Little Chickadee*

18.21 LE CREUSET SCREWPULL FOIL CUTTER & 18.22 MUNINI FOIL CUTTER

You can cut foil or plastic from a bottle with a knife, but a dedicated foil cutter works better. The 2¾" by 1¾" Screwpull foil cutter is easy to squeeze around the top of a bottleneck. Sharp little steel wheels set in a plastic body slice the foil or other sealing material, allowing it to come off in a neat sheet. The Munini cutter is the best of its class. It has the same round-topped palm-friendly shape as Munini's other paraphernalia. You just pop the 2¼"-tall cutter over the bottle, squeeze, and turn. More ergonomic than the Screwpull, it comes in bodacious blue, green, red, white, black, yellow, and colors that look like wood.

18.23 THE WINE ENTHUSIAST MINIATURE DISTILLING MACHINE

Ever the coy old coot, the Wine Enthusiast insists that his elegant, all-glass still is *not*, repeat *not*, intended to make distillate spirits. Nevertheless, following the semiopaque instructions provided in English and Italian, we risked federal jail time and turned some leftover wine into a quite passable grappa brandy. The burner that makes the thing go runs on rubbing alcohol and takes its own good time to heat the wine until the alcohol vaporizes. One run produces two tiny glasslets of hooch.

18.24 EVERGREEN LABS INC. WINE AWAY RED WINE STAIN REMOVER

We never had much luck getting wine stains out of double damask tablecloths with Perrier and salt, so we were glad to hear about Evergreen Labs Inc.'s Wine Away. It's a secret all-natural fruit and vegetable extract that really did get red wine out of a beige high-pile carpet without much hassle. Just spray it on and wipe the stain out.

19

COFFEE- & TEA-MAKING EQUIPMENT

COFFEE

A TASTE FOR COFFEE first took hold in Ethiopia but, curiously, it was not consumed as a beverage; by all historical accounts, coffee appears to have been used as a food before it became a drink. Possibly as early as the sixth century, North Africans discovered that the seeds of the fruit of the wild coffee tree could be chewed whole or crushed with fat to make a paste and then molded into balls. These balls, like an early version of quick-energy trail mix, were carried on short forays as well as into battle.

Sometime later, the entire fruit was steeped to make a drink, but it was not until the thirteenth century that the seeds were cleaned, roasted, and infused into water to make coffee. The new beverage first achieved popularity among Muslims who used it to keep the pious awake during nocturnal devotions. Though there was much debate among Islamic scholars as to whether coffee, with its stimulating effects, was lawful, it was eventually accepted. In fact, the word *coffee* derives, via the Turkish *kahveh,* from the Arabic *qahwah,* one of the words that meant "wine."

In the fourteenth century, Arab colonists in east Africa and those on the nearby Arabian peninsula began cultivating coffee trees (hence one of their botanical names, *coffea arabica*). Enterprising Arab merchants, taking advantage of their central position between Asia and Europe, introduced coffee to border-ing countries by adding the beans to shipments of spices from the Orient. Through these exports, the use of coffee quickly spread outward—first to Persia and Syria, then to Cairo, and a few years later, to Venice. Thereafter it passed to Constantinople, where the first coffeehouse was established in 1554.

During the next hundred years, coffee made its conquest of the Mediterranean countries, then quickly headed toward England, where a coffeehouse opened in Oxford in 1650. Local purveyors, promoting the exotic brew, made the usual exaggerated claims. In an advertisement in the London *Publick Adviser,* dated May 19, 1657, coffee was described as "a very whole-some and Physical drink" that "closes the Orifice of the Stomack, fortifies the heat within, helpeth Digestion, quickeneth the Spirits, maketh the heart lightsom, is good against Eye-sores, Coughs, or Colds, Rhumes, Consumption, Headach, Dropsie, Gout, Scurvy, King's Evil, and many others."

Marseilles appears to have had the first coffeehouse on the continent, which opened in 1671. The first successful coffeehouse in Paris was called Café Procope and opened in 1686. Offering customers a clean and luxurious enviroment, Café Procope is still in business. Coffeehouses and cafés quickly multiplied in London, Paris, Vienna, and other European centers. First drawn by curiosity, residents began frequenting these establishments as much for their congenial atmosphere as for the coffee. Coffeehouses became meeting points for the fashionable, literary, and political classes of the day.

Until the end of the seventeenth century, the world was almost entirely dependent on coffee beans from Africa and the nearby peninsula of what is now called Yemen. Turkish merchants held a monopoly on the supply until early in the eighteenth century, when the Dutch brought coffee trees to their colonies in Indonesia, quickly establishing large successful plantations, and incidentally adding the term *Java* to the coffee lex-

icon. Soon after, a single *arabica* tree made a voyage under the care of marine captain Gabriel Mathieu de Clieu to the French Caribbean colony of Martinique where, presumably under instructions from Louis XV, the lone bush was experimentally planted on the island. It thrived, and eventually the French became major coffee merchants. By the end of the 1800s, Central and South American coffee growers had achieved the dominant market position they maintain today, followed by the other principal coffee-growing regions, Africa and Indonesia.

GRINDING EQUIPMENT

HOME GRINDING USED TO BE a laborious chore requiring some elbow grease and several minutes spent turning a hand-cranked mill. With today's electric coffee grinders, all you need is a few seconds and the ability to press a button. There are basically two kinds of grinders in the appliance universe—burr mills and blade grinders. An ideal grinder should hold at least 8 ounces of beans (though many hold less), produce an evenly textured grind and very little coffee "dust," allow for easy removal of the grounds, be easy to clean after each use, heat the beans only minimally, and be relatively quiet. If you use various kinds of coffeemakers, the grinder you select should have a wide range of adjustments, from ultrafine to coarse.

WHY YOU SHOULD GRIND YOUR OWN COFFEE

If you care about good coffee, you must care about grinding. Matching the right grind of coffee beans to your particular brewing method is essential for achieving the correct "extraction of soluble solids"—that which the experts tell us makes one cup of coffee full-bodied and flavorful and another weak as dishwater, or muddy and bitter. Even the best equipment, the finest beans, and a careful measure of pure water cannot guarantee a delicious brew if the coffee that goes into making it is not properly ground. Delicious results depend on an ideal ratio of time to grind—that is, the shorter the brewing time, the finer the grind must be for a flavorful, balanced extraction. Espresso,

for example, requires a very fine, almost powdery grind because it has a brewing time of 30 seconds or less. Conversely, plunger-pot coffee, in which the grounds steep in water for a full 4 to 6 minutes, demands a very coarse grind. Medium grinds work best for various kinds of drip or percolated coffee.

So if proper grinding is critical, why not just buy preground beans from a coffee boutique? Because once a coffee bean has been ground, its fragrant compounds and aromatic oils begin to dissipate. Grinding breaks apart thousands of cells, releasing the aromatics that give coffee its strength and nuance; the longer you wait before brewing, the more potential flavor is lost. Coffee

aficionados emphatically agree: to ensure the best brew, buy freshly roasted beans and grind them just before you need them.

Grinding at home also lets you experiment with different blends and brewing methods. In one day you could brew a quick-start cup of espresso in the morning, make a pot of drip coffee for an afternoon klatch, and steep a plunger pot of half-decaf after dinner. All these methods need a particular grind, and having the equipment at home allows you to custom-grind for each one so that what ends up in your cup will please your mouth. After all, there are few good things in life you can count on—a fine cup of coffee should be one of them.

BURR MILLS

Burr mills (also called burr grinders) use metal plates or stones to grind a few coffee beans at a time, working on the same principle by which people have ground wheat, corn, and other grains for centuries. Hand-cranked burr mills are still produced by a few manufacturers, but unless you have plenty of time or don't like to use electricity, today's wide range of press-a-button machines are much more practical. You simply put beans into a hopper, set a knob for the desired consistency, and turn on the machine. The hopper sends a controlled amount of beans onto two metal plates, one of which is stationary. When the other turns, a series of grooves snag and grind the beans into evenly sized granules that are then sent into a removable container.

With precision and consistency, the burr mill will usually produce a uniform grind of beans regardless of how many or few beans you feed it, or which of the different grind settings you choose. This means that you end up with an even bed of ground coffee for hot water to pass through; there's no coffee dust to trap the liquid, or coarse particles to form channels that make the water drip too fast. Another benefit of burr mills is that they generate little heat during the grinding process, so the beans stay cool, preventing the loss of flavorful aromatics that otherwise evaporate when exposed to heat. With this type of machine you may also be able to grind a larger amount of coffee at one time. Blade grinders produce between 12 and 21 tablespoons of ground coffee depending on their bean capacity. If you use a full 2 tablespoons of coffee per cup, this may not be enough for an entire pot.

While they are the grinder of choice for many coffee drinkers, home burr mills are not perfect. For one thing, they tend to be quite noisy. Some models also take up a precious chunk of counter or cabinet space. Finally, burr mills can be costly, especially the top-rated models. Nevertheless, experts say, they're well worth the investment. There are plenty of cheap and effective brewing methods, but as Corby Kummer, author of *The Joy of Coffee,* says, "There's no substitute for a grinder that will produce the same result time after time and give you a superior cup of coffee."

refill and empty them. Over time the wood in the drawer will absorb oil from the coffee, and since there's no real way to clean it, it has the potential to become rancid. But in this age of supercomputerized touch-pad appliances, there's a certain nostalgic charm in owning a gadget like this and knowing it performs as well as some high-tech applicances.

19.2 STARBUCKS BARISTA BURR GRINDER

Elegantly designed, this model has ten grind settings with icons depicting which ones to use for various coffee-making methods: a drawing of an espresso filter and cup appears above the finest setting, a drip filter and pot indicates the medium setting, and a French press designates the coarsest. As it is only 6" wide, 5½" deep, and 11½" high, the machine doesn't demand too much valuable countertop space. While the hopper holds 10 ounces of coffee beans, the ground coffee container only holds 18 tablespoons of ground coffee, so you may have to empty and refill it more than once if you use 2 tablespoons of coffee per cup and are making a full pot. For periodic cleaning, this grinder is easy to take apart and put back together.

19.1 PEUGEOT MANUAL COFFEE GRINDER

Hand-cranking this wooden mill rewards you with a consistently even grind that isn't subjected to any heat. Although not as effortless as using an electric grinder, it's not as strenuous or time-consuming as you would expect. If you use a coarse grind—let's say for a French press—you can grind your coffee just as quickly and easily as with a blade grinder. However, because the hopper holds only about an ounce of coffee and the drawer doesn't hold much more, you'll need to continually

19.3 CAPRESSO BURR GRINDER

Our top choice for grinding coffee beans, the Capresso gives a perfectly even grind *quickly* and holds a generous 8 ounces of beans in the hopper and 30 tablespoons in the ground coffee container. There's a choice of seventeen grind settings. Rather than select an arbitrary time for grinding, you're given a choice of grinding enough coffee for 4, 8, or 12 cups—but keep in mind that the manufacturer is allowing one tablespoon of coffee per cup. It is 4½" wide, 6" deep, and stands 9½" high, and the plastic body comes in both black and white. The burr grinder lifts out so you can brush it off occasionally, but the plastic hopper doesn't come off for cleaning so you can only wipe it out. One more negative, but a very minor one: There's no cord storage.

CHOOSING A FILTER

Whether you choose a manual or electric drip coffeemaker, the question of what kind of filter to use inevitably comes up: permanent metal or throwaway paper? If paper, bleached or unbleached?

The choice between metal or paper depends on whether you like a bit of texture and sediment in your cup. Paper filters trap every bit of colloids and most of the coffee oils during brewing, whereas gold-plated, fine mesh filters let some through. Those in favor of the metal say it makes coffee with more body and nuance; paper filter users boast that their coffee has more clarity and keeps better since it doesn't have particles that can become overextracted. Metal filters are a benefit in that they never run out and can save you money in the long run. But unlike paper filters that go easily from brewer to garbage bin, with the spent grounds neatly trapped inside them, metal filters must be washed after each use.

Shopping for paper filters used to be simple—they were all made of the same chlorine-bleached material and you picked your filter according to the size and shape you needed. Then consumers became informed about the dangers to their health and the planet from chlorine-bleached paper, and they demanded a new choice. Hence the advent of unbleached brown-colored filters. These were hardly safer though, because untreated paper has its own measure of harmful resins and impurities—and in addition, coffee drinkers complained that the filters added woody and tarlike notes to their brew. Fortunately, the industry came up with a third choice that seems to endanger neither the drinker's health nor the coffee taste: oxygen-bleached filters. These have now become the standard in commercial filter brewing, making them the best choice if you prefer paper.

BLADE GRINDERS

These small, canister-shaped gizmos are essentially bean choppers, comprised of a motorized base and a metal container on top. You place the beans inside the container, cover it with the fitted lid, and press down on the top or on a button to activate the propeller-like blades; the beans are chopped by the blades until you stop pressing. Blade grinders are fast, easy to use, and can be had for a fraction of the price of burr mills, but, not surprisingly, you pay dearly in sacrificed coffee flavor.

Chopping beans, rather than milling them, results in granules that can vary greatly in size, from coarse and rocky at the top of the container to fine and dusty beneath the blades. When brewing, the dust can dam up the works, slowing the passage of water so that it extracts too many bitter compounds. The oversize granules do the opposite, creating sluices for water to pass through too quickly, preventing it from picking up the soluble solids that constitute a good cup of coffee. Other drawbacks of the blade grinders include the heat that is often created by chopping, hastening the escape of flavorful aromatics, plus the guesswork involved in knowing the quantity of beans to use and when to stop pressing.

19.4 BRAUN COFFEE GRINDER

This blade grinder pulled ahead of the pack—it ground beans well and relatively evenly, keeping them cool in the process, and didn't make a terrible racket. In one shot it grinds 2½ ounces of coffee, producing about 15 tablespoons of freshly ground coffee ready to brew. You control the fineness of the grinds by how long you press the top button. The cord wraps neatly in a crevice in the base. Along with the machine comes a tool with a 1-tablespoon scoop on one end and a cleaning brush on the other.

BREWING EQUIPMENT

THE SIMPLEST WAY to make coffee is to throw a handful of roasted ground coffee into a potful of near-boiling water, turn off the heat, cover the pot, and steep it like tea. Minutes later strain it through a cloth, and you've got the stuff of cowboy legends. This is called the open-pot method and it mostly appeals to those who love campfire cuisine or scorn fancy appliances. The rest of us generally seek a neater, more precise way of infusing water with coffee. To that end, there are dozens of coffeemakers—from manual and electric drip machines to plunger pots to percolators—but not one of them can call itself "the best." Just as there is no superior bean, there is no single way to brew coffee. Much depends on how you like your coffee and on how much effort you're willing to invest in making it. Some believe that the best brewing method is the one that's the most convenient to use. Others are willing to fuss a bit more if it means better flavor. Whatever your coffee needs, there is undoubtedly a particular coffeemaker that can satisfy you.

MANUAL DRIP COFFEEMAKERS

Low-tech and low-priced, manual drip coffeemakers consist of a filter holder that fits snugly over a glass carafe, thermal jug, or individual coffee cup. Measure the ground coffee into the filter, bring water to boil, let it cool slightly, and then pour into the filter. The water and ground beans steep briefly before the extracted coffee flows through a spout into the vessel underneath. The water passes over the beans just once, ideally with enough time to produce a full-bodied brew, but not so long that it picks up bitterness.

When you're making a potful, you have to pour the water in batches, which requires that you hang around during the brewing process. Some consider this an annoying inconvenience, which is why the electric drip machine was developed. But many experts swear by the hands-on method because it avoids all the pitfalls of electric brewing. For one, you can be sure the water temperature is correct (195°F to 205°F) by pausing a few seconds between boiling and pouring. Then you can ensure that there is even saturation by premoistening the grounds. Finally, unlike some of their electric counterparts, manual drip systems don't subject brewed coffee to the "burn" of burner plates—a built-in fixture intended to preserve the heat of brewed coffee but one that also *cooks* the coffee as it sits, thereby destroying the brew's flavor and aroma. For the same reason, one should avoid placing the glass carafe of manual drip makers over a low flame on the stove to keep the contents hot for any length of time beyond that needed to brew and quickly serve, for that too will hurt the flavor. The smart way to maintain the temperature and taste of your coffee is to pour it immediately into a thermal carafe that has been preheated with hot water. Note also that the less airspace at the top of the carafe, the longer the liquid will stay hot. However, even in a thermal carafe the flavor of your coffee will deteriorate after several hours. We've found that microwaving coffee will reheat it without ruining the flavor. Just be sure to heat it in a microwave-safe mug or container until just hot enough to drink, but not boiling.

For making one perfect cup of coffee, choose this set consisting of a #2 plastic filter cone and 10-ounce ceramic mug. The mug is microwave safe. If you like, you can also use the filter on the mug of your choice.

An elegant, hourglass-shaped vessel made of one piece of handblown glass, the original Chemex manual drip coffeemaker was considered a peerless model of clean form and sound function when it was introduced in 1941 by German chemist-inventor and member of the Bauhaus art movement Peter Schlumbohm. Indeed, the Chemex design has earned an honored place in the permanent collection of New York's Museum of Modern Art as well

19.5 MELITTA CAFÉ-EURO 6-CUP COFFEEMAKER

As simple as it is, for some coffee lovers, this is all you need to produce the ultimate brew. Place a paper filter into the #4 plastic filter cone, measure in your coffee, pour in water, and in a few minutes and with a minimum of work you have a small pot—25.4 ounces, or about 4 cups—of perfection. The glass carafe can be popped into the microwave for reheating and both sections can be cleaned in the dishwasher. If you find the server not quite elegant enough to bring to the table, you can use the filter to drip coffee into a ceramic or fine china coffeepot.

as the Smithsonian Institution in Washington, D.C. Today, in addition to the handblown original, there is a less expensive version (shown here) made of machine-made glass fitted at the waist with the same handsome wooden girdle and leather thong as the older model. And it's used exactly the same way: measure medium-ground coffee into the paper-filter-lined glass cone on top, boil water, cool it slightly, pour a small amount over the grounds until they're evenly moistened and swell slightly, or "bloom," then pour in the remaining water and let drip.

With its spare, laboratory look, Chemex seduces buyers of that aesthetic, but when it comes to brewing, this model is very similar to other manual drip coffeemakers. Some coffee critics claim that the heavier triple-layer filters used with the Chemex produce a brew that is too pure, too refined. The manufacturer claims that such filtering is essential to remove the acids, sediment, and bitter elements that spoil a good cup of coffee. And so it goes, with debate being the only sure thing in all coffee-making discussions. If you do choose a Chemex, you'll want to purchase an S-shaped bottle brush to go along with it for cleaning the bottom half of the pot.

RECIPE FOR COFFEE

Black as the devil,
Hot as hell,
Pure as an angel,
Sweet as love.

—CHARLES MAURICE DE
TALLYRAND-PÉRIGORD

PLUNGER POTS

A plunger pot, also called a French press, is the method that *cuppers*—professional coffee testers—use to brew coffee. With the plunger pot, coarse-ground coffee is infused with near-boiling water inside the device's spouted heat-resistant glass cylinder. After about 4 to 6 minutes, a screen made of plastic, nylon, or metal is slowly pushed from the top of the glass chamber to the bottom, thereby straining the coffee and trapping the grounds on the floor of the pot. The result is a rich brew with a varying amount of sediment, depending on the fineness of the strainer mesh and the grounds. Not surprisingly, this invention can also be used to make tea.

Some critics of the plunger pot complain that by the time the coffee is fully infused, it has cooled too much. To lessen this effect, fill the glass pot with very hot tap water until just before brewing, or wrap a thick handtowel around the cylinder during brewing. There are now also metal insulated plunger pots.

A plunger pot worth your time and money will have a fine screen that leaves no room at the sides of the carafe for particles to sneak through, plus a strong middle spindle that makes it easier to keep the plunger perfectly straight while pushing it down; capacities range from 3 to 12 cups.

19.8 BODUM CHAMBORD COFFEE PRESS

This charming French press consists of a glass container with a Bakelite handle and knob and stainless steel frame, lid, and strainer. It makes 32 ounces of coffee. Inside the lid there's a plastic seal to help keep heat from escaping and to prevent hot coffee from spilling out, although you'll still want to serve the coffee quickly, as you would with any glass plunger pot.

19.9 THERMOS NISSAN VACUUM-INSULATED COFFEE PRESS

Because this stainless steel plunger pot is vacuum-insulated, it solves the most common complaint about plunger pots—coffee that's not hot enough. Not only will your brew be significantly higher in temperature, but it will stay hot for a good hour. There's no glass lining, and so no need to worry about breakage, the usual problem with this type of coffeemaker. It has a capacity of 1 quart—enough for three or four mugs or eight small cups.

395

THE VACUUM POT

Want a coffeemaker that entertains as well as brews a good cup? The odd-looking vacuum pot does both quite well, though you have to serve as a diligent assistant. First you must set water to boil in a kettle (if you have an eternity, there is an alcohol-burning heating stand available as an accessory that will eventually boil the water). Then attach the filter provided—either metal, glass, or plastic depending on the manufacturer—onto the base of the upper glass globe. Measure the recommended amount of ground coffee into the globe. Next fill the lower glass globe with hot water; fit the upper globe, which has a tube emerging from the filter, neatly into the lower globe, creating an airtight seal. Set this whole superstructure over a low flame and watch as steam pressure forces the water up through the tube into the top globe, where it meets with the coffee. Stir briefly, then let the coffee steep for 2 minutes or more. Finally, extinguish the flame and prepare for the drama: Air in the lower globe will cool and contract, forming a strong vacuum that sucks the coffee-water slurry through the filter and back into the bottom globe with a fascinating burbling swoosh. Remove the upper globe and triumphantly pour the coffee. Your exacting effort will be rewarded with a brew that has much to offer: properly hot temperature, a rich flavor that highlights the complex acidity in fine coffee without any bitterness, and a full body without sediment.

The obvious disadvantage of this method is that it's not convenient—to use or to clean up. In addition, the glass globes are delicate and liable to break sooner or later. But as a grand finale to a special meal, the vacuum pot will steal the show.

19.10 BODUM SANTOS VACUUM POT

Coffee brewed in this model is, as promised, among the best you will ever taste. Fully assembled on your range, the Santos stands a dramatic 11½" high. For best results, use a medium grind of coffee, the same that is used for electric drip machines. After you've completed the brewing process, or about 5 minutes after you've added boiling water to the bottom globe, you can place the top chamber in the tall plastic stand that's provided and top the carafe with the plastic lid. There's also a special plastic stand to slip on the bottom of the coffeepot to protect your table from heat. This coffeemaker yields ten 5-ounce cups and is dishwasher safe.

Coffee is the
favorite drink
of the civilized world.

—THOMAS JEFFERSON,
1823

BREWING PROPORTIONS

The proper proportion of coffee to water is 2 tablespoons of coffee per 6 ounces of water, which will yield a 5-ounce serving. (This is considered a standard serving of coffee because until the last twenty years or so coffee was generally served in a traditional teacup, which measures 6 ounces; 1 ounce of headroom is allowed for the addition of milk or cream.) This has been scientifically proven to bring out the maximum number of pleasant flavor compounds from coffee, providing a well-rounded, full-bodied beverage. Using less ground coffee will result in a thinner, less strong brew but risks overextraction or release of the bitter and unpleasant-tasting compounds in coffee that come out when too much water passes over the same grinds. For weaker coffee, you are better off using the full amount of ground coffee and diluting the finished brew.

However, in the last two decades it has become standard to use only 1 tablespoon of coffee per coffee "cup," and many coffeemakers come with a coffee measure that holds 1 tablespoon. It is speculated that among the reasons many people find the coffee served in Starbucks and other specialty coffee shops better than the brew they make at home is that these stores use the proper ratio of coffee to water.

ELECTRIC DRIP MACHINES

For some, making coffee is a comforting ritual, while for others it's a chore to be done with as soon as possible. It is for those folks in the latter category that the electric drip machine exists. These push-a-button coffeemakers only require you to feed them the proper amount of water and medium-ground coffee, then you're free to walk away until the last drip has dropped. With preprogrammable settings, these machines can even be set to brew moments before the morning alarm rings, so you can literally wake up and smell the coffee. Likewise, some models have built-in clocks, grinders, adjustable brew cycles, temperature controls, and automatic shut-off switches. For all their bells and whistles, electric coffeemakers don't guarantee a brew that is any better, and can often be worse than the simple manual drip method. But they do take care of heating the water and passing it over the coffee grounds so you needn't bother. And they are one of the best ways of making a lot of coffee quickly.

When choosing from the mind-boggling selection of electric automatic drip machines, budget and personal preferences are big considerations. The two factors that are most likely to guarantee you superior coffee—fast brewing times and water temperatures between 195°F and 205°F—are impossible to determine when shopping. However, you can check that the filter basket is large enough to hold a 2-tablespoon coffee measure per cup and provide ample headroom for the grinds to be agitated and swollen by the water passing through. If you'll be keeping coffee hot for longer than an hour, choose a coffeemaker with a thermal carafe rather than a burner plate. For convenience, look for a water reservoir that lifts out for easy filling and determine if the machine is easy to clean.

charcoal filter for removing chlorine from the water and a permanent gold filter come with the machine. There's room to store the cord in the back of the plastic housing. It comes in black and white.

19.12 CAPRESSO ELEGANCE THERM

We think this is as good as it gets if you want the automation of an electric drip machine without much compromise in the quality of your coffee. Thanks to superior engineering, the Capresso quickly heats water to the optimum brewing temperature and then makes 8 cups in 7½ minutes, directly into an insulated carafe. As the glass-lined carafe remains covered during the brewing process—coffee drips down through the lid—there's a minimum loss of heat. You can remove the water container for filling at the sink, which means you don't use the thermal container—subjecting it to cold water would also detract from its ability to keep the coffee hot. The carafe keeps your coffee at serving temperature for about 4 hours. As you'd expect from a model in this price category, it can be programmed to have your coffee ready in the morning and allows you to interrupt

19.11 CAPRESSO COFFEETEAM PLUS

Here you get ultimate convenience and a good cup of coffee. This machine heats the water to the ideal brewing temperature quickly, although it takes about 10 minutes to brew a full pot. Pour your coffee beans into the built-in burr grinder, program the number of cups and the fineness of the grind, and when the coffeemaker starts, the grinder will automatically grind beans and transfer them to the filter. The hopper will hold about 5 ounces of beans—enough for about 30 tablespoons of ground coffee depending on the grind setting. While this large 10-cup model (width 11½", length 10", and height 15½") is for those who insist on grinding their own beans, preground coffee can be used. Other sophisticated features include the ability to program it to brew in the morning, a pause function that allows you to grab a cup before all the coffee's ready, and an automatic shut-off after 2 hours. A

the cycle if you're too impatient to wait for the whole pot to be ready. Included with the Elegance Therm are a chlorine filter and a permanent gold filter. In the base of the plastic unit there's a place to neatly stash the cord. This coffeemaker is fairly compact—it's only 7½" by 12¼" and 14" in height—and comes in both black and white.

19.13 KRUPS CRYSTAL AROME PLUS TIME

The undeniably beautiful design of the original version of the Crystal Arome was fatally flawed by a carafe that dribbled when pouring. So the folks at Krups tried again, and this time they got it right. Now it won't spill even when you're pouring out the last drop. You can depend on this 10-cup model for a smooth, full-bodied beverage whether you brew a pot after dinner or wake up to one that you've programmed the night before. And yes, you can sneak a cup before it's ready if you're impatient. While this machine will shut off automatically after one hour, you can program it to stay on for up to 5 hours. There's a water filter that's designed to remove chlorine from the water and prevent scale from forming inside the machine. When the filter needs replacing, a light

flashes. All this classy style is contained in a package that's 7" wide, 9" deep, and 13" high and is complemented by a matte finish in either black or white; there's even a place to stow the excess cord so nothing can detract from the Crystal Arome's good looks.

19.14 BRAUN FLAVORSELECT 12-CUP CAPPUCCINO COFFEEMAKER WITH FROTHING ATTACHMENT

Love a good full-size cup of American-style coffee? Don't really care for espresso or the fuss involved in making it, but find the frothy topping on a cappuccino comforting? If you answered yes to all the preceding questions, the FlavorSelect is for you. It makes 12 cups of rich and full-bodied coffee because it brews with water that's the proper temperature. True to its name, this model allows you to select the flavor of your coffee, from robust to mild. It adjusts the strength the correct way, by using the maximum amount of coffee for brewing and then adding hot water directly into the carafe to make it milder. On the side of the plastic housing, there's a nozzle for foaming milk. Other notable features are automatic shut-off after 2 hours, and "pause and serve" for stealing a cup before brewing's com-

pleted. A water filter for reducing chlorine and preventing calcification is included, and there's an indicator to remind you when to change it. Any excess cord length can be tucked in the back of the machine. On your countertop it needs a space that's 11" wide, 10½" deep, and 14" high.

19.15 KITCHENAID 12-CUP ULTRA COFFEEMAKER

With a sterling reputation to maintain, KitchenAid has been careful to bring a high level of performance to every product it introduces. What's the newest KitchenAid on the block? This 12-cup automatic drip coffeemaker which features two heating elements, one that makes sure the water is hot enough for proper extraction, and one that keeps the coffee on the warming plate within 3° of the ideal 174°F holding temperature. In fact, the company's so concerned about the way coffee's kept hot that when you brew only 1 to 3 cups, it decreases the temperature of the plate to prevent the small quantity of coffee from overheating. On the side of the machine there is a lighted display that tells you how much time has elapsed since the coffee was brewed—if it's been more than an hour you can opt to discard it and make a fresh pot. This brewer allows you to choose the strength of your coffee and still get maximum flavor.

For milder brews, it drips some of the water through the full amount of ground coffee and diverts the rest directly into the carafe. Of course, like all others in its price range, it allows you to sneak a cup during the brew cycle, turns off automatically after 2 hours, and has a place to stash the cord. A charcoal water filter for eliminating chlorine is included along with a spoon for measuring your coffee grinds. The coffeeemaker measures 8½" wide, 9½" deep, and 13½" high. The plastic housing is available in black and white.

PERCOLATORS

Picture a small fountain inside a covered jug and there you have the basic design of a percolator coffeepot. This old-fashioned device forces hot water up through a center tube and then sprays it over the coffee that rests just below in a metal filter basket insert. A weak brew quickly flows out, collects at the bottom of the percolator, and is then forced back up the tube, to be sprayed over the grinds yet again. The water passes over the coffee several times during brewing, much to the horror of many aficionados who claim that this results in overextraction, bringing out too many soluble substances and bitter flavors and leaving the brew an acrid, unbalanced casualty.

Despite these indictments, the percolator was widely adopted in the United States in the early 1900s and its popularity remained strong for several decades, until the advent of automatic drip coffeemakers. A cup of percolated coffee is much less common now, but it still endures as the brewing method of choice for a small but die-hard group of coffee drinkers. These fans also boast, correctly, that the percolator system makes one of the fastest and hottest cups of coffee around.

Percolators are available in both stovetop and electric models. The first consists of a stainless steel or glass pot with a percolator insert and a 2- to 12-cup capacity. The plug-in versions have a pitcher made of stainless steel, glass, or heat-resistant plastic equipped with a heating element on the bottom. They automatically brew and keep coffee warm. Small (2 to 4 cups) and large capacities (10 cups or more) are available.

19.16 FARBERWARE MILLENNIUM 12-CUP CORDLESS PROGRAMMABLE PERCOLATOR

Farberware has been producing versions of their percolator for a long time, and we have a fondness for its handsome and now-classic design. Perhaps it's the good old retro appeal that made us find that, even though it violates all the principles of good coffee-making, this speedy brewer doesn't make a half-bad cup of joe. It delivers 12 cups of piping hot coffee in just 9 minutes, and will keep the coffee hot until it shuts itself off automatically after 2 hours. What has changed is that the percolator now sits on a base containing a clock and a timer, so you can program it to start brewing just as you wake up.

19.17 FARBERWARE MILLENNIUM STAINLESS STEEL SUPERFAST COFFEE URN

We can't lie—this giant percolator doesn't make the best coffee we've ever tasted. However, we're not aware of any other that makes coffee for a crowd as quickly and looks this good. And it can't be beat for convenience—just add water (cup markings are easy to read), measure out the grinds, and plug it in. A red light indicates when coffee's ready to serve: about 30 minutes later for a full urn of 36 cups. On your buffet table it will stand 17" high and take up about 13" in diameter. The stainless steel loops on the end of the plastic handles stay perfectly cool, so it's easy to move if necessary, and the spigot doesn't dribble. Urns that make up to 22 and 55 cups are also available from this manufacturer.

His most frequent ailment
was the headache which
he used to relieve by inhaling
the steam of coffee.

—DR. JOHNSON,
The Life of Pope

NEAPOLITAN COFFEEMAKERS

Here we have the gymnastic event in coffee-making. Invented by the French (who call it *café filtre*) but cherished by the Italians, the Neapolitan coffeemaker (aka *neapolitana* and *macchinetta*) consists of two latched metal pots, one atop the other with a metal-screened coffee chamber in between. The user flips over this coffeemaker at just the right moment to somersault near-boiling water in one pot into the coffee compartment and through the grounds to end up in the other, spouted, pot. It's essentially a single-pass manual drip method like the others described, but one that produces a more full-bodied brew because the water passes through the ground coffee at a slower pace, drawing out more of the coffee's essential oils. Also, as the water is heated, steam collects within the pot, which moistens the coffee grounds and begins the oil extraction. There is controversy over which are better: stovetop coffee and espresso makers made of aluminum or those made of stainless steel. Aluminum is more porous than stainless steel, and over time it absorbs the coffee's oils, which gives the brew a characteristic taste and aroma that is highly desired among some coffee drinkers. Those who do not like the effect aluminum has on their coffee can opt for the stainless steel models. However, we confess to a sentimental attachment to the inexpensive aluminum versions found in so many Italian-American homes and restaurants. Their capacities range from two to twelve 2-ounce servings.

19.18 ILSA NAPOLETANA COFFEEPOT

Made of 99.5 percent of pressed aluminum, this traditional Italian-made coffeemaker makes a delicious strong brew without bitterness. It's billed as a six-serving size, which means it holds 1 cup of water, enough to make six very "short" (less than 2-ounce) servings.

MIDDLE EASTERN COFFEE

THE PREPARATION AND SERVICE of coffee is surrounded by tradition and ceremony in the lands of the Eastern Mediterranean. Middle Easterners, many of whom are forbidden alcoholic beverages by their religion, drink coffee in situations where Westerners would more likely opt for wine or cocktails. In the Middle East it is coffee, not the martini, that lubricates social interchange. Coffee is served on all special occasions and whenever a distinguished visitor comes to call. Neither business transactions nor serious conversations can take place without the accompaniment of numerous tiny cups of coffee.

19.19 LA PAVONI TURKISH *CEZVE* (OR GREEK *BRIKI*)

Turkish coffee is entirely different from American coffee; the rules of coffee-making discussed earlier in the chapter don't apply. For instance, Turks, as well as Greeks and other Middle Easterners, do the one thing our brew experts warn against: they boil the coffee. But they boil it in such a precise way, with a particular pot and a specific type and grind of coffee, that the result is something quite enjoyable—although unlike any other coffee you've ever had.

They start with a small tapered pot like this one made out of tin-lined copper, which allows substantial metal-to-liquid contact to hasten boiling. Its spouted collar facilitates neat pouring, and a 6¼" riveted extra-long brass handle keeps hands away from the heat. The base is 4" in diameter. A special kind of coffee, lightly roasted and ground as fine as flour, is mixed with an equal amount of sugar and the right proportion of water (2 teaspoons of grind to about ½ cup water). Over a medium flame, the mixture is brought to a frothing simmer. The moment before it is about to boil over, the pot is removed from the heat and the prized foam at the top is distributed among the cups. (Getting the foam perfect is a rite of passage for each generation of coffee makers.) To finish, the coffee is brought back to a simmer once or twice more and then poured. After the thick silt of coffee particles settles to the bottom of each cup, the remaining liquid can be surprisingly mild and pleasantly sweet—not at all muddy and harsh as most people expect. But many an inexperienced drinker of Turkish coffee who downs a cupful is surprised by the nasty silt in the bottom. It must be sipped carefully and never to the last drop. This *cezve* holds 6 demitasse cups.

19.20   TURKISH COFFEE GRINDER

It looks like a particularly treasured and elegant pepper mill, and it operates on the same principle. This 9½"-tall brass mill has incised abstract decoration (Islam traditionally forbids representations of living things) and is made up of four different parts. To grind coffee, remove the handle and little domed lid, put the beans in the upper section, and replace the dome and handle. As you grind, powdery fine coffee drops into the bottom section. A screw at the base of the upper section can be turned to control the fineness of the grind.

19.21   BEDOUIN COFFEEPOT

Bedouin coffee is a heady, aromatic brew that actually tastes as good as it smells. Nomads, of necessity, have few material possessions; but pride of place is given to coffee-making equipment. The preparation, serving, and drinking of coffee is a serious business. Green coffee beans are roasted to a velvety chocolate brown, cooled in a special container, and then pulverized in a mortar. Coffee and water are boiled briefly; the grounds are allowed to settle, and the finished brew—sometimes spiced with cardamom—is poured into a gleaming serving pot, like the one shown here. The handmade brass pot is lined with tin, and has an insulating handle-cover of woven simulated-leather strips. Rows of stamped designs encircle the body and lid. The pot is 8½" high and holds 1½ cups. The spout is 3" long, giving the server more control when pouring.

"Is that decaf?"

TURKISH COFFEE ICE CREAM

1½ quarts

I love the ritual of making Turkish coffee. So much so that I let the coffee boil up an odd number of times—three, five, or seven, as tradition demands. There is less mystery involved in making the ice cream, but it has all the taste of a good rich cup of Turkish coffee. The only drawback is that after eating it, there are no coffee grounds to tell your fortune.

7 cups heavy cream	9 large egg yolks
2½ cups espresso coffee beans	1 tablespoon rosewater
1 cup sugar	½ teaspoon ground cardamom

1 Heat the cream to boiling in a large saucepan. Remove from the heat and stir in the coffee beans. Let steep 2 to 2½ hours. Strain the cream into another saucepan, add ½ cup sugar, and reheat to boiling, stirring to dissolve the sugar.

2 Lightly whisk the egg yolks and the remaining ½ cup sugar until blended. Whisk in about 1 cup of the hot cream mixture, then whisk into the remaining cream mixture. Cook over medium heat, stirring constantly, until thick enough to coat the back of a spoon, 3 to 5 minutes. Do not boil.

3 Strain the custard into a mixing bowl and place immediately in a larger bowl filled with ice water. Stir in the rosewater and cardamom. Chill the custard well. Freeze in an ice cream maker according to the manufacturer's instructions.

The Mediterranean Kitchen, by Joyce Goldstein

ESPRESSO MAKERS

IN ITALY, A TINY CUP OF ESPRESSO is not merely a beverage—it is an elixir. Dark and intense, harmonious and stimulating, a single gulp of espresso is a delicious restorative that Italians stop for almost religiously. Each day they make a trip to the altar of their local *caffè*, where the *barista*—high priest of the espresso machine—brings the bittersweet miracle of espresso to bear with cup after cup of the rich brew. If properly blessed, each serving will be crowned with *crema*, fine burnished amber foam that floats on top and adds a smoothness and creaminess to the drink. Producing *crema* is a combination of using the proper machinery and the right grind of freshly roasted coffee (note: you'll never get *crema* with stale coffee), and possessing the skill and intuition to know exactly how to fill the filter and tamp the grinds. When present, the ethereal *crema* signifies that the *barista* knows the precise ritual of espresso-making.

Though espresso came to its glory in Italy, it now has a worldwide fan club. The hissing and grinding of high-performance espresso machines in bustling cafés are sounds heard round the globe. Coffee drinkers have developed a thirst not just for espresso, but for its progeny: *caffè macchiato*, cappuccino, and *caffè latte*. Because so many have been smitten with the flavor of these beverages, home espresso machines are hot items. There is an enormous range in price, quality, and performance, so you'll want to consider the choices carefully.

There are basically three types of espresso machines, distinguished by the mechanism they use to force hot water rapidly through the coffee grounds: steam pressure, a manual piston, or an electric pump. Most machines hold enough water to make at least four demitasse-size cups, plus extra for steaming milk, but some models can make close to fifty little cups. The machines heat the water in 2 to 3 minutes, during which time you can measure the coffee into the filter holder—a removable part that looks something like a flat-bottomed ice-cream scoop. Generally coffee for espresso should be ground very fine, but not to a powder.

Steam espresso machines can make up to four 2- to 3-ounce cups at once, while piston and pump machines usually make 1 or 2 cups at a time—but they're ready to make the next batch almost immediately. With a steam machine, the user can flip a switch and then walk away if not frothing milk; the espresso automatically streams into a glass carafe just like regular electric drip coffee-makers. Piston and pump machines are more complicated. First you must tamp, meaning pack, the coffee evenly and firmly into the filter holder to prevent the pressurized water from rushing through any loose spots. Then it's necessary to watch as the brew dispenses into the waiting cups so you can manually stop the flow of espresso when finished; these machines can't stop themselves.

If the selection of a model is overwhelming, keep in mind that it needs to accomplish just two tasks—make hot, flavorful espresso and froth milk for cappuccino and *latte*. That's why we recommend either a piston or a pump machine. Steam machines are not equipped with a strong pump to create the driving pressure that forces water rapidly through coffee, producing a true espresso. Instead, they use steam pressure, which fails to extract all the flavor and texture from the beans. The result is an espresso with little or no *crema*—one that's probably more like the brew from a moka pot than that from a serious espresso machine.

When deciding between a piston or pump espresso machine, you must first consider whether you enjoy interacting with the machine or whether you prefer a machine that performs some or all of the tasks automatically. Check out the capacity of the water tank. If you'll be making an occasional cup of coffee for your own pleasure, choose a machine with a small capacity, but if you and your family drink multiple cups in a day or you entertain often, look for a larger tank. Also determine whether it can produce enough pressure to make *crema*. Typically a machine needs between nine and eleven bars of pressure, but a good espresso maker should have more power than it needs. Therefore we recommend that you look for a machine with eleven to eighteen bars of pressure. In addition to brewing espresso, the machine should be able to produce steam for frothing milk and should reheat quickly. The higher the wattage of the machine, the faster it will recover. Also, see if the filter holder is solid and heavy; judge whether the machine and steaming device are easy to clean; finally, find out what kind of maintenance it requires.

MOKA EXPRESS STOVETOPS

Before you head off into the arena of espresso machines, consider the option of a coffee-making method that's been in Italian households for more than half a century. It is called the moka express, so named in the 1930s by its first large-scale manufacturer, Bialetti. A simple stovetop brewer, the moka is made of upper and lower faceted metal chambers joined by a cinched band where the metal coffee filter goes. It works by the forces of steam pressure and gravity: water boils in the closed lower chamber with enough headroom to allow a cloud of steam to collect. The pressure from the steam forces hot water out of the chamber and through the medium-fine coffee grounds, where it drips into the upper, handled chamber. The resulting beverage essentially tastes like drip coffee, but one with some of the texture and emulsion that give espresso its characteristic mouth feel and flavor. This brew can't compare with espresso from a high-powered pump machine, and it's almost never crowned by *crema,* but many fans, including Italians, say it's just fine for mixing with steamed milk to make *lattès.* Stovetop mokas are also convenient to use, easy to clean, and take up little space.

There is a coffee-drinking community that swears by the classic moka models, made of aluminum. Over time the aluminum absorbs the coffee's oils and aroma and imparts a distinctive taste to the coffee. Always thoroughly dry the interior of the espresso maker to avoid pitting due to buildup of mineral deposits from the water. Stainless steel versions are increasingly available, but they often come in smaller sizes—1- to 9-cup capacities whereas the classic can come as large as 18-cup capacity.

19.22 BIALETTI MOKA EXPRESS 3-CUP COFFEEMAKER

This is the original Italian aluminum stovetop espresso maker. It makes three cups, but keep in mind that the cup size indicates little more than a 2-ounce swallow of espresso. Other sizes include 1-, 2-, 6-, 9-, 12-, and 18-cups. Aluminum pots can darken and become pitted if not thoroughly rinsed and dried after every use, so if you use the moka express, take proper care of it.

PISTON MACHINES

Though espresso first became popular around the turn of the twentieth century, it was virtually reinvented in 1948, when Giovanni Achille Gaggia mounted a spring-powered piston over the filter holder of an espresso machine. This manually operated apparatus created a mechanical source of pressure that could push hot water through the coffee at more than 100 pounds per square inch. Moreover, it made it possible to use water that was heated to 192°F to 198°F—the ideal temperature for extraction—rather than the boiled water of existing steam machines. The result of Gaggia's invention was a sweeter, more intense cup of coffee than the steam models could make—and a revolution in espresso machine technology.

Today's piston-powered home machine is a reproduction of vintage technology. Though impressive in appearance, the system is notoriously difficult to operate. Success depends on when, how hard, and how fast the user raises and depresses the pull lever. The perfect grind size is also crucial; use only a fine but not powdery grind of coffee from a high-quality burr grinder, or preground espresso. Then prepare yourself for a challenge.

If you're a hands-on person in the truest sense of the word, this is the machine for you. It uses electricity to heat the water and build up pressure, but by pressing down on the lever, you provide the actual force that pushes the water through the ground coffee. If you put in the armwork to figure just how hard you have to press down, and use the proper grind of coffee (neither too fine nor too coarse) you will be rewarded with a fine cup of espresso burnished with *crema*. It comes with two attachments for turning it into cappuccino: a standard arm that froths milk in a cup, and an automatic attachment that dispenses frothed milk into a container. Made of chrome, it measures 11″ by 7″ and stands 12″ high. Along with your machine you get 1- and 2-cup filters, a tamper, a measuring spoon, and an instructional video.

A SCIENTIST'S FORMULA
FOR PERFECT ESPRESSO

❧ DR. ERNESTO ILLY ❧

Illycaffè is considered by many experts to be the world's leading brand of espresso, and Dr. Ernesto Illy, the leading scientific authority on the subject. He built a multimillion-dollar laboratory in which he and a group of fellow chemists study the procedures that produce a perfect cup of espresso. Here are his suggestions:

You can buy your espresso coffee in the form of ground coffee or whole bean. If the coffee is vacuum-packed, you can buy it ground and it will be perfect. If it's not vacuum-packed, you are better off buying the whole bean and grinding it yourself. Just make sure you grind it very fine.

Start with 7 grams of carefully roasted and ground Arabica coffee. Each grain should be no smaller than one micron but no larger than one millimeter. Thirty cubic centimeters of water at 90°C should pass through the grinds at 9 atmospheres of pressure. This passage should take place during a 25-second period.

It is disgusting to note the increase in the quantity of coffee used by my subjects and the amount of money that goes out of the country in consequence. Everybody is using coffee. If possible this must be prevented. My people must drink beer. His Majesty was brought up on beer, and so were his officers. Many battles have been fought and won by soldiers nourished on beer; and the King does not believe the coffee-drinking soldiers can be depended upon to endure hardships or to beat his enemies in case of the occurrence of another war.

—FREDERICK THE GREAT (1777)

ELECTRIC PUMP MACHINES

Now we come to the darling in the category of home espresso makers, electric pump machines. Italian engineering wizard Ernesto Valento is credited with introducing the first successful prototype in 1961. This new kid on the *strada* featured an electric pump to force water through coffee rather than Gaggia's manually operated spring piston. The pump pushed tap water through a copper spiral pipe fixed inside a boiler full of hot water. This quickly heated the water, and with continued pressure from the pump, the water was forced rapidly through ground coffee into a waiting cup.

The same system of boiler/pump mechanics is now the most popular design in modern home espresso machines—and for good reason. The espresso and steamed milk that these pumps produce rival the best coffee bar versions. And because many have large water reservoirs, pump systems let you make cup after cup without having to wait. Though each model has its own idiosyncrasies, pump machines are generally easy to use (providing you've first been tutored by a salesperson, instruction manual, or video). With a little practice, almost anyone can make very good espresso and cappuccino. For the mechanically disadvantaged, some newer models offer simplified procedures, such as prepacked pods or capsules of espresso so there's no need to measure and tamp—and clean-up is merely a rinse—and devices that fit over the steaming wand to make frothing more successful.

When shopping, look for heavy, solid equipment; an adjustable steam wand rather than one fixed in position, so it can accommodate pitchers of varying sizes; and preferably a large-capacity, removable water reservoir for convenience in filling and continuous brewing.

19.24 STARBUCKS BARISTA

Whether or not you're a fan of the coffee from Starbucks, we guarantee you'll be satisfied with the *crema*-topped cup of espresso delivered by this pump-driven machine. It's our top choice for those of you who enjoy the acts of filling, tamping, and timing but want the machine to exert the pressure. To operate, you press large buttons that clearly indicate with green and red lights whether they are on or off. The tank can be

---

STEAMING WANDS

As any good witch will tell you, a wand is only as powerful as the force behind it. The same is true of steaming wands on home espresso machines. All models have wands—a projecting tube fixed to the machine—but they don't all have the power to make steamy, foamed milk. This is especially true of inexpensive steam-powered systems. The ability to froth and foam depends on the capacity of the machine's water boiler—not the wand. All the wand does is deliver steam from the boiler to the cup, so the bigger the boiler, the stronger and longer-lived will be the foaming steam. Heating the milk will also be easier if the steaming wand is movable, allowing you to position the pitcher where it will get the most steaming.

If frothing milk is more important to you than the quality of your coffee, you can look for a machine that comes with a "sleeve" or similar device for making foaming easier. It fits over the wand and draws air into the milk while the wand ejects steam. Without this accessory, the user must be careful to keep the nozzle of the wand just under the surface of the liquid, so it can emit steam and mix air into the milk. If buried, you simply get steamed milk—no foam. If raised too high, you get bubbly froth—not velvety foam—and milk that is warm but not hot and steamy.

Many machines come with automatic frothing attachments. Some have internal compartments that can be filled with milk, and others come with hoses that connect from a container of milk on the counter to the machine. The milk is heated and frothed inside the machine and then dispensed into a cup or pitcher. The automatic attachments emit a continuous flow of frothy milk and require little expertise, but have more parts to clean than traditional wands.

removed so you can fill it at the sink. As it holds a generous 96 ounces, enough for forty-eight 2-ounce shots, the Barista is clearly designed for frequent use. You'll need to clear a moderate amount of counterspace for it; it measures 9" wide, 12" deep, and 12" high. In addition to 1- and 2-cup filters, there's one that can accommodate preportioned, pretamped pods of ground coffee that you can purchase at Starbucks or from other manufacturers. The steam arm rotates to accommodate various size pitchers. A how-to video is included that compensates for the lack of clarity in the owner's manual.

19.25 CAPRESSO FULLY AUTOMATIC COFFEE & ESPRESSO CENTER

The ultimate machine if you're fussy about the quality of your espresso but don't like the fuss involved in making it. Before you use it for the first time, you'll have to sit down and carefully read the operating instructions (plan on spending a good hour doing so), but once you've mastered them, there's not much work other than pouring in coffee beans and placing cups beneath the spout. This behemoth of a machine (11" wide, 14½" deep, and 14" high) grinds, tamps, and then dispenses perfect espresso, and also cleans itself up afterward. For complete customization to your personal preferences, it allows you to choose the fineness

---

> # MAKING CAPPUCCINO
>
> The recipe for a classic cup of cappuccino consists of a single shot of espresso (about 1½ ounces) topped with equal amounts of steamed milk and frothed milk—ideally about ¼ cup each, though Americans generally prefer more milk.
>
> Getting the right combination of steamy milk and dense, fine foam is usually the most challenging part of the formula, since frothing requires more finesse than brewing. For best results, start with very cold milk in a cold container—stainless steel is most common, but ceramic can work too. Ideally, its opening should be narrower than its base, to prevent milk from spraying out. The size of your container depends on the number of servings you want; keep in mind that during steaming, the milk will at least double in volume. Low-fat and skim milk foam more readily than whole milk.
>
> When your machine indicates that it's ready to steam, place the wand nozzle into the milk just below the surface; open the valve gradually, and gently move the container in a slow, circular path, creating small even bubbles rather than big ones. After 20 to 30 seconds, depending on volume, there should be a nice head of foam on top of steamed milk. Use a large spoon to trap the foam while the hot milk pours out over the espresso, then spread the foam on top. A convex 6-ounce cup or mug is just right for a cappuccino of standard proportions.
>
> Always steam the milk first, then make the espresso so the coffee is hot when you add the froth.

and amount of ground coffee and the quantity of water—you can "order" anything from a ½-ounce of intensely flavored *ristretto* (a short espresso) to a mellow 8 ounces of coffee. The spout glides easily up and down (sorry, you have to do this yourself) to accommodate tiny espresso cups or large mugs. The water tank, which lifts out to be filled at the sink, holds 64 ounces, and the burr grinder accommodates 10 ounces of beans. These large capacities, combined with complete automation, allow you to serve espresso efficiently to a large party. Used grounds are automatically transferred to a container inside the machine. On the side there's a frothing attachment and you do have to hold the cup under the nozzle yourself. Program the machine to shut itself off between 2 and 5 hours after it's turned on. When the used coffee container is full (after about 10 to 16 servings) or there's not enough water in the tank, lights will alert you to attend to them, and the machine won't operate until you do. When the machine is turned both on and off, it will rinse itself automatically. If for some reason you prefer it, you can use pre-ground coffee instead of letting the machine do the grinding. You can either adjust the machine to the level of water hardness in your area or install the filter that comes with the machine—it reduces water hardness as well as removing chlorine, and eliminates the need to decalcify.

19.26 THE NESPRESSO SYSTEM

It never fails to amaze us that even though it uses prepacked coffee, this easy-to-use machine delivers a delicious cup of *crema*-topped espresso. To operate it, you fill the removable 1¼-quart water tank and heat the water by activating a switch as you would with any manually operated machine; but instead of filling the filter with grounds, you pop in a small aluminum capsule of coffee. Once you put the filter in place, the machine punctures the capsule and then forces water through it. It's up to you to determine the length of brewing time and consequent amount of espresso in the cup, so perhaps it takes a tiny bit of technique after all. After brewing, it's easy to knock out the capsule and quickly insert another for a second cup. And yes, it does have a frothing nozzle, another hands-on feature that may take some practice to perfect. With your machine you receive a set of two demitasse cups and an assortment of forty capsules. Nine blends of coffee, including two decaffeinated selections, are available. Worried about buying more capsules? You can order them by mail, phone, fax, or Internet 24 hours a day, 7 days a week, and delivery is guaranteed within 2 business days. The approximate cost is 45¢ per serving. The housing is black plastic with stainless steel accents and measures 8″ wide, 11″ deep, and 11″ high.

COFFEE & ESPRESSO ACCESSORIES

19.27 ILSA STAINLESS STEEL MILK JUG

This jug holds 2¼ full cups of milk, enough for four to six cappuccinos, depending on the size of your cup and the frothing ability of your machine. Because the opening is narrower than the base, the milk can swirl and aerate in the pitcher without spraying out the top. A metal jug is better to use than a ceramic one because you can actually feel the milk getting hot. The Ilsa jug is also available in a 9-ounce (3-cup), 27-ounce (9-cup), or 36-ounce (12-cup) size.

19.28 PROGRESSIVE INTERNATIONAL PROFESSIONAL COFFEE TAMPER

Tamping is an important step in making good espresso because it ensures even extraction of the coffee grinds when water passes through the filter. A good tamper should be made of a light metal, and the diameter of the tamper should fit snugly into the filter holder of your espresso machine. This aluminum tamper from Progressive International has a different-size tamper on each end. To use, grip the tamper with your palm flat against the base of the handle and your fingers wrapped around the cylindrical middle. With a straight arm, gently press down on the coffee to form the "pellet." Release and tap the handle of the filter to remove any grounds stuck to the side of the filter. With added pressure, press once again on the pellet with the tamper, then turn it at least 360° to smooth the surface.

19.29 BONJOUR CAFFE FROTH TURBO

If you don't have an espresso machine equipped with a steaming wand, this battery-operated mini

When we drink coffee, ideas march in like the army.
—HONORÉ DE BALZAC

blender is the best alternative we've found for frothing milk. You place the frothing disc just under the surface of your milk, press a button on the top of the handle, and in seconds you'll triple the volume of the milk. If you use a microwave-safe pitcher, you can zap the milk briefly to heat it up first—when warmed, the froth turns into a stiff foam. You'll need to purchase four AA batteries. When not in operation, slip the plastic sheath over the rod to keep it clean.

19.30 ROYAL ENTERPRISES INC. CLEANCAF

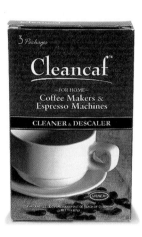

When your coffeemaker is taking an excessively long time to brew, it's most likely the result of scale buildup inside the machine. While you can run white vinegar through the machine to remove mineral deposits, we like to use a dissolved packet of Cleancaf instead. At the same time that it descales, this commercial product will rid the machine of those brown stains, caused by oils from the coffee, that not only look unsightly but can affect the taste of the brew. After Cleancaf's been used in the machine it requires several rinses of water. As Cleancaf is tinted blue and bubbles up, it's easy to see when it hasn't been thoroughly rinsed out—just swirl some water in your coffeemaker again.

19.31 THERMOS NISSAN VACUUM CARAFE

Slim and elegant, this 1-quart insulated carafe will keep coffee hot enough to serve for a whopping 24 hours! (Not that we suggest that you keep it hot *that* long. You're bound to notice a deterioration in flavor.) All metal with a plastic handle and lid, it's virtually unbreakable. To pour, you merely need to twist the lid to the open position without removing the stopper.

19.32 BODUM BISTRO VACUUM JUG

With a clean modern design executed in plastic and the ability to keep beverages at an acceptable serving temperature for more than 6 hours, this is a good choice for holding coffee hot if you like to refill your cup throughout the day. You turn the lid to the open position for pouring—

no need to remove it and expose the entire pot to air and/or risk misplacing it. Its bulky appearance belies the fact that it only holds slightly less than one quart. One more negative: The liner is made of glass so it does have to be handled with care.

19.33 THERMOS NISSAN VACUUM-INSULATED TRAVEL TUMBLER

When you're traveling, depend on this stainless steel mug to keep your coffee steaming for a full hour. Although it's not leakproof, it has features designed to minimize spills: the plastic cover dips lower than the rim to allow some headroom for splashes; a mini lid flips up when you're sipping and snaps down when you're not; and a textured rubber grip helps you keep a tight hold. The tumbler will fit in any car drink holder that can accommodate a can of soda. Filled to capacity, it holds 14 ounces.

19.34 TAYLOR CAPPUCCINO FROTHING THERMOMETER

The folks at Starbucks clued us in to the fact that between 140°F and 160°F is the ideal temperature range for frothing milk to top a cappuccino.

A lower temperature produces a soft cloud rather than a foam, a higher one, milk with a scalded taste. Specifically designed for frothing, this thermometer only measures between 120°F and 180°F, and the desired range is colored in yellow so it's easy to identify. Use the adjustable clip on the stem to attach the thermometer to a frothing pitcher.

19.35 BRAUN GOLD SCREEN COFFEE FILTER

If you prefer using a permanent metal filter instead of disposible paper ones, this filter made by Braun fits all coffeemakers that use a #4 filter. It has a plastic handle and indentations for easy removal from the filter basket.

SOUR CREAM COFFEE CAKE

Makes 1 9" cake; 10 to 12 servings

Coffeehouses were popular in the colonies before they caught on in Europe. In the City Tavern Coffee Room, cakes were served as an accompaniment to what was a relatively newfangled drink, coffee.

CRUMB TOPPING
½ cup granulated sugar
½ cup chopped walnuts
2 tablespoons all-purpose flour
2 tablespoons unsalted butter, melted
1 teaspoon ground cinnamon

CAKE
1 cup granulated sugar
¼ pound (1 stick) unsalted butter
2 cups all-purpose flour, sifted
1½ teaspoons baking powder
½ teaspoon baking soda
½ teaspoon salt
2 large eggs
1 teaspoon vanilla extract
8 ounces (1 cup) sour cream

1 Preheat the oven to 350°F. Lightly coat one 9 by 2½" round cake pan with vegetable cooking spray and dust lightly with flour.
2 PREPARE THE CRUMB TOPPING In a small bowl, combine the ½ cup sugar, nuts, 2 tablespoons flour, 2 tablespoons melted butter, and cinnamon. Set aside.
3 PREPARE THE CAKE In the bowl of an electric mixer, cream the 1 cup sugar and the ¼ pound butter on medium until light and fluffy, scraping side of bowl often.
4 In a separate bowl, sift together the 2 cups flour, baking powder, baking soda, and salt.

5 Add the eggs and vanilla slowly and beat well, scraping down the side of the bowl often.
6 With the electric mixer on low, slowly add the dry ingredients, alternating with the sour cream.
7 Pour the batter into the prepared pan. Sprinkle the crumb topping on the top of the batter. Bake for 45 to 50 minutes, until golden brown and a toothpick inserted in the center comes out clean.
8 Cool cake in pan on wire rack for 10 minutes. Remove from pan. Cut into slices and serve.

City Tavern Cookbook, by Walter Staib

TEA

ACCORDING TO CHINESE LEGEND, tea was discovered more than five thousand years ago by Emperor Shen Nung, who insisted upon drinking only boiled water because he felt it was healthier. When leaves from a tea plant fell into his pot of water, he drank the infusion, enjoyed it, and initiated the practice of drinking tea in China. But it took more than three thousand years for it to become popular throughout the Chinese Empire. And although the Dutch introduced tea to Europe and America in the seventeenth century, it wasn't until two hundred years later that large quantities of tea were imported from China to both London and New York.

The most common kinds of tea are green, oolong, and black which all come from the same plant. What differentiates them is the degree of processing that the leaves undergo. Green tea is the least processed—it's minimally oxidized, rolled, and dried. Black tea is the most processed. The leaves that become black tea are rolled and then oxidized by being exposed to the air while fermenting before they're dried. Oolong, which tastes somewhere between black and green tea, is semi-fermented. The majority of tea consumed in the world is black tea. The greater the degree of processing or fermentation the hotter the water and the longer the steeping time necessary for extraction.

MAKING THE PERFECT POT OF TEA

❦ MIRIAM NOVALLE ❦

There are short answers and long answers—even entire books—on how to brew the perfect pot of tea. Here is a short answer, based on techniques we use at the T Salon.

The number one component of great tea is cold filtered water. It will give you a fine, pure cup of tea, the essence of which is not tainted by too much calcium, iron, or the other minerals present in tap water. The teapot you use depends upon the type of tea you're brewing: green tea likes a cast-iron pot that retains its heat; traditional black teas, such as Assam, Darjeeling, and Salaam, like small unglazed Yixing clay pots, porcelain pots, or glazed terra-cotta pots. Glass teapots, resistant to residual odors or flavors, are the most versatile, suitable for use with a variety of teas and with flavored teas.

To brew the tea, you can put the tea leaves directly in the pot where they can totally unfurl, then use a strainer over the cup to catch the leaves as you pour. Or you can use an infuser—a wire-mesh ball, an infusion basket, or a natural fiber bag—to hold the tea leaves in the pot. The infuser must be large enough not to cramp the swelling of the leaves; when you add the dried leaves they should fill half the infuser at most, since they easily swell to twice their size.

Fill the pot with hot filtered water and let it sit until you're ready to brew the tea. Bring the filtered water to a gentle boil, then remove it immediately from the heat. Drain the teapot and add the tea—one level teaspoon per cup in most cases, a little more if the tea leaves are large or include flowers. Most black teas brew best in water that's about 200°F, but 195°F is pre-

ferred for oolong, and 180°F for jasmine. Green teas brew best in somewhat cooler water, from 125°F for Japanese Gyokuro, 125°F to 175°F for Sencha, up to 200°F for Bancha. Steep black teas for 3 to 5 minutes, green teas from 2 (Sencha) to 4 (Chinese green tea) minutes. Remove the infuser or strain the tea as soon as the proper steeping time is reached so that the tannin in the leaves doesn't make the tea too bitter.

Once your tea is perfectly brewed, enjoy it straight and unadulterated. If you must, you could add a little warm milk to your Darjeeling or Assam. But never, ever add lemon or sugar to your tea. These are bad old habits. You wouldn't add lemon juice or sugar to a fine wine. Why should you change the flavor of a beautiful, freshly brewed gourmet tea?

TEAKETTLES

AS IT IS USUALLY KEPT in view on the rangetop, your choice of teakettle will most likely depend on your own individual sense of style. However, as it's also an item that will be used frequently, we encourage you to pick up and handle a kettle before you make a purchase. Remember, if it feels heavy empty, it will seem even more so when it's filled. Make sure the handle is comfortable even when you lift it high, as if you were pouring out the very last drops of water. Generally we find that when the handle is placed slightly back from the center, or is on the side of the pot, it is easier to grasp. However, a side handle should not be attached so low that it risks coming into contact with the heat source. You should also make sure that the handle is not made of a material that will heat up during use.

To ensure that a kettle is not allowed to boil dry, we recommend ones with a whistle. However, they often have a lid with a whistle hole over the spout, requiring you to either flip up or remove the lid before pouring. Our top choices allow the whistle to come through without making it necessary for you to fiddle with the spout and risk coming in contact with escaping steam. If for aesthetic reasons you prefer a kettle that has a lid on the spout, check out how easy it is to open or take off the spout lid. Many designs have triggers or other mechanisms in the handle that you activate to pull open the spout. Kettle lids should be easy to remove for filling and cleaning yet stay in place when you're pouring. The opening should be large enough to allow you to clean inside.

"Darjeeling, Earl Grey, blackberry, sassafras, chamomile, rose hip, cranberry, orange pekoe, spicy cinnamon, peppermint, licorice, strawberry patch, sesame, mint, Chinese, or carob?"

19.36 COPCO ULTIMO ARIA 2000 TEAKETTLE

You'd never guess that this cheery yellow enameled steel number represents the state of the art in stovetop kettles. By ingeniously putting the whistle in the lid, the Copco design team has solved the problem of how to open the spout without risking a steam burn. The soft-to-the-touch handle is not only exceptionally comfortable to hold, but stays completely cool to the touch. Thanks to the pointy plastic spout you can pour without spilling a drop. And that's not all—in under 7 minutes this 2½-

quart kettle is one of the quickest we tested at bringing water to a boil. For a subtler statement, you can choose a black or white finish.

19.37 OXO GOOD GRIPS UPLIFT TEAKETTLE

While not speedy (it takes about 9 minutes to boil a full pot of water at high heat), this handsome 2-quart stainless steel model has a big advantage over many other whistlers in that the spout opens automatically when you lift the handle of the kettle. It has a Santoprene handle that is comfortable to hold, won't slip from your grasp, and, best of all, stays cool enough to lift without a pot holder. The loud harmonic whistle is hard to ignore. Other colors include white, black, cream, orange, red, blue, and yellow.

19.38 SIMPLEX TEAKETTLE

This English kettle, crafted of tin-lined copper, has a chrome exterior,

CARDAMOM TEA (*ILAICHI CHAH*)

This tea is mellower than *masala* tea. It is flavored only with pods of green cardamom, which lend a tasty sweetness.

8 6-ounce servings

6 cups cold water
12 green cardamom pods
6 heaping teaspoons leaf tea, or 9 tea bags (orange pekoe)
1 piece of lemon, lime, or orange peel (1" by ½")
scalded milk and sugar, to be served on the side

1 Combine water and cardamom pods in a deep saucepan, and bring to a boil. Reduce heat and simmer, covered, for 5 minutes. Turn off heat, and let soak, covered, for 10 minutes.
2 While the cardamom is soaking, rinse the teapot with boiling water. Add the tea leaves or bags and the peel to the pot.
3 Bring the cardamom water to a full boil, and pour it, pods and all, into the teapot. Let the tea brew for 2 to 3 minutes before serving. Pass the scalded milk and sugar on the side.

This is the way Indians enjoy cardamom tea. You may, if you wish, omit the milk and sugar altogether, in which case reduce the tea to 2 heaping teaspoons or 3 tea bags, or else the brewed tea will be too strong and bitter.

Classic Indian Cooking, by Julie Sahni

so you get superb heat conductivity without a cleaning nightmare. While an all-copper version is available, trust us, you don't want it. This is an item you'll be keeping on top of the stove and using often, and you'll find maintaining the copper in a pristine state next to impossible. Choose from two designs: one has a solid bottom and the other a coiled copper wire in the base. The wire version, designed exclusively for use on a gas burner, brings water to a boil about two-thirds faster than the flat-bottomed one. Be careful not to boil the kettle dry or place it off center on the burner to simmer since you'll risk damaging the coils. The spout narrows at the opening, allowing a whistle to come through. With its wooden handle and its traditional shape, this kettle is a classic beauty.

GRADES OF TEA

Whole leaf Also called orange pekoe and pekoe, this is the best tea to use for brewing. Pekoe has nothing to do with flavor, but refers to the size of the tea leaves. Orange pekoe is made from the smallest and youngest leaves. Pekoe is made from slightly larger young leaves.
Broken leaf A smaller grade, it's also called broken pekoe and broken orange pekoe.
Fannings Tiny bits of leaf that are used in cheap blends and teabags.
Dust The lowest grade, used in teabags and instant blends.

ELECTRIC KETTLES

IN GREAT BRITAIN, electric kettles are a household staple, keeping hot water always at the ready. Purists may object to the fact that after the first cup or pot is made, subsequent ones will be made from water that is reboiled and therefore contains less of the oxygen needed for a perfectly made cup of tea. However, for casual tea drinking throughout the day, or to free up the burners on your stove, an electric kettle is a perfectly fine way to boil water. Models are available in both plastic and stainless steel. Needless to say, the metal ones are handsomer, but they're also pricier and, unlike the plastic kettles, do not have indicators telling you exactly how much water remains in the kettle. We can recommend either material, as we have not been able to taste a difference between water boiled in them. You can also choose between corded and cordless kettles. With a cordless model you can remove the kettle from its base and bring it into the dining room for pouring.

Regardless of what they're made of or whether or not they have cords, all electric kettles should turn off automatically when the water comes to a boil and should have a feature to prevent them from boiling dry. Like stovetop kettles, they should not be excessively heavy and should have comfortable handles and lids that are easy to remove for filling and cleaning. Some plastic models have water level indicators with quantities given in liters, not cups. If you aren't comfortable with the metric system, this may be a disadvantage. The higher the wattage, the faster the water is brought to a boil. Look for a kettle that shuts off once the water has boiled and that has a light that indicates when it's in the process of heating. An electric kettle is likely to remain on the countertop to be used whenever some boiling water is needed, for bouillon, soaking dried mushrooms or chiles, or for instant hot cereal, so a place in the base to store excess cord length is a particularly handy feature.

19.39 BRAUN AQUAEXPRESS

From all the moderately priced electric kettles with plastic bodies that we tested, the Braun emerged at the top of the class. The cup markings are clearly readable on see-through water level indicators on both sides of the kettle. On the control, there's a marking to tell you whether it's in the on or off position and there's a light that signals when the kettle is heating up the water. A filter sits behind the spout to prevent mineral deposits from the water that calcify in the kettle from falling into your cup. It takes 7 minutes to boil the full capacity of 1¾ quarts, about the same amount of time on average it takes a stovetop kettle. As we prefer, the kettle detaches from the base, and as we insist, it has an automatic shut-off feature. In the base there's a place to store the excess cord.

19.40 RUSSELL HOBBS CLASSIC SOVEREIGN STAINLESS STEEL CORDLESS KETTLE

Here we have state of the art technology along with traditional teakettle styling. With 1800 watts of power and a proprietary heating system, this kettle is about as fast as any you can find. A full pot, or about 2 quarts, takes just a tad over 6 minutes. There are markings for minimum and maximum water levels, but none for specific cup amounts. A filter for mineral deposits pops in behind the spout; we found it sometimes popped out of place, so if you don't have hard water, you may want to consider not bothering with it. When the water's boiled or there's none remaining in the kettle, it shuts off automatically. The kettle detaches from the base, which has room to wrap any excess cord length. The whole appliance requires 12″ of counterspace, and, of course, it won't take up a burner on the stove.

If this is coffee, then please— bring me some tea. But if this is tea, please bring me some coffee.
—ABRAHAM LINCOLN

TEAPOTS

As it will be used for serving, your choice of a teapot will undoubtedly depend on what looks good to you. However, there are some things to look for that will make it easier to use. Most importantly, the teapot should be easy to pour and not very heavy. The spout should be well defined, so that it won't dribble, and the lid should remain in place even when the pot is held at a 90° angle to pour out the very last drops of liquid. If you prefer using a strainer, look for a pot that comes with either an ample-sized one that will allow the water to circulate freely around the leaves or has an opening in the top that is generous enough to allow you to use your own strainer. A large opening will also make it easy to empty it of used tea leaves.

19.41 UPTON TEA IMPORTS CHATSFORD TEAPOT

Perfect! That sums up our feelings about this British-designed 4-cup earthenware teapot. It pours elegantly and the chubby shape keeps the brew hot. It comes with an easy to remove plastic mesh strainer insert that's quite roomy, so the tea leaves have plenty of room to circulate during steeping. It comes glazed inside and out in white, brown, blue, green, and yellow in 2-, 4-, and 6-cup sizes, and in white and blue in a 10-cup version (in this instance a cup is 6 ounces).

19.42 APRIL CORNELL STACKING TEAPOT

Solitary tea drinkers will take comfort from this attractive ceramic mini pot decorated with pictures of chamomile flowers. The pot steeps enough tea for about one and a half servings of the matching extra-large 12-ounce cup. For storage, the pot sits on top of the cup. Our only complaint: There's a relatively small opening in the teapot, so it can be a little tricky to clean out loose tea leaves—you might want to use a strainer or tea bags.

19.43 JOYCE CHEN JAPANESE *TETSUBIN* (CAST-IRON) HOBNAIL TEAPOT

While this traditional handcast Japanese 24-ounce teapot cries out for green tea, it's such a joy to use that it would be a shame to limit its use to Japanese tea. It's easy to pour from, and the lid won't fall off even when you're pouring out the very last drops of tea. Along with the pot, you get a stainless steel infuser, so you can remove the leaves after

---

A WORD ABOUT TEA PRESSES

A press is a convenient way to separate tea leaves from the liquid after brewing. However, it is not our method of choice precisely because it presses—by pressing the tea leaves you risk extracting the bitter tannins remaining in the leaves after the tea has been brewed. However, if you do favor this method we suggest avoiding those tea presses which require that you slowly add the water to the pot over several minutes, much the way you do when brewing coffee with a manual filter pot. With this type of press, you are violating another principle of tea-making, namely that the water swirl around all of the tea leaves for a set period of time. Any coffee plunger pot can be used for tea as well, but we advise keeping separate pots for tea and coffee to prevent crossover of flavors.

steeping—something you'll want to do especially if you're preparing delicate green teas. As it's made of cast iron, it keeps brewed tea extremely hot but also gets quite hot to the touch itself. Inside, it's lined with porcelain enamel, so the iron won't interact with tea or impart a metallic taste. Be sure to dry the inside and outside of the pot after washing to prevent rusting, especially on the rim, where moisture gets trapped under the lid.

19.44 IMPERIAL TEA YIXING CLAY TEAPOT

As far back as the year A.D. 960, artists have crafted diminutive teapots from the so-called "purple" sand found only in the Jiangsu province of China. Often the reddish purple sand is blended with natural pigments into clays of various colors, most commonly shades of umber, terra cotta, and ochre, so teapots are available in many hues. They also vary in design from round shapes to squares and pyramids, from plain to highly decorated, with Chinese motifs of all kinds including bamboo, tree branches, and dragons. Both inside and out, Yixing teapots are always left unglazed so that the porous clay absorbs the flavor, smell, and color of tea brewed in it and becomes "cured" after repeated use. They impart distinctiveness to subsequent brews, which is maintained by dedicating a single flavor of tea to a specific Yixing teapot. Likewise to preserve the seasoning, pots are never cleaned with soap but merely

In Japan, when tea is served, whether to family or to guests, it is generally the responsibility of one person, usually the woman of the house or her daughter. The grace and attention with which it is performed is impressive. No matter how many people are being served, or how lively and distracting the conversation, as soon as a cup is empty, the server notices and offers to refill it.

—JOHN & JAN BELLEME,
Cooking with Japanese Foods

THE JAPANESE TEA CEREMONY

The traditional tea ceremony, or *cha-no-yu*, is a social ritual rooted in Zen Buddhism, with rules laid down by the great tea masters of the fifteenth and sixteenth centuries. In short, it is the brewing and drinking of tea in the company of friends, while contemplating objects of beauty. Politics and business are never discussed. The heart of the experience is to strive for harmony with nature and self.

The ritual itself is carefully choreographed: once the guests have arrived, the host or hostess—a trained "tea master"—brings in the utensils and arranges them in an artistic pattern around the *furo* (brazier) and *okama* (teakettle). The bamboo teaspoon and tea caddy are ceremoniously wiped by the host with a silk napkin called a *fukusa*. A bamboo dipper, *hishaku*, is used to transfer a small amount of hot water from the iron kettle to the tea bowl, which is then wiped with a *chakin*, a small oblong cloth of pure linen. The public washing of these objects honors the guests.

Using the bamboo tea spoon, the tea master gently transfers a few measures of brilliant green powdered tea, called *matcha* or *hiki-cha*, from the caddy to the tea bowl, lightly tapping the spoon against the bowl's rim after the last spoonful. The tapping not only shakes off any specks of tea but is also the call to contemplate the ritual. The tea master continues by lowering the bamboo dipper into the teakettle, rotating it gracefully as it sinks into the water, and then tips out the water over the tea bowl. The final step: The tea is whipped into a jade froth with a bamboo whisk. The tea bowl is then placed on another silk napkin, where the first guest picks them up. Before and during the slow sips of tea, the guest remarks on the tea's froth, color, taste, and aroma. The ritual is then repeated, and the tea bowl is passed from guest to guest. Formal tea ceremonies can last as many as four hours and are preceded by a special *kaiseki ryori*, or tea ceremony meal. While the tea ceremony utensils are the finest the host can provide, they are never ostentatious; the Zen principles of simplicity, serenity, withdrawal, and contemplation prevail.

---

rinsed with hot water. As they're intended for individual use, the Chinese would carry their own personal teapots and drink directly from the spouts. When you use this 4-ounce pot, you'll notice that in spite of its tiny size, it has all the attributes we feel make a superior teapot.

TEA FILTERS

FILTERS OF ALL TYPES, including balls and infusers, are designed to make it easy to remove tea leaves from brewed tea, thereby preventing overextraction of the tea leaves and residue from floating in your cup. However, we weigh heavily against tea balls because they impede the brewing process and over time the clasps loosen and the rims bend, letting tea escape into your cup. When tea is properly made, the water is free to circulate around the tea leaves; therefore any product in this category should allow for maximum contact between the water and the tea at the same time that it prevents leaves from escaping into the water. We prefer items made of a fine mesh or porous paper; the water can penetrate these thoroughly yet, because of the small openings, they do not allow tea to escape. These gizmos should also be able to hold an ample amount of tea without compacting the leaves and be easy to fill, as well as easy to open and clean.

19.45 SWISS GOLD CUP O' TEA PERMANENT FILTER

This 23-karat-gold-plated filter sits neatly inside a mug or teacup, where it allows water to circulate freely around tea leaves so they can unfurl for maximum infusion. When topped with the plastic lid that comes with the filter, your cup becomes a single-serving teapot. Steep tea to your satisfaction, then remove the filter and place it on the inverted lid to protect the table from dribbles.

> Thank God for tea! What would the world do without tea?—how did it exist? I am glad I was not born before tea.
>
> —SIDNEY SMITH,
> *Lady Holland's Memoir*

19.46 SWISS GOLD POT O' TEA PERMANENT TEA FILTER

If you want to be able to remove tea leaves from a pot before they steep too long, turning your tea bitter, this 23-karat-gold-plated filter is a good option. It's ample enough to allow water to fully infuse the tea and is easy to pull out of the pot. Along with the filter you get a plastic cover to use during steeping in case the lid of your teapot doesn't fit with the filter in place. Invert the lid after brewing and it becomes a small trivet for the filter.

19.47 t-SAC CUP & TEAPOT FILTERS

If you love the convenience of tea bags but prefer to use your own fresh whole tea leaves, make your own tea bags with these unbleached paper filters. Because they're completely porous, they'll expose more of the tea to water than a tea ball. They're easy to fill and they don't leave any leaves behind in the cup. Hang the flap over the side of your cup and it will remain dry, so you can pull the bag out after steeping. Sold in packages of a hundred in four sizes, from a single-cup serving to one that holds enough leaves for a 12-cup teapot. Keep these filters in mind for summer. The larger bags are excellent for making pitchers of iced tea. You could even steep a mixture of black or green tea with an herbal or fruit infusion.

19.48 SAMOVAR

Tea and the samovar were introduced to Russia by the Mongols, the "Golden Horde" who conquered all of southern Russia and held northern Russia at bay for more than two centuries until Ivan the Terrible drove them out. The samovar is an ornate brass urn for preparing and serving tea that has become an integral part of Russian life. From early morning to late evening, at every meal and between meals, Russians gather around the samovar for a cup or glass of hot tea. There is even a verb in Russian meaning "to pass the time in drinking tea." This samovar, although made in Germany, has the authentic Russian shape and decoration. It is 15" tall and 11½" in diameter, made of chrome, stainless steel, and heavy brass decorated with cutout designs at the top. It has two large brass handles with ceramic grips by which the whole samovar may be lifted. Fill the urn with cold water (it will easily hold 3 gallons) then turn on the thermostat. When the water boils, a strong essence of tea is brewed in the stainless teapot; the pot is then placed atop the urn. Cutout designs on the teapot holder permit steam and hot air to escape while warming the teapot. To serve the tea, pour a bit of the strong essence into a cup and dilute it with boiling water drawn from the elegant brass-handled spigot.

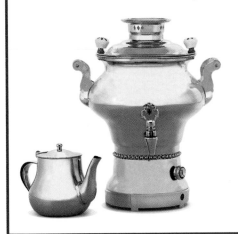

ELECTRIC TEA MAKERS

Ideally, electric steepers, whether designed to make hot or cold tea, should replicate the traditional tea-making method. That is, they should bring water to a boil before releasing it onto the tea and should allow all of the water to circulate around all of the tea. We know of only one that actually boils water and steeps the tea leaves—the Chef'sChoice TeaMate. Virtually all of the other models on the market function more like an automatic drip coffeemaker: they heat water, which then drips through the tea leaves. If convenience is more important to you than the quality of your tea, you may find these machines useful.

19.49 MR. COFFEE THE ICED TEA POT

Right up front we have to say that this product is not for tea purists, and it doesn't fill the requirements for producing a perfect cup of tea. Basically, it's a drip coffee machine that drips hot water through tea into an ice-filled plastic pitcher instead of a carafe. Throughout the dripping process, the temperature of the water is not consistently just below boiling, and all of the tea leaves never have a chance to steep in all of the water. However, having said that, we can report that it makes a decent 2-quart pitcher of iced tea with a minimum of fuss in under ten minutes. You can even throw sugar, lemon, mint, or other seasonings right in with the tea—leaves or bags of your choice—so you don't have to doctor it up before serving. And if you prefer, you can just as easily make iced coffee instead of tea. Because it's a space eater at 11" by 6¼" with a height of 13", we recommend this specialized machine to hard-core iced tea drinkers who aren't overly fussy about the quality of their tea or the appearance of their serving ware. One way to guarantee that the ice in the pitcher does not dilute the tea is to keep a couple of trays of "tea cubes" on hand in the freezer.

19.50 CHEF'S CHOICE INTERNATIONAL TEAMATE ELECTRIC TEA MAKER

As far as we're concerned, if you don't want to take the kind of care that's necessary to make an absolutely perfect cup of tea, and prefer the automation of an electric machine, this is the only one to consider. The TeaMate is not simply a coffeemaker with a teapot instead of a carafe. It works much like a Russian samovar. As water is heated, steam enters the steeping chamber (or filter basket) containing the tea leaves or bags, causing the leaves to swell, so that more of their surface area is exposed, which allows greater release of flavor. When the water is just at the boiling point, a portion of it is released into the steeping chamber, forming a tea concentrate. At the end of the steeping time, which you can program according to your preference at anywhere from 2 to 15 minutes, the concentrate and the remaining near-boiling water are released simultaneously into the carafe. The heating element turns on at the same time that the water begins heating, so the glass carafe is preheated to help keep the tea hot. It brews 2 to 8 cups. In the back of the 8" wide by 7½" deep and 12½" high TeaMate, there's cord storage. A permanent gold filter to hold the tea is included.

19.51 *MATE* GOURD WITH *BOMBILLA*

If any beverage rivals coffee in Latin America it is *yerba mate,* a tealike brew made from the dried leaves of a shrub of the *Ilex,* or holly, genus. Since ancient times, long before the arrival of the white man, South American Indians made a drink from these plants, which grow wild along the banks of the Paraguay River. Today, millions of Argentines, Uruguayans, Chileans, Brazilians, and Paraguayans, of every ethnic background and every walk of life, quaff the caffeine-loaded potion daily and constantly. *Mate,* as it is commonly called, is made by pouring about 2 teaspoons of the crushed leaves—the *yerba*—into a special fist-size gourd cup—the *mate.* The gourd is filled with hot, not boiling, water, and is allowed to steep for a bit, after which the infusion is slowly sipped through a special metal or wooden strawlike tube called a *bombilla.*

The elegant, 4"-high Uruguayan *mate* cup shown here is a classic example of these traditionally hand-decorated utensils. The hollowed-out and dried gourd has a 1¼"-wide opening at one end with a silvery metal rim, embossed with delicate curlicues and gold-tinted flowers. Inside, the gourd still bears rough traces of the dried pulp; outside, the seashell-like, tortoise-colored vegetable is adorned with natural blond markings resembling spokes. Because the gourd does not have a flat bottom, it is designed to be kept cupped in the palm of the hand, and custom dictates that the gourd be passed from person to person as long

as the supply lasts, a ritualistic practice not unlike smoking an Indian peace pipe.

This mate comes with a handy embossed stand. The 8"-long *bombilla's* hollow stem is twisted at the top, producing a decorative, braided effect. And as always, the "straw" comes equipped with a flat, spoon-shaped strainer, perforated with tiny holes, at the bottom end. An oval-shaped, brass-covered mouthpiece is provided at the top end. The strainer, which can be opened for cleaning, sits at the bottom of the *mate* gourd and keeps the crushed leaves from being sipped up the tube. Aficionados collect *bombilla* and *mate* gourd sets, particularly antiques, which are sometimes embellished with pure gold.

"Take some more tea," the March Hare said to Alice, very earnestly.

"I've had nothing yet," Alice replied in an offended tone: "so I can't take more."

"You mean you can't take *less,*" said the Hatter: "it's very easy to take *more* than nothing."

—LEWIS CARROLL,
Alice's Adventures in Wonderland

20

PRESERVING & CANNING DEVICES

WHEN *THE COOKS' CATALOGUE* was first published in 1975, interest in home canning and preserving had been declining. Increasingly, women—who had traditionally done most canning and preserving—were working outside the home, with less time to spend preparing food from scratch. Manufacturers filled the gap, making products available on store shelves that were once only put up in jars at home. Canning became old-fashioned and nostalgic, a waste of time.

Indeed, the reality of home canning in earlier times could be summed up in one word: drudgery. Apron-clad women spent endless hours peeling, slicing, dicing, and chopping raw food with rust-prone carbon steel knives and tin graters in kitchens that often lacked running water, good lighting, and adequate refrigeration. Commercially prepared products were not yet common and cheap, and many households lacked the means to buy enough of them to supplement fresh food during the winter, so home canning, pickling, salting, smoking, and drying were a necessity. However, the old preserving methods yielded foods of dubious, and sometimes deadly, quality.

Today, more women than ever are in the workforce, and they are more hard-pressed to fit food shopping and cooking into busy schedules. New prepared foods are being introduced all the time. Fast-food takeout has become so popular that supermarkets, and even the corner delis in big cities, have expanded their salad bars to include prepared dishes of every kind. Many also offer prepacked heat-and-serve meals and home-catering, and stock their shelves with fancy preserves and other items, such as pickles and tomato sauces, which were once the pride of the home canner.

So why would anyone today spend time and effort canning and preserving food at home? The most important reason is superior flavor and quality. Anyone who has ever tasted homemade strawberry jam can tell you that not even the most expensive commercial version can match it for taste, aroma, and color. The home canner whose main concern is quality, not economy—make no mistake, home canning and preserving today is no money-saver—is able to select the raw materials with care, at peak season. Those who are concerned about pesticides and the environment can put organic produce in the preserving kettle. Putting up food at home also means that there are no hidden ingredients, no unwanted additives and preservatives like those used in commercial products, and no excess sugar, salt, or fat. And, like home bakers who take pride in serving warm, crusty loaves fresh from the oven, today's recreational canners delight in offering homemade preserves and pickles to family and friends. Moreover, new safety guidelines have been set, new equipment has made it quicker and easier to can, preserve, freeze, and dry foods at home, allowing us to transform previously onerous chores into pleasurable leisure activities that enrich our lives and our palates.

CANNING

The Development of Canning

Canning as we know it is a scant two centuries old, although people had learned to store food much earlier. In colonial times, women packed foods into handmade stone and pottery containers and wooden barrels. Old cookbooks recommended methods that we now understand are extremely risky. Not until the early nineteenth century did science enter the picture, preparing the way for commercial canning and improving the safety of home-canned foods. Credit for developing modern canning methods usually goes to two Frenchmen and a tinsmith from Brooklyn, New York. The seeds of canning technology had been planted in the seventeenth century by Otto von Guericke, a German scholar, engineer, and politician, and Denis Papin, a French scholar and physicist. Von Guericke discovered a way to seal canning jars under pressure, and Papin's experiments led to the forerunner of today's pressure canners-cookers.

Speaking of pressure, in 1795 Napoléon Bonaparte offered a prize of twelve thousand gold francs to anyone who could come up with a method for preserving food to feed his increasingly far-flung troops. Nicolas Appert, an obscure Parisian confectioner, began work on a method of vacuum packing. By 1804, Appert had established a factory for vacuum packing foods—boiling foods in glass jars and sealing them with corks and tar—and he finally picked up the prize in 1809. Improvements were soon on the way. In 1810, Peter Durand, an Englishman, invented a tin-plated steel container for vacuum-packed foods; soon the more practical tin cans began replacing jars in factories (but not in homes). Yet the armed forces were still seeking better products. Several decades later, Gail Borden's canned condensed milk, perfected in 1854, sustained Union troops during the Civil War, many years before the product was sold in stores.

But that's getting ahead of the story. Roughly forty years after Nicolas Appert's invention, enter the Brooklyn tinsmith, John Landis Mason. His surname became the generic term for the canning jar he invented: a straight-sided glass container with a shoulder topped by a threaded rim, which permits the user to secure the lid by screwing on a threaded metal ring. All the parts were reusable, and canning became possible at home.

It was long thought that canning kept food from spoiling by eliminating oxygen, but by 1895, American scientists, basing their work on the theories of the French chemist Louis Pasteur, proved that it was actually the destruction of bacteria by heating that preserved the food. It is now known that the vacuum seal created by removing oxygen from the jars protects the sterility of their contents.

As with the development in canning inspired by Napoléon's challenge, the military continues to influence advances in food preservation. Changes in military chow and the rations available for high-endurance exploration have contributed to the trend. In the 1970s and 1980s the U.S. armed forces switched from the much-maligned C rations to MREs—meals ready to eat—which are based on freeze-dried foods. NASA's astronauts have come to include everything from freeze-dried Thanksgiving turkey to chocolate pudding in their zero-gravity repasts.

Canning Equipment

More than fifty cookbooks in print focus on the subjects of home canning, drying, freezing, and preserving, and more are being written each year. Kerr and Ball, America's two major manufacturers of canning jars and supplies, have joined forces under license to Alltrista Corporation, while French, German, and Italian canning jars are competing with the classic mason jar design, the standard in this country for more than a century.

Food processors, slicers, thermometers, and other utensils and appliances have simplified home canning. Multipurpose tools have largely eliminated drudgery from home food preservation, and you will find dozens of them as you read this book. When a recipe tells us to peel, slice, dice, shred, julienne, or purée an ingredient, the tools we reach for include a swivel-blade peeler, a mandoline, a blender, a food processor, a food mill, and a clamp-on hand-cranked fruit and vegetable strainer with attachments to screen out seeds from all sorts of fruits and vegetables. One model is designed to make chunks suitable for salsas, relishes, and chutneys.

Other staples of canning equipment include colanders and wire-mesh strainers, long-handled skimmers (for removing foam from the surface of jams), scales, timers, and large stainless steel spoons and slotted spoons for removing fruit from scalding water before peeling. There are also optional but useful items such as apple parers, apple corers, strawberry hullers, cherry pitters, melon ballers, corn cutters, cabbage cutters, tomato juicer-pulpers, zesters or strippers for citrus peel, and citrus reamers. Other handy utensils for serious canners include jar lifters, lid wands, bubble releasers, canning funnels, and jelly bags with metal stands.

A stoneware pickle crock with a food-safe glaze is handy for summer pickles, and a fine-mesh stainless steel teabag is convenient for whole spices that will be removed from pickles or relishes before they are packed into jars. Pitcher-shaped ovenproof and microwavable glass measures are indispensable, as are sets of dry measures and measuring spoons. A 2-quart glass measure is useful for precooking small quantities of berries or other fruit for jam in a microwave oven before adding sugar and finishing them in a flameproof pot on the stovetop. A Baumé hydrometer can tell you when you've added just enough sugar to fruit juice to make it gel properly, and a candy and deep-fry thermometer will indicate to you when the gelling point has been reached.

For making fruit butters, it's a good idea to use a slow-cooker in order to avoid the volcanic eruptions that occur when these thick mixtures are cooked in a saucepan on a rangetop. The butters can be slow-cooked from start to finish, or the mixture may be preheated in a microwave oven, then transferred to a slow-cooker for unattended final cooking. You can also microwave fruit for jam, jelly, preserves, and marmalades with no added pectin; the speed of the cooking process helps retain color and flavor, and the fruit can then be mixed with sugar and finished in a saucepan or wok on the rangetop.

Those interested in preserving food at home do need some specialized equipment. The list consists mostly of products that make canning safer and sometimes, easier. The essentials include a traditional porcelain-enameled steel preserving kettle that can double as a water-bath canner. If you make jams, jellies, preserves, and marmalades infrequently or have limited storage space, a pasta pot or stockpot with a secure lid makes a good substitute for a traditional water-bath canner

and, without the lid, for a preserving kettle. Choose a pot whose capacity is at least three or four times the volume of the largest mixture you will cook in it, to allow for expansion of the ingredients as they boil. A stainless steel replacement jar rack for the traditional canning kettle has an extra wire in the bottom to hold 4-ounce jelly jars, but a round cake rack set in the bottom of the pot can substitute for a canning rack. A traditional 14-quart unlined copper French preserving kettle is still advertised in some housewares catalogues, although it is not recommended by the U.S. Department of Agriculture (USDA) or Cooperative Extension agents for any type of home food preparation because the metal can affect some foods adversely. Is this an overreaction? For the small amounts of preserving and jam-making that some cooks delight in today, perhaps.

An alternative to the stovetop kettle/water-bath canner is a thermostatically controlled, stainless steel electric appliance that can be set for temperatures up to 212°F. Pressure canners are necessary for safe processing of low-acid foods, like most vegetables, and they make a handy substitute for restaurant-size pots when you're cooking for a crowd. Steam canners, another alternative to water-bath canners, are sometimes available from mail-order catalogues or at garage and yard sales, but they are not recommended by the USDA because food processed in them may spoil. Ovens, microwave ovens, and dishwashers are not acceptable substitutes for stovetop water-bath sterilizers: filled, sealed jars would explode as pressure inside the jars increased when heated. In a water-bath the jars are fully covered by boiling water which not only equalizes the pressure inside the jars, but also protects them from airborne bacteria. Processed high-acid foods like pickles, or foods with heavy sugar content, like jams, rarely present a safety problem, but low-acid foods not properly processed can spoil and be dangerous. It is best to consult a manual published by the USDA or one of the canning-jar companies.

Canning jars come in a variety of sizes and shapes from American, French, German, and Italian manufacturers. Can-and-freeze mason jars are widely available in several sizes, and lids for them come in two sizes—regular and wide mouth—and two types: two-part self-sealing metal lids (required for water-bath and pressure canning) and one-piece white plastic lids for refrigerator and freezer storage. Many of today's canning jars and lids have had a makeover. The plain jar with the manufacturer's name on it is being challenged by jars embossed with fruit and garden designs or decorative patterns. Instead of straight sides, some now have voluptuous bodies, the better to show off the jewel-like jellies or jams within. Utilitarian-looking two-part self-sealing lids that we used to cover with rounds of fabric when we gave jams as gifts now need no disguise; they come in fruit patterns, gingham plaids, and seasonal motifs of poinsettia, pine, and holly. We like glass jars for jams and other sweet spreads, because they can be sterilized, and sweet spreads packed in them tend to resist mold longer than the same foods packed in plastic containers. Because they resist breakage, however, freezer-safe plastic containers may be preferred for some foods.

20.1 BALL JAR LIFTER

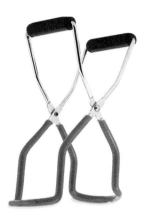

Made of stainless steel with heat-resistant handles and plastic-coated grips, this item is an absolute necessity for anyone canning anything. Its design has varied only slightly over the years. Some early models were all metal; the plastic coating is a twentieth-century improvement. Traditional kitchen tongs cannot get a good grip on empty jars without compromising their sterility because one side of the tongs has to go inside the jar. Traditional tongs are also a bad choice for lifting filled, sealed jars because their shape won't grip the round containers as securely as canning tongs. If a jar is too tall to be sterilized in an upright position, as sometimes happens, the canning tongs can safely grab it on its side.

20.2 BALL CANNING FUNNEL

Pouring a hot, sticky liquid like jam or jelly into a jar with a narrow opening is easy with a jar funnel. We show the Ball brand, made of heat-resistant plastic. Funnels are available in plastic or stainless steel, depending on the brand. Sizes also differ slightly from brand to brand, but all have stems designed to fit the openings on standard and wide-mouth canning jars. The length of the stem helps you estimate the amount of air space remaining at the top before sealing the jars.

20.3 BUBBLE FREER SPATULA

No matter how carefully you fill a jar, air bubbles often appear around the sides. To get rid of them, you need to release them with a flat-edged device. Metal is a poor choice because it could scratch the glass and weaken it dangerously during processing in a

---

APPLE BUTTER

About 2 cups

If you use a single sweet apple variety such as Cortland, you may need no additional sugar. If you mix sweet and tart varieties (McIntosh, Northern Spies, Winesaps, Cortlands), you may want to add a little sugar or one of the Native Americans' typical sweeteners—honey or maple syrup.

2 pounds apples
1 (6-ounce) can frozen apple juice concentrate, thawed, or ¾ cup boiled apple cider (see note)
sugar or maple syrup (optional)
ground cinnamon, ginger, mace, or coriander (optional)

Peel and core apples and purée them in a food processor with the thawed apple juice concentrate or boiled cider. Empty the purée into a 2-quart slow cooker, and cook, covered, on high for about 8 hours, or until very thick. Taste for sweetness, and add sugar or maple syrup, if desired. This will thin down the butter somewhat. Cover, and continue to cook on high until thick. Stir in spices of your choice, starting with ¼ to ½ teaspoon of one or more, and tasting after each addition. Divide among hot, sterilized jars or freezer containers, cool, cover tightly, label, and refrigerate or freeze. Keeps at least 1 month in refrigerator, or 6 months or more in freezer.

NOTE: Boiled apple cider is regular-strength fresh (unpasteurized) cider that has been boiled rapidly to measure half its original volume. This concentrates the flavor and sweetness.

Preserving in Today's Kitchen, by Jeanne Lesem

water-bath or pressure canner. Wood, being porous, can harbor germs. A plastic model, like the one we show here, is long enough to reach the bottom of your deepest jar while keeping your hand safely above the hot food. This one is 12″ long.

20.4 BALL CANNING LID WAND

A canning lid wand is a 7″-long plastic stick with a magnet on one end and a hanging hole on the other—a design so simple you wonder why it didn't occur to anyone long before the last quarter of the twentieth century. This inexpensive tool is far superior to kitchen tongs or even a jar lifter in allowing you to remove flat jar lids, one by one, from hot water without burning your fingers or compromising the cleanliness of the sealant side of the lid.

20.5 BALL JELLY BAG STAND

Although the shape of this modern jelly bag with stand may remind you of a space-age moon lander, it actually works on the same principle as the old-fashioned floor models from the early twentieth century. The stands were usually about 3′ high and made of wood. The jelly bag would hang from a frame at the top of the stand suspended several feet above a bowl. The cook poured the contents of the pot directly into the bag. The bag was often made of cotton flannel, a better choice, we think, than the nylon mesh used by some contemporary manufacturers, because closely woven cotton produces a clearer juice.

This stand is 11½″ high, made of chrome-plated steel, and it has feet designed to clamp on the sides of a large bowl or a 2-quart heatproof glass measure. It comes with one 4½″ by 8½″ standard-size washable nylon strainer bag and can be used also with large, 4½″ by 11½″ bags. Extra bags in both sizes are available in pairs.

20.6 GRANITE WARE BOILING-WATER-BATH CANNER

This old-fashioned 21½-quart enameled steel pot with lid and wire rack is 14″ in diameter and 12½″ high with the lid on. It has a jar capacity of 7 quarts, 7 pints, seven 12-ounce jelly jars, 7 half pints, or seven 4-ounce jelly jars. Without its rack, this time-honored porcelain-on-steel pot becomes a perfect preserving kettle for large recipes. Because its bottom and sides are thinner than those of today's high-quality cookware, how-ever, jams and preserves made without added pectin tend to stick and burn unless they are stirred often during the final stages of cooking.

20.7 BALL REPLACEMENT RACK

Stainless steel and rustproof, this rack is 12″ wide at the top. An extra wire in the bottom keeps 4-ounce jelly jars safely in place during processing. It holds twelve such jars in a single layer, or twice as many if you separate the second layer with a large cake rack.

20.8 PRESTO PRESSURE CANNER

Anyone who plans on canning low-acid foods (including vegetables, a few fruits, and all sorts of prepared dishes) will need a pressure canner. Today's pressure canners have several built-in safety devices such as a vent pipe with a regulator that automatically releases any excess pressure, an airvent-cover lock that vents air while indicating pressure in the canner, an overpressure plug in the cover that automatically releases steam if the vent pipe should become clogged, and a locking bracket inside the canner

THE OLD BACHELOR'S FRUIT PRESERVES

½ gallon

These preserves are not really preserves in the traditional sense, but rather a mélange of sun-drenched fruit soaked in alcohol. The heady confiture is not served at breakfast or teatime, but with coffee, after the evening meal. Fruit and alcohol are served together in a glass or cup or, more informally, in a still-hot coffee cup. These are a traditional treat in Provence at the end of Christmas or New Year's Eve dinner.

No matter the quantity, you always use the same weight of sugar as fruit, so if you would like to make a little more, for example, with 5 pounds of fruit, use 5 pounds of sugar. Increase the brandy proportionately as well. Choose four to six of the following fruits, depending on market availability; you don't necessarily need equal amounts of each fruit. Once the confiture is begun, you can continue replenishing it, adding more sugar, fruit, and alcohol. Be sure to cover the fruit with the alcohol or it will spoil.

3 pounds granulated sugar
3 cups marc de Provence, pear or raspberry eau-de-vie, Armagnac, or kirsch

FOR THE FRUIT, enough of four to six different kinds
  to equal 3 pounds:
medium strawberries, rinsed, hulled, and halved
blackberries, rinsed and patted dry
raspberries
blueberries, rinsed
peaches, peeled, pitted, and sliced into ⅛ sections
ripe but firm pears, peeled, halved, cored, and cut into ½" slices

1 Combine the sugar and marc de Provence in a large saucepan and heat over medium-low heat, stirring occasionally, until the sugar completely dissolves, about 5 minutes. Remove from the heat and set aside to cool.

2 Layer the fruits in a wide-mouth ½-gallon canning jar or a ½-gallon ceramic pot with a tight-sealing lid. Arrange the fruits in the following order: strawberries, blackberries, raspberries, blueberries, peaches, and pears. Pour in enough of the sugar mixture to cover the fruit and almost fill the jar; leave about 1" empty to allow for the slight expansion of the mixture as it ferments. (If you have any marc de Provence left over, save it for another use, such as poaching fruit.) Seal the jar and set in a cool dark place. Let macerate for at least two months, turning the jar upside down every week or two, so that any sugar settled on the bottom will permeate the fruits.
3 Serve in small stemmed glasses, generously dispensing the liquid in the jar along with the fruit.

From *Ducasse Flavors of France,* by Alain Ducasse with Linda Dannenberg

---

body that prevents the cover from being opened until the pressure inside has been reduced to zero.

This weighted-gauge canner has a 17-quart liquid capacity, and it can hold twenty-four half-pint mason jars, ten pint jars, or seven 1-quart jars. The inside height is 8⅞", and the inside diameter is 12". It's also available in a 22-quart liquid capacity. The Presto pressure canners can be used as pressure cookers but are recommended mainly for soups, stews, poultry, and meat. For safety reasons, they should never be filled more than half full for soups and stews or two-thirds full for poultry and meat. Similarly, do not try to use your regular pressure cooker as a pressure canner.

20.9 ROBINSON RANSBOTTOM SAUERKRAUT CROCK

Sauerkraut aficionados will want to ferment cabbage themselves the old-fashioned way, in this handsome, glazed, beige crock with its rich brown interior and soft blue crown decoration. Five quarts of finely shredded white cabbage can be layered in the crock with salt (2 teaspoons for each pound of cabbage). Some people assume there's vinegar in sauerkraut, but the pickling is only salt. As the layers are built up they should be pounded down with a wooden mallet, and finally covered with a clean cloth and some heavy rocks or other weights. During the fermentation process, the crock should be stored at 60°F, and the brine that rises above the cloth removed every few days. In a month you will have a generous supply of sauerkraut, ready to be spiced as you wish—with juniper berries, peppercorns, bay leaves, caraway seeds, or allspice—and steamed with your favorite sausages or pork.

20.10 ALLTRISTA CORPORATION BALL & KERR CANNING JARS

The preferred design in the United States is the mason jar, with threaded rim and two-part self-sealing lids. Ball and Kerr are the major manufacturers of mason jars. Jar sizes are: 4 ounces, ½ pint, 12 ounces, pint, quart, and ½ gallon. All except the 4-ounce, 12-ounce, and ½-gallon sizes come in both regular and wide-mouth designs. Prices vary, depending on brand, size, and whether you buy them individually or prepacked in boxes with lids and labels included.

Before you shop for jars, bear in mind that USDA and state Cooperative Extension Services recommend only mason jars for foods that should be processed in a water-bath or a pressure canner. They also recommend ½-gallon mason jars only for canning high-acid juices. Two-part self-sealing metal lids with a sealant ring around the outer edge are the preferred closure for mason jars to be water-bath or pressure canned. They come in two sizes, standard (or regular) and wide mouth, in boxes of twelve flat lids and twelve rings (rings are reusable if they are not bent or rusty). Replacement lids come in boxes of twelve. Plastic caps for refrigerator or freezer storage come in regular and wide mouth sizes in boxes of eight. The one-part caps are dishwasher-safe.

Once a jar is opened, you may want to substitute rustproof plastic caps for metal lids. One-piece plastic caps are the perfect solution.

20.11 BORMIOLI ROCCO "QUATTRO STAGIONI" CANNING JAR

The ½-liter Bormioli Rocco canning jar shown here is a mason jar design from Italy. The maker's lids are the one-piece design, and not reusable, but the ½-liter and ¼-liter sizes accept regular two-part self-sealing lids.

20.12 WECK CANNING JAR

The tulip-shaped Weck jar we show comes in a variety of designs and sizes, with glass lids, rubber rings, and stainless steel clamps for water-bath and pressure canning. Founded in Oflingen, Germany, on January 1, 1900, Weck provides detailed direc-

"Dear Diary: Today I picked a peck of pickled peppers."

tions for canning with its jars, as well as how to test for a vacuum seal. Each set comes with snap-on plastic lids for refrigerator and freezer storage.

20.13 LUMINARC CANNING JAR

Though French confiture jars like this 14-ounce example from Luminarc cannot be processed at all because they are closed only with snap-on plastic lids, they can, and should, be sterilized before using. They are our first choice for jams, jellies, preserves, marmalades, and any other

acid mixtures prepared for short-term storage in the refrigerator or freezer, because they can double as good-looking serving dishes.

PICKLED OKRA

Approximately 2 pints

This recipe is better if small, tender okra pods are used. Watch out, though: these are hot!

1 pound young okra
½ small *habanero* or other hot chile, sliced thin, or to taste
1 small onion, sliced thin
2 cloves garlic, sliced thin
1 cup water
3 cups distilled white vinegar
1 tablespoon pickling spice
2 teaspoons salt

Wash the okra and pick it over, removing any pods that are hard and woody and any with soft spots. Pack the okra into hot sterilized pint canning jars, stem ends down. Place the remaining ingredients in a nonreactive saucepan and bring them to a boil over medium heat. Remove the liquid from the heat and slowly pour it over the okra in the jars. Seal the jars according to proper canning procedures and store them in a cool dark place for 4 weeks, then serve as a condiment with virtually everything.

The Welcome Table, by Jessica B. Harris

DRYING

THOUGH PRESERVING MAY BRING to mind that lovely jar of strawberry jam or fresh corn chutney, drying is an equally important method of food preservation. Commercially made solar dehydrators and racks for oven drying are history, but sales of electric dehydrators are booming, and many basic canning books provide plans and directions for sun-drying food.

Dehydration may be the world's oldest method of food preservation. Pulses and legumes, as well as strips of meat, were dried and stored for future meals. Dried grain could be ground. Dried and salted fish could be reconstituted. Early settlers in America learned the techniques of drying fish and corn from Native Americans. Campers, hikers, and other outdoor enthusiasts still rely on GORP (good old raisins and peanuts), jerky, and other dried or freeze-dried foods. Currently, Americans eat an estimated 20 pounds of dried foods a year (not counting ingredients like grains), or about 1 percent of our total food consumption. Though one food dehydration expert credits the counterculture of the

1960s and 1970s for helping to introduce dried foods to mainstream America, that opinion may be oversimplified. What child has not grown up eating raisins?

Electric dehydrators are the most efficient and cost-effective equipment for anyone who uses a lot of dried foods as snacks or recipe ingredients. There are other choices beyond state-of-the-art electric dehydrators, although these appliances have virtually eliminated the market for commercial solar dryers and racks for oven drying. Although their capacity is small, compared with countertop dehydrators, and fuel use may be greater, the second most efficient way to dry food indoors is in convection ovens. Because not all convection oven-makers recommend their units for drying food, we suggest you investigate the ones you are considering before making a purchase.

General canning and preserving cookbooks often provide directions for building solar dryers, and a few cookbooks tell you how to dry food in the oven. Experts do not recommend oven drying of any fruit or vegetable with very high water content. This category would include things like tomatoes, bell peppers, and chilies, to name a few (though professional chefs sometimes semi-dry these vegetables in the oven to concentrate their flavors). Also, many ovens today cannot be set to a temperature low enough (below 200°F) for effective drying. Microwave ovens are not recommended because they dry foods unevenly.

A word of caution about jerky: precooking had always been recommended for pork and poultry because of the risk of food-borne diseases, but since 1997 the Oregon State University Extension Service has recommended precooking all meat jerky in a boiling marinade. This change was made after a local outbreak of *E. coli* in that state was traced to undercooked venison jerky. The service says many home dehydrators today are not designed to bring raw meat to a safe temperature during the time in the drying cycle allotted for bacterial destruction. The only way to be sure your jerky will be safe is to precook it.

Properly dried fruits and vegetables will keep as long as a year if they are stored in airtight containers in a dark, dry pantry, and even longer when refrigerated or frozen.

20.14 NESCO AMERICAN HARVEST GARDENMASTER PROFESSIONAL FOOD DEHYDRATOR AND JERKY MAKER

At 1,000 watts, this is the most powerful food dehydrator we could find. In an informal test by one state Cooperative Extension Service, the Gardenmaster ranked first in ability to reach higher temperatures, an important safety factor. Once food was prepped, it was a quick and easy process to fill and stack the trays, set the thermostat, and flip the on-off switch. The machine is easy to clean, has a moderate noise level, and has cool operation.

Almost everything we dried tasted better than store-bought counterparts. Cilantro leaves and flat-leaf parsley remained green when fully dried, and quickly regained their characteristic scent and flavor when rehydrated in water (though the parsley took more than 24 hours to dry). Vegetable chips, tomatoes, jalapeno chilies, apple rings, and strawberry-rhubarb fruit leather (i.e., a fruit roll) turned out great. Juice- and syrup-packed canned pineapple slices dried into chewy confections that tasted like pricey glazed fruit but without the excess sugar and calories. Canned applesauce made good fruit leather. Overripe fresh fruit made extra-sweet snacks as its natural sugar content was concentrated by drying. You can also dry cherries and blueberries for a fraction of the cost of store-bought ones and avoid the additives, preservatives, artificial colors, and sweeteners used by some manufacturers.

The Gardenmaster is 15″ in diameter, 9½″ high, and comes with four trays, but it can be expanded to hold up to thirty trays. The Snackmaster Pro, a 500-watt model, has many of the same features and is only 13″ in diameter, about 9″ high, and fits twelve trays. Accessories for both include extra trays, fruit-roll sheets, fine-mesh screens, an assortment of spices, and a jerky kit for use with ground meat.

FREEZING

THE ANCIENT INCAS freeze-dried their potatoes by stamping on frozen potatoes to remove the moisture, then storing them in stone warehouses in the high Andes. Although some of their descendants still freeze-dry potatoes and use them to prepare stews, it is not possible to carry out the process in most homes. Instead, freezing has become the method of choice for preserving food today.

Freezing is mostly a twentieth-century development whose popularity began increasing rapidly after World War II. For home gardeners it is an excellent way of saving what you cannot eat within a few days. No special tools are needed. Vegetables and fruits that require blanching to prevent enzymatic changes (mostly to do with texture) can be prepared in any saucepan or stockpot. In addition to can-and-freeze jars, we have many choices of plastic storage containers with tight lids and food-grade freezer bags, most of which can be hand-washed and reused. The wide-mouth can-and-freeze jar is a twentieth-century invention, developed after World War II when home freezers became popular. It is a straight-sided jar that flares outward at the top, so that frozen foods need not be fully defrosted to be emptied.

VACUUM SEALING

FOR THE LONGEST STORAGE of all you will need a vacuum-packaging appliance. Vacuum packaging significantly extends the storage time and quality of dried and frozen foods. A basic kit includes a selection of precut bags and rolls of heavy-duty bag-making material designed to withstand the stress of removing the air that surrounds bagged foods. Optional accessories vary from brand to brand; one possibility is seal-ers that can be attached by hose to the base unit and used to reseal commercial cans and jars, oil and wine bottles, special rigid plastic canisters, and even mason jars. However, please note that vacuum-sealing systems are not a substitute for traditional canning or freezing. Any food that requires refrigerator or freezer storage before vacuum packing must be stored the same way, even after packing.

20.15 TILIA'S FOODSAVER PRO-FESSIONAL II VACUUM SEALER

With one touch of a button, this sealer will press and release to vacuum-pack and seal food. It comes in a kit that includes precut plastic bags and rolls of bag material. It has a port for jar-sealer attachments that fit regular and wide-mouth mason jars, as well as VacuTop universal lids to replace the original lids from cans or jars and create a vacuum at the same time. VacuTop bottle stoppers can also be used to reseal open bottles of wine and oils; eliminating the air keeps wine fresh and delays the onset of rancidity in oil that is stored for long periods at room temperature.

Whether you use precut bags or make your own from the manufacturer's material, you will first need to freeze prepared foods in a rigid container lined with food-grade plastic. Once frozen, the food can be unwrapped, transferred to a FoodSaver bag, and then vacuum sealed. All precut bags, and those cut from rolls of bag materials can be washed by hand or in a dishwasher and reused several times. An instruction manual and a 30-minute how-to video come with the kit. This sealer weighs 5 pounds and is 15″ by 5½″ by 4″.

VINEGARED GINGER

2 cups

½ pound (225 grams) fresh ginger root
2 teaspoons salt

FOR THE MARINADE:
1 cup rice vinegar
7 tablespoons water
2½ tablespoons sugar

1 Clean ginger knobs well with damp cloth. Sprinkle lightly with salt and leave for 1 day.
2 Mix marinade in crockery bowl, making sure sugar is dissolved. Drain the ginger, then pickle in marinade for 7 days. Keeps in covered container in refrigerator at least several months. The ginger will turn pinkish in the vinegary marinade.
3 Cut into paper-thin slices along the grain. Set a small mound on every individual plate. Two tablespoons per person throughout the course of a sushi meal is about average. Eat with fingers.

Japanese Cooking: A Simple Art, by Shizuo Tsuji

APPENDICES

UNIVERSAL TOOLS

THE AUTOMATIC GARAGE DOOR OPENER, the television remote control, the lever door handle, and a host of other "necessities" are all examples of the benefits of a design philosophy intended to enable people with disabilities to lead full lives. Although Universal Design has only been around since the early 1970s, when it was started at the University of North Carolina as a project for assistive technology, it has had an immense impact on daily life for all of us, not just for the 54 million Americans with disabilities, for whom accessibility and the adaptation of tools is a path to independent living. Just as the Americans with Disabilities Act set the architectural standards for public buildings in 1990, Universal Design has addressed the needs of home design. In this appendix, we spotlight products that have emerged from this important program, which has transcended the status of being just a design movement. As with other design movements, it has been through many phases.

At first, "accessibility" meant building unwieldy structural modifications and installing metal grab bars that made a home look more like a hospital. Since then, the concept of accessibility has shifted toward the creation of objects designed specifically for the needs of people with disabilities. There has also been a progression from scruffy prototypes banged together from off-the-shelf appliances with the addition of "assistive" components fashioned from poor materials, to sleek, beautifully forged or modeled utensils that use the best

materials and are produced on a scale that allows for competitive pricing. The movement has also progressed from mechanical solutions to design problems to high-technology automation; levers and handles have been replaced with push-buttons, automated timers, and, in some cases, completely voice-activated computerized control systems. In Cambridge, the Massachusetts Institute of Technology Media Lab is at work creating "smart" rooms, including kitchens that are fully automated, while a range of automated appliances is being tested at Xerox's Palo Alto Research Center (PARC) in California.

Research and development programs like these arose largely as a result of economics. The $1 trillion in consolidated buying power of people with disabilities represents one of America's largest untapped markets. The graying of America and the growing recognition of the importance of people with disabilities as consumers has prompted many major corporations, including the Big Three automakers (Ford, General Motors, and DaimlerChrysler), Johnson & Johnson, IBM, and Microsoft, to launch aggressive research and marketing divisions to explore new products and re-jigger old ones to meet demand. Obviously one of the most significant sectors in this consumer trend are the two areas of the home that most require modification when disability is in the picture: the kitchen and the bathroom. The new products that emerge minimize the strength needed to accomplish the most mundane of movements. Within the last three years, major manufacturers like General Electric, Whirlpool, Black & Decker, Miles Homes, American Standard, and Farberware have invested hundreds of millions of dollars in design projects aimed at creating or improving products to meet the needs of this important market.

The most important contributions to the field have accompanied the development of objects for the use of those with mobility impairments, often from arthritis and strokes, as well as from cerebral palsy, multiple sclerosis, muscular dystrophy, Lou Gehrig's disease, polio, Guillain-Barré (walking polio), and Huntington's disease. Consider the case of a person who has had a stroke and goes from being right-handed, and nearly ambidextrous, to left-handed without much strength or coordination on the right side. Creating kitchen implements for such an individual is one of the challenges of Universal Design.

For those who are blind, or have partial sight that permits them to discern the differences between light and shadow, kitchen redesign must incorporate strong contrast between materials or colors and glare-free but strong lighting. A bright circular burner against a dark surrounding surface can help prevent burns. A shift from one surface material (wood) to another (Corian) allows for "way finding" along the countertop or shelf. Many of the best products available from The Lighthouse, a nonprofit organization in New York that serves thousands of blind clients every year, are reinventions of everyday utensils with features that allow those with limited vision to use them.

True to the philosophy of Universal Design, the innovations that were made on behalf of wheelchair users have led many with leg or back conditions that make standing for long periods difficult to consider cooking from a seated position. A modular kitchen has been designed with power controls that adjust shelf, counter, and sink heights. It has a host of timers and push-button controls that reduce to an absolute minimum the strength and effort needed by a cook.

In the kitchen, where safety as well as convenience are necessities, Universal Design is now in its heyday, offering products that are more comfortable, more fun, and safer to use. The utensils created according to its principles have become some of the smartest and smartest-looking items in the chef's repertory, combining utility with beauty in a way that completely dispels the old stereotypes of assistive technology. For example, the elegant Black & Decker Ergo line of appliances has the swift curves of a sculpture by Constantin Brancusi and looks good enough to keep out on the counter between uses. The new Ergo electric knife features an offset handle that fits any hand size and keeps your knuckles from hitting the cutting board. Additionally, the knife's ergonomic shape offers a fresh visual approach to a common household appliance. By now, most cooks are familiar with the Good Grips utensils originally designed by OXO, the ones with the black rubber handles that are easily gripped by those with arthritis—and welcomed by those who don't have a disability.

There are many universally designed pieces of equipment from different manufacturers featured throughout this book. The following are examples of products that meet the most demanding needs of cooks with a range of disabilities.

A.1 OXO MEASURING CUP SET

Here is a set of measuring cups that is great for people with limited vision. They are black plastic, the perfect color to set off the white of flour or sugar by contrast. The standard 1-, ½-, ⅓-, ¼- measurement markings are large and easy to see in bright orange, green, blue, and red. They have an oversized, tapered hole that almost finds the hook for the user, making them particularly easy to store. These measuring cups are the handiest and smartest-looking we've tried.

> Food is our common ground, a universal experience.
> —JAMES BEARD

A.2 FARBERWARE MILLENNIUM PRESSURE COOKER

The pressure cooker is already a godsend in terms of convenience, and now Farberware has taken it a step further by making a fully programmable model that cooks quickly and cleans up easily. This 4-quart-capacity cooker, made of heavy-duty, nonstick aluminum, can be operated with the push of a few buttons. It has "cool-to-the-touch" molded housing and is notable for its quick cooking and ability to keep food warm. It can be used for steaming, as well as for pressure-cooking stocks, sauces, and large cuts of meat. Because it is light and the controls are easily activated (they do not require much strength) we found this a terrific product for people with arthritis or limited mobility.

A.3 HOMECRAFT TWISTER JAR OPENER

Grip and turn. How many times a day do we perform these simple operations in the kitchen as we open jars, bottles, and storage containers? How difficult would they be if arthritis, a stroke, or another disability reduced our ability to grip or make a turning motion? This astonishingly simple device, literally just a soft cone of rubber, can help people with a weak or painful grip. It can accommodate lids from ¾" to 1½" in diameter.

A.4 EMSON SPEED PEELER

Using a back and forth action much like an automatic carving knife, this lightweight, high-speed peeler, with its rechargeable battery, eliminates the repetitive motions that are necessary to peel vegetables or fruits by traditional means. As those who work with computers a great deal may know, any repetitive motion, no matter how small or easy, can eventually lead to a cumulative injury known as repetitive stress disorder that affects the joints and muscles and results in chronic pain. This peeler will protect you from such a hazard and is a pleasure to use.

A.5 & A.6 HOMECRAFT HI-D PARING BOARD & FOOD PREP BOARD

These boards were devised for amputees or those who have had a stroke and have use of only one hand. The 11" square Hi-D paring board uses aluminum nails to hold food in place, freeing the hand to manipulate a knife. Corner guards keep food such as bread in place for spreading and cutting, and four rubber slip-resistant feet secure the board to the counter for safe cutting. Made of high-density polyethylene, this paring board is easy to clean and will wear well. The 8¾" Food Prep Board with its patterned surface and raised edges serves the same function as the guards on the paring board; it keeps food from moving.

A curved lip hangs over and hugs the countertop edge to prevent the board from moving while in use. These boards are low-tech, inexpensive ways to solve a frustrating problem, but use caution: the nails on the paring board can be dangerous.

A.7 MARKTIME BRAILLE TIMER

A deft variation on a classic theme, this small, easily handled braille timer has all its markings in raised type, a real plus for those who have no vision. (Limited-vision chefs can use large-character digital timers.) Although only about 5 percent of blind people use braille (it is difficult to learn later in life), it is interesting that this timer can be useful even to those who don't read braille fluently, since the numbers can be easily mastered.

A.8 SMARTBOARD CUTTING BLOCK

To minimize the lifting and carrying of bowls, plates, and pots when cooking, American Clipper has created an ingenious cutting board. Made of Canadian rock maple, this 1"-thick board sits on raised nonslip feet and has an inset semicircular opening at the front edge for a bowl or plate to slide up to it. Once you have finished prepping the food, you need only push it into the bowl or onto a plate underneath. This board is useful for people with arthritis or limited mobility and strength. The board's raised feet give it increased elevation and relieve some of the strain of bending over the board. Please note that this feature may make things difficult for wheelchair users, for whom many countertops are already too high.

A.9 BLACK & DECKER ERGO ELECTRIC KNIFE

This is one of the first products out of the gate for an important new line of ergonomically designed kitchen tools from Household Products, Inc. Lightweight but powerful, the motor of the Ergo electric knife sets it apart, as does its easily grasped, rubber-accented handle and the power it puts at the fingertips of someone who may not be able to carve meat or slice bread easily.

"No, I don't want to play chess. I just want you to reheat the lasagna."

B

THE COOKS' LIBRARY

For the compiler of a bibliography or reading list, the most important thing to consider is who will be using the list, and for what purpose. We asked Nach Waxman of Kitchen Arts & Letters, Inc., in New York City to compile a list of the books he thinks are indispensable to a serious culinary library. Though the list doesn't encompass every great book written, all the books, in one way or another, make an important contribution to our understanding of food growing and raising, marketing, preparation, and consumption. Nearly all are twentieth-century publications, with a strong bias toward more recent and more accessible works. The titles that are marked with an asterisk are suggested as the core works of a cook's reference shelf.

GENERAL

Kamman, Madeleine. *The New Making of a Cook* (Morrow, 1997)
This massive revised edition of *Making of a Cook* (1971) is a "scientific" examination of cooking methods by one of the finest thinkers in the food world and teacher of hundreds of chefs.

Pépin, Jacques. *The Art of Cooking,* two volumes (Knopf, 1987, 1988—out of print)
The magnum opus of the highly popular chef and teacher. A hefty two-volume work dealing with cooking techniques for virtually every food used by cooks today in Europe and America. Thousands of detailed color photographs show the methods that are used by our leading chefs. There are recipes, but they're not the point.

*Peterson, James. *Essentials of Cooking* (Artisan, 1999)
A fine compendium of cooking techniques, accompanied by outstanding step-by-step photographs. The author is a well-known teacher and chef. Similar to Jacques Pépin's *Art of Cooking*, but more tightly focused and essentially done without any recipes. Most useful for the intermediate cook.

*Rombauer, Irma and Marion Becker. *The All-Purpose Joy of Cooking* (Plume, 1997)
The massive revision of America's great encyclopedic cookbook, first published in 1931. No longer Irma Rombauer's book but still a tremendously useful source for recipes, reference, instruction, and advice. From storing asparagus to constructing a standing rib roast to making Greek pastry, everything you need (or most of it) is here.

Rosso, Julee and Sheila Lukins. *The New Basics* (Workman, 1989)
The modern answer to *Fannie Farmer, Joy of Cooking,* and the other great books. A collection of recipes and information for the turn-of-the-century set—stylish and useful. Cocktail party goodies right through to turkey-roasting charts.

NATIONAL & ETHNIC CUISINES

AFRICAN

Abdenour, Samia. *Egyptian Cooking: A Practical Guide* (American University, Cairo, 1984)
Although part of a Middle Eastern tradition, Egyptian food has much that is its own. This conscientious book is a serious effort to record a variety of "modern" (as opposed to ancient) Egyptian recipes. A useful collection.

Africa News. *Africa News Cookbook* (Africa News, 1985; Penguin, 1986) A very serviceable anthology of recipes from all over the continent, with a better-than-ordinary selection from the sub-Saharan regions. Notes provide background on ingredients, traditions.

Mesfin, Daniel. *Exotic Ethiopian Cuisine* (Exotic Ethiopian, 1993) A good, sound book, utterly lacking in pretense, about a lesser-known cuisine. Self-published—probably the only way such a book could see the light of day.

Wolfert, Paula. *Couscous and Other Good Food from Morocco* (Harper & Row, 1973) Wolfert's first book, based on long-term residence in Morocco, is surely her best. A prize example of simple, authentic cooking, this is better than other, more glamorous-looking works on the region.

AMERICAN

Anderson, Jean. *American Century Cookbook* (Clarkson Potter, 1997) Splendid, informal history of American eating in the twentieth century—from Steak Diane to Rice Krispies to Jell-O mold marvels, a warm, dizzying tour. Great nostalgia with a scholarly core.

Beard, James. *James Beard's American Cookery* (Little, Brown, 1972) The best of Beard's works, this hefty survey demonstrates that there is no standard American cooking, no central location for our cuisine. America's food is the inspired sum of its many regional traditions. An epic work.

Bertolli, Paul. *Chez Panisse Cooking* (Random House, 1994) Alice Waters had a lot of fine cooks working in her kitchen, and Paul Bertolli, a talented Italian-American, was one of the best. Sturdy food with an Italian bent, but far different from Waters's own ethereal California fare. Nonetheless, her principles are the inspiration for this book, and her name appears as well.

Dent, Huntley. *Feast of Santa Fe* (Simon & Schuster, 1995) Old-style Southwest food, showing its Spanish and Native American roots. Not the fancified nouvelle and fusion cooking we know too well, but rather a region's low-key, authentic food.

*Egerton, John. *Southern Food* (Knopf, 1987; paper, University of North Carolina Press, 1993) Less a cookbook than a near-encyclopedia of Southern ingredients and dishes. From grits to Country Captain, this loving book presents basic definitions, history, lore, comparative notes, and more.

Harris, Jessica B. *The Welcome Table* (Simon & Schuster, 1995) More than two hundred recipes from the African American community. A bright, lively book that gives a slightly modern, healthier twist to popular down-home food, from Southern pork chops to turnip greens to pickled peaches.

*Mariani, John. *Encyclopedia of American Food and Drink* (Lebhar-Friedman, 1999) (Originally published as *Dictionary of American Food and Drink,* Ticknor & Fields, 1983) A valuable collection of fact and folklore about America's foods and beverages. From the origin of shoofly pie to the definition of hobo eggs and recipes for dirty rice and Senate bean soup, the book provides entertaining entries and a good level of reliable information.

Ogden, Bradley. *Breakfast, Lunch, and Dinner* (Random House, 1991) A fine West Coast chef offers some simple recipes with a distinctly American feel. Using largely familiar ingredients, Ogden creates dishes that makes palates leap and propels daily meals to the realm of the memorable.

Trotter, Charlie. *Charlie Trotter's Cookbook* (Ten Speed, 1994) A chef, and a book, representing the American high-end cooking of the 1990s and beyond. Inventive, stylish, and highly commercial.

Worthington, Diane. *Cuisine of California* (J. P. Tarcher, 1983; paper, Chronicle, 1997) The best work on the new food of California from the time before it became pretentious, undisciplined, and even a little silly. Simple ideas, clean tastes, and, in the forefront, fresh ingredients—before *talking* about them became a fashionable cliché.

ASIAN

Batmanglij, Najmiah. *New Food of Life* (Mage, 1992) The major work on Persian food—fresh, exotic, elegant. A beautifully made book, with stunning color photographs of the food, and very helpful culinary and cultural notes.

Brennan, Jenifer. *Original Thai Cookbook* (Putnam, 1981; paper, Perigee, 1984) There are more spectacular Thai cookbooks, filled with color photos and high-level recipes, but there is no better introduction to Thai cuisine than this. Ingredients, methods, and menus are explained with care to launch every beginner on the way to understanding this exciting, exotic cooking tradition.

*Cost, Bruce. *Bruce Cost's Asian Ingredients* (Morrow, 1988; HarperCollins, 2000) Coverage of the major Asian and Southeast Asian food products, including (and this is much of the book's value) packaged ingredients, such as soy sauce and preserved black beans. How the products are made, the varieties available, packaging information, and suggestions for use. Outstanding.

*Dahlen, Martha. *Cook's Guide to Chinese Vegetables* (Hong Kong; published in U.S. as *Popular Guide to Chinese Vegetables,* Crown, 1983; revised under new title, China Books, 1995) Excellent drawings, useful descriptions, tips, hints, and a few recipes for each vegetable, along with Chinese characters so you can take the book into the market and get more than a glassy look when you ask for tree ears.

Duong, Binh and Marcia Kiesel. *Simple Art of Vietnamese Cooking* (Simon & Schuster, 1991—out of print) Large, authoritative work on the highly varied cuisines of Vietnam, representing a number of different regions and traditions. The authors are a restaurateur and a food writer.

*Hosking, Richard. *Dictionary of Japanese Food* (Charles Tuttle, 1996) A dictionary that not only defines the vocabulary of Japanese food and cooking but through that vocabulary, reveals much of the cultural underpinnings of Japanese food traditions. There should, by law, be a book like this for every one of the world's major cuisines.

Lo, Eileen Yin-Fei. *The Chinese Kitchen* (Morrow, 1999)
A cookbook and a manual of technique and instruction by a master teacher. One of the definitive Chinese cookbooks.

Owen, Sri. *Indonesian Food and Cookery* (Prospect Books, 1986)
Owen, an Asian food scholar living and working in Britain, has provided an outstanding ethnographic cookbook, integrating in a single text recipes and social and cultural information related to food and food preparation. A model for books of this sort.

Roden, Claudia. *Book of Middle Eastern Food* (Knopf, 1974; revised edition, Knopf, 2000)
One of the few books to integrate and explore the entire breadth of Mediterranean and West Asian food. Roden, a major food authority, offers comments and history, as well as great recipes.

Sahni, Julie. *Classic Indian Cooking* (Morrow, 1980)
This book is a superb introduction to the food of India, especially valuable for its first ninety pages—a short course on Indian ingredients, equipment, techniques, and the basic pantry. The recipes are clear and authentic.

Solomon, Charmaine. *Complete Book of Asian Cooking* (Landsdowne [Australia], 1976; Periplus, 1992)
Solomon, who has lived and traveled in virtually every corner of south and southeast Asia, takes us on a country by country tour, providing a brief essay on the food of each national culinary tradition and then serving up ten to fifteen good recipes to illustrate the character of the food.

*Solomon, Charmaine. *Encyclopedia of Asian Food* (New Holland [Australia], 1996; Periplus, 1998)
A masterful reference work on Asian ingredients by the woman who is arguably the final authority for this huge region and its foods. Precise, informative, and essential for anyone who cooks, writes, or eats Asian.

Tropp, Barbara. *The Modern Art of Chinese Cooking* (Morrow, 1982; paper, Morrow, 1996)
Chinese cooking at a high level by an outstanding restaurateur and teacher. Tropp, a Chinese-speaking American, writes with awesome confidence and clarity.

Tsuji, Shizuo. *Japanese Cooking: A Simple Art* (Kodansha, 1980)
An important work, both cookbook and reference, by one of Japan's best-known teachers. It includes coverage of every major Japanese culinary tradition, from soba noodles and sushi to rarified temple meals. Good reading, great cooking.

EUROPEAN

Anderson, Jean. *The Food of Portugal* (Morrow, 1994)
A fine introduction—warm, knowledgeable, reliable—by one of America's soundest and most prolific food writers, based on her dozens of trips to Portugal and an obvious affection for the people and their food.

Boyd, Lizzie. *British Cookery* (British Tourist Authority, 1976; revised edition, Helm Publishers, 1988—out of print)
Widely held to be the authoritative work on British regional cookery, this huge collection of recipes and notes demonstrates the very best of British cooking. From Lancastershire potato pie to the Osborne pudding in Norfolk, this is a delight to browse through and cook from.

Casas, Penelope. *Foods and Wines of Spain* (Knopf, 1982)
The best basic book, both for orientation and for recipes on the Spanish culinary tradition. The author has also written separate works on two special subjects: *Tapas* (1985) and *Paella* (1999).

Hess, O. and A. *Viennese Cookbook* (Crown, 1952—out of print)
This translation from the German appears to be the book of choice for Austrians seeking their favorite old-time recipes. Good, solid treatment—no bells and whistles, no light touch.

Kochilas, Diane. *Food and Wine of Greece* (St. Martin's Press, 1990)
A Greek-American who has returned to Greece to live, Kochilas has conscientiously recovered hundreds of traditional recipes from Greece—mainland and islands. She does very little to "improve" them, preferring a somewhat ethnographic approach. The result is a huge, useful success.

Lang, George. *Cuisine of Hungary* (Atheneum, 1971)
The magnificent cooking tradition of Hungary is described, presented, and embraced in a loving hug by the great restaurateur, consultant, scholar, and humanist. Every country should be blessed with such an exponent.

Root, Waverley. *The Food of France* (Knopf, 1958; paper, Vintage, 1977) and *The Food of Italy* (Atheneum, 1971; paper, Vintage, 1992)
Superb studies/guides for two leading culinary traditions of Europe. Historically oriented and arranged by region, these two books provide an education for travelers and a course for cooks. There should be books like this for every country.

Scharfenberg, Horst. *The Cuisines of Germany* (German edition, 1980; English translation, Simon & Schuster, 1989—out of print)
A worthy statement of the many regional cuisines of Germany—recipes ranging from Thuringian Cabbage Rolls to Fluffy Swabian Muffins. Rigorously authentic recipes, along with good historical and gastronomic notes. A rich and authoritative work.

Shulman, Martha Rose. *Mediterranean Light* (Bantam Books, 1989)
The pleasure-giving foods of the Mediterranean region are covered with a light spin by one of our most skilled food writers. Not quite vegetarian, this outstanding book dishes up good, healthy, unpretentious food.

Toomre, Joyce (trans. and ed.). *Classic Russian Cooking* (University of Indiana Press, 1992; paper, University of Indiana Press, 1998)
Translation of a monumental nineteenth-century Russian cookbook, *A Gift to Young Housewives* by Elena Molokhovets (1861). The book is in the grand tradition of Russian food, although it is hardly short on the cabbages, root vegetables, mushrooms, and meats that make Russian cuisine one of Europe's sturdiest.

VanWaerebeck, Ruth. *Everybody Eats Well in Belgium* (Workman, 1996)
A Belgian-born food writer provides a zesty introduction to what seems perennially to be called "Europe's best-kept secret." The prize dishes are presented appealingly; both French and Flemish Belgium are well represented.

FRENCH

Child, Julia. *Mastering the Art of French Cooking,* two volumes (Knopf, 1961 [paper, Knopf, 1983], 1970)
This monumental work written with Simone Beck and Louisette Bertholle started America down the path of serious international cooking. Friendly, but a good deal more rigorous than Julia ever was on TV. An approach to cooking that goes far beyond French food.

Grausman, Richard. *At Home with French Classics* (Workman, 1988)
A prominent culinary educator gives us French cooking stripped to its essentials— the classic dishes without the usual thick coating of elitist mystique. Refreshingly no-nonsense.

*Lang, Jenifer (ed.). *Larousse Gastronomique* (3rd English-Language Edition) (Crown, 1988)
This one-volume encyclopedia of French food is an essential for anyone concerned with classic European cooking. Not a cookbook (although it contains some recipes) but an important reference work, with advice on everything from technical details to cultural and historical facts.

Marshall, Lydie. *Cooking with Lydie Marshall* (Knopf, 1982—out of print)
A longtime teacher in New York City, Provence-born Lydie Marshall offers, in the guise of a cookbook, marvelous lessons in French cooking, every recipe representing a point of culinary theory or practice.

Olney, Richard. *Simple French Food* (Atheneum, 1974; paper, Macmillan, 1992)
The basic work by the great American cook who lived nearly half his life in France. A thoughtful treatment of cooking and pantry fundamentals.

Roberts, Michael. *Parisian Home Cooking* (Morrow, 1999)
Not just another French cookbook, but rather a treatment of the way Parisians, using the many fine food resources they have available in their noble city, cook for themselves at home. Eye-opening for its simplicity and its artlessness—a surprise from a former cutting-edge chef.

*Temmerman, Genevieve. *A–Z of French Food* (Scribo [France], 1988)
A compact dictionary of French cooking terminology, including ingredients, cooking methods, equipment, and finished dishes.

Wolfert, Paula. *Cooking of Southwest France* (Harper & Row, 1983)
A dazzling cookbook on the vigorous food of Périgord and Gascony, ever so much more than the sum of its recipes. Wolfert's protracted visits to the region, her bent for scholarship, and her passion for great cooking combine to give us her monumental work.

ITALIAN

Bugialli, Giuliano. *Fine Art of Italian Cooking* (Times Books, 1977; 2nd edition, Random House, 1990)
The renowned teacher's first book and, many feel, still his best. Fine recipes from many historical periods and many regions are embedded in a highly readable text that provides rich cultural details. From the culinary heritage of the Medicis to contemporary disputes about matters of taste, this book is an education as well as a significant cookbook.

Hazan, Marcella. *The Essentials of Classic Italian Cooking* (Knopf, 1992)
The compounding of two earlier general works on Italian cooking, this important volume is an inventory of authoritative recipes for the full range of the Italian culinary repertoire. Hazan, for years a great teacher, has given us a bible for the food she knows and loves.

Kasper, Lynn Rosetto. *The Splendid Table* (Morrow, 1992)
A splendid work about the food and cuisine in the northern Italian region of Emilia-Romagna, by an American who traced her culinary tradition to its roots. Rich in every dimension, the book features the region's subtle flavorings and its cultural history.

LaPlace, Viana and Evan Kleiman. *Cucina Fresca* (Harper & Row, 1985), *Cucina Rustica* (Morrow, 1990), and *Pasta Fresca* (Morrow, 1988)
This brilliant trilogy represents some of the best writing ever on Italian home cooking. All three provide simple, nonprescriptive recipes written to encourage spontaneity, thoughtfulness, and flexibility. The first volume deals with cold and room-temperature foods, the second with plain country food, the third, clearly, with pasta.

*Mariani, John. *Dictionary of Italian Food and Drink* (Broadway Books, 1998)
A good Italian-English food dictionary, whose somewhat expanded entries make it almost a mini-encyclopedia. A very useful little book. Also useful, with a larger number of entries, but shorter ones, is *Dictionary of Italian Cuisine* by Maureen Fant and Howard M. Isaacs (Ecco Press, 1998).

Schwartz, Arthur. *Naples at Table* (HarperCollins, 1998)
The food and culture of Naples and Campania, treated with energy and respect by the highly admired writer and radio personality. An outstanding example of what a regional book should be.

JEWISH

Nathan, Joan. *Jewish Holiday Kitchen* (Schocken, 1979; revised edition, Schocken, 1988)
A fine kosher cookbook, organized by the festivals of the Jewish year. Good summaries of each holiday, showing how the traditional foods become part of the celebrations, plus a lot of strongly authentic recipes.

Roden, Claudia. *Book of Jewish Food* (Knopf, 1996)
A magnificently assembled history and recipe collection covering the entire world of Jewish cooking, from Europe to the exotic cuisines of North Africa and the Far East. Fascinating stories, excellent historical illustrations, and great recipes.

Sheraton, Mimi. *From My Mother's Kitchen* (Harper & Row, 1979; revised edition, Harper & Row, 1991—out of print)
A wonderfully annotated collection of recipes from central and eastern Europe, as reestablished in America. All the old flavors and traditions are delightfully presented in a quasi-memoir by the former restaurant critic of the *New York Times.*

WESTERN HEMISPHERE

Bayless, Rick and Deanna. *Authentic Mexican* (Morrow, 1987)
From the owners of the celebrated Frontera Grill and Topolobampo in Chicago, a lucid exposition of Mexican home cooking, packed with richly informative sidenotes and good, open-minded recipes.

438

Idone, Christopher. *Brazil: A Cook's Tour* (Clarkson Potter, 1995)
A conscientious attempt to take on one of the most bewilderingly varied cuisines in the world. From region to region, the foods of Brazil are revealed to be fresh, innovative, and highly accessible. An intelligent, attractive book, long on history and good tastes.

Kennedy, Diana. *The Art of Mexican Cooking* (Bantam Books, 1989—out of print)
A little looser and more permissive than the author's highly influential *Cuisines of Mexico* (1972; revised 1986), this book explores a wide range of Mexican styles of cooking and is a big, useful reference work.

MacKie, Cristine. *Life and Food in the Caribbean* (New Amsterdam, 1991—out of print)
A near-perfect integration of the food of a region with the history and the natural history from which it sprang. Recipes, yes, but even more valuable, a portrait of nature and culture that gave rise to a vigorous, richly varied food tradition.

Umana-Murray, Mirtha. *Three Generations of Chilean Cuisine* (Lowell House, 1996)
A national tradition of South American food, sliced longitudinally to reveal its roots and its slow but inexorable evolution. Many dishes appear to be European, until, examined closely, they reveal their solid attachment to the land and the coast of their adopted country. Good stories, good recipes, good food for thought.

SINGLE SUBJECT

Alford, Jeffrey and Naomi Duguid. *Seductions of Rice* (Morrow, 1998)
An admirable examination of the world of rice, from cultivation right through to its spectacularly varied uses in kitchens in every part of the globe. A fine cookbook, but even more, a piece of accessible scholarship that could well serve as a model for any ingredient-inspired work.

Bittman, Mark. *Fish: The Complete Guide* (Macmillan, 1994)
Writer-editor Bittman provides a wide-ranging introduction to fish cookery, offering good background information and many, many highly reliable recipes.

Cunningham, Marion. *The Breakfast Book* (Knopf, 1987—out of print)
One of America's finest bakers takes on the meal Americans seem to like best. Steering clear of gimcrackery, Cunningham deals with the good, plain baked goods and other specialties that make the morning meal a nostalgic focus.

*Davidson, Alan. *North Atlantic Seafood* (Viking, 1980—out of print)
Britain's great scholar-cook provides definitive profiles of the major cold-water species and tells us about their uses as food. It has a limited number of recipes, but massive quantities of information. A companion volume, *Mediterranean Seafood* (Viking, 1981—out of print), covers European warm-water species.

*Dewitt, Dave. *Chile Pepper Encyclopedia* (Morrow, 1999)
Dewitt, founder of *Chile Pepper Magazine* and author of a dozen or so books, has based an entire career on the capsicum family, and here he provides a full-scale reference work on every imaginable pepper variety and the foodstuffs that are made from them. Good clear entries, useful book.

Ellis, Merle. *The Great American Meat Book* (Knopf, 1996)
From the popular TV series host, a thorough guide to the world of meat, from the farm to the meat packer to steaks sizzling on the grill. Excursions into health questions, dealing with your butcher, cutting your own meat, and much more.

*Illy, Francesco. *The Book of Coffee* (Abbeville, 1989)
A large, handsome coffee-table book on every aspect of the beverage, from growing to brewing. It contains an ample history, information on coffee-making machines, serving and consuming, science, traditions, and much more. Not a true reference book, but a fact-packed companion.

Jamison, Sheryl and Bill. *Smoke and Spice* (Harvard Common Press, 1994)
The techniques of grilling and barbecuing for those with some experience in this type of cooking. These excellent food writers have done three books on cooking with fire and smoke.

*Jenkins, Steve. *Cheese Primer* (Workman, 1996)
This is an informal but fact-jammed reference book on the cheeses of the world—and on cheese in general. The author, a longtime cheese department manager and an accomplished retailer, sheds light on the many mysteries of this great food, enabling all of us to become cheese-literate.

Kafka, Barbara. *Soup: A Way of Life* (Artisan, 1998)
A roaring cataract of great recipe ideas from one of the finest writers in the business. The recipes are all straightforward and cook-friendly—a Kafka trademark.

King, Shirley. *Fish: The Basics* (Simon & Schuster, 1990; paper, Houghton Mifflin, 1999)
A highly admired chef and teacher provides not only recipes but all the background one could hope for in selecting fish and cooking it by appropriate methods. An eye-opener for those who have limited themselves to cooking salmon and flounder.

*McClane, A. J. *McClane's Encyclopedia of Fish Cookery* (Holt, 1977—out of print)
An important reference work, now somewhat in need of an update. Covers fish and seafood—descriptions, information on availability by range and season, uses, alternative names, and other information. Not totally systematic, but by far the best there's been.

Peterson, James. *Splendid Soup* (Bantam Books, 1993; revised edition, Wiley, 2000)
An outstanding teacher presents an entire course on soup, offering not only recipes but an excellent treatment of the theory and principles of soup-making.

Raichlin, Steven. *The Barbecue! Bible* (Workman, 1997)
A talented chef with a bent for snappy flavors offers recipes, threaded through with first-rate information on grill and barbecue methods. Simple, accessible.

Rance, Patrick. *Book of French Cheese* (Macmillan [UK], 1989—out of print)
The late Berkshire cheesemonger describes in detail and analyzes critically several hundred cheeses from every region of France. Done with perception and good common sense, this guide, although out of date in some respects, will be the basic work for some years to come.

Schlesinger, Chris and John Willoughby. *Thrill of the Grill* (Morrow, 1990)
Restaurateur Schlesinger and writer Willoughby take on grilling at its highest level—as an advanced method comparable to broiling, frying, or roasting, not merely as a way of doing hamburgers on the patio. Great recipes, lively flavors.

*Stewart, Martha. *Martha Stewart's Hors D'Oeuvres* (Clarkson Potter, 1999)
An astonishingly fertile collection of ideas and suggestions for finger foods and other appetizers. This is an encyclopedia of ideas more than it is a cookbook. A model of clarity and good looks.

BAKING & DESSERTS

Alford, Jeffrey and Naomi Duguid. *Flatbreads and Flavors* (Morrow, 1995)
Among the finest achievements of modern culinary writing. The authors have produced a masterful study of a single food, which is made and used differently in dozens of cultures. Cooking, reference, and travel are combined in this work that every food writer should be required to read.

Beranbaum, Rose Levy. *The Cake Bible* (Morrow, 1988)
One of America's most important bakers offers what can only be called her wisdom on the entire range of cakes and cake production. Much more than a recipe book, *The Cake Bible* offers detailed discussions, charts, and tables on variations in ingredients, conditions, and other parameters of high-level baking. Essential for those advanced in the field.

Clayton, Bernard. *New Complete Book of Bread* (Simon & Schuster, 1987)
A hobbyist-become-master baker who understands the needs of the amateur, Clayton provides well-studied, well-tested recipes for a huge range of breads; reliable and comprehensive.

Field, Carol. *The Italian Baker* (Harper & Row, 1991)
Breads and sweet baking from one of the leading figures of her generation. It is no small compliment to Field that this book was translated into Italian and published in Italy. A very important work.

Healy, Bruce and Paul Bugat. *Art of the Cake* (Morrow, 1999)
These teachers and bakers, one American, the other French, wrote *Mastering the Art of French Pastry* (1984), which they are now replacing with three books—*The French Cookie Book* (1994), *Great Cakes* (1999), and a work-in-progress on French pastry technique. These are innovative, authoritative works, required reading for all serious bakers.

MacLauchlan, Andrew. *The Making of a Pastry Chef* (Wiley, 1999)
Essays, interviews, observations about creativity and career in the world of professional baking. It offers useful revelations for the prospective baker or pastry cook, for whom it should be required reading. The author is a prominent pastry chef.

Ortiz, Joe. *The Village Baker* (Ten Speed, 1993)
A fine California baker teaches the fundamentals of rough, crusty peasant breads. Containing both home recipes and recipes geared to professional bakers, this book is a rare prize.

Silverton, Nancy. *Desserts* (Harper & Row, 1986; hardcover reprint, Biscuit Books, 2000)
The highly admired pastry chef who spent the early part of her career at Spago offers a stunning range of baked and unbaked desserts, many featuring powerful fruit flavors.

Van Over, Charles. *The Best Bread Ever* (Broadway Books, 1997)
This is a revolutionary book about bread baking that recommends the food processor and temperature controls every step of the way for what they can do to help the home baker come up with loaves that are not only somewhat easier to make, but have exceptional depth of flavor and great textures.

VEGETABLES & VEGETARIAN

Greene, Bert. *Greene on Greens* (Workman, 1988)
The immensely popular food writer profiles twenty-odd vegetables, adding delightful personal notes, and providing a fistful of recipes for each. It's as much fun to read as to cook from—and it's a *lot* of fun to cook from.

Grigson, Jane. *Jane Grigson's Fruit Book* (Michael Joseph [UK], 1980; paper, Penguin, 1981)
A highly regarded work by one of England's all-time greats, it features history, lore, a little horticulture, and a lot of quality recipes for different kinds of fruit

Grigson, Jane. *Jane Grigson's Vegetable Book* (Michael Joseph [UK], 1978; paper, Penguin, 1980)
The masterful English food writer offers a near-definitive treatment of the major species of vegetables, combining informative essays and exemplary recipes. An important resource.

Jaffrey, Madhur. *Madhur Jaffrey's World-of-the-East Vegetarian Cookbook* (Knopf, 1981)
A staple for the adventuresome vegetarian—a fascinating exploration of meatless foods, from the Middle East all the way to Japan. Exciting.

LaPlace, Viana. *Verdura* (Morrow, 1991)
Italian vegetable cooking, the homestyle way. The exemplary recipes are more suggestions than they are prescriptions. A truly inspirational book.

Madison, Deborah and Edward Brown. *Greens* (Bantam Books, 1987)
Probably the most sophisticated vegetarian cookbook of the modern era—stunning, hugely flavorful dishes. Few of them are easy or effortless, but the time and energy are well rewarded.

Moosewood Collective. *Sundays at Moosewood* (Simon & Schuster, 1990)
Perhaps the most interesting of the many Moosewood books because it draws on a wide range of ethnic traditions. Rather than offering made-up recipes with vegetable ingredients, the compilers provide sturdy dishes, authentic in style, from about twenty national traditions.

CHEFS

Blanc, Georges. *The Natural Cuisine of Georges Blanc* (Stewart, Tabori & Chang, 1987—out of print)
Blanc is among the first contemporary French chefs to stress fresh and seasonal ingredients. These words may be cliché by now, but Blanc's work is anything but that.

This is a book of lively, sparkling flavors and richly varied textures. A highly influential contribution.

Boulud, Daniel and Dorie Greenspan. *Café Boulud Cookbook* (Scribner, 1999)
A chef's simple philosophy of fresh, seasonal ingredients has been translated into an extremely user-friendly cookbook chock-full of excellent recipes. This is a book that deserves to be kept in the kitchen, at the ready.

Dornenberg, Andrew and Karen Page. *Becoming a Chef* (Van Nostrand Reinhold, later Wiley, 1995)
A chef and a writer—husband and wife—explore the ways in which the chef's career is established. A skilled blending of practical advice and extremely well done interviews with dozens of chefs and others in the food business, this book is both informative and inspiring.

Dornenberg, Andrew and Karen Page. *Culinary Artistry* (Wiley, 1996)
A worthy companion to *Becoming a Chef,* this volume explores the process of culinary invention—how chefs get their ideas, how they elaborate and develop concepts and temper them with the practicalities of restaurant production. Based heavily on interviews.

*Escoffier, George Auguste. *Culinary Guide* (*Le Guide Culinaire*) (1907; current edition, William Heinemann [UK], 1979)
The masterwork on classic cuisine by one of the most important figures of modern cookery. More of an aide-mémoire than a step-by-step cookbook, this large volume provides condensed working descriptions of more than five thousand dishes and other preparations.

Portale, Alfred. *Gotham Bar and Grill Cookbook* (Broadway Books, 1997)
A prominent New York chef shows not only his food but an outstanding restaurant. Tips, hints, and penetrating explanations make this book an education as well as a collection of recipes.

Robuchon, Joël. *L'Atelier of Joël Robuchon* (Wiley, 1996)
One of his generation's best-known chefs, the brilliant Robuchon exposes his own innovative ideas to the creativity of cooks who have worked in his kitchen. Presenting a particular dish, he invites some of his

younger colleagues to give their own take on the basic concept. Exciting.

Vongerichten, Jean-Georges. *Simple Cuisine* (Prentice-Hall, 1991)
A pioneering and important book by a major chef. Vongerichten introduces the principles of flavor intensification through the use of such concentrates as juices, broths, and infusions. An original, highly influential book.

White, Marco Pierre. *White Heat* (Pyramid, 1990; paper, Mitchell Beazley [UK], 1999)
The culinary enfant terrible of early 1980s London struts his stuff. Bold, imaginative, self-indulgent—this book, White's first, helped kick off the British food explosion of the ensuing decade. An inspiration for many professionals.

REFERENCE

Corriher, Shirley. *CookWise* (Morrow, 1997)
This book explains how and why things happen in the kitchen and what you can do to control your results. You'll learn how to create recipes that work and how to correct ones that don't. Corriher is the Sherlock Holmes of cooking and her book will stand by you like Dr. Watson. In addition, there are 230 excellent recipes, which prove her points.

*Davidson, Alan. *The Oxford Companion to Food* (Oxford University Press, 1999)
Davidson, perhaps the twentieth century's leading scholar of food and food history, served as general editor of this volume of Oxford's great reference program. Sixteen years in the making, this huge work, incorporating the specialized knowledge of many dozens of experts, is in general a triumph—good for reference and often a delight to read.

*Herbst, Sharon Tyler. *Food Lover's Companion* (paper, Barrons, 1990; revised edition, Barrons, 1995)
An outstanding little dictionary of food and cooking. More than terms parsimoniously but accurately defined. Get one for the kitchen, one for the study.

*Johnson, Hugh. *Hugh Johnson's Encyclopedia of Wine* (Simon & Schuster, annually since 1977)
Each year, Johnson, Britain's best-known wine writer, offers in this packed little book

information on wines from around the world, on estates and vineyards, on wine regions, and all the background relevant to anyone who wants to buy and consume wine knowledgeably.

*McGee, Harold. *On Food and Cooking* (Scribners, 1984)
The scientific underpinnings of the cooking process. A massive, highly readable work that helps cooks understand what is actually going on in their mixing bowls, their pots and pans, their freezers and ovens. Stimulating, informative—how cooking really works.

*Ortiz, Elizabeth Lambert. *Encyclopedia of Herbs, Spices, and Flavorings* (Dorling Kindersley, 1992)
An intelligently done, beautifully illustrated reference work, providing material that ranges from botany through culinary uses for nearly two hundred plants used around the world for flavoring. Outstanding coverage.

*Peterson, James. *Sauces: Classical and Contemporary Sauce-Making* (Van Nostrand Reinhold, 1991; revised edition, Wiley, 1998)
A chef and longtime teacher's massive work on understanding these staples of the cooking repertoire. From classic French to contemporary fruit sauces, the major text.

*Root, Waverley. *Food* (Simon & Schuster, 1980)
A totally delightful, sometimes reliable treasure trove of information about food that happens to interest this highly admired writer. A quintessential "personal encyclopedia," wonderful to read and to use—if you approach it with a grain of salt.

*Schneider, Elizabeth. *Uncommon Fruits and Vegetables* (Harper & Row, 1986; revised edition, Morrow, 1998)
A treatment of about a hundred "exotic" edible flora—basic background, some botanical detail, information on preparation and uses, a few illustrated recipes. Best of all is the writing: Schneider, a scholar, describes taste and texture better than any writer we know.

*Stobart, Tom. *Herbs, Spices, and Flavorings* (International Food and Wine Society, 1970; reprint, Overlook, 2000)
The best concise reference on the world of flavoring ingredients—basic botany, extraction and fabrication, uses, and names in

441

eight or ten different languages. A highly respected work.

*Time-Life Books. *The Good Cook* (1979-1983—out of print)
One of the great cooking works of the twentieth century—twenty-eight volumes, arranged by subject (from "Beef and Veal" to "Wine"). Edited brilliantly by Richard Olney, each of these volumes contains a fully illustrated course on the subject at hand, including excellent introductions, cooking methods, and even theory. The second part of each volume is a fine recipe collection.

*Trager, James. *The Food Chronology* (Holt, 1995; paper, Holt, 1997)
Food history and food facts by the thousands, somewhat zanily organized into a year-by-year chronology (from prehistory to the present). Still fascinating, and, thanks to a good index, fairly usable for research.

*Willan, Anne. *La Varenne Pratique* (Crown, 1989)
One of the most important culinary books of the twentieth century—covers food, food handling, and appropriate cooking methods and is packed with instructional color photos. Know what this book has to teach, and you'll practically never need a cookbook.

HISTORY

Beeton, Isabella. *Mrs. Beeton's Book of Household Management* (Ward Lock [UK], 1861; Southover Press, reprint 1998)
Everything on the orderly household and the accomplished kitchen by a sadly short-lived young woman (1836–1865) whose name has been adapted for generations of books. A fascinating look at the early Victorian world, and in particular its ways with food.

Flandrin, J.-L. and Massimo Montanari, eds. *Food: A Culinary History* (original French publication, 1996; English translation, Columbia University Press, 1999)
A large, substantial collection of papers by a number of academics on various aspects of food history. The editors, both culinary historians, have produced a book covering dozens of topics, some highly specialized, others of broader application. A serious work, but sporadically entertaining.

Giacosa, Ilyria. *A Taste of Ancient Rome* (University of Chicago Press, 1992)
This account of the food of ancient Rome is popularly written, but the scholarship is sound. Not just recipes (mostly from Apicius), but excellent background on everything from agricultural production to markets to the organization of cooking in different households. Outstanding.

Harris, Jessica B. *Iron Pots and Wooden Spoons* (Macmillan, 1989; paper, Simon & Schuster, 1999)
The author, a respected academic, writes quite unacademically about African American food. This book explores the influences of Africa on foods around the world, especially in the Western Hemisphere. An eye-opening delight.

Tannahill, Ray. *Food in History* (Stein & Day, 1973; revised edition, Crown, 1988)
An accessible world history of food with lots of good anecdotal material. Especially useful because it goes beyond European traditions. Not super-scholarly, but very conscientious.

Wheaton, Barbara Ketcham. *Savoring the Past* (University of Pennsylvania Press, 1983—out of print; revised edition, Scribners, 1996—out of print)
A very important work about the French kitchen and table from 1300 to 1789. Wheaton's enthusiastic, full-frontal approach makes this a book that goes far beyond gastronomy to examine the society and the institutions that shaped the world of food in pre-Revolutionary France.

READING

David, Elizabeth. *French Provincial Cooking* (Michael Joseph [UK], 1960; paper [revised edition], Penguin [U.S.], 1970)
A cookbook, but placed here under "Reading" because that is how Britain's greatest-ever food writer works her magic: cook a dish by learning about the world and the culture from which it springs. David's self-conscious imprecision stimulates more good cooking than a thousand "accurate" recipes.

Fisher, M. F. K. *The Art of Eating* (World Publishing, 1954; paper, Macmillan, 1990)
Five short books in one volume by America's greatest writer about food. Belles lettres, not cookbooks, *The Gastronomical Me* and others demonstrate Fisher's postulate that food and autobiography are inseparable.

Grey, Patience. *Honey from a Weed* (Harper & Row, 1987; paper, Lyons Books, 1997)
A longtime denizen of the islands of the western Mediterranean, Grey examines the peculiar juncture of geography, gastronomy, topography, horticulture, mythology, literature, and the culinary arts. Not many could pull all these under one roof—but she does, and the result is great, elevating reading.

Liebling, A. J. *Between Meals* (Simon & Schuster, 1959; paper, North Point, 1986)
The acclaimed *New Yorker* writer recounts his gastronomic coming of age in Paris as a young man. In a magnificently controlled style that combines journalistic and literary craft, Liebling simultaneously enlarges our experience and tickles our funny bones.

Trillin, Calvin. *The Tummy Trilogy* (Farrar, Straus & Giroux, 1994)
A three-in-one of humorist Trillin's *American Fried, Alice, Let's Eat,* and *Third Helpings.* Wry, clever—a dangerous book for the crackup-prone.

Visser, Margaret. *Much Depends on Dinner* (McClelland and Stewart [Canada], 1986; paper, Grove Press, 1999)
Built around a simple menu—corn on the cob with salt and butter, roast chicken with rice, salad dressed in lemon juice and olive oil, and ice cream—Visser presents the extraordinary history and mythology, allure and obsessions, perils and taboos of an ordinary meal in a way that is witty, funny, and fascinating.

Wechsberg, Joseph. *Blue Trout and Black Truffles* (Knopf, 1954; paper, Academy Chicago, 1985)
Word sketches about food and the good life in mid-twentieth-century Europe and America by the urbane Vienna-born writer for *Gourmet* and *The New Yorker.*

C

PRODUCT INDEX

CATALOGUE NUMBER	ITEM DESCRIPTION	MANUFACTURER/ U.S. DISTRIBUTOR	MANUFACTURER MODEL NUMBER
1.1	Endurance Spice Spoons	R.S.V.P. International Inc.	6206
1.2	Measuring Spoons	OXO International	76281
1.3	Measuring Cups	OXO International	76381
1.4	Measuring Cups	Amco	864
1.5	Odd-Size Measuring Cups	Amco	824
1.6	Measure-Batter Bowl	Catamount Housewares	TB2000
1.7	Pyrex Stackable Measuring Cup Set	Corning Consumer Products Company/ World Kitchen	6021001
1.8	Perfect Beaker	Emsa/Frieling USA, Inc.	2206 990096
1.9	Adjustable Tablespoon	KitchenArt	13100
1.10	Endurance Handy Scoops	R.S.V.P. International Inc.	SCOOP-SM
1.10	Endurance Handy Scoops	R.S.V.P. International Inc.	SCOOP-MD
1.10	Endurance Handy Scoops	R.S.V.P. International Inc.	SCOOP-LG
1.11	Vita Scale	Soehnle/Frieling USA, Inc.	8020 63
1.12	Baker's Dream Scale	Salter Housewares	3007
1.13	Mechanical Scale	Pelouze Scale Company	A22R
1.14	Scaleman	Component Design Northwest, Inc.	DS10
1.15	Mechanical Scale	EKS, USA	53CR
1.16	Baker's Scale	Pelouze Scale Company	BD8SC
1.17	Antique Scale	Salter Housewares	060
1.17	Imperial Brass Weight Set	Salter Housewares	063
1.18	Pyrex Oven Thermometer	Robinson Knife Company	17001
1.19	Bulb-Type Mercury Thermometer	Component Design Northwest, Inc.	OT-600
1.20	Sunbeam Large-Face Refrigerator-Freezer Thermometer	Springfield Precision Instruments	90303
1.21	Refrigerator-Freezer Dial Thermometer	Taylor Precision Products, L.P.	5923
1.22	SuperFast Thermapen	Thermoworks, Inc.	THS211-076
1.23	Professional Digital Test Thermometer	Cooper Instrument Corporation	DFP450
1.24	Digital Cooking Thermometer-Timer	Taylor Precision Products, L.P.	1470
1.25	Preprogrammed Cooking Thermometer	Polder, Inc.	307

PRODUCT INDEX

CATALOGUE NUMBER	ITEM DESCRIPTION	MANUFACTURER/ U.S. DISTRIBUTOR	MANUFACTURER MODEL NUMBER
1.26	Acu-Rite Sure-Grip Instant-Read Thermometer	Chaney Instruments Company	00669
1.27	Commercial Test Thermometer	Cooper Instrument Corporation	CT220
1.28	RediChek Thermometer	Maverick Industries, Inc.	ET-3
1.29	Noncontact Thermometer	Cooper Instrument Corporation	460
1.30	Candy-Jelly-Deep-Fry Mercury Thermometer	Taylor Precision Products, L.P.	5983
1.31	Candy Thermometer-Celsius	Matfer, Inc.	111355
1.32	Candy-Deep-Fry Thermometer	Acme International, Inc.	99830
1.33	Chocolate Thermometer	Cordon Rose/New York Cake & Baking	NONE
1.34	Thermomètre Boulanger	Matfer, Inc.	250305
1.35	Salometer	Matfer, Inc.	072285
1.36	Syrup Density Meter	Matfer, Inc.	111350
1.36	Test Tube for Syrup Density Meter	Matfer, Inc.	250112
1.37	Egg Timer	Progressus Company, Inc.	16
1.38	Square Mechanical Timer	Polder, Inc.	51-90
1.39	Sunbeam Digi-Master Deluxe	Springfield Precision Instruments	90373
1.40	Portable Timer	Polder, Inc.	898-90
1.41	Triple Timer Clock	Polder, Inc.	891-90
1.42	Clock-Double Timer	The West Bend Company	40031X
1.43	Voicecraft Talking Digital Timer & Clock	Component Design Northwest, Inc.	TM102
2.1	Heavy Copper Bowl; 6 qt.	Kitchen Supply Company	2256
2.2	All-Steel Mixing Bowl	Hackman Tabletop, Inc.	444 080-2
2.3	Nonskid Mixing Bowls, 2 qt., 4 qt. and 6 qt.	Amco	875RBB
2.4	Deep Bowl Set & Lids, 16cm, 20 cm and 24 cm	Rösle USA	SP15671
2.4	Bowl Lid, 24 cm	Rösle USA	SP91464
2.4	Bowl Lid, 20 cm	Rösle USA	SP91460
2.4	Bowl Lid, 16 cm	Rösle USA	SP91456
2.5	Mixing Bowls with Hand Grip	Gourmet Standard	B20G
2.6	Pinch Bowls	Amco	237
2.7	Pyrex 3-Piece Mixing-Bowl Set	Corning Consumer Products Company/ World Kitchen	6001001
2.8	Nonskid Mixing Bowl, 2 qt.	OXO International	70581
2.8	Nonskid Mixing Bowl, 4 qt.	OXO International	70481
2.9	Batter Bowl	Frieling USA, Inc.	2249 251200
2.10	Ceramic Bowl Set	Chantal Cookware	90-5BL
2.11	Mixing Bowl, 4½″	Mason Cash of England	080069
2.11	Mixing Bowl, 8″	Mason Cash of England	010301
2.11	Mixing Bowl, 10″	Mason Cash of England	010189
2.12	Pudding Basin	Mason Cash of England	080342
2.13	Rubberwood Salad Bowl	Woodard + Charles Ltd.	WC902
2.14	Herb Bowl with Mezzaluna Chopper	J. K. Adams Company, Inc.	HB-1010
3.1	Classic Cook's Knife	Wüsthof-Trident of America	4584⁄26
3.2	LamsonSharp Gold Cook's Knife	Lamson & Goodnow Mfg. Co	39850
3.3	Four-Star Cook's Knife	Zwilling J. A. Henckels Inc.	31071-230
3.4	Infinity Edge Cook's Knife	Regent-Sheffield/World Kitchen	5191009
3.5	Au Carbone Cook's Knife	Sabatier–A Division of Excel	80805
3.6	Four Star Paring Knife	Zwilling J. A. Henckels Inc.	31070-080
3.7	Diva Paring Knife	Seshin USA, Inc.	DIVA
3.8	Paring Knife	Global/Sointu, Inc.	GSF-15
3.9	Grand Prix Paring Knife	Wüsthof-Trident of America	4063
3.10	LamsonSharp Wide Paring Knife	Lamson & Goodnow Mfg. Co	39610

CATALOGUE NUMBER	ITEM DESCRIPTION	MANUFACTURER/ U.S. DISTRIBUTOR	MANUFACTURER MODEL NUMBER
3.11	Five-Star Paring Knife	Zwilling J. A. Henckels Inc.	30040-060
3.12	LamsonSharp Fluting Parer	Lamson & Goodnow Mfg. Co	39709
3.13	Classic Cleaver	Wüsthof-Trident of America	4680/16
3.14	Four-Star Cleaver	Zwilling J. A. Henckels Inc.	31095-150
3.15	Commercial Cleaver	Sabatier–A Division of Excel	80320
3.16	All-in-One Knife	Joyce Chen	50-0751
3.17	Dexter Chinese Chef's Knife	Russell Harrington Cutlery	S5198
3.18	Grand Prix *Santoku*	Wüsthof-Trident of America	4189
3.19	*Deba*	Global/Sointu, Inc.	G-7
3.20	Kasumi *Yanagi*	Masamoto Sohoten/Korin	HMA-KK0427
3.21	Kasumi *Usuba*	Masamoto Sohoten/Korin	HMA-KK0619
3.22	Sani-Safe Butcher Knife	Russell Harrington Cutlery	S112-10
3.23	Collezione Maître Butcher Knife	Montana	120736
3.24	Sani-Safe Scimitar Knife	Russell Harrington Cutlery	S132-10
3.25	Sani-Safe Boning Knife	Russell Harrington Cutlery	S136F
3.26	Chef'sChoice Trizor Professional 10x Boning Knife	EdgeCraft Corporation	2000300
3.27	Ham Boning Knife	Victorinox/R. H. Forschner & Co.	5.6900.19
3.28	Au Carbone Boning Knife	Sabatier–A Division of Excel	80801
3.29	Sani-Safe Fillet Knife	Russell Harrington Cutlery	S133-7
3.30	Collezione Maître Fillet Knife	Montana	120712
3.31	Slicer	Global/Sointu, Inc.	GSF-24
3.32	Infinity Edge Slicer	Regent-Sheffield/World Kitchen	519101901
3.33	Grand Prix Slicer	Wüsthof-Trident of America	4527/23
3.34	Ham Rack	J. B. Prince	R109
3.35	Commercial Ham Slicer	Sabatier–A Division of Excel	80318
3.36	Collezione Maître Salami Slicer	Montana	120718
3.37	Four-Star Roast Beef Slicer	Zwilling J. A. Henckels Inc.	31081-2601
3.38	Classic Salmon Slicer	Wüsthof-Trident of America	4543
3.39	Sani-Safe Narrow Slicer	Russell Harrington Cutlery	S140N-10GE
3.40	Commercial Steak Knives	Sabatier–A Division of Excel	84303
3.41	Optima Dough Knife	Montana	170185
3.42	Optima Adjustable Bread Knife	Montana	M170006
3.43	Four-Star Bread Knife	Zwilling J. A. Henckels Inc.	31076-200
3.44	LamsonSharp Gold Bread Knife	Lamson & Goodnow Mfg. Co	39855
3.45	Good Grips Bread Knife	OXO International	23381
3.46	Sandwich Spatula	Best Manufacturers, Inc.	B-288
3.47	LamsonSharp Tomato Knife	Lamson & Goodnow Mfg. Co	39717
3.48	Classic Tomato Knife	Wüsthof-Trident of America	4109/14
3.49	Collezione Maître Citrus Knife	Montana	120704
3.50	Ming Tsai Ceramic Fruit Knife	Kyocera America, Inc./Harold Import Co., Inc.	KC35
3.51	Grapefruit Knife	Wüsthof-Trident of America	3044
3.52	LamsonSharp Grapefruit Knife	Lamson & Goodnow Mfg. Co	32604
3.53	Frozen-Food Knife	Wüsthof-Trident of America	4191
3.54	Arrow-Shaped Oyster Knife	Wüsthof-Trident of America	4280
3.55	Sani-Safe Oyster Knife	Russell Harrington Cutlery	S121
3.56	Good Grips Clam Knife	OXO International	35781
3.57	Sani-Safe Bay Scallop Knife	Russell Harrington Cutlery	S124
3.58	Oyster Glove	Savoir Vivre	NONE
3.59	Crab Knife	Wüsthof-Trident of America	3330

CATALOGUE NUMBER	ITEM DESCRIPTION	MANUFACTURER/ U.S. DISTRIBUTOR	MANUFACTURER MODEL NUMBER
3.60	Offset Cheese Knife	Wüsthof-Trident of America	4800
3.61	Offset Cheese Knife	Zwilling J. A. Henckels Inc.	38027-151
3.62	Parmesan Knife	Montana	241330
3.63	Gorgonzola Knife	Montana	241334/14
3.64	Double-Handled Cheese Knife	Matfer, Inc.	090345
3.65	Mezzaluna	Zwilling J. A. Henckels Inc.	31750-140
3.66	Double-Bladed Mezzaluna	Rösle USA	96 190
3.67	Decorating Knife	Wüsthof-Trident of America	4200
3.68	Commercial Straightening Steel	Sabatier–A Division of Excel	2180323
3.69	Zip Zap	The Zanger Company	40047 54325
3.70	Diamond Sharpener	EZE-LAP Diamond Products, Inc.	D10F
3.71	Pocket Sharpener	EZE-LAP Diamond Products, Inc.	ST
3.72	Carborundum Stone	Privately Owned	NONE
3.73	Ceramic Whetstone	Global/Sointu, Inc.	MS5/O & M
3.74	Chef'sChoice Serrated Blade Diamond Hone Knife Sharpener	EdgeCraft Corporation	430
3.75	Knife Sharpener	Chantry-Victor, Inc.	1000
3.76	Chef'sChoice EdgeSelect Diamond Hone Sharpener-Plus	EdgeCraft Corporation	120
3.77	Knife Sharpener	EZ Sharp	90621 11433
3.78	Super Magnet Knife Rack	Messermeister/DAMCO	DSM-18D
3.79	Knife Block	J. K. Adams Company, Inc.	HKG-1
3.80	In-Drawer Knife Tray	J. K. Adams Company, Inc.	IDW-06
3.81	Knife Sheath	Messermeister/DAMCO	EGS-08
3.82	PCA Butcher Block	John Boos & Company	PCA
3.83	Wooden Cutting Board	J. K. Adams Company, Inc.	TBT-2014
3.84	Plasti-tuff Cutting Board	Teknor Apex Company	173-070
3.85	Sani-tuff Cutting Board	Teknor Apex Company	159-905
3.86	Chop & Chop Cutting Mat	New Age Products	10
4.1	Spice Cutter	Küchenprofi-USA	13.7006.22.00
4.2	Chopper	Zyliss USA Corporation	10-020
4.3	Bron Classic Mandoline	SCI Cuisine International	R6100
4.4	Professional Mandolin	Matfer, Inc.	215060
4.5	Performance Shield Cut-Resistant Gloves	R. H. Forschner & Co.	83503
4.6	Asian Mandoline Plus	Joyce Chen	51-0555
4.7	Benriner Cook Help Upright Turning Slicer	NY Mutual Trading Company	655 25 90592
4.8	Le Rouet Turning Slicer	Mouli Manufacturing Corp.	TLR7001
4.9	Chef'sChoice Professional Electric Food Slicer	EdgeCraft Corporation	640
4.10	Radimax Spiral Cutter	Westmark/Norpro	W5135
4.11	Good Grips Multi Grater	OXO International	32780
4.12	Microplane Cheese Grater-Zester	Grace Manufacturing	30020S
4.13	ProGrip Ultra Tower Grater	Progressive International Corp.	GT-7436
4.14	Microplane Spice Grater	Grace Manufacturing	30018
4.15	Drum Cheese Grater with Bowl	Mouli Manufacturing Corp.	VV6100
4.16	Grattalo Cheese Scraper	ILSA/Gary Valenti, Inc.	286
4.17	Deluxe Cheese Grater Set (Drum for Cheese Grater)	Zyliss USA Corporation	11 225
4.17	Deluxe Cheese Grater Set (Cheese Collector for Grater)	Zyliss USA Corporation	11 240
4.17	Deluxe Cheese Grater Set (Cheese Grater)	Zyliss USA Corporation	11 220

CATALOGUE NUMBER	ITEM DESCRIPTION	MANUFACTURER/ U.S. DISTRIBUTOR	MANUFACTURER MODEL NUMBER
4.18	Good Grips Rotary Cheese Grater	OXO International	32880
4.19	Porcelain Ginger Grater	Kyocera America, Inc.	P-1
4.20	Rotating Coconut Grater	Foods of India	NONE
4.21	Grater Brush	Mouli Manufacturing Corp.	AC2010
4.22	Swivel Peeler	Messermeister/DAMCO	800-58
4.23	Peelz-it	iSi North America	8685
4.24	Stationary Peeler	Wüsthof-Trident of America	4034
4.25	Y Peeler	OXO International	21081
4.26	Swiss Peeler	Kuhn Rikon Corp.	2212
4.27	Citrus Knife	Frieling USA, Inc.	0073
4.28	Lemon Zester	Wüsthof-Trident of America	3088
4.29	Citrus Peeler	iSi North America	8587
4.30	Channel Knife	Wüsthof-Trident of America	3066
4.31	Microplane Zester	Grace Manufacturing	30001S
4.32	Potato Chipper	Zyliss USA Corporation	13 030
4.33	Butter Curler	Rösle USA	12740
4.34	Lee Corn Cutter & Creamer	Norpro	5402
4.35	Radish Rose Cutter	Westmark/Matfer	073145
4.36	Hong Kong Vegetable Cutters	NY Mutual Trading Company	VARIOUS
4.37	Bean Slicer	VillaWare	583
4.38	Butter Slicer	Westmark/Matfer	073085
4.39	Pickle Slicer	Matfer, Inc.	120903
4.40	Peel-Star Asparagus Peeler	Westmark/Matfer	090395
4.41	E-Z-Roll Garlic Peeler	Elan	NONE
4.42	Chestnut Peeler	Matfer, Inc.	121030
4.43	Avocado Skinner	Amco	747
4.44	Peel-Away Apple & Potato Peeler	Back to Basics	A505
4.45	Garnish Kit	Amco	248
4.46	Baller, 1.5 cm	Rösle USA	12 702
4.46	Baller, 2.2 cm	Rösle USA	12 706
4.46	Baller, 3.0 cm	Rösle USA	12 710
4.47	Good Grips Double Melon Baller Cutter	OXO International	39781
4.48	Cheese, Chocolate, & Truffle Shaver	Mouli Manufacturing Corp.	AU 7164
4.49	12-Piece Cutter Set	J. B. Prince	T200
4.50	Vegetable Corer	Rösle USA	12 748
4.51	Apple Corer	OXO International	20181
4.52	Tomato Shark	Messermeister/DAMCO	800-151
4.53	Pineapple Corer & Slicer	Vacu Vin USA, Inc.	4880250
4.54	Apple Divider	OXO International	32681
4.55	Cherry Pitter	Leifheit International	36704
4.56	Olive Pitter	Westmark /Matfer	073090
4.57	Plum Pitter	Leifheit International	36602
4.58	Strawberry Huller	Norpro	5126
4.59	Twin Lissi Kitchen Shears	Zwilling J. A. Henckels, Inc.	43943-000
4.60	LamsonSharp Forged Kitchen Shears	Lamson & Goodnow Mfg. Co	758
4.61	Poultry Shears	Kretzer Scheren Solingen/ Helco Ltd. European Imports	60624
4.62	Fish Shears	Wüsthof-Trident of America	5562
4.63	Dual-Purpose Egg Slicer	Pedrini USA, Inc.	2271
4.64	Egg Topper	Zyliss USA Corporation	21 100 PA

CATALOGUE NUMBER	ITEM DESCRIPTION	MANUFACTURER/ U.S. DISTRIBUTOR	MANUFACTURER MODEL NUMBER
4.65	Egg Piercer	Zyliss USA Corporation	23-000
4.66	Cheese Plane	Rösle USA	12 738
4.67	Cheese Wire	Matfer, Inc.	072569
4.68	Cheese Cutter	Leifheit International	21416
4.69	Lobster Cracker	Zyliss USA Corporation	20 300
4.70	Good Cook Shrimp Tool	Bradshaw International	24298
4.71	French Fish Scaler	J. B. Prince	U658
4.72	Stainless Fish Pliers	Messermeister/DAMCO	FP-998
4.73	Nut & Seafood Cracker	OXO International	35581
4.74	Lobster-Nutcrackers	Mouli Manufacturing Corp.	GH34
4.75	Reed's Rocket Nutcracker	Harold Import Company, Inc.	1710
4.76	Betel Nut Slicer	Foods of India	G42
5.1	*Tamis*	Mouli Manufacturing Corp.	CM605
5.1	Coarse *Tamis* Screen	Mouli Manufacturing Corp.	CM608
5.2	Perforated *Chinois*	De Buyer/World Cuisine, Inc.	335020
5.3	Mesh *Chinois*	SCI Cuisine International	R2618
5.4	*Chinois*	Mouli Manufacturing Corp.	TL3018
5.4	Stainless *Chinois* Holder	Mouli Manufacturing Corp.	FL3020
5.5	Wooden Pestle for *Chinois*	Mouli Manufacturing Corp.	TL3019
5.6	*Champignon*	Küchenprofi-USA	08.7008.10.00
5.7	Food Mill	Foley	5404513
5.8	Victorio Food Strainer	VillaWare	200
5.9	Food Mill, 2 qt.	Moulinex	103186
5.10	Good Grips Potato Masher	OXO International	34581
5.11	Potato Masher	Calphalon Corp.	UN19
5.12	Potato Masher	Rösle USA	12780
5.13	Good Grips Potato Ricer	OXO International	26981
5.14	King Potato Ricer	VillaWare	365
5.15	Susi Deluxe Garlic Press	Zyliss USA Corporation	12-036
5.16	Good Grips Garlic Press	OXO International	28181
5.17	Vitrified Ceramic Mortar & Pestle	Mason Cash of England	380381
5.18	*Suribachi*	Joyce Chen	90-2001
5.18	*Suribachi* Pestle	Joyce Chen	90-2004
5.19	Marble Mortar & Pestle	Norpro	694
5.20	Lava Stone Mortar & Pestle	Kitchen Market	NONE
5.21	Lava Stone Corn Grinder	Dance of the Ancestors	200-413
5.22	Indian Brass Mortar and Pestle	Foods of India	NONE
5.23	Unicorn Magnum Plus	Tom David, Inc.	NONE
5.24	Millenium Chef's Peppermill	William Bounds Ltd.	04711
5.25	Auberge Peppermill	Peugeot/Swissmar Imports, Ltd.	P809-1
5.26	Good Grips Pepper Mill	OXO International	32180
5.27	Perfex Pepper Mill	Mouli Manufacturing Corp.	HY7339
5.27	Perfex Salt Mill	Mouli Manufacturing Corp.	HY7335
5.28	Salt Ceramill	WMF USA Headquarters	06 5358 7730
5.29	Nut Twister	William Bounds Ltd.	07000
5.30	Poppyseed Grinder	VillaWare	635
5.31	Our Best Grain Mill	Lehman's	C17A
5.32	Grain Master Whisper Mill	Lehman's	71550
5.33	Deluxe Food Grinder	Maverick Industries, Inc.	MM6386

CATALOGUE NUMBER	ITEM DESCRIPTION	MANUFACTURER/ U.S. DISTRIBUTOR	MANUFACTURER MODEL NUMBER
5.34	Magic Mill Assistant Meat Grinder Attachment	Magic Mill	322
5.35	Meat Grinder Attachment	Kenwood/Maverick Industries, Inc.	A920
5.36	Porkert No. 10 Meat Grinder	VillaWare	265-10
5.37	Sausage Stuffer	The Sausage Maker	E55000
5.38	Large Flat Pounder	Mouli Manufacturing Corp.	AU71525
5.39	Large Vertical Pounder	Mouli Manufacturing Corp.	AU71510
5.40	Round Meat Pounder	Norpro	6211
5.41	Meat Hammer	Norpro	153
5.42	CitrusMate Plus	Black & Decker	CJ525
5.43	Mighty OJ	Metrokane, Inc.	3501
5.44	Mexican Lime Press	Best Manufacturers, Inc.	B-185
5.45	Ceramic Lemon Juicer	Kotobuki	113931
5.46	Limona Citrus Press	Westmark /Norpro	W5000
5.47	Metal Citrus Juicer	Küchenprofi-USA	13.6600.28.00
5.48	Lemon Juicer	OXO International	28281
5.49	Wooden Reamer	SCI Cuisine International	W12
5.50	Pleated Citrus Reamer	OXO International	39281
5.51	Citrus Trumpet	Frieling USA, Inc.	0061
5.52	Juicer	Champion	MAR-48C
5.53	Omega 4000 Juice Extractor	Omega Products Inc.	4000
5.54	OptiFruit	Krups North America, Inc.	291
5.55	Wheat Grass Juicer	Back to Basics	SJ-27
5.56	Juice Extractor	Braun North America	MP80
6.1	Colander	Danesco International, Inc.	16630
6.2	Colander	All-Clad Metalcrafters	5605C
6.3	Colander	Rösle USA	16 324
6.4	Mini Colander	Metro Marketing	0056
6.5	Over-The-Sink Colander	Norpro	2157
6.6	Long-Handled Colander	Danesco International, Inc.	16520
6.7	Spaghetti Colander	The Vollrath Company	47960
6.8	6-Qt. All-Purpose Insert	Calphalon Corp.	APC-8706
6.9	Scoop Colander	Sitlax, Ltd.	CO-6
6.10	Colander-Strainer	Norpro	2142
6.11	Salad Drier	Zyliss USA Corporation	15-112
6.12	Salad Spinner	OXO International	32480
6.13	Mini Salad Spinner	Copco	2555-4924
6.14	Tea Strainer	Rösle USA	ST95158
6.15	Double Rod Strainer	OXO International	38891
6.16	Shallow Strainer	Amco	816
6.17	Strainer	Mouli Manufacturing Corp.	KN1766
6.18	Fat Separator	Catamount Housewares	SP600
6.19	Gravy Separator	Pedrini USA, Inc.	5303
6.20	Cromargan Skimming Ladle	WMF USA Headquarters	18 7252 6030
6.21	Egg Separator	BOJ/USA	12120
7.1	French Mixing Spoon	H. A. Mack	F53
7.2	Italian Cooking Spoon	H. A. Mack	H22
7.3	Spanish Mixing Spoon	H. A. Mack	Z19
7.4	Portuguese Cooking Spoon	H. A. Mack	P35
7.5	All-Purpose Spatula	Joyce Chen	33-0021

CATALOGUE NUMBER	ITEM DESCRIPTION	MANUFACTURER/ U.S. DISTRIBUTOR	MANUFACTURER MODEL NUMBER
7.6	Shovall	Paul Oliver Woodware	22
7.7	Serving Spoon	Zwilling J. A. Henckels Inc.	39721-000
7.8	Nylon Kitchen Spoon	Zwilling J. A. Henckels Inc.	12400-000
7.9	Kitchen Spatula	Matfer, Inc.	113035
7.10	Classic Cooking Spoon	Rösle USA	95671
7.11	Slotted Spoon	H. A. Mack	Z112
7.12	Large Slotted Spoon	Calphalon Corp.	US-02
7.13	Blunt-End Perforated Spoon	Best Manufacturers, Inc.	B-6P
7.14	Stir-Fry Scoop	Calphalon Corp.	UN16
7.15	Pasta Fork	Calphalon Corp.	UN07
7.16	Porcelain Tasting Spoon	Apilco/Cuthbertson Imports	040 001
7.17	Polish Chocolate Spoon	H. A. Mack	PL26
7.18	Portuguese Egg Spoon	H. A. Mack	P43B
7.19	Horn Caviar Spoon & Server	Savoir Vivre	NONE
7.20	Ladle with Pouring Rim	Rösle USA	10 010
7.21	Scoop Ladle	Rösle USA	10 020
7.22	Coconut Ladle	Coconut Cookery	NONE
7.23	Sauce Ladle	WMF USA Headquarters	18 7184 6040
7.24	Extra-Deep Skimmer	Rösle USA	10 030
7.25	Stainless Steel Chinese Ladle	Kam Man Food Products, Inc.	NONE
7.26	Wire Skimmer	Le Creuset of America	F1410
7.27	Skimmer	Rösle USA	10 052
7.28	Fine Mesh Skimmer	Mouli Manufacturing Corp.	P17105
7.29	Brass Strainer	Joyce Chen	30-0028
7.30	Silicone Spatula	OXO International	73091
7.31	Silicone Spatula (Red)	OXO International	72791
7.32	Revereware Dura-Spatula Set	Acme International, Inc.	55114
7.33	Spoon-Spatula, 11¼″	Le Creuset of America	FB102
7.34	Spoon-Spatula, 10½″	Le Creuset of America	FB107
7.35	Super Spatula	Le Creuset of America	FB103
7.36	All-Purpose Spatula	Trudeau Corporation	099-924
7.37	Solid Pelton Spatula	Matfer, Inc.	112430
7.38	Solid Spatula	Global/Sointu, Inc.	GS-25
7.39	LamsonSharp Slotted Turner	Lamson & Goodnow Mfg. Co	39572
7.40	Turner-Spatula	Global/Sointu, Inc.	GS-27
7.41	Slotted Pelton Spatula	Matfer, Inc.	112420
7.42	Wide-Blade Spatula	Amco	876
7.43	Asian Turner	OXO International	29691
7.44	Taiwan Cooking Chopsticks	H. A. Mack	T71/18
7.45	Stainless Steel–Tipped Chopsticks	NY Mutual Trading Company	685 30 91685
7.46	Locking Tongs	Messermeister/DAMCO	800-90
7.47	Tongs	Cuisinart	SFTL-11
7.48	Pot Fork	OXO International	79391
7.49	Cooking Fork	OXO International	21781
7.50	Curved Carving Fork	Wüsthof-Trident of America	4411
7.51	Bayonet Chef's Fork	Sabatier–A Division of Excel	80516
7.52	Balloon Whisk	Best Manufacturers, Inc.	1416B
7.53	Round Balloon Whisk	Rösle USA	WH95591
7.54	French Whisk	Best Manufacturers, Inc.	12-SW

CATALOGUE NUMBER	ITEM DESCRIPTION	MANUFACTURER/ U.S. DISTRIBUTOR	MANUFACTURER MODEL NUMBER
7.55	Standard Whisk	Chantal Cookware	KT-WS12
7.56	Heat-Resistant Whisk	Amco	8091
7.57	Two-Wire Batter Whisk	Amco	8028
7.58	Flat Whisk	OXO International	74391
7.59	Spiral Whisk	Rösle USA	WH95541
7.60	Light Design Whisk	Best Manufacturers, Inc.	820
7.61	Molinillo	Kitchen Market	UT06
7.62	Hand Beater	Frieling USA, Inc.	0060
8.1	Heavy-Duty Mixer	KitchenAid	KSM5PS
8.2	Major Classic Mixer	Kenwood/Maverick Industries, Inc.	KM-800
8.3	ChefMix	Hamilton Beach	60690
8.4	DLX 2000 Assistant	Magic Mill	DLX 2000
8.5	Smartpower Count-Up 9-Speed Hand Mixer	Cuisinart	HTM-9LT
8.6	7-Speed Ultra Power Plus Hand Mixer	KitchenAid	KHM7T
8.7	Smartpower Duet Blender–Food Processor	Cuisinart	BFP-703
8.8	Ultra Power Blender	KitchenAid	KSB5
8.9	Professional Bar Blender	Waring	PBB25
8.10	Power Xtreme Blender	Krups North America, Inc.	572
8.11	Chrome Classic DrinkMaster Drink Mixer	Hamilton Beach	730C
8.12	SmartStick Extendable Shaft Hand Blender & Chopper-Grinder	Cuisinart	CSB-55
8.13	Cordless Rechargeable Hand Blender	Cuisinart	CSB-44
8.14	Multiquick Deluxe Hand Blender & Chopper	Braun North America	MR430HC
8.15	Pro Food Prep Center	Cuisinart	DLC-7SFP
8.16	Power Prep Plus Food Processor	Cuisinart	2014
8.17	Professional Food Processor	KitchenAid	KFP670
8.18	R2 Ultra Food Processor	Robot Coupe USA	700R2U
8.19	Blixer BX3 Food Processor	Robot Coupe USA	700BX3
8.20	PowerPro Food Processor	Black & Decker	FP1000
8.21	MiniPrep Processor	Cuisinart	DLC-1
9.1	Cast-Iron Frying Pan	Lodge Manufacturing Co.	8SK2
9.2	Copper Fry Pan with Stainless Steel Lining	Bourgeat USA, Inc.	3690.24
9.3	Copper Fry Pan with Tin Lining	De Buyer/World Cuisine, Inc.	660324
9.4	Carbon Steel Frying Pan	De Buyer/World Cuisine, Inc.	511024
9.5	Millennium Stainless Steel Covered French Skillet	Farberware Cookware	52011
9.6	Hi*Density Skillet	KitchenAid Cookware	85324
9.7	Stainless Steel Nonstick Skillet	All-Clad Metalcrafters	5110NS
9.8	Cast Aluminum Nonstick Frypan	ScanPan USA, Inc.	4501/26
9.9	Tradition Skillet	Berndes Cookware, Inc.	671056
9.10	Skillet with Dome Cover	Farberware Electrics	FSS344
9.11	Deep Dutch Skillet	Black & Decker	SK500
9.12	Copper Oval Pan	Bourgeat USA, Inc.	3700.36
9.13	Professional Hard-Anodized Oval Sauté Pan	Calphalon Corp.	G192HC
9.14	LTD Oval Pan	All-Clad Metalcrafters	3612
9.15	Carbon Steel Crepe Pan	De Buyer/World Cuisine, Inc.	512020
9.16	Cuprinox Crepe Pan	Mauviel/Matfer, Inc.	6535-25
9.17	Oval Flambé Pan	Mauviel/Fante's	5660
9.18	Round Flambé Pan	Mauviel/Fante's	5661
9.19	Nonstick Omelet Pan	All-Clad Metalcrafters	5108NS

CATALOGUE NUMBER	ITEM DESCRIPTION	MANUFACTURER/ U.S. DISTRIBUTOR	MANUFACTURER MODEL NUMBER
9.20	Commercial Hard-Anodized Omelet Pan	Calphalon Corp.	D1388
9.21	Millennium Stainless Steel Nonstick Skillet	Farberware Cookware	53012
9.22	Endurance II Triple-Ply Omelet Pan	R.S.V.P. International Inc.	E-10F
9.23	Japanese *Tamago* Pan	Korin	TK 301 01A
9.24	Carbon Steel Paella Pan	De Buyer/World Cuisine, Inc.	511328
9.25	Aluminum Nonstick Paella Pan	Bourgeat USA, Inc.	6645.40
9.26	Paella Pan with Domed Lid	All-Clad Metalcrafters	5413
9.27	Copper Sauté Pan	Mauviel/Matfer, Inc.	032026
9.28	Copper *Sauteuse*	Bourgeat USA, Inc.	3721.20
9.29	Five-Ply Stainless Steel Clad Sauté Pan with Helper Handle	KitchenAid Cookware	75908
9.30	LTD Sauté Pan	All-Clad Metalcrafters	3403
9.31	Commerical Hard-Anodized Sauté Pan	Calphalon Corp.	D5005
9.32	Commerical Stainless Sauté Pan	Calphalon Corp.	Q5003
9.33	Cast-Iron Chicken Fryer	Lodge Manufacturing Co.	10CF2
9.34	Deep Covered Sauté Pan	Le Creuset of America	L2556-27
9.35	Splatter Guard	Le Creuset of America	N4070-28
9.36	Cast-Iron Deep-Fryer	Lodge Manufacturing Co.	10DO2
9.37	Fry Basket	Lodge Manufacturing Co.	10FB2
9.38	Black Steel Frying Bowl with Basket	Matfer, Inc.	062060
9.39	*Karhai*	Foods of India	NONE
9.40	Birds' Nest Basket	Matfer, Inc.	112321
9.41	Rosette Iron Set	Nordic Ware	01306
9.42	Tempura Cooker	River Light Company/Williams-Sonoma	1286962
9.43	FryDaddy Electric Deep Fryer	Presto	05420
9.44	RotoFryer	DeLonghi America, Inc.	F895
9.45	Round-Bottom Wok Set	Allied Metal Spinning Company	WS14BX
9.46	Pro Chef Carbon-Steel Wok	Joyce Chen	22-0060
9.47	Professional Hard-Anodized Stir-Fry Pan	Calphalon Corp.	G165HC
9.48	Peking Pan	Joyce Chen	22-9930
9.49	LTD Stir-Fry Pan	All-Clad Metalcrafters	3410
9.50	Maxim High Performance Electric Wok	Salton, Inc	EW70
9.51	Endurance Crescent Pot-Edge Strainer	R.S.V.P. International Inc.	PT-15
9.52	Hammered Copper Saucepan	Mauviel/Matfer, Inc.	032004
9.53	Hammered Saucepan	De Buyer/World Cuisine, Inc.	660018
9.54	Copper Saucepan	Bourgeat USA, Inc.	3601.18
9.55	Krona Pot	Norpro	601
9.56	Five-Ply Stainless Steel Clad Saucepan	KitchenAid Cookware	75900
9.57	Nouvelle Stainless Steel Saucepan	Anolon	72013
9.58	Stainless Steel Nonstick Saucepan	All-Clad Metalcrafters	5202NS
9.59	Phenolic Handle Saucepan	Le Creuset of America	L2939-18
9.60	Stainless Steel Saucier	All-Clad Metalcrafters	5212
9.61	Commercial Hard-Anodized Saucepan	Calphalon Corp.	D8702 1/2
9.62	Centurion Brushed Stainless Steel Saucepan	Lincoln Foodservice Products, Inc.	822 3702
9.63	*Sauteuse Evasée*	Bourgeat USA, Inc.	3731.24
9.64	Commercial Hard-Anodized Chef's Pan	Calphalon Corp.	D-141
9.65	High*Density Hard-Anodized Aluminum Saucier	KitchenAid Cookware	85331
9.66	*Marmitout* (Multifunction) Pan	Le Creuset of America	L2531-22

CATALOGUE NUMBER	ITEM DESCRIPTION	MANUFACTURER/ U.S. DISTRIBUTOR	MANUFACTURER MODEL NUMBER
9.67	Professional Hard-Anodized Butter Warmer	Calphalon Corp.	G710 1/2 HC
9.68	LTD Windsor Pan	All-Clad Metalcrafters	3212.5
9.69	Stainless Steel Pressure Cooker with BiMetal-Clad Base	Presto	01362
9.70	Clipso Pressure Cooker	T-Fal	4103000
9.71	Copper *Bain-Marie*	Mauviel/Swissmar Imports, Ltd.	M2703.12
9.72	Glass *Bain-Marie*	Catamount Housewares	DB2000
9.73	Heat Diffuser	ILSA/Harold Import Company	255
9.74	3-Quart Double Boiler Insert	All-Clad Metalcrafters	5703DB
9.75	Stockpot with Spigot	Bourgeat USA, Inc.	7122.24
9.76	Five-Ply Stainless Steel Clad Stockpot	KitchenAid Cookware	75903
9.77	Marmite	Ceraflame, Inc.	C45020
9.78	Commercial Stainless Saucepan	Calphalon Corp.	QL8706 1/2
9.79	Commercial Hard-Anodized Nonstick Stockpot	Calphalon Corp.	C812S
9.80	Enamel Stockpot	Chantal Cookware	33-2405
9.81	Topstar Low Casserole with Lid	WMF USA Headquarters	17 5020 6040
9.81	Topstar *Bain-Marie*	WMF USA Headquarters	17 5902 6040
9.81	Topstar Steamer Insert	WMF USA Headquarters	17 5906 6040
9.81	Topstar Stock Pot with Lid	WMF USA Headquarters	17 5220 6040
9.81	Topstar Broth Colander	WMF USA Headquarters	17 5922 6040
9.81	Topstar Rice Insert	WMF USA Headquarters	17 5942 6040
9.82	Thermos Hot Pot	Thermos Nissan	RPA4500S
9.83	Double Steamer Basket	Norpro	172
9.84	Endurance Steamer Basket	R.S.V.P. International Inc.	FSS-9
9.85	Tiered Bamboo Steamers	Joyce Chen	26-0013
9.86	Steamer Insert	All-Clad Metalcrafters	5703ST
9.87	EveryDay Stainless Steel Steamer	Cuisinart	99-35
9.88	Charleston Rice Cooker	FRED	NONE
9.89	*Couscoussière*	De Buyer/World Cuisine, Inc.	070455
9.90	Artichoke Cooker	Amco	675
9.91	Asparagus Cooker	Amco	680
9.92	*Pommes Vapeur* Pot	Matfer, Inc.	031231
9.93	Deluxe Rice Cooker & Warmer	Zojirushi America Corp.	NRC-10
9.94	Fish Poacher	De Buyer/World Cuisine, Inc.	344862
9.95	Turbot Poacher	De Buyer/World Cuisine, Inc.	898150
9.96	Fish Poacher	Calphalon Corp.	G-1420HCB
9.97	18/10 Stainless Steel Lid	KitchenAid Cookware	75908
9.98	Nouvelle Long Handle Lid	Anolon	SEE 72013
9.99	Round French Oven Lid	Le Creuset of America	L2501-26
9.100	Tradition Glass Domed Lid	Berndes Cookware, Inc.	604424
9.101	Glass Lid	Chantal Cookware	210N
9.102	Strainer Lid	Norpro	SEE 601
9.103	Flat Lid	Calphalon Corp.	G308B
9.104	Flat Copper Lid	Mauviel/Matfer, Inc.	031120
9.105	Copper Lid	De Buyer/World Cuisine, Inc.	651024
9.106	Domed Lid	Calphalon Corp.	G140CB
9.107	Endurance Universal Lid	R.S.V.P. International Inc.	UNIV
9.108	Round French Oven	Le Creuset of America	L2501-24

CATALOGUE NUMBER	ITEM DESCRIPTION	MANUFACTURER/ U.S. DISTRIBUTOR	MANUFACTURER MODEL NUMBER
9.109	Tradition Dutch Oven	Berndes Cookware, Inc.	674026
9.110	Dutch Oven	ScanPan USA, Inc.	8001/56
9.111	Inca Gold Multipurpose Pan	Demeyere	12828
9.112	Stainless Steel Dutch Oven	All-Clad Metalcrafters	5500
9.113	Oval French Oven	Le Creuset of America	L2502-29
9.114	Copper Oval Stew Pan	De Buyer/World Cuisine, Inc.	634624
9.115	Dinner-Is-Served Pan	Chantal Cookware	61-380S BL
9.116	Professional Hard-Anodized Oval Braiser	Calphalon Corp.	G6916HCB
9.117	Copper Braising Pan	Bourgeat USA, Inc.	3741.24
9.118	Stainless Steel Casserole	Cuisinart	955-24
9.119	Stainless Steel Braiser	All-Clad Metalcrafters	5400
9.120	*Tagine*	Le Creuset of America	L7473-00
9.121	Copper *Cataplana*	The Spanish Table	NONE
9.122	Black-Iron *Sukiyaki-Nabe*	NY Mutual Trading Company	640 25 91327
9.123	Covered *Nabe*	NY Mutual Trading Company	640 15 93675
9.124	Removable Crock Pot	Rival	3656 FO
9.125	Classic Fondue Set	Chantal Cookware	50-18ENS
9.126	Fondue *Bourguignonne* Set	De Buyer/World Cuisine, Inc.	670101
9.127	Copper & Porcelain Fondue Pot	Old Dutch International, Ltd.	763
9.128	Cheese Fondue Set	Swissmar Imports, Ltd.	KF-66530
9.129	Cuisipro Chocolate Fondue Set	Browne & Company	78 8636
9.130	Mongolian Copper Fire Pot	Fante's	98357
9.131	Copper Polenta Pot	Ruffoni Copper USA	6230/25
9.132	Zabaglione Pot	Mauviel/Swissmar Imports, Ltd.	2195.16
9.133	Sugar Pot	De Buyer/World Cuisine, Inc.	657120
9.134	Bean Pot	Ceraflame, Inc.	C30018
9.135	Chinese Earthenware Casserole	Kam Man Food Products, Inc.	NONE
9.136	*Römertopf*	Reco International Corp.	113
9.137	*Schlemmertopf*	Reston Lloyd, Ltd.	863-34
9.138	Cassoulet Dish	Matfer, Inc.	051799
9.139	*Etruria*	Chef Walter	NONE
9.140	*Tegamaccio*	Chef Walter	NONE
10.1	Professional Hard-Anodized Round Griddle	Calphalon Corp.	GR1213HC
10.2	Old-Style Cast-Iron Griddle	Lodge Manufacturing Co.	100G2
10.3	Copper-Banded Soapstone Griddle	Woodstock Soapstone Company	NONE
10.4	Commercial Hard-Anodized Square Griddle	Calphalon Corp.	D-1211
10.5	Chef'sDesign Maxi Griddle	Wisconsin Aluminum Foundry	3230
10.6	LTD Nonstick Grande Griddle	All-Clad Metalcrafters	3020NS
10.7	*Tava* Griddle	Hawkins Cookers, Ltd.	NONE
10.8	Earthenware *Comal* Griddle	Casa Puebla	NONE
10.9	Jumbo Cool Touch Electric Griddle	Presto	07035
10.10	Grillit Pan	Le Creuset of America	L2027-30
10.11	Corona Range Grill	Universal Trading Products	190
10.12	Five-Ply Clad Grill Pan	KitchenAid Cookware	75912
10.13	Professional Grill Pan	Anolon	81070
10.14	Commerical Hard-Anodized Square Grill Pan	Calphalon Corp.	D-1111
10.15	Chef'sDesign Ribbed Griddle	Wisconsin Aluminum Foundry	3540
10.16	Mini Reversible Grill-Griddle	Le Creuset of America	L2092
10.17	Giant Reversible Grill-Griddle	Le Creuset of America	L0053
10.18	Alfredo Healthy Grill	DeLonghi America, Inc.	BG16

CATALOGUE NUMBER	ITEM DESCRIPTION	MANUFACTURER/ U.S. DISTRIBUTOR	MANUFACTURER MODEL NUMBER
10.19	Deluxe Health Grill	T-Fal	1335
10.20	George Foreman's Lean Mean Fat-Reducing Grilling Machine	Salton, Inc	GR20
10.21	Raclette with Grill	Swissmar Imports, Ltd.	KF 77034
10.22	Chef'sChoice WafflePro	EdgeCraft Corporation	MODEL 830
10.23	Uno Belgian Waffler	VillaWare	2000
10.24	Belgian Waffler	Nordic Ware	15040
10.25	Swedish *Plätt* Pan	SCI Cuisine International	C4107
10.26	Danish *Aebleskive* Pan	Lodge Manufacturing Co.	32D2
10.27	Scandinavian Waffle Iron	Skeppshult/EKS, Inc.	10
10.28	Norwegian *Goro* Iron	Bethany Housewares, Inc.	375
10.29	Norwegian *Krumkake* Iron	Nordic Ware	01540
10.30	*Krumkake* Roller	SCI Cuisine International	W27
10.31	Prima *Pizzelle* Baker	VillaWare	5000-NS
10.32	*Pizzelle* Iron	SCI Cuisine International	A606
11.1	Avante Deluxe Electronic Toaster	T-Fal	8747
11.2	Two-Slice Toaster	Dualit	A2BR/87
11.3	Two-Slice IntelliToast Toaster	Hamilton Beach	22505
11.4	Two-Slice Toaster with Toast Logic	Sunbeam	3806
11.5	Custom Control Total Touch 4-Slice Electronic Toaster	Cuisinart	CPT-65
11.6	Digital Ultra Power Plus Toaster	KitchenAid	KTT2610B
11.7	Intellitoast Toaster Oven-Broiler	Hamilton Beach	31450
11.8	Convection Oven Toaster-Broiler	Cuisinart	TOB-175
11.9	Dining-In Convection Countertop Oven-Broiler	Black & Decker	CTO9000
12.1	"Pots & Pans" Roaster	Calphalon Corp.	P1830
12.2	Stainless Roti Pan	All-Clad Metalcrafters	5016
12.3	Rectangular Roaster	Circulon	88962
12.4	Cuprinox *Plat à Rotir* Roasting Pan	Mauviel/Matfer, Inc.	6509-35
12.5	Oval Covered Roaster	Circulon	88975
12.6	Granite Ware Covered Roaster	Columbian Home Products, LLC.	0510-4
12.7	Non-Stick Roast Rack	Adam Industries	81616
12.8	Adjustable Roast Rack	Amco	734
12.9	Large Roast Rack	Calphalon Corp.	RR1115
12.10	Cradle Roast Rack	Amco	749
12.11	Chestnut Pan	De Buyer/World Cuisine, Inc.	529028
12.12	Vertical Poultry Roaster	Spanek, Inc.	SVR-311-3
12.13	Stainless Steel Bulb Baster	Fox Run Craftsmen	5679
12.14	Heat-Resistant Glass Baster	Fox Run Craftsmen	5678
12.15	Spiridoso	Pedrini USA, Inc.	2340
12.16	Lamsonsharp Basting Brush	Lamson & Goodnow Mfg. Co	589
12.17	Turkey Lacers	Matfer, Inc.	120840
12.18	Trussing Needle	Wüsthof-Trident of America	4385
12.19	Larding Needle	Wüsthof-Trident of America	4380
12.20	Larding Needle	Matfer, Inc.	120842
12.21	Good Grips Turkey Lifter	OXO International	38780
12.22	Turkey-Roaster Lifter Chain	Norpro	837
12.23	Showtime Rotisserie & BBQ	Ronco Inventions	STO7
12.24	Cool Side 5 Roaster Oven	Nesco	4005-04-30

CATALOGUE NUMBER	ITEM DESCRIPTION	MANUFACTURER/ U.S. DISTRIBUTOR	MANUFACTURER MODEL NUMBER
13.1	Oval Baking Dish	Le Creuset of America	PG1040-28
13.2	Baking Dish	Matfer, Inc.	980851
13.3	Ceramika Artystyckna Boleslawiec Baking Dish	The King Arthur Flour Baker's Catalogue	5148
13.4	Rectangular Baking Dish	Emile Henry USA	271903
13.5	Baking Dish	Pillivuyt of North America	250429 BL
13.6	14″ *Cazuela*	The Spanish Table	NONE
13.7	Quiche/Pizza Dish	Le Creuset of America	PG1020-24
13.8	Natural Scallop Shell	Sweet Celebrations	47597
13.9	Porcelain Scallop Shell	Browne & Company	56 4000
13.10	Escargot Dish	Browne & Company	74 4044
13.11	Snail Fork	Harold Import Company, Inc.	2734
13.11	Snail Tongs	Harold Import Company, Inc.	4004
13.12	Round Copper Gratin Pan	Old Dutch International, Ltd.	737
13.13	Stainless Steel Gratin Pan	All-Clad Metalcrafters	5812
13.14	Oval Au Gratin	Le Creuset of America	L0013-28
13.15	Salamander	Matfer, Inc.	242085
13.16	Porcelain Gratin Dish	Apilco/Cuthbertson Imports	264001
13.17	*Pommes Anna* Pan	Mauviel/Matfer, Inc.	214716
13.18	Round-Eared Egg Dish	Pillivuyt of North America	230312 BL
13.19	Egg Cocotte with Ears	Pillivuyt of North America	260309 BL
13.20	Egg Coddlers	Privately Owned	NONE
13.21	Ramekin	Pillivuyt of North America	260415 BL
13.22	Ramekins	Emile Henry USA	616120
13.23	Cheflamme Butane Culinary Torch	Messermeister/DAMCO	FT911
13.24	Custard Cup	B.I.A. Cordon Bleu, Inc.	900010
13.25	Pyrex Custard Cups	Corning Consumer Products Company/ World Kitchen	6001142
13.26	Japanese Custard Cup	Korin	CMU 103
13.27	*Pots de Crème* Set	Apilco/Cuthbertson Imports	085 001
13.28	Crème Brûlée Dish	Apilco/Cuthbertson Imports	099 001
13.29	Individual Soufflé Dish	B.I.A. Cordon Bleu, Inc.	900013
13.29	Multiquart Soufflé Dish	B.I.A. Cordon Bleu, Inc.	900018
13.30	Extra-High Individual Soufflé Dish	Apilco/Cuthbertson Imports	576 001
13.30	Extra-High Multiquart Soufflé Dish	Apilco/Cuthbertson Imports	575 001
13.31	Glass Soufflé Dish	Catamount Housewares	S2000
13.32	Octagonal Terrine	Matfer, Inc.	051480
13.33	Oval Terrine	Apilco/Cuthbertson Imports	027001
13.34	Pâté Terrine	Le Creuset of America	L0524-32
13.35	Galantine Mold	J. B. Prince	R101 10
13.36	*Pâté en Croûte* Mold	Matfer, Inc.	340902
13.37	Nonstick Paté Mold	Matfer, Inc.	331291
13.38	Round Fluted Pâté Ring	Matfer, Inc.	331265
13.39	Fish Mold	Copper Products of Italy	125
13.40	Pudding Mold	A. Metalúrgica	44083
13.41	Charlotte Mold	De Buyer/World Cuisine, Inc.	012514
13.41	Charlotte Mold Lid	De Buyer/World Cuisine, Inc.	006714
13.42	Aspic Mold	SCI Cuisine International	B310
13.43	Round Mold	Copper Products of Italy	49

CATALOGUE NUMBER	ITEM DESCRIPTION	MANUFACTURER/ U.S. DISTRIBUTOR	MANUFACTURER MODEL NUMBER
13.44	Timbale	Piazza/J. B. Prince	M184-B
13.45	Pyramid Ice Cream Mold	Matfer, Inc.	341103
13.46	La Bombe Ice Cream Mold	A. Metalúrgica	44260
13.47	Falafel Shaping Kit	Nouri's	NONE
13.48	NonStick Fluted Mold	A. Metalúrgica	14600
13.49	Individual Turk's Head Mold	J. B. Prince	M301
13.50	Endurance Stacks-The Kit	R.S.V.P. International Inc.	STACK
13.51	Round Bottomless Form, 2½″ in diameter	Matfer, Inc.	375072
13.51	Round Bottomless Form, 2⁷⁄₁₆″ in diameter	Matfer, Inc.	375071
13.52	Hemisphere Mold	De Buyer/World Cuisine, Inc.	313309
13.53	*Coeur à la Crème* Mold	Apilco/Cuthbertson Imports	084 001
13.54	Butter Paddles	SCI Cuisine International	W17
13.55	Table Art Pig Butter Mold	Sweet Celebrations	510238
13.55	Table Art Rose Butter Mold	Sweet Celebrations	653977
13.56	Butter Mold	SCI Cuisine International	W11-910
13.57	Wood *Battera* Sushi Mold	Korin	TK-612-01
13.58	*Makizushi* Mat	Korin	TK-601-04
13.59	*Hangiri* Tub	Korin	TK 602 01/60
13.59	Paddle	Korin	TK 603 01/48
14.1	Butcher Block Counter Board	J. K. Adams Company, Inc.	BBCB-16
14.2	Rolling Pin	H. A. Mack	H50/20
14.3	Drying Screen	Bartelt Design & Manufacturing	216
14.4	2½″ Square Pasta Stamp	SCI Cuisine International	A113
14.5	2½″ Round Pasta Stamp	Fox Run Craftsmen	5746
14.6	2″ Round Pasta Stamp	SCI Cuisine International	E28
14.7	Pasta Jagger	VillaWare	420
14.8	*Chitarra*	E. Rossi & Company	NONE
14.9	Fusilli Pin	E. Rossi & Company	NONE
14.10	2½″ Square Ravioli Mold	VillaWare	5500
14.11	2″ Round Ravioli Mold	VillaWare	5700
14.12	2″ Square Ravioli Mold	VillaWare	5400-01
14.13	Ravioli Mold	SCI Cuisine International	P756
14.14	Gnocchi Paddles	VillaWare	581
14.15	Trattorina Pasta Machine	Belpasta Corporation	TPM 0200
14.16	Pasta Roller Set	KitchenAid	SNFGA
14.17	Pasta Machine	Atlas/Gary Valenti, Inc.	V190
14.18	Pastadrive Motor for Atlas Pasta Machine	Atlas/Gary Valenti, Inc.	V177
14.19	Trattorina *Raviolera*	Belpasta Corporation	TRM 004
14.20	BeeBo *Cavatelli* Maker	VillaWare	5300
14.21	Brass Noodle Press	Foods of India	NONE
14.22	Kull Swabian Spaetzle Press	J. B. Prince	U545
14.23	Austrian Spaetzle-Maker	VillaWare	350
14.24	Spaetzle Maker	SCI Cuisine International	Z327
14.25	Zenker Spaetzle Maker	SCI Cuisine International	B2402
15.1	Half-Sheet Loaf-Rising Cover	The King Arthur Flour Baker's Catalogue	4096
15.2	Camwear CamSquare Dough-Rising Container	Cambro Manufacturing Company	6SFSCW
15.2	Cover for CamSquare Container	Cambro Manufacturing Company	SFC6
15.3	Adjustable Bread *Couche*	The King Arthur Flour Baker's Catalogue	6100
15.4	26″ *Couche* Linen Canvas	FBM	32100025

CATALOGUE NUMBER	ITEM DESCRIPTION	MANUFACTURER/ U.S. DISTRIBUTOR	MANUFACTURER MODEL NUMBER
15.5	Dough Proofing Basket	FBM	310.01
15.6	Reed Bread Form	FBM	AX290110
15.7	Professional Nonstick French Bread Pan	Chicago Metallic	69610
15.8	Professional Nonstick Baguette Pan	Chicago Metallic	69609
15.9	2-Channel Metal Baguette Pan	Matfer, Inc.	311120
15.10	Silform Baguette Mold	Demarle, Inc.	80-042295
15.11	*Pain de mie* Pan	Matfer, Inc.	340841
15.12	Brioche Mold	Matfer, Inc.	330135
15.13	Individual Brioche Mold	Matfer, Inc.	334027
15.14	*Brioche Mousseline* Mold	Bridge Kitchenware	NONE
15.15	Vienna Roll Stamp	Wooley Electric Supply, Inc	NONE
15.16	*Babas au Rhum* Molds	Matfer, Inc.	331596
15.17	Pizza Serving/Cooking Tray	Allied Metal Spinning Company	TA12
15.18	Commercial Perforated Pizza Crisper	Chicago Metallic	77014
15.19	Pizza Crisper	Best Manufacturers, Inc.	UC-214
15.20	Twine Knife	Victorinox/R. H. Forschner & Co.	40990
15.21	Razor Blade Holder	FBM	32100035
15.22	Lame with Plastic Cover	Matfer, Inc.	120005
15.23	Bron Bread Cutter	Mouli Manufacturing Corp.	TLN7002
15.24	Crumb Tray	Mountain Woods, Inc.	CTC
15.25	HearthKit Oven Insert	Breadways, Inc.	NONE
15.26	Superstone La Cloche	Sassafras	1005
15.27	Superstone Deep-Dish Baking Stone	Sassafras	2522
15.28	Baking Stone	Kitchen Supply Company	4467
15.29	Good Grips Pizza Wheel	OXO International	26681
15.30	Pizza Cutter	Allied Metal Spinning Company	PCP4
15.31	Aluminum Peel	Allied Metal Spinning Company	P1235
15.32	Baker's Peel	Allied Metal Spinning Company	WP 1222
15.33	Metal Tortilla Press	VillaWare	406
15.34	Chapati Press	Spice and Sweet Corner	NONE
15.35	Automatic Bread- & Dough-Maker	The West Bend Company	41093
15.36	Bread Bakery	Panasonic	YD-205
16.1	Magic Line Cookie Sheet	Parrish's Cake Decorating Supplies , Inc.	PCS-121810
16.2	Millennium Cookie Sheet	Farberware Millenium Bakeware/World Kitchen	5198002
16.3	Oven Baking Sheet	Matfer, Inc.	310101
16.4	Extraordinaire Cookie Sheet	Kaiser Bakeware	751382
16.5	Commercial Standard Jelly Roll Pan	Chicago Metallic	77813
16.6	Commercial Non-Stick Jelly Roll Pan	Chicago Metallic	61813
16.7	Perforated Baking Pan	Chicago Metallic	69318
16.8	8½″ x 12½″ Cook-Eze Reusable Pan Liners	KatchAll Industries International, Inc.	CE-3504
16.9	9″ Round Cook-Eze Reusable Pan Liners	KatchAll Industries International, Inc.	CE-3506
16.10	8½″ Square Cook-Eze Reusable Pan Liners	KatchAll Industries International, Inc.	CE3503
16.11	Half-Size Silpat Liner	Demarle, Inc.	80-042295
16.12	Magic Line Square Baking Pan	Parrish's Cake Decorating Supplies , Inc.	PSQ
16.13	La Forme Rectangular Pan	Kaiser Bakeware	730400
16.14	Pyrex Oblong Baking Pan	Corning Consumer Products Company/ World Kitchen	6001012
16.15	Magic Line Loaf Pan	Parrish's Cake Decorating Supplies , Inc.	PLM-5
16.16	Pyrex Loaf Pan	Corning Consumer Products Company/ World Kitchen	6001005

CATALOGUE NUMBER	ITEM DESCRIPTION	MANUFACTURER/ U.S. DISTRIBUTOR	MANUFACTURER MODEL NUMBER
16.17	Professional Loaf Pan	Chicago Metallic	60042
16.18	La Forme Nonstick Mini-Loaf Pan Set	Kaiser Bakeware	730387
16.19	Mini-Loaf Strapped Set	Chicago Metallic	30440
16.20	Magic Line Cake Pan	Parrish's Cake Decorating Supplies , Inc.	PRD 9"
16.21	Professional Cake Pan	Chicago Metallic	60629
16.22	Cake Pan	All-Clad Metalcrafters	9002
16.23	Baker's Secret Round Cake Pan	EKCO/World Kitchen	64970
16.24	Mini Round Cake/Flan Pan	J. B. Prince	M484-10
16.25	Magi-Cake Strips	Norpro	3583
16.26	Entremet Ring	J. B. Prince	M246-9.5
16.27	Quadrant Cake Form	J. B. Prince	M477
16.28	Adjustable Tart Ring	Matfer, Inc.	371490
16.29	La Forme Gâteau Pan	Kaiser Bakeware	630243
16.30	*Obstorte* Pan	Dr. Oetker/Leifheit International	02246 2
16.31	"Saddle of Venison" *Rehrücken* Mold	Frieling USA, Inc.	3424
16.32	Handle-It Glass Bottom Springform Pan	Frieling USA, Inc.	3850
16.33	La Forme Leakproof Springform Pan	Kaiser Bakeware	730035
16.34	Nonstick Two-Piece Tube Pan	Chicago Metallic	26183
16.35	Angel Food Cake Pan	J. B. Prince	M361-4
16.36	Tin-Plate *Kouglof* Mold	Matfer, Inc.	340642
16.37	Simax Glass *Kugelhopf* Mold	Kavalier Glassworks of North America	2050
16.38	Aluminum Bundt Pan	Nordic Ware	51122
16.39	Cast-Aluminum Bundt Pan	Nordic Ware	51224
16.40	*Savarin* Mold	Matfer, Inc.	341186
16.41	Silverstone 12-cup Muffin Tin	Chicago Metallic	06212
16.42	Mini Muffin Tin	Chicago Metallic	60012
16.43	6-Hole Fluted Muffin Pan	Lodge Manufacturing Co.	19M2
16.44	6-Hole Giant Muffin Tin	Norpro	3772
16.45	6-Cup Puffy Crown Pan	Norpro	3973
16.46	"Ear of Corn" Pan	Lodge Manufacturing Co.	27C2
16.47	Corn Bread Skillet	Lodge Manufacturing Co.	8CB2
16.48	Cast-Iron Popover Pan	Lodge Manufacturing Co.	10P2
16.49	Madeleine Tin	J. B. Prince	M139
16.50	Ladyfinger Tin	J. B. Prince	M444
16.51	Silpat Flexipan Madeleine Mold	Demarle, Inc.	FLX03511
16.52	Cannelé Mold, Large	J. B. Prince	M480-45
16.53	Cannelé Mold, Small	J. B. Prince	M480-35
16.54	*Gefu Christstollen* Pan	Sweet Celebrations	79367
16.55	Brown Bag Cookie Art Ceramic Shortbread Mold	Sweet Celebrations	538507
16.56	Pyrex Traditional Pie Pan	Corning Consumer Products Company/ World Kitchen	6001003
16.57	Baker's Secret Covered Pie Pan	EKCO/World Kitchen	64231
16.58	Pie Partners	Fasmodea	9009
16.59	Pie Dish	Emile Henry USA	623166
16.60	Ceramic Pie Pan Set	Mason Cash of England	380749
16.61	Fluted Tart Mold	Matfer, Inc.	334215
16.62	Tinned Steel Loose-Bottomed Tart Mold	Matfer, Inc.	341773
16.63	Blued-Steel Loose-Bottomed Tart Mold	Matfer, Inc.	341783
16.64	Nonstick Steel Loose-Bottomed Tart Mold	Matfer, Inc.	332225
16.65	Rectangular Tart Mold	J. B. Prince	M331

CATALOGUE NUMBER	ITEM DESCRIPTION	MANUFACTURER/ U.S. DISTRIBUTOR	MANUFACTURER MODEL NUMBER
16.66	Square Tart Mold	J. B. Prince	M346
16.67	Tarte Tatin Pan	Matfer, Inc.	341222
16.68	Plain Barquette Mold	Matfer, Inc.	342131
16.69	Fluted Barquette Mold	Matfer, Inc.	342121
16.70	Removable Bottom Tartlet	J. B. Prince	M295-4.75
16.71	Petits Four Pastry Set	Matfer, Inc.	341001
16.72	Plain Tart Ring	Matfer, Inc.	371615
16.73	Flower Tart Ring	Matfer, Inc.	371302
16.74	Round Quiche Pan	Apilco/Cuthbertson Imports	101 001
16.75	*Tourtière*	Emile Henry USA	276000
16.76	Cornet Mold	J. B. Prince	B882
16.77	Lady Lock Form	J. B. Prince	B621
16.78	*Croquembouche* Form	Matfer, Inc.	340463
16.79	Cannoli Forms	Ateco/August Thomsen Corp.	924S
16.80	Bowl Scraper	J. B. Prince	B634
16.81	Bench Scraper	J. B. Prince	B635-PL
16.82	Flour Sifter	OXO International	73481
16.83	Pastry Blender	Browne & Company	65506 06246
16.84	Blending Fork	Norpro	3249
16.85	Rolling Pin Cover & Pastry Cloth Set	Norpro	3093
16.86	Marble Pastry Board	SCI Cuisine International	G1218
16.87	Wooden Rolling Pin	Matfer, Inc.	112360
16.88	Nylon Rolling Pin	Matfer, Inc.	140010
16.89	Tapered Rolling Pin	J. K. Adams Company, Inc.	FRP-4
16.90	Rolling Pin	Thorpe Rolling Pin Company	D
16.91	Fluted Puff Pastry Rolling Pin	Matfer, Inc.	140025
16.92	Flour Wand	Best Manufacturers, Inc.	FD-1
16.93	Endurance Fine Mesh Shaker	R.S.V.P. International Inc.	ST-12
16.94	Baking Spatula with Plastic Handle	Ateco/August Thomsen Corp.	1309
16.95	Baking Spatula with Wooden Handle	Ateco/August Thomsen Corp.	1375
16.96	Straight-Blade Icing Spatula	Ateco/August Thomsen Corp.	1384
16.97	Offset Baking Spatula	Ateco/August Thomsen Corp.	1385
16.98	Trowel-Shaped Icing Spatula	Ateco/August Thomsen Corp.	1383
16.99	Baker's Knife	Wüsthof-Trident of America	4831
16.100	Roller Docker	J. B. Prince	B716
16.101	Flat Pastry Brush	Matfer, Inc.	116016
16.102	Natural White Bristle Grease Brush	Ateco/August Thomsen Corp.	1612
16.103	Baking Beans	Matfer, Inc.	340001
16.104	Pastry Crimper	New York Cake & Baking	NONE
16.105	Pie Bird	Boston Warehouse Trading Corp.	74303
16.106	Cake Tester	Ateco/August Thomsen Corp.	1444
16.107	Plain Pastry Wheel	J. B. Prince	B690
16.108	Fluted Pastry Wheel	J. B. Prince	B69
16.109	12-piece Pastry Cutter Set	Ateco/August Thomsen Corp.	5457
16.110	Puff Pastry Cutters	Matfer, Inc.	150102
16.111	Lattice Dough Cutter	J. B. Prince	B629
16.112	Lattice Dough Roller	J. B. Prince	B715
16.113	Star Pastry Cutter Set	Ateco/August Thomsen Corp.	7805
16.114	Heart Pastry Cutter Set	Ateco/August Thomsen Corp.	7804
16.115	Trick Or Treat Cutter Set	Ateco/August Thomsen Corp.	1430

CATALOGUE NUMBER	ITEM DESCRIPTION	MANUFACTURER/ U.S. DISTRIBUTOR	MANUFACTURER MODEL NUMBER
16.116	Rolling Cookie Cutter	Norpro	3298
16.117	Eiffel Tower Cutter	Sur La Table	16871
16.118	Croissant Cutter	J. B. Prince	B624C
16.119	Endurance Biscuit Cutters	R.S.V.P. International Inc.	BC-4
16.120	English Muffin Rings	Norpro	3775
16.121	Square Vol-au-Vent Cutter	Bridge Kitchenware	NONE
16.122	Doughnut Cutter	Ateco/August Thomsen Corp.	14423
16.123	*Springerle* Rolling Pin	The House On The Hill	1551
16.124	*Springerle* Cookie Roller	The House On The Hill	1550
16.125	*Springerle* Board	The House On The Hill	4128
16.126	Stackable Cooling Racks	Wilton Industries	2305-F-151
16.127	Nonstick Square Cooling Grid	Wilton Industries	2305-F-228
16.128	Chrome-Plated Round Cooling Grid	Wilton Industries	2305-F-130
16.129	Cake Stencils	J. B. Prince	B868
16.130	Cake & Pastry Decorating Set	Ateco/August Thomsen Corp.	701
16.131	Cookie Press	Kuhn Rikon Corp.	2460
16.132	Easy Whip	iSi North America	6670US
16.133	Decorating Stand	Ateco/August Thomsen Corp.	612
16.134	Universal EZ Disher	Zeroll	2040
16.135	Decorating Combs	J. B. Prince	B647
16.136	Cake Decorating Set	Norpro	3562
16.137	Dura Cloth Canvas Pastry Bag	Ateco/August Thomsen Corp.	3212
16.138	Sure-Grip Plastic-Coated Pastry Bag	Ateco/August Thomsen Corp.	3112
16.139	Flex Nylon Pastry Bag	Ateco/August Thomsen Corp.	3012
16.140	Bismarck Tube	Ateco/August Thomsen Corp.	230
16.141	55-Piece Decorating Set	Ateco/August Thomsen Corp.	783
16.142	12-Piece Pastry Tube Set	Ateco/August Thomsen Corp.	786
16.143	Disposable Pastry Bags	Ateco/August Thomsen Corp.	462
16.144	Parchment Triangles	Ateco/August Thomsen Corp.	50
17.1	Il Gelataio Magnum, II	Simac/Lello Appliances Corp.	4050
17.2	Lussino Pro	Musso/Lello Appliances Corp.	4080
17.3	The PacoJet	PacoJet AG	NONE
17.4	La Glacière	Krups North America, Inc.	358
17.5	Big Chill	Salton, Inc	ICM-21
17.6	White Mountain Hand-Crank Ice Cream Freezer	The Rival Company	F64304-X
17.7	White Mountain Electric Ice Cream Freezer	The Rival Company	F69206
17.8	Ice Cream Scoop	Zeroll	3030
17.9	Ice Cream Spade	Zeroll	1050-ZT (SET)
17.10	Ice Cream Scoop	OXO International	21381
17.11	Pointed Nonstick Scoop	OXO International	26481
17.12	Spring Scoop	Norpro	677
17.13	Ice Cream Scoop	Zwilling J. A. Henckels Inc.	13070-001
17.14	Yogurt Maker	Salton, Inc	YM9
18.1	Bordeaux Grand Cru Wineglass	Riedel Crystal	400/00
18.1	Bourgogne Grand Cru Wineglass	Riedel Crystal	400/16
18.1	Champagne Glass	Riedel Crystal	400/8
18.1	Alsace Wineglass	Riedel Crystal	400/5
18.2	Bottle Funnel with Removable Screen	The Wine Enthusiast	D5047
18.3	Kea Corkscrew	BOJ/USA	17002
18.4	Cork Pops II Wine Opener	Cork Pops	12244

CATALOGUE NUMBER	ITEM DESCRIPTION	MANUFACTURER/ U.S. DISTRIBUTOR	MANUFACTURER MODEL NUMBER
18.5	Screwpull Lever Model	Le Creuset of America	S1600
18.6	Wall-Mounted Corkscrew	BOJ/USA	09923
18.7	Ah So Cork Puller	Monopol/Swissmar Imports, Ltd.	IM1625.21
18.8	Cork Lift Cork Retriever	International Wine Accessories	CC00-001
18.9	Champagne Chiller	Oenophilia	184017
18.10	Quick Chill Wine & Beverage Wrap	Sierra Housewares, Inc.	2112
18.11	Screwpull Champagne Star	Le Creuset of America	S1300
18.12	Champagne Key	Mouli Manufacturing Corp.	GH46
18.13	Bott Champagne Cork Remover	Munini/Massimo Italian Treasures	10114
18.14	Nutcracker & Champagne Opener	Monopol/Swissmar Imports, Ltd.	G09081B
18.15	Champagne Saber	The Wine Enthusiast	M4222
18.16	Elmo Wine Stopper	Munini/Massimo Italian Treasures	10214
18.17	Screwpull Champagne Crown Resealer	Le Creuset of America	S1800
18.18	Champagne Bottle Stopper	BOJ/USA	12138
18.19	Private Preserve Wine Preserver	Oenophilia	074000
18.20	Anti-Drip Ring	BOJ/USA	12155
18.21	Screwpull Foil Cutter	Le Creuset of America	S1400
18.22	Foil Cutter	Munini/Massimo Italian Treasures	M10320BT
18.23	Miniature Distilling Machine	The Wine Enthusiast	1492
18.24	Wine Away Red Wine Stain Remover	Evergreen Labs, Inc.	66008
19.1	Manual Coffee Grinder	Peugeot/Bridge Kitchenware	NONE
19.2	Barista Burr Grinder	Starbucks	144349
19.3	Burr Grinder	Capresso, Inc.	551
19.4	Aromatic Coffee Grinder	Braun North America	KSM4
19.5	Café-Euro 6-Cup Coffeemaker	Melitta USA	ECM 6/4B
19.6	Café-Euro 1-Cup Coffeemaker	Melitta USA	ECM 1/2B
19.7	10-Cup Classic Series	Chemex	CM-10A
19.8	Chambord Coffee Press	BODUM, Inc.	1928
19.9	Vacuum-Insulated Coffee Press	Thermos Nissan	NCI 1000
19.10	Santos Vacuum Pot	BODUM, Inc.	1208
19.11	CoffeeTeam Plus	Capresso, Inc.	452
19.12	Elegance Therm	Capresso, Inc.	439.04
19.13	Crystal Arome Plus Time Coffeemaker	Krups North America, Inc.	467
19.14	FlavorSelect 12-Cup Cappuccino Coffeemaker with Frothing Attachment	Braun North America	KF 190
19.15	12-Cup Ultra Coffeemaker	KitchenAid	KCM200
19.16	Millennium 12-Cup Cordless Programmable Percolator	Farberware Electrics	FCP-512S
19.17	Millennium Stainless Steel Superfast Coffee Urn	Farberware Electrics	FSU236
19.18	Napoletana Coffeepot	ILSA/Gary Valenti, Inc.	V15
19.19	Turkish *Cezve* (Greek *Briki*)	La Pavoni/European Gift & Housewares	280-4
19.20	Turkish Coffee Grinder	Nouri's	NONE
19.21	Bedouin Coffeepot	Nouri's	NONE
19.22	Moka Express 3-Cup Coffeemaker	Bialetti/Gary Valenti, Inc.	V21
19.23	Professional	La Pavoni/European Gift & Housewares	PC-16
19.24	Barista	Starbucks	131714
19.25	Fully Automatic Coffee & Espresso Center	Capresso, Inc.	C1000
19.26	The Nespresso System	Krups North America, Inc.	583
19.27	Stainless Steel Milk Jug	ILSA/Harold Import Company	8866

CATALOGUE NUMBER	ITEM DESCRIPTION	MANUFACTURER/ U.S. DISTRIBUTOR	MANUFACTURER MODEL NUMBER
19.28	Professional Coffee Tamper	Progressive International Corp.	GMCT-01
19.29	Caffe Froth Turbo	BonJour	74766000770255
19.30	Cleancaf Cleaner and Descaler	URNEX	CLCF1/12
19.31	Vacuum Carafe	Thermos Nissan	TGB 1000
19.32	Bistro Vacuum Jug	BODUM, Inc.	1601
19.33	Vacuum-Insulated Travel Tumbler	Thermos Nissan	JMH400
19.34	Capuccino Frothing Thermometer	Taylor Precision Products, L.P.	5997
19.35	Gold Screen Coffee Filter	Braun North America	UGSF4
19.36	Ultimo Aria 2000 Teakettle	Copco	2502-4025
19.37	Good Grips Uplift Teakettle	OXO International	71180
19.38	Copper Teakettle	Simplex	4
19.39	Aquaexpress	Braun North America	WK200
19.40	Classic Sovereign Stainless Steel Cordless Kettle	Russell Hobbs	3181US
19.41	Chatsford Teapot	Upton Tea Imports	AP44C
19.42	Stacking Teapot	April Cornell	PYCHMST5
19.43	Japanese *Tetsubin* (Cast-Iron) Hobnail Teapot	Joyce Chen	90-0046
19.44	Yixing Clay Teapot	Imperial Tea Court	00305
19.45	Cup O' Tea Permanent Filter	Swiss Gold	TF500
19.46	Cup O' Tea One Cup Permanent Tea Filter	Swiss Gold	TF300B
19.47	t-Sac Cup & Teapot Filters	Alexander Gourmet Imports, Ltd.	0910
19.48	Samovar	Widerview, Inc.	GG2314
19.49	The Iced Tea Pot	Mr. Coffee	TM1
19.50	Chef'sChoice International Tea Mate Electric Tea Maker	EdgeCraft Corporation	690
19.51	*Mate* Gourd	Antique loaned by The Argentine Pavillion, NY, NY	NONE
19.52	*Bombilla*	Antique loaned by The Argentine Pavillion, NY, NY	NONE
20.1	Ball Jar Lifter	Alltrista Corporation	10200
20.2	Ball Canning Funnel	Alltrista Corporation	10400
20.3	Ball Bubble Freer Spatula	Alltrista Corporation	10300
20.4	Ball Canning Lid Wand	Alltrista Corporation	10100
20.5	Ball Jelly Bag Stand	Alltrista Corporation	00600
20.6	Granite Ware Boiling-Water-Bath Canner	Columbian Home Products, LLC.	0707-3
20.7	Ball Replacement Rack	Alltrista Corporation	00701
20.8	Pressure Canner	Presto	01750
20.9	Sauerkraut Crock	Robinson Ransbottom Pottery	179
20.10	Ball Half-Gallon Wide Mouth Mason Jar	Alltrista Corporation	68000
20.10	Ball Quart Regular Mason Jar	Alltrista Corporation	62000
20.10	Kerr Pint Regular Mason Jar	Alltrista Corporation	00503
20.10	Ball 4 oz Deluxe Quilted Crystal Jelly Jars	Alltrista Corporation	80400
20.10	Ball 8 oz Deluxe Quilted Crystal Jelly Jar	Alltrista Corporation	81200
20.10	Kerr 8 oz Decorated Jelly Jar	Alltrista Corporation	00105
20.10	Ball Pint Regular Mason Jar	Alltrista Corporation	61000
20.11	"Quattro Stagioni" Canning Jar	Bormioli Rocco Glass Company	3.88330-1. LID ¢70
20.12	Mini Tulip-Shaped Jar	J. Weck/Glashaus, Inc.	762
20.13	14 oz Working Glass	Luminarc	13297
20.14	American Harvest GardenMaster Professional Food Dehydrator and Jerky-Maker	Nesco	FD-1000
20.15	Foodsaver Professional II Vacuum Sealer	Tilia, Inc.	TIL-00-0311

CATALOGUE NUMBER	ITEM DESCRIPTION	MANUFACTURER/ U.S. DISTRIBUTOR	MANUFACTURER MODEL NUMBER
App A-1	Measuring Cup Set	OXO International	30581
App A-2	Millennium Pressure Cooker	Farberware Electrics/Salton, Inc.	FPC400
App A-3	Speed Peeler	Emson	NONE
App A-4	Homecraft Twister Jar Opener	Smith & Nephew	AA500-0
App A-5	HiD Paring Board	Sammons Preston	3099
App A-6	Food Prep Board	Sammons Preston	3023
App A-7	Marktime Braille Timer	Maxi-Aids	7059711
App A-8	Smartboard Cutting Block	American Clipper	SB1216
App A-9	Ergo Electric Knife	Black & Decker	EK600

Up-to-date prices for the equipment in
The New Cooks' Catalogue
can be found online at
www.burtwolf.com

D

MANUFACTURERS & DISTRIBUTORS

A

A. METALÚRGICA
c/o Mr. Tiago Pinto
The Bristol Group
1900 L St., N.W., Suite 407
Washington, DC 20036
(202) 293-3454

ACME INTERNATIONAL, INC.
1006 Chancellor Ave.
Maplewood, NJ 07040
(973) 416-0400
info@acme-usa.com

ADAM INDUSTRIES
P.O. Box 14335
Chicago, IL 60614
(312) 274-0485

**ALEXANDER GOURMET
IMPORTS, LTD.**
5630 Timberlea Blvd.
Mississauga, Ontario L4W 4M6
Canada
(800) 265-5081

ALL-CLAD METALCRAFTERS
424 Morganza Rd.
Canonsburg, PA 15317
(800) ALL-CLAD
info@allclad.com

ALLIED METAL SPINNING COMPANY
808 Cauldwell Ave.
Bronx, NY 10456

ALLTRISTA CORPORATION
345 South High St., Suite 201
Muncie, IN 47305
(765) 281-5077
(800) 428-8150
www.homecanning.com

AMCO
North Lakeview Pkwy.
Vernon Hills, IL 60061
(877) 310-9102

AMERICAN CLIPPER
202 South William St.
Johnstown, NY 12095
(518) 762-6860
(877) 966-3468
clipper@superior.net

ANOLON COOKWARE
Consumer Relations
One Meyer Plaza
Vallejo, CA 94590
(800) 326-3933
karen@anolon.com

APILCO,
see Cuthbertson Imports.

APRIL CORNELL
458 Hurricane Ln.
P.O. Box 1710
Williston, VT 05495
(802) 879-5100

ATECO,
See August Thomsen Corporation.

ATLAS,
See Gary Valenti, Inc.

AUGUST THOMSEN CORPORATION
36 Sea Cliff Ave.
Glen Cove, NY 11542
(516) 676-7100
(800) 645-7170

B

B.I.A. CORDON BLEU, INC.
867 American St.
San Carlos, CA 94070
(650) 595-2400
(800) 242-2210

BACK TO BASICS
11660 South State St.
Draper, UT 84020
(801) 571-7349
(800) 688-1989

**BARTELT DESIGN
& MANUFACTURING**
1206 East MacArthur St.
Sonoma, CA 95476
(707) 938-0517
(800) 428-0538

BELPASTA CORPORATION
1085 Commonwealth Ave. PMB194
Boston, MA 02215
(617) 923-4696
moulay@belpasta-trattorina.com

BERNDES COOKWARE INC.
1200-G Westinghouse Blvd.
Charlotte, NC 28273
(704) 588-8090
(800) 966-3009
www.berndes.com

BEST MANUFACTURERS, INC.
6105 N.E. 92nd Dr.
Portland, OR 97220
(503) 253-1528
(800) 500-1528
bestmfrs@ix.netcom.com

BETHANY HOUSEWARES, INC.
P.O. Box 199
Cresco, IA 52136
(319) 547-5873
sales@bethanyhousewares.com

BIALETTI,
See Gary Valenti, Inc.

**BLACK & DECKER
HOUSEHOLD PRODUCTS INC.**
6 Armstrong Rd.
Shelton, CT 06484
(800) 323-1946

BODUM, INC.
c/o Federal Wholesale Group
125 Lena Dr.
Aurora, IL 44202
(800) 232-6386
www.bodum.com

BOJ/USA
P.O. Box 464
Cedar Crest, NM 87008
(505) 286-4050
rsmcg@highfiber.com

BONJOUR
80 Berry Dr., Suite A
Pacheco, CA 94553
(925) 676-1300
(800) 226-6568

BORMIOLI ROCCO GLASS COMPANY
1185 Avenue of the Americas, 17th Floor
New York, NY 10036
(212) 719-0606

**BOSTON WAREHOUSE
TRADING CORP.**
59 Davis Ave.
Norwood, MA 02062
(781) 769-8550
(888) 923-2982

BOURGEAT USA, INC.
20 Fernwood Rd.
Boston, MA 02132
(617) 469-0189
(800) 469-0188
bourgeat@earthlink.net
www.bourgeat.fr

BRADSHAW INTERNATIONAL
9409 Buffalo Ave.
Rancho Cucamonga, CA 91730
(909) 476-3884
(800) 421-6290

BRAUN NORTH AMERICA
800 Boylston St.
Boston, MA 02199
(800) 272-8611
www.braun.com

BREADWAYS, INC.
149 Georgetown Rd.
Weston, CT 06883
(877) 432-7845

BRIDGE KITCHENWARE
214 East 52nd St.
New York, NY 10022
(212) 688-4220
s.bridge@ix.netcom.com

BROWNE & COMPANY
100 Esna Park Dr.
Markham, Ontario L3R 1E3
Canada
(905) 475-6104

C

CALPHALON CORPORATION
P.O. Box 583
Toledo, OH 43697
(419) 666-8700

**CAMBRO MANUFACTURING
COMPANY**
7601 Clay Ave.
Huntington Beach, CA 92647
(714) 848-1555
(800) 854-7631

CAPRESSO, INC.
81 Ruckman Rd.
Closter, NJ 07624
(201) 767-3999
contact@capresso.com
www.capresso.com

CASA PUEBLA
2710 Broadway, 2nd Floor
New York, NY 10025
(212) 531-0552

CATAMOUNT HOUSEWARES
309 Country St.
Bennington, VT 05201
(802) 442-5438
mkvt@sover.net

CERAFLAME INC.
230 Fifth Ave., 7th Floor
New York, NY 10001
(212) 679-5060
info@ceraflame.com
www.ceraflame.com

CHAMPION
Plastatek Manufacturing Co. Inc.
6220 E. Highway 12
Lodi, CA 95240

CHANEY INSTRUMENTS COMPANY
P.O. Box 70
965 Wells St.
Lake Geneva, WI 53147
(262) 248-4449
(800) 777-0565
chanins@geneva.com

CHANTAL COOKWARE
2030 W. Sam Houston Pkwy.
Houston, TX 77043
(713) 467-9949
(800) 365-4354
www.chantalcookware.com

CHANTRY-VICTOR, INC.
P.O. Box 3039
Clearwater, FL 33767
(800) 242-6879
chantry123@aol.com

CHEF WALTER
265 Atwells Ave.
Providence, RI 02903
(401) 273-2652
(800) 344-6311
feedback@chefwalter.com
www.chefwalter.com

CHEMEX
69 South Church St.
Pittsfield, MA 01201
(413) 499-2370
(800) 243-6399
chemexcof@aol.com

CHICAGO METALLIC
800 Ela Rd.
Lake Zurich, IL 60047
(847) 726-5218
(800) 238-2253
retailpans@aol.com
www.bakingpans.com

CIRCULON COOKWARE
Consumer Relations
One Meyer Plaza
Vallejo, CA 94590
(800) 326-3933
Dan@circulon.com

COCONUT COOKERY
P.O. Box 953
Volcano, HI 96785
(888) 444-0448

COLUMBIAN HOME PRODUCTS, LLC.
1600 Beech St.
Terre Haute, IN 47804
(812) 232-0500

**COMPONENT DESIGN
NORTHWEST, INC.**
5254 S.W. Humphrey Blvd.
Portland, OR 97221
(800) 338-5594
info@cdnw.com

COOPER INSTRUMENT CORPORATION
33 Reeds Gap Rd.
Middlefield, CT 06455
(860) 347-2256
(800) 835-5011

COPCO
A division of Wilton Industries, Inc.
2240 West 75th St.
Woodridge, IL 60517
(630) 963-7100
(800) 772-7111
copco@wilton.com

COPPER PRODUCTS OF ITALY
1861 Dillon Rd.
Maple Glen, PA 19002
(877) 646-0967
www.cpi-inc.net

CORDON ROSE,
See New York Cake & Baking.

CORK POPS
20 Mariposa Rd.
San Rafael, CA 94901
(415) 485-0360
(800) 322-6757

**CORNING CONSUMER
PRODUCTS COMPANY,**
See World Kitchen.

CUISINART
One Cummings Point Rd.
Stamford, CT 06904
(203) 975-4600
(800) 726-6247
cuisinart@conair.com

CUTHBERTSON IMPORTS
P.O. Box 3098
Noroton, CT 06820
(203) 834-0506
(800) 607-8733

D

**DAMCO (DRESSLER AMERICAN
MARKETING COMPANY)**
418 Bryant Circle, Suite A
Ojai, CA 92023
(805) 640-0051
(800) 426-5134

DANCE OF THE ANCESTORS
1306 Fourth St.
El Sobrante, CA 94710
(510) 528-3262
(800) 471-2250

DANESCO INTERNATIONAL INC.
18111 Trans-Canada
Kirkland, Quebec H9J 3K1
Canada
(514) 694-9111
(800) 667-6543

DE BUYER,
See World Cuisine, Inc.

DELONGHI AMERICA, INC.
Park 80 West
Plaza One
Saddle Brook, NJ 07663
(201) 909-4000
(800) 322-3848
consumer@delonghiusa.com

DEMARLE, INC.
2666 B Rte. 130 N
Cranbury, NJ 08512
(609) 395-0219
info@Demarleusa.com
www.demarleusa.com

DEMEYERE-A.S.C., N.A.
3 Dorchester Dr.
Westport, CT 06880
(203) 255-2402
(800) 338-7304
info@demeyere.be
www.demeyere.be

DR. OETKER,
See Leifheit International.

DUALIT
16–28 Penarth St.
London, SE15 1TU
United Kingdom
(44) 0 171639 5271
info@dualit.com

E

EDGECRAFT CORPORATION
825 Southwood Rd.
Avondale, PA 19311
(610) 268-0500
(800) 342-3255

EKCO,
See World Kitchen.

EKS, USA
700 Industrial Dr.
Cary, IL 60013
(847) 462-8033
(877) 462-8033
info@eksusa.com
www.eks.nu.

ELAN
The Omessi Group, Ltd.
11710 Doral Ave.
Northridge, CA 91326
(818) 831-0748

EMILE HENRY USA
204 Quigley Blvd.
New Castle, DE 19720
(302) 326-4800
www.emilehenryusa.com

EMSON
E. Mishan & Sons, Inc.
230 Fifth Ave., Suite 800
New York, NY 10001
(800) 423-4248

EUROPEAN GIFT & HOUSEWARES
514 South Fifth Ave.
Mount Vernon, NY 10550
(914) 664-3448

EVERGREEN LABS, INC.
P.O. Box 1298
Walla Walla, WA 99362
(888) WINEAWAY
cheryl@innw.net

EZ SHARP
Creative Products International, Inc.
8811 Tradeway
San Antonio, TX 78217
(800) 368-3882
info@ez-sharp.com
www.ez-sharp.com

EZE-LAP DIAMOND PRODUCTS, INC.
3572 Arrowhead Dr.
Carson City, NV 89706
(800) 843-4815

F
FANTE'S
1006 S. Ninth St.
Philadelphia, PA 19147
(215) 922-5557

FARBERWARE COOKWARE
Consumer Relations
525 Curtola Parkway
Vallejo, CA 94590
(707) 551-2800
(800) 809-7166
John@farberwarecookware.com

FARBERWARE MILLENNIUM BAKEWARE,
See World Kitchen.

FARBERWARE ELECTRICS,
See Salton, Inc.

FASMODEA
169 Jonas St.
Lyndhurst, Ontario KOE 1NO
Canada
(800) 463-8783

FBM
2666 Route 130
Cranbury, NJ 08512
(609) 860-0577
fbmbongard@aol.com

FOLEY
A Division of The Mirro Company
1512 Washington St.
Manitowoc, WI 54221
(920) 684-4421
(800) 518-6245
moreinfo@mirro.com
www.mirro.com

FOODS OF INDIA
121 Lexington Ave.
New York, NY 10016
(212) 683-4419

FOX RUN CRAFTSMEN
P.O. Box 2727
1907 Stout Dr.
Ivyland, PA 18974
(215) 675-7700
(800) 372-0700

FRED
237 King St.
Charleston, SC 29401
(843) 723-5699

FRIELING USA, INC.
1920 Center Park Dr.
Charlotte, NC 28217
(704) 357-1080
(800) 827-2582
mail@frieling.com
www.frieling.com

G
GARY VALENTI, INC.
54–56 Flushing Ave.
Maspeth, NY 11378
(718) 386-0896

GLASHAUS, INC.
450 Congress Parkway, Suite E
Crystal Lake, IL 60014
(815) 356-8440
glashaus@glashaus.com

GLOBAL,
See Sointu, USA.

GOURMET STANDARD
20220 87th Ave., S. Bldg. 1
Kent, WA 98051
(253) 395-7770

GRACE MANUFACTURING
614 SR 247
Russellville, AR 72802
(800) 555-2767
info@microplane.com
www.microplane.com

H
H.A. MACK
P.O. Box 2827
Woburn, MA 01888
(781) 938-5461
(800) 441-4027

HACKMAN TABLETOP, INC.
27 Danbury Rd., 3rd Floor
Wilton, CT 06897
(203) 834-1825
(800) 448-8252
customerservice@hackmantabletop.com

HAMILTON BEACH
4421 Waterfront Dr.
Glen Allen, VA 23060
(804) 273-9777
(800) 851-8900
www.hamiltonbeach.com

HAROLD'S KITCHEN
Harold Import Company, Inc.
140 Lehigh Ave.
Lakewood, NJ 08701
(732) 367-2800

HAWKINS COOKERS LTD.
Bay City International
P.O. Box 11706
Green Bay, WI 54307
(920) 339-0510

HELCO LTD. EUROPEAN IMPORTS
P.O. Box 69
Mt. Vernon, VA 22121
(703) 360-5766

THE HOUSE ON THE HILL
P.O. Box 7003
Villa Park, IL 60181
(630) 969-2588
houshill@flash.net

I

ILSA,
See Gary Valenti, Inc.

IMPERIAL TEA COURT
1411 Powell St.
San Francisco, CA 94133
(415) 788-6080
(800) 567-5898
imperial@imperialtea.com
www.imperialtea.com

**INTERNATIONAL WINE
ACCESSORIES (IWA)**
10246 Miller Rd.
Dallas, TX 75238-1206
(800) 527-4072

ISI NORTH AMERICA INC.
P.O. Box 616
30 Chapin Rd.
Pine Brook, NJ 07058
(973) 227-2426
(800) 447-2426
www.isinorthamerica.com

J

J. B. PRINCE
36 East 31st St.
New York, NY 10016
(212) 683-3553

J. K. ADAMS COMPANY, INC.
1430 Route 30
Dorset, VT 05251
(800) 451-6118

J. WECK,
See Glashaus, Inc.

JOHN BOOS & COMPANY
315 South First St.
Effingham, IL 62401
(217) 347-7701
sales@johnboos.com
www.johnboos.com

JOYCE CHEN
6 Fortune Dr.
Billerica, MA 01821
(978) 671-9500
info@joycechen.com
www.joycechen.com

K

KAISER BAKEWARE
1200-G Westinghouse Blvd.
Charlotte, NC 28273
(704) 588-8090
(800) 966-3009
sales@kaiserbakeware.com

KAM MAN FOOD PRODUCTS, INC.
200 Canal St.
New York, NY 10013
(212) 571-0330

**KATCHALL INDUSTRIES
INTERNATIONAL, INC.**
5800 Creek Rd.
Cincinnati, OH 45242
(800) 533-6900

**KAVALIER GLASSWORKS
OF NORTH AMERICA**
1301 Brummel Ave.
Elk Grove Village, IL 60007
(847) 364-7303
(800) 746-2948
www.simax.com

KENWOOD,
See Maverick Industries, Inc.

**THE KING ARTHUR FLOUR
BAKER'S CATALOGUE**
P.O. Box 876
Norwich, VT 05055-0876
(800) 827-6836

KITCHEN MARKET
218 Eighth Ave.
New York, NY 10011
(212) 243-4433
(888) HOT-4433
mail@kitchenmarket.com

KITCHEN SUPPLY COMPANY
7333 West Harrison St.
Forest Park, IL 60130
(708) 383-5990
(800) 793-6244
ksc@wwa.com

**KITCHENAID
APPLIANCES DIVISION**
750 Monte Rd.—MD 5207
Benton Harbor, MI 49022
(616) 923-3045
(800) 541-6390
www.kitchenaid.com

KITCHENAID COOKWARE
Consumer Relations
One Meyer Plaza
Vallejo, CA 94590
(888) 801-1707
Jane@kitchenaidcookware.com
www.kitchenaid.com

KITCHENART
A Division of Robbins Industries, Inc.
4420 Helton Dr.
Florence, AL 35630
(256) 760-8900
(800) 239-8090
info@kitchenart.com
www.kitchenart.com

KORIN
57 Warren St.
New York, NY 10007
(800) 626-2172
www.korin.com

KOTOBUKI
320 Victory Ave.
S. San Francisco, CA 94080
(650) 588-8593

KRETZER,
See Helco Ltd. European Imports.

KRUPS NORTH AMERICA, INC.
7 Reuten Dr.
Closter, NJ 07624
(201) 767-5500
(800) 526-5377
www.krups.com

KÜCHENPROFI-USA
1023 S. Pines Rd.
Spokane, WA 99206
(509) 928-8873
(800) 336-6693
marpachouse@worldnet.att.net

KUHN RIKON CORPORATION
350 Bon Air Center, Suite 240
Greenbrae, CA 94904
(415) 461-3927
(800) 662-5882
kuhnrikon@kuhnrikon.com
www.kuhnrikon.com

KYOCERA AMERICA, INC.
8611 Balboa Ave.
San Diego, CA 92123
(858) 576-2600
kaicorp@kyocera.com
www.kyocera.com

L

LA PAVONI,
See European Gift & Housewares

LAMSON & GOODNOW MFG. CO.
45 Conway St.
Shelburne Falls, MA 01370
(413) 625-6331
(800) 872-6564

LE CREUSET OF AMERICA
One Bob Gifford Blvd.
Early Branch, SC 29916
(803) 943-4308
(877) CREUSET
cservice@lecreuset.com
www.lecreuset.com

LEHMAN'S
P.O. Box 41
Kidron, OH 44636
(877) 438-5346
info@lehmans.com

LEIFHEIT INTERNATIONAL
510 Broad Hollow Rd., Suite 209
Melville, NY 11747
(516) 501-1054
usleifheit@aol.com
www.leifheit.de

LELLO APPLIANCES CORPORATION
355 Murray Hill Parkway
East Rutherford, NJ 07073
(201) 939-2555

LINCOLN FOODSERVICE PRODUCTS, INC.
1111 N. Hadley Rd.
Fort Wayne, IN 46804
(219) 459-8200
(888) 417-5462

LODGE MANUFACTURING CO.
204 E. Fifth St.
South Pittsburg, TN 37380
(423) 837-7181
info@lodgemfg.com
www.lodgemfg.com

LUMINARC-ARC INTERNATIONAL
Wade Blvd., P.O. Box 5001
Millville, NJ 08332
(856) 825-5620

M

MAGIC MILL
382 Route 59, Sec. #338
Monsey, NY 10952
(914) 368-2532
info@ magicmillusa.com
www.magicmillusa.com

MASAMOTO SOHOTEN,
See Korin.

MASON CASH OF ENGLAND
1901 Route 130
North Brunswick, NJ 08902
(732) 940-8300

MASSIMO ITALIAN TREASURES
P.O. Box 835
Woodbridge, CA 95258
(209) 365-0868
www.massimotreasures.com

MATFER, INC.
16249 Stagg St.
Van Nuys, CA 91406
(818) 782-0792
(800) 766-0333

MAUVIEL,
See Matfer, Inc. or Swissmar Imports, Ltd.

MAVERICK INDUSTRIES, INC.
94 Mayfield Ave.
Edison, NJ 08837
(732) 417-9666
(800) 526-0954
mavind@aol.com

MAXI-AIDS
42 Executive Blvd.
Farmingdale, NY 11735
(516) 752-0521
(800) 522-6294

MELITTA USA
13925 58th St. N.
Clearwater, FL 33760
(727) 535-2111

MESSERMEISTER,
See DAMCO

METRO MARKETING
2851 E. Las Hermanas St.
Rancho Dominguez, CA 90221
(310) 898-1888
(800) 367-0845

METROKANE, INC.
964 Third Ave.
New York, NY 10155
(212) 759-6262
(800) 724-4321

MONOPOL,
See Swissmar Imports, Ltd.

MONTANA
c/o Fiskars Consumer Products Inc.
636 Science Dr.
Madison, WI 53711
(608) 233-1649

MOULI MANUFACTURING CORP.
One Montgomery St.
Belleville, NJ 07109
(973) 751-6900

MOULINEX
20 Caldari Rd.
Concord, Ontario L4K 4N8
Canada
(905) 669-0114

MOUNTAIN WOODS, INC.
20631 Highway 2
East Glacier Park, MT 59434
(406) 226-9309
(800) 835-0479
mtwoods@mountainwoods.com
www.mountainwoods.com

MR. COFFEE
A Division of the Sunbeam Corporation
P.O. Box 948389
Maitland, FL 32794-8389
(800) 672-6333
www.sunbeam.com

MUSSO,
See Lello Appliances Corporation.

N

NESCO—THE METAL WARE CORPORATION
P.O. Box 237
1700 Monroe St.
Two Rivers, WI 54241
(920) 793-1368
www.nesco.com

NEW AGE PRODUCTS
3060 Industry St., Suite 108
Oceanside, CA 92054
(800) 886-2467
napchop@aol.com
www.chop-chop.com

NEW YORK CAKE & BAKING
56 West 22nd St.
New York, NY 10010
(212) 675-2253

NORDIC WARE
Highway 7 at 100
Minneapolis, MN 55416
(612) 920-2888
(800) 328-4310
info@nordicware.com
www.nordicware.com

NORPRO
2215 Merrill Creek Pkwy.
Everett, WA 98203
(425) 261-1000
(800) 722-0202
www.norpro.com

NOURI'S
Nouri Brothers Shopping Center
999 Main St.
Patterson, NJ 07503
(973) 279-2388

NY MUTUAL TRADING COMPANY
25 Knickerbocker Rd.
Moonachie, NJ 07074
(201) 933-9555

O

OENOPHILIA
P.O. Box 17115
Chapel Hill, NC 27516
(919) 644-0555
(800) 899-6366
oenophilia@oenophilia.com
www.oenophilia.com

OLD DUTCH INTERNATIONAL, LTD.
421 N. Midland Ave.
Saddle Brook, NJ 07663
(201) 794-6262

OMEGA PRODUCTS INC.
6291 Lyters Ln.
Harrisburg, PA 17111
(717) 561-1105
(800) 633-3401
omegaus@aol.com
www.omegajuicers.com

OXO INTERNATIONAL
75 Ninth Ave., 5th Floor
New York, NY 10011
(212) 242-3333
(800) 545-4411
info@oxo.com
www.oxo.com

P

PACOJET AG
Bundesstrasse 9
CH-6300 Zug
Switzerland
[41] 417102522
pacojet.ag@bluewin.ch

PANASONIC
One Panasonic Way
Secaucus, NJ 07094
(800) 211-7262
consumerproducts@panasonic.com

PARRISH'S CAKE DECORATING SUPPLIES, INC.
225 West 146th St.
Gardena, CA 90248
(310) 324-225

PAUL OLIVER WOODWARE
Oliverhill, MS/368
Gin Gin, 4671
Australia
[61] 07 4157 4321
oliverr@ozemail.com.au

PEDRINI USA INC.
125 Cartwright Loop
Bayport, NY 11705
(516) 472-4501

PELOUZE SCALE COMPANY
7400 W. 100th Place
Bridgeview, IL 60455
(800) 654-8330
www.healthmeter.com

PEUGEOT,
See Swissmar Imports, Ltd.

PILLIVUYT OF NORTH AMERICA
2620 W. Beltline Highway
Middleton, WI 53562
(262) 886-2753
pillivuyt@pillivuytna.com
www.pillivuyt.com

POLDER, INC.
8 Slater St.
Port Chester, NY 10573
(914) 937-8200
(800) 431-2133
polderwire@aol.com

PRESTO
National Presto Industries, Inc.
3925 N. Hastings Way
Eau Claire, WI 54703
(715) 839-2121
contact@gopresto.com
www.gopresto.com

PROGRESSIVE INTERNATIONAL CORPORATION
6111 S. 228th St.
Kent, WA 98032
(253) 850-6111
(800) 426-7101
picl@progressiveintl.com

PROGRESSUS COMPANY INC.
100 Merrick Rd.
Rockville Centre, NY 11570
(516) 255-0245

R

REGENT SHEFFIELD,
See World Kitchen.

R. H. FORSCHNER & CO.
One Research Dr.
Shelton, CT 06484
(203) 929-6391
www.swissarmybrands.com

R.S.V.P. INTERNATIONAL INC.
4021 13th Ave., W.
Seattle, WA 98119
(206) 282-1037
(800) 275-7787
rsvpintl@earthlink.net

RECO INTERNATIONAL CORPORATION
138 Haven Ave.
Port Washington, NY 11050
(516) 767-2400
recoint@aol.com

RESTON LLOYD, LTD.
22880 Glenn Dr.
Reston, VA 22090
(703) 437-0003
info@restonlloyd.com

RIEDEL CRYSTAL
24 Aero Rd.
Bohemia, NY 11716
(800) 642-1859
riedel.crystal@kufstein.netwing.at

THE RIVAL COMPANY
800 E. 101st Terrace
Kansas City, MO 64131
(800) 557-4825
www.rivco.com

RIVER LIGHT COMPANY,
See Williams-Sonoma.

ROBINSON KNIFE COMPANY
2615 Walden Ave.
Buffalo, NY 14225
(716) 685-6300
(800) 245-2433

ROBINSON RANSBOTTOM POTTERY
P.O. Box 7
Roseville, OH 43777
(740) 697-7355
(800) 730-5166
bbennett@ransbottompottery.com
www.rrpco.com

ROBOT COUPE U.S.A.
280 South Perkins St.
Jackson, MS 39236
(800) 824-1646

RONCO INVENTIONS
21344 Superior St.
Chatsworth, CA 91311
(818) 775-4602

RÖSLE USA
204 Quigley Boulevard
New Castle, DE 19720
(302) 326-4801
www.rosleusa.com

RUFFONI COPPER USA
1108 A Edgehill Dr.
Burlingame, CA 94010
(650) 375-0803
kahndotkahn@aol.com

**RUSSELL HARRINGTON
CUTLERY COMPANY**
44 Green River St.
Southbridge, MA 01550
(508) 765-0201
sales@rhcutlery.com
www.russell-harrington.com

RUSSELL HOBBS
29039 Clayton Ave.
Wickliffe, OH 44092
(440) 944-3500
(800) 669-7434

S

SABATIER
A Division of Excel
100 Andrews Rd.
Hicksville, NY 11801
(516) 794-3355
customerservice@excelimporting.com

SALTER HOUSEWARES
15 Gardner Rd.
Fairfield, NJ 07004
(973) 227-3057
salesdesk@salterhousewares.com
www.salterhousewares.com

SALTON, INC.
550 Business Center Dr.
Mount Prospect, IL 60056
(847) 803-4600
(800) 272-5629
salton@saltonusa.com
www.salton-maxim.com

SAMMONS PRESTON
An AbilityOne Company
P.O. Box 5071
Bolingbrook, IL 60440
(800) 323-5547

SASSAFRAS ENTERPRISES, INC.
1622 West Carroll Ave.
Chicago, IL 60612
(312) 226-2000
(800) 537-4941
sassinc@aol.com

THE SAUSAGE MAKER
Niagara Frontier Food Terminal
1500 Clinton St., Bldg. 123
Buffalo, NY 14206
(716) 824-6510

SAVOIR VIVRE
P.O Box 40145
Philadelphia, PA 19106
(215) 625-7964
carovivre@aol.com

SCANPAN USA INC.
49 Walnut St.
Norwood, NJ 07648
(201) 767-6252
scanpan@scanpan.com
www.scanpan.com

SCI CUISINE INTERNATIONAL
PO Box 659
Camarillo, CA 93011
(805) 482-0791

SESHIN USA INC.
603-G Country Club Dr.
Bensenville, IL 60106
(630) 238-1882
maxhahn@msn.com

SIERRA HOUSEWARES, INC.
4115 West Ogden Ave.
Chicago, IL 60623
(773) 522-5600
(888) 212-0302
chillzon@aol.com

SIMAC,
See Lello Appliances Corporation

SIMPLEX
1354 Ester Dr.
Burlington, Ontario
Canada L7P 1L3
(905) 331-2707
kmalleret@home.com
www.simplexkettles.co.uk

SITLAX LTD.
381 Blair Rd.
Avenel, NJ 07001
(732) 596-9393
sitlax@ix.netcom.com
www.sitlax.com

SKEPPSHULT,
See EKS USA.

SMITH & NEPHEW
One Quality Dr.
P.O. Box 1005
Germantown, WI 53022
(800) 228-3693

SOEHNLE,
See Frieling USA, Inc.

SOINTU, USA
443 Greenwich St.
New York, NY 10013
(212) 219-8585
(800) 428-9595

SPANEK, INC.
19135 Brook Ln.
Saratoga, CA 95070
(408) 867-4500

THE SPANISH TABLE
15427 Western Ave.
Seattle, WA 98101
(206) 682-2827

SPICE AND SWEET CORNER
135 Lexington Ave.
New York, NY 10016
(212) 689-5182

**SPRINGFIELD PRECISION
INSTRUMENTS**
76 Passaic St.
Wood Ridge, NJ 07075
(973) 777-2900
(888) 809-3284

STARBUCKS
Customer Relations
PO Box 3717
Seattle, WA 98124
(206) 447-1575 ext. 82900

**SUNBEAM TIMERS
AND THERMOMETERS,**
See Springfield Precision Instruments.

**SUNBEAM CORPORATION
CONSUMER SERVICE**
P.O. Box 948389
Maitland, FL 32794
www.sunbeam.com
(800) 438-8407

SUR LA TABLE
1765 Sixth Avenue S.
Seattle, WA 98134
(800) 243-0852

SWEET CELEBRATIONS
P.O. Box 39426
Edina, MN 55439
(800) 328-6722

SWISS GOLD
elfo USA inc.
1855-F Beaver Ridge Circle
Norcross, GA 30071
(678) 969-0001
elfousa@aol.com
www.swissgold.com

SWISSMAR IMPORTS, LTD.
35 E. Beavercreek Rd., Unit #6
Richmond Hill, Ontario L4B 1B3
Canada
(905) 764-1121
info@swissmar.com
www.swissmar.com

T

TAYLOR PRECISION PRODUCTS, L.P.
2220 Entrada del Sol
Las Cruces, NM 88001
(505) 526-0944
info@taylorusa.com

TEKNOR APEX COMPANY
505 Central Aveune
Pawtucket, RI 02861
(800) 556-3864

T-FAL
25 Riverside Dr.
Pine Brook, NJ 01058
(800) 395-8325
consumerservice@t-fal.com
www.t-fal.com

THERMOS NISSAN
300 N. Martingale Rd., Suite 200
Schaumburg, IL 60173
(800) 831-9242
www.thermos.com

THERMOWORKS, INC.
221 S. Country Manor Ln.
Alpine, UT 84004
(801) 756-7705

THORPE ROLLING PIN COMPANY
336 Putnam Ave.
Hamden, CT 06517
(203) 787-0281

TILIA, INC.
568 Howard St., 3rd Floor
San Francisco, CA 94105
(415) 543-9136
(800) 777-5452
cust_service@tilia.com
www.tilia.com

TOM DAVID, INC.
P.O. Box 541
Nantucket, MA 02554
(800) 634-8881

TRUDEAU CORPORATION
10440 Woodward Avenue
Woodridge, IL 60517
(800) 878-3328
usorder@trudeaucorp.com

U

**UNIVERSAL TRADING
PRODUCTS, INC.**
311 N. Walnut St.
Wood Dale, IL 60191
(888) 545-1582

UPTON TEA IMPORTS
231 South St.
Hopkinton, MA 01748
(800) 234-8327
uptontea@tiac.net
www.uptontea.com

URNEX
Royal Enterprises, Inc.
Yonkers, NY 10705
(800) 222-2826
info@urnex.com
www.urnex.com

V

VACU VIN USA, INC.
P.O. Box 5489
Novato, CA 94948
(415) 382-1241
www.vacuvin.com

VILLAWARE
3615 Superior Ave., No. 44
Cleveland, OH 44114
(216) 391-6650
pdittoe@villaware.com

THE VOLLWRATH COMPANY
1236 N. 18th St.
Sheboygan, WI 53081
(920) 457-4851

W

WARING
283 Main St.
New Hartford, CT 06057
(800) 988-1000

THE WEST BEND COMPANY
400 Washington St.
West Bend, WI 53095
(262) 334-2311
housewares@westbend.com
www.westbend.com

WESTMARK,
See Matfer, Inc. or Norpro.

WIDERVIEW, INC.
131 Liberty St.
Petaluma, CA 94952
www.widerview.com.

WILLIAM BOUNDS LTD.
3737 W. 240th St.
Torrance, CA 90505
(800) 473-0504

WILLIAMS-SONOMA
Mail Order Department
P.O. Box 7456
San Francisco, CA 94120
(800) 541-1262

WILTON INDUSTRIES
2240 W. 75th St.
Woodridge, IL 60517
(630) 810-2205
(800) 794-5866
info@wilton.com
www.wilton.com

THE WINE ENTHUSIAST
8 Saw Mill River Rd.
Hawthorne, NY 10532
(914) 345-9463

**WISCONSIN ALUMINUM
FOUNDRY CO., INC.**
838 S. 16th St.
Manitowoc, WI 54220
(920) 682-8627

WMF USA HEADQUARTERS
85 Price Parkway
Farmingdale, NY 11735
(631) 293-3990

WOODARD + CHARLES LTD.
485-21 S. Broadway
Hicksville, NY 11801
(516) 932-1122
(800) 645-8264

WOODSTOCK SOAPSTONE COMPANY
66 Airpark Rd.
West Lebanon, NH 03784
(800) 866-4344

WOOLEY ELECTRIC SUPPLY, INC.
1023 W. 7th St.
Little Rock, AR 72201
(501) 372-3887

WORLD CUISINE, INC.
2316 Cotner Avenue
Los Angeles, CA 90064
(310) 445-0909
www.world-cuisine.com

THE WORLD KITCHEN HELP CENTER
140 Washington Ave.
P.O. Box 7369
Endicott, NY 13761
(800) 999-3436

**WÜSTHOF-TRIDENT
OF AMERICA, INC.**
200 Brady Ave.
Hawthorne, NY 10532
(914) 773-0200
(800) 289-9878
info@wusthof.com

Z

THE ZANGER COMPANY
7 Moody Rd.
Enfield, CT 06083
(203) 749-1880
(800) 229-4687

ZEROLL
P.O. Box 999
Ft. Pierce, FL 34954
(561) 461-3811
(800) 872-5000
lennyv@zeroll.com
www.zeroll.com

ZOJIRUSHI AMERICA CORPORATION
6259 Bandini Blvd.
Commerce, CA 90040
(800) 733-6270
jh@zojirushi.com
www.zojirushi.com

ZWILLING J. A. HENCKELS INC.
171 Saw Mill River Rd.
Hawthorne, NY 10532
(914) 747-0300
www.j-a-henckels.com

ZYLISS USA CORP.
19751 Descartes
Foothill Ranch, CA 92610
(949) 699-1884
www.zylissusa.com

CONTRIBUTORS' BIOGRAPHIES

BRUCE AIDELLS is the owner of Aidells Sausage Company (San Francisco) and the author of nine cookbooks, including (with coauthor Denis Kelly) *Bruce Aidells' Complete Sausage Book* (Ten Speed Press, 2000), *The Complete Meat Cookbook* (Houghton Mifflin, 1998), *Flying Sausages* (Chronicle Books, 1995), and *Real Beer and Good Eats* (Knopf, 1992).

EMILY ARONSON was part of the original team that produced *The Cooks' Catalogue* and has edited more than fifty books relating to food and travel. For more than twenty years, she has been the executive producer and director of television programs seen on public television, Discovery's Travel Channel, and Cable News Network.

NANCY VERDE BARR is an Italian food authority and author. A former executive chef for Julia Child in charge of live demonstrations and TV, she was culinary producer for the *Baking with Julia* series on PBS and an assistant writer for *Cooking with Master Chefs* and *In Julia's Kitchen with Master Chefs*. The author of *We Called It Macaroni* (Knopf, 1991 & 1996) and the forthcoming *Simply Italian* (Knopf, 2001), she contributes articles to *Gourmet, Food & Wine*, and *Bon Appétit*. As a food consultant, producer, and writer, she has worked on *Good Morning America* and The Food Network. She also teaches cooking classes around the country.

LIDIA MATTICHIO BASTIANICH is an authority on the cooking of her native Italy. She is the author of *Lidia's*

Italian Table (with Christopher Styler; William Morrow, 1998), companion to her twenty-six-part PBS series of the same name, and *La Cucina di Lidia* (Doubleday, 1990). She lectures widely on Italian cuisine and is the co-owner of three New York restaurants: Felidia, Becco, and Frico Bar.

MARIO BATALI, the host of *Molto Mario* on The Food Network, is the author of two books, *Mario Batali's Simple Italian Food* (Clarkson Potter, 1998) and *Mario Batali Holiday Food: Family Recipes for the Most Festive Time of the Year* (Clarkson Potter, 2000). He is chef and co-owner of four New York City restaurants: Po, Lupa, Esca, and Babbo, which was named Best New Restaurant of 1998 by the James Beard Foundation.

MICHAEL & ARIANE BATTERBERRY, the founders of *Food & Wine* and *Food Arts,* have authored eighteen books on food, entertaining, art, and social history. Considered experts and trend spotters in the world of food and drink, the Batterberrys have appeared on television and lectured on food and wine at institutions around the country.

RICK BAYLESS is chef and owner of Chicago's Topolobampo and Frontera Grill, which was chosen by Patricia Wells at the *International Herald Tribune* as one of the best casual restaurants in the world. Named Chef of the Year by the James Beard Foundation in 1995, he is the author of *Authentic Mexican* (William Morrow, 1987); *Rick Bayless's Mexican Kitchen* (Scribner, 1996), which was named Best

Cookbook of the Year by the International Association of Culinary Professionals; and *Mexico One Plate at a Time* (Scribner, 2000).

DANIEL BOULUD is a native of Lyon, France. Owner of Daniel and Café Boulud (New York), he is regarded as one of America's greatest chefs. Named Chef of the Year by *Bon Appétit* and winner of the Top Table award from *Gourmet* for his restaurant Daniel, he is the author of two books: *Daniel Boulud's Café Boulud Cookbook* (Scribner, 1999) and *Cooking with Daniel Boulud* (Random House, 1993).

TERRANCE BRENNAN, one of the finest chefs and restaurateurs in the United States, is chef and proprietor of Picholine (New York). Formerly of Le Cirque, Montrâchet, Annabelle's, and the Polo Restaurant in the Hotel Westbury, he was cited by *Food & Wine* as one of the eight Best New Chefs in America in 1995. Picholine has consistently won the Zagat Survey's top rating for Mediterranean cuisine.

GIULIANO BUGIALLI is a popular Italian cooking teacher and demonstrator who draws record-breaking audiences. He is author of *The Fine Art of Italian Cooking* (Times Books, 1990), *Bugialli's Italy* (William Morrow, 1998), and *Bugialli on Pasta* (Stewart, Tabori & Chang, 2000), among others. His weekly television show, in Italian, aired around the world for more than five years.

DAVID BURKE is Executive Chef at Park Avenue Café (New York) and the first non-Frenchman ever to win France's highest cooking honor, the Meilleurs Ouvriers de France Association medal and diploma. He is author of *Cooking with David Burke* (Knopf, 1995) and currently at work on a plan to revive the Edwardian Room in New York's Plaza Hotel.

FRED E. CARL JR. is CEO and founder of Viking Range Corporation (Ultraline in Canada), originator of commercial-style appliances for the home. He was inducted into the National Kitchen and Bath Association Hall of Fame in 1994.

PENELOPE CASAS is an authority on Spanish food and travel. Her books include *Foods and Wines of Spain* (Random House, 1982), *Tapas: The Little Dishes of Spain* (Random House, 1985), *Discovering Spain* (Knopf, 1996), and *Paella!: Spectacular Rice Dishes from Spain* (Henry Holt, 1999). She is an adjunct professor at New York University and leads tours to Spain each year.

HELEN CHEN is CEO and Chairman of Joyce Chen Products and Keilen, Inc. (suppliers of Asian and ethnic cookware and products) and an expert on Chinese cooking. *Peking Cuisine* (Orion Books, 1997) and *Helen Chen's Chinese Home Cooking* (Hearst Books, 1994) are among her six cookbooks. She teaches Chinese cuisine at Boston University.

JULIA CHILD, the doyenne of food and wine in America, brought classical cuisine to suburban America's kitchens with her many popular PBS television series. She is author or coauthor of eleven books, including *The Way to Cook* (Knopf, 1989), *Baking with Julia* (William Morrow, 1996), and her latest, *Julia's Kitchen Wisdom* (Knopf, 2000). Mrs. Child won Emmy awards for her work in 1995 and 1997. She began her culinary career at Paris's famed Le Cordon Bleu in 1949 and is a cofounder of The American Institute of Wine & Food.

BERNARD CLAYTON is one of America's premier bakers and writers on the subject of breads. He has written *Bernard Clayton's New Complete Book of Breads* (Simon & Schuster, 1995), which won the coveted Tastemaker Award for Best Cookbook and was praised by Craig Claiborne as perhaps the best book on the subject in the English language; *Bernard Clayton's Complete Book of Small Breads* (Simon & Schuster, 1998); and *The Complete Book of Soups and Stews* (Simon & Schuster, 1997).

ANDY COE is a food and travel writer who has coauthored *Foie Gras: A Passion* (Wiley, 1999). He has also written guidebooks to Cuba and Mexico.

SHIRLEY CORRIHER is a cooking teacher, food scientist, and consultant. She is author of *CookWise: The Hows and Whys of Successful Cooking* (William Morrow, 1997), which won the James Beard Award for Food Reference and Technique in 1998. Her students have included the editors of *Bon Appétit*, *Food & Wine*, and *Gourmet*.

MARJORIE CUBISINO is a home economist and consultant who works with housewares and major and small appliances. A former editor for *Good Housekeeping* and *McCall's* magazines, she has been doing extensive product testing in the Food Appliances Department at the Good Housekeeping Institute.

MARION CUNNINGHAM, known for her acclaimed work on the *Fannie Farmer* cookbooks, is the author of *Learning to*

Cook with Marion Cunningham (Knopf, 1999), *Cooking with Children* (Knopf, 1995), and *The Breakfast Book* (Knopf, 1987), among others. Her food column has appeared in the *San Francisco Chronicle* and the *Los Angeles Times*. She assisted James Beard in his many cooking classes for eleven years and today writes and teaches in California.

ARIANE DAGUIN is owner and cofounder of D'Artagnan, which in 1985 became the first purveyor of foie gras in the United States and now supplies organic game and fowl of the highest quality to restaurants and the public. She is a native of Gascony, France, and author (with George Faison and Joanna Pruess) of *D'Artagnan's Glorious Game Cookbook* (Little, Brown, 1999).

LINDA DANNENBERG, a journalist specializing in French cuisine and lifestyle, is a contributor to *Wine Spectator, Town & Country, House Beautiful,* and *Victoria* magazines. Her books include *Paris Bistro Cooking* (Clarkson Potter, 1991), *Ducasse Flavors of France* (with Alain Ducasse; Artisan, 1998), and her latest, *Perfect Vinaigrettes* (Stewart, Tabori & Chang, 1999).

ROCCO DISPIRITO is the chef and owner of Union Pacific (New York). Known for his creative combinations of French and Asian foods, he was named one of America's Best New Chefs by *Food & Wine* in 1999. Trained at the Culinary Institute of America and the revered Jardin de Cygne in Paris, he has worked at Lespinasse (New York) and Aujourd'hui (Boston).

ALAIN DUCASSE is a master chef and the only chef with six Michelin stars to his credit. He heads Louis XV–Alain Ducasse in Monaco and the Restaurant Alain Ducasse in Paris, France. He is author of *Ducasse Flavors of France* (Artisan, 1998), *L'Atelier of Alain Ducasse* (Wiley, 2000), and the forthcoming *Harvesting Excellence* (Editions Assouline, 2000). In June 2000 his new (self-titled) restaurant Alain Ducasse opened to acclaim in New York City.

CAROL EINHORN is a writer at Organic, Inc., an Internet services company in New York, where she develops editorial content for client websites. Her profiles of musicians and music industry executives have appeared in a variety of print and online publications, including *Billboard* and www.grammy.com. Her songwriting has been recognized with numerous awards from ASCAP and The Songwriters' Guild of America. She is also editor of *WIM,* the quarterly magazine published by Women in Music, Inc.

FLORENCE FABRICANT, a regular food and restaurant columnist for the *New York Times* dining section, also contributes features about food, wine, and travel to the *Times*. She has written five cookbooks, including *New Home Cooking: Feeding Family, Feasting Friends* (Clarkson Potter, 1991), which was named Best General Cookbook by the International Association of Culinary Professionals and Best Special Occasion Cookbook by the James Beard Foundation in 1992. She worked on the original *Cooks' Catalogue* and was the editor for the revised paperback edition. Fabricant was elected to the Who's Who of Cooking in America and is a member of Les Dames d'Escoffier.

AMY FARGES is the co-owner of Marche aux Delices, a wild and exotic mushroom mail order company. A graduate of La Varenne in Paris, she has written articles for *Food & Wine, Fine Cooking,* and *Bride's* magazines. She is the author of *The Mushroom Lovers' Cookbook and Primer* (with Christopher Styler; Workman, 2000).

RONNIE FEIN is a freelance food writer and author of *The Complete Idiot's Guide to Cooking Basics, 3rd Ed.* (Macmillan, 2000). Her articles have appeared in *Cook's Illustrated, The Advocate, Newsday,* Hersam-Acorn Newspapers, *Consumer's Digest, Consumer Guide,* and *Connecticut, Westport,* and *Greenwich* magazines. She gives demonstrations and teaches small hands-on cooking classes at her School of Creative Cooking.

SUSANNA FOO is the chef and owner of Susanna Foo Chinese Cuisine (Philadelphia) and author of *Susanna Foo Chinese Cuisine* (Chapters Publishing Ltd., 1995). An expert on Chinese cuisine, she is a native of Taiwan and graduate of the Culinary Institute of America.

LARRY FORGIONE is the proprietor of New York's An American Place, The Beekman 1766 Tavern, The Coach House, and Rosehill. He is author of *An American Place* (William Morrow, 1996), which won a James Beard Foundation Award. In 1999 he received the Silver Spoon Award from *Food Arts* magazine.

SHARON FRANKE is director of the Food Appliances Department at the Good Housekeeping Institute and spokesperson on issues relating to appliances and other cooking equipment for *Good Housekeeping* magazine.

EDWARD GIOBBI is a well-known artist and author of *Pleasures of the Good Earth* (Knopf, 1991) and *Eat Right, Eat Well—The Italian Way* (with Richard N. Wolff; Knopf, 1998).

DORIE GREENSPAN, the "Tools of the Trade" columnist for *Bon Appétit* magazine, has written six cookbooks, including *Baking with Julia* (William Morrow, 1996), winner of a James Beard Foundation Award and *Desserts by Pierre Hermé* (Little, Brown, 1998), named Cookbook of the Year by the International Association of Culinary Professionals. Her most recent work, *The Café Boulud Cookbook* (Scribner, 1999), is a collaboration with Chef Daniel Boulud. She is at work, with Pierre Hermé, on a chocolate dessert book.

CAROL GUBER is director of food programs at New York University's Department of Nutrition & Food Studies. She formerly managed the retail sales division of the caviar company Petrossian.

JESSICA B. HARRIS is a culinary historian and author of seven cookbooks on the foods of the African Diaspora, including *Sky Juice and Flying Fish* (Fireside, 1991), *Iron Pots and Wooden Spoons* (Fireside, 1999), and *The Welcome Table* (Fireside, 1996). Dr. Harris has lectured on African American foodways at institutions across the country. She is currently at work on *Beyond Gumbo: Creole Fusion Food.*

MARCELLA HAZAN is credited with making true Italian cuisine accessible for American home cooks. Her works include *The Classic Italian Cookbook* (1973), *Essentials of Classic Italian Cooking* (Knopf, 1992), *Marcella's Italian Kitchen* (Knopf, 1986), and *Marcella Cucina* (HarperCollins, 1997). For years she conducted weeklong cooking classes in her home, part of a sixteenth-century palazzo, in Venice. She and her wine-authority husband, Victor, are natives of Cesenatico in Emilia-Romagna, Italy.

MAIDA HEATTER is the author of several classic dessert cookbooks, including *Maida Heatter's Cakes* (Andrews Mc-Meel, 1997), *Maida Heatter's Pies & Tarts* (Andrews McMeel, 1997), and *Maida Heatter's Brand-New Book of Great Cookies* (Random House, 1995). Her first book, *Maida Heatter's Book of Great Chocolate Desserts* (Random House, 1995), was a *New York Times* bestseller and has been inducted into the James Beard Foundation's Cookbook Hall of Fame. *Maida Heatter's Book of Great Desserts* (Andrews McMeel, 1999) is her latest creation.

PIERRE HERMÉ, dubbed the Picasso of pastry in *Vogue* magazine, is the author of *Desserts by Pierre Hermé* (with Dorie Greenspan; Little, Brown, 1998). He apprenticed to the legendary Gaston Lenôtre when he was only fourteen. In 1997, he was decorated as a Chevalier of Arts and Letters and named France's Chef of the Year. The Pierre Hermé Salon de Thé, his second site in Japan, opened in July 2000.

KEN HOM, an authority on Chinese cuisine, hosts the *Ken Hom Travels with a Hot Wok* series on BBC and PBS. His books include *Ken Hom's Hot Wok* (West One Hundred Seventy Five, 1999), *Easy Family Recipes from a Chinese-American Childhood* (Knopf, 1997), *The Taste of China* (Trafalgar Square, 1997), *Ken Hom's Asian Ingredients* (Ten Speed Press, 1996), and *Ken Hom's Chinese Kitchen* (Hyperion, 1995). He is the chef and owner of Yellow River Café (London, England).

ERNESTO ILLY is the president of Illycaffè S.P.A., renowned makers of espresso coffee and products, in Trieste, Italy. Serving 3 million espresso coffees daily, Illycaffè sets the quality standard for coffee throughout the world. A chemist and inventor by training, Dr. Illy is well respected in the coffee industry for his expertise. He is founder and senior vice president of the prestigious ASIC—Association Scientifique International du Café—Paris, which studies the biological, chemical, and physical properties of coffee.

STEVEN JENKINS, one of the country's top cheese specialists, is the author of the *Cheese Primer* (Workman, 1996), which won the James Beard Foundation Award in 1997. A regular contributor to National Public Radio's *The Splendid Table* with Lynn Rossetto Kasper, his "The Jenkins Chronicles" can be heard weekly.

THOMAS KELLER is the chef and owner of The French Laundry (Yountville, California), named the number-one restaurant in America by *Esquire, Zagat's Guide, Gourmet, Bon Appétit,* the *New York Times,* and *Wine Spectator.* He has written *The French Laundry Cookbook* (with Deborah Jones and Susie Heller; Artisan, 1999) and was named Best Chef in California in 1996 and Outstanding Chef in America in 1997 by the James Beard Foundation.

ELAINE KHOSROVA is a food writer and cooking enthusiast whose work has appeared in *Country Living, Ladies Home Journal, Classic American Home,* and *Parenting* magazines. Her life's ambition is to preach the gospel of good home cooking from her kitchen pulpit.

GRAY KUNZ is the former Executive Chef of the four-star Lespinasse at the St. Regis Hotel (New York). Known for his use of Asian, Middle Eastern, and Indian ingredients in his modern French cuisine, he grew up in Singapore and trained in the Lausanne kitchen of France's Fredy Girardet.

DANIEL LEADER is the owner of Bread Alone Bakery in Woodstock, New York, and the author of *Bread Alone* (with Judith Blahnik; William Morrow, 1993). He is known for his belief in the age-old tradition of using only the finest organic nuts, fruits, and stone-ground grains to make his bread.

DAVID LEITE is a frequent contributor to the *Chicago Sun-Times* and writes for Culinary.com and his own website, leitesculinaria.com.

SARABETH LEVINE is the owner of New York's three Sarabeth's restaurants. The James Beard Foundation named her Pastry Chef of the Year in 1996. Her restaurants are known for her award-winning handmade fruit preserves and jams, as well as for the lines at their famous weekend brunches.

MICHAEL LOMONACO is the chef and director of Windows on the World and Wild Blue (at the top of the World Trade Center in New York). Formerly of Le Cirque and the '21' Club, he now hosts two television food programs: *Epicurious* on the Discovery Channel and *Michael's Place* on The Food Network. He is coauthor of *The '21' Club Cookbook* (Doubleday, 1995), and is currently at work on two new cookbooks.

PRISCILLA MARTEL is a chef and food writer who specializes in healthful cuisine, baking, and the foods of the Mediterranean. Her work has appeared in *Cooking Light, Fine Cooking,* and the *Hartford Courant* newspaper. Formerly proprietor of Connecticut's Restaurant du Village and Restaurant au Musée and Executive Chef at the Norwich Inn & Spa in Vermont, she is coauthor of the award-winning *Best Bread Ever* (Broadway Books, 1997). Her latest project is a book on rustic hearth baking.

NOBUYUKI MATSUHISA was named one of America's ten Best Chefs and is known for his revolutionary sushi and seafood dishes. He is the owner of Matsuhisa in Beverly Hills and (with actor Robert DeNiro and restaurateur Drew Nieporent) Nobu and Next Door Nobu in New York, Nobu London, and Nobu Las Vegas.

MICHAEL MCCARTY, the chef and owner of Michael's (Santa Monica, California, and New York) is author of *Michael's Cookbook* (Macmillan, 1989). He received the Grande Dîplome at Le Cordon Bleu in Paris.

DANNY MEYER is the creator and owner of four New York restaurants: Union Square Cafe, ranked "New York's Most Popular Restaurant" (*Zagat* 1997–2000), Gramercy Tavern (with chef and partner Tom Colicchio), Eleven Madison Park, and Tabla. He is coauthor, with Michael Romano, of *The Union Square Cafe Cookbook* (HarperCollins, 1994).

JOAN NATHAN is the author of *Jewish Cooking in America* (Knopf, 1998), the companion to her twenty-six-part PBS series, *Jewish Cooking in America with Joan Nathan*. She regularly contributes articles on international ethnic food and special holiday features to the *New York Times, Food Arts, Gourmet,* and the *B'nai B'rith International Jewish Monthly.* Founder of the Ninth Avenue Food Festival in New York City, her other books include *The Jewish Holiday Kitchen* (Schocken, 1998) and *The Children's Jewish Holiday Kitchen* (Schocken, 2000).

MARION NESTLE is Professor and Chair of the Department of Nutrition and Food Sciences at New York University. Formerly senior nutrition policy advisor at the Department of Health and Human Services, she chaired the American Cancer Society committee that issued dietary guidelines for cancer prevention in 1996. Professor Nestle is currently a member of the Food and Drug Administration's Science Board.

DUC BERNARD DE NONANCOURT descends from two distinguished champagne-making families. As a member of the French Résistance, he came to understand the value of single-minded determination, which (after the Second World War) he brought to the making of champagne. Under his direction, Laurent-Perrier has become one of the most respected champagne houses in the world.

MIRIAM NOVALLE is an entrepreneur and owner of T Salon and T Emporium (New York), which carries more than 250 different loose-leaf teas, including her unique black and green tea blends. She supplies restaurants and hotels worldwide and has gained recognition from the *New York Times,* Lifetime TV, and numerous magazines.

FRANÇOIS PAYARD is the chef and owner of Payard Pâtisserie and Bistro (New York). Both the James Beard Foundation and *Bon Appétit* have named him Pastry Chef of the Year. A native of Nice, France, and a third-generation pâtissier, he is the author of *Simply Sensational Desserts* (Broadway Books, 1999).

JACQUES PÉPIN is a master chef, host of award-winning cooking shows on PBS, food columnist, teacher, and author of eighteen cookbooks, including *Jacques Pépin's Table* (Bay

Books, 1997), *Jacques Pépin's Kitchen: Cooking with Claudine* (Bay Books, 1996), and *Julia and Jacques Cooking at Home* (with Julia Child and David Nussbaum; Knopf, 1999). In 1996, his works earned him a place in the James Beard Foundation's Cookbook Hall of Fame. He grew up in his parents' restaurant in Bourg-en-Bresse (near Lyon), France, and writes a quarterly column for *Food & Wine*.

JAMES PETERSON is a chef and the author of *Vegetables* (William Morrow, 1998), winner of a 1999 James Beard Award; *Essentials of Cooking* (Artisan, 2000); *Fish & Shellfish* (William Morrow, 1996); and *Sauces: Classical and Contemporary Sauce Making* (Wiley, 1998). He is a sought-after teacher, writer, consultant, and speaker.

ALFRED PORTALE is the executive chef and co-owner of Gotham Bar and Grill (New York). Considered one of the best chefs in America, he is the author of *Alfred Portale's Gotham Bar and Grill Cookbook* (Doubleday, 1997) and *Alfred Portale's 12 Seasons Cookbook* (Broadway Books, 2000). Chef Portale graduated first in his class from the Culinary Institute of America.

PAUL PRUDHOMME, a Louisiana chef, CEO of Magic Seasoning Blends, Inc., and owner of K-Paul's Louisiana Kitchen (New Orleans), brought Cajun and Creole cuisine to the attention of home cooks with his three PBS cooking series. He is author of *Chef Paul Prudhomme's Louisiana Kitchen* (William Morrow, 1984), *Fork in the Road* (William Morrow, 1993), *Fiery Foods That I Love* (William Morrow, 1995), and most recently, *Louisiana Tastes* (William Morrow, 2000).

WILLIAM RICE, food and wine columnist of the *Chicago Tribune,* is the author of the *Steak Lover's Cookbook* (Workman, 1997), *Feasts of Wine and Food* (William Morrow, 1987), and coeditor of three editions of the restaurant guide *Where to Eat in America* (with Burt Wolf and Barbara Goldman; Macmillan, 1987).

CHARLES A. RILEY II is the editor-in-chief and co-founder of *We* magazine, the first lifestyle magazine for people with disabilities. Dr. Riley has authored seven books on art, policy, and design, including *High Access* (Rizzoli, 1999), *Color Codes* (University Press of New England, 1996), and *The Saints of Modern Art* (University Press of New England, 1984).

ERIC RIPERT is chef and partner at New York's Le Bernardin, named Best Restaurant in America by *GQ* maga-zine in 1997 and awarded four stars by the *New York Times* in 1994. He honed his skills in Paris at Jamin (which holds three Michelin stars) and the four-hundred-year-old La Tour D'Argent, prior to arriving in the United States. The coauthor, with Maguy Le Coze, of *Le Bernardin Cookbook* (Doubleday, 1999), he is a native of Antibes, France.

CLAUDIA RODEN, a native of Cairo, Egypt, has written several cookbooks, including *The New Book of Middle Eastern Food* (Knopf, 2000); *Mediterranean Cookery* (Knopf, 1987), which accompanied her BBC and PBS series of the same name; *Invitation to Mediterranean Cooking* (Rizzoli, 1997); and *The Book of Jewish Food* (Knopf, 1996), winner of the James Beard Best Cookbook Award in 1997. She has worked as a "gastronomic foreign correspondent" for several newspapers and teaches courses in Middle Eastern cooking.

DOUGLAS RODRIGUEZ is an acclaimed chef at Chicama (New York) and was formerly at Patria (New York). He has written *Latin Flavors on the Grill* (with Andrew Dicataldo; Ten Speed Press, 2000), *Latin Ladles* (Ten Speed Press, 1998), and *Nuevo Latino* (with John Harrison; Ten Speed Press, 1995).

MICHAEL ROMANO is chef and partner at the three-star Union Square Cafe (New York), voted "New York's Most Popular Restaurant" (Zagat 1997–2000) and named Outstanding Restaurant of the Year by the James Beard Foundation in 1997. He is coauthor of *The Union Square Cafe Cookbook* (HarperCollins, 1994) and has been named one of *Food & Wine* magazine's Top Ten Chefs in the United States.

MIRIAM RUBIN is a professional chef, food writer, and the author of *Grains* (Collins, 1995) and the editor of *Victoria Sweet Baking* (Hearst Books, 1997). She has worked as food editor for *Weight Watchers* magazine and developed recipes for several books.

JULIE SAHNI, a chef and authority on Indian cooking, is the author of *Classic Indian Cooking* (William Morrow, 1980), *Classic Indian Vegetarian and Grain Cooking* (William Morrow, 1985), and *Julie Sahni's Introduction to Indian Cooking* (Ten Speed Press, 1998), among others.

MARCUS SAMUELSSON is the executive chef of Aquavit (New York); he won three stars from the *New York Times* in 1995, when he was only twenty-four. Born in Ethiopia and raised in Sweden, he has been named one of the Great Chefs of America by the Culinary Institute of America and a Rising Star Chef by the James Beard Foundation.

HILARIE SHEETS is a freelance writer and contributing editor of *ARTnews* magazine. She is the author of *New York's 100 Best Party Places* (City & Co., 2000).

NANCY SILVERTON is an award-winning pastry chef and baker. She is the owner of Campanile restaurant and La Brea Bakery (Los Angeles). A graduate of Le Cordon Bleu in London and former head pastry chef at Wolfgang Puck's Spago, she has written several cookbooks, including *Nancy Silverton's Breads from the La Brea Bakery* (Villard Books, 1996) and *The Food of Campanile* (with Mark Peel; Villard Books, 1997). *Nancy Silverton's Pastries from the La Brea Bakery* (Villard Books, 2000) is her most recent book.

RAYMOND SOKOLOV is Leisure & Arts Editor for the *Wall Street Journal*. His books include *With the Grain* (Knopf, 1996), *The Saucier's Apprentice* (Knopf, 1976), and *Fading Feast* (David R. Godine, 1998). A graduate of Harvard and a former Fulbright Scholar, he has worked as a foreign correspondent and book critic for *Newsweek,* a feature writer for *Natural History* magazine, and as the food editor for the *New York Times*.

ANDRÉ SOLTNER is coauthor of *The French Culinary Institute's Salute to Healthy Cooking* (Rodale Press, 1998) and *The Lutèce Cookbook* (with Seymour Britchky; Knopf, 1995). A native of France, he was for thirty-four years chef and owner of Lutèce (New York). He now teaches as a Master Chef and Senior Lecturer at the French Culinary Institute in New York.

LYN STALLWORTH is a freelance food writer, editor, and instructor in the New School Culinary Arts program. She has written four cookbooks, among them *The Country Fair Cookbook* (Hyperion, 1994) and *The Brooklyn Cookbook* (Knopf, 1991), coauthored with Rod Kennedy Jr. She worked on numerous volumes of the Time-Life Books *Foods of the World* series, edited books for the Beard/Glaser/Wolf Great Cooks series, was senior editor of *The Pleasures of Cooking* magazine, and an editor of *Microwave Cooking* and *Light and Easy* magazines. She attended cooking schools in France, Mexico, and New York.

JANE & MICHAEL STERN write culinary guides and travel the United States in search of good regional restau-

rants. They are authors of *Eat Your Way Across the U.S.A.* (Broadway Books, 1999), *Chili Nation* (Broadway Books, 1999), and *Square Meals* (Lebhar-Friedman, 2000). They can be heard on National Public Radio's *The Splendid Table* each week and their column "Two for the Road," winner of two James Beard Awards, appears monthly in *Gourmet*.

CHRISTOPHER STYLER has been a chef, restaurant consultant, and author for more than twenty years. He is editor of *Lidia's Italian Table* (with Lidia Mattichio Bastianich; William Morrow, 1998), and coauthor of *Sylvia's Soul Food* (with Sylvia Woods; Hearst Books, 1992) and the upcoming *Mushroom Lovers' Cookbook and Primer* (with Amy Farges; Workman, 2000). He has served as associate or culinary producer for four PBS food series, including *Lidia's Italian Table* and *Julia and Jacques Cooking at Home.*

JEAN TIBBETTS is the coauthor of *The Well-Tooled Kitchen* (with Fred Bridge; William Morrow, 1991) and author of *Erté* (Bison Books, 1995). She also contributed to *Erté: The Last Works* (Dutton, 1992) and *Cooking with Daniel Boulud* (Random House, 1993). Her work has also appeared in the *New York Times, Martha Stewart Living,* and *Food & Wine.*

JACQUES TORRES, formerly of New York's Le Cirque, is a renowned pastry chef and the youngest chef ever to win the prestigious Meilleurs Ouvriers de France competition. He has also been named James Beard Pastry Chef of the Year. He now devotes his time to Jacques Torres Chocolate, a wholesale and retail chocolate manufacturing business in Brooklyn, New York, and MrChocolate.com. A native of Bandol, France, in southern Provence, his PBS series *Dessert Circus at Home* premiered in 1998. He is author of *Dessert Circus* (William Morrow, 1998) and the award-winning *Dessert Circus at Home* (William Morrow, 1999).

BARBARA TROPP is the author of *China Moon Cookbook* (Workman, 1992) and *The Modern Art of Chinese Cooking* (William Morrow, 1982), regarded as the classic text in English on Chinese cooking techniques. A China scholar and former owner of the Ivy Award–winning China Moon Café in San Francisco, she has received the Silver Spoon Award from *Food Arts.*

JILL VAN CLEAVE is a cookbook author and food consultant. Her books include *Big, Soft, Chewy Cookies* (Contemporary Books, 1995); *The Neighborhood Bakeshop* (William

Morrow, 1997); and *Icing the Cake* (Contemporary Books, 1990).

CHARLES VAN OVER is a chef, cookbook author, food consultant, and owner of a wholesale bread bakery. His book *The Best Bread Ever* (Broadway Books, 1997) is the award-winning guide to his unique technique for making flavorful breads at home. Former owner of the award-winning French bistro Restaurant du Village (Chester, Connecticut), he has toured America teaching grilling and barbecuing as spokesperson for the Beef Industry Council.

MARGARET VISSER is an award-winning food writer and historian. Her books include *The Rituals of Dinner* (Penguin USA, 1992), which won the International Culinary Professionals' Literary Food Writing Award and was a *New York Times* Notable Book of the Year; *Much Depends on Dinner* (Grove Press, 1999); and *The Way We Are* (Faber & Faber, 1996). Born in South Africa, she studied at the Sorbonne and holds a doctorate in Classics from the University of Toronto.

JEAN-GEORGES VONGERICHTEN is the chef and owner of the New York City restaurants JoJo, Vong, Jean Georges, and The Mercer Kitchen, for which he holds an unprecedented total of twelve stars from the *New York Times*. In 1998 he became the first chef ever to win both the James Beard Best New Restaurant and Outstanding Chef awards in the same year. He has written *Jean-Georges: Cooking at Home with a Four-Star Chef* (with Mark Bittman; Broadway Books, 1998), *Simple Cuisine* (IDG, 1998), and *Simple to Spectacular* (with Mark Bittman; Broadway Books, 2000). He is a native of Strasbourg, France.

ALICE WATERS, the chef and owner of Chez Panisse and Café Fanny (San Francisco), is known for her commitment to serving only the highest-quality, organically grown products. She is author of *Chez Panisse Café Cookbook* (HarperCollins, 1999) and *Chez Panisse Vegetables* (HarperCollins, 1996), among others. Currently at work on *Chez Panisse Fruits* (HarperCollins, 2000), Waters is collaborating on a restaurant in the Louvre's Musée des Arts Decoratifs in Paris. It is to serve as both a café and art installation expressing the sensuousness of food.

NACH WAXMAN is the founder and owner of Kitchen Arts & Letters, the premier bookstore for food and wine professionals, opened in New York City in 1983. A book edi-

tor in the culinary arts for many years, he was associated with the original *Cooks' Catalogue*.

JASPER WHITE is a chef and the former co-owner of Boston's award-winning Jasper's Restaurant. Named Best Chef in the Northeast in 1990, he is the author of *Jasper White's Cooking from New England* (HarperCollins, 1989), *Lobster at Home* (Scribner, 1998), and *Fifty Chowders* (Scribner, 2000). His new restaurant, Summer Shack, opened in May 2000.

BURT WOLF is the host and writer of seven internationally syndicated television series that deal with food, travel, and cultural history. He was the first recipient of the James Beard Foundation Award for Best Television Food Journalism, and has been nominated for two CableAce Awards and a national Emmy in connection with travel and cultural history. During his thirty years as a journalist, he has written or edited more than sixty books.

PAULA WOLFERT is the author of six cookbooks, including *The Cooking of Southwest France* (HarperCollins, 1988), *Mostly Mediterranean* (Penguin USA, 1996), *Mediterranean Grains and Greens* (HarperCollins, 1998), and the much-praised *Cooking of the Eastern Mediterranean* (HarperCollins, 1994). She has been awarded the Julia Child, James Beard, and the M. F. K. Fisher awards, among others.

SUSAN WYLER is food editor for TV Guide Celebrity Dish and president of King Hill Productions. She has worked with editors of major publishing houses to package and produce more than seventy cookbooks. Her own books include *Great Books for Cooks* (Ballantine, 1999), *Cooking from a Country Farmhouse* (HarperCollins, 1993), and *Simply Stews* (HarperCollins, 1995). She is a former food editor of *Food & Wine*.

JANE ZIEGELMAN is a food writer who has coauthored *Foie Gras: A Passion* (Wiley, 1999). She has also developed many recipes for *Jane* magazine's "Eat" page.

KEVIN ZRALY has been wine director of the world-renowned Windows on the World (New York) since 1976 and is the creator of their famous wine list. He has written *Windows on the World Complete Wine Course* (Sterling Publications, 1999) and is the founder/instructor of the acclaimed Windows on the World Wine School.

ACKNOWLEDGMENTS

THE EDITORS of *The New Cooks' Catalogue* are indebted to hundreds of people who have been involved with this project. However, we would like to express our special appreciation to the following:

⑥

Jennifer Arago-Shechter, Merry Aronson, Lise Belle-feuille, Alan Berger, Matt Bunn, Diana Cadogan, Andy Cope, David Dean, Dalton Delan, Laura di Bonaventura, John Fulvio, Marc Goldstein, Dave Hodess, Kenneth Jackier, Mort Janklow, Joel Kleiman, Kip Knight, Mike La Bonia, Roy Lampe, Gérard and Madeleine Lorentz, Caroline McCool, Raymond W. Merritt, Ellen Mai, Merrideth Miller, Anita Michael, Pattie Newi, Gene Nichols, Jack Norris, Larry Ossias, Janet Pappas, John Peaslee, Jeff Powell, Tracy Randall, David Romeike, Amy Rosen, Steven J. Ross, Glen Senk, David Shechter, Stuart and Judy Shechter, Cullen Stanley, Bruce Stark, Ted Turner, Susan Van Velson, Paul Waide, Marjorie Wolff, Jose Pedro Zanoniani, and Susan Ziegler.

⑥

Leyla Aker, Peter Andersen, Paul Bogaards, Roméo Enriquez, Kathleen Fridella, Katherine Hourigan, and Andy Hughes of Alfred A. Knopf.

⑥

Patrick F. Moran and Carolyn M. Sands of North Market Street Graphics.

⑥

Michael Bynoe, Cynthia De Jesus, Carlos Gonzalez, Tommy Hind, Maria Quezada, Herbert Sulker, and Nathaniel Washington for their assistance "managing the pots."

⑥

Representatives of the cooking equipment manufacturers who generously shared their time and expertise.

Bill Ackerman, Debbie Adrion, Joseph Agnes, Rick Agresta, Cecilia Aguillon, Anne Bruce Ahearn, Moulay Alaoui, Gayle Allen-Grier, David Alvo, Robin Anderson, Karen Anello, Jeff Armstrong, Mary Ayers, Mary Ellen Barnett, Amelia Barrett, Melanie C. Batalis, David Bean, Brad Beasley, Arnie Beiss, George F. Bente, Margo Beren, Dominique Besson, Christina Bevacqua, Jack Bevington, Knud Bisgard, Greg Bittner, Bob Boney, Katherine Boury, Kristen Brady, Peter Braley, Richard Braun, Conrad Brazzale, Jack Breeden, Wayne Brinkley, Liz Bristol, Liz Burns, Rikki Byers, Lisa Byrne, Lou Cahn, Robert Candler, Elizabeth Carmel, Sandy Castellow, Michelle Caverlengo, Simone Chance, Peter A. Chapman, Helen Chen, Jason Chin, Donna Colavito, Carolyn Coley, Joy Collins, John Paul H. Cook, John Cooper, Cheryl A. Corn, Beth Corwin, Susie Cover, Neil J. Crumley, Sharon Cunningham, Sheila D'Amore, Fran De Lallo, Terry Delaney, Kim Delmore, Rick Denham, Tracey Denig, Lacey Devereaux, Josh Dick, Thomas and Diane DiNicola, Patrick Dittoe, Susan Doctor, Karen

Dorion, Malcolm Douglas, Craig Dreilinger, Bernd Dressler, Stephanie DuQuette, Lillian Ehrenhauf, Susan Federighi, Eliane Feiner, Michelle Fernez, Linda Field, Tim Fields, Tim Finnegan, ML First, Deborah Fitzgerald, Hope Flamm, Deborah A. Flynn, Kim Forbes, Joe Ford, Alecia Fowler, Marilyn Frates, Olivier Frot, Marie Ganguzza, Dan Garasich, Gabriella Garcia, Chris Gimble, Joan Gioiella, Tracy Glass, Candice Gohn, Abigail A. Goodman, Patrick Gordon, Jeff Grace, Sharon Graham, Beth De Grandis, John Granelli, Eliza Grassy, Katie Gray, Jill Gurley, Max Hahn, Jared A. Hall, P. J. Hamel, Robert Harris, Robin Harris, Judy Harrold, Mariko Hashimoto, Gail Hawes, Barbara A. Hayward, Catherine Heller, Brenda Heltsley, Steve Herbert, Doug Herrmann, Barb Hezel, Darlene J. Hines, Karl Hipp, Gretchen Holt, Scott Horlbogen, Eric Horn, Beth Horne, Christopher E. Hubbuch, Steve Hudon, Lars Inderwisch, Stacey Inglis-Baron, Michelle Izzo, Philip Jacobs, Angela Jannusch, Susan Jardina, Christian Jarry, Mike Jayroe, Jane Jerger, Michele Johann, Eric Johnson, Hope Johnson, Joel Johnson, Russell Johnson, Heather Jones, April Joyce, Mara Levy Kahn, Ken Kandall, Ricki Kane, Alain Karyo, Michael Karyo, Beverly Burger Kastel, Saori Kawano, Darren Keller, Bob Kellermann, Lisa Kerrister, Brian Kileff, Simon Kirby, Kathryn E. Kloppenberg, Jack Knippel, Ann Knutson, Dan E. Koch, Rick Komas, Bjorn Kunz, Tim LaFrancis, Nancy A. Lang, Alan Langer, David Lanzillo, Robert Laub, Yvette Laugier, Carolyn LeFavor, Alex Lee, Glenda Lehman-Ervin, Bob Leiberman, Karen Leitza, Joanne M. Lenweaver, Jan Levean, Lisa Lim, Rachel Litner, Donna Long, Ginnie Mackell, Karen Mahaffey, Karen Malleret, Anne Manlow, Nadege Marini, Rita Marquette, Larry Marsh, Annie Marshall, Norma Mathewson, Melissa Mauro, Brian J. Maynard, Shawn McBride, Melinda McDonald, Kathleen McDonnell, Bob McGuire, Tom McPeck, Francisco Méndez, Jeff Merrifield, Jim Meshes, Marvin R. Mick, Monica Minadeo, Steven Mishan, Chris Mitchell, Luisella Monastero, Carlos Monteiro, Olympia Moretti, Nancy Moylan, John V. Murnahan, David J. Murphy, Daphne Murray, Georgie Murray, Hugh Musick, Tammy Nadler, Willard Neese, Sharon Nelson, Georgie Nickell, Masumi Nishimura, Howard Noel, Shane Nolan, Melanie Northfield, Albert Nouri, Diane O'Connell, Suzen O'Rourke, Denby Olcott, Raewyn & Paul Oliver, Hetty Oppman, MaryAnne Ostrowski, Tim Pagnum, Jose Pagum, Faith Paris, Sharon Parker, Susan Parker, Tamara J. Parker, Norma Parrish, Gil Paul, Bobbi Pauline, Julie Peluski, Alan S. Peppel, John Perks, Esther Perman, John Peterson, Rob Peterson, Dawn Pierce, Peter Pike, Todd Piker, Tiago Mota Pinto, Michael Plaum, Jay Powell, Jasmine Prezeau, Judy Prince, Lou Radecki, Gary Ragan, Henry Read, Laurie Reed, Heio W. Reich, Judith Reinhard, Joia Ricci, Kim Rice-Maccubbin, Walter Rich, Phillippe Rimbert, Greg Rindik, Robert Rios, John Roberts, Doreen Robideaux, Jim Rogers, Libby Rogers, Mary M. Rodgers, Lori Rooney, Leslie Russell, Rick Sadowsky, Bob Saia, Andrea Sanchez, Frank Sanchez, Donald Sanders, Steve Sanders, Jeff Sanelli, Jack Saunders, Gunter Scheible, Michel Scheinmann, Jim Schnabel, Bernard Schnacke, Monika Schnacke, Doug Schneider, Linda Schultz, Nanci Schultz, Sam Schwartzberg, Joan Scire, Don Scott, Laura Scott, Greg Scribner, Steve Scribner, Tracy Sellman, Alan Senior, Heather Larson Shaw, Florence Sheffer, Lynn Sherwin, Marcy Sherwin, Nancy Siler, Enrico Simpatico, Gloria Smith, Margot Smith, Holly Smith-Berry, Amy Snyder, Sharon Somers, Denis Spanek, Doug Stein, Amy Stern, Margaret Stern, Crista Stiernelof, Jozef B. Tomichek, Nancy Thompson, Marie Tommassello, Bob Topazio, Chris Tracy, Jody Tullos, Anne Unger, Boris Unwalla, Grace Valenti, Lenny Van Valkenburg, Carla M. Vallone, Chris Varkala, Magda Vigoni, Kim de la Villefromoy, Kevin Vining, Robert Vitantonio, Gail Volpi, Katey Von Hagel, Jeana M. Vranich, Mike Wallace, Laura Wanazek, Barry Wax, Julie Weidenheft, Diane S. Weiss, Erik Weiss, Barbara Westfield, Margaret White, Todd Whitten, Pamela Wittenberg, Cathy Wilson, Steve Winston, Gina Woman, Charles Wooley, Beatrice Yang, Kim Yearick, and Linda Yost.

486

RECImPE INDEX

A

anchovy butter, grilled beef cross rib with, 100

anise-flavored biscuits (*biscotti all' anice*), 149

apples
  apple butter, 422
  beer-baked beans with apples & sausage, 230
  warm applesauce with cream, 80

apricot sherbet, 125

Asian pear dipping sauce, 238

avocados
  romaine, tomato, & avocado salad with corn bread croutons, with creamy chipotle vinaigrette, 123

B

beans
  beer-baked beans with apples & sausage, 230
  bessara (fava bean purée), 164
  tortellini with navy bean sauce, 293

beef
  Bolognese meat sauce, 131
  bool kogi (Korean sesame-grilled beef), 238
  grilled beef cross rib with anchovy butter, 100
  sauerbraten, 219

beer-baked beans with apples & sausage, 230

bessara (fava bean purée), 164

biscotti all' anice (anise-flavored biscuits), 149

Bolognese meat sauce, 131

bool kogi (Korean sesame-grilled beef), 238

bread
  best bread ever: epis, 306
  pâte à brioche surfine (brioche dough), 309
  pizza dough, 314

brioche dough (*pâte à brioche surfine*), 309

buttercream, traditional vanilla, 330

buttermilk
  buttermilk sorbet, 371
  currant–dried cherry buttermilk scones, 4

C

cakes
  Fannie Abzug's cheesecake, 120
  Kugelhopf Lenôtre, 335
  pear-walnut coffee cake, 154
  pound cake, 8
  sour cream coffee cake, 409
  traditional vanilla birthday cake, 330
  warm, soft chocolate cake, 22

calvados
  grenadins de porc normande (pork chops with cream and calvados), 176

capers, veal scaloppine with tomato, oregano, &, 110

cardamom tea (*ilaichi chah*), 412

champagne
  salade de fruits au sabayon de champagne (fruit salad with champagne sabayon sauce), 384

cheese
  cheese soufflé, 275
  grilled cheese sandwich, 235

cheesecake, Fannie Abzug's, 120

cherries
  currant–dried cherry buttermilk scones, 4

chicken
  chicken & herb salad with red pepper oil, 117
  fond blanc de volaille (chicken stock), 91
  lemon chicken: the authentic version, 194
  roasted chicken, 251

chicken (*cont'd*)
  stuffed chicken breasts, 60

chili powder
  winter squash soup with red chili & mint, 205

chipotle peppers
  romaine, tomato, & avocado salad with corn bread croutons, with creamy chipotle vinaigrette, 123

chocolate
  chocolate leaves, 19
  New York super fudge chunk, 374
  warm, soft chocolate cake, 22

chowder, roasted corn & lobster, 76

cinnamon
  cinnamon-sugar, 357
  cinnamon toast, 249

coffee
  Turkish coffee ice cream, 402

coffee cakes
  pear-walnut coffee cake, 154
  sour cream coffee cake, 409

cookies, Granny's old-fashioned sugar, 357

corn
  corn tortillas, 318
  roasted corn & lobster chowder, 76

corn bread
  romaine, tomato, & avocado salad with corn bread croutons, with creamy chipotle vinaigrette, 123

cornmeal batter, oysters fried in, 54

cream
  classic cream puff pastry, 367
  grenadins de porc normande (pork chops with cream and calvados), 176
  warm applesauce with cream, 80

crème brûlée, 273

croutons
  romaine, tomato, & avocado salad with cornbread croutons, with creamy chipotle vinaigrette, 123
currant–dried cherry buttermilk scones, 4
custard
  crème brûlée, 273

E

eggplant and pasta timbale (*timballo alle melanzane*), 283
eggs
  cheese soufflé, 275
  egg spaetzle, 300
  old-fashioned egg sauce, 254
  omelet, 182
epis bread, 306

F

fava bean purée (*bessara*), 164
figs, poached spiced, 137
fish and shellfish
  bay scallop and tomato gratin, 266
  cedar-planked salmon, 254
  cherry tomatoes filled with smoked salmon mousse, 79
  gravlax with mustard sauce, 49
  grilled beef cross rib with anchovy butter, 100
  lobster rolls, 87
  open-faced brook trout, 46
  oysters fried in a cornmeal batter, 54
  oysters in a pot, 223
  roasted corn & lobster chowder, 76
  shrimp *remoulade*, 155
  shrimp sambal, 59
foie gras, classic terrine of, 276
fond blanc de volaille (chicken stock), 91
fruit
  old bachelor's fruit preserves, 424
  salade de fruits au sabayon de champagne (fruit salad with champagne sabayon sauce), 384
  see also specific fruits
  fuzi, 297

G

garlic paste, 96
ginger
  ginger ice cream, 372
  vinegared ginger, 428
gratin dishes
  bay scallop and tomato gratin, 266
gravlax with mustard sauce, 49
greens, tangle of tart, 67
grenadins de porc normande (pork chops with cream and calvados), 176
grilled cheese sandwich, 235

H

herbs
  chicken & herb salad with red pepper oil, 117
hollandaise sauce, 146

I

ice cream
  ginger ice cream, 372
  New York super fudge chunk, 374
  Turkish coffee ice cream, 402
ilaichi chah (cardamom tea), 412

K

Kugelhopf Lenôtre, 335

L

lamb
  shoulder of lamb, 260
  tagine el lahm felfla matisha (*tagine* of lamb with green peppers and tomatoes), 221
lemons
  lemon chicken: the authentic version, 194
  lemon tart, 343
lobsters
  lobster rolls, 87
  roasted corn & lobster chowder, 76

M

marinade, "wild boar," 379
mint, winter squash soup with red chili &, 205
mousse
  cherry tomatoes filled with smoked salmon mousse, 79
mustard sauce, gravlax with, 49

N

navy bean sauce, tortellini with, 293

O

okra, pickled, 426
omelet, 182
oregano, veal scaloppine with tomato, capers, &, 110
oysters
  oysters fried in a cornmeal batter, 54
  oysters in a pot, 223

P

paella, Valencia's traditional (*paella a la Valenciana*), 185
pancakes
  Bridge Creek heavenly hots, 234
pappardelle, 297
parsley
  tabbouleh (cracked wheat salad with parsley and tomatoes), 33

pasta
  pasutice, fuzi, pappardelle, 297
  timballo alle melanzane (eggplant and pasta timbale), 283
  tortellini with navy bean sauce, 293
pasutice, 297
pâte à brioche surfine (brioche dough), 309
pears
  Asian pear dipping sauce, 238
  pear-walnut coffee cake, 154
  poires au vin rouge (pears braised in red wine), 387
peppers
  chicken & herb salad with red pepper oil, 117
  romaine, tomato, & avocado salad with cornbread croutons, with creamy chipotle vinaigrette, 123
  tagine el lahm felfla matisha (*tagine* of lamb with green peppers and tomatoes), 221
piri-piri sauce, 222
pizza dough, 314
plum pudding, steamed, 30
poires au vin rouge (pears braised in red wine), 387
pork
  grenadins de porc normande (pork chops with cream and calvados), 176
  Nan's extra special marinated spareribs, 28
  pork marinated to taste like wild boar, 379
  roast pork loin, 16
potatoes, mashed, 95
pound cake, 8
preserves, old bachelor's fruit, 424
pudding, steamed plum, 30
puff pastry, classic cream, 367

R

ratatouille (Provençal vegetables), 35
remoulade sauce
  shrimp *remoulade*, 155
rice
  perfect rice, 288
  risotto Milanese, 135
  Valencia's traditional paella (*paella a la Valenciana*), 185
risotto Milanese, 135
romaine, tomato, & avocado salad with corn bread croutons, with creamy chipotle vinaigrette, 123
rosettes, 191

S

salads
  chicken & herb salad with red pepper oil, 117
  romaine, tomato, & avocado salad with cornbread croutons, with creamy chipotle vinaigrette, 123

salads (*cont'd*)
  salade de fruits au sabayon de champagne (fruit salad with champagne sabayon sauce), 384
  tabbouleh (cracked wheat salad with parsley and tomatoes), 33
salmon
  cedar-planked salmon, 254
  cherry tomatoes filled with smoked salmon mousse, 79
  gravlax with mustard sauce, 49
sandwiches
  grilled cheese sandwich, 235
  lobster rolls, 87
sauces
  Asian pear dipping sauce, 238
  Bolognese meat sauce, 131
  gravlax with mustard sauce, 49
  hollandaise sauce, 146
  for lemon chicken, 194
  old-fashioned egg sauce, 254
  piri-piri sauce, 222
  salade de fruits au sabayon de champagne (fruit salad with champagne sabayon sauce), 384
  shrimp *remoulade*, 155
  tortellini with navy bean sauce, 293
sauerbraten, 219
sausage, beer-baked beans with apples &, 230
scallops
  bay scallop and tomato gratin, 266
scones, currant–dried cherry buttermilk, 4
sesame oil
  bool kogi (Korean sesame-grilled beef), 238
sherbet, apricot, 125
shrimp
  shrimp *remoulade*, 155
  shrimp sambal, 59
sorbet, buttermilk, 371
soufflé, cheese, 275

soups
  roasted corn & lobster chowder, 76
  winter squash soup with red chili & mint, 205
sour cream coffee cake, 409
spaetzle, egg, 300
spareribs, Nan's extra special marinated, 28
squash
  winter squash soup with red chili & mint, 205
strawberries with zabaglione in red wine, 25
sugar
  cinnamon-sugar, 357
  Granny's old-fashioned sugar cookies, 357

T

tabbouleh (cracked wheat salad with parsley and tomatoes), 33
tagine el lahm felfla matisha (tagine of lamb with green peppers and tomatoes), 221
tarts
  lemon tart, 343
  sweet tart dough, 351
tea, cardamom (*ilaichi chah*), 412
timballo alle melanzane (eggplant and pasta timbale), 283
toast, cinnamon, 249
tomatoes
  bay scallop and tomato gratin, 266
  cherry tomatoes filled with smoked salmon mousse, 79
  romaine, tomato, & avocado salad with corn bread croutons, with creamy chipotle vinaigrette, 123
  tabbouleh (cracked wheat salad with parsley and tomatoes), 33
  tagine el lahm felfla matisha (tagine of lamb with green peppers and tomatoes), 221
  veal scaloppine with tomato, oregano, & capers, 110
tortellini with navy bean sauce, 293

tortillas, corn, 318
trout, open-faced brook, 46
Turkish coffee ice cream, 402

V

vanilla
  traditional vanilla birthday cake, 330
  traditional vanilla buttercream, 330
veal scaloppine with tomato, oregano, & capers, 110
vinaigrettes
  romaine, tomato, & avocado salad with cornbread croutons, with creamy chipotle vinaigrette, 123
vinegared ginger, 428

W

waffles, 243
walnuts
  pear-walnut coffee cake, 154
wheat
  tabbouleh (cracked wheat salad with parsley and tomatoes), 33
"wild boar" marinade, 379
wine
  poires au vin rouge (pears braised in red wine), 387
  pork marinated to taste like wild boar, 379
  salade de fruits au sabayon de champagne (fruit salad with champagne sabayon sauce), 384
  zabaglione with strawberries in red wine, 25
  winter squash soup with red chili & mint, 205

Z

zabaglione with strawberries in red wine, 25

INDEX

A

Acme
  Candy–Deep-Fry Thermometer, 18
acorns, 165
Acu-Rite
  Sure-Grip Instant-Read Thermometer, 15
Adams Industries
  Nonstick Roast Pan, 255
aebleskive pans, 243
Aeschylus, 383
African words in American culinary usage,
    221
Ah So
  Cork Puller, 380–1
Aidells, Bruce, 108, 379
All-Clad
  Cake Pan, 329–30
  Colander, 119
  construction of individual subbrands,
    180
  LTD Oval Pan, 179
  LTD Sauté Pan, 188
  LTD Stir-Fry Pan, 195–6
  LTD Windsor Pan, 201
  Nonstick Grande Griddle, 234–5
  Nonstick Omelet Pan, 183
  Paella Pan with Domed Lid, 184
  Stainless Roti Pan, 252
  Stainless Steel Braiser, 220
  Stainless Steel Dutch Oven, 218
  Stainless Steel Gratin Pan, 268
  Stainless Steel Nonstick Saucepan, 199
  Stainless Steel Nonstick Skillet, 177
  Stainless Steel Saucier, 199
  Steamer Insert, 209
  3-Quart Double Boiler Insert, 203–4
Allen, Herbert, 379

Allied Metal
  Aluminum Peel, 317
  Baker's Peel, 317
  Pizza Cutter, 316
  Pizza Serving/Cooking Tray, 311
  Round-Bottom Wok Set, 194
Alltrista Corporation
  Canning Jars, 425
aluminum pots and pans, 170–1, 173,
    196–7, 204
Amco
  Adjustable Roast Rack, 255–6
  Artichoke Cooker, 211
  Asparagus Cooker, 211
  Avocado Skinner, 78
  Cradle Roast Rack, 256
  Garnish Kit, 78
  Heat-Resistant Whisk, 147
  Measuring Cups, 3
  Nonskid Mixing Bowls, 26
  Odd-Size Measuring Cups, 4
  Pinch Bowl, 27
  Shallow Strainer, 125
  Two-Wire Batter Whisk, 147
  Wide-Blade Spatula, 141
A. Metalúrgica
  Bombe, 283–4
  Nonstick Fluted Mold, 284
  Pudding Mold, 280–1
Anderson, Jean, 87, 300
Andoh, Elizabeth, 288
angel food cake pans, 334
anodized aluminum, 171
Anolon
  Nouvelle Long-Handle Lid, 215
  Nouvelle Stainless Saucepan, 199
  Professional Grill Pan, 238

Apilco
  Coeur à la Crème Mold, 285
  Crème Brûlée Dish, 274
  Extra-High Individual & Multiquart Soufflé
    Dishes, 275
  Oval Terrine, 277–8
  Porcelain Gratin Dish, 269
  Porcelain Tasting Spoon, 133
  Pots de Crème Set, 272
  Round Quiche Pan, 345
Appel, Jennifer, 330
Appert, Nicolas, 420
apple corers, 80
apple dividers, 81
apple peelers, 78
April Cornell
  Stacking Teapot, 414
artichoke cookers, 211
Asian knives, 42–4
asparagus cookers, 211
asparagus peelers, 77
aspic molds, 282
Ateco
  Bismarck Tube, 366
  Cake & Pastry Decorating Set, 363
  Cake Tester, 356
  Cannoli Forms, 346–7
  Decorating Stand, 364
  Disposable Bags, 368
  Doughnut Cutter, 360
  Dura Cloth, Sure-Grip Plastic-Coated, &
    Flex Nylon Pastry Bags, 365–6
  Fifty-Five-Piece Decorating Set, 366, 368
  Long Baking Spatulas with Plastic &
    Wooden Handles, 353–4
  Natural White Bristle Grease Brush, 355
  Parchment Triangles, 368

Ateco (*cont'd*)
  Small Straight-Blade, Offset, & Trowel-Shaped Icing Spatulas, 354
  Star & Heart Cutters, 358
  Trick or Treat Cutter Set, 358
  Twelve-Piece Pastry Cutter Set, 356–7
  Twelve-Piece Pastry Tube Set, 368
Atlas
  Pasta Machine, 296–7
avocado skinners, 78

B

babas au rhum molds, 310
Back to Basics
  Peel-Away Apple & Potato Peeler, 78
  Wheat-Grass Juicer, 117
baguette pans and molds, 307–8
Bailey, Lee, 80
bains-marie, 202–4
baking and pastry equipment, 321–68
  baking knives, 354
  baking pans, 325–8
  baking sheets, 322–4
  baking spatulas, 353–4
  basic pastry tools, 347–53
  cooling racks, 361–2
  cutters, 356–61
  decorating tools, 362–8
  dredgers, 352–3
  flour wands, 352
  jelly-roll pans, 324
  liners and baking mats, 325
  minor pastry tools, 354–6
  nonstick finishes, 327
  pastry bags and tubes, 365–8
  pastry blenders, 348–9
  pastry boards and cloth, 349
  pie pans, 339–42
  quiche pans, 345
  rolling pins, 350–2, 360–1
  scrapers, 347
  shapes of pans, 322
  sifters, 348
  specialty baking frames and forms, 337–9
  specialty pastry forms, 346–7
  standards for, 321–2
  tart pans, 342–5
  see also cake pans
baking and pizza stones, 313–15
baking dishes, 263–75
  custard cups, 271–2, 274
  gratin pans, 267–9
  oven dishes for eggs, 269–75
  ramekins, 270–1
  scallop shells, 265–6
  snail-serving equipment, 266–7
  soufflé dishes, 274–5
baking powder, 336
baking-roasting relationship, 250–1
balances and scales, 6–10

Ball
  Canning Funnel, 422
  Canning Jars, 425
  Canning Lid Wand, 423
  Jar Lifter, 422
  Jelly Bag Stand, 423
  Replacement Rack, 423
ballers, 78–9
Balzac, Honoré de, 407
bannetons, 304–6
barbecue thermometers, 17
barquette molds, 344
Barr, Nancy Verde, 245
Bartelt
  Drying Screen, 290–1
Bastianich, Lidia Matticchio, 297, 301
basting equipment, 257–8
Batali, Mario, 135, 296
Batterberry, Michael and Ariane, 162
batter bowls, 28
batter whisks, 147
Baumé scale, 20
Bayless, Rick, 98, 318
bean pots, 228
bean slicers, 77
Beard, James, 16, 204, 250, 253
Becker, Marion Rombauer, 30
Bedouin Coffeepot, 401
Beebo
  Cavatelli Maker, 298–9
Beeton, Isabella, 280
Belgian wafflers, 242
Belleme, John and Jan, 415
Benriner
  Cook Help Upright Turning Slicer, 68
Beranbaum, Rose Levy, 367
Berndes
  Tradition Dutch Oven, 217
  Tradition Glass Domed Lid, 215
  Tradition Skillet, 178
Berra, Yogi, 315
Best Manufacturers
  Balloon Whisk, 145
  Blunt-End Perforated Spoon, 133
  Flour Wand, 352
  French Whisk, 145
  Light Design Whisk, 148
  Mexican Lime Press, 113
  Pizza Crisper, 311
  Sandwich Spatula, 51
betel nut slicers, 88
Bethany
  Norwegian *Goro* Iron, 244
B.I.A. Cordon Bleu
  Custard Cup, 272
  Individual & Multiquart Soufflé Dishes, 274
Bialetti
  Moka Express 3-Cup Coffeemaker, 403
biscuit cutters, 359
Bismarck tubes, 366

Bittman, Mark, 22, 117
Black & Decker
  CitrusMate Plus, 113
  Deep Dutch Skillet, 178–9
  Dining-In Convection Countertop Oven-Broiler, 249
  Ergo Electric Knife, 432
  Power Pro, 164
blade grinders, 393
blenders
  countertop, 154–7
  immersion, 158–60
blow-dryers, 137
Bodum
  Bistro Vacuum Jug, 408
  Chambord Coffee Press, 395
  Santos Vacuum Pot, 396
BOJ
  Anti-Drip Ring, 387
  Champagne Bottle Stopper, 386
  Egg Separator, 127
  Kea Corkscrew, 377–81
  Wall-Mounted Corkscrew, 380
bombe molds, 283–4
Bonaparte, Napoléon, 86, 420
boning knives, 46–7
Bonjour
  Caffe Froth Turbo, 407–8
Borden, Gail, 420
Bormioli Rocco
  "Quattro Stagioni" Canning Jar, 425
Boston Warehouse Trading Co.
  Pie Bird, 355–6
Botticelli, Sandro, 265
bottle stoppers, 385–6
Boulud, Daniel, 188, 266
Bourgeat
  Aluminum Nonstick Paella Pan, 184
  Copper Braising Pan, 220
  Copper Fry Pan with Stainless Steel Lining, 176
  Copper Oval Pan, 179
  Copper Saucepan, 198
  Copper *Sauteuse*, 186
  Sauteuse Evasée, 200
  Stockpot with Spigot, 205–6
bowls, 24–33
  ceramic, 29
  copper, 24–5
  glass, 27
  holding a bowl steady, 27
  minibowls, 27
  pastry-making, 32
  plastic, 28
  pudding, 30
  salad, 32, 33
  stainless steel, 26–7
  very large, 26
  wooden, 32–3
braille timers, 431
braising pans, 220

Brass Noodle Press, 300
Braun
    AquaExpress, 413
    Aromatic Coffee Grinder, 393
    flavorSelect 12-Cup Cappuccino
        Coffeemaker with Frothing
        Attachment, 398
    Gold Screen Coffee Filter, 408
    Juice Extractor, 117
    Multiquick Deluxe Hand Blender &
        Chopper, 159–60
bread
    dough preparation, 302–4
    sourdough starter, 319
bread- and pizza-making equipment, 302–20
    baking and pizza stones, 313–15
    bread machines, 319–20
    couches and bannetons, 304–6
    peels, 316–17
    pizza cutters, 315–16
    pizza dishes, 265
    pizza pans, 310–11
    scoring and slicing tools, 312–13
    specialty bread pans, 306–8, 310–11
    tortilla and chapati presses, 317, 319
bread knives, 50–1
Brearley, Harry, 169
Brennan, Terrance, 64
Brillat-Savarin, Jean-Anthelme, 163, 336
brioche molds, 308, 310
Brioche Mousseline Mold, 310
Britchkey, Seymour, 91
Bron
    Bread Cutter, 312
    Classic Mandoline, 66
Brown, Ed, 46
Brown, Edward Espe, 205
Brown Bag
    Cookie Art Ceramic Shortbread Pan, 339
Browne & Co.
    Escargot Dish, 267
    Pastry Blender, 348–9
    Porcelain Scallop Shell, 266
Bubble Freer Spatula, 422–3
Bugialli, Giuliano, 291
Bulkin, Rena, 120
Bundt pans, 335
Burke, David, 137, 372
burr mills, 391–2
butchering knives, 44–5
butcher's needles, 258–9
butter curlers, 75–6
butter molds, 285–6
butter slicers, 77
butter warmers, 201

C

cake pans, 328–36
    cake rings, 331–2
    with designs, 332–3
    layer cake pans, 329–31

cake pans (cont'd)
    muffin tins, 336–7
    springform pans, 333
    tube pans, 334–6
cakes, large and small, 324
cake testers, 356
Calphalon
    Commercial Hard-Anodized Chef's Pan,
        200
    Commercial Hard-Anodized Nonstick
        Stockpot, 207
    Commercial Hard-Anodized Omelet Pan,
        183
    Commercial Hard-Anodized Saucepan,
        199–200
    Commercial Hard-Anodized Sauté Pan, 188
    Commercial Hard-Anodized Square
        Griddle, 233
    Commercial Hard-Anodized Square Grill
        Pan, 239
    Commercial Stainless Saucepan, 206–7
    Commercial Stainless Sauté Pan, 188–9
    construction of individual subbrands, 180
    Domed Lid, 216
    Fish Poacher, 214
    Flat Lid, 216
    Large Roast Rack, 256
    Large Slotted Spoon, 132–3
    Pasta Fork, 133
    Potato Masher, 94
    "Pots & Pans" Roaster, 252
    Professional Hard-Anodized Butter
        Warmer, 201
    Professional Hard-Anodized Oval Braiser,
        219
    Professional Hard-Anodized Oval Sauté
        Pan, 179
    Professional Hard-Anodized Round
        Griddle, 231–2
    Professional Hard-Anodized Stir-Fry Pan,
        195
    6-Quart All-Purpose Inset, 121
    Stir-Fry Scoop, 133
Camwear
    Camsquare Dough-Rising Container, 305
candy thermometers, 17–19
cannelé molds, 339
canning equipment, 420–6
cannoli forms, 346–7
Capote, Truman, 348
cappuccino formula, 406
cappuccino makers, 398, 408
Capresso
    Burr Grinder, 392
    Coffeeteam Plus, 397
    Elegance Therm, 397–8
    Fully Automatic Coffee & Espresso Center,
        406
carbon steel, 36
carborundum stone, 58–9
Carême, Antonin, 281, 360, 362

Carl, Fred E., Jr., 172
Carlin, George, 380
Carroll, Lewis, 418
carving (slicing) knives, 47–9
Casas, Penelope, 185
cassava, 165
casseroles, 217–23, 228
cassoulet dishes, 229
casting process, 168
cast-iron cookware, seasoning of, 234
Catamount
    Fat Separator, 126
    Glass Bain-Marie, 203
    Glass Soufflé Dish, 275
    Measure-Batter Bowl, 4–5
cataplana pans, 222
cavatelli makers, 298–9
caviar spoons and servers, 134
cazuelas, 265
Ceraflame
    Bean Pot, 228
    Marmite, 206
Ceramika Artystyczna Boleslawiec
    Baking Dish, 264
cezve coffeemakers, 400–1
champagne bottle stoppers, 386
champagne chillers, 383
champagne openers, 384–5
champagne-opening technique, 386
champagne saber, 385
Champion
    Juicer, 115
Chantal
    Ceramic Bowl Set, 29
    Classic Fondue Set, 224
    Dinner-Is-Served Pan, 219
    Enamel Stockpot, 207
    Glass Lid, 215
    Standard Whisk, 146
Chantry
    Knife Sharpener, 59–60
chapati presses, 317, 319
Charleston
    Rice Cooker, 210–11
charlotte molds, 281–2
"Châteauneuf"
    Bottle Funnel with Removable Screen, 377
cheese cutters, 83–4
cheese graters, 70, 71–2
cheese knives, 54–6
cheese shavers, 79
cheese storage, 85
Chef'sChoice
    Edgeselect Diamond Hone Sharpener-
        Plus, 60
    International TeaMate Electric Tea Maker,
        418
    Professional Electric Food Slicer, 68–9
    Serrated Blade Diamond Hone Knife
        Sharpener, 59
    Trizor Professional 10x Boning Knife, 46

Chef'sChoice (*cont'd*)
Wafflepro, 242
Chef Walter
Etruria, 229–30
Tegamaccio, 230
Chemex
10-Cup Classic Series, 394–5
Chen, Helen, 209
Cheney, Gertrude Louise, 77
cherry pitters, 81
chestnut pans, 256
chestnut peelers, 78
Chicago Metallic
Commercial Perforated Pizza Crisper, 311
Commercial Standard & Nonstick Jelly-Roll Pans, 324
Mini-Loaf Strapped Set, 328
Mini Muffin Pan, 336–7
Nonstick Two-Piece Tube Pan, 334
Perforated Baking Pan, 324
Professional Cake Pan, 329
Professional Loaf Pan, 327
Professional Nonstick Baguette Pan, 307
Professional Nonstick French Bread Pan, 307
Silverstone Twelve-Cup Muffin Tin, 336
chicken fryers, 189
Child, Julia, 2, 29, 162, 166, 275
Chinese cooking, 43, 58, 193
Chinese Earthenware Casserole, 228
Chinese spatula-turners, 141
chinois, 89–92
chitarra, 293
Choate, Judith, 371
chocolate shavers, 79
chocolate spoons, 133–4
chocolate swizzles (*molinillos*), 148
chocolate thermometers, 19
Chop & Chop
Cutting Mat, 64
chopping blocks and boards, 62–4
chopsticks, cooking, 141–3
Christmas pudding, 31
Circulon
Oval Covered Roaster, 255
Rectangular Roaster, 253
citrus juicers, 112–15
citrus knives, 51
citrus peelers and zesters, 74–5
cladding, 172
clam knives, 53–4
clarity in cooking, 144
Clause, Jean-Pierre, 278
Clayton, Bernard, 32
cleavers, 42, 43
Clieu, Gabriel Mathieu de, 390
Coconut Cookery
Coconut Ladle, 135
coconut graters, 73
coeur á la crème molds, 285
coffee
grinding concerns, 390

coffee (*cont'd*)
history of, 389–90
proper proportion of coffee to water, 396
roasts, 393
coffee-making equipment, 389–409
accessories, 407–9
brewing equipment, 393–400
cappuccino makers, 398, 408
electric drip machines, 397–9
filters, 393
grinding equipment, 390–3, 401
manual drip coffeemakers, 394–5
Middle Eastern coffee, 400–1
Neapolitan coffeemakers, 400
percolators, 399
plunger pots, 395
vacuum pots, 396
see also espresso makers
Cohen, Ben, 374
colanders, 118–22
comal griddles, 235–6
Component Design
Bulb-Type Mercury Thermometer, 11
Scaleman, 8
Voicecraft Talking Digital Timer & Clock, 23
composing a dish, 281
conduction cooking, 167
Confucius, 42
convection cooking, 167
cookie cutters, 358–9
cookie presses, 363
cookie sheets, 322–4
cooking chopsticks, 141–3
cooking forks, 143–4
cooking process, 167–8
cooking spoons, 129–36
perforated and slotted, 132–3
solid, 129–32
specialty, 133–4
cook's knives, 38–40
cookware, *see* pots and pans
cooling racks, 361–2
Cooper
Commercial Test Thermometer, 15
Noncontact Thermometer, 16–17
Professional Digital Test Thermometer, 14
Copco
Mini Salad Spinner, 124
Ultimo Aria 2000 Teakettle, 411–12
copper pots and pans, 169–70, 173, 196, 204
specialty pots, 226–7
Copper Products of Italy
Fish Mold, 280
Mold, 282
Cordon Rose
Chocolate Thermometer, 19
corers, 80–2
Cork Lift
Cork Retriever, 381
Corkpops II
Wine Opener, 378–9

cork retrievers, 381
corkscrews, 377–81
corn bread skillets, 338
corn cutters, 76
corn grinders, 99–100
cornucopia forms, 346
Corriher, Shirley, 250, 272
Cortés, Hernán, 148
couches, 304–6
couscous, 210
couscoussières, 211
crab knives, 54
crème brûlée dishes, 274
crenulated knives, 56–7
crepe pans, 181–2
crock pots, 223
croissant cutters, 359
croquembouche forms, 346
Cuisinart
Convection Oven Toaster-Broiler, 249
Cordless Rechargeable Hand Blender, 159
Custom Control Total Touch Four-Slice Electronic Toaster, 248
Everyday Stainless Steel Steamer, 209–10
MiniPrep Processor, 164
Power Prep Plus Food Processor, 160–2
Pro Food Prep Center, 160, 163
SmartPower Count-Up Nine-Speed Hand Mixer, 153
SmartPower Duet Blender-Food Processor, 155
SmartStick Extendable Shaft Hand Blender & Chopper-Grinder, 158–9
Stainless Steel Casserole, 220
Tongs, 143
Cuisipro
Chocolate Fondue Set, 225
culinary torches, 271
Cunningham, Marion, 5, 234, 249
curlers, 75–6
curved knives, 33, 56–7
custard cups, 271–2, 274
cutting boards, 62–4
cutting instruments, 65–88
baking cutters, 356–61
cheese cutters, 83–4
corers and pitters, 80–2
fish equipment, 85–6, 87
graters, 69–73
ham racks, 48
mandolines, 66–7
mincing devices, 65–7
nutcrackers, 87–8, 385
shears, 82–3
slicing machines, 68–9
see also knives; peelers
cutting techniques, 43

D

Daguin, Ariane, 276, 278

Dance of the Ancestors
    Lava Stone Corn Grinder, 99
Danesco
    Colander, 119
    Long-Handled Colander, 120
Dannenberg, Linda, 424
David, Tom, 101
De Buyer
    Carbon Steel Crepe Pan, 181
    Carbon Steel Frying Pan, 177
    Carbon Steel Paella Pan, 184
    Charlotte Mold, 281–2
    Chestnut Pan, 256
    Copper Fry Pan with Tin Lining, 176–7
    Copper Lid, 216
    Copper Oval Stew Pan, 218–19
    Couscoussière, 211
    Fish Poacher, 213
    Fondue *Bourguignonne* Set, 224–5
    Hammered Copper Saucepan, 198
    Hemisphere Mold, 285
    Perforated *Chinois*, 90
    Sugar Pot, 227
    Turbot Poacher, 214
decorating tools, 362–8
deep fat, skimming in, 136
deep-fat fryers and frying accessories, 190–3
deep-fat thermometers, 17–19
deep-frying, oils for, 18
dehydrators, 426–7
Delonghi
    Alfredo Healthy Grill, 240
    Rotofryer, 192–3
Demarle
    Half-Size Silpat Liner, 325
    Silform Baguette Mold, 308
    Silpat Flexipan Madeleine Mold, 338–9
Demeyere
    Inca Gold Multipurpose Pan, 218
Dexter/Russell's
    Sani-Safe Bay Scallop Knife, 54
    Sani-Safe Boning Knife, 46
    Sani-Safe Butcher Knife, 44
    Sani-Safe Fillet Knife, 47
    Sani-Safe Narrow Slicer, 49
    Sani-Safe Oyster Knife, 53
    Sani-Safe Scimitar Knife, 45
DiSpirito, Rocco, 286
Dr. Oetker
    Obsttorte Pan, 332–3
Doherty, John, 293
double boilers, 202–4
dough knives, 49
doughnut, invention of the, 360
doughnut cutters, 360
dough thermometers, 19
Douglas, Malcolm, 13
drawn utensils, 168
dredgers, 352–3
Dualit
    Two-Slice Toaster, 247

Ducasse, Alain, 98, 144, 424
Durand, Peter, 420
Dutch ovens, *see* casseroles

E

"ear of corn" pans, 337
earthenware, 165–6, 227–30
Earthenware
    Comal Griddle, 235–6
ecology-mindedness in food preparation, 304
eggbeaters, rotary, 148
egg coddlers, 270
egg-cracking technique, 272
egg piercers, 83
eggs, oven dishes for, 269–75
egg separators, 127
egg slicers, 83
egg spoons, 134
egg timers, 21
egg toppers, 83
eighth of a teaspoon, measurement of, 3
Ekco
    Baker's Secret Round Cake Pan, 330–1
    Covered Pie Pan, 341
Eks
    Mechanical Scale, 9
Elan
    E-Z-Roll Garlic Peeler, 77–8
Emile Henry
    Pie Dish, 341
    Ramekins, 271
    Rectangular Baking Dish, 264
    Tourtière, 345
EMSA
    Perfect Beaker, 5
Emson
    Speed Peeler, 431
enameled-iron saucepans, 197
Endurance
    Biscuit Cutters, 359
    Crescent Pot-Edge Strainer, 197
    Fine Mesh Shaker, 353
    Handy Scoops, 6
    Spice Spoons, 3
    Stacks the Kit, 284
    Steamer Basket, 209
    II Triple-Ply Omelet Pan, 183
    Universal Lid, 216
English muffin rings, 359–60
escargot equipment, 266–7
espresso makers, 402–7
    accessories, 407–9
    electric pump machines, 405–7
    moka express, 403
    piston machines, 404
    steaming wands, 405
espresso formula, 404
ETL mark on appliances, 157
Evergreen Labs Inc.
    Wine Away Red Wine Stain Remover, 388

Eze-Lap
    Diamond Sharpener, 58
    Pocket Sharpener, 58
EZ Sharp
    Knife Sharpener, 60–1

F

Fabergé, Peter Carl, 134
Fadiman, Clifton, 84
Faison, George, 276
fait-tout pans, 196
Falafel Shaping Kit, 283
family and restaurant cooking, difference
    between, 301
family meals, 236
fantasy kitchens, 170
Farberware
    Millennium Cookie Sheet, 323
    Millennium Pressure Cooker,
        430–1
    Millennium Stainless Steel Covered
        |French Skillet, 177
    Millennium Stainless Steel Nonstick
        Skillet, 183
    Millennium Stainless Steel Superfast
        Coffee Urn, 399
    Millennium 12-Cup Cordless
        Programmable Percolator, 399
    Skillet with Dome Cover, 178
Farmer, Fannie, 5
Fasmodea
    Pie Partners, 341
fat separators, 126
FBM
    Couche Linen Canvas, 305
    Dough Proofing Basket, 305–6
    Razor Blade Holder, 312
    Reed Bread Form, 306
Feldeisen, Bruno, 154
Fields, W. C., 387
filleting knives, 46–7
firepots, 225–6
fish cutting instruments, 85–6, 87
fish doneness, testing for, 142
Fisher, M. F. K., 179, 269
fish molds, 280
fish poachers, 213–14
fish shears, 83
fish slicers, 48–9
flambé pans, 182
flan pans, 331
flan rings, 345
flat slicing, 43
fløtevafler irons, 244
flour wand, 352
foie gras, 278
Foley
    Food Mill, 92–3
fondue pots, 224–6
Foo, Susanna, 72
food mills, 92–3

food processors, 155, 160–4
accessories for, 163
food thermometers, 12, 13–17
forging process, 168
Forgione, Larry, 254
forks, cooking, 143–4
Forschner
Performance Shield Cut-Resistant Gloves, 67
Fox Run
Heat-Resistant Glass Baster, 258
Round Pasta Stamp, 292
Stainless Steel Bulb Baster, 257
Franey, Pierre, 384
Frederick the Great, 404
freezer thermometers, 11–12
freezing foods, 427–8
Frieling
Batter Bowl, 28
Citrus Knife, 74
Citrus Trumpet, 114–15
Hand Beater, 148
Handle-It Glass Bottom Springform Pan, 333
"Saddle of Venison" *Rehrücken* Mold, 333
frozen-food knives, 52
fruit knives, 51–2
fryers, deep-fat, 190–3
frying pans, 175–9
Furnas, J. C., 10
fusilli pins, 293

G

garlic peelers, 77–8
garlic presses, 96–7
Garrick, David, 108
Gefu
Christstollen Pan, 339
ginger graters, 72–3
gingerroot, 72
Giobbi, Edward, 292
Global
Ceramic Whetstone, 59
Deba, 44
Paring Knife, 41
Slicer, 47
Solid Spatula, 139–40
Turner-Spatula, 140
gloves
cut-resistant, 67
oyster, 54
gluten, 302
gnocchi paddles, 294
Goldsmith, Oliver, 386
Goldstein, Joyce, 402
Good Cook
Shrimp Tool, 86
Gorgonzola knives, 55
goro irons, 244
Gourmet Standard
Mixing Bowls with Hand Grip, 27

Grace, Richard and Jeff, 70
Grahame, Kenneth, 247
Grain Master
Whisper Mill, 106
grain mills, 105–6
Granite Ware
Boiling-Water-Bath Canner, 423
Covered Roaster, 255
grapefruit knives, 52
graters, 69–73
gratin pans, 267–9
Greenfield, Jerry, 374
Gregory, Hanson Crockett, 360
griddles, grill pans, and irons, 175, 231–45
electric griddles, 236
electric indoor grills, 240–1
grill pans, 237–9
pizzelle makers, 245
raclette–makers, 241
Scandinavian specialty griddles and irons, 243–4
seasoning cast-iron cookware, 234
waffle irons, 242, 244
what to look for, 232–3
grill thermometers, 17
Guber, Carol, 14
Guericke, Otto von, 420

H

Hackman Tabletop
All-Steel Mixing Bowl, 26
Hall, Charles Martin, 170
H. A. Mack
French Mixing Spoon, 129
Italian Mixing Spoon, 129
Polish Chocolate Spoon, 133–4
Portuguese Egg Spoon, 134
Portuguese Mixing Spoon, 130
Rolling Pin, 290
Slotted Spoon, 132
Spanish Mixing Spoon, 129–30
Taiwan Cooking Chopsticks, 141–2
Hamel, P. J., 303
Hamilton Beach
Chefmix, 152
Chrome Classic DrinkMaster Drink Mixer, 157
IntelliToast Toaster Oven Broiler, 248
Two-Slice IntelliToast Toaster, 247
ham racks, 48
ham slicers, 48
hand mixers, 153–4
hands as kitchen tools, 130
Hangiri Tub with Paddle, 288
Harold's Kitchen
Escargot Fork & Tongs, 267
Harrington, Henry, 50
Harris, Jessica B., 221, 426
Hawkins
Tava Griddle, 235
Hazan, Marcella, 110, 111, 131

Hazelton, Nika, 243
Hearon, Reed, 25
Hearthkit
Oven Insert, 314
heat diffusers, 4, 203
Heatter, Maida, 350, 357
Henry VIII, king of England, 280
herb assortment (*mezze*), 25
herb cutters, 66
Herbert, George, 334
Hermé, Pierre, 331, 353
Hirigoyen, Gerald and Cameron, 100
Hofstadter, Douglas R., 356
Hom, Ken, 43, 194
Homecraft
Twister Jar Opener, 431
Hong Kong
Vegetable Cutters, 77
horizontal slicing, 43
House on the Hill
Springerle Board, 361
Springerle Cookie Roller, 361
Springerle Rolling Pin, 360–1
hydrometers, 20

I

ice cream makers, 369–73
ice cream molds, 283
ice creams and frozen desserts, 372
ice cream scoops, 374–5
Illy, Ernesto, 404
Ilsa
Heat Diffuser, 203
Napoletana Coffeepot, 400
Stainless Steel Milk Jug, 407
Ilsa Grattalo
Cheese Scraper, 71
Imperial Tea
Yixing Clay Teapot, 414–15
Indian Brass Mortar & Pestle, 99–100
induction cooking, 167
Ingber, Sandy, 54
iron, 34–5
iron pots and pans, 168–9, 173
irons, *see* griddles, grill pans, and irons
iSi
Citrus Peeler, 75
Easy Whip, 363–4
Peelz-It, 74

J

J. A. Henckels
Five-Star Paring Knife, 41
Four-Star Bread Knife, 50
Four-Star Cleaver, 42
Four-Star Cook's Knife, 39
Four-Star Paring Knife, 41
Four-Star Roast Beef Slicer, 48
Mezzaluna, 56
Nylon Kitchen Spoon, 131

J. A. Henckels (*cont'd*)
    Offset Cheese Knife, 55
    Scoop, 375
    Serving Spoon, 130–1
    Twin Lissi Kitchen Shears, 82
Japanese Black-Iron *Sukiyaki-Nabe,*
    222
Japanese Covered *Nabe,* 222–3
Japanese Custard Cups, 272
Japanese knives, 44
Japanese *Tamago* Pan, 183
Japanese tea ceremony, 415
jar openers, 431
J. B. Prince
    Angel Food Cake Pan, 334
    Bench Scraper, 347
    Bowl Scraper, 347
    Cake Stencils, 363
    Cornet Mold (French Cornucopia Form),
        346
    Croissant Cutter, 359
    Decorating Combs, 364–5
    Entremet Ring, 331–2
    Fluted Pastry Wheel, 356
    French Fish Scaler, 86
    Galantine Mold, 278–9
    Individual Turk's Head Mold, 284
    Ladyfinger Tin, 338
    Lady Lock Form, 346
    Lattice Dough Cutter, 358
    Lattice Dough Roller, 358
    Madeleine Tin, 338
    Mini Round Cake/Flan Pan, 331
    Plain Pastry Wheel, 356
    Quadrant Cake Form, 332
    Rectangular & Square Tart Molds, 344
    Removable Bottom Tartlet, 344
    Roller Docker, 354–5
    Small & Large *Cannelé* Molds, 339
    Twelve-Piece Cutter Set, 80
Jefferson, Thomas, 289, 369, 396
jelly-roll pans, 324
jelly thermometers, 17–19
Jenkins, Steven, 85
jerky makers, 427
Jewish cooking, 71
J. K. Adams
    Butcher Block Counter Board, 290
    Herb Bowl with Mezzaluna Chopper, 33
    In-Drawer Knife Tray, 61
    Knife Block, 61
    Tapered Rolling Pin, 351
    Wooden Cutting Board, 63
John Boos
    PCA Butcher Block, 63
Johnson, Samuel, 105
Joyce, James, 212
Joyce Chen
    All-Purpose Spatula, 130
    Asian Mandoline Plus, 67
    Brass Strainer, 137

Joyce Chen (*cont'd*)
    Chinese All-in-One Knife, 43
    Japanese *Tetsubin* (Cast-Iron) Hobnail
        Teapot, 415
    Peking Pan, 195
    Pro Chef Carbon-Steel Wok, 194–5
    Suribachi, 98
    Tiered Bamboo Steamers, 209
juice extractors, 115–17
juicers, citrus, 112–15

K

Kafka, Barbara, 250, 260
Kaiser
    Extraordinaire Cookie Sheet, 323–4
    La Forme *Gâteau* Pan, 332
    La Forme Leakproof Springform Pan, 333
    La Forme Nonstick Mini-Loaf Pan Set, 328
    La Forme Rectangular Pan, 326
karhai pans, 190–1
Katchall
    Cook-Eze Reusable Round, Square &
        Rectangular Pan Liners, 325
Kavalier
    Simax Glass *Kugelhopf* Mold, 335
Keller, Thomas, 152
Kelly, Denis, 379
Kennedy, Diana, 98
Kennedy, Rod, Jr., 219
Kenwood
    Major Classic Mixer, 150, 151–2
    Meat Grinder Attachment, 109
Kerr
    Canning Jars, 425
King Arthur flour
    Adjustable Bread *Couche*–Multiloaf
        Banneton, 305
    Half-Sheet Loaf-Rising Cover, 305
KitchenAid
    construction of individual subbrands, 180
    Digital Ultra Power Plus Toaster, 248
    18/10 Stainless Steel Lid, 215
    Five-Ply Clad Grill Pan, 237–8
    Five-Ply Stainless Steel Clad Saucepan,
        198–9
    Five-Ply Stainless Steel Clad Sauté Pan
        with Helper Handle, 186–7
    Five-Ply Stainless Steel Clad Stockpot, 206
    Heavy-Duty Mixer, 150–1
    Hi*Density Hard-Anodized Aluminum
        Saucier, 200–1
    Hi*Density Hard-Anodized Clad Skillet,
        177
    Pasta Roller Set, 295–6
    Professional Food Processor, 162–3
    Seven-Speed Ultra Power Plus Hand Mixer,
        154
    12-Cup Ultra Coffeemaker, 398–9
    Ultra Power Blender, 155–6
Kitchenart
    Adjustable Tablespoon, 5–6

Kitchen Market
    Lava Stone Mortar & Pestle, 99
Kitchen Supply Company
    Baking Stone, 315
    Heavy Copper Bowl, 25
Knickerbocker, Peggy, 25
knife storage units, 61–2
knife straighteners and sharpeners,
    57–61
knives, 34–57
    Asian, 42–4
    baking, 354
    blades of, 36, 37
    boning and filleting, 46–7
    brand names of, 37–8
    bread, 50–1
    butchering, 44–5
    care of, 38
    cheese, 54–6
    cleavers, 42, 43
    cook's, 38–40
    curved and crenulated, 33, 56–7
    cutting techniques with, 43, 58
    electric, 432
    frozen-food, 52
    fruit and vegetable, 51–2
    as gifts, 41
    handles of, 37
    history of, 34
    Japanese, 44
    judging the quality of, 36–7
    metals used in making, 34–6
    paring, 40–1
    safety precautions for, 37
    scimitar, 45
    serrated, 50–2
    shellfish, 53–4
    slicing (carving), 47–9
    for sushi preparation, 45
    table, 52
    tang sections of, 37
    twine, 312
    "wardrobe" of, 38
Kotobuki
    Ceramic Lemon Juicer, 113
Kretzer
    Poultry Shears, 82–3
krumkake irons and rollers, 244
Krups
    Crystal Arome Plus Time, 398
    La Glacière, 372–3
    Optifruit, 116–17
    Power Xtreme Blender, 156–7
Küchenprofi
    Champignon, 91–2
    Metal Citrus Juicer, 114
    "Spice Cutter," 66
Kugelhopf molds, 284, 335
Kuglof molds, 334
Kuhn Rikon
    Cookie Press, 363

Kuhn Rikon (*cont'd*)
  Swisspeeler, 74
Kull
  Swabian Spaetzle Press, 300
Kummer, Corby, 391
Kunz, Gray, 371
Kuralt, Charles, 239
Kyocera
  Ginger Grater, 72–3
Kyocera Ming Tsai
  Ceramic Fruit Knife, 51–2

L

lacing equipment, 258–9
ladles, 134–6
ladyfinger tins, 338
lady lock forms, 346
LamsonSharp
  Basting Brush, 258
  Forged Kitchen Shears, 82
  Gold Bread Knife, 50
  Gold Cook's Knife, 39
  Gold Line fluting parer, 41
  Grapefruit Knife, 52
  Slotted Turner, 140
  Tomato Knife, 51
  Wide Paring Knife, 41
Lang, Jenifer, 324
La Pavoni
  Professional, 404
  Turkish *Cezve* (or Greek *Briki*), 400–1
Lappé, Frances Moore, 123
larding needles, 259–60
layer cake pans, 329–31
Leader, Daniel, 304
Lebewohl, Sharon, 120
Le Creuset
  Deep-Covered Sauté Pan, 189
  Grillit Pan, 237
  Marmitout (Multifunction) Pan, 201
  Mini & Giant Reversible Grill-Griddle, 239
  Oval au Gratin, 268
  Oval Baking Dish, 264
  Oval French Oven, 218
  Pâté Terrine, 278
  Phenolic Handle Saucepan, 199
  Quiche/Pizza Dish, 265
  Round French Oven, 217
  Round French Oven Lid, 215
  Screwpull Champagne Crown Resealer, 386
  Screwpull Champagne Star, 384
  Screwpull Foil Cutter, 388
  Screwpull Lever Model, 379
  Splatter Guard, 189
  Spoon-Spatulas, 138–9
  Super Spatula, 139
  Tagine, 221-2
  Wire Skimmer, 136
Lee
  Corn Cutter & Creamer, 76
Lee, Lorraine, 70

Lehman's
  Our Best Grain Mill, 106
Leifheit
  Cheese Cutter, 84
  Cherry Pitter, 81
  Plum Pitter, 81–2
Leite, David, 222
lemon juicers, 113, 114
lemon zesters, 74–5
Lenôtre, Gaston, 309, 335
Le Rouet
  Turning Slicer, 68
Lesem, Jeanne, 422
Levine, Sarabeth, 341
lids for pots and pans, 174, 214–16
Liebling, A. J., 119
lifters, 139–41
lime presses, 113
Lincoln Centurion Brushed Stainless Steel Saucepan, 200
liqueurs for cooking, 383
lobster cookery, 206
lobster crackers, 85, 87
Lodge
  Cast-Iron Chicken Fryer, 189
  Cast-Iron Deep Fryer & Basket, 190
  Cast-Iron Frying Pan, 176
  Cast-Iron Popover Pan, 338
  Corn Bread Skillet, 338
  Danish *Aebleskive* Pan, 243
  "Ear of Corn" Pan, 337
  Old-Style Cast-Iron Griddle, 232
  Six-Hole fluted Muffin Pan, 337
Lomonaco, Michael, 40, 76
Luminarc
  Canning Jars, 426
Lu Yu, 69

M

mace, 104
madeleine tins, 338–9
Madison, Deborah, 205
Maggio, Salvatore, 149
Magi-Cake Strips, 331
Magic Line
  Cake Pan, 329
  Cookie Sheet, 322–3
  Loaf Pan, 326–7
  Square Baking Pan, 326
Magic Mill
  Assistant Meat Grinder Attachment, 108
  DLX 2000 Assistant, 150, 152
Makizushi Mat, 287–8
Malgieri, Nick, 149
mandolines, 66–7
manioc, 165
Marktime
  Braille Timer, 431
Marshall, Lydie, 93
Masamoto Sohonten Kasumi
  Usuba, 44
  Yanagi, 44

Mason, John Landis, 420
Mason Cash
  Ceramic Pie Pan Set, 342
  Mixing Bowls, 29
  Pudding Basins, 30
  Vitrified Ceramic Mortar & Pestle, 97–8
Mate Gourd with *Bombilla*, 418
Matfer
  Adjustable Tart Ring, 332
  Babas au Rhum Molds, 310
  Baking Beans, 355
  Baking Dish, 264
  Birds' Nest Basket, 191
  Black Steel Frying Bowl with Basket, 190
  Brioche Mold & Individual Brioche Mold, 308, 310
  Candy Thermometer, 18
  Cassoulet Dish, 229
  Cheese Wire, 84
  Chestnut Peeler, 78
  Croquembouche Form, 346
  Double-Handled Cheese Knife, 55–6
  Flat Pastry Brush, 355
  Flower Tart Ring, 345
  Fluted Puff Pastry Rolling Pin, 352
  Fluted Tart Mold, 342–3
  Kitchen Spatula, 131–2
  Lame with Plastic Cover, 312
  Larding Needle, 260
  Nonstick Pâté Mold, 279
  Octagonal Terrine, 277
  Oven Baking Sheet, 323
  Pain de Mie Pan, 308
  Pâté en Croûte Mold, 279
  Petits Fours Pastry Set, 344–5
  Pickle Slicer, 77
  Plain & Fluted Barquette Molds, 344
  Plain Tart Ring, 345
  Pommes Vapeur Pot, 212
  Professional Mandoline, 66–7
  Puff Pastry Cutters, 357–8
  Pyramid Ice Cream Mold, 283
  Round Bottomless Forms, 284–5
  Round Fluted Pâté Ring, 279
  Salamander, 268
  Salometer, 20
  Savarin Mold, 336
  Slotted Pelton Spatula, 140–1
  Solid Pelton Spatula, 139
  Syrup Density Meter, 20
  Tarte Tatin Pan, 344
  Thermométre Boulanger, 19
  Tinned-Steel, Blued-Steel, & Nonstick Steel Tart Molds, 343
  Tin-Plate *Kuglof* Mold, 334
  Turkey Lacers, 258–9
  Two-Channel Metal Baguette Pan, 307–8
  Wooden & Nylon French Rolling Pins, 350–1
Matsuhisa, Nobu, 45
Mauviel
  Copper *Bain-Marie*, 203

Mauviel (*cont'd*)
  Copper Sauté Pan, 186
  Cuprinox Crepe Pan, 181
  Cuprinox *Plat à Rotir* Roasting Pan, 253
  Flat Copper Lid, 216
  Hammered Copper Saucepan, 198
  Oval Flambé Pan, 182
  Pommes Anna Pan, 269
  Round Flambé Pan, 182
  Zabaglione Pot, 227
Maverick Industries
  Deluxe Food Grinder, 107
  RediChek Thermometer, 16
Maxim
  High Performance Electric Wok, 196
McCarty, Michael, 382
McGee, Harold, 250
McRae, Carmen, 316
measuring devices, 1–23
  dry and liquid ingredients, differences in
    measuring, 2
  eighth of a teaspoon, measurement of, 3
  Farmer's influence on measuring, 5
  measuring cups and spoons, 2–6
  salometers and hydrometers, 20
  scales and balances, 6–10
  timers, 21–3, 431
  see also thermometers
meat, 14
meat grinders, 107–9
meat slicers, 48–9
Melitta
  Café-Euro 1-Cup Coffeemaker, 394
  Café-Euro 6-Cup Coffeemaker, 394
Mencken, H. L., 208
mercury thermometers, 10, 11
Messermeister
  Cheflamme Butane Culinary Torch, 271
  Fish Pliers, 86
  Knife Sheath, 62
  Locking Tongs, 142
  Super Magnet Knife Rack, 61
  Swivel Peeler, 73–4
  Tomato Shark, 81
metric system, 1–2
Metro
  Mini Colander, 119–20
Metrokane
  Mighty OJ, 113
Meyer, Danny, 95
mezzaluna knives, 33, 56–7
mezze (herb assortment), 25
Microplane
  Cheese Grater-Zester, 70
  Spice Grater, 70
  Zester, 75
microwave cooking, 167
Middle Eastern coffee equipment,
    400–1
mincing devices, 65–7
mincing technique, 43
mise en place, 64

Mr. Coffee
  Iced Tea Pot, 417
mixers
  attachments for, 150
  hand, 153–4
  stand, 150–2
moka express espresso machines, 403
molds, 276–86
  bread, 308, 310
  butter, 285–6
  cake, 333, 334–6
  charlotte, 281–2
  fish, 280
  open, 282–5
  pasta, 293–4
  pastry, 346–7
  pâté, 277–9
  pudding, 280–1
  specialty baking, 338–9
  sushi, 287
  tart, 342–5
  terrines, 277–9
molinillos (chocolate swizzles), 148
Mongolian Copper Firepot, 225–6
Monopol
  Nutcracker & Champagne Opener, 385
Montaigne, Michel, 45
Montana
  Collezione Maître Butcher Knife, 44–5
  Collezione Maître Citrus Knife, 51
  Collezione Maître Fillet Knife, 47
  Collezione Maître Salami Slicer, 48
  Gorgonzola Knife, 55
  Optima Adjustable Bread Knife, 50
  Optima Dough Knife, 49
  Parmesan Knife, 55
Montezuma, Aztec emperor, 148
mortars and pestles, 97–100
Mouli
  Champagne Key, 384
  Cheese, Chocolate, & Truffle Shaver, 79
  Chinois with Custom Stand, 91
  Drum Cheese Grater with Bowl, 71
  Fine Mesh Skimmer, 137
  Grater Brush, 73
  Large Flat Pounder, 111
  Large Vertical Pounder, 111
  Lobster-Nutcrackers, 87
  Strainer, 125
  Tamis with Coarse Screen, 90
  Wooden Pestle for *Chinois*, 91
Moulinex
  Food Mill, 93
Mountain Woods
  Crumb Tray, 312–13
muffin tins, 336–7
Munini
  Bott Champagne Cork Remover, 385
  Elmo Wine Stopper, 385
  Foil Cutter, 388
Musso
  Lussino Pro, 370–1

Mutual Trading Company
  Stainless Steel–Tipped Chopsticks, 142

N

nabe pots, 222–3
Nald, Leo, 219
Nathan, Joan, 71
National Museum of Pasta Foods (Rome),
    296
Natural Scallop Shell, 265
Neapolitan coffeemakers, 400
Nesco
  American Harvest Gardenmaster
    Professional Food Dehydrator and
    Jerky-Maker, 427
  Cool Side 5 Roaster Oven, 262
Nespresso System, 407
Nestle, Marion, 14
N.Y. Cake & Baking
  Pastry Crimper, 355
Nonancourt, Duc de, 386
nonstick bakeware, 327
nonstick cookware, 171–2, 175, 197
noodle presses, 300
Nooteboom, Cees, 265
Nordic Ware
  Aluminum & Cast-Aluminum *Bundt* Pans,
    335
  Belgian Waffler, 242
  Norwegian *Krumkake* Iron, 244
Norpro
  Blending Fork, 349
  Cake Decorating Set, 365
  Colander-Strainer, 122
  Double Steamer Basket, 208
  English Muffin Rings, 359–60
  Krona Pot, 198
  Marble Mortar & Pestle, 98–9
  Meat Hammer, 112
  Over-the-Sink Colander, 120
  Rolling Cookie Cutter, 358–9
  Rolling Pin Cover & Pastry Cloth Set,
    349
  Round Pounder, 111
  Scoop, 375
  Six-Cup Puffy Crown Pan, 337
  Six-Hole Giant Muffin Tin, 337
  Strainer Lid, 216
  Strawberry Huller, 82
  Turkey-Roaster Lifter Chain, 260–1
Novalle, Miriam, 410
nutcrackers, 87–8, 385
nutmeg, 104
nutmeg graters, 104–5

O

obsttorte pans, 332–3
O'Connell, Patrick, 67
Oenophilia
  Champagne Chiller, 383
  Private Preserve Wine Preserver, 387

Oetker, August, 336
oils for deep-frying, 18
Old Dutch
    Copper Gratin Pan, 268
    Copper & Porcelain Fondue Pot, 225
olive pitters, 81
Omega
    4000 Juice Extractor, 116
omelet pans, 182–3
organizing the workspace, 64
Osius, F. J., 154
oval pans, 179
oven thermometers, 10–11
Over, Charles Van, 306
OXO
    Apple Corer, 80
    Apple Divider, 81
    Asian Turner, 141
    Cooking Fork, 143
    Double Rod Strainer, 124–5
    Flat Whisk, 147
    Flour Sifter, 348
    Good Grips Bread Knife, 51
    Good Grips Clam Knife, 53–4
    Good Grips Double Melon Baller Cutter, 79
    Good Grips Garlic Press, 97
    Good Grips Multi Grater, 70
    Good Grips Pepper Mill, 103
    Good Grips Pizza Wheel, 315
    Good Grips Potato Masher, 94
    Good Grips Potato Ricer, 95
    Good Grips Rotary Cheese Grater, 72
    Good Grips Turkey Lifter, 260
    Good Grips Uplift Teakettle, 412
    Lemon Juicer, 114
    Measuring Cups, 3
    Measuring Cup Set, 430
    Measuring Spoons, 3
    Nonskid Mixing Bowls, 28
    Nut & Seafood Cracker, 87
    Pleated Citrus Reamer, 114
    Pot Fork, 143
    Salad Spinner, 123
    Scoop and Nonstick Scoop, 374–5
    Silicone Spatulas, 138
    Y Peeler, 74
oyster gloves, 54
oyster knives, 53

P

Pacojet, 371–2
paella pans, 184
pain de mie pans, 308
Palmer, Charlie, 371
Panasonic
    Bread Bakery, 320
pan heat, testing for, 16–17
Papin, Denis, 420
parchment cones, 364, 368
paring knives, 40–1
Parmesan knives, 55
Passmore, Jacki, 223

pasta
    cooking technique, 298
    dried and fresh, 289–90, 292
    flavored varieties, 296
    handmade vs. machine pasta, 291
    history of, 289
    museum dedicated to, 296
    ravioli, 294
    shaping and cutting techniques, 292
Pastadrive
    Motor for Atlas Pasta Machine, 297
pasta forks, 133
pasta-making equipment, 289–301
    hand tools, 290–4
    machines, 294–9
    noodle presses, 300
    spaetzle makers, 299–301
Pasteur, Louis, 420
pastry equipment, see baking and pastry
        equipment
pastry-making, 32, 323
pâté molds, 277–9
Paul Oliver
    Shovall, 130
Payard, François, 323, 343, 351
Pedrini
    Dual-Purpose Egg Slicer, 83
    Gravy Separator, 126
    Spiridoso, 258
peelers, 73–80
    citrus, 74–5
    electric, 431
    specialized, 75–8
    truffle, 79–80
peels, 316–17
Pelouze
    Baker's Scale, 9
    Scale, 8
Pépin, Jacques, 176, 279, 387
peppercorns, 102
pepper mills, 100–4
pepper-roasting technique, 259
Pepys, Samuel, 112
percolators, 399
Perfex
    Pepper & Salt Mills, 103–4
pestles, 91
    see also mortars and pestles
Peterson, James, 146
petits fours pastry sets, 344–5
Peugeot
    Auberge Pepper Mill, 102–3
    Manual Coffee Grinder, 391
Piazza
    Timbale, 282–3
pickles, 20
pickle slicers, 77
pie pans, 339–42
Pillivuyt
    Dish, 264–5
    Egg Cocotte with Ears, 270
    Ramekin, 270

Pillivuyt (cont'd)
    Round-Eared Egg Dish, 270
pineapple corer/slicers, 81
pitters, 80–2
pizza-making equipment, see bread- and
        pizza-making equipment
pizzelle makers, 245
plätt pans, 243
Plotkin, Fred, 299
plum pitters, 81–2
plunger pots, 395
poachers, fish, 213–14
Point, Fernand, 147
Polder
    Portable Timer, 22
    Preprogrammed Cooking Thermometer, 15
    Square Mechanical Timer, 21
    Triple Timer Clock, 22–3
polenta pots, 226–7
Pollack, Bunny, 219
pommes Anna pans, 269
Popeil, Ron, 261
popover pans, 338
poppyseed grinders, 105
porcelain, 166
porcelain-enamel coatings for pots and pans,
        171, 173
Portale, Alfred, 281
potato chippers, 75
potato mashers and ricers, 94–6
potato peelers, 78
potato steamers, 212
Potenza, Walter, 229
pots and pans, 165–230
    baking pans, 325–8
    bottoms of, 168, 172
    braising pans, 220
    bread pans, 306–8, 310–11
    building a collection, 174–5
    care and cleaning of, 173
    casseroles, 217–23, 228
    cataplana pans, 222
    chestnut pans, 256
    chicken fryers, 189
    choosing pots and pans for your kitchen,
        174
    coatings for, 171–2, 173
    construction of individual subbrands, 180
    cooking process and, 167–8
    crepe pans, 181–2
    deep-fat fryers and frying accessories,
        190–3
    double boilers and bains-marie, 202–4
    earthenware pots, 227–30
    electric deep fryers, 192–3
    electric pots and skillets, 174, 178–9
    electric rice cookers, 212–13
    fish poachers, 213–14
    fondue pots, 224–6
    form and function concerns, 173–4
    frying pans, 175–9
    gratin pans, 267–9

pots and pans (*cont'd*)
    handles of, 167–8, 173–4
    history of, 165–7
    jelly-roll pans, 324
    lids for, 174, 214–16
    manufacture of, 168
    metals used for making, 168–71, 196–7, 204
    multipiece sets, 174
    must-haves, 175
    nabe pots, 222–3
    omelet pans, 182–3
    oval pans, 179
    paella pans, 184
    pie pans, 339–42
    pizza pans, 310–11
    pressure cookers, 201–2, 430–1
    quiche pans, 345
    roasting pans, 252–3, 255
    sandwich bottoms, 172
    saucepans, 196–201
    sautéing pans, 186–9
    seasoning cast-iron cookware, 234
    slow cookers, 223
    specialty baking forms, 337–9
    specialty copper pots, 226–7
    steamers and steaming baskets, 208–13
    stockpots, 204–8
    tagines, 221–2
    tart pans, 342–5
    "tri-ply" and "five-ply," 172
    woks, 193–6
    see also cake pans
poultry roasters, 256
poultry shears, 82–3
pounders, 110–12
presenting a meal, 286
preserving equipment, 419–28
    for canning, 420–6
    dehydrators, 426–7
    for freezing, 427–8
    vacuum sealers, 428
pressure canners, 423–4
pressure cookers, 201–2, 430–1
Presto
    FryDaddy Electric Deep Fryer, 192
    Jumbo Cool Touch Electric Griddle, 236
    Pressure Canner, 423–4
    Stainless Steel Pressure Cooker with
        Bimetal-Clad Base, 202
Progressive
    ProGrip Ultra Tower Grater, 70
Progressive International
    Professional Coffee Tamper, 407
Progressus
    Egg Timer, 21
Proust, Marcel, 214, 338
Prudhomme, Paul, 236
Pruess, Joanna, 276
Puck, Wolfgang, 314
pudding
    Christmas, 31
pudding bowls, 30

pudding molds, 280–1
Purdy, Susan, 4
Pyrex
    Custard Cups, 272
    Loaf Pan, 327
    Oblong Baking Pan, 326
    Oven Thermometer, 10–11
    Stackable Measuring Cup Set, 5
    Three-Piece Mixing-Bowl Set, 27
    Traditional Pie Pan, 340
Pythagoras, 100

Q

quiche dishes, 265
quiche pans, 345

R

raclette-makers, 241
radiation cooking, 167
radish rose cutters, 76–7
Raichlen, Steven, 238
ramekins, 270–1
ravioli, 294
ravioli makers, 297–8
ravioli molds, 293–4
Reco International
    Römertopf, 229
Redon, Odile, 260
Reed's
    Rocket Nutcracker, 87–8
refrigerator thermometers, 11–12
Regent-Sheffield
    Infinity Edge Cook's Knife, 39
    Infinity Edge Slicer, 47–8
Rehrücken molds, 333
Reingold, Carmel Berman, 372
restaurant and family cooking, difference
        between, 301
restaurant stoves, 166, 172
Reston Lloyd
    Schlemmertopf, 229
Revereware
    Dura-Spatula Set, 138
rice cookers, 210–11, 212–13
Richelieu, Cardinal, 52
Riedel glasses, 376
Ripert, Eric, 142
Rival
    Removable Crock Pot, 223
River Light
    Tempura Cooker, 191–2
roast beef slicers, 48
roasting-baking relationship, 250–1
roasting equipment, 250–62
    basting equipment, 257–8
    chestnut pans, 256
    electric roasters, 262
    electric rotisseries, 261
    high covered roasters, 253
    history of, 250
    lacing equipment, 258–9
    larding needles, 259–60

roasting equipment (*cont'd*)
    roasting pans, 252–3, 255
    roasting racks, 255–6
    turkey lifters, 260–1
    what to look for, 252–3
Roberts, Julia, 266
Robinson Ransbottom
    Sauerkraut Crock, 424
Robot Coupe
    Blixer R2 Ultra Food Processor, 163–4
    BX3 Commercial Food Processor, 163–4
Robuchon, Joël, 35, 35, 94
Roden, Claudia, 25, 33, 283
Rodriguez, Douglas, 259
roll-cutting, 43
rolling pin covers, 349
rolling pins, 290, 350–2, 360–1
Romano, Michael, 95
Rombauer, Irma S., 30
Ronald, Mary, 251
Ronco
    Showtime Rotisserie & BBQ, 261
Rosette Iron Set, 191
Rösle
    Ballers, 78–9
    Butter Curler, 75–6
    Cheese Slicer, 83–4
    Classic Cooking Spoon, 132
    Colander, 119
    Deep Bowl Set & Lids, 26
    Double-Bladed Mezzaluna, 56–7
    Extra-Deep Skimmer, 135
    Ladle with Pouring Rim, 134–5
    Potato Masher, 94–5
    Round Balloon Whisk, 145
    Scoop Ladle, 135
    Skimmer, 136–7
    Spiral Whisk, 147
    Tea Strainer, 124
    Vegetable Corer, 80
Rotating Coconut Grater, 73
rotisseries, electric, 261
Royal Enterprises Inc.
    Cleancaf, 409
Rozin, Elizabeth, 230
Ruffoni
    Copper Polenta Pot, 226–7
Russell, John, 50
Russell Harrington's
    Dexter Chinese Chef's Knife, 43
Russell Hobbs
    Classic Sovereign Stainless Steel Cordless
        Kettle, 413

S

Sabatier
    Au Carbone Boning Knife, 47
    Au Carbone Cook's Knife, 40
    Bayonet Chef's Fork, 144
    Commercial Cleaver, 42
    Commercial Ham Slicer, 48
    Commercial Steak Knives, 49

Sabatier (cont'd)
   Commercial Straightening Steel, 57
Sabbon, Françoise, 260
Sahni, Julie, 231, 412
salad bowls, 32, 33
salad greens, washing technique for, 123
salad spinners, 122–4
salamander metal tool, 268
salami slicers, 48
salmon, beverages to serve with, 377
salmon slicers, 49
salometers, 20
salt density, 20
Salter
   Antique Scale, 9–10
   Baker's Dream Scale, 7–8
salt mills, 100–1, 103–4
Salton-Maxim
   Big Chill, 373
   George Foreman's Lean Mean Fat-
      Reducing Grilling Machine, 241
   Yogurt Maker, 375
Sammons Preston
   Hi-D Paring Board & Food Prep Board, 431
samovar, 417
Samuelsson, Marcus, 377
Sandburg, Carl, 118
sandwich, origin of the, 52
sandwich spatulas, 51
Sassafras
   Superstone Deep-Dish Baking Stone, 315
   Superstone La Cloche, 314–15
saucepans, 196–201
sauce whisks, 145–7
sauerkraut crocks, 424
Sausage Maker Sausage Stuffer, 109
sausage meals, 108
sausage stuffers, 109
sautéing pans, 186–9
savarin molds, 336
Savoir-Vivre
   Horn Caviar Spoon & Server, 134
scales and balances, 6–10
scallop knives, 54
scallop shells (baking and serving dishes),
   265–6
Scandinavian specialty griddles and irons,
   243–4
ScanPan
   Cast Aluminum Nonstick Frypan, 178
   Dutch Oven, 217–18
Schlesinger, Chris, 123
Schumpf, Brownie, 87
SCI
   Aspic Mold, 282
   Butter Mold, 286
   Butter Paddle, 285
   Krumkake Roller, 244
   Marble Pastry Board, 349
   Mesh Chinois, 90–1
   Pizzelle Iron, 245
   Ravioli Mold, 294

SCI (cont'd)
   Round and Square Pasta Stamps, 292
   Spaetzle Maker, 301
   Swedish Plätt Pan, 243
   Wooden Reamer, 114
scimitar knives, 45
scoring and slicing tools, 312–13
scrapers, 347
seasoning cast-iron cookware, 234
separators, 118
   egg, 127
   fat, 126
serrated knives, 50–2
Serventi, Silvano, 260
Seshin
   Diva Paring Knife, 41
Seuss, Dr., 233
Shakespeare, William, 216
shears, 82–3
shellfish knives, 53–4
Shen Nung, Emperor, 410
Shere, Lindsey Remolif, 137
shortbread pans, 339
shrimp tools, 86
Sierra Housewares
   Quick Chill Wine & Beverage Wrap, 383
sieves, 89–92, 125
sifters, 348
silver coatings for pots and pans, 171, 173
Silverton, Nancy, 125, 319
Simac
   Il Gelataio Magnum II, 370
Simonds, Nina, 59
Simplex
   Teakettle, 412
Sitlax
   Scoop Colander, 121–2
Skeppshult
   Scandinavian Waffle Iron, 244
skillets, 175–9, 338
skimmers, 136–7
slicers, 77, 79
slicing knives, 47–9
slicing machines, 68–9
slicing technique, 43
slow cookers, 223
Smartblock
   Cutting Block, 431–2
Smith, Sydney, 416
snail-serving equipment, 266–7
Soehnle
   Vita Scale, 7
Soltner, André, 91, 251
soufflé dishes, 274–5
sourdough starter, 319
spaetzle makers, 299–301
spaghetti colanders, 120–1
Spanek
   Vertical Poultry Roaster, 256
Spanish Table
   Cazuela, 265
   Copper Cataplana, 222

spatulas
   baking, 353–4
   bubble freer, 422
   cooking spoons, 130, 131–2
   lifters and turners, 139–41
   for mixing, blending, folding, scraping,
      and spreading, 138–9
   sandwich, 51
spice graters, 70
spice grinders, 100–1, 104–5
spices, roasting of, 231
spirits for cooking, 383
splatter guards, 189
spoons, see cooking spoons
Springerle tools, 360–1
springform pans, 333
square vol-au-vent cutter, 360
Staib, Walter, 409
stainless steel, 36
Stainless Steel Chinese Ladle, 135–6
stainless steel pots and pans, 169, 173, 197,
   204
Stallworth, Lyn, 219
stand mixers, 150–2
Starbucks
   Barista, 405–6
   Barista Burr Grinder, 391
steak knives, 49
steamers and steaming baskets, 208–13
steaming wands, 405
steel, 35–6
steel pots and pans, 168–9, 173, 197, 204
Stern, Jane and Michael, 235
Stevens, Nancy J., 374
Stewart, Martha, 79
stew pans, 218–19
Stilton cheese, cutting and serving, 56
stir-frying, 193
stir-fry scoops, 133
stockpots, 204–8
Stollen pans, 339
stoneware, 166, 227
stoves, 166, 172
strainers, 118, 124–5
   crescent pot-edge, 197
strawberry hullers, 82
Styler, Christopher, 170
sugar density, 20
sugar pots, 227
Sunbeam
   Digimaster Deluxe, 22
   Large-Face Refrigerator-Freezer
      Thermometer, 12
   Two-Slice Toaster with Toast Logic,
      247
suribachi, 98
Sur la Table
   Eiffel Tower Cutter, 359
sushi equipment, 45, 287–8
Swiss Gold
   Cup o' Tea Permanent Tea Filter, 416
   Pot o' Tea Permanent Tea Filter, 416

Swissmar
  Cheese Fondue Set, 225
  Raclette with Grill, 241

T

Table Art
  Butter Mold, 285–6
table knives, 52
tagines, 221–2
Talleyrand-Périgord, Charles Maurice de, 395
tamago pans, 183
tart pans, 342–5
tava griddles, 235
Taylor
  Candy-Jelly–Deep-Fry Mercury Thermometer, 18
  Cappuccino Frothing Thermometer, 408
  Digital Cooking Thermometer-Timer, 15
  Refrigerator-Freezer Dial Thermometer, 12
tea
  brewing technique, 410
  history of, 410
  Japanese tea ceremony, 415
tea-making equipment, 410–18
  electric kettles, 413
  electric tea makers, 417–18
  samovars, 417
  tea filters, 416
  teakettles, 411–12
  teapots, 414–15
  tea presses, 414
  tea strainers, 124
Teknor Apex
  Plasti-Tuff Cutting Board, 63
  Sani-Tuff Cutting Board, 63–4
tempura cookers, 191–2
tenderizers, 112
terrines, 277–9
T-Fal
  Avante Deluxe Electronic Toaster, 246–7
  Clipso Pressure Cooker, 202
  Deluxe Health Grill, 240
thermometers, 10–19
  accuracy testing of, 11
  candy, jelly, and deep-fat, 17–19
  cappuccino frothing, 408
  chocolate, 19
  dough, 19
  food, 12, 13–17
  grill, 17
  mercury, 10, 11
  oven, 10–11
  for pan heat, 16–17
  refrigerator and freezer, 11–12
Thermos
  Hot Pot, 208
  Nissan Vacuum Carafe, 408
  Nissan Vacuum-Insulated Coffee Press, 395
  Nissan Vacuum-Insulated Travel Tumbler, 408

Thermoworks
  Superfast Thermapen, 14
Thompson, Flora, 225
Thorpe
  Rolling Pin, 351
Tilia's FoodSaver
  Professional II Cacuum Sealer, 428
timbales, 282–3
timers, 21–3, 431
tin coatings for pots and pans, 171, 173
toast, 247
toaster ovens, 248–9
toasters, 246–8
tomato corers, 81
tomato knives, 51
tongs, 142–3
torches, 271
Torey, Allysa, 330
Torres, Jacques, 271, 273
tortilla presses, 317, 319
Trattorina
  Pasta Machine, 295
  Raviolera, 297–8
Tropp, Barbara, 58
Trudeau
  All-Purpose Spatula, 139
truffle slicers and cutters, 79–80
trussing needles, 258–9
t-sac
  Cup & Teapot Filters, 416
Tsuji, Shizuo, 428
tube pans, 334–6
turbot poachers, 214
turkey lacers, 258–9
turkey lifters, 260–1
Turkish coffee equipment, 400–1
Turkish Coffee Grinder, 401
turners, 139–41
twine knives, 312

U

UL symbol on appliances, 157
Unicorn
  Magnum Plus, 101–2
Universal
  Corona Range Grill, 237
Universal Design kitchen tools, 429–32
Upton Tea Imports
  Chatsford Teapot, 414

V

vacuum pots, 396
vacuum sealers, 428
Vacu Vin
  Pineapple Corer & Slicer, 81
Valento, Ernesto, 405
vegetable knives, 51–2
Vespucci, Amerigo, 20
Victorinox
  Ham Boning Knife, 46–7
  Twine Knife, 312
Vienna roll stamps, 310

Viking ranges, 172
Villas, James, 155
Villaware
  Austrian Spaetzle Maker, 300–301
  Bean Slicer, 77
  Gnocchi Paddle, 294
  King Potato Ricer, 96
  Metal Tortilla Press, 317, 319
  Pasta Jagger, 292
  Poppyseed Grinder, 105
  Porkert No. 10 Meat Grinder, 109
  Prima *Pizzelle* Baker, 245
  Ravioli Molds, 293
  Uno Belgian Waffler, 242
  Victorio Food Strainer, 93
Visser, Margaret, 31, 326
vol-au-vent cutters, 360
Vollrath
  Spaghetti Colander, 120–1
Vongerichten, Jean-Georges, 22, 115, 117

W

waffle irons, 242, 244
Waring
  Professional Bar Blender, 156
Waring, Fred, 154
Waters, Alice, 97, 123
Weck
  Canning Jar, 425–6
Weir, Joanne, 164
welding process, 168
Wells, Patricia, 35
West Bend
  Automatic Bread- & Dough-Maker, 320
  Clock–Double Timer, 23
Westmark
  Butter Slicer, 77
  Limona Citrus Press, 114
  Olive Pitter, 81
  Peel-Star Asparagus Peeler, 77
  Radimax Spiral Cutter, 69
  Radish Rose Cutter, 76–7
wet-clay cookers, 228
wheat-grass juicers, 117
whipped cream makers, 363–4
whisks, 144–8
  balloon, 145
  coiled, 147
  flat, 147
  miniwhisks, 148
  rotary eggbeaters, 148
  sauce, 145–7
White, Jasper, 206
White Mountain
  Hand-Crank & Electric Ice Cream Freezers, 373
Wilde, Oscar, 145
Willan, Anne, 8
William Bounds
  Millennium Chef's Pepper Mill, 102

William Bounds (*cont'd*)
   Nut Twister, 104–5
Willoughby, John, 123
Wilton Industries
   Nonstick & Chrome-Plated Cooling Grids, 362
   Stackable Cooling Racks, 362
Wine Enthusiast
   Miniature Distilling Machine, 388
wineglasses, 376
wines for a menu, 382
wines for cooking, 383
wine tools, 376–88
   absurd items, 380
   bottle stoppers, 385–6
   champagne openers, 384–5
   cork retrievers, 381
   corkscrews, 377–81
   handy equipment, 387–8
   wine coolers, 382–3
   wine funnels, 377
   wine preservation equipment, 386–7
Wisconsin Aluminum Foundry
   Chef's Design Maxi Griddle, 234
   Chef's Design Ribbed Griddle, 239
WMF
   Cromargan Skimming Ladle, 126
   Salt Ceramill, 104
   Sauce Ladle, 135
   Topstar Multipot, 207–8
woks, 193–6
Wolfert, Paula, 210, 221

Wood *Battera* Sushi Mold, 287
wooden utensils, 128
Woods, Sylvia, 28
Woodstock Soapstone Company
   Copper-Banded Soapstone Griddle, 232–3
Woodward & Charles
   Rubberwood Salad Bowl, 32
Wooley
   Vienna Roll Stamp, 310
Wright, Steven, 10
Würz, Hedy, 300
Wüsthof, Wolfgang, 143–4
Wüsthof-Trident
   Arrow-Shaped Oyster Knife, 53
   Baker's Knife, 354
   Channel Knife, 75
   Classic Cleaver, 42
   Classic Cook's Knife, 39
   Classic Salmon Slicer, 49
   Classic Tomato Knife, 51
   Crab Knife, 54
   Curved Carving Fork, 143–4
   Decorating Knife, 57
   Fish Shears, 83
   Frozen-Food Knife, 52
   Grand Prix Paring Knife, 41
   Grand Prix Santoku, 43
   Grand Prix Slicer, 48
   Grapefruit Knife, 52
   Larding Needle, 259–60
   Lemon Zester, 74–5
   Offset Cheese Knife, 55

   Stationary Peeler, 74
   Trussing Needle, 259

Y

yerba mate makers, 418
Yin-Fei Lo, Eileen, 193
Yixing teapots, 415
yogurt makers, 375

Z

zabaglione pots, 227
Zanger
   Zip Zap, 58
Zenker
   Spaetzle Maker, 301
Zeroll
   Scoop and Spade, 374
   Universal EZ Disher, 364
zesters, 74–5
Zojirushi
   Deluxe Rice Cooker & Warmer, 212–13
Zraly, Kevin, 380
Zyliss
   Chopper, 66
   Deluxe Cheese Grater Set, 71–2
   Egg Piercer, 83
   Egg Topper, 83
   Lobster Cracker, 85
   Potato Chipper, 75
   Salad Drier, 122
   Susi Deluxe Garlic Press, 96

PERMISSIONS ACKNOWLEDGMENTS

Grateful acknowledgment is made to the following for permission to reprint copyrighted material. Every reasonable effort has been made to trace the ownership of all copyrighted material included in this volume. Any errors that may have occurred will be corrected in subsequent editions provided notification is sent to the publisher.

ⓖ

Cunningham. "Roast Pork Loin" from *James Beard's Theory & Practice of Good Cooking* by James Beard. Copyright © 1977 by James Beard. "Granny's Old-Fashioned Sugar Cookies" from *Maida Heatter's Book of Great American Desserts* by Maida Heatter. Copyright © 1985 by Maida Heatter. "Cheese Soufflé" from *The Way to Cook* by Julia Child. Copyright © 1989 by Julia Child. "*Timballo Alle Melanzane* (Eggplant and Pasta Timbale)" from *The Good Food of Italy* by Claudia Roden. Copyright © 1990 by Claudia Roden. "Cutting with a Chinese Cleaver" and "Lemon Chicken" from *Easy Family Recipes from a Chinese-American Childhood* by Ken Hom. Copyright © 1997 by TAUROM Incorporated. "Bolognese Meat Sauce" and "Veal Scaloppine with Tomato, Oregano, and Capers" from *Essentials of Classic Italian Cooking* by Marcella Hazan. Copyright © 1992 by Marcella Hazan. "Ginger Ice Cream" from *Cooking with David Burke* by David Burke and Carmel Berman Reingold. Copyright © 1994 by David Burke and Carmel Berman Rheingold. "*Salade de Fruits au Sabayon de Champagne* (Fruit Salad with Champagne Sabayon Sauce)" from *Pierre Franey's Cooking in France* by Pierre Franey and Richard Flaste. Copyright © 1994 by Pierre Franey and Richard Flaste. "Cinnamon Toast" from *Learning to Cook* by Marion Cunningham. Copyright © 1999 by Marion Cunningham. "*Fond Blanc de Volaille* (Chicken Stock)" from *The Lutèce Cookbook* by André Soltner. Copyright © 1995 by André Soltner. "Tabbouleh" from *The Book of Jewish Food* by Claudia Roden. Copyright © 1996 by Claudia Roden. "Sauerbraten" from *The Brooklyn Cookbook* by Lyn Stallworth and Rod Kennedy Jr. Copyright © 1991 by Lyn Stallworth and Rod Kennedy Jr. "Shrimp Sambal" from *A Spoonful of Ginger* by Nina Simonds. Copyright © 1999 by Nina Simonds. "Beer-Baked Beans with Apples and Sausage" from *Blue Corn and Chocolate* by Elizabeth Rozin. Copyright © 1992 by Elizabeth Rozin. Reprinted by permission of Alfred A. Knopf, a division of Random House, Inc.

"Buttermilk Sorbet" from *Great American Food* by Charlie Palmer. Copyright © 1996 by Charlie Palmer and Judith Choate. "Pizza Dough" from *The Wolfgang Puck Cookbook* by Wolfgang Puck. Copyright © 1986 by Wolfgang Puck. "Poached Spiced Figs" from *Chez Panisse Desserts* by Lindsay Remolif Shere. Copyright © 1995 by Lindsay Shere. "A Tangle of Tart Greens" from *The Inn at Little Washington* by Patrick O'Connell. Copyright © 1996

by Patrick O'Connell. Reprinted by permission of Random House, a division of Random House, Inc.

"Fanny Abzug's Cheesecake" from *The 2nd Avenue Deli Cookbook* by Sharon Lebewohl and Rena Bulkin. Copyright © 1999 by Sharon Lebewohl and Rena Bulkin. Reprinted by permission of Villard, a division of Random House, Inc.

Running Press:
"Sour Cream Coffee Cake" from *City Tavern Cookbook* by Walter Staib. Copyright © 1999 by Walter Staib. Reprinted by permission of Running Press Book Publishers

Simon & Schuster:
"Classic Cream Puff Pastry" from *The Pie and Pastry Bible* by Rose Levy Beranbaum. Text copyright © 1999 by Cordon Rose, Inc. "Traditional Vanilla Birthday Cake" and "Traditional Vanilla Buttercream" from *The Magnolia Bakery Cookbook* by Jennifer Appel and Allysa Torey. Copyright © 1999 by Jennifer Appel and Allysa Torey. "Waffles" from *The Belgian Cookbook* by Nika Hazelton. Copyright © 1970 by Nika Hazelton. "Bay Scallop and Tomato Gratin" from *Daniel Boulud's Cafe Boulud Cookbook* by Daniel Boulud and Dorie Greenspan. Copyright © 1999 by Daniel Boulud and Dorie Greenspan. "Steamed Plum Pudding" from *The Joy of Cooking* by Irma S. Rombauer and Marion Rombauer. Copyright © 1975 by Simon & Schuster Inc. Reprinted with the permission of Scribner, a division of Simon & Schuster Inc.

"Pickled Okra" from *The Welcome Table* by Jessica B. Harris. Copyright © 1995 by Jessica B. Harris. Reprinted with the permission of Simon & Schuster Inc.

Stewart, Tabori, & Chang:
"Oysters Fried in a Cornmeal Batter" from *The Grand Central Oyster Bar and Restaurant Complete Seafood Cookbook,* by Sandy Ingber. Copyright © 1999 by Gallagher's Steakhouse and Grand Central Oyster Bar Franchising Corporation. Reprinted by permission of agent and packager, Freundlich Communications.

University of Chicago Press:
"Shoulder of Lamb" from *The Medieval Kitchen* by Odile Redon, François Sabbam and Silvano Serventi. Copyright © 1998 by The University of Chicago. Reprinted by permission of the University of Chicago Press.

PERMISSIONS ACKNOWLEDGMENTS

Workman Publishing Company, Inc.:

"New York Super Fudge Chunk" from *Ben & Jerry's Homemade Ice Cream and Dessert Book* by Ben Cohen and Jerry Greenfield with Nancy J. Stevens. Copyright © 1987. "Korean Sesame-Grilled Beef (*Bool Kogi*)" and "Asian Pear Dipping Sauce" from *The Barbecue! Bible* by Steven Raichlen. Copyright © 1998 by Steven Raichlen. "Picky About Size" from *China Moon Cookbook* by Barbara Tropp. Copyright © 1992 by Barbara Tropp. Reprinted by permission of Workman Publishing Company, Inc. All rights reserved.

"The Old Bachelor's Fruit Preserves" from *Ducasse Flavors of France* by Alain Ducasse with Linda Dannenberg. Copyright © 1998 by Alain Ducasse. Reprinted by permission of Artisan, a division of Workman Publishing Company, Inc. All rights reserved.

The authors and publisher also wish to thank the following for use of material from their titles:

Elizabeth Andoh, *At Home with Japanese Cooking;* Mario Batali, *Mario Batali's Simple Italian Food;* Helen Chen, *Helen Chen's Chinese Home Cooking;* Bernard Clayton, *The Complete Book of Pastry: Sweet & Savory;* Shirley Corriher, *Cookwise;* Alain Ducasse, *Ducasse Flavors of France;* Edward Giobbi, *Pleasures of the Good Earth;* Marcella Hazan, *Essentials of Classic Italian Cooking,* Pierre Hermé, *Desserts;* Daniel Leader, *Bread Alone: Bold Fresh Loaves from Your Own Hands;* Claudia Roden, *A Book of Middle Eastern Food;* Douglas Rodriguez, *Nuevo Latino.*

As well as:

Larry Forgione, David Leite, Michael Lomonaco, James Peterson, Jane and Michael Stern, and André Soltner.

The text and titling of this book was set in Chaparrel, an Adobe Original typeface, designed by Carol Twombly. The original inspiration for Chaparral was a page of "humanist" style lettering from a sixteenth-century manuscript. While digitizing the lettering, Twombly saw that it could be adapted into a readable slab serif design. Because it is a multiple master typeface its varying proportions give it a lively vitality in all weights and sizes.

Cronos, a finely crafted sans serif typeface by Robert Slimbach, is used for the setting of recipes and various sidebars. Also an Adobe Original multiple master typeface, it is unique among sans serif types for its warmth, versatility, and reference to old style text faces.